Introduction to Digital Systems

Introduction to Digital Systems

Miloš D. Ercegovac
Computer Science Department
University of California Los Angeles

Tomás Lang
Department of Electrical and Computer Engineering
University of California at Irvine

Jaime H. Moreno
IBM T.J. Watson Research Center

John Wiley & Sons, Inc.
New York • Chichester • Weinheim • Brisbane • Singapore • Toronto

ACQUISITION EDITOR Regina Brooks
MARKETING MANAGER Katherine Hepburn
PRODUCTION EDITOR Patricia McFadden
DESIGNER Ann Marie Renzi
ILLUSTRATION EDITOR Sigmund Malinowski
ILLUSTRATION STUDIO Pro Image

The book was set in 10/12 Times Roman by Eigentype Compositors, and was printed and bound by R. R. Donnelley. The cover was printed by Lehigh Press.

This book is printed on acid-free paper. 

The paper in this book was manufactured by a mill whose forest management programs include sustained yield harvesting of its timberlands. Sustained yield harvesting principles ensure that the number of trees cut each year does not exceed the amount of new growth.

Library of Congress Cataloging-in-Publication Data

Ercegovac, Miloš D.
Introduction to digital system / Miloš D. Ercegovac, Tomás Lang, Jaime H. Moreno.
p. cm.
Includes index.
ISBN 0-471-52799-8 (cloth, alk. paper)
1. Electronic digital computers. 2. Digital integrated circuits.
I. Lang, Tomás. II. Moreno, Jaime H., 1954– . III. Title.
TK7888.3.E73 1999
004 – dc21 98-24462
CIP

ISBN 0-471-57299-8

Printed in the United States of America

10 9 8 7 6 5 4 3 2

Preface

GOAL AND AUDIENCE

This textbook covers the specification, analysis, and design of digital systems. The theory and practice of these systems have developed over the last 50 years and have received a dramatic impulse because of the rapid growth of digital communications, digital instruments, digital entertainment technology, and especially of general-purpose computers. Basic theoretical knowledge about digital systems has consolidated over this period, and methods for their specification, analysis, and design have evolved. However, the field continues changing very rapidly, as technological advances make possible ever more complex and powerful systems.

The rapid pace of change in the field of digital systems constantly outdates some topics and creates new ones, making the field a very dynamic one. As a result, a study of these systems that provides relatively long-lasting knowledge must rely on basic concepts and on a general methodology that can be adapted to the rapidly evolving characteristics. To satisfy such goals, this book distinguishes among the specification of a system and its implementation, and introduces analysis and design methods that are hierarchical and structured. In this way, the specification techniques remain relatively stable throughout time, whereas the implementation of the systems changes according to the technology.

The choice of material and the sequence of exposition was guided by the desire to present well-established concepts and notation, as well as analysis and design techniques, in a concise and comprehensive manner. As a result of that intention, several important topics could not be covered; missing topics include asynchronous circuits and systems, and testing and design for testability. For the same reason, no detailed discussion of specific CAD tools is presented, although the related concepts are introduced and simple examples of their use are given. A WWW site, discussed later, contains material on these and other related topics that instructors may wish to use.

The textbook is suitable for a first course in digital systems, usually taught in the sophomore year to computer engineering, electrical engineering, and computer science majors. The complete book can be covered in a one-semester course, and the most important topics can be covered in a one-quarter course, as outlined later in this Preface. A concurrent laboratory experience is possible, especially one that relies on analysis and design tools and programmable modules. However, we favor a laboratory that follows the course so that it can make immediate use of *all* the material in this course. To provide students with some hands-on experience with CAD tools for design entry and simulation, we developed a set of homework problems for several CAD platforms suited for academic use. These are available from the WWW site.

The book has no specific prerequisite, only the general knowledge obtained from the usual mathematics and physics courses at the freshman level. Basic "electronics" background is given in Chapter 3.

This textbook prepares students for a design-oriented course as well as for specialized courses in VLSI design, testing, implementation of digital signal processing systems, computer design, and microprocessor-based design.

CHARACTERISTICS OF THE PRESENTATION

The presentation emphasizes the concepts, illustrating such concepts for present-day technology. The book stresses a variety of description methods, such as tables, maps, expressions, and description languages. A subset of the language VHDL is introduced and used in the last sections of the relevant chapters, but these sections could be omitted or replaced with the discussion and use of some other hardware description language.

Each chapter contains an outline of the concepts covered. Moreover, each chapter contains a large number of exercises that help students grasp the corresponding material.

ORGANIZATION

The book is divided into two parts. The first part (Chapters 1 through 12) presents the specification and implementation of simple combinational and sequential systems. Chapters 2 through 6 deal with combinational systems: Chapter 2 discusses specification forms, Chapter 3 reviews the related technology, focusing on CMOS circuits and emphasizing the parameters needed for analysis and design, and Chapters 4 through 6 present general methods to analyze combinational networks and discuss their implementation using basic combinational modules (gates), programmable logic devices (PLAs and PALs), and 2-input multiplexers.

Chapters 7 and 8 are dedicated to simple sequential systems, and follow the same ordering as for combinational systems. Chapter 7 defines sequential systems and discusses their specification, whereas Chapter 8 discusses canonical sequential networks, the technology as related to sequential systems, focusing again on CMOS circuits, and the basic approaches for the analysis and design of sequential systems using basic modules (flip-flops).

Chapters 9 through 12 deal with the analysis and design of modular digital systems, that is, systems that are based on complex modules rather than on basic gates and flip-flops. Chapter 9 presents standard combinational modules such as decoders, encoders, multiplexers, and shifters. Arithmetic modules (adders, comparators, ALUs, and multipliers) are covered in Chapter 10, together with the the representation of signed integers and the implementation of the corresponding basic operations. Chapter 11 introduces basic sequential modules: registers, shift registers, and counters. We discuss the use of counters in the implementation of sequential systems, and the implementation of large modules as networks of smaller ones. Chapter 12 discusses programmable modules, some of which were already introduced in Chapter 5.

In the second part of the book, Chapter 13 discusses the organization, analysis, and design of systems at the register-transfer level (RTL), and introduces methods for their specification using a subset of VHDL. Chapter 14 presents the organization of the data and control subsystems, and gives a complete design example. The chapter finishes with a discussion of microprogramming and describes a microprogrammed control unit. Finally, Chapter 15 utilizes the techniques introduced in previous chapters to describe the specification and implementation of a simple microcomputer.

The book also contains an appendix presenting a short treatment of Boolean algebras.

CAD Tools

Exposing students to computer-aided design tools for digital systems is desirable for introducing them to modern design processes. Because the range of CAD tools available is quite wide, from industrial systems such as ViewLogic PowerView to academic packages such as LogicWorks, we have not included the use of any specific tool in the text. Instead, we provide sets of design problems together with a brief discussion of a suitable tool on our WWW site (`http://www.cs.ucla.edu/Logic_Design`). These problems range from basic ones intended to familiarize students with the use of minimization tools such as Espresso and SIS, schematic entry, simulation, and timing analysis, to more challenging ones exposing the use of complex modules. The problems in the sets come from the book; they can be used selectively as homeworks or within a laboratory course.

Companion CD-ROM

The book comes with a CD-ROM containing Altera's MAX+PLUS II software (student edition), a complete CAD environment for the design and synthesis of digital systems using Altera's programmable logic devices. MAX+PLUS II includes tools for design and simulation of digital systems, ranging from schematic capture to synthesis based on hardware description languages (Altera HDL and VHDL). The CD-ROM has documentation describing the features and use of the various tools.

The VHDL source code of the examples used throughout the book is available on our WWW site. Several of those examples use VHDL packages from the standard IEEE library (ieee.std_logic_1164), which are included in the MAX+PLUS II support libraries. It should be noted that some of the VHDL examples in the book correspond to high-level behavioral descriptions; although these are valid descriptions in a VHDL compiling environment, certain constructs used might not be allowed in a synthesis environment such as MAX+PLUS II; consequently, those examples might not be accepted by the MAX+PLUS II VHDL compiler. This is the case, in particular, for some of the descriptions in the later chapters of the book.

Typical Sequences

The book could be used in any of the following course settings:

a. One-quarter course: Chapters 1 through 11, and a choice of problem sets from the WWW site for hands-on experience.
b. One-semester course: All chapters and a choice of problem sets from the WWW site for hands-on experience. In the case of a course with laboratory, only Chapters 1 through 11.
c. One-quarter/semester elective course: Follows (a) or (b). It also covers Chapters 12 through 15, and μVHDL sections in all chapters. May include supplemental topics from the WWW site. Design project.

SUPPLEMENTAL MATERIAL

Supplemental material for this textbook consists of the following:

Instructor's Manual containing solutions to all the exercises, as well as sample tests with answers, available from the publisher.

Lecture viewgraphs (in Postscript form), available from the WWW site, containing lecture material used at UCLA.

ACKNOWLEDGMENTS

We thank the many people who have helped us in developing this book; in particular, our colleagues at UCLA Al Avizienis, Leon Alkalaj, John Harding, Miodrag Potkonjak, and David Rennels, for their comments and patience while enduring numerous "last" versions of the book. We are indebted to Al for many constructive suggestions. We are also grateful to professors Douglas Blough from University of California at Irvine, and Jordi Cortadella from Polytechnic University of Catalonia, Barcelona, for their constructive comments. We thank our many teaching assistants and students for their comments, suggestions, and correction of errors; in particular, we acknowledge Eric Gouriou, Yutao He, Huan Liu, Robert McIlhenny, Marcelo Moraes de Azevedo, Alberto Nannarelli, Brian Park, Alexandre F. Tenca, Tatsuhiro Torii, Li-Yu Sung, and Alex Wong.

We also received helpful comments from reviewers. The editorial assistance and patience of the staff at Wiley has been invaluable.

June 1998 Miloš D. Ercegovac, Tomás Lang, Jaime H. Moreno

Contents

Chapter 1

Introduction

In this chapter, we discuss

- What a digital system is and how it differs from an analog system.
- Why digital systems are important and where are they used.
- The basic types of digital systems: combinational and sequential.
- The specification and implementation of digital systems.
- The processes of analysis and design.
- The use of CAD tools.

1.1 ABOUT DIGITAL SYSTEMS

What Is a Digital System?

A **digital system** is a system in which signals have a **finite** number of **discrete** values. This contrasts with **analog systems,** in which signals have values from a continuous (infinite) set. As an elementary example, a digital scale measures weight through discrete signals indicating pounds and ounces (or kilograms and grams); on the other hand, an analog scale measures weight through a continuous signal corresponding to the position of a pointer (the hand) over a scale.

Analog and digital signals are illustrated in Figure 1.1. In the digital case, time may also be discretized (as shown in Figure 1.1*c*), so that signals may change only at discrete instants; these instants are labeled with integer values. Systems with this type of digital signals are called **synchronous**, whereas those in which changes may occur at any instant are called **asynchronous.** In this text, we focus on synchronous systems because they are more widely used. Figure 1.1*d* illustrates the representation of digital signals by sequences of values.

Why Are Digital Systems Important?

Digital systems are used in information processing (also called data processing and signal processing, depending on the specific application), wherein they have become prevalent and have displaced the earlier analog systems. Some of the benefits of digital systems are:

1. Digital representation is well suited for both numerical and nonnumerical information processing. An example of digital nonnumeric information is the written language in which the letters have values from the finite alphabet A,B,C. . . , and so on.

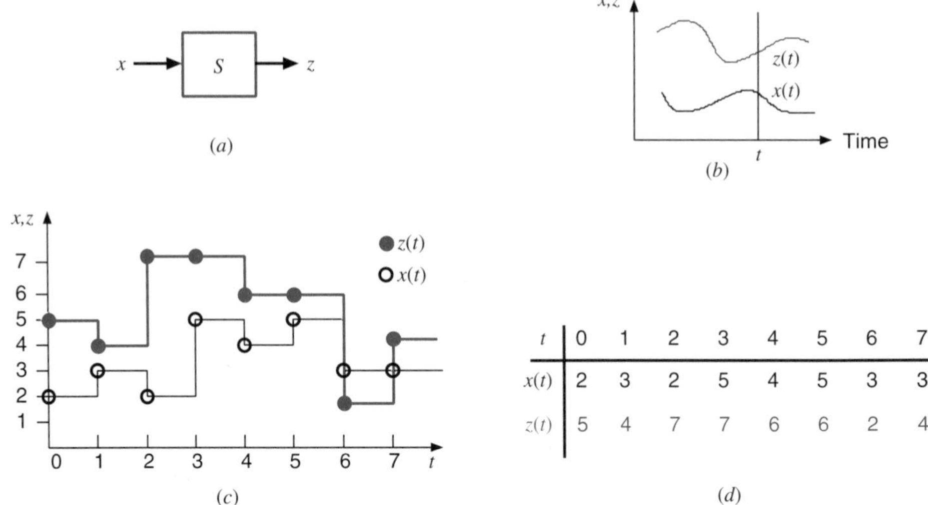

t	0	1	2	3	4	5	6	7
$x(t)$	2	3	2	5	4	5	3	3
$z(t)$	5	4	7	7	6	6	2	4

Figure 1.1 (*a*) Block representation of system *S*. (*b*) Analog input and output signals. (*c*) Synchronous digital input and output signals. (*d*) Pair of input-output sequences.

2. Information processing can use a general-purpose system (a **computer**) that is programmed for a particular processing task, eliminating the need to have a different system for each task. The representation of the program and its interpretation can use the same techniques employed for the representation and transformation of the data.
3. The finite number of values in a digital signal can be represented by a vector of signals with just two values (**binary signals**). For example, the 10 values of a decimal digit can be represented by a vector of four binary signals as follows:

digit	0	1	2	3	4	5	6	7	8	9
vector	0000	0001	0010	0011	0100	0101	0110	0111	1000	1001

   This representation allows implementations in which all signals are binary; as a result, the devices that process these signals are very simple (essentially, just switches with two states: open and closed).
4. Digital signals are quite insensitive to variations of component parameter values (such as operating temperature). As illustrated in Figure 1.2, the physical representation of the values are sufficiently separated so that small variations do not change the value. This is especially true for binary signals.
5. Numerical digital systems can be made more accurate by simply increasing the number of digits used in the representation. For example, the time of day can be represented with a low-precision signal as 12:35 (hours and minutes), or more precisely as 12:35:07 (hours, minutes, and seconds).
6. The advances of microelectronics technology in recent years have made possible the fabrication of extremely complex digital systems that are small, fast, and cheap. Complex digital systems are built as **integrated circuits** composed of a large number of very simple devices.
7. It is possible to select among different implementations of systems that trade off speed and amount of hardware. For example, if we want to add two integers represented by six decimal digits, we can choose among a parallel implementation (see Figure 1.3*a*) which simultaneously adds all six digits, or a serial implementation (Figure 1.3*b*) in

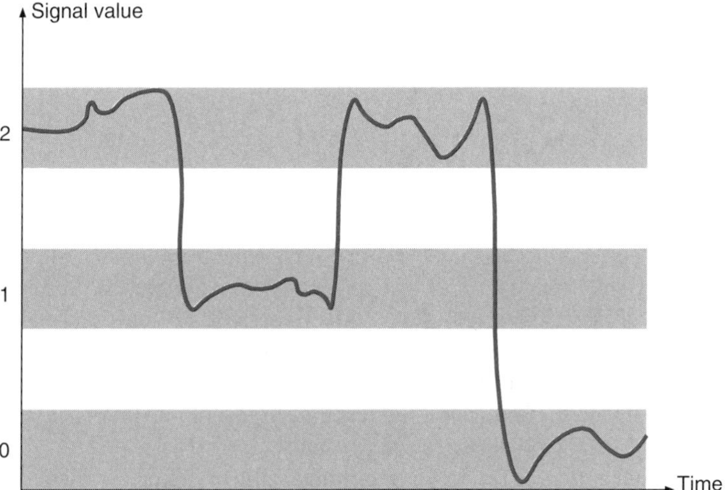

Figure 1.2 Separation of digital signal values.

which the digits of the result are obtained in sequence. In the parallel case, the system is faster but uses more hardware (a six-digit adder), whereas in the serial case it is slower but uses a one-digit adder six times.

When Are Digital Systems Used?

Digital representation and processing methods have been used for a long time. The adding machine and typing machine are just two examples. The development of digital artifacts underwent a dramatic increase with the invention of the digital computer circa 1940. According to today's standards, at that time computers were few, very expensive, not very powerful, not very reliable, and hard to program and use. Since then, extraordinary progress has been made in all these aspects, making the computer indispensable in almost every aspect of modern society.

The development of computer technology, and digital microelectronics in particular, has made possible the cost-effective production of a large variety of specialized digital systems. Some examples are digital watches and timers, calculators, instruments, controllers, video games, cameras, locks, communication equipment, digital music recording, and digital video recording. This trend continues as new applications for digital systems are constantly developed; in some cases the new applications are replacing analog systems, but in many others they are making possible applications that did not previously exist. As a consequence,

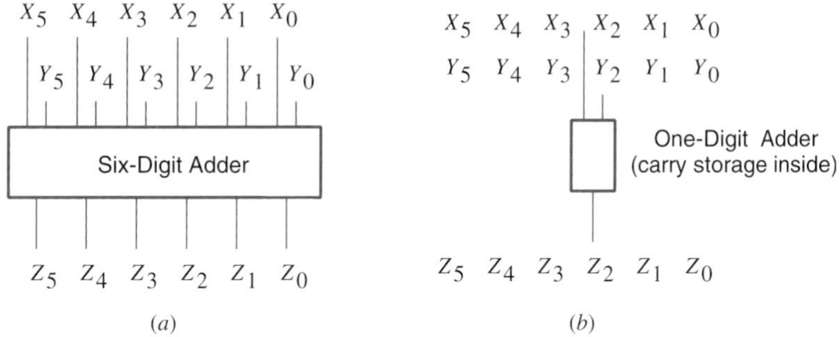

Figure 1.3 Six-digit adder. (*a*) Parallel implementation. (*b*) Serial implementation.

knowledge about the design and use of digital systems is required in a large variety of human activities.

Analog and Digital Signals

Because signals in the physical world are analog, it is necessary to convert from an analog signal to a digital signal and vice versa whenever digital systems have to interact with these physical signals. As an example, consider a system for processing voice signals produced by a singer (see Figure 1.4*a*). Analog signals are generated and transmitted through the air, until a microphone converts them into electric signals (still analog). Then, an analog-to-digital converter transforms the signals to digital, and these digital signals are processed and stored. To transmit the resulting signals to an audience, they are converted to analog and then applied to a speaker system.

The process for converting from analog to digital is called **quantization** or **digitization.** For example, the analog signal in Figure 1.4*b* is sampled at periodic intervals and quantized into four levels, and then the digital representation is conveyed by the sequence of digits. The accuracy with which the conversion is done depends on the number of levels and on the frequency of the samples (this singer has unusually limited voice!).

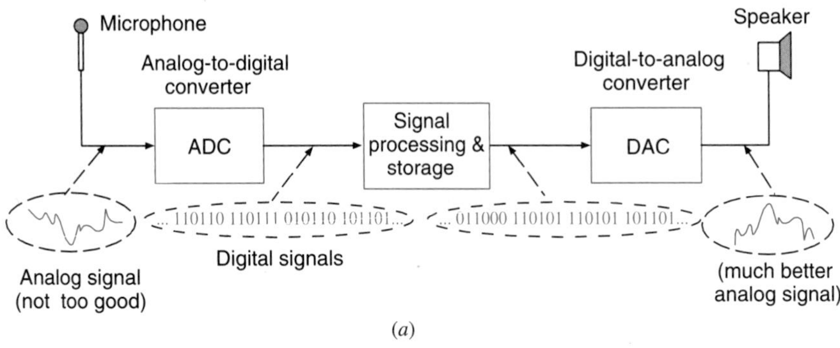

(*a*)

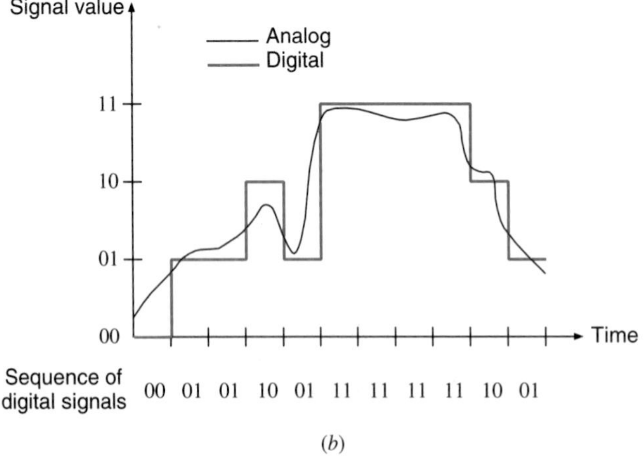

(*b*)

Figure 1.4 (*a*) A system with analog and digital signals. (*b*) Analog-to-digital conversion.

Combinational and Sequential Systems

Digital systems are divided into two classes: **combinational systems** and **sequential systems.** In combinational systems, the output at time t depends **only** on the input at time t (see Figure 1.5a). That is,

$$z(t) = F(x(t))$$

In this case, we can say that the system has no **memory** because the output does not depend on previous inputs. In sequential systems, on the other hand, the output at time t depends on the input at time t and possibly also depends on the input at time prior to t (as shown in Figure 1.5b). This can be written for the general case as

$$z(t) = F(x(0, t))$$

where $x(0, t)$ is the input sequence from time 0 to time t.

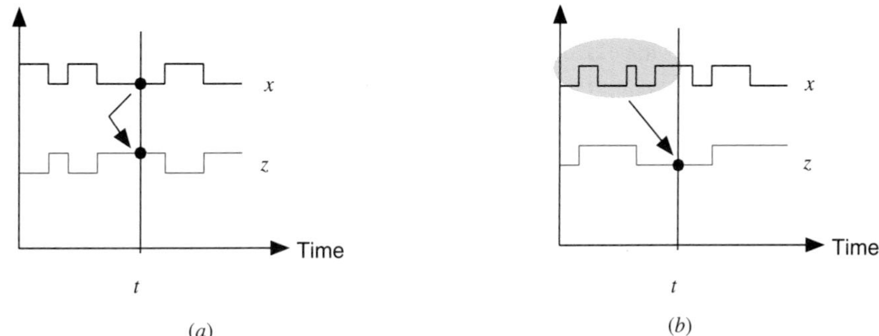

Figure 1.5 Input-output functions for (a) a combinational system and (b) a sequential system.

Example 1.1 and Example 1.2 illustrate a sequential system and a combinational system, respectively.

EXAMPLE 1.1

A digital system S has an input x with values 0,1, or 2, and an output z with values 0 or 1. The function is defined as follows:

$$z(t) = \begin{cases} 1 & \textbf{if } \text{the input sequence } (x(0), x(1), \ldots, x(t)) \text{ has} \\ & \quad \text{an even number of 2's and an odd number of 1's} \\ 0 & \textbf{otherwise} \end{cases}$$

This system is sequential because the output at time t depends on previous inputs. The function description makes it possible to determine the output sequence for a given input sequence. For example, the following is a pair of input-output sequences:

t	0	1	2	3	4	5	6	7	8	9	10	11
x	1	2	2	0	1	2	0	0	0	2	1	1
z	1	0	1	1	0	0	0	0	0	0	1	0

■

EXAMPLE 1.2

A digital system has two input signals. Input $x(t)$ has values from the set of letters (upper and lower case) and input $y(t)$ has values 0 and 1. The function of the system is to change $x(t)$ to opposite case when $y(t) = 1$ and leave it unchanged when $y(t) = 0$. This is a combinational system because the output at time t depends only on the input at time t. An example of a pair of input-output sequences is

t	0	1	2	3	4	5	6
x	E	X	A	M	P	L	E
y	0	1	0	0	0	1	0
z	E	x	A	M	P	l	E

■

The essential difference between combinational and sequential systems is apparent by looking at the output functions from Examples 1.1 and 1.2. In the first example, the output might have different values even if inputs are identical because the output depends on the previous input values (see, for example, the input/output values for $t = 2$ and $t = 5$). In the second example, on the other hand, the output is the same whenever inputs are the same.

This classification is useful in the study of digital systems, because the simpler combinational systems can be studied first.

1.2 SPECIFICATION AND IMPLEMENTATION, ANALYSIS, AND DESIGN

The study of any system involves its specification and implementation (see Figure 1.6). The **specification** of a system refers to a description of its function and of other characteristics required for its use, such as speed, technology, and power consumption. Specification is related to **what** the system does without reference to **how** it performs the operation. A specification should be as complete and as simple as possible; all required details must be included, but no irrelevant ones. Moreover, a specification should be formal in the sense that its interpretation is unambiguous.

The specification of a system must describe its function in a way that is adequate for two purposes:

- to use the system as a component in more complex systems; and
- to serve as the basis for the implementation of the system by a network of simpler components.

Several specification methods for digital systems are presented in this text. The most appropriate method for a given system depends on the complexity of the system and on the intended use of the specification. In Chapter 2 we introduce high-level and binary-level specification of combinational systems. Specification of sequential systems is discussed in Chapter 7. Specification of complex digital systems that require a register-transfer model is the subject of Chapter 13.

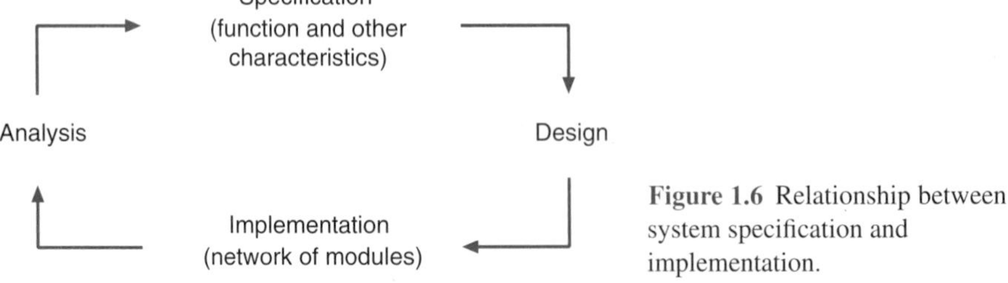

Figure 1.6 Relationship between system specification and implementation.

On the other hand, an **implementation** of a system refers to **how** the system is constructed from simpler components. In the case of digital systems, the implementation is a **digital network** that consists of the interconnection of digital modules. This network can be defined at several levels depending on the complexity of the primitive modules used, which can range from very simple **gates** to complex **processors.**

At the physical level, all digital systems are implemented by a complex interconnection of elementary electronic elements such as transistors, resistors, and so on (these elements are described in Chapter 3). Therefore, the implementation of any digital system could be described as an electronic circuit by indicating these components and their connections. This is impractical, however, because of the complexity of most digital systems. It would be like describing the human body by giving the characteristics of each cell and their relative positions. It is necessary, therefore, to define intermediate levels of modules of increasing complexity, whose description includes only the characteristics that are relevant for their use as components in a more complex system (see Figure 1.7). This corresponds to a **hierarchical implementation**.

Modules are more than just conceptual entities used to simplify the description of an implementation. They are most often designed and built separately and then assembled together to form the final system. Moreover, there exist standard modules of several levels of complexity that can be used in the design of large numbers of different systems. This fact has been important in the cost-effectiveness of digital systems.

The interconnection of modules in an implementation has to follow certain rules for the network to perform adequately. These rules are, in general, specified independently from the definition of the modules, so that they can be used with any type of module at all levels of the implementation.

In this text, we emphasize the separation of the specification of a system from its implementation. This distinction is very important in complex systems because

- it shields the description required to use the system from implementation details; and
- it allows choosing an implementation from different alternatives, without influencing the description required for using the system.

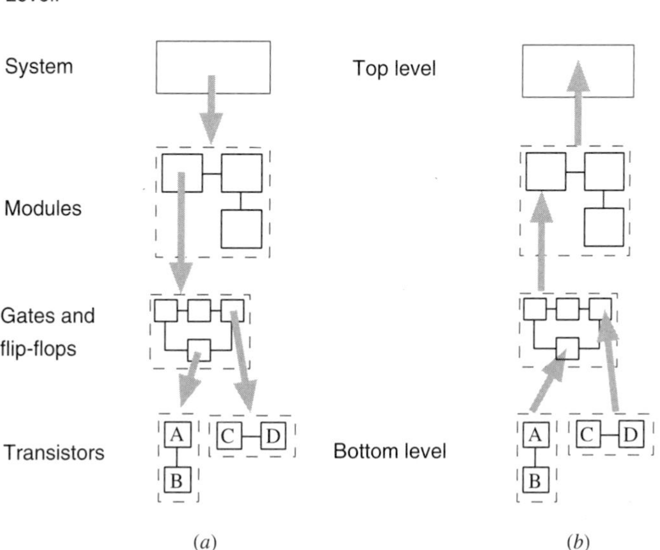

Figure 1.7 Hierarchical implementation. (*a*) A top-down approach. (*b*) A bottom-up approach.

The implementation of combinational systems at the gate level is discussed in Chapters 4, 5, and 6, and at the module level in Chapters 9, 10, and 12. The implementation of sequential systems is the subject of three chapters: implementation of elementary sequential systems is discussed in Chapter 8, and implementations of more complex sequential modules are covered in Chapters 11 and 12. Implementation of register-transfer level systems is presented in Chapters 13 and 14.

Structured Analysis and Design

The **analysis** of a system has as objective the determination of its specification from an implementation (see Figure 1.6). The system thus analyzed can be a module in a larger system, resulting in a multilevel analysis process. For complex systems, this multilevel approach is indispensable to have a manageable analysis.

On the other hand, the **design** process consists of obtaining an implementation that satisfies the specification of a system (see Figure 1.6). If the system is complex, it is also necessary to use a multilevel approach; two variants of this approach have been proposed:

The top-down approach, illustrated in Figure 1.7*a*, decomposes the system into subsystems that themselves are decomposed into simpler subsystems, until a level is reached at which the subsystems can be realized directly with available modules.

This method has the disadvantage that no systematic procedure exists to assure that the decomposition at a particular level optimizes the final implementation. The success of the approach depends on the experience of the designer to choose an adequate decomposition at each level. (An inadequate decomposition in the top-down approach leads to a "bottomless implementation," as one of our colleagues remarked once.)

The bottom-up approach, illustrated in Figure 1.7*b*, connects available modules to form subsystems, and these subsystems are connected to other subsystems until the required functional specification is fulfilled.

This approach has a similar disadvantage to that discussed for the top-down case. The composition of subsystems should be done in a way that results in the correct system specification. Again, in general, there is no systematic procedure that assures that this will occur.

Consequently, a combination of the two approaches should be used: the system is decomposed into subsystems (top-down) but the specific decomposition depends on which subsystems can be cost-effectively composed from primitive modules (bottom-up).

In this book, analysis and design are discussed at several levels. In Chapters 1 to 12, we consider combinational and sequential systems; we develop a bottom-up approach, in which we begin with the use of primitive building blocks, that is, gates and flip-flops, and then introduce standard modules, such as decoders, adders, and counters. Then, in Chapters 13 to 15, we present, in a top-down manner, the implementation of a register-transfer level system consisting of a data subsystem and a control subsystem, each of which is composed of the modules studied in earlier chapters.

Levels of an Implementation: Module, Logical, Physical

The implementation of a system may be described at different levels. To illustrate these levels, let us consider the system depicted in Figure 1.8, which computes

$$Z(t) = \sum_{i=0}^{t} X(i)$$

At the **module level,** the system consists of two registers and an adder (Figure 1.8*a*). At the **logical level**, as illustrated in Figure 1.8*b*, these modules are implemented with **gates** and **flip-flops** (elementary combinational and sequential components, respectively), and signals are binary (have two values, called 0 and 1). Components of these types are then connected to form networks that implement more complex functions (such as the registers and the adder).

Underneath the logical level is the **physical level,** in which the components are realized in some technology. For the most part, digital systems are electronic systems, although there are other technologies that are sometimes used, resulting in mechanical systems, hydraulic systems, optical systems, biochemical systems, etc.

In the electronic technology, as shown in Figure 1.8*c*, signals are electric signals (voltages, currents, charges) and the basic components are transistors (electrically controlled switches) and power supplies. Gates and flip-flops are formed by connecting several of these

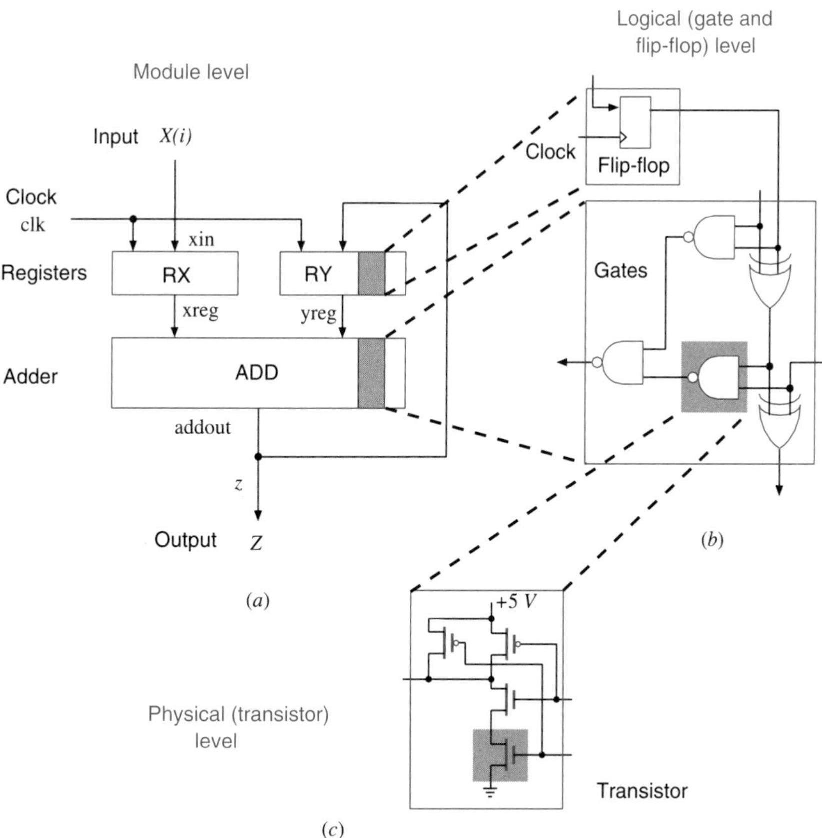

Figure 1.8 Digital system. (*a*) Module level. (*b*) Logical level. (*c*) Physical level.

transistors; networks of gates and flip-flops are realized by connecting the components with some conducting material.

It would be possible to study digital systems completely at the logical level. However, this could lead to systems that might not have the desired characteristics when actually built. Consequently, in the study at the logical level, it is necessary to incorporate characteristics that are abstracted from the physical level. For example, if we are designing a system that will be realized in the popular CMOS technology, we need to know what components are effectively realized in this technology (type of gates, number of inputs, speed, area, etc.). Such aspects are addressed in Chapter 3 of this book.

1.3 COMPUTER-AIDED DESIGN TOOLS

The design of digital systems is an involved and laborious process. Various computer-aided design (CAD) tools are available to help making this process efficient, timely, and economical. We now briefly overview the subject of CAD tools, which, in its details, is beyond the scope of this textbook.

CAD tools are intended to support all phases of digital design: (1) description (specification), (2) design (synthesis), including various optimizations to reduce cost and improve performance, and (3) verification (by simulation or formally) of the design with respect to its specification. These three phases typically require several passes to obtain a suitable implementation.

Description of digital systems is performed in a hierarchical manner, as discussed in the previous section. The "traditional" way to describe digital systems consists of a description of its structure through a graphical form (a drawing), as depicted in Figure 1.8. This description provides a **logic diagram** of the system at different levels, showing the modules and their interconnections. Such diagrams used to be drawn manually, but nowadays there are tools that allow generating and editing these drawings on a computer; this process is called **schematic capture** because the tool is used to capture the **schematic** description of the digital system. The process is supported by **libraries** of standard components, so a system can be "built" by using standard parts that are placed together to compose an implementation.

An alternative approach, which is becoming widely accepted and is replacing schematic capture, is the use of a **hardware-description language** (HDL). Several languages of this type have been proposed in the past, with the recent standardization of two of them: Verilog and VHDL. In this text, we use a subset of VHDL (which we call μVHDL) for the description of systems. Figure 1.9 gives a structural μVHDL description of the system depicted in Figure 1.8*a*, assuming that additional descriptions exist for the modules used in it (`BitReg8, Adder`); such lower level modules can be described in terms of their behavior rather than as the interconnection of even lower level components. Note that generating this description only requires a text editor in a computer, although there are tools that allow other types of input such as a drawing of the description at the top-most level.

We should note that these two description approaches can coexist; for example, there are tools that convert from a HDL description to a logic diagram, as well as tools that generate VHDL code from a schematic diagram.

Logic diagrams and HDL descriptions also provide information such as module types, signal names, wire type, and pin numbers, which are needed in later phases of a design.

```
USE WORK.ALL;
ENTITY sample_system IS
  PORT (xin: IN  BIT_VECTOR;
        z  : OUT BIT_VECTOR;
        clk: IN  BIT       );
END sample_system;

ARCHITECTURE structural OF sample_system IS
  SIGNAL xreg, yreg, addout: BIT_VECTOR(7 DOWNTO 0);

BEGIN
  RX: ENTITY BitReg8 PORT MAP(xin,xreg,clk);
  RY: ENTITY BitReg8 PORT MAP(addout,yreg,clk);
 ADD: ENTITY Adder   PORT MAP(xreg,yreg,addout);
      z <= addout;
END structural;
```

Figure 1.9 μVHDL-based description of a system.

Synthesis and optimization tools help in obtaining an implementation from a given description, and in improving some characteristics such as the number of modules and the network delays. These tools use transformation techniques such as the ones discussed in this text.

Simulation tools are used to verify the operation of the system. These tools use the description of the system to produce the values of the signals (internal and external) for a given input. The simulation is used to detect errors in a design and to determine characteristics, such as delay and power consumption, which are hard to obtain analytically. Evidently, the accuracy of the simulation depends on the accuracy of the model used to describe the components.

In addition to tools for the design at the logical level, there are others for the physical implementation of chips and boards, such as for VLSI layout, printed-circuit board layout and routing, thermal and mechanical analysis of chips and boards, and so on.

1.4 FURTHER READINGS

The literature on digital systems, computers in particular, and their applications is readily available as books, technical magazines, and popular articles. For a comprehensive introduction to the basic aspects of computing systems (hardware, software, and applications) we suggest *The Mystical Machine*, by J. E. Savage, S. Magidson, and A. M. Stein, Addison-Wesley, Reading, MA, 1986. A popular book on background topics in electronics is *Intuitive Digital Computer Basics* by T. Fredericksen, McGraw-Hill, New York, 1988. For current reviews of the state-of-the-art in digital technologies, design tools, and applications, a good source is the January issue of *IEEE Spectrum*, published by the Institute of Electrical and Electronics Engineers, New York.

Chapter 2

Specification of Combinational Systems

In this chapter, we present and discuss

- The high-level and binary-level specifications.
- The representation of data elements (signal values) by binary variables (signals) and the standard codes for positive integers and characters.
- The representation by switching functions and switching expressions.
- The NOT, AND, OR, NOR, XOR, and XNOR switching functions and their representation. Gate symbols.
- The sum of products (SOP) and product of sums (POS) expressions.
- The transformation of switching expressions using the switching algebra.
- The use of various specification methods in some examples.
- The use of the μVHDL description language.

2.1 COMBINATIONAL SYSTEMS: DEFINITION AND SPECIFICATION LEVELS

A **combinational system** is a digital system in which the value of the output at any instant depends only on the value of the input at that same instant (and not on previous values). As depicted in Figure 2.1, this is expressed as

$$z(t) = F(x(t))$$

Because the function F is not time dependent, there is no need to have an explicit time dependency in the variables and we can write

$$z = F(x)$$

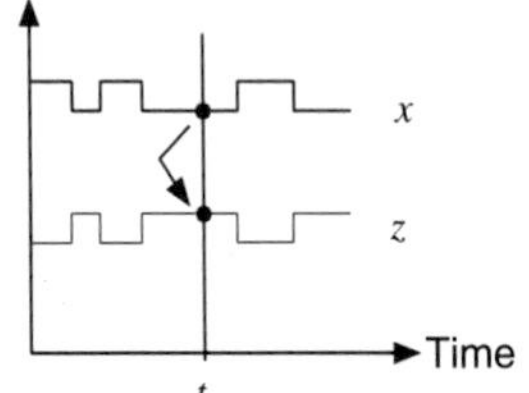

Figure 2.1 Combinational system.

Combinational systems are specified at two levels, as illustrated in Figure 2.2: **high level** and **binary level.** In a **high-level specification,** the system is described by a function on finite sets and represented by tables or expressions. In contrast, in a **binary-level specification** all variables are binary, that is, each variable has only two values, denoted 0 and 1. This is expressed by

$$\underline{z}_b = F_b(\underline{x}_b)$$

wherein $\underline{x}_b$ and $\underline{z}_b$ are **vectors** (ordered collections) of binary variables, and F_b is a **binary function.** Each binary variable is called a **bit** (**bi**nary digi**t**), and a vector of binary variables is called a **bit-vector.**

The correspondence between these two specification levels is given by the **coding** and **decoding** functions (see Figure 2.2). The coding function describes how each value of the input x is represented by a different combination of values of the bits in $\underline{x}_b$. Similarly, the decoding function describes the relationship among z and $\underline{z}_b$. For a variable of v values, a bit-vector of at least $\lceil log_2 v \rceil$ bits is needed to represent these v values. This is so because k binary variables (taken as a vector) have 2^k different values.

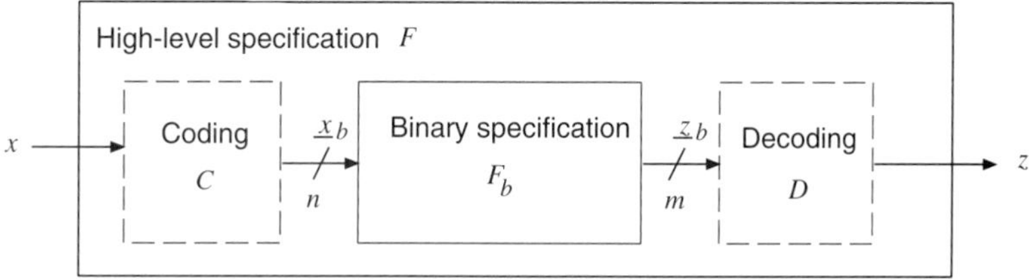

Figure 2.2 High-level and binary-level specification.

EXAMPLE 2.1

A combinational system has as input a decimal digit and as output the remainder when the input is divided by three. The high-level specification of this system is

Input: $x \in \{0, 1, 2, 3, 4, 5, 6, 7, 8, 9\}$
Output: $z \in \{0, 1, 2\}$

Function: F is described by the following table:

x	0	1	2	3	4	5	6	7	8	9
$z = F(x)$	0	1	2	0	1	2	0	1	2	0

or by the arithmetic expression

$$z = x \bmod 3$$

where $a \bmod b$ is the remainder obtained when dividing integer a by integer b.

To obtain a binary specification, the input x is encoded into the bit-vector $\underline{x}_b$ and the output z into the bit-vector $\underline{z}_b$. Moreover, the function F is mapped onto the function F_b.

Many alternative codes are possible. Because the number of values of x is ten, at least four binary variables are needed. We use the standard code discussed in the next sections, which in this case is as follows:

x	0	1	2	3	4	5	6	7	8	9
$\underline{x}_b = C(x)$	0000	0001	0010	0011	0100	0101	0110	0111	1000	1001

$\underline{z}_b$	00	01	10
$z = D(\underline{z}_b)$	0	1	2

The function F_b is obtained by replacing the values in the table of the high-level specification. The resulting binary specification is

Input: $\underline{x}_b = (x_3, x_2, x_1, x_0),\ x_i \in \{0, 1\}$
Output: $\underline{z}_b = (z_1, z_0),\ z_i \in \{0, 1\}$

Function: F_b is described by the following table:

$\underline{x}_b$	0000	0001	0010	0011	0100	0101	0110	0111	1000	1001
$\underline{z}_b = F_b(\underline{x}_b)$	00	01	10	00	01	10	00	01	10	00

■

As will be apparent throughout the text, a high-level specification is preferable whenever possible because it is easier to understand and use. The binary level is primarily used for implementation purposes because, due to technological considerations, the implementation of digital system uses binary variables.

In this chapter, we limit the discussion to the **functional specification** of a system. Other aspects of a system required for a complete specification, such as delay and size constraints, are discussed in following chapters.

2.2 HIGH-LEVEL SPECIFICATION OF COMBINATIONAL SYSTEMS

We address now in more detail the high-level specification of combinational systems. This specification consists of the following three components:

- The set of values for the input, called the **input set;**
- The set of values for the output, called the **output set;** and
- The specification of the **input-output function.**

Input and Output Sets

The finite input and output sets can be described by listing their elements or by some condition (property) that uniquely identifies the elements. For example,

{ UP, DOWN, LEFT, RIGHT, FIRE }

describes a set of five elements, whereas the conditional form

$$\{x \mid (5 \leq x \leq 10^4) \quad \text{and} \quad (x \bmod 3 = 0)\}$$

describes the finite set of integers between 5 and 10^4 that are multiples of 3.

In the most general case, the input and output sets contain arbitrary elements, such as in the preceding example. On the other hand, some frequently used sets correspond to the values taken by physical quantities (numerical values) and to representation of the written language (characters).

In many cases, it is convenient to define input and output sets consisting of **composite** elements, which are constructed as **structures** of primitive elements. The simplest, and most used of these structures, is the **vector** (or one-dimensional array), which is an ordered set of primitive elements. The number of elements is the **length** of the vector. A particular element within the vector is identified by an **index,** which is usually an integer in the range from 1 to 'length' (or from 0 to 'length − 1'). The elements in a vector are of the same type and have the same set of values. Depending on the type of the primitive element, we can have **integer-vectors** (also called digit-vectors), **character-vectors** (also called character strings), **set-vectors,** and **bit-vectors.** Examples of these vector types are given in Figure 2.3.

In general, the elements of a vector are written separated by a comma, as depicted in Figure 2.3; for simplicity, whenever it is clear from the context, vector elements may also be written without the commas, and the entire vector without the parenthesis, as illustrated for the bit-vector case in Figure 2.3.

Vector Type		Example
Digit	$\underline{x} = (x_{n-1}, x_{n-2}, \ldots, x_0)$ $x_i \in \{0, 1, 2, \ldots, 9\}$	$\underline{x} = (7, 0, 6, 3)$
Character	$\underline{c} = (c_{n-1}, c_{n-2}, \ldots, c_0)$ $c_i \in \{A, B, \ldots, Z\}$	$\underline{c} = (B, O, O, K)$
Set	$\underline{s} = (s_{n-1}, s_{n-2}, \ldots, s_0)$ $s_i \in \{\text{red, blue, white}\}$	$\underline{s} = (\text{red,blue,blue})$
Bit	$\underline{y} = (y_{n-1}, y_{n-2}, \ldots, y_0)$ $y_i \in \{0, 1\}$	$\underline{y} = (1, 1, 0, 1, 0, 0)$ $\underline{y} = 110100$

Figure 2.3 Examples of vectors.

Input-output Function

The input-output function can be defined in the following alternatives ways:

1. A **table,** since the input set is finite. This representation is useful only if the input set has few elements. For example,

x	z
A	65
B	66
C	67
D	68
E	69

2. An **arithmetic expression,** if the elements of the input and output sets are numeric values. For example,

$$z = 3x + 2y - 2$$

3. A **conditional expression,** if the function can be partitioned into subfunctions. Each of the subfunctions can be represented by any of the methods presented here. For example,

$$z = \begin{cases} a+b & \textbf{if} \quad c > d \\ a-b & \textbf{if} \quad c = d \\ 0 & \textbf{if} \quad c < d \end{cases}$$

4. A **logical expression** (a proposition), if the output set of the function is {T, F} (True, False). For example,

$$z = (\text{SWITCH1} = \text{CLOSED}) \textbf{ and } (\text{SWITCH2} = \text{OPEN})$$
$$\textbf{or } (\text{SWITCH3} = \text{CLOSED})$$

5. A **composition of simpler functions.** The primitive functions used in the composition should be defined by one of the other methods. For example, the maximum of four elements is obtained by the following composition of the primitive function GREATER:

$$\text{MAX}(v, w, x, y) = \text{GREATER}(v, \text{GREATER}(w, \text{GREATER}(x, y)))$$

in which

$$\text{GREATER}(a, b) = \begin{cases} a & \textbf{if} \quad a > b \\ b & \textbf{otherwise} \end{cases}$$

The choice among these representations depends on the type of system being described and on the use to be given to the representation. In general, one should use the most expressive and compact representation which is compatible with the desired objective.

EXAMPLE 2.2

A combinational system has as input a string (vector) of four characters, a single character, and an integer with range from 0 to 3. The output also consists of a string of four characters. The system performs character replacement. A high-level description is

Inputs: $\underline{x} = (x_3, x_2, x_1, x_0),\ x_i \in \{\text{A,B}, \ldots, \text{Z,a,b}, \ldots, \text{z}\}$
$y \in \{\text{A,B}, \ldots, \text{Z,a,b}, \ldots, \text{z}\}$
$k \in \{0, 1, 2, 3\}$

Outputs: $\underline{z} = (z_3, z_2, z_1, z_0),\ z_i \in \{\text{A,B}, \ldots, \text{Z,a,b}, \ldots, \text{z}\}$

Function:
$$z_j = \begin{cases} x_j & \textbf{if} \quad j \neq k \quad j \in \{0, 1, 2, 3\} \\ y & \textbf{if} \quad j = k \end{cases}$$

That is, the output of the system corresponds to the input string vector $\underline{x}$ whose k-th character is replaced by the character in y. An input-output pair is

Input: $\underline{x} = (\text{C,A,S,E})$, $y = \text{R}$, $k = 1$
Output: $\underline{z} = (\text{C,A,R,E})$

In this case, a tabular specification is impractical due to the large input set. ■

2.3 DATA REPRESENTATION AND CODING

To obtain a binary description of a combinational system it is necessary to represent the elements of the input and output sets by vectors of binary variables (bit-vectors) according to codes. These **codes** establish a correspondence between the high-level sets of values and those of the binary vectors.

Different codes can be used for a given set of elements. Some codes have **fixed length**, that is the same number of bits for all high-level elements, whereas other codes have **variable length**. A fixed-length code using bit-vectors of k bits can represent $n = 2^k$ elements. The following example illustrates some codes.

EXAMPLE 2.3

Consider a set with the following elements:

$$\{AL, BERT, DAVE, JERRY, LEN\}$$

Because the set has five elements, the bit-vector representing them using a fixed-length code must have at least three bits. Three possible codes are shown as follows

	Fixed Length		Variable Length
Element	Code 1	Code 2	Code 3
AL	000	0110	01
BERT	010	0101	001
DAVE	100	0011	0001
JERRY	110	1001	00001
LEN	111	1111	000001

Note that in this case we have written the bit-vectors without the commas separating the elements, and without the parentheses. ■

Some **standard codes** are used for the representation of characters and integers; they are of the fixed-length type. We now present some examples of such codes.

2.3.1 Representation of Characters

The early codes used for the representation of **alphanumeric characters** had five bits, so that only 32 characters could be represented. Currently, the standard codes have seven or eight bits per character, resulting in sets of 128 or 256 characters, respectively. Table 2.1 lists the representation of several upper-case letters, digits, and special signs for two standard codes. ASCII (American Standard Code for Information Interchange) is a seven-bit code representing a 128-character set. Its code words are extended to eight bits by inserting an extra bit at the left end. This extra bit, unless used for error detection, is set to 0. EBCDIC (Extended Binary-Coded Decimal Interchange Code) uses eight-bit code words to encode a 256-character set.

For example, the 6-character string "A CAB." is represented in 8-bit ASCII as follows:

A	blank	C	A	B	.
01000001	00100000	01000011	01000001	01000010	00101110

2.3.2 Representation of Positive Integers

We consider only positive integers for the time being (signed integers are discussed in Chapter 10). The representation of these integers is done at two levels (see Figure 2.4):

Table 2.1 Examples of alphanumeric codes

Character	Codes ASCII	EBCDIC
A	100 0001	1100 0001
B	100 0010	1100 0010
C	100 0011	1100 0011
⋮	⋮	⋮
Y	101 1001	1110 1000
Z	101 1010	1110 1001
0	011 0000	1111 0000
1	011 0001	1111 0001
2	011 0010	1111 0010
⋮	⋮	⋮
8	011 1000	1111 1000
9	011 1001	1111 1001
blank	010 0000	0100 0000
.	010 1110	0100 1011
(	010 1000	0100 1101
+	010 1011	0100 1110
⋮	⋮	⋮

Level 1: the integer is represented by a **digit-vector**, which is composed of **digits** that take values from a reduced set of integers.

Level 2: each of the digits is represented by a **bit-vector.**

Representation by Digit-vector

An integer is represented by a digit-vector using a **number system.** The most used one is the **radix-*r* conventional number system** (or just radix-r system). In this system, the digit-vector

$$\underline{x} = (x_{n-1}, x_{n-2}, \ldots, x_1, x_0)$$

represents the integer x such that

$$x = \sum_{i=0}^{n-1} x_i r^i$$

where the digit x_i takes values from the set $\{0, 1, \ldots, r-1\}$ and r is the radix. Each digit in this system is called a radix-r digit. The set of representable values is

$$0 \leq x \leq r^n - 1$$

<table>
<tr><td>Level 1: Integer (digit-vector)</td><td colspan="4">5</td><td colspan="3">6</td><td colspan="3">3</td><td colspan="3">0</td></tr>
<tr><td>Level 2: Bit-vector</td><td>1</td><td>0</td><td>1</td><td>1</td><td>1</td><td>0</td><td>0</td><td>1</td><td>1</td><td>0</td><td>0</td><td>0</td></tr>
</table>

Figure 2.4 Two-level representation of integers.

In the radix-2 case (also called a binary representation) each digit has two values, 0 and 1. For example, the digit-vector

$$\underline{x} = (1, 0, 0, 1, 0, 1)$$

represents the integer **thirty-seven** because

$$1 \times 2^5 + 0 \times 2^4 + 0 \times 2^3 + 1 \times 2^2 + 0 \times 2^1 + 1 \times 2^0 = (37)_{10}$$

where the subscript 10 indicates that it corresponds to the radix-10 representation (also called the decimal representation).

As another example, the digit-vector

$$\underline{x} = (1, 2, 1, 0)$$

represents the integer **one-hundred** in the radix-4 number system.

A particular digit-vector represents different integers for representations with different radices. For example, the digit-vector

$$\underline{x} = (7, 3, 2, 2)$$

represents the integer **seven-thousand-three-hundred-twenty-two** in the radix-10 system and the integer **three-thousand-seven-hundred-ninety-four** in the radix-8 system because

$$\begin{aligned} x_{10} &= 7 \times 10^3 + 3 \times 10^2 + 2 \times 10^1 + 2 = (7322)_{10} \\ x_8 &= 7 \times 8^3 + 3 \times 8^2 + 2 \times 8^1 + 2 \quad = (3794)_{10} \end{aligned}$$

Note that here we write the name of the integer in words to distinguish it from its many representations and that, by convention, the name is associated to the decimal representation. When no radix is specified, we assume a radix-10 or radix-2 representation and distinguish between the two by the context.

In digital systems, the most frequently used radices are of the form $r = 2^k$, because this simplifies the representation by a bit-vector and produces more efficient implementation of the operations. The representation is **binary** for $r = 2$, **quaternary** for $r = 4$, **octal** for $r = 8$, and **hexadecimal** for $r = 16$. Also used is $r = 10$ (**decimal**) due to the advantages for a human user in having decimal input and output.

Representation of Digits

In the second level of the representation, each of the digits in the digit-vector is represented by a bit-vector according to a **code**. We now consider these codes.

- For radix-2, the digit is directly represented by one bit, so no code is needed and there is no difference between the digit-vector and the bit-vector.
- For radix 2^k, a bit-vector of at least k bits is needed to represent a digit. The most used code is the **binary code** in which the digit is represented in the radix-2 number system. That is, the bit-vector $(d_{k-1}, d_{k-2}, \ldots, d_0)$ represents the digit value

  $$d = \sum_{i=0}^{k-1} d_i 2^i$$

  as depicted in Table 2.2. The digit-vector is then represented by the concatenation of the bit-vectors for each digit, as illustrated in Figure 2.5.

  Other ways of encoding the digits are used in some special cases. For example, the **Gray code** has the property that the bit-vectors corresponding to consecutive digit values differ only in one bit, as shown in Figure 2.6 for hexadecimal digits. This

Table 2.2 Binary codes for digits with $r = 2^k$ values

Digit Value (Symbol)	Binary $k=1$	Quaternary $k=2$	Octal $k=3$	Hexadecimal $k=4$
d	d_0	$d_1 d_0$	$d_2 d_1 d_0$	$d_3 d_2 d_1 d_0$
0	0	00	000	0000
1	1	01	001	0001
2		10	010	0010
3		11	011	0011
4			100	0100
5			101	0101
6			110	0110
7			111	0111
8				1000
9				1001
10 (A)				1010
11 (B)				1011
12 (C)				1100
13 (D)				1101
14 (E)				1110
15 (F)				1111

5			6			3			0		
1	0	1	1	1	0	0	1	1	0	0	0

Figure 2.5 Bit-vector representation using the binary code.

property leads to simpler and more reliable implementations of some systems such as analog-to-digital converters.

- For decimal digits, a minimum of four bits is needed to represent a digit. Several codes that use this minimum are described in Table 2.3. The first two are **weighted codes**

Digit	Gray code
0	0000
1	0001
2	0011
3	0010
4	0110
5	0111
6	0101
7	0100
8	1100
9	1101
10	1111
11	1110
12	1010
13	1011
14	1001
15	1000

(*a*)

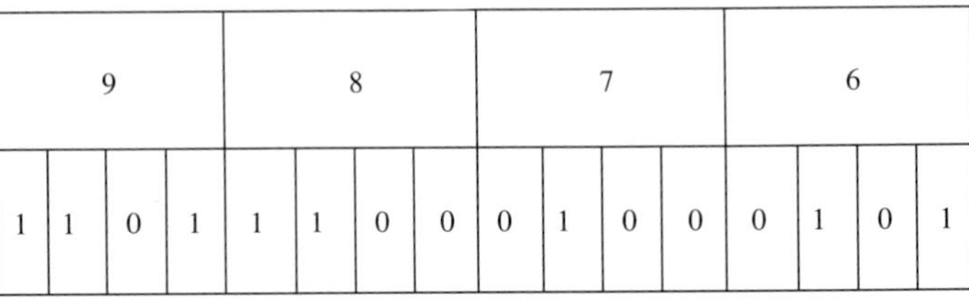

(*b*)

Figure 2.6 (*a*) Gray code. (*b*) Gray-code bit-vector representation of a digit-vector.

Table 2.3 Codes for decimal digits

Digit Value	BCD 8421	2421	Excess-3	2-Out-of-5
0	0000	0000	0011	00011
1	0001	0001	0100	11000
2	0010	0010	0101	10100
3	0011	0011	0110	01100
4	0100	0100	0111	10010
5	0101	1011	1000	01010
6	0110	1100	1001	00110
7	0111	1101	1010	10001
8	1000	1110	1011	01001
9	1001	1111	1100	00101

and the integers over the corresponding columns are the weights. A code is **weighted** when the digit value is obtained as

$$d = \sum_{i=0}^{k-1} d_i w_i$$

where the w_i's are the **weights** and k is the number of bits. For the BCD (Binary-Coded-Decimal) code, the weights are 8,4,2,1 (and, therefore, is also called the 8-4-2-1 code). Because this is the same as for the hexadecimal code, some systems used for operations for the radix-16 representation can also be used for radix-10. This is one of the reasons for the popularity of the BCD code.

The 2-4-2-1 code, which is also weighted, has the property that to obtain the complement of the digit with respect to 9 (i.e., the value $9 - d$) each bit of the representation is complemented with respect to 1 $(1 - d_i)$. This simple complementation is useful when performing operations such as subtraction.

The Excess-3 code is not weighted, but it has the same complementation property as the 2-4-2-1 code.

The 2-out-of-5 code uses five bits and represents each value by a bit-vector that has two 1's. The inefficiency of using five bits, instead of the minimum of four, is counterbalanced by the property that an error in a single bit can be detected; if a single 0(1) is changed to 1(0), the resulting vector does not represent a digit because it does not have two 1's.

Because the decimal representation requires 4 bits to represent each digit (10 values instead of the 16 values available), the decimal representation is less efficient than a radix-2^k representation. That is, for the same range of integers, more bits are needed in a decimal representation than in a radix-2^k representation. For example, the decimal representation of an integer ranging from 0 to $10^6 - 1$ requires 24 bits (4 bits per digit), whereas a binary representation requires only 20 bits because $(2^{20} - 1) > 10^6$.

2.4 BINARY SPECIFICATION OF COMBINATIONAL SYSTEMS

We now discuss the specification of combinational systems at the binary level. This level is obtained by applying coding functions to the inputs and outputs of a high-level specification. The resulting binary systems are implemented by combinational networks, as illustrated later in this chapter and discussed in detail in Chapters 4, 5, and 6.

2.4.1 Switching Functions

A combinational system with n (binary) inputs and m (binary) outputs (see Figure 2.7*a*) is represented by a set of m functions, each having as domain the set of binary n-tuples and as range the set $\{0, 1\}$. Example 2.1 illustrates the representation using two of these functions.

The foregoing functions are called **switching functions** and are central to the study of combinational systems. A switching function of n variables $f(x_{n-1}, \ldots, x_1, x_0)$ is a mapping from the set $\{0, 1\}^n$ (the set of binary n-tuples) into the set $\{0, 1\}$. This is illustrated for $n = 3$ in Figure 2.7*b*.

Note that 0 and 1 are generic names for the two elements of the set and do not necessarily represent the corresponding integers.

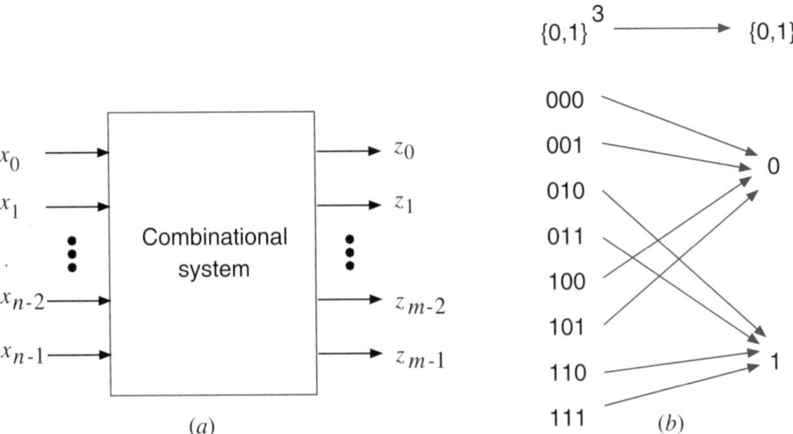

Figure 2.7 (*a*) Binary combinational system. (*b*) A switching function for $n = 3$.

Tabular Representation of Switching Functions

Like any function with a finite domain, a switching function can be represented by a table (which for switching functions is sometimes called a **truth table**). The table has one row for each value of the domain (input set), so that for n variables the table has 2^n rows.

To simplify the notation in the table, an integer j is associated with each binary n-tuple in such a way that the n-tuple is the binary representation of j (where the elements 0 and 1 correspond to the integers 0 and 1). That is, for the n-tuple $(x_{n-1}, \ldots, x_0)$, $x_i \in \{0, 1\}$, we have

$$j = \sum_{i=0}^{n-1} x_i 2^i$$

EXAMPLE 2.4

The following table depicts a switching function of three variables, both in the binary and in the simplified notation.

n-tuple notation		Simplified notation	
$x_2\,x_1\,x_0$	$f(x_2, x_1, x_0)$	j	$f(j)$
0 0 0	0	0	0
0 0 1	0	1	0
0 1 0	1	2	1
0 1 1	1	3	1
1 0 0	0	4	0
1 0 1	0	5	0
1 1 0	1	6	1
1 1 1	1	7	1

■

Due to the number of rows, the table representation is useful only for functions with a small number of variables. A more manageable representation is obtained when the table is converted into a two-dimensional array by partitioning the variables into two groups.

EXAMPLE 2.5

The following two-dimensional array represents a switching function of five variables.

	$x_2x_1x_0$							
x_4x_3	000	001	010	011	100	101	110	111
00	0	0	1	1	0	1	1	1
01	0	1	1	1	1	0	1	1
10	1	1	0	1	1	0	1	1
11	0	1	0	1	1	0	1	0

$f(x_4, x_3, x_2, x_1, x_0)$

■

One-set and Zero-set Representations

Because the range of the function is the set {0, 1}, it is redundant to specify the whole table; it is sufficient to list the set of values of j for which the function has value 1. This set is called the **one-set** of the function. Similarly the **zero-set** is defined as the set of values of j for which the function has value 0. The most compact of the two can be used; moreover, an arithmetic expression that represents the set is also possible in some cases.

For instance, the function in Example 2.4 can be represented by

$$f(x_2, x_1, x_0) = \textit{one-set}\ (2, 3, 6, 7)$$

or by

$$f(x_2, x_1, x_0) = \textit{zero-set}\ (0, 1, 4, 5)$$

An example of an arithmetic expression to describe a one-set is

$$f(x_9, \ldots, x_0) = \textit{one-set}\ \{j \mid (j+1) \bmod 3 = 0,\ 0 \leq j \leq 1023\}$$

This expression represents the function that has value 1 for $j = 2, 5, 8, \ldots, 1022$. It is a very compact representation of a function whose table has 1024 rows.

The one-set and zero-set are also referred to as **on-set** and **off-set**, respectively. Other useful representations for functions with large n are discussed later in this chapter.

Important Switching Functions

We now present some important switching functions. The four functions of one variable are defined in Table 2.4. The most interesting of them is the **complement** (or NOT) function, which has value 1 when the input has value 0, and value 0 when the input has value 1. The 16 switching functions of two variables are shown in Table 2.5; because of their importance, some of these functions have special names, as indicated in the table.

Table 2.4 Switching functions of one variable

x	f_0 0-CONSTANT (always 0)	f_1 IDENTITY (equal to x)	f_2 COMPLEMENT (NOT)	f_3 1-CONSTANT (always 1)
0	0	0	1	1
1	0	1	0	1

Table 2.5 Switching functions of two variables

	x_1x_0				
Function	00	01	10	11	Name
f_0	0	0	0	0	
f_1	0	0	0	1	AND
f_2	0	0	1	0	
f_3	0	0	1	1	
f_4	0	1	0	0	
f_5	0	1	0	1	
f_6	0	1	1	0	EXCLUSIVE-OR (XOR)
f_7	0	1	1	1	OR
f_8	1	0	0	0	NOR
f_9	1	0	0	1	EQUIVALENCE (XNOR)
f_{10}	1	0	1	0	
f_{11}	1	0	1	1	
f_{12}	1	1	0	0	
f_{13}	1	1	0	1	
f_{14}	1	1	1	0	NAND
f_{15}	1	1	1	1	

The two-variable functions named in Table 2.5 generalize as follows for n variables:

- the AND function of n variables has the value 1 only when all input variables are 1;
- the OR function of n variables has the value 1 when at least one input variable is 1;
- the XOR (Exclusive-OR) function of n variables has the value 1 when an odd number of input variables is 1. Its name for two variables comes from the fact that it has value 1 whenever one input has value 1 (but not both).
- The NAND and NOR functions are the complement of the AND and OR functions, respectively.
- The XNOR function is the complement of the XOR function, that is, it has value 1 when an even number of inputs is 1. The name of EQUIVALENCE for the two-variable case comes from the fact that it has value 1 when both inputs have the same value.

Incomplete Switching Functions

An **incomplete switching function** is a switching function that is undefined for some n-tuples of the domain. The value of the function for these n-tuples is called a **don't care** and is indicated by a – (a dash) in the tabular representation.[1] More formally, an incomplete switching function is a mapping from the set $\{0, 1\}^n$ into the set $\{0, 1, -\}$.

EXAMPLE 2.6

The following table describes an incomplete switching function:

$x\,y\,z$	f
0 0 0	0
0 0 1	1
0 1 0	0
0 1 1	–
1 0 0	1
1 0 1	0
1 1 0	–
1 1 1	1

■

In a similar fashion as for completely specified functions, incomplete functions can be described by the one-set, zero-set, and **dc-set.** Because the function now has three possible values, two of the three sets are required. For instance, function $f(x, y, z)$ in Example 2.6 can be represented by any of the following pairs of sets:

[*one-set* (1,4,7), *zero-set* (0,2,5)]
[*one-set* (1,4,7), *dc-set* (3,6)]
[*zero-set* (0,2,5), *dc-set* (3,6)]

Incomplete switching functions occur whenever some n-tuple value is not allowed at the input of a combinational system.

EXAMPLE 2.7

Consider a system whose input set is a decimal digit represented in the BCD code. That is, the input set consists of the bit-vectors $I = \{0000, 0001, \ldots, 1001\}$. The output z is equal to 1 if the input digit is odd and is 0 otherwise. The switching function corresponding to this system is incomplete because the values of the domain 1010, 1011, 1100, 1101, 1110, and 1111 do not represent any value of the input set and, therefore, never occur. ■

Composition of Switching Functions

Complicated switching functions can be represented by combining several elementary functions. Such combinations are called **compositions**. Because the values 0 and 1 in the range of the function are also the values of the components of the argument $\underline{x}$, a composition of switching functions is also a switching function. For example:

[1] Other symbols used in the literature for the **don't care** value are x, d, dc, and ϕ.

$$\begin{aligned}\text{AND}(x_3, x_2, x_1, x_0) &= \text{AND}(\text{AND}(x_3, x_2), \text{AND}(x_1, x_0))\\ \text{XOR}(x_1, x_0) &= \text{OR}(\text{AND}(\text{NOT}(x_0), x_1), \text{AND}(x_0, \text{NOT}(x_1)))\\ \text{MAJ}(x_3, x_2, x_1, x_0) &= \text{OR}(\text{AND}(x_3, x_2, x_1), \text{AND}(x_3, x_2, x_0),\\ &\quad \text{AND}(x_3, x_1, x_0), \text{AND}(x_2, x_1, x_0))\end{aligned}$$

The majority function MAJ has value 1 when more than half of the variables have value 1. Consequently, for four variables it can be described by the OR function of the AND functions of all combinations of three variables.

These identities can be checked by constructing the tables of the functions. Composition of switching functions is also the basis for the network implementation of combinational systems, as discussed in Chapter 4.

2.4.2 Switching Expressions

Switching expressions (also called **formulas** or **forms**) are used to represent completely specified switching functions in a way similar to that in which arithmetic expressions represent numerical functions. In structure these switching expressions are almost the same as arithmetic expressions, except for the inclusion of the additional operator COMPLEMENT. This is shown by the following rules for construction of a valid switching expression.

A **switching expression** (SE) of n variables is a string of symbols for the variables, the binary operators $+$ and $\cdot$, the unary operator $'$, and (). It is formed as follows:

1. The symbols 0 and 1 are SEs.
2. A symbol representing a binary variable is a SE.
3. If A and B are SEs, then
   - $(A)'$ is a SE. This is referred to as "A complement." An alternative symbol to denote A complement is $\overline{A}$.
   - $(A) + (B)$ is a SE. This is referred to as "A OR B"; it is also called "A plus B" or "sum" due to the similarity with the corresponding arithmetic symbol.
   - $(A) \cdot (B)$ is a SE. This is referred to as "A AND B"; it is also called "A times B" or "product" due to the similarity with the corresponding arithmetic symbol.

Some parentheses can be eliminated from a SE due to

- **precedence rules** for the operations: $'$ precedes $\cdot$ which precedes $+$;
- the associativity of $\cdot$ and of $+$; that is, $(a \cdot b) \cdot c$ can be written $a \cdot b \cdot c$, and $(a + b) + c$ can be written as $a + b + c$.

Also, the $\cdot$ can be omitted to simplify the notation. For example, the expression

$$((x_1)' \cdot x_2) + (x_3 + ((x_4 \cdot x_5) \cdot (x_6)')) \cdot x_7$$

can be written as

$$(x_1' x_2 + x_3 + x_4 x_5 x_6') x_7$$

To determine whether a given string is a switching expression, it is necessary to check whether it can be constructed by application of the rules. The following are well-formed switching expressions:

$$x_0 \qquad x_1 + x_2 x_3' \qquad 1 + 0(x + y)$$

whereas the following ones are not:

$$(x_1 + {}'x_2 +)x_3 \qquad \text{“This is a switching expression.”}$$

As we mentioned, the syntactic rules are very similar to those used for arithmetic expressions with $+$ and $\times$ (or $\cdot$). The only difference is that the symbol $'$ is also included in switching expressions. Because both arithmetic and switching expressions appear in the text, the symbol $+$ denotes addition, whereas **+** is used in switching expressions.

The preceding definition is syntactical: it gives rules for the construction of switching expressions but does not assign any meaning to the string. The semantics are obtained by relating a switching expression with a switching function. To do this, we introduce a particular Boolean algebra (see Appendix) called **switching algebra**, which is used to evaluate switching expressions.

Switching Algebra and Expression Evaluation

The **switching algebra** consists of two elements 0 and 1, and the operations **+**, $\cdot$, and $'$ which are called OR, AND, and NOT (COMPLEMENT), respectively. These operations are defined by the following tables, in which the columns correspond to the values of one operand, the rows to the values of the other, and the entries to the result of the operation:

+	0	1
0	0	1
1	1	1

·	0	1
0	0	0
1	0	1

′	
0	1
1	0

Note the correspondence between these operations and the switching functions OR, AND, and NOT.

The switching algebra is used to evaluate switching expressions. Each of the variables appearing in an expression is assigned a value from the set $\{0, 1\}$ and the evaluation is done using the definition of the operators in the switching algebra.

To assign values unambiguously, the variables appearing in the switching expression are ordered to form a vector. For example, $E(x, y, z) = xyz' + y'z$ is evaluated for assignment $(0, 1, 1)$ by making $x = 0$, $y = 1$, and $z = 1$. We call $E(0, 1, 1)$ the **value of the expression** E for assignment $(0, 1, 1)$.

EXAMPLE 2.8

Consider the switching expression

$$E(x_2, x_1, x_0) = x_2 + x_2'x_1 + x_1x_0'$$

The value of E for assignment $(1, 0, 1)$ is

$$E(1, 0, 1) = 1 + 1' \cdot 0 + 0 \cdot 1' = 1 + 0 + 0 = 1$$

■

Representing Switching Functions by Switching Expressions

When an expression is evaluated for all the possible assignments of values to the variables, the set of pairs (assignment, value) is a switching function. We say that the expression **represents** the resulting function.

EXAMPLE 2.9

The switching expression $E(x_2, x_1, x_0) = x_2 + x_2'x_1 + x_1x_0'$ represents the switching function f:

$x_2\ x_1\ x_0$	f
000	0
001	0
010	1
011	1
100	1
101	1
110	1
111	1

■

In particular, the following expressions represent the switching functions described in Table 2.5. These can be checked by comparing the function definition in Table 2.5 with the tables obtained by evaluating the expressions.

Function	2 variables	n variables
AND	x_1x_0	$x_{n-1}x_{n-2}\cdots x_0$
OR	$x_1 + x_0$	$x_{n-1} + x_{n-2} + \ldots + x_0$
XOR	$x_1x_0' + x_1'x_0$	
XNOR	$x_1'x_0' + x_1x_0$	
NAND	$(x_1x_0)'$	$(x_{n-1}x_{n-2}\cdots x_0)'$
NOR	$(x_1 + x_0)'$	$(x_{n-1} + x_{n-2} + \ldots + x_0)'$

Switching Functions and Gates

As discussed in Chapter 3, a **gate** is a module implementing a simple switching function. These gates are the basic building blocks used for implementing more complex combinational modules. Figure 2.8 shows the symbols for gates corresponding to the basic switching functions of one and two variables. The corresponding switching expressions are also given. The symbols generalize for more inputs, as illustrated for AND and OR gates in Figure 2.9.

Equivalent Switching Expressions

Two switching expressions are **equivalent** if they represent the same switching function. We write $E_1 = E_2$ to denote that E_1 and E_2 are equivalent.

EXAMPLE 2.10

The following two switching expressions are equivalent:

$$W = x_1x_0 + x_1'$$

$$Z = x_1' + x_0$$

Gate type	Symbol	Switching expression
NOT	x → z or x → z	$z = x'$
AND	x_1, x_0 → z	$z = x_1 x_0$
OR	x_1, x_0 → z	$z = x_1 + x_0$
NAND	x_1, x_0 → z	$z = (x_1 x_0)'$
NOR	x_1, x_0 → z	$z = (x_1 + x_0)'$
XOR	x_1, x_0 → z	$z = x_1 x_0' + x_1' x_0 = x_1 \oplus x_0$
XNOR	x_1, x_0 → z	$z = x_1' x_0' + x_1 x_0$

Figure 2.8 Gate symbols.

Gate type	Symbol	Switching expression
AND	x_{n-1}, x_{n-2}, …, x_0 → z	$z = x_{n-1} x_{n-2} \cdots x_0$
OR	x_{n-1}, x_{n-2}, …, x_0 → z	$z = x_{n-1} + x_{n-2} \cdots + x_0$

Figure 2.9 n-input AND and OR gate symbols.

The corresponding switching functions are

$x_1 x_0$	W	Z
00	1	1
01	1	1
10	0	0
11	1	1

■

Because of the definition of equivalence, the set of switching expressions is divided into classes and all switching expressions in a class represent the same function, as shown in Figure 2.10. Equivalence of expressions is important because it allows us to choose from a

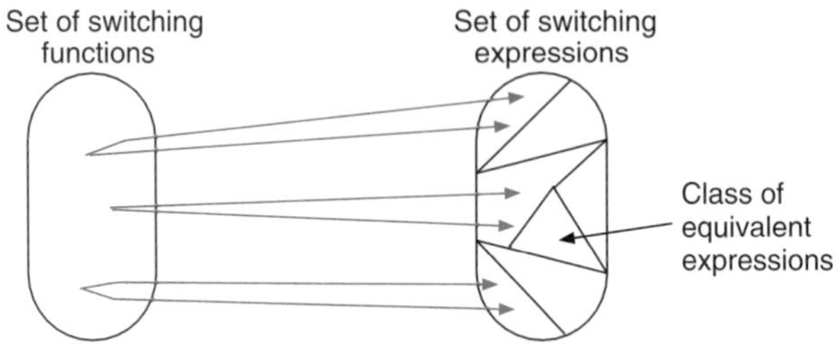

Figure 2.10 Correspondence between switching functions and switching expressions.

class the expression that is most suitable for a specification. In addition, because switching expressions are related to some implementations, it is possible to choose the expression that results in the best implementation.

Algebraic Method of Obtaining Equivalent Expressions

Because the switching algebra is a Boolean algebra, all Boolean algebra identities can be used to transform a switching expression without changing its value. Consequently, we can apply an algebraic method to obtain equivalent expressions. Table 2.6 lists the identities that are most useful for this purpose; proofs of these identities are provided in the Appendix.

Table 2.6 The principal identities of Boolean algebra

1.	$a + b = b + a$	$ab = ba$	Commutativity
2.	$a + (bc) = (a + b)(a + c)$	$a(b + c) = (ab) + (ac)$	Distributivity
3.	$a + (b + c) = (a + b) + c$	$a(bc) = (ab)c$	Associativity
	$= a + b + c$	$= abc$	
4.	$a + a = a$	$aa = a$	Idempotency
5.	$a + a' = 1$	$aa' = 0$	Complement
6.	$1 + a = 1$	$0a = 0$	
7.	$0 + a = a$	$1a = a$	Identity
8.	$(a')' = a$		Involution
9.	$a + ab = a$	$a(a + b) = a$	Absorption
10.	$a + a'b = a + b$	$a(a' + b) = ab$	Simplification
11.	$(a + b)' = a'b'$	$(ab)' = a' + b'$	DeMorgan's law

EXAMPLE 2.11

The following expressions are equivalent:

$$E_1(x_2, x_1, x_0) = x_2x_1 + x_2x_1' + x_2x_0$$

$$E_2(x_2, x_1, x_0) = x_2$$

Applying the transformations allowed in the Boolean algebra, we get

$$\begin{aligned}
x_2x_1 + x_2x_1' + x_2x_0 &= x_2(x_1 + x_1') + x_2x_0 && \text{using } ab + ac = a(b + c) \\
&= x_2 \cdot 1 + x_2x_0 && \text{using } a + a' = 1 \\
&= x_2(1 + x_0) && \text{using } ab + ac = a(b + c) \\
&= x_2 \cdot 1 && \text{using } 1 + a = 1 \\
&= x_2 && \text{using } a \cdot 1 = a
\end{aligned}$$

■

Sum of Products and Sum of Minterms

We now consider a special form of switching expression, called the **sum of products** (SOP) form. Moreover, we define **minterms** and show that each switching function is uniquely represented by a sum of minterms.

- A **literal** is either an uncomplemented or a complemented variable.
- A **product term** (P) is either a single literal, or the AND (product) of literals.
- A **sum of products** (SOP) is a switching expression consisting either of a single product term, or the OR (sum) of product terms.

These definitions are illustrated by the following examples:

Literals	x, y, z', x'
Product terms	$x_0, x_2x_1, x_3x_1x_0'$
Sum of products	$x_2' + x_3'x_1 + x_3'x_1'x_0$

The correspondence among sums of products and AND-OR gate networks is illustrated in Figure 2.11.

A **minterm** of n variables is a product term of n literals, in which each variable appears exactly once either in uncomplemented or complemented form. For example, for $n = 3$, $x_2x_1'x_0'$ and $x_2'x_1'x_0$ are minterms, whereas x_2x_1' and $x_1x_1x_1x_0$ are not.

There are 2^n minterms of n variables. These minterms are denoted $m_0, m_1, \ldots, m_j, \ldots, m_{2^n-1}$, where j is the integer whose binary representation is obtained when a 1 is associated with each uncomplemented variable and a 0 with each complemented variable in the minterm. For example, the minterm $x_3x_2'x_1'x_0$ is denoted m_9 because 1001 represents the integer 9. This representation is called the **m-notation**.

Each minterm has value 1 only for one assignment of the variables. This is so because the product has value 1 only when all literals have value 1 and this occurs only for one assignment, as all other assignments produce at least one literal with value 0. For example, consider the minterm

$$m_{11} = x_3x_2'x_1x_0$$

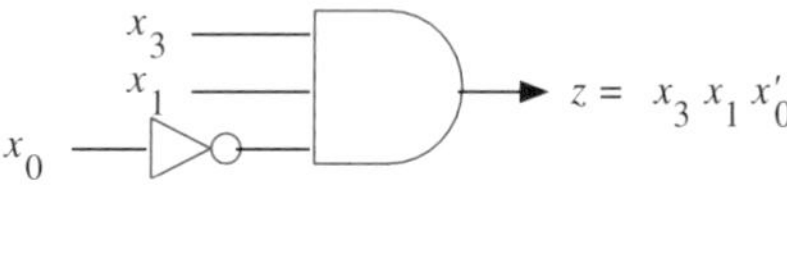

(*a*)

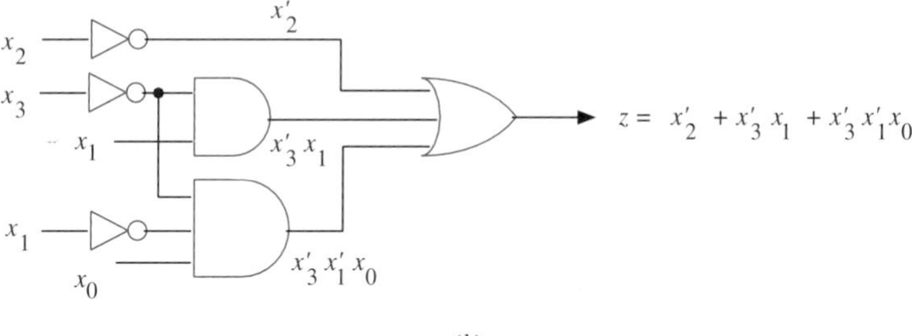

(*b*)

Figure 2.11 Sum of products and AND-OR gate network. (*a*) Product term. (*b*) Sum of products.

This has value 1 for the assignment $(x_3 = 1, x_2 = 0, x_1 = 1, x_0 = 1)$ and value 0 for all other assignments.

As a consequence, minterm m_j represents the switching function whose one-set has only element j; that is, the function has only one 1 in its table and this 1 is in row j. This is illustrated for $n = 3$ as follows:

	m_0	m_1	m_2	m_3	m_4	m_5	m_6	m_7
$x_2x_1x_0$	$x_2'x_1'x_0'$	$x_2'x_1'x_0$	$x_2'x_1x_0'$	$x_2'x_1x_0$	$x_2x_1'x_0'$	$x_2x_1'x_0$	$x_2x_1x_0'$	$x_2x_1x_0$
000	1	0	0	0	0	0	0	0
001	0	1	0	0	0	0	0	0
010	0	0	1	0	0	0	0	0
011	0	0	0	1	0	0	0	0
100	0	0	0	0	1	0	0	0
101	0	0	0	0	0	1	0	0
110	0	0	0	0	0	0	1	0
111	0	0	0	0	0	0	0	1

A **sum of minterms** is a sum of products in which all products are minterms and no minterm is repeated. For example,

$$E(x_2, x_1, x_0) = x_2'x_1'x_0 + x_2'x_1x_0' + x_2x_1x_0'$$

is a sum of minterms of three variables. This can be written as

$$E(x_2, x_1, x_0) = m_1 + m_2 + m_6$$

or in the compact notation

$$E(x_2, x_1, x_0) = \sum m(1, 2, 6)$$

Note that, because the order of the products does not change the value of the expression, we put the minterms in ascending order. A gate network for this expression is shown in Figure 2.12.

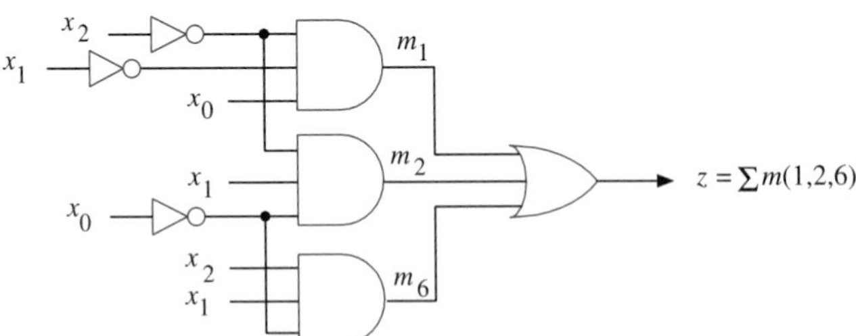

Figure 2.12 Gate network corresponding to $E(x_2, x_1, x_0) = \sum m(1, 2, 6)$.

Because each of the minterms has value 1 for one assignment, the sum of minterms has value 1 for as many assignments as minterms in the expression. In the foregoing example, the sum of minterms has value 1 for three assignments, that is, for $(x_2 = 0,\ x_1 = 0,\ x_0 = 1)$, for $(x_2 = 0,\ x_1 = 1,\ x_0 = 0)$, and for $(x_2 = 1,\ x_1 = 1,\ x_0 = 0)$. Consequently, this sum of minterms represents the function that has value 1 for those same assignments.

Any switching function can be represented by a sum of minterms. This expression is the sum of the minterms corresponding to the elements in the one-set representation of the function. That is, if

$$E(\underline{x}) = \sum m(\{j \mid f(j) = 1\})$$

then E represents f because

- the sum evaluates to 1 whenever one of the minterms evaluates to 1; and
- minterm m_j evaluates to 1 only when the assignment corresponds to $x = j$.

The minterms that appear in the sum of minterms that represents function f are called the minterms of f.

EXAMPLE 2.12

The sum of minterms that represents the following function

j	$x_2x_1x_0$	f
0	000	0
1	001	0
2	010	1
3	011	1
4	100	0
5	101	1
6	110	0
7	111	0

is

$$E = \sum m(2, 3, 5) = x_2'x_1x_0' + x_2'x_1x_0 + x_2x_1'x_0$$ ■

The sum of minterms that represents a function is unique, so it is a canonical representation; such an expression is also called a **canonical sum of products** (CSP).

Because every function is represented by a sum of minterms, **every switching expression has an equivalent sum of minterms.** The equivalent sum of minterms of a given expression can be obtained by first constructing the tabular representation of the function or by applying algebraic transformations as shown in the following example.

EXAMPLE 2.13

The sum of minterms equivalent to the expression

$$E(x_2, x_1, x_0) = x_2(x_1x_0)' + x_1x_0'$$

is obtained by application of algebraic identities as follows:

$$\begin{aligned}
E(x_2, x_1, x_0) &= x_2x_1' + x_2x_0' + x_1x_0' \\
&= x_2x_1'(x_0 + x_0') + x_2x_0'(x_1 + x_1') + x_1x_0'(x_2 + x_2') \\
&= x_2x_1'x_0 + x_2x_1'x_0' + x_2x_0'x_1 + x_2x_0'x_1' + x_1x_0'x_2 + x_1x_0'x_2' \\
&= x_2'x_1x_0' + x_2x_1'x_0' + x_2x_1'x_0 + x_2x_1x_0' \\
&= \sum m(2, 4, 5, 6)
\end{aligned}$$

Alternatively, the sum of minterms can be obtained by constructing the table of the function. This is done by evaluating the expression for all assignments, as follows:

	implies that the function is 1 for assignments
$x_1x_0' = 1$	010 and 110
$x_2(x_1x_0)' = 1$	100, 101, and 110

The corresponding tabular representation is

j	$f(j)$
0	0
1	0
2	1
3	0
4	1
5	1
6	1
7	0

Because the table of the function has value 1 for rows 2, 4, 5, and 6, the sum of minterms is $E(x_2, x_1, x_0) = \sum m(2, 4, 5, 6)$. ■

Product of sums and product of maxterms

In an analogous way to the sum of products and sum of minterms, we now define **product of sums** (POS) and **product of maxterms.** All the development in this part can be obtained from the discussion in the previous one by replacing product by sum (and vice versa), 0 by 1 (and vice versa), and uncomplemented by complemented (and vice versa). This is due to the duality properties of the operations AND and OR in Boolean algebras (see Appendix). We follow the same sequence as in the earlier discussion but with less explanation.

- A **sum term** (S) is either a literal or a sum of literals. For example, x_2, $(x_5 + x_6)$, and $(x_1 + x_2' + x_4)$ are sum terms.
- A **product of sums** (POS) is a switching expression consisting of a single sum term or several sum terms connected by the AND operator (product). An example is $x_0(x_3' + x_2)(x_3' + x_2' + x_1)$.

The correspondence between products of sums and OR-AND gate networks is illustrated in Figure 2.13.

A **maxterm** of n variables is a sum term in which each variable appears exactly once either in uncomplemented or complemented form. For example, for $n = 3$, $x_2' + x_1 + x_0$ and $x_2 + x_1' + x_0'$ are maxterms whereas $x_2 + x_1$ is not.

There are 2^n maxterms of n variables. These maxterms are denoted by $M_0, M_1, \ldots, M_j, \ldots, M_{2^n-1}$, where j is the integer whose binary representation is obtained when a 0 is associated with each uncomplemented variable and a 1 with each complemented variable. For example, the maxterm $(x_3 + x_2' + x_1' + x_0)$ is denoted M_6 because 0110 represents the integer six. This representation is called the ***M*-notation**. Note the difference with respect

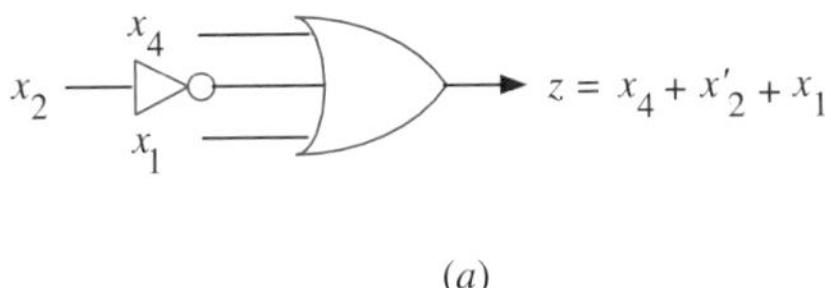

(*a*)

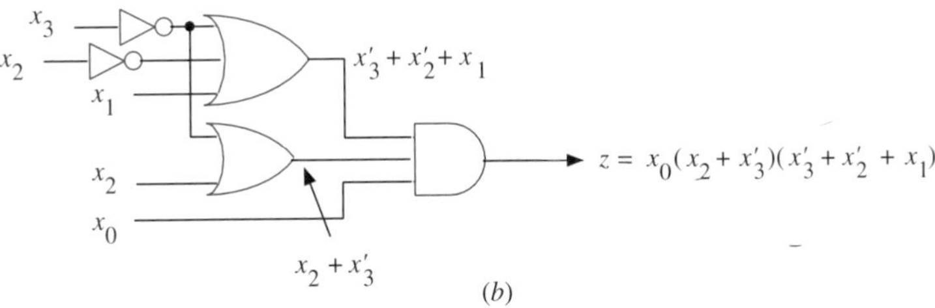

(*b*)

Figure 2.13 Product of sums and OR-AND gate network. (*a*) Sum term. (*b*) Product of sums.

to the notation for minterms, in which uncomplemented variables are associated with 1 and complemented with 0.

Each maxterm has value 0 only for one assignment of the variables. This is so because the sum has value 0 only when all literals have value 0. For example, the maxterm $M_{10} = x'_3 + x_2 + x'_1 + x_0$ has value 0 only for the assignment $x_3 = 1,\ x_2 = 0,\ x_1 = 1,\ x_0 = 0$.

Maxterm M_j represents the function whose zero-set contains only element j, that is, the function has only one 0 in its table and this 0 is in row j.

A **product of maxterms** is a product of sums in which each product is a maxterm and there are no repeated terms. The compact notation for a product of maxterms is

$$E(\underline{x}) = \prod M(\{j \mid f(j) = 0\})$$

EXAMPLE 2.14

The product of maxterms

$$E(x_2, x_1, x_0) = (x_2 + x_1 + x_0)(x'_2 + x_1 + x'_0)(x'_2 + x'_1 + x_0)$$

can also be denoted using M-notation by

$$\begin{aligned} E(x_2, x_1, x_0) &= M_0 \cdot M_5 \cdot M_6 \\ &= \prod M(0, 5, 6) \end{aligned}$$

A gate network for this expression is shown in Figure 2.14.

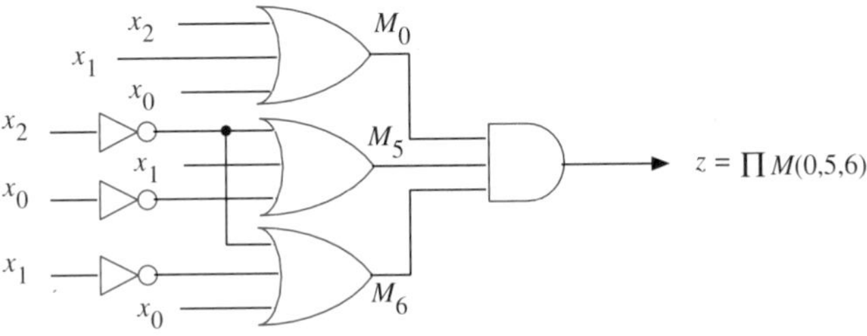

Figure 2.14 Gate network corresponding to $E(x_2, x_1, x_0) = \prod M(0, 5, 6)$.

■

A product of k maxterms represents a switching function that has value 0 for k assignments. The representation of a function by a product of maxterms is unique; this is a canonical representation also called a **canonical product of sums** (CPS). This representation is more compact than sum of minterms when the number of zeros is small.

EXAMPLE 2.15

The product of maxterms that represents the following function

j	$x_2x_1x_0$	f
0	000	0
1	001	1
2	010	1
3	011	0
4	100	1
5	101	1
6	110	1
7	111	0

is

$$E(x_2, x_1, x_0) = \prod M(0, 3, 7)$$
$$= (x_2 + x_1 + x_0)(x_2 + x_1' + x_0')(x_2' + x_1' + x_0')$$ ■

Switching Expressions for Incompletely Specified Functions

Incompletely specified switching functions can be represented by two expressions: one corresponding to the 1's (or 0's) of the function and the other to the don't cares. Similarly to the notation $\sum m$ and $\prod M$, we use the notation $\sum dc$ and $\prod dc$ for the don't care values.

EXAMPLE 2.16

The following incompletely specified function

$x_2x_1x_0$	$f(x_2, x_1, x_0)$
000	1
001	0
010	–
011	–
100	1
101	1
110	0
111	0

is described by $\sum m(0, 4, 5)$ and $\sum dc(2, 3)$. ■

Conversion among Canonical Forms

The conversion among canonical forms is straightforward; the sum of minterms corresponds to the one-set of the function, whereas the product of sums corresponds to the zero-set.

Therefore, obtaining one canonical form knowing the other consists of including the non-appearing indices. That is,

$$\sum m(\{j \mid f(j) = 1\}) = \prod M(\{j \mid f(j) = 0\})$$

EXAMPLE 2.17

The m-notation representing a function $f(x, y, z)$ is

$$\sum m(0, 4, 7)$$

Because the function has three variables, the equivalent expression in M-notation is

$$\prod M(1, 2, 3, 5, 6)$$

■

2.5 EXAMPLES OF SPECIFICATIONS

We now give three examples of binary specification of combinational systems, illustrating the various description methods discussed in the previous sections.

EXAMPLE 2.18

The high-level specification of a lock control is

Inputs: $CLASS \in \{0, 1, 2, 3\}$
$GROUP \in \{\text{A, B, C}\}$
Outputs: $LOCK \in \{\text{OPEN, CLOSED}\}$

$$\text{Function:} \quad LOCK = \begin{cases} \text{OPEN} & \textbf{if } CLASS \geq 2 \textbf{ and } GROUP = \text{A} \\ \text{CLOSED} & \textbf{otherwise} \end{cases}$$

This function can also be given by the following table:

	GROUP		
CLASS	A	B	C
0	CLOSED	CLOSED	CLOSED
1	CLOSED	CLOSED	CLOSED
2	OPEN	CLOSED	CLOSED
3	OPEN	CLOSED	CLOSED
		LOCK	

To obtain a binary description, we code the input and output. A possible coding is

LOCK	L	*GROUP*	G_1G_0	*CLASS*	C_1C_0
OPEN	1	A	11	0	11
CLOSED	0	B	10	1	10
		C	00	2	01
				3	00

Using these codes, the corresponding switching function is

	$G_1\ G_0$			
$C_1\ C_0$	00	01	10	11
00	0	–	0	1
01	0	–	0	1
10	0	–	0	0
11	0	–	0	0
		L		

and a switching expression for the output is

$$L = G_0 C_1'$$

■

EXAMPLE 2.19

A radix-4 digit-comparator module compares two radix-4 digits and produces one output with values G(reater), E(qual), and S(maller). The high-level specification is

Inputs: $x, y \in \{0, 1, 2, 3\}$
Output: $z \in \{\text{G, E, S}\}$

$$\text{Function:} \quad z = \begin{cases} \text{G} & \textbf{if } x > y \\ \text{E} & \textbf{if } x = y \\ \text{S} & \textbf{if } x < y \end{cases}$$

The tabular description of this function is

	y			
x	0	1	2	3
0	E	S	S	S
1	G	E	S	S
2	G	G	E	S
3	G	G	G	E
		z		

To obtain a binary description we have to code the input and output values on bit-vectors. As discussed in Section 2.3, the most used code is the binary code in which the radix-4 digit is represented by the corresponding radix-2 bit-vector. That is,

$$x = 2x_1 + x_0 \quad \text{and} \quad y = 2y_1 + y_0$$

where (x_1, x_0) and (y_1, y_0) are the bit-vectors representing x and y, respectively.

The three-valued output requires at least two binary variables. To simplify the binary description, we use three binary variables and the following code:

z	$z_2\ z_1\ z_0$
G	100
E	010
S	001

The resulting binary system can be described by the following logical expressions:

$$z_2 = \begin{cases} 1 & \textbf{if } x_1 > y_1 \textbf{ or } (x_1 = y_1 \textbf{ and } x_0 > y_0) \\ 0 & \textbf{otherwise} \end{cases}$$

$$z_1 = \begin{cases} 1 & \textbf{if } x_1 = y_1 \textbf{ and } x_0 = y_0 \\ 0 & \textbf{otherwise} \end{cases}$$

$$z_0 = \begin{cases} 1 & \textbf{if } x_1 < y_1 \textbf{ or } (x_1 = y_1 \textbf{ and } x_0 < y_0) \\ 0 & \textbf{otherwise} \end{cases}$$

From these logical expressions, we can obtain the switching functions described by the following table:

	$y_1\ y_0$			
$x_1\ x_0$	00	01	10	11
00	010	001	001	001
01	100	010	001	001
10	100	100	010	001
11	100	100	100	010
	$z_2\ z_1\ z_0$			

The sum of minterms are described in m-notation by

$$z_2(x_1, x_0, y_1, y_0) = \sum m(4, 8, 9, 12, 13, 14)$$

$$z_1(x_1, x_0, y_1, y_0) = \sum m(0, 5, 10, 15)$$

$$z_0(x_1, x_0, y_1, y_0) = \sum m(1, 2, 3, 6, 7, 11)$$

■

EXAMPLE 2.20

A combinational system has two 8-bit inputs, representing alphanumeric characters, and a binary output. The system performs matching of the input characters. The high-level specification is

Inputs: $x, y \in \{A, B, \ldots, Z, a, b, \ldots, z, 0, 1, \ldots, 9, *, +, /, \ldots\}$
Outputs: $z \in \{0, 1\}$

Function: $z = \begin{cases} 1 & \textbf{if } x = y \\ 0 & \textbf{if } x \neq y \end{cases}$

The input bit-vectors are $\underline{x} = (x_7, \ldots, x_0)$ and $\underline{y} = (y_7, \ldots, y_0)$. Because there are 16 binary input variables, a table is impractical. We can obtain a switching expression directly by noticing that the output is 1 only when the two bit-vectors are bitwise equal. That is,

$$z = (x_7y_7 + x_7'y_7')(x_6y_6 + x_6'y_6')(\cdots)(x_0y_0 + x_0'y_0')$$

■

2.6 SPECIFICATION USING μVHDL

As stated earlier, the specification of a combinational system consists of the input set, output set, and the input-output function. In principle, any way of describing these components is acceptable. However, to be able to communicate these specifications, and to have a version that can be used to simulate the behavior of the system in a computer, some standard languages have been developed. These languages are called **hardware description languages** (HDL) because they are used to describe hardware.

Several hardware description languages have been proposed in the past, with capabilities to describe the specification and implementation of hardware systems at different levels. Two such languages — VHDL and Verilog — have recently become standards; both are widely used nowadays. These languages have become popular among designers, vendors, and developers as a medium to describe and communicate hardware designs for the purposes of specification, simulation, description of implementation, and synthesis (automatic realization); with them, a single notation is used throughout the entire design process, including simulation driven by the HDL-based description.

Languages such as VHDL or Verilog support **behavioral** specifications at a high level as well as at the binary level. In other words, using the language one can first provide a simple specification of the system (its overall behavior), which can be refined later. Moreover, at any time the specification is "complete" in the sense that it can be used for other phases in the design process (such as simulation).

In this section we present specifications using the language μVHDL (a subset of VHDL), which has been derived with the objective of providing a simpler language suitable as an introduction to the field, but which follows the features of its ancestor. Indeed, the μVHDL descriptions used in this book are suitable for compiling them using a VHDL compiler. Only some VHDL statements and constructs are available in μVHDL; VHDL features not used in this book are not included in μVHDL (i.e., VHDL has capabilities that we will not explore). Some elements of VHDL are quite intuitive and can be inferred from programming languages, so we use them without formal introduction. We focus first on the elements of the language required for behavioral specification of combinational systems. (Additional features of the language suited only for describing the implementations are given later.)

Elements of μVHDL

Modules: Entity and Architecture

The basic component described in μVHDL is a **module** (see Figure 2.15), which is specified by:

- inputs;
- outputs;
- function; and
- delays.

Because for the time being we are concerned only with the functional specification, we omit the delays.

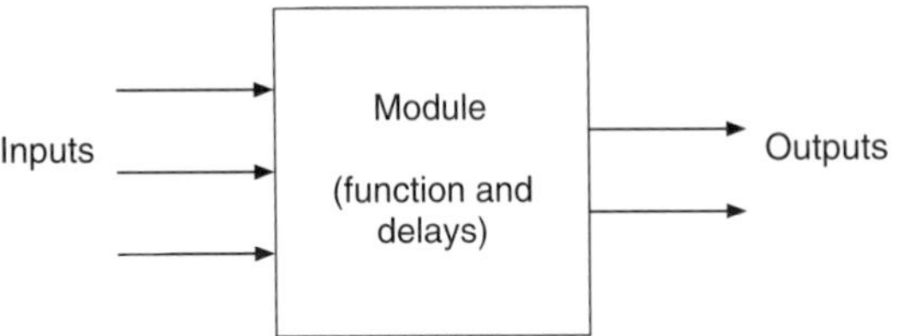

Figure 2.15 Basic component in μVHDL.

The inputs and outputs are specified by a design `ENTITY`, composed by an **entity name** and an **entity declaration**, in which each input and each output is represented by a `PORT` declaration (we use uppercase characters to represent reserved words in the language, although the language is case insensitive). An example of an entity is as follows:

```
ENTITY adder IS
  PORT(x,y: IN  BIT;
       z  : OUT BIT);
END adder;
```

This declaration specifies a design entity named `adder`, which has two input ports (`x,y`) and one output port (`z`), all of them of type `BIT` (the concept of **type** is described later in this section). Input ports are identified by the keyword `IN`, whereas output ports are identified by the keyword `OUT`.

The function of the module is described by `ARCHITECTURE` bodies; a given module may have several architecture bodies, which may correspond to different levels of detail in the description, or to alternative versions of the module. There are two types of architecture bodies:

Behavioral architecture: the functionality of the entire module is described as a whole, using high-level expressions and language constructs. The **behavior** of the module is described as a **process** whose body consists of a set of **statements**.

Structural architecture: the module is described as the interconnection of simpler modules (hierarchical description); the simpler modules are described independently. The functionality of the higher-level modules is determined from the behavior of the simpler modules and their interconnection.

We consider now only behavioral architectures; structural architectures are discussed in the chapters on implementation.

The overall format of a behavioral architecture body is

```
ARCHITECTURE arch_name OF module_name IS
BEGIN
  PROCESS
      process_declarations
    BEGIN
      behavioral_description_statements;
    END PROCESS;
END arch_name;
```

This declaration specifies an architecture named `arch_name` of a module (design entity) called `module_name`; `arch_name` is an arbitrary name, whereas module_name is the name given to the module in the `ENTITY` declaration. The architecture consists of a `PROCESS`, which contains the statements describing the behavior of the module.

Before addressing the details of μVHDL, let us illustrate the language with an example; the specific language constructs used in this example, as well as general concepts regarding the language, are described later in this section.

EXAMPLE 2.21

Specification of a Radix-4 Digit-comparator

Let us consider the behavioral description of the radix-4 digit-comparator specified in Example 2.19, both at a high-level as well as at the binary level.

High-level Specification

The following entity declaration describes a radix-4 digit-comparator module which consists of two input ports of type Radix4 (integers in the range 0 to 3), as well as an output port of type MagnComp={G,E,S}:

```
USE WORK.BitDefs_pkg.ALL;          -- package contains definition of
                                   -- Radix4 and MagnComp
ENTITY radix4_comp IS
  PORT(x,y : IN  Radix4;           -- inputs
       z   : OUT MagnComp);        -- outputs
END radix4_comp;
```

A corresponding architecture body is

```
ARCHITECTURE behavioral OF radix4_comp IS
BEGIN
  PROCESS (x,y)
  BEGIN
    IF    (x > y) THEN z <= G;
    ELSIF (x = y) THEN z <= E;
    ELSE               z <= S;
    END IF;
  END PROCESS;
END behavioral;
```

This architecture body contains a **signal assignment statement** to z, which depends on the result from comparing the input operands.

Binary Specification

Let us consider now a binary behavioral description of the radix-4 digit-comparator. At this level, the operands and result are represented in the radix-2 number system by bit-vectors. In such a case, the entity declaration indicates that ports are bit-vectors, as follows:

```
USE WORK.BitDefs_pkg.ALL;          -- package contains definition of
                                   -- BitVector2 and BitVector3
ENTITY binradix4_comp IS
  PORT(x,y : IN  BitVector2;       -- inputs
       z   : OUT BitVector3);      -- outputs
END binradix4_comp;
```

The corresponding architecture body consists of a process whose statements operate on bit-vectors, as follows:

```
ARCHITECTURE behavioral OF binradix4_comp IS
BEGIN
  PROCESS (x,y)
  BEGIN
    IF    (x > y) THEN z <= "100";
    ELSIF (x = y) THEN z <= "010";
    ELSE               z <= "001";
    END IF;
  END PROCESS;
END behavioral;
```

The behavior of the module is described by a conditional statement that compares the value of the input signals, and assigns the corresponding code of the result to the output signal. ■

The descriptions given above use user-defined elements (constructs which are not part of μVHDL), such as BitVector2; these elements must be specified separately through a construct called PACKAGE, as follows:

```
-- ---------------------------------------------------------------
-- PACKAGE
-- ---------------------------------------------------------------
PACKAGE BitDefs_pkg IS
-- ---------------------------------------------------------------
-- Subtypes
-- ---------------------------------------------------------------
   SUBTYPE  BitVector   IS BIT_VECTOR;
   SUBTYPE  BitVector2  IS BIT_VECTOR( 1 DOWNTO 0);
   SUBTYPE  BitVector3  IS BIT_VECTOR( 2 DOWNTO 0);

   SUBTYPE  Radix4      IS INTEGER RANGE 0 TO 3;
   TYPE     MagnComp    IS (G,E,S);

END BitDefs_pkg;

-- ---------------------------------------------------------------
-- PACKAGE BODY
-- ---------------------------------------------------------------
PACKAGE BODY BitDefs_pkg IS
-- ---------------------------------------------------------------
END BitDefs_pkg;
-- ---------------------------------------------------------------
```

With these examples in mind, let us now address the features of the language. As already stated, in this chapter we only describe features required for the specification of combinational systems; features used for other types of descriptions are introduced in later chapters, as needed.

Signals, Variables, and Constants

Values are represented in μVHDL by SIGNALS, which are time functions. Ports are the physical channels through which input/output values are transmitted into and out from a module; input and output signals are attached to the input and output ports, respectively. Input signals are "used" inside the modules, whereas output signals are "assigned" values inside the modules. In particular,

- a signal is used in a behavioral architecture when it appears in the right-hand side of an expression;
- a behavioral architecture assigns values to an output signal through a **signal assignment statement** denoted by the symbol <=, such as

```
x <= '1';      -- binary value 1 is assigned to x
x <= u + y;    -- value of (u+y) is assigned to x
```

(the symbol "--" denotes the start of a comment which ends at the end of the line)

VARIABLEs are used to aid in the description of a module, such as in the decomposition of a complex function into steps using variables to keep intermediate results. For example, a function that counts the number of bits set to 1 in a bit-vector can keep the partial count in a variable as a loop traverses the vector. Variables receive values by **variable assignments**, denoted by the symbol ":=". An example is

```
a := x + y;
```

In addition to signals and variables, μVHDL descriptions may use CONSTANTs, which maintain a constant value.

Data Types and Object Declarations

The values of signals, variables, and constants can correspond to different data TYPEs, such as INTEGER, REAL, BIT, and nonnumeric sets. Data types are characterized by a name, a set of values, and a set of operations. μVHDL has the following classes of types:

scalar types: includes integer, floating point, types defined by an enumeration of their values, and physical types; and

composite types: these correspond to arrays of scalar types.

Predefined μVHDL scalar types are

```
TYPE INTEGER   IS RANGE -2,147,483,647 TO 2,147,483,647;
                                  -- -(2**31 - 1)  to  2**31 - 1
TYPE REAL      IS RANGE -1.0E+38 TO 1.0E+38;
TYPE BOOLEAN   IS (FALSE, TRUE);
TYPE BIT       IS ('0', '1');
TYPE CHARACTER IS (....,'A','B','C',...,'a','b','c',...'0','1',...)
TYPE TIME      IS RANGE 0 TO 2,147,483,647
                  UNITS ps; ns; us; sec; min; hr; END UNITS;
```

Note that type BIT is defined as the enumeration of characters '0' and '1', not the integers with the same name. The predefined type CHARACTER corresponds to the enumeration of all the characters available in the ASCII set. Individual characters are enclosed in single quotes, whereas a string of characters is enclosed in double quotes (i.e., 'a',"abc"). Values of type TIME must be specified in any of the units indicated.

Predefined array types in μVHDL are

```
TYPE STRING     IS ARRAY(POSITIVE RANGE <>) OF CHARACTER;
TYPE BIT_VECTOR IS ARRAY(NATURAL  RANGE <>) OF BIT;
```

Note that the definition of type STRING and BIT_VECTOR do not specify the size of the corresponding array; this is known as an **unconstrained** array specification. The definition of a signal of this type must specify the range.

In addition to the predefined types, it is possible to define types (called user-defined types). Examples of user-defined enumerated types are

```
TYPE FivePrimes  IS (1,3,5,7,11);
TYPE Vowels      IS ('a','e','i',o','u');
TYPE Colors      IS (blue, green, red, yellow);
```

Examples of user-defined array types are

```
TYPE BitVector4 IS ARRAY (3 DOWNTO 0) OF BIT;
TYPE BitVector8 IS ARRAY (7 DOWNTO 0) OF BIT;
TYPE Memory     IS ARRAY(INTEGER RANGE <>) OF BitVector8;
```

A SUBTYPE is a subset of a type obtained by constraining its range; μVHDL predefined subtypes are

```
SUBTYPE NATURAL  IS INTEGER RANGE 0 TO 2,147,483,647;
SUBTYPE POSITIVE IS INTEGER RANGE 1 TO 2,147,483,647;
```

Examples of user-defined subtypes are

```
SUBTYPE ByteInt        IS INTEGER RANGE 0 TO 255;
SUBTYPE TComplByteInt  IS INTEGER RANGE -128 TO 127;
SUBTYPE LowerCase      IS CHARACTER RANGE 'a' TO 'z';
```

The data type of signals, variables, and constants are specified with **object declarations,** which also assign an initial value to the object; by default, integer objects are assigned the smallest value, whereas enumerated type objects are assigned the first value in the enumeration list. For example:

```
SIGNAL   clk         : BIT    ;
SIGNAL   m,n         : INTEGER;
SIGNAL   x_in        : BitVector4:= ('0','1','0','0');
SIGNAL   y_in        : BitVector4:= ("0101");
CONSTANT count_limit: INTEGER:= 20;
VARIABLE count       : INTEGER:= 1;
VARIABLE z           : BitVector8:= (1=>'1',3=>'1',others=>'0');
```

In these examples, signal `clk` is assigned the initial default value `'0'` and `m,n` are assigned the default value `-2,147,483,647`; all other objects have initial values assigned explicitly. In the case of `x_in, y_in`, the initial value of the elements of the arrays are indicated in left-to-right order, either as a set of characters (enclosed in single quotes) or as a string (enclosed in double quotes); on the other hand, in `z` the elements are given in arbitrary order.

Expressions

Expressions are built from data objects and operators. The operators must be defined for the type of the corresponding data objects, otherwise the expression is illegal. The result of an expression is a data object of the type generated by the expression, which can be assigned to a signal or variable of the same type. Examples are

```
SIGNAL   x,y,z: INTEGER;
VARIABLE a,b,c: BitVector4;

x + y + z     -- produces an INTEGER result
a OR b        -- produces a result of type BitVector4,
              -- according to the definition of the
              -- operator OR for this type
```

```
func(x)         -- produces a result of the type defined by
                -- operator func for operand of type INTEGER
a op x          -- produces a result of the type defined by
                -- operator op for operands of type BitVector4
                -- and INTEGER; illegal if such a definition does
                -- not exist
```

Basic arithmetic operators (such as +, -, *, /) are defined for the different data types, including operations on digit-vectors. These operators accept operands of a given type and produce a result also of the same type. For example, the operator + is predefined for operands of type BIT_VECTOR, in which case these operands (and the result) are interpreted as the radix-2 representation of integers.

The basic logic operations (such as AND,OR,XOR) are used with operands of type BIT or BOOLEAN; bit operands are normally used for binary (hardware related) expressions, whereas Boolean operands are used for logic (language related) expressions. These operators also accept operands of type BIT_VECTOR, in which case the operation is performed on the corresponding bits of the operands. These are referred as **bitwise** operations. For example,

```
VARIABLE a: BitVector4 := ('0','1','1','1');
VARIABLE b: BitVector4 := ('1','1','0','0');
VARIABLE c: BitVector4;

c := a AND b;   -- produces c:=('0','1','0','0')
```

Subtypes use the operators defined for the corresponding type, and generate a result of the type. For example, if x,y are signals of subtype ByteInt, then x+y produces a result of type INTEGER; such a result may also be of subtype ByteInt if it fulfills the corresponding range constraint.

Control Flow Statements

Control flow statements used to describe the behavior of modules include

- IF statement, such as

```
IF (clk = '1') AND (x = '1') THEN
    z := a OR b;
ELSIF (clk = '0') THEN
    z := '0';
END IF;
```

- CASE statement, such as

```
CASE Data IS
  WHEN "000"  => k := 1;
  WHEN "111"  => k := 0;
  WHEN others => k := k+1;
END CASE;
```

  in which the different values of Data appear preceded by the keyword WHEN; the default case is indicated by the line WHEN others, which, if it exists, must be the last entry of the CASE statement.

- FOR LOOP statement, such as

```
FOR i IN 1 TO 20 LOOP
  count := count + a(i);
END LOOP;

FOR i IN 20 DOWNTO 1 LOOP
  count := count + a(i);
END LOOP;
```

- `WHILE LOOP` statement, such as

```
WHILE (a = b) LOOP
  i:= i+1;
  a:= x(i);
  b:= y(i);
END LOOP;
```

The execution of loop statements can be interrupted with statements `NEXT` and `EXIT`. `NEXT` forces execution to continue with the next iteration of a loop, whereas `EXIT` forces execution to continue at the statement that follows the loop.

Functions and Procedures

Functions and procedures are used to encapsulate specific functionalities, in the same way as in programming languages. These constructs are useful to represent specific hardware functions that are part of a module, or to contain some functionality needed by the description. Functions return a single result, whereas procedures may return more than one result. The format of these constructs is:

```
FUNCTION func_name(parameter_list)
       RETURN return_type
IS
  function_declarations;
BEGIN
  function_statements;
  RETURN(return_variable);
END FUNCTION;

PROCEDURE proc_name(parameter_list)
IS
  procedure_declarations;
BEGIN
  procedure_statements;
END PROCEDURE;
```

The declarations section of these statements defines types, variables and constants used by the function or procedure; the statements section contains the statements that describe the corresponding behavior. Functions contain a `RETURN` statement with a single argument of the type specified in the function header. The following example illustrates these features.

EXAMPLE 2.22

The structure of functions and procedures in μVHDL, as well as their use, is as follows:

```
USE WORK.BitDefs_pkg.ALL;

FUNCTION compare(x,y: Radix4)
```

```
    RETURN MagnComp;
IS
  VARIABLE t: MagnComp;
BEGIN
  IF    (x > y) THEN t:= G;
  ELSIF (x = y) THEN t:= E;
  ELSE               t:= S;
  END IF;
  RETURN(t);
END compare;

PROCEDURE comp_two(w,x,y: IN  Radix4;
                   z1,z2: OUT MagnComp)
IS
BEGIN
  IF    (w > x) THEN z1 := G;
  ELSIF (w = x) THEN z1 := E;
  ELSE               z1 := S;
  END IF;

  IF    (w > y) THEN z2 := G;
  ELSIF (w = y) THEN z2 := E;
  ELSE               z2 := S;
  END IF;
END comp_two;
```

A function is used as part of an expression, whereas a procedure is a statement by itself. For example,

```
res := compare(a,b);
comp_two(a,b,c,r1,r2);
```

■

Processes

The PROCESS statement is used to encapsulate the behavior of a module; an architecture body containing the behavioral description of a module may have only one process which embodies its entire functionality, or may have multiple processes. In this chapter, we consider only the case of a single PROCESS in an architecture body.

The format of the PROCESS statement is illustrated in the following example.

EXAMPLE 2.23

The following architecture body describes the PROCESS statement:

```
ENTITY recode IS
  PORT(x_in   : IN   INTEGER RANGE  0 TO 9;
       z0_out : OUT  INTEGER RANGE -5 TO 5;
       z1_out : OUT  BIT);
END recode;

ARCHITECTURE behavioral OF recode IS
BEGIN
  PROCESS (x_in)
  -- process declarations
    VARIABLE d_0 : INTEGER;
    VARIABLE d_1 : BIT;
  BEGIN
```

```
  -- process body
    IF (x_in < 5) THEN
      d_0 := x_in;
      d_1 := '0';
    ELSE                  -- x_in >=  5
      d_0 := x_in - 10;
      d_1 := '1';
    END IF;
    z0_out <= d_0;
    z1_out <= d_1;
  END PROCESS;
END behavioral;
```

■

The action of a process consists of the interpretation of its statements whenever any of the signals listed next to the `PROCESS` are assigned a value. The statements are then interpreted sequentially. The declarations section defines types, variables, and constants used by the `PROCESS`. In the foregoing example, the process is interpreted each time the input signal `x_in` is assigned a value; when that occurs, the statements in the body of the process are interpreted, assigning values to output signals `z0_out, z1_out`.

Packages and Libraries

μVHDL-based descriptions are VHDL compliant, so they can be used in a VHDL environment to simulate the behavior of the system. In addition to the language constructs presented earlier, μVHDL defines some other facilities that are helpful for simulation. Such facilities are described now.

A `PACKAGE` is a collection of elements, such as data types, subprograms, and constants. A package can be regarded as a collection of tools used to build modules. Packages allow sharing (globally) these tools among different modules. A package consists of two parts:

Package declaration, which defines the interface for the package (in a similar way to an entity defining the interface for a module); and

Package body, which specifies the details of the package (in a similar way to an architecture body defining the behavior of a module).

Subprograms declared in a package declaration must have a corresponding subprogram body in the package body. The package body may contain local declarations that are used only within the package body; these declarations are not visible outside the package.

A μVHDL-based simulation environment uses a **library** called `WORK` to store representations of facilities that can be used by the modules. For example, the elements of a `PACKAGE` are placed in library `WORK`, so they become part of the library. The components of library `WORK` are visible to any module that **uses** the library through a `USE` clause. In a system with multiple modules, the `USE` clause must precede the entity declaration of each module; in other words, the scope of the `USE` clause extends only to the end of the entity that follows the clause.

EXAMPLE 2.24

The following illustrates a package declaration and package body:

```
PACKAGE sample_pkg IS
  CONSTANT max : INTEGER := 255 ;

  FUNCTION check_max(a: INTEGER) RETURN BIT;
END sample_pkg;
```

```
PACKAGE BODY sample_pkg IS
  FUNCTION check_max(a: INTEGER)
    RETURN BIT
  IS
    VARIABLE t: BIT;
  BEGIN
    IF (a > MAX) THEN t:= '1';
    ELSE              t:= '0';
    END IF;
    RETURN(t);
  END check_max;
END sample_pkg;
```

This package declares a constant of type INTEGER and a function; these elements are available to be used in a module after accessing the package, as follows:

```
USE WORK.sample_pkg.ALL;     -- uses all elements of package sample_pkg
                             -- which are stored in library WORK
ENTITY use_sample_pkg IS
  PORT(x : IN  INTEGER;
       z : OUT BIT);
END use_sample_pkg;

ARCHITECTURE behavioral OF use_sample_pkg IS
BEGIN
  PROCESS (x)
    BEGIN
      z  <= check_max(x);
  END PROCESS;
END behavioral;
```

The clause USE WORK.sample_pkg.ALL specifies that this module uses all the declarations in the package sample_pkg, which is stored in library WORK. As a consequence, the elements of the package can be used in the module, without further declaration. ■

In addition to the predefined 2-valued types BIT, BIT_VECTOR in μVHDL, there exist standard packages for describing multi-valued signals; in particular, the package ieee.std_logic_1164 defines a standard 9-valued logic for signal values, which also includes the definition of bit-vectors and operations on 9-valued signals. This package is contained in the LIBRARY ieee which can be used by a μVHDL description. The logic values defined in the ieee.std_logic_1164 are a combination of five *states* and three signal *strengths*, wherein some logic values have only an associated state, others have only an associated strength, and others have an associated state and strength. The values are:

Logic Value	State	Strength
U	Uninitialized	–
0	0	Forcing
1	1	Forcing
X	Unknown	Forcing
L	0	Resistive
H	1	Resistive
W	Unknown	Resistive
Z	–	High impedance
–	Don't care	–

Signals having these values are defined as of TYPE STD_ULOGIC and STD_ULOGIC_VECTOR. SUBTYPEs derived from STD_ULOGIC are STD_LOGIC and STD_LOGIC_VECTOR which restrict the logic values to the set {'U','X','0','1','Z'}. The package also includes the definition of logic operators and conversion functions among these types and types BIT, BIT_VECTOR. Additional standard packages are

- ieee.std_logic_arith, which defines the bit-vector types SIGNED, UNSIGNED as well as arithmetic functions on these types, STD_LOGIC_VECTOR and INTEGER, and conversion functions among them;
- ieee.std_logic_signed, which defines arithmetic functions on STD_LOGIC_VECTOR and INTEGER, and conversion functions, assuming that the STD_LOGIC_VECTORs are **signed** values;
- ieee.std_logic_unsigned, which defines arithmetic functions on STD_LOGIC_VECTOR and INTEGER, and conversion functions, assuming that the STD_LOGIC_VECTORs are **unsigned** values.

Functional μVHDL-based Specification of Combinational Systems

The behavior of a combinational module, that is, its output changing as a consequence of a change in any of the inputs, is described directly using the elements of μVHDL already presented in this chapter. In fact, the examples given in this section correspond to specifications of this type.

As stated earlier, the description of systems may use variables as an aid to simplify complex functions; such functions can be decomposed into partial terms or steps, using variables to save the intermediate results. In the case of combinational systems, the value of those variables is **generated and used in the same interpretation** of the PROCESS describing the behavior of the system.

Simulating the Specification

As also stated earlier, one of the advantages of using a hardware-description language is the ability to simulate the specification of a system and verify that its behavior is as expected. This level of "testing" can be performed directly with a specification as the ones described in this chapter, by providing values to the input signals and observing the values of the output signals. The details of the mechanisms for this objective are dependent on the specific compiler/simulator environment used. Typically, these mechanisms consist of simulation statements such as

```
force x 1      assign value 1 to input signal x
list y         observe the output signal y
run            simulate for the given input
```

or statements such as

```
start 0;        set starting time
stop 100;       set ending simulation time
inputs x y;     define inputs
pattern         define sequence of input values
0> 0 0          input values at time 0
22> 3 1         input values at time 22
57> 1 2         input values at time 57
;
outputs z;      define outputs
```

2.7 FURTHER READINGS

A more detailed discussion of switching theory and some aspects of the specification methods for combinational systems is given in books on switching theory, such as *Switching and Automata Theory*, by Z. Kohavi, New York: McGraw-Hill, 1978; *Logic Design Principles* by E. McCluskey, Englewood Cliffs, NJ: Prentice-Hall, 1986; and *Introduction to Digital Logic Design* by J. P. Hayes, Reading, MA: Addison-Wesley, 1993. They concentrate on the binary specification methods without giving much attention to the high-level techniques.

The more mathematical aspects are treated in textbooks on discrete mathematics such as *Discrete Mathematical Structures* by H. S. Stone, Chicago: Science Research Associates, 1973; and *Introduction to Discrete Structures* by F. P. Preparata and R. T. Yeh, Reading, MA: Addison-Wesley, 1973.

For an historical perspective on the development of data representation see *Coded Character Sets, History and Development* by C. E. Mackenzie, Reading, MA: Addison-Wesley, 1980.

VHDL and its use in digital design are discussed in *The Designer's Guide to VHDL* by P. Ashenden, San Franciso: Morgan Kaufmann Publishers, Inc., 1996; *VHDL* by D. L. Perry, New York: McGraw-Hill, 1991; *VHDL Analysis and Modeling of Digital Systems* by Z. Navabi, New York: McGraw-Hill, 1993; and *Structured Logic Design with VHDL* by J. P. Armstrong and F. G. Gray, Englewood Cliffs, NJ: Prentice-Hall, 1993, to mention few of many available books.

EXERCISES

High-level Description

Exercise 2.1 A combinational system has one input x, which represents a decimal digit. The output z is the square of x if x is greater than 4; otherwise, the output z is two times x.

a. Give a high-level description of the system using expressions.
b. Show a table of the function.

Exercise 2.2 A combinational system has two inputs, $\underline{x} = (x_{15}, \ldots, x_0)$ and $\underline{y} = (y_1, y_0)$, with x_i and y_i having values 0, 1, or 2. There is one output $\underline{z} = (z_{13}, \ldots, z_0)$ obtained by deleting the leftmost instance of the pattern $\underline{y}$ from the input $\underline{x}$. If $\underline{x}$ does not contain the pattern specified by $\underline{y}$, the output $\underline{z}$ has all elements $z_i = 0$. For example, if $\underline{x} = (0, 1, 2, 1, 2, 0, 1, 2, 0, 0, 0, 1, 2, 2)$ and $\underline{y} = (1, 2)$ then $\underline{z} = (0, 1, 2, 0, 1, 2, 0, 0, 0, 1, 2, 2)$

Give a high-level specification of this system. How many rows would a tabular description have?

Exercise 2.3 Give a high-level specification of a combinational system that computes the distance between two 1's in the input bit-vector $\underline{x} = (x_{n-1}, \ldots, x_0)$. Assume that $\underline{x}$ has exactly two 1's. For instance, if $\underline{x} = (1, 0, 1, 0, 0)$ then the distance is 2.

Exercise 2.4 A pattern detector has as input a 4×4 matrix whose elements take values a, b, c, or d. The output is 1 if the matrix contains one b surrounded by eight a's and 0 otherwise.

Give a high-level description of the system in terms of conditional logic expressions. How many rows would a tabular description have?

Exercise 2.5 A combinational incrementer/decrementer has as inputs an integer in the range 0 to $2^{16} - 1$ and a binary control signal. If the control signal has value 1, the system increments modulo-2^{16} (i.e., it computes $z = (x + 1) \bmod 2^{16}$), otherwise it decrements modulo-2^{16}.

Give a high-level description of the system in terms of a conditional arithmetic expression. Can you give a tabular representation of the function?

Exercise 2.6 The table shown below defines two three-valued functions. Determine the table for the function $f(a, b) = f_2(b, f_1(a, b))$.

	a				a		
b	0	1	2	b	0	1	2
0	2	0	2	0	2	0	0
1	0	1	1	1	0	2	0
2	2	1	0	2	0	0	2
		f_1				f_2	

Codes for Data Representation

Exercise 2.7 What is the minimum number of binary variables required to represent a variable that can take integer values from 10 to 25? Write a table describing a possible coding function.

Exercise 2.8

a. Give a binary code to represent the month of a year.
b. How many bits is the minimum needed to represent the date (month, day, year)? Use a vector of three components and represent each component in the binary number system. Consider dates up to the year 2500.
c. What is the minimum needed for the date of (b) if the representation of the day and of year are done in decimal (two digits for the day and four digits for the year)?
d. What is the minimum number of bits required for the date of (b) if just one component is used? What is the disadvantage of this representation?

Exercise 2.9 Is there a unique code for representing the decimal digits using the weight vector 2-4-2-1? If not, give two such codes and determine how many different codes there are.

Exercise 2.10 Consider a weighted code for decimal digits using four bits. For weights that are positive integers, determine conditions that the weights have to satisfy,

Exercise 2.11

a. For the integer with decimal representation 34567, give the corresponding bit-vectors for the BCD code and for the Excess-3 code.
b. Perform the subtraction of $z_{10} = (99999_{10} - 34567_{10})$ for the integers represented in BCD and in the 2-4-2-1 codes. Use the fact that in the 2-4-2-1 code the complement with respect to 9 is obtained by complementing each bit.

Exercise 2.12 Consider a five-bit vector $\underline{x}$ that represents a decimal digit in a 2-out-of-5 code:

a. Give a table of the 32 possible values of $\underline{x}$ and indicate which values are valid representations of decimal digits.
b. Give a high-level description of a combinational system that has an output of 1 when the vector $\underline{x}$ represents a valid digit in a 2-out-of-5 code.

Exercise 2.13

a. Determine the radix-16 representation of the integer whose radix-2 representation is 1001010100011110.
   Hint: Partition the radix-2 vector into groups of four bits and determine the radix-16 digit values that are coded by each group (using the binary code).
b. Determine the radix-2 representation of the integer whose radix-8 representation is 3456.
   Hint: Code each radix-8 digit using the binary code and concatenate the resulting groups of three bits.
c. Using the foregoing hints, give a procedure to convert from radix-2 to radix-2^k and vice-versa.

Binary Description – Switching Functions

Exercise 2.14 The majority switching function $M(x, y, z)$ is equal to 1 when two or three of its arguments are 1. By comparison of the tabular descriptions, show that

$$M[a, b, M(c, d, e)] = M[M(a, b, c), d, M(a, b, e)]$$

Because the tables of the five-variable functions are quite large, a simpler approach might be to consider separately the cases $a = b = 0$, $a = b = 1$, and $a \neq b$.

Exercise 2.15 Prove or disprove the following equalities, by constructing the corresponding tables.

a. $f_{XOR}(f_{AND}(x_1, x_0), f_{AND}(x_1, x_0)) = f_{EQUIVALENCE}(x_1, x_0)$
b. $f_{NAND}(f_{NAND}(x_1, x_0), f_{NAND}(x_1, x_0)) = f_{AND}(x_1, x_0)$

Exercise 2.16 Determine the number of different switching functions of n variables.

Exercise 2.17 A **symmetric switching function** is a function whose value does not change when its arguments are permuted.

a. Give a table of a symmetric switching function of three variables.
b. Determine how many symmetric switching functions of three variables exist.
c. Show that a symmetric switching function must have the same value for all arguments that have the same number of 1's. Using this fact, show that a symmetric switching function of n variables can be described by a subset A of the set of integers $\{0, 1, ..., n\}$ such that integer i is in A if the function has value 1 whenever i variables are 1.
d. Give the table of the symmetric switching function of four variables whose set A is $\{0,2,3\}$.
e. Using the result of part (c), determine how many symmetric functions of n variables exist.
f. Is the composition of symmetric switching functions a symmetric function? Consider, for instance, the function $f(x, y, z) = \text{AND}(\text{OR}(x, y), z)$.
g. Determine the table of the function $f = f_1(f_2(a, b, c), f_1(b, c, a), c)$ wherein f_1 and f_2 are the symmetric switching functions with sets $A_1 = \{0, 1\}$ and $A_2 = \{0, 3\}$, respectively.
h. Given the set A of a symmetric function f, determine the set A_c of the complement of f. Illustrate for the 4-variable symmetric function with $A = \{0, 1\}$.

Exercise 2.18 A **threshold switching function** is a function that has value 1 whenever $\sum w_i x_i > T$ and 0 otherwise; the values w_i's are integers called the weights, x_i is a binary variable interpreted as the integers 0 and 1, and T is an integer called the threshold.

a. Write a table that represents the threshold function of three variables with $w_1 = 1$, $w_2 = 2$, $w_3 = -1$, and $T = 2$. Also give the one-set or the zero-set.
b. Determine a set of weights and a threshold for the switching function of three variables described by *one-set* (3,5,7).
Hint: Write the inequalities (in terms of the weights and the threshold) for each value of (x_2, x_1, x_0) and find a solution to the system of inequalities.
c. Show that the XOR function of two variables is not a threshold function; that is, show that no weights and threshold can be found to describe this function. *Hint:* Show that the system of inequalities does not have a solution.
d. Determine the weights and threshold for the majority function of four variables, that is, the function that has the value 1 whenever three or four variables have the value 1.

Exercise 2.19 A combinational system computes the distance between two 1's in the input bit-vector $\underline{x} = (x_3, x_2, x_1, x_0)$, which has exactly two 1's. For example, for $\underline{x} = (0, 1, 0, 1)$ the distance is 2. That is, if the two 1's are at positions i and j, distance is $|j - i|$.

a. Give a description in terms of switching functions.
b. Give the one-set, the zero-set, and the dc-set.

Exercise 2.20 In Exercise 2.1, obtain the description in terms of incompletely specified switching functions for the BCD code presented in Table 2.3. Use the simplified notation of Example 2.4, two-dimensional tables of Example 2.5, and give the one-set and dc-set description.

Exercise 2.21 In Exercise 2.1, obtain the description in terms of incompletely specified switching functions for the Excess-3 code presented in Table 2.3. Use the simplified notation of Example 2.4, two-dimensional tables of Example 2.5, and give the one-set and dc-set description.

Exercise 2.22 In Exercise 2.1, obtain the description in terms of incompletely specified switching functions for the 2-out-of-5 code presented in Table 2.3. Use the simplified notation of Example 2.4, two-dimensional tables of Example 2.5, and give the one-set and dc-set description.

Exercise 2.23 Determine the number of incompletely specified switching functions of n variables.

Boolean Algebra

Exercise 2.24 Using the postulates of Boolean algebra and the theorems given in the Appendix, prove each of the following:

a. $a'b' + ab + a'b = a' + b$
b. $a' + a(a'b + b'c)' = a' + b + c'$
c. $(a'b' + c)(a + b)(b' + ac)' = a'bc$
d. $ab' + b'c' + a'c' = ab' + a'c'$
e. $wxy + w'x(yz + yz') + x'(zw + zy') + z(x'w' + y'x) = xy + z$
f. $abc' + bc'd + a'bd = abc' + a'bd$

Exercise 2.25 Given that $xy' + x'y = z$, show that $xz' + x'z = y$. *Hint:* Replace z by $xy' + x'y$ and simplify.

Exercise 2.26 Simplify algebraically the following expression:

$$a + a'b + a'b'c + a'b'c'd + a'b'c'd'e$$

Exercise 2.27 An operation $*$ is defined for two-valued variables a and b as follows:

$$a * b = ab + a'b'$$

Let $c = a * b$. Determine which of the following identities are valid:

a. $a = b * c$
b. $a * bc = 1$

Exercise 2.28 Show that $ab = ac$ does not imply that $b = c$.

Exercise 2.29 Consider the system consisting of three elements 0, 1, and 2 and the operators # and & defined by the tables below. Determine whether this system is a Boolean algebra (see Appendix). If not, indicate which postulates are not satisfied.

#	0	1	2
0	0	0	0
1	0	1	1
2	0	1	2

&	0	1	2
0	0	1	2
1	1	1	2
2	2	2	2

Exercise 2.30 Show the operation tables for a Boolean algebra of four elements. *Hint:* Call the elements a, b, c, d; choose among them the two identity elements; and construct tables so all the postulates are satisfied.

Exercise 2.31 Show that the NAND and NOR operators are not associative.

Exercise 2.32 The XOR operator is denoted by the symbol $\oplus$ and defined by the identity $x_1 \oplus x_0 = x_1'x_0 + x_1x_0'$ (i.e., $x_1 \oplus x_0$ represents the XOR function).

a. Show that XOR operator is (i) commutative, (ii) associative, and, (iii) distributive with respect to AND.
b. Prove or disprove the following:

- if $x \oplus y = 0$ then $x = y$
- $x' \oplus y = (x \oplus y)'$
- $x \oplus y = x' \oplus y'$
- if $x \oplus y = z \oplus y$ then $x = z$
- $x \oplus x \oplus \ldots \oplus x$ is 0 for an even number of x's and x for an odd number of x's.

Description by Switching Expressions

Exercise 2.33 Determine whether the following are switching expressions:

a. $(a + b' + c)(d' + e') + f'g + k'i'$
b. $(a + b + c)(d' + e)$
c. $a + 1' + (a'ba'b + c(b' + a)b'$

Exercise 2.34 Evaluate the following switching expressions for the assignments (0,1,1,0) and (1,1,1,0):

a. $E(w, x, y, z) = w + x' + (x + y)(w + z)'$
b. $E(x_3, x_2, x_1, x_0) = x_2 x_1 + x_3$

Exercise 2.35 Prove the following equivalence for switching expressions by evaluating them for all possible assignments.

$$xyz + yw + x'z' + xy' = y'z' + yw + xz + x'yz'$$

Exercise 2.36 Determine the switching function represented by the following switching expressions (show a truth table):

a. $E(x, y) = xy + xy'$
b. $E(x, y, z) = xyz + x'y + xyz'$

Exercise 2.37 Using tables, determine all pairs of equivalent switching expressions from the set of expressions given as follows:

a. $x'y' + xz + x'z'$
b. $xy + x'y' + yz'$
c. $xyz + x'y'z + x'z' + xyz'$
d. $y'z + x'z' + xyz$
e. $x'y' + x'z' + xyz$

Exercise 2.38 Reduce the following switching expressions to the number of literals specified:

a. $abc'd + ab'c + bc'd + ab'c' + acd + a'bcd$ 4 literals
b. $acb + ac'd + bc'd' + a'b'c' + ab'c'd' + bc'd$ 3 literals

Exercise 2.39 Find the canonical expressions for the following switching function:

a	b	c	f
0	0	0	0
0	0	1	1
0	1	0	1
0	1	1	1
1	0	0	0
1	0	1	1
1	1	0	0
1	1	1	0

Exercise 2.40 Obtain the equivalent sum of minterms and product of maxterms for the following expressions. Use m- and M-notation.

a. $a'b + ac + bc$
b. $(ab + c)(d'e + f)$
c. $a'b(ab + c)(b + c'd)$

Exercise 2.41 Determine the sum of minterms and product of maxterms that are equivalent to

$$E(x, y, z) = x' + x(x'y + y'z)'$$

Exercise 2.42 Convert the following SEs into sums of minterms:

a. $\{[(a + b + a'c')c + d]' + ab'\}$
b. $\{[w' + (xy + xyz' + (x + z)')'](z' + w')\}'$

Exercise 2.43 Convert the following SEs into product of maxterms without obtaining the sum of minterms first:

a. $xyz + yw + x'z' + xy'$
b. $(abc + ab')'(a'b + c')$

Exercise 2.44 Convert the following canonical expressions of (w, x, y, z) into the other canonical forms.

a. $\sum m(0, 1, 3, 4, 11, 12, 14, 15)$
b. $\prod M(0, 1, 3, 5, 6, 9, 10, 13)$

Exercise 2.45 Express the complement of $E(x, y, z) = \prod M(0, 1, 4, 6, 7)$ as a sum of minterms and a product of maxterms.

Examples of Systems

Exercise 2.46 Describe an adder whose inputs A and B are integers in the range 0 to 3. The adder should have a carry-in and a carry-out to connect several of these modules to construct a multidigit (radix 4) adder. Give the following descriptions:

a. High-level using arithmetic expressions.
b. A table of the arithmetic function.
c. A tabular description of the switching functions, with inputs and outputs coded in the binary code. Give also the corresponding one-set.

Exercise 2.47 Describe an incrementer/decrementer system whose input is an integer in the range 0 to 15. A control input determines whether the system increments or decrements. Give the following descriptions:

a. High-level using arithmetic expressions.
b. A table of the arithmetic function.
c. A tabular representation of the switching functions, with the inputs and outputs in a binary code. Give also the zero-set.

Exercise 2.48 Describe a system that counts the number of 1's in a four-bit vector $\underline{x}$. Give the following descriptions, if practical:

a. High-level using arithmetic expressions.
b. Table of the arithmetic function.
c. A tabular representation of the switching functions, with the inputs and outputs in a binary code. Give also the one-set.

Exercise 2.49 Describe a 2×2-bits multiplier, that is, each operand represents an integer in the range 0 to 3. Give the following descriptions:

a. High-level using arithmetic expressions.

b. Table of the arithmetic function.
c. A tabular representation of the switching functions, with the inputs and outputs in a binary code. Give also the one-set.

Exercise 2.50 An open stairwell has four floors and one switch per floor to control the light. If all switches are off, the light is off; any single change in the position of any switch changes the "state" of the light. Describe the combinational system required to control the light. Give

a. High-level description.
b. Table of switching functions.
c. Switching expressions.

Exercise 2.51 A combinational system has as input a decimal digit and as output the 9's complement of the input. Describe the system giving

a. A high-level description.
b. Tabular and (one-set, dc-set) description of the functions for one of the following codes:

- Excess-6 (defined in a similar manner as the Excess-3 code, that is, 0 is represented by 0110, etc.)
- 2-out of-5
- weighted with weights 4,3,2,1 and with weights 8,-4,2,-1. These codes are defined using the expression of Section 2.3.2.

c. Switching expressions for the functions in (b).

Exercise 2.52 Describe a binary-to-decimal converter that has a four-bit input vector and the output in the BCD representation (two digits).

a. Give a high-level description.
b. Give switching expressions.

Exercise 2.53 Describe a combinational system that has two hexadecimal digits as inputs and the same digits ordered by magnitude as outputs.

a. Give a high-level description.
b. Give switching expressions when the digits are represented in the binary code. Use the intermediate variables g, e, and s obtained from the comparison of the hexadecimal digits.

Exercise 2.54 A priority encoder has eight binary inputs and an integer output. The inputs are numbered 0 to 7, whereas the value of the output is the integer that corresponds to the largest index of the input having value 1. For example, for input $\underline{x} = (0, 1, 0, 1, 1, 1, 0, 0)$ the output is $z = 6$. Describe the system giving:

a. A high-level specification.
b. Switching expressions for a binary representation of the output.
c. Switching expressions for a Gray-code representation of the output.

To simplify the description, decompose the system into two cascaded subsystems, as shown in Figure 2.16. The first system is a priority-resolution system that gives a 1 output corresponding to the highest-priority input that has value 1 (all other outputs are 0); the second system is an encoder, that is, its output is an integer representing the index of the input with value 1.

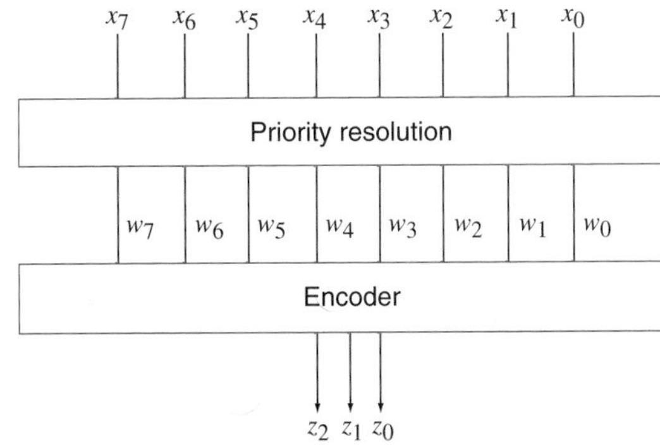

Figure 2.16 Cascaded subsystems for priority encoder.

Exercise 2.55 Describe a combinational comparator, similar to Example 2.19, for hexadecimal input digits. *Hint:* Generalize the following description of the two-bit comparator:

$$
\begin{aligned}
z_2 &= x_1 y_1' + e_1 x_0 y_0' \\
z_1 &= e_1 e_0 \\
z_0 &= x_1' y_1 + e_1 x_0' y_0
\end{aligned}
$$

where $e_i = x_i y_i + x_i' y_i'$.

Specification Using μVHDL

Any of the exercises under the heading "Examples of Systems" can be done using μVHDL.

Chapter 3

Combinational Integrated Circuits: Characteristics and Capabilities

In this chapter, we discuss

- The representation of binary variables at the physical level.
- The basic switch structure of gates and their operation.
- The realization of gates using CMOS[1] circuits.
- The characteristics of circuits: input load factors and fanout factors, propagation delays, transition times, and effect of load.
- Three-state gates (drivers) and buses.
- The effect of noise and noise margins.
- The evolution of integrated circuits (ICs).
- VLSI circuit-level design styles.
- Packaging levels: chips, boards, and cabinets.
- The μVHDL description of gates.

The realization of combinational digital systems involves two levels:

a. The **logic level,** at which the primitive components are called **gates.** These gates implement basic switching functions, such as AND, OR, NOT, XOR, NAND, and NOR.
b. The **circuit level,** which corresponds to the physical realization of the gates.

Combinational systems specified by sets of switching functions (as discussed in Chapter 2) are implemented as **networks** of gates. This "functional" implementation is independent of the circuit level. However, there are some characteristics of the realization of the gates that determine whether a given gate network –which is functionally correct– can be physically realized or not. Moreover, the selection of the most suitable gate network in terms of measures such as speed, cost, and packaging size depends on circuit characteristics. Consequently, the important issues at the circuit level cannot be ignored.

[1]CMOS – Complementary Metal Oxide Semiconductor circuit technology.

Digital systems could be realized by designing directly at the circuit level. However, that option is too complex and time consuming for large systems because there are too many interacting factors. A hierarchical approach is a more adequate strategy, in which the circuit characteristics of simple modules are abstracted and then used in the design at the logic level. The approach used in this book follows the hierarchical strategy just mentioned. For those purposes, in this chapter we provide an elementary discussion of the circuits used to realize gates as integrated circuits (ICs). Later chapters use these gates to construct digital networks. We consider gates at the electrical-circuit level, without going into details of the associated electronics and solid-state physics. The objective of this chapter is to describe the basic characteristics and parameters at the circuit level, which are needed to determine the feasibility of a given system as well as to select a suitable design at the logic level.

The circuits presented here are intended to illustrate the concepts, structure, and behavior that are typical; they do not necessarily correspond in all details to actual circuits. We define and briefly discuss the circuit characteristics that are used in the analysis/design at the logic level, and illustrate them for realizations in the CMOS technology. The concepts related to electrical circuits are discussed in basic physics courses.

3.1 REPRESENTATION OF BINARY VARIABLES

The realization of gates by electronic circuits is based on

- the **representation** of the binary values 0 and 1 by the values of electrical signals (voltages, currents, or electrical charges); and
- the **realization of circuits** that operate on these signals to implement the desired switching functions.

In the following discussion we illustrate these concepts using voltages. The voltages that represent the two binary values are called V_H (high) and V_L (low), where $V_H > V_L$, as shown in Figure 3.1. The actual values of these voltages depend on the specific technology; moreover, a range of voltages is used to represent each value: the high region is defined by the range $[V_{Hmin}, V_{Hmax}]$ and the low region is defined by the range $[V_{Lmin}, V_{Lmax}]$. To discriminate properly among these ranges, there should exist a suitable forbidden region in the range $[V_{Lmax}, V_{Hmin}]$. Typical values for a 3.3 V CMOS technology are

V_{Hmax}	3.3 V	V_{Lmax}	0.8 V
V_{Hmin}	2.0 V	V_{Lmin}	0.0 V

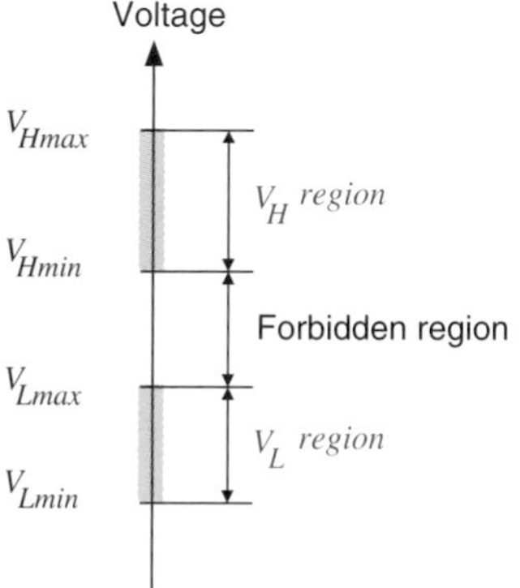

Figure 3.1 Voltage regions.

There are two possible correspondences among the voltages and the values 0 and 1, as follows:

Positive logic	V_H is associated with 1 V_L is associated with 0
Negative logic	V_H is associated with 0 V_L is associated with 1

Different switching functions are implemented by the same circuit, depending on the logic used (either positive or negative). For example, a circuit whose input and output voltages are as indicated in the leftmost columns in the table depicted in Figure 3.2 can implement either the AND or the OR logic function. In this text we assume positive logic, so we use interchangeably V_H and 1 as well as V_L and 0.

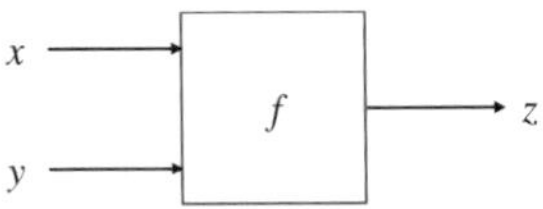

Input Voltages		Output Voltage	Positive Logic			Negative Logic		
x	y	z	x	y	z	x	y	z
V_L	V_L	V_L	0	0	0	1	1	1
V_L	V_H	V_L	0	1	0	1	0	1
V_H	V_L	V_L	1	0	0	0	1	1
V_H	V_H	V_H	1	1	1	0	0	0
			f = AND			f = OR		

Figure 3.2 Positive and negative logic.

3.2 STRUCTURE AND OPERATION OF CMOS GATES

As stated earlier, the primitive modules used in the design at the logic level are called **gates** and they implement basic switching functions, such as NOT, AND, OR, XOR, NAND, and NOR. The actual circuit realization of these gates depends on the technology. We now consider the structure and operation of gates in terms of switches.

3.2.1 n-type and p-type Switches

The basic component used in the realization of gates is the **controlled switch**. As shown in Figure 3.3*a*, such a switch has three terminals *A*, *B*, and *C*; the voltage between the control terminals determines whether the switch is OPEN or CLOSED; when OPEN the resistance between terminals *A* and *B* is very high, whereas when CLOSED the resistance is very low. In the models used here, these resistances are approximated by zero for the closed switch and by infinity for the open switch. The boundary between the two regions of the control voltage is called the **threshold voltage**.

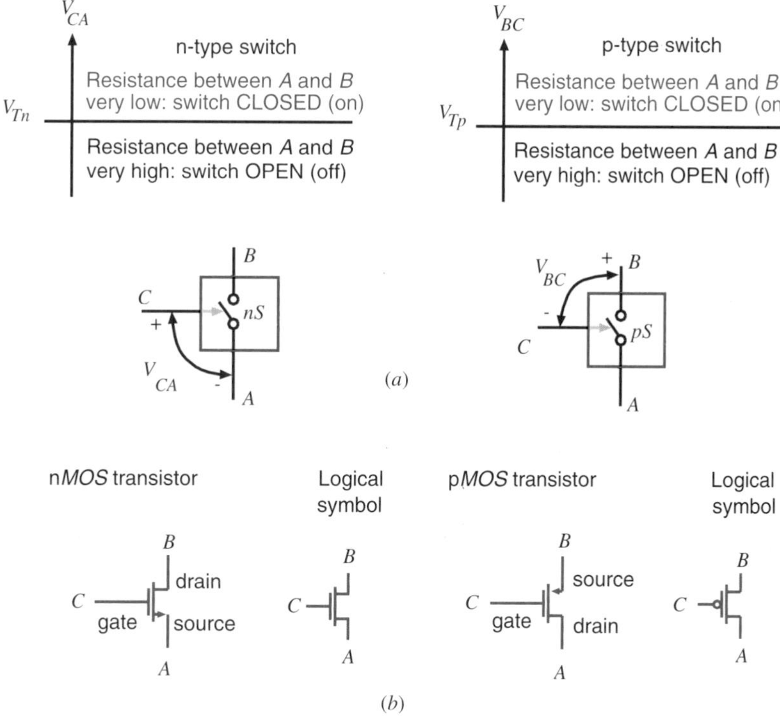

Figure 3.3 (*a*) n-type and p-type controlled switches. (*b*) nMOS and pMOS transistors.

Two types of switches exist (which are denoted as *nS* and *pS*, respectively, in the figures):

n-type: the switch is OPEN (OFF) if $V_{CA} < V_{Tn}$ and CLOSED (ON) if $V_{CA} > V_{Tn}$, where V_{Tn} is the threshold voltage for an n-type switch.

p-type: the switch is OPEN (OFF) if $V_{BC} < V_{Tp}$ and CLOSED (ON) if $V_{BC} > V_{Tp}$, where V_{Tp} is the threshold voltage for a p-type switch.

In CMOS technology, the switch is realized by a transistor, as shown in Figure 3.3*b*. Moreover, an n-channel (nMOS) transistor realizes an n-type switch, whereas a p-channel (pMOS) transistor realizes a p-type switch. Figure 3.3*b* also shows the symbols for the transistors when they are used as switches.

3.2.2 NOT Gate

The simplest CMOS gate is the NOT gate, formed by one nMOS and one pMOS transistor connected to the power supply voltage V_{DD} and to ground (0 V). This structure is depicted in Figure 3.4 together with the corresponding switch network. V_{Tn} and V_{Tp} are the threshold voltages of nMOS and pMOS transistors, respectively.

Because $V_{BC} = V_{DD} - v_{in}$ ($V_{DD} = V_{BC} + v_{in}$), the following two situations exist:

1. $v_{in} < V_{Tn}$. Then $V_{CA} < V_{Tn}$ and the n-switch is open. Moreover, if $V_{DD} > V_{Tn} + V_{Tp}$ then $V_{BC} > V_{Tp}$ and the p-switch is closed. This results in $v_{out} = V_{DD}$.
2. $v_{in} > V_{DD} - V_{Tp}$. Then $V_{BC} < V_{Tp}$ and the p-switch is open. Moreover, if $V_{DD} > V_{Tn} + V_{Tp}$ then $V_{CA} > V_{Tn}$ and the n-switch is closed. This results in $v_{out} = 0$.

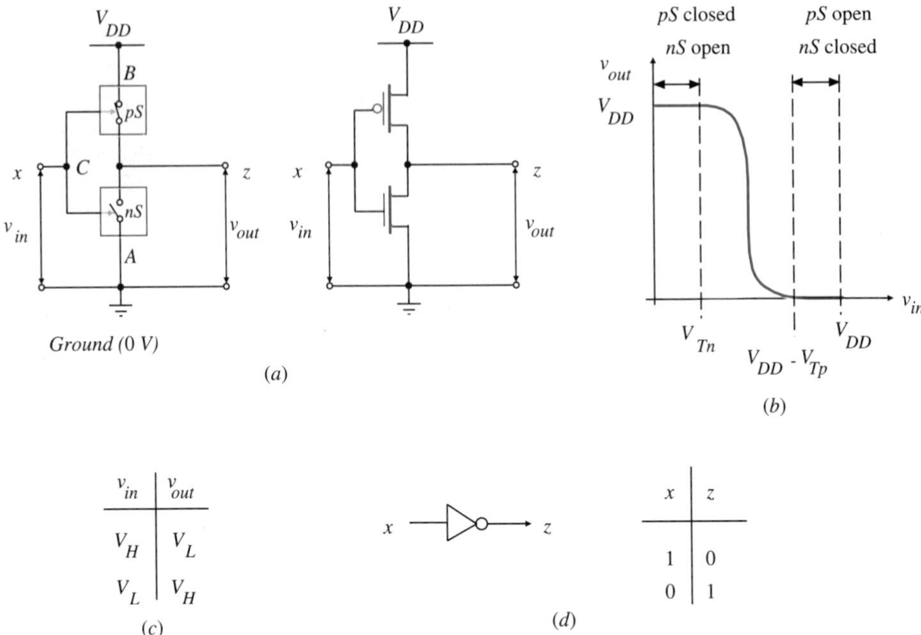

Figure 3.4 Circuit for NOT gate. (*a*) Switch and transistor networks. (*b*) Input-output voltage characteristic. (*c*) Input-output function. (*d*) Logic symbol and switching function.

This behavior is depicted in the input-output characteristic shown in Figure 3.4*c*. Consequently, the circuit performs the NOT function if the following conditions are satisfied:

$$V_{L_{max}} < V_{Tn}, \qquad V_{H_{min}} > V_{DD} - V_{Tp}, \qquad V_{DD} > V_{Tn} + V_{Tp}$$

Note that for $V_{Tn} < v_{in} < V_{DD} - V_{Tp}$, both switches are closed, and the resistance between V_{DD} and Ground is very low, producing a large current. Consequently, this condition can only be present for a short time, and the rise and fall times of v_{in} should be small.

For CMOS, the traditional value of V_{DD} has been 5 V. However, recent implementations have lowered this value to 3.3 V and below; this is mainly done to reduce the power consumption.

3.2.3 NAND and NOR Gates

The basic NOT circuit can be extended by connecting several switches in **series** or in **parallel**, as shown in Figure 3.5. Note that CMOS switches come always in pairs: one n-type and one p-type. The n-type switches form the **n-net**, which produces the output 0, whereas p-switches form the **p-net**, which produces the output 1. The p-net and n-net functions are complementary: when the p-net is off, the n-net is on, and vice versa. The corresponding tables in Figure 3.5 indicate that the circuits realize the NAND and NOR functions, respectively. Gates with a larger number of inputs are obtained by including additional switch pairs.

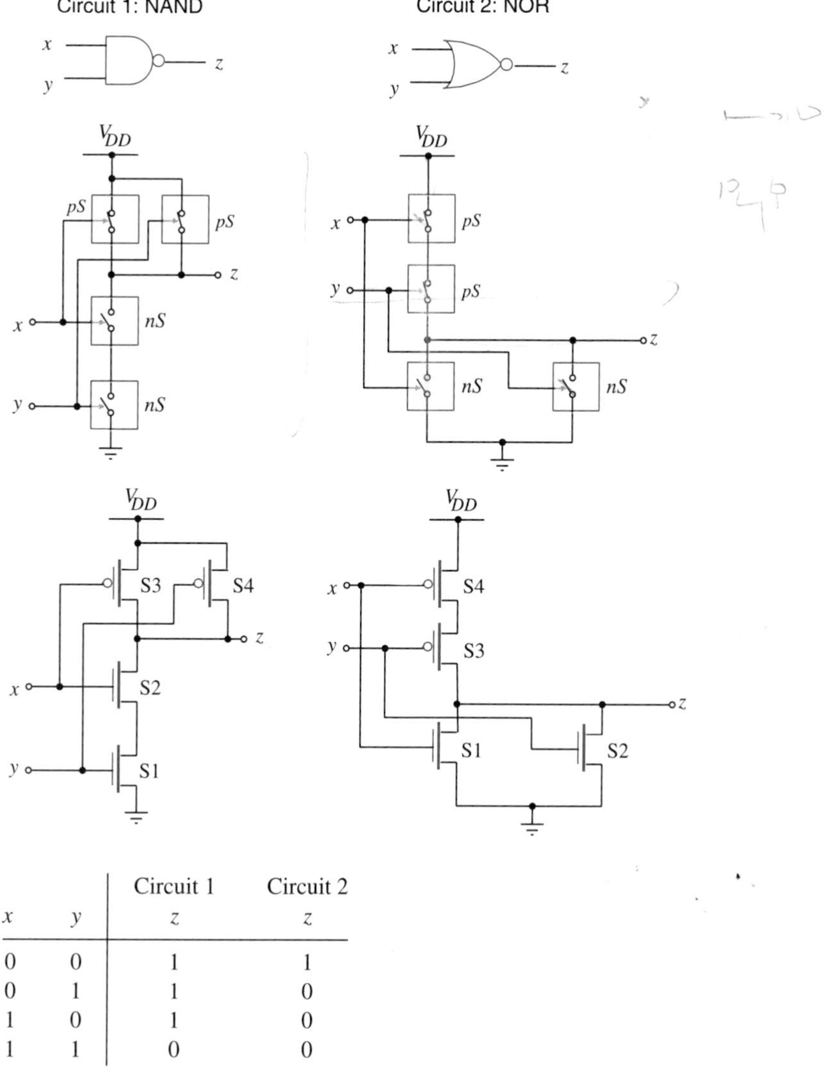

x	y	Circuit 1 z	Circuit 2 z
0	0	1	1
0	1	1	0
1	0	1	0
1	1	0	0

Figure 3.5 Circuits for NAND and NOR gates.

3.2.4 AND and OR Gates

As shown in Figure 3.6, AND and OR gates are realized by adding an inverter (NOT gate) to the output of the NAND and NOR, respectively. This illustrates that, in CMOS technology, inverting gates (NAND and NOR) are simpler than noninverting gates, such as AND and OR.

3.2.5 Complex Gates

Although any combinational system can be implemented by a gate network using only a subset of the gates presented up to now (as discussed in Chapter 4), having transistor structures that implement more complex switching functions might help reducing the overall transistor count and the delay of a network. These structures are called **complex gates**; two typical examples are the AND-NOR structure (also called AND-OR-INVERT, AOI) and

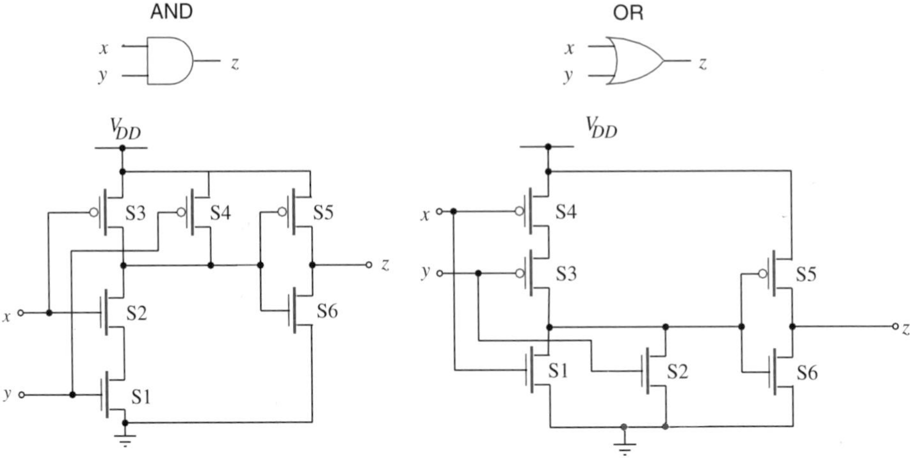

Figure 3.6 Circuits for AND and OR gates.

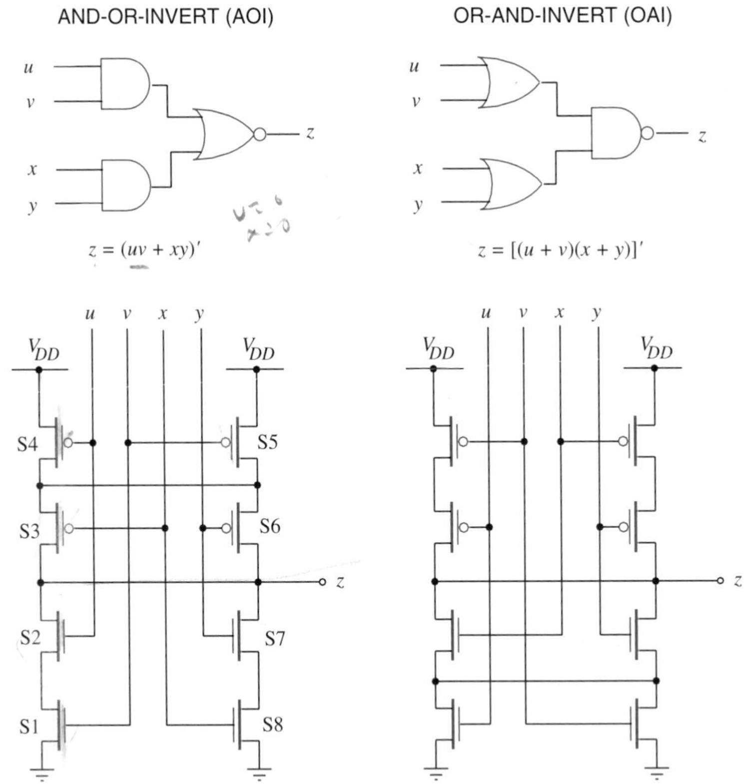

Figure 3.7 Examples of complex gates.

the OR-NAND structure (also called OR-AND-INVERT, OAI). These structures are shown in Figure 3.7. In the AOI gate, switches S_1, S_2, S_7, and S_8 form the n-net which is ON when $uv + xy = 1$ (i.e., there is a path of closed switches to 0 V), producing $z = 0$. The remaining switches form the p-net, which produces the output 1 when $uv + xy = 0$. Consequently, the network implements the expression $z = (uv + xy)'$. A similar analysis shows that the circuit on the right implements $z = [(u + v)(x + y)]'$.

3.2.6 Transmission Gate, XOR gate, and Two-input Multiplexer

Figure 3.8*a* depicts a switch constructed with a pair of complementary transistors, which is known as a **transmission gate.** Note that the controlling signal for one transistor is the complement of the signal controlling the other transistor. When $C = 1$ (and $C' = 0$) the switch is CLOSED, whereas when $C = 0$ the switch is OPEN. The pair of complementary transistors are needed so that both values, 0 and 1, can be transmitted without degrading the corresponding signal; the n-channel transistor transmits a 0 without degradation, whereas the p-channel transmits a 1 without degradation. When the switch is open, the output of the transmission gate is disconnected from the input (i.e., its value corresponds to a high impedance). For this reason, such a value is denoted with Z (a standard label for impedance). Note that the output signal of the transmission gate (z) has three possible values: 0, 1, or Z. A transmission gate can be used for internal parts of complex gates but not for a gate output.

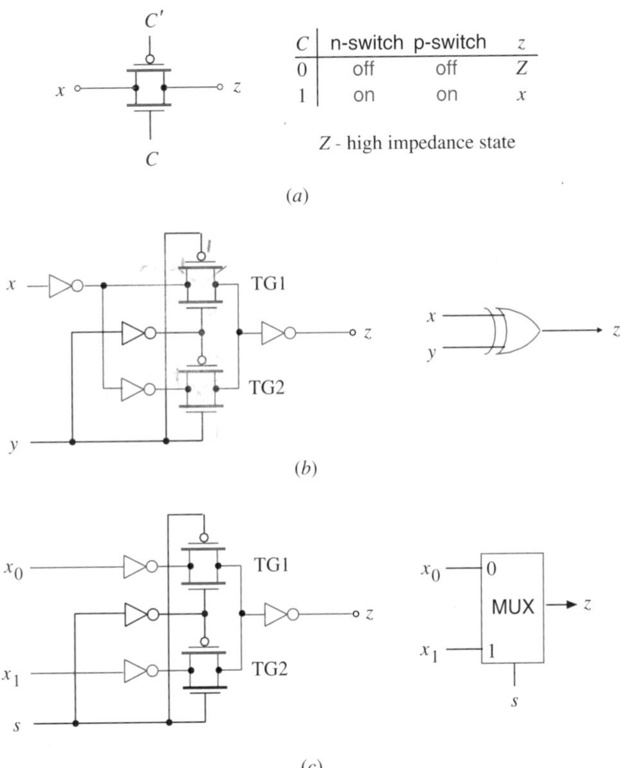

Figure 3.8 (*a*) Transmission gate. (*b*) Implementation of XOR with transmission gates. (*c*) Implementation of two-input MUX with transmission gates.

An example of a network that uses transmission gates is the XOR gate shown in Figure 3.8*b*; this network, which has fewer transistors than a structure without transmission gates, implements $z = x'y + xy'$ as follows:

y	$TG1$	$TG2$	z
0	ON	OFF	x
1	OFF	ON	x'

Another example of a network that uses transmission gates is the MUX **(multiplexer)** module. This module, shown in Figure 3.8*c*, has two binary data inputs x_1 and x_0, one binary control input s, and one binary output z. It implements the function described by

$$z = \text{MUX}(x_1, x_0, s) = x_1 s + x_0 s'$$

as follows:

s	$TG1$	$TG2$	z
0	ON	OFF	x_0
1	OFF	ON	x_1

As shown in these circuits, the outputs from several transmission gates can be connected together as long as exactly only one of them is closed and defines the value of the output.

3.3 PROPAGATION DELAYS, TRANSITION TIMES, AND EFFECT OF LOAD

The output voltage of a gate does not attain its final value instantaneously in response to a change of voltage at any of its inputs. The corresponding **time delay** is due to

- the delay of the switch; and
- the capacitance of the circuit elements and of the connections.

Such a noninstantaneous change defines the following timing characteristics of a gate, as illustrated in Figure 3.9 for a NOT gate:

Propagation delay is the time between predefined points on the input and output signals (usually 50% of the signal change). Two cases exist:

- t_{pHL}: propagation delay when the output signal changes from high to low; and
- t_{pLH}: propagation delay when the output signal changes from low to high.

Sometimes the average of t_{pHL} and t_{pLH}, denoted by t_p, is used as a simpler (but less precise) measure of the timing characteristics of a gate.

Transition time is the time taken by a signal to change between predefined points during a transition (usually 10% and 90% of the signal change). Two cases exist:

- t_r: transition time for low-to-high change (rise time); and
- t_f: transition time for high-to-low change (fall time).

The propagation delay of the gates determines the speed of a network. This speed is an important performance measure for digital systems, and in some cases is a fundamental factor in assuring the correct operation (the system not only has to perform a function but it is essential that it responds within a time interval).

Effect of Load: Input Load Factor, Total Load, and Fanout Factor

A combinational system is implemented by a network of gates, which is constructed by connecting the output of one gate to the inputs of other gates (see Figure 3.10). The gate inputs to which a gate output is connected affect the voltage of the output signal as well as its timing characteristics. We now give a simplified explanation of the circuit basis for this influence, and present a standardized method to determine its effect.

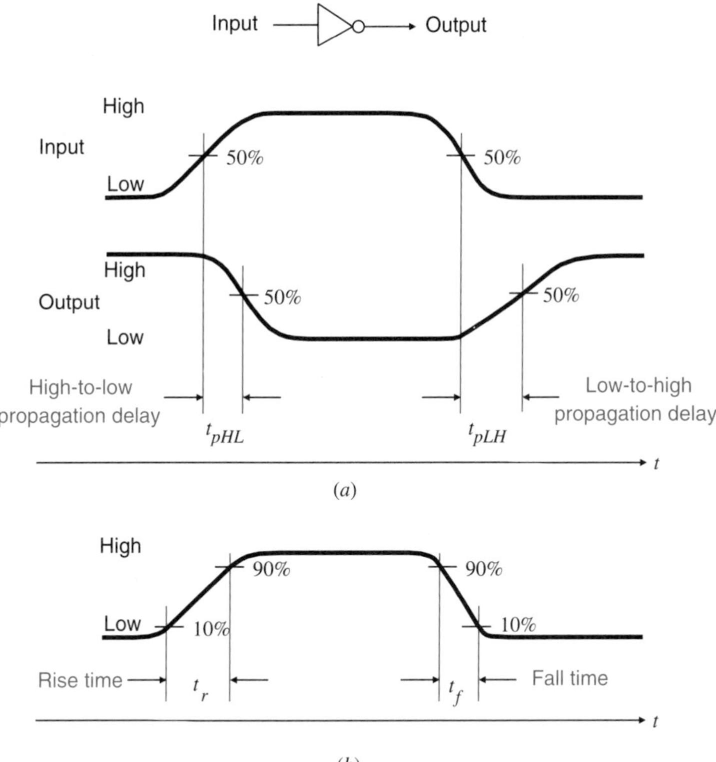

Figure 3.9 Timing parameters. (*a*) Propagation delay. (*b*) Rise and fall times.

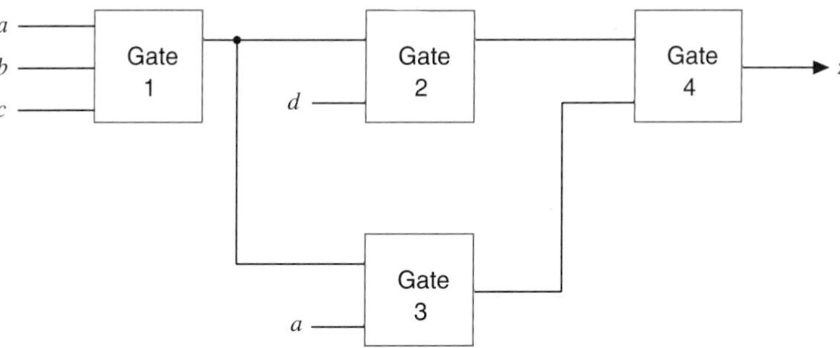

Figure 3.10 A gate network.

In its simplest form, the **load** imposed on a gate output by a gate input can be described by an equivalent resistance R_{in} and by an equivalent capacitance C_{in} connected in parallel, as shown in Figure 3.11. The resistance corresponds to the static load (effect when the voltage at the input does not change) and the capacitance to the dynamic load (effect during a voltage transition). When several inputs are connected to an output, the **total load** (or just load) on that output is obtained by combining the loads of each input.

In CMOS, the input resistance is very high compared with the resistance of a closed switch. Therefore, the effect of the static load can be neglected. On the other hand, the dynamic load (capacitance) has a significant effect on the timing characteristic, as illustrated in Figure 3.12 for the low-to-high transition, where load *B* corresponds to a larger equivalent capacitance than that of load *A*.

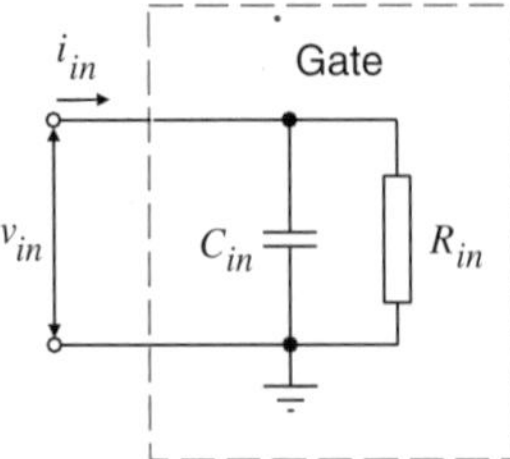

Figure 3.11 Equivalent circuit for gate input.

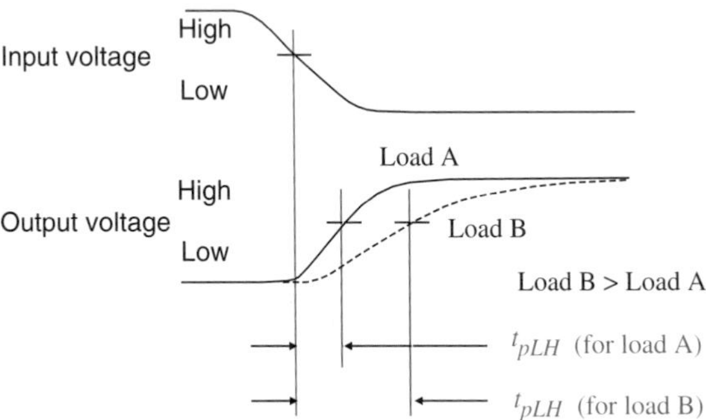

Figure 3.12 Effect of load on propagation delay.

The gates that are connected together to form a network usually belong to the same family, so the calculation of the timing characteristics of a gate output is simplified by using the following procedure:

1. A **standard load** unit is defined for the family. This standard load usually corresponds to the load of the input of a basic gate, such as a NOT.
2. The load of the gate inputs is given in terms of this unit. This measure is called the **load factor** of the input (I).
3. The **total load** of an output (L) is calculated as the sum of the load factors of all the inputs connected to the output, as depicted in Figure 3.13.

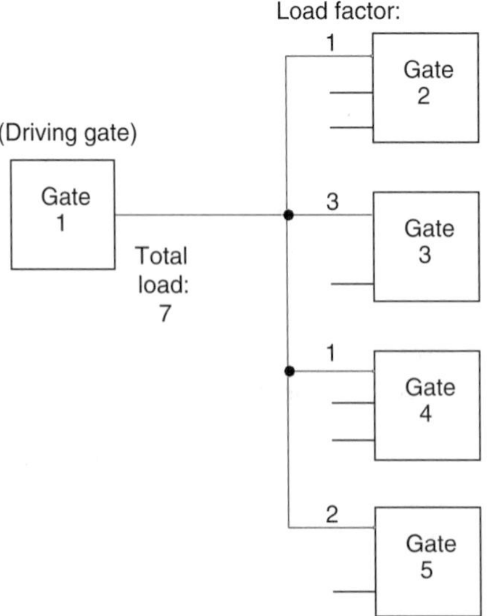

Figure 3.13 Output load of gate 1.

4. The timing characteristics of the gate output are given in terms of this total load. Usually, the propagation delays are linearly dependent on the load; for example, if L is the output load, the low-to-high propagation delay is specified as

$$t_{pLH} = 0.10 + 0.04L \text{ ns}$$

In the case of gate 1 in Figure 3.13, because the total load is $L = 7$, we get

$$t_{pLH} = 0.10 + 0.04 \times 7 = 0.38 \text{ ns}$$

Due to the effect of the load on the transition times, and to assure acceptable rise and fall times, the maximum load on an output gate is limited. This maximum value is called the **fanout factor** of the output. For example, a typical value of the fanout factor is 12 standard loads.

Special modules called **buffers** are used to reduce the effect of the load on the propagation delay. Basically, buffers correspond to NOT gates with larger transistors.

Fanin and its Effect on Timing and Voltages

The number of inputs to a gate is called its **fanin**. The fanin also influences the output voltage and timing characteristics of a gate. The details of this dependence are specific to each technology, but usually a larger fanin produces larger rise and fall times, and a smaller difference between the high and low voltages. Because these properties are undesirable, it is convenient to use gates with low fanin. Moreover, to get acceptable timing characteristics, gates are constructed up to a maximum number of inputs; for example, a typical maximum value is eight inputs.

3.4 VOLTAGE VARIATIONS AND NOISE MARGINS

As indicated earlier, the two voltage values V_H and V_L must be reasonably separated to adequately discriminate among them (see Figure 3.1). Because variations in the circuits' properties as well as in their loading can make the voltages vary from one gate to another, the circuits must operate correctly within a range of voltage values. Moreover, to tolerate **noise** (undesired changes in signal voltages caused by electromagnetic radiation, sudden changes in power supply voltage, etc.), it is essential that the voltage ranges at the input and output sides of the circuit differ as indicated in Figure 3.14. The difference $V_{Hmin}(\text{OUT}) - V_{Hmin}(\text{IN})$ represents the **noise margin** for the high voltage. The noise margin for the low voltage is defined in a similar manner. For example, typical values for a CMOS family of circuits are

Logical Level	Signal Voltage		Noise Margin
High	$V_{Hmin}(\text{OUT})$ $V_{Hmin}(\text{IN})$	2.4 V 2.0 V	0.4 V
Low	$V_{Lmax}(\text{OUT})$ $V_{Lmax}(\text{IN})$	0.4 V 0.8 V	0.4 V

3.5 POWER DISSIPATION AND DELAY-POWER PRODUCT

Power is consumed in electronic components as a result of the current flowing through (equivalent) resistances. The amount of power consumption per component is a characteristic of each technology. This power has to be generated by power supplies and must be dissipated from chips, boards, etc. to keep the temperature at acceptable values. This

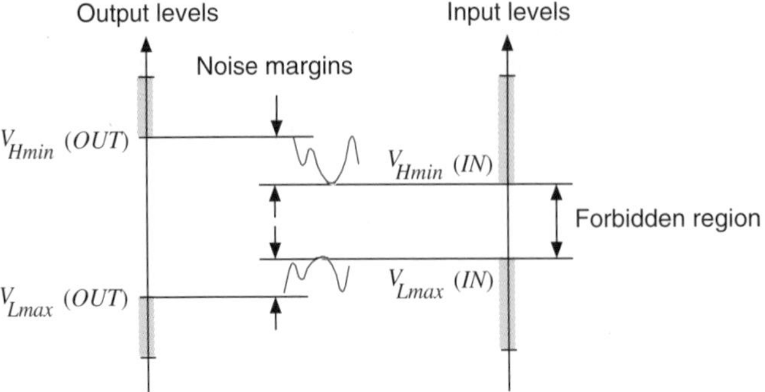

Figure 3.14 Noise margins.

dissipation requirement limits the density of components in a system. Moreover, usually there is a relationship among power consumption and speed of a circuit. This relationship has motivated the use of a combined measure called the **delay-power product,** which is the product of the delay of the circuit times the power consumed. Lower values correspond to circuits that achieve a given speed with lower power dissipation.

In CMOS, due to the large resistance of gate inputs, the power dissipated when the voltages are not changing can be neglected. That is, practically all the power is dissipated when the signals are changing. Consequently, one of the main advantages of CMOS is that the static power dissipation for this technology is inherently small; however, such an advantage decreases for high-frequency circuits.

3.6 BUSES AND THREE-STATE DRIVERS

Some digital systems consist of several modules (see Figure 3.15) in which, at a given time, the output of only one of the modules is selected for transmission and/or further processing. This selection can be implemented by a network such as the one depicted in Figure 3.15, where the output of module M_i is selected when $s_i = 1$ and $s_j = 0$, for all $j \neq i$. This implementation has the disadvantage that, if the number of modules is large, the OR gate has many inputs; due to the limitations in the maximum number of inputs, such an OR gate has to be implemented by a network of OR gates.

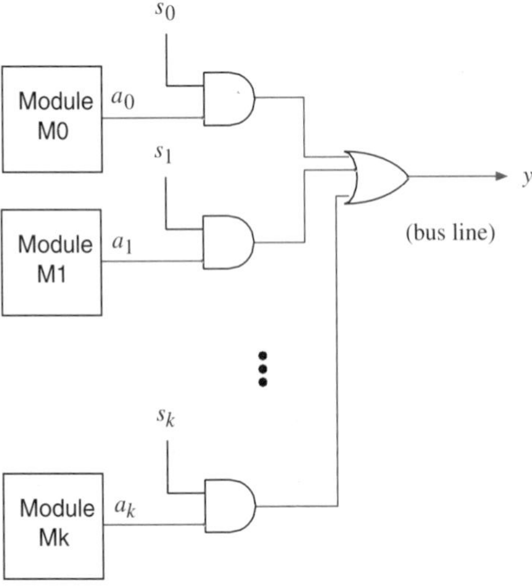

Figure 3.15 Gate network for selecting a module output.

The OR gate in Figure 3.15 can be eliminated by using **three-state gates (drivers)**. These gates have the following characteristics:

- The output has three possible values. That is, in addition to the two normal values 0 and 1, the output can also take a third value called Z.
- The gate has two binary inputs (see Figure 3.16*a*): a data input x and an enable input e. Its operation is such that when the enable signal is 1 the output corresponds to the data input (noninverting driver), whereas when the enable input is 0 the output has value Z.

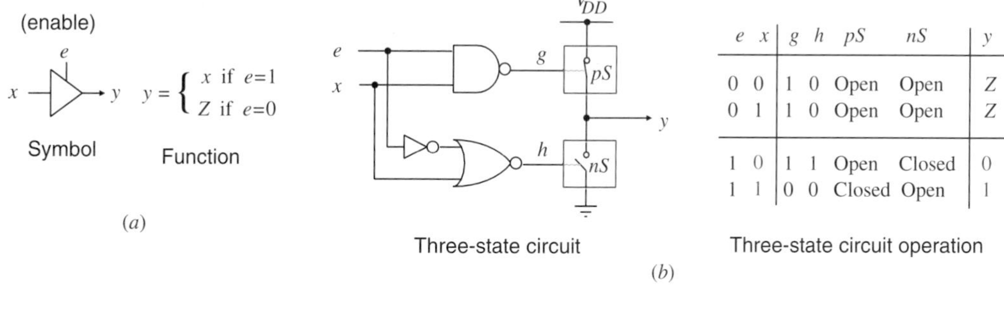

e	x	g	h	pS	nS	y
0	0	1	0	Open	Open	Z
0	1	1	0	Open	Open	Z
1	0	1	1	Open	Closed	0
1	1	0	0	Closed	Open	1

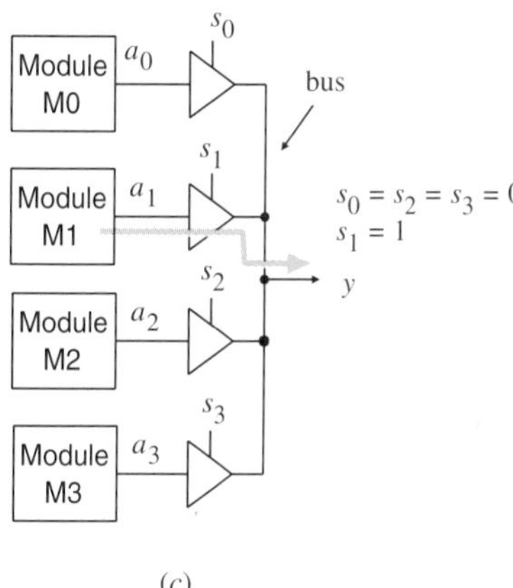

Figure 3.16 (*a*) Three-state gate: symbol and function. (*b*) Circuit and operation. (*c*) Example of use.

- The value Z corresponds to a high impedance (like an open switch).[2] As a result, the outputs of several three-state drivers can be connected together as long as only one driver is enabled at a time. Figure 3.16*c* shows an example of such a connection. The output corresponds to the switching expression

$$y = a_0 \cdot s_0 + a_1 \cdot s_1 + a_2 \cdot s_2 + a_3 \cdot s_3$$

Note that, for the network to operate properly, exactly one of the signals s_0, s_1, s_2, s_3 should have value 1 at a given time. The line connecting the output of the three-state gates is called a **bus**, and the three-state gates are called **bus drivers**.

[2]This is the reason for calling this value Z, the usual label for impedance. In some texts and data sheets, the third value is called Hi-Z.

A CMOS realization of the three-state driver is shown in Figure 3.16*b*, together with a table describing the circuit operation. Note that, in contrast to transmission gates, three-state gates are used at the output of a module.

3.7 CIRCUIT CHARACTERISTICS OF A CMOS FAMILY

Effective physical implementation of basic gates exists for most semiconductor technologies. These gates are produced by semiconductor manufacturers in small-scale integrated circuits (SSI packages) which contain a small number of gates, and are also used in the implementation of medium-scale (MSI), large-scale (LSI), and very large-scale (VLSI) modules.

The prevalent technology today is CMOS due to its simple processing, good static and dynamic characteristics, and low power consumption. As an illustration, Table 3.1 gives the main parameters of a family of CMOS gates; this family is a representative example of the gate-array technology available in 1995.[3] These characteristics are used later in some of the analysis and design examples. Note that the delays and the size of the gates increase with the number of inputs, the delay is a linear function of the gate output load, and the maximum number of inputs is four for the AND and OR gates, eight for NAND and NOR, and three for XOR and XNOR.

The maximum load (fanout factor) of the gates is limited because the load affects the characteristics of the signals, such as rise time and fall time. A typical fanout factor for this family is 12.

The delay characteristics given in Table 3.1 serve to make approximate delay calculations of gate networks. For more accurate calculations, electrical models of the gates are used in circuit simulators such as SPICE. These simulators also take into account the loading and delay effects of the interconnections.

Table 3.1 gives nominal (or typical) values of delay. However, these values vary with parameters of the process used to manufacture the chips, as well as with environmental parameters such as temperature and voltage. To take into account these variations, the nominal delay is multiplied by delay derating factors. These factors depend on the operating environment where the chip is utilized; there are three standard operating environments, called **commercial, industrial,** and **military.** The values of these factors are obtained from the manufacturer.

3.8 EVOLUTION IN THE IMPLEMENTATION OF DIGITAL SYSTEMS

It is of interest at this point to describe briefly the historical evolution of digital modules and their implementation. Initially, all designs had to be done using elementary electronic devices. Soon it was apparent that some simple networks of these devices were frequently utilized, so modules having several of these elementary devices were made available for use in many designs. These modules were implemented as a card with inputs and outputs going to a connector. To build a system, several of these cards were connected through a backplane. To make these cards compatible and useful for many designs, their electrical characteristics such as voltage and impedance were standardized. This was the origin of standard modules.

---

[3]The characteristics are an approximation to those of the LSI Logic's LCA500K process technology. LCA is a gate array technology that features 0.5 μm, 3.3 V technology. More details on this gate-array family can be found in LCA500K Preliminary Design Manual, LSI Logic Corporation, Milpitas, CA 1994.

Table 3.1 Characteristics of a family of CMOS gates

Gate Type	Fan-in	Propagation Delays t_{pLH} (ns)	Propagation Delays t_{pHL} (ns)	Load Factor I (standard loads)	Size (equivalent gates)
AND	2	$0.15 + 0.037L$	$0.16 + 0.017L$	1.0	2
AND	3	$0.20 + 0.038L$	$0.18 + 0.018L$	1.0	2
AND	4	$0.28 + 0.039L$	$0.21 + 0.019L$	1.0	3
OR	2	$0.12 + 0.037L$	$0.20 + 0.019L$	1.0	2
OR	3	$0.12 + 0.038L$	$0.34 + 0.022L$	1.0	2
OR	4	$0.13 + 0.038L$	$0.45 + 0.025L$	1.0	3
NOT	1	$0.02 + 0.038L$	$0.05 + 0.017L$	1.0	1
NAND	2	$0.05 + 0.038L$	$0.08 + 0.027L$	1.0	1
NAND	3	$0.07 + 0.038L$	$0.09 + 0.039L$	1.0	2
NAND	4	$0.10 + 0.037L$	$0.12 + 0.051L$	1.0	2
NAND	5	$0.21 + 0.038L$	$0.34 + 0.019L$	1.0	4
NAND	6	$0.24 + 0.037L$	$0.36 + 0.019L$	1.0	5
NAND	8	$0.24 + 0.038L$	$0.42 + 0.019L$	1.0	6
NOR	2	$0.06 + 0.075L$	$0.07 + 0.016L$	1.0	1
NOR	3	$0.16 + 0.111L$	$0.08 + 0.017L$	1.0	2
NOR	4	$0.23 + 0.149L$	$0.08 + 0.017L$	1.0	4
NOR	5	$0.38 + 0.038L$	$0.23 + 0.018L$	1.0	4
NOR	6	$0.46 + 0.037L$	$0.24 + 0.018L$	1.0	5
NOR	8	$0.54 + 0.038L$	$0.23 + 0.018L$	1.0	6
XOR	2*	$0.30 + 0.036L$	$0.30 + 0.021L$	1.1	3
		$0.16 + 0.036L$	$0.15 + 0.020L$	2.0	
XOR	3*	$0.50 + 0.038L$	$0.49 + 0.027L$	1.1	6
		$0.28 + 0.039L$	$0.27 + 0.027L$	2.4	
		$0.19 + 0.036L$	$0.17 + 0.025L$	2.1	
XNOR	2*	$0.30 + 0.036L$	$0.30 + 0.021L$	1.1	3
		$0.16 + 0.036L$	$0.15 + 0.020L$	2.0	
XNOR	3*	$0.50 + 0.038L$	$0.49 + 0.027L$	1.1	6
		$0.28 + 0.039L$	$0.27 + 0.027L$	2.3	
		$0.19 + 0.036L$	$0.17 + 0.025L$	1.3	
2-OR/NAND2	4	$0.17 + 0.075L$	$0.10 + 0.028L$	1.0	2
2-AND/NOR2	4	$0.17 + 0.075L$	$0.10 + 0.028L$	1.0	2

L: Load on the gate output.

* Different characteristics for each input.

As the devices became smaller and the design methods matured, more complex modules were built on a card. Functions such as adders, decoders, multiplexers, registers, and counters were included in one card. At the same time, individual primitive modules (gates and flip-flops) were packaged together, although not connected together, so that they could be incorporated by a designer in the implementation of more complex functions.

The next step was the introduction of integrated circuits. Early examples of such circuits contained several gates or flip-flops in one semiconductor component, and were actually **integrated** implementations of what formerly was built on a printed-circuit card. All gates inputs and outputs were available at the pins of the package (chip). Some chips contained interconnections among the gates, implementing simple functions. Initially, just a few gates (less than ten) could be included in one package, resulting in what is today called **small-scale integration** (SSI) technology. The effect of this development was the reduction in volume, power consumption, and cost of the implementation of these simple functions.

The technology continued evolving, making it possible to have more electronic devices per chip. This led to the introduction of more complex functions, such as decoders, adders, and comparators on a single chip. These chips are called **medium-scale integrated** (MSI) modules, containing up to 100 gates. At this level of complexity, one of the major problems is the determination of which functions should be implemented in a chip. These functions should be useful for many systems because MSI modules are cost effective only if they are mass produced. Another important factor is the number of inputs and outputs of the module, because there is a severe limitation on the number of pins of an integrated package and because external connections are costly. A few dozen standard MSI modules have evolved.

The density of devices on a chip continued to increase, leading to **large-scale integration** (LSI) modules with up to several hundreds or a few thousands gates. The problem of cost-effectiveness and mass production is even more critical in this case, due to the larger complexity of the function that can be implemented. This led to the introduction of **programmable modules**, such as read-only memories (ROMs) and programmable logic arrays (PLAs). These modules have a regular structure and can be used to implement a large class of functions, the specific function being "programmed" in the last step of production or in the field.

Finally, a new increase in density has given rise to **very-large-scale integrated** (VLSI) modules containing many thousands of gates. Complete processors can be put in a single chip using this technology. As of 1998, there are VLSI chips containing several million devices, which implement the functionality formerly available in large systems. Moreover, the density of VLSI chips continues to increase, doubling the capacity every 18 to 24 months.

The level of integration (number of transistors on a chip) has been increasing dramatically in the last years; this increase is illustrated in Table 3.2.

In summary, in just a few years there has been a revolution in the implementation of digital systems. This has resulted in an explosive expansion of their use, and in a drastic modification in the specification and design methods. In the 1950s, technology produced gates at great cost, so designs tended to minimize the number of gates. Integration has changed the situation because thousands of gates can be fabricated together in a single chip, which costs much less than one 1950-type gate. As a consequence, the minimization of the number of gates is not always the primary design objective. Moreover, the constant demand for higher performance of the systems requires that functions are implemented using structures with shorter delays, which usually means using more gates.

In addition, the development of a complex integrated chip is very expensive, so that a particular chip design is profitable only if the chip is used in many applications and is produced in large volumes. Consequently, a design challenge is to use standard modules in

Table 3.2 Levels of integration of digital chips

Level of integration	Technology	Number of transistors	Typical functions
SSI	bipolar	≈ 10	Individual gates, flip-flops
MSI	MOS, bipolar	10–100	Adders, counters, registers
LSI	MOS, bipolar	100–10,000	ROMs, PLAs, small memories
VLSI	MOS, bipolar	$> 10{,}000$	large memories, microprocessors, complex systems

the systems. This might change in the future, if the development cost of an integrated chip is dramatically reduced.

The technological changes have also had a large impact on the way digital systems have to be studied. At this time, many of the traditional methods of specification and design are being discarded or modified in order to adapt them to the higher complexity of the systems and the different implementation constraints. Because no definitive specification and design techniques have evolved yet (and may never do so), it is necessary to concentrate on the conceptual background that will almost certainly serve as the basis for new methods; today's methods should be used only as illustrations of the application of the concepts to specific constraints. The student will then be equipped to develop and use new methods under different constraints.

Due to the complexity of the systems being designed nowadays, suitable development tools are necessary. These are **computer-aided design** (CAD) tools, which help in the specification, design, simulation, and implementation of a system. Some of the tools mimic the design process traditionally used (drawing the schematics of the systems) but in a hierarchical manner; others use a register-transfer level approach, in which the system is represented in a **hardware description language** (HDL). In all cases, the tools include simulation capabilities. Moreover, there are synthesis tools that transform a high-level description into an implementation, using specific technologies.

3.9 VLSI CIRCUIT-LEVEL DESIGN STYLES

The circuit-level design of a VLSI chip consists essentially in the determination of the characteristics of the circuit components (basically, transistors), their placement and their connection (routing). Several styles have evolved for this design level; among other aspects, they differ in the primitive modules used in the design at the logic level, and in the flexibility allowed for the placement of modules on a chip.

Full-custom design, which was the first style to evolve, uses circuit elements such as transistors and connections as the primitive components; a designer has complete freedom regarding the placement of these components on a chip and on their interconnection, as long as certain design rules are satisfied. The determination of the characteristics of the chip, such as speed, area and power dissipation, is done at the circuit level. This design style is the most flexible and permits the optimization of particular characteristics. However, for complex chips it is very time consuming and requires a full knowledge of the operation of the components at the circuit level.

To simplify the design process, several more restricted design styles have been introduced; they are characterized by the basic components that a designer can use, and by the ways that these components can be placed on the chip. In **semicustom** design, a library of cells (**standard cells**) is designed at the circuit level; these cells are specified by their function and some circuit characteristics. The use of the cells at the logic level simplifies considerably the design process, but reduces the flexibility and the possibility of optimizing specific characteristics. In some instances, a combination of full-custom and semicustom design is best, wherein the critical portions of the system are designed using full-custom.

A third style is called **gate-array** design. In this approach, basic components (usually basic gates) are placed on a regular structure within a chip, and the design consists of determining the connections between the gates. Figure 3.17 illustrates a segment of a gate array consisting of three-input NAND gates surrounded by vertical and horizontal channels for routing wires.

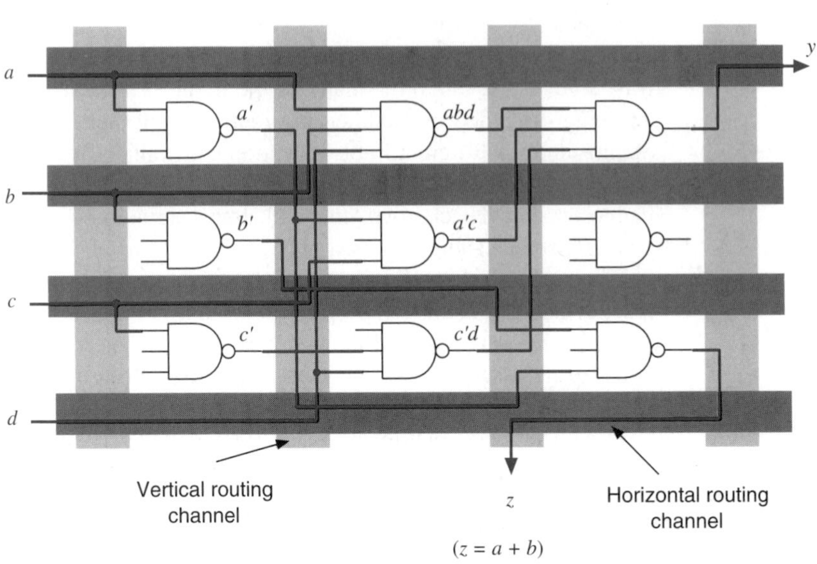

Figure 3.17 Example of a gate array.

3.10 PACKAGING LEVEL: CHIPS, BOARDS, AND CABINETS

Complex digital systems are implemented in a hierarchical manner. From the point of view of the circuit realization, the main levels are integrated circuits (chips), boards, and subsystems. A chip is the primitive packaging unit for integrated circuits (see Figure 3.18). Several chips are put together on a (printed circuit) board (Figure 3.19*a*); this is necessary whenever the complexity of a system is greater than what can be put on a single chip and/or when the volume of production of the system does not warrant the design and construction of a specialized chip, so that it is more cost effective to put together several chips (however, this results in a larger as well as slower system because the propagation time of signals between chips is significantly larger than between circuits inside a chip). Finally, several boards are put together in a cabinet (rack) to form the system (or a subsystem). The boards are connected through a backplane (Figure 3.19*b* and 3.19*c*).

The following table indicates the type and number of packaging levels in the IBM 3081 central processing unit.

Level of Packaging	Number of Components	Size (mm × mm)
Module	100–133 chips	90 × 90
PC board	6 – 9 modules	600 × 700
Subsystem (processor)	3 boards	
System (CPU)	2 subsystems	

Source H. B. Bakoglu (1990).

3.11 μ VHDL DESCRIPTION OF GATES

We now address the description of basic gates and their characteristics using the hardware description language μVHDL. The functional description of the gates follows the definitions

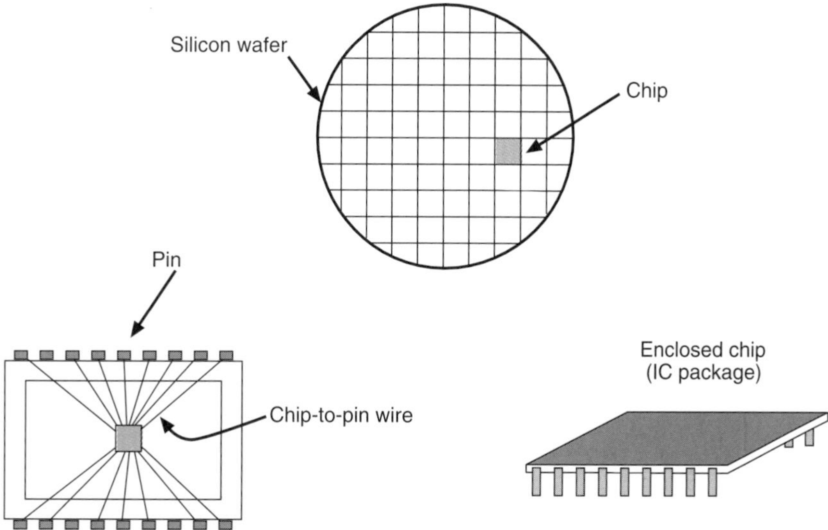

Figure 3.18 Silicon wafer, chip, and integrated circuit package.

and examples given in Chapter 2 for combinational systems. However, because the functionality of basic gates is quite simple, the corresponding behavioral descriptions are also quite simple. We now introduce additional features of the language, which allow incorporating the other characteristics of the basic gates into the μVHDL-based descriptions, and illustrate the use of such features with some examples.

When a μVHDL description is used as a complete specification of a module, then the description should contain the specification of the characteristics of the module such as delays, load factors, and so on. This is accomplished using the language constructs described in this section (such as the clause AFTER). In contrast, when a μVHDL description is used as the specification for the synthesis of a module, then the characteristics of a module are determined by the physical components used in the synthesis process, their interconnection, and so on. This is the case, for example, when the μVHDL description is used to specify the functionality of a programmable logic device (see Chapter 12), wherein the delays and load factors are determined by the logic devices and their interconnection. Consequently, the specification of the characteristics of a module depends on the intended use of the μVHDL description. In this section, we assume that the explicit specification of the characteristics of a module is necessary.

Specification of Delays

In μVHDL, signals are continuous functions of time (time functions) that are generated through signal assignments. As discussed in Chapter 2, values assigned to input signals represent the external stimuli to a module, whereas assignments to output signals are generated by a module.

In μVHDL, a signal assignment may include a **delay**, represented by an AFTER clause, which indicates when the assigned value appears at the signal with respect to the time when the assignment is made. This is specified as follows:

```
y <= '0';
x <= '1' AFTER 5 ns;
z <= '0','1' AFTER 10 ns;
```

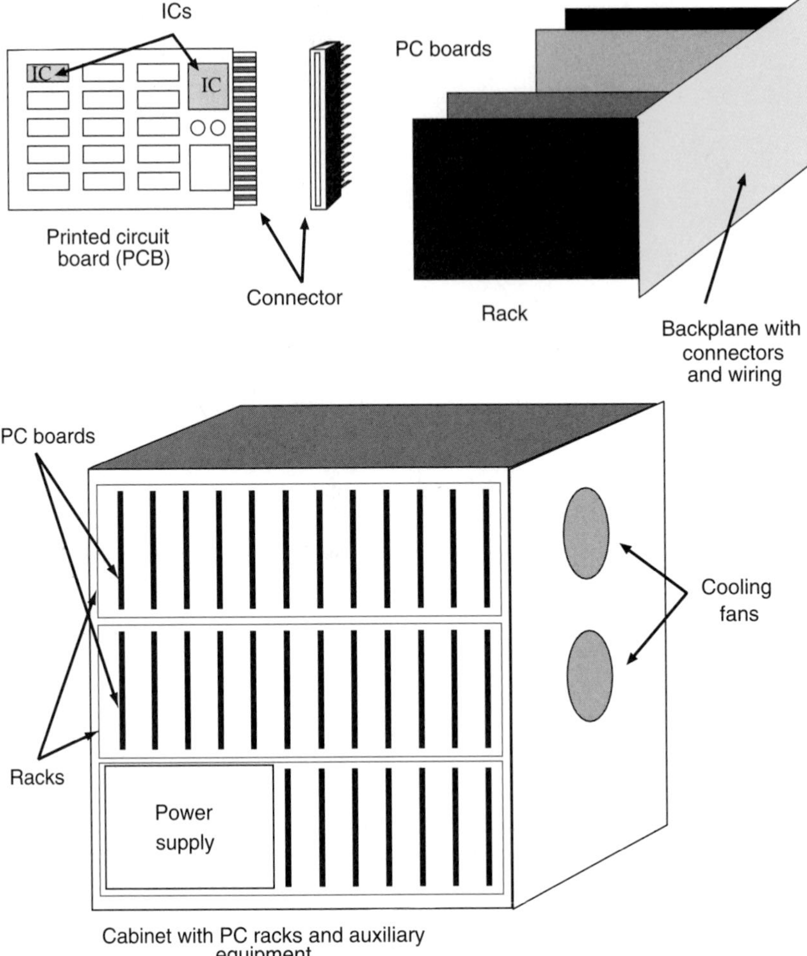

Figure 3.19 Packaging levels.

The first assignment states that signal y is assigned the value '0' immediately; on the other hand, the second assignment states that signal x is assigned the value '1' with a delay of 5 ns. That is, the value assigned to x will appear on the signal 5 ns later than the value assigned to y. The last assignment combines the notation used in the other two cases: signal z is assigned the value '0' immediately, and the value '1' with a delay of 10 ns.

The delay specified in the AFTER clause may be the result of an expression; for instance,

```
x <= '1' AFTER (base_delay + delay_factor * L)
```

The use of delays in signal assignments is illustrated in the following example.

EXAMPLE 3.1

An AND gate with a constant delay of 0.15 ns is described as follows:

```
ENTITY and_gate IS
  PORT(x,y : IN  BIT;
       z   : OUT BIT);
END and_gate;
```

```
ARCHITECTURE const_delay OF and_gate IS
BEGIN
  PROCESS (x,y)
    CONSTANT delay   : TIME := 150 ps;
  BEGIN
      z <= (x AND y) AFTER delay;
  END PROCESS;
END const_delay;
```

This description consists of a PROCESS containing a single statement, which gives the functionality of the gate as well as its delay with respect to a change in either of the inputs. ■

The following example corresponds to a refinement of the AND gate given in Example 3.1, in which there are different delays depending on the type of output transition.

EXAMPLE 3.2

An AND gate with transition-dependent delays is described as follows:

```
ENTITY and_gate IS
  PORT(x,y: IN  BIT;
       z  : OUT BIT);
END and_gate;

ARCHITECTURE trans_dep_delay OF and_gate IS
BEGIN
  PROCESS (x,y)
    SUBTYPE  BitVector2 IS BIT_VECTOR(1 DOWNTO 0);
    VARIABLE vold, vnew : BIT;
    VARIABLE both : BitVector2 ;
    CONSTANT TpHL : TIME := 160 ps;
    CONSTANT TpLH : TIME := 150 ps;
  BEGIN
    vnew := x AND y;
    both := vold & vnew;              -- & : concatenate operator
    CASE both IS
      WHEN "00" | "11" => null;       -- | : logic or
      WHEN "10"        => z <= vnew AFTER TpHL;
      WHEN "01"        => z <= vnew AFTER TpLH;
    END CASE;
    vold:= vnew;
  END PROCESS;
END trans_dep_delay;
```

This description uses variables to represent the new and previous values produced by the gate. The gate output is assigned the new value, which depends only on the current input. The previous value of the output signal is preserved by the process only to determine the delay, as described by the entries to the CASE statement. ■

Specification of Load

The description of a gate usually does not contain a specification of the load imposed on it because such a load depends on the network attached to the gate output. Moreover, it is desirable to have a single description for a given type of gate in which the load is a parameter. This functionality can be described in μVHDL using the statement GENERIC, which appears in the ENTITY declaration of a module; this statement specifies the name and type of each parameter, and its default value. The use of this statement for describing the load imposed on a gate is illustrated in the following example.

EXAMPLE 3.3

The following description corresponds to the two-input AND gate given in Table 3.1, with delay depending on the load imposed on the gate. The value of such a load is provided to the module as a generic parameter.

```
PACKAGE factors_pkg IS
  SUBTYPE load_value IS REAL RANGE 0.0 TO 12.0;
END factors_pkg;

USE WORK.factors_pkg.ALL;

ENTITY and_gate IS
  GENERIC (L: load_value:= 1.0);     -- default value for gate load
  PORT(x,y: IN  BIT;
       z  : OUT BIT);
END and_gate;

ARCHITECTURE load_dep_delay OF and_gate IS
BEGIN
  PROCESS (x,y)
    CONSTANT base_delay   : TIME:= 150 ps;
    CONSTANT delay_factor: TIME:=  37 ps;
  BEGIN
    z <= (x AND y) AFTER (base_delay + delay_factor * L);
  END PROCESS;
END load_dep_delay;
```

This entity declaration indicates that the gate has one GENERIC parameter (which in this case represents the number of standard loads connected to the gate), and provides the default value L=1.0 for it. The delay of this gate is determined by the value of L; in the default case (no value specified for the parameter), the delay is 0.187 ns. ■

The descriptions given in the last two examples can be combined so that the delay of the gate depends on its load as well as on the type of transition.

Additional aspects in the description of gates are the load factor of each input (input load factor), the fanout factor, and the size of the gate (in terms of equivalent gates). This type of information is used, for example, to determine the actual load imposed on other gates, to determine the equivalent size of an entire network, or to verify that the load on a gate does not exceed its fanout factor. Such information can be provided with the ATTRIBUTE declaration, as illustrated in the following example.

EXAMPLE 3.4

A two-input XOR gate as the one given in Table 3.1 is characterized by having a different load factor for each input. Assuming the same delay for low-to-high and high-to-low transitions in response to changes in either input, the description of such a gate including its equivalent size is

```
PACKAGE factors_pkg IS
  SUBTYPE load_value IS REAL    RANGE 0.0 TO 12.0;
  SUBTYPE size_value IS INTEGER RANGE 1 TO 10;

  ATTRIBUTE load_factor: load_value;
  ATTRIBUTE equiv_size : size_value;
END factors_pkg;

USE WORK.factors_pkg.ALL;

ENTITY xor_gate IS
  GENERIC (L   : load_value:= 1.0);
  PORT    (x,y : IN  BIT;
           z   : OUT BIT);
END xor_gate;

ARCHITECTURE with_attribs OF xor_gate IS
  ATTRIBUTE load_factor OF x:SIGNAL IS 2.0;
  ATTRIBUTE load_factor OF y:SIGNAL IS 1.1;
  ATTRIBUTE equiv_size  OF xor_gate:ENTITY IS 3;
BEGIN
  PROCESS (x,y)
    CONSTANT base_delay   : TIME := 300 ps;
    CONSTANT delay_factor : TIME :=  36 ps;
  BEGIN
     z <= (x XOR y) AFTER (base_delay + delay_factor * L);
  END PROCESS;
END with_attribs;
```

In this description, the intrinsic properties of the gate are specified by using the ATTRIBUTE declaration. The difference between an ATTRIBUTE and a GENERIC declaration is that the ATTRIBUTE describes a characteristic of the gate itself, whereas the GENERIC describes a characteristic imposed on the gate. ■

Gates as the ones described in this section are used in the next chapters to form part of networks of gates that implement combinational systems.

3.12 FURTHER READINGS

Analysis and Design of Integrated Circuits by D. A. Hodges and H. G. Jackson, New York: McGraw-Hill, 1983; *Microelectronics: Digital and Analog Circuits* by J. Millman, New York: McGraw-Hill, 1979; and *Digital Design: Principles and Practices* by J. F. Wakerly, Englewood Cliffs, NJ: Prentice-Hall, 1994 provide a thorough treatment of the electronic aspects of digital circuits. Regarding theory and design of MOS circuits (nMOS and CMOS), among the many books written on the subject the reader may consult *Introduction to VLSI Design* by C. Mead and L. Conway, Reading, MA: Addison-Wesley, 1980, *Introduction to nMOS and CMOS VLSI Systems Design* by A. Mukherjee, Englewood Cliffs, NJ: Prentice-Hall, 1986; and *Basic VLSI Design: Systems and Circuits* by D. A. Pucknell and K. Eshraghian, New York: Prentice-Hall, 1988; CMOS in particular is discussed in *Principles of CMOS VLSI Design: A Systems Perspective* by N. Weste and K. Eshraghian, 2nd ed., Reading, MA: Addison-Wesley, 1993.

For a comprehensive discussion of VLSI circuits, process technologies, design methodologies, and computer-aided design (CAD) tools, see, for example, *VLSI Engineering* by

T. E. Dillinger, Englewood Cliffs, NJ: Prentice-Hall, 1988. A comprehensive treatment of digital integrated circuits from a circuit and system design point of view is provided in *Digital Integrated Circuits: A Design Perspective* by J. M. Rabaey, Upper Saddle River, NJ: Prentice-Hall, 1996.

Circuits, interconnections, and packaging for VLSI are discussed in depth in *Circuits, Interconnections, and Packaging for VLSI* by H. B. Bakoglu, Reading, MA: Addison-Wesley, 1990. Information about particular integrated circuits can be obtained from data books provided by the manufacturers.

EXERCISES

Representation of binary variables

Exercise 3.1 A logic family has the following ranges of voltages to represent the high and low values: HIGH = 3.5 V to 5.0 V, LOW = 0.0 V to 1.5 V.

a. For the following signal values, determine the corresponding logic values for positive and for negative logic:
   i. 1.0 V.
   ii. 4.5 V.
   iii. 2.0 V.
   iv. −1.0 V.
b. For a module with inputs x_1 and x_0 and output z you have performed the following set of measures (all in volts):

x_1	x_0	z
0.3	0.2	0.5
0.3	4.5	4.4
4.5	0.2	4.4
4.5	4.5	0.2

What type of gate does this circuit implement for positive and for negative logic?

Basic gate structure

Exercise 3.2 As stated in Section 3.2.3, the p-net is the complement of the n-net; that is, when the n-net has a path to ground the p-net should not have a path to V_{DD}, and vice versa. Show that this requirement is not satisfied for the network in Figure 3.20. (*Hint:* Consider the case $a = b = 1$ and $c = d = 0$). Consequently, this network is not satisfactory to implement the expression $z = (a' + b')c'd'$.

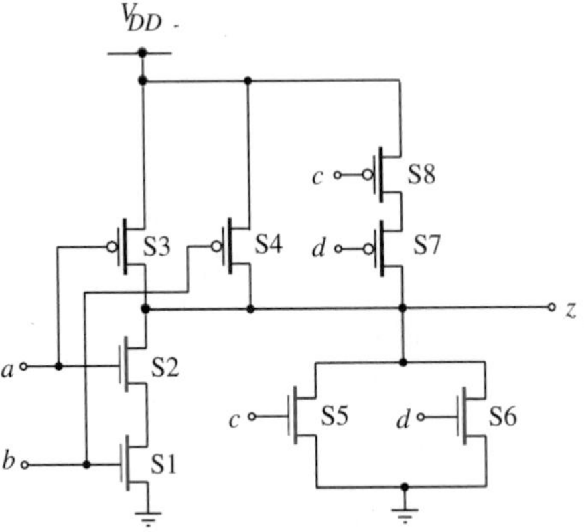

Figure 3.20 Network for Exercise 3.2.

Exercise 3.3 Show a CMOS circuit for the network depicted in Figure 3.21 using:

a. AND and NOR circuits;
b. one complex gate.

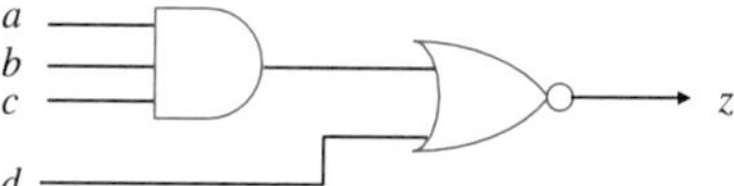

Figure 3.21 Network for Exercise 3.3.

Exercise 3.4 Show a CMOS circuit that implements the following function for positive logic:

x_1	x_0	z
0	0	0
0	1	1
1	0	0
1	1	0

Exercise 3.5 Determine the function of the circuit shown in Figure 3.22.

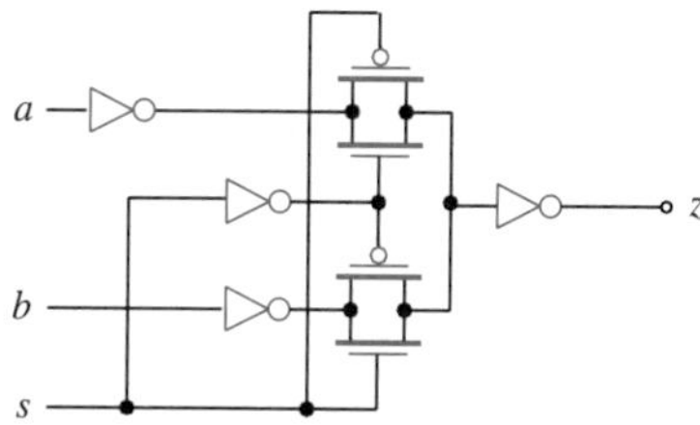

Figure 3.22 Network for Exercise 3.5.

Driving capabilities: load factors and output load

Exercise 3.6 For the network shown in Figure 3.23,

a. determine the output load of gate 1;
b. how many additional gate inputs with load factor of 1 can be connected to the output of gate 6?

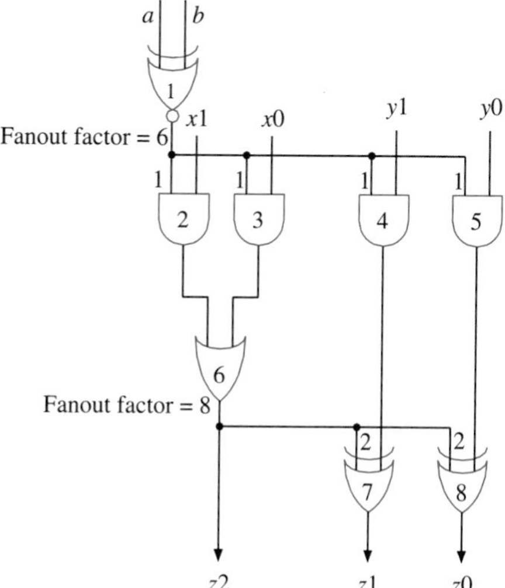

Figure 3.23 Network for Exercise 3.6.

Propagation delays

Exercise 3.7 Determine the propagation delays for a NOR gate that has the input and output waveforms depicted in Figure 3.24.

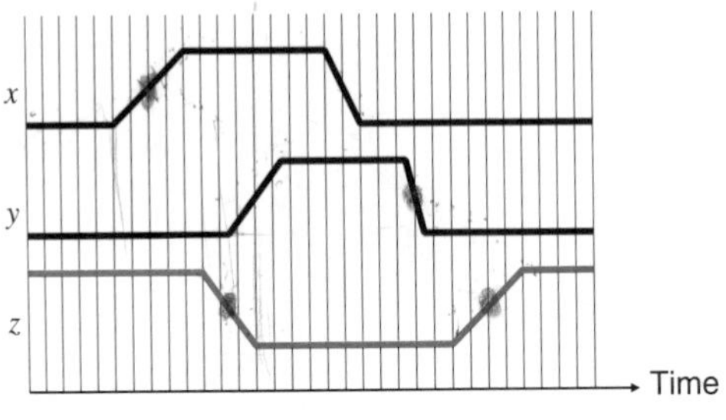

Figure 3.24 Waveform for Exercise 3.7.

Exercise 3.8 For a gate, the propagation delays are given by the expressions

$$t_{pHL} = 0.43 + 0.15L \text{ (ns)}$$

$$t_{pLH} = 0.35 + 0.25L \text{ (ns)}$$

Show a possible pair of input-output waveforms for $L = 1$ and for $L = 2$.

Exercise 3.9

a. A gate in a network has a load $L = 70$. Determine the propagation delays for the expressions given in Exercise 3.8.

   This delay can be reduced by putting a buffer at the output of the gate. The load factor of the buffer is $I = 2$ and its propagation delay is described by the expressions

$$t_{pHL} = t_{pLH} = 0.6 + 0.02L \text{ (ns)}$$

b. Determine the propagation delay of the gate followed by one buffer (the buffer feeding the $L = 70$ load).
c. Connect to the output of the gate two buffers, each feeding half of the load. Determine the delay.
d. Determine the optimal number of buffers to connect in parallel.

Exercise 3.10 Determine the rise and fall times in the timing diagram depicted in Figure 3.25.

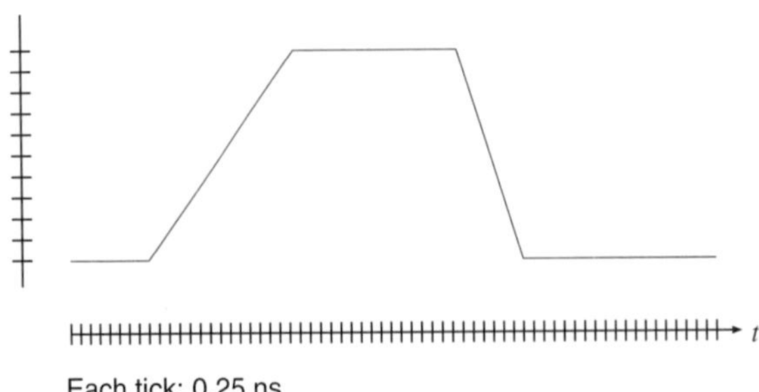

Figure 3.25 Waveform in Exercise 3.10.

Noise margins

Exercise 3.11 Determine the noise margins for a gate with the following voltage ranges

$$\begin{aligned} a &\leq V_H(\text{IN}) &\leq b \\ c &\leq V_L(\text{IN}) &\leq d \\ e &\leq V_H(\text{OUT}) &\leq f \\ g &\leq V_L(\text{OUT}) &\leq h \end{aligned}$$

μVHDL descriptions

Exercise 3.12 Write a μVHDL description for the three-input AND and OR gates given in Table 3.1; include gate delay that depends on the transition and the load.

Exercise 3.13 Write a μVHDL description for the three-input NAND and NOR gates given in Table 3.1; include gate delay that depends on the transition and the load.

Exercise 3.14 Write a μVHDL description for the three-input XOR gate given in Table 3.1; include gate delay that depends on the transition and the load.

Chapter 4

Description and Analysis of Gate Networks

In this chapter, we discuss

- The definition, description, and characteristics of gate networks.
- Alternative sets of gates that compose networks.
- The analysis of gate networks: determination of the function and of other characteristics.
- The description of gate networks using μVHDL.

As indicated in Chapter 3, the realization of a combinational system involves the circuit level and the logic level. The circuit level, which was the subject of the previous chapter, deals with the physical realization of gates. In contrast, the logic level consists of the realization of a combinational system by a collection of simpler systems (called **combinational modules**) in a structure known as a **combinational network**. This network concept can be used at several levels in a hierarchical manner (see Figure 4.1) because a module in a network can itself be realized as a network of simpler modules. Such a realization is referred to as a **hierarchical implementation** of a combinational system.

In this chapter we study the lowest level of the hierarchical implementation — **gate networks** — that is, combinational networks in which the modules are the gates described in Chapters 2 and 3. These networks are important because they provide the interface between the circuit level and the logic level, and they represent the foundation on which more complex systems are developed. Moreover, this study allows us to introduce concepts and

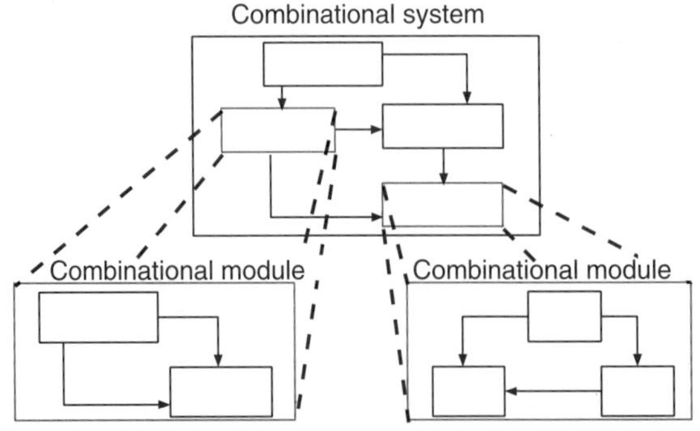

Figure 4.1 Hierarchical implementation of a combinational system.

procedures that are useful at all levels of the hierarchy. This chapter addresses the description and analysis of gate networks, whereas design methods are presented in Chapter 5.

4.1 DEFINITION OF GATE NETWORKS

A **gate network** is an interconnection of gates that implements a (binary) combinational system. As shown in Figure 4.2, it consists of

- gates;
- external inputs and outputs; and
- connections (**from** external inputs and gate outputs **to** gate inputs and external outputs).

The **connections** in a network carry **signals** (values), and have the following restrictions:

1. Each gate input is connected either to a constant value (0 or 1), to a network (external) input, or to a gate output. Only one connection to a gate input is allowed; an undefined value might result if two or more signals (with different values) are connected simultaneously to a single gate input. Exceptions to this rule are the three-state connections discussed in Chapter 3.

   Figure 4.3*a* shows an invalid connection from the outputs of gates G_1 and G_2 to the lower input of gate G_3.

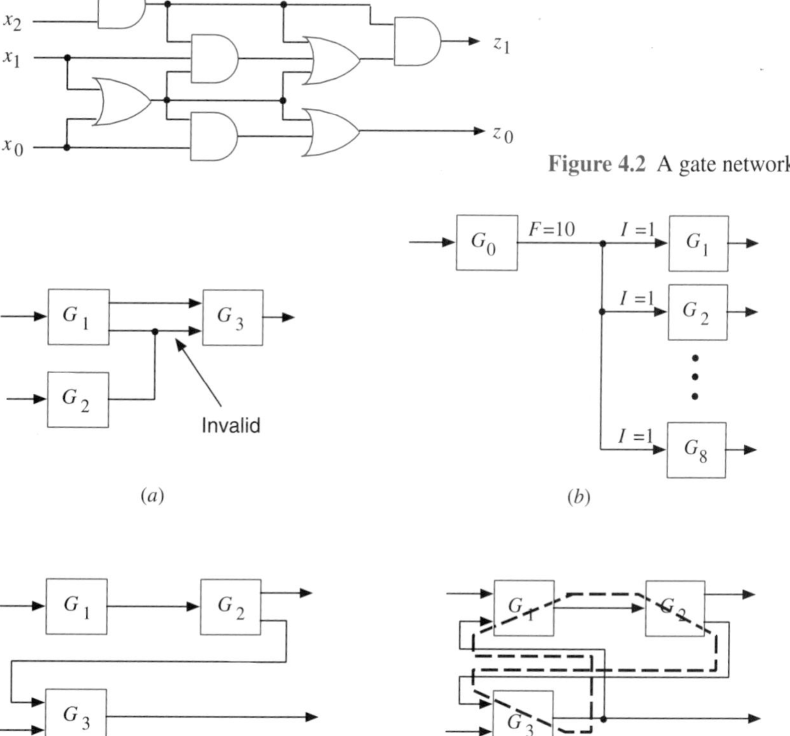

Figure 4.2 A gate network.

Figure 4.3 (*a*) Invalid network connection. (*b*) Acceptable output load. (*c*) Loop-free network. (*d*) Network with loop.

2. The **output load** imposed on a gate output should not be greater than its fanout factor. This load is computed as the sum of the input load factors I of all the gates inputs which are connected to the gate output.

   Figure 4.3*b* shows a valid connection: the input load factor of the gates is $I = 1$ so that the output load of gate G_0 is 8. Because the fanout factor is $F = 10$, this is valid.

In addition, gates have to be electrically compatible, that is, they must belong to the same or a compatible logic family.

A combinational network is **loop-free** (cycle-free) if, when starting at any point in the network and going through the gates in the direction from input to output, it is not possible to reach the input to any gate twice. For example, the network in Figure 4.3*c* is loop-free, whereas the network in Figure 4.3*d* has a loop ($G_1 \rightarrow G_2 \rightarrow G_3 \rightarrow G_1$).

Gate networks without loops are combinational, that is, they implement a switching function. In contrast, networks with loops might have a sequential instead of a combinational behavior if there is signal feedback (this subject is discussed in Chapter 7).

The network shown in Figure 4.2 is a valid gate network because it does not have loops and the two rules listed above are met. These conditions are necessary to obtain a **valid network**; however, they are not sufficient to obtain a good design. The corresponding design methods are discussed in Chapter 5.

4.2 DESCRIPTION AND CHARACTERISTICS OF GATE NETWORKS

The **description of a gate network** consists of the description of the gates and the interconnections. The description of gates has already been discussed in Chapters 2 and 3. For the description of the interconnections, the following approaches are typically used:

- graphical representation (**a logic diagram**);
- tabular representation (**a net list**); and
- representation based on a hardware description language (**a set of language statements**).

As depicted in Figure 4.4*a*, gates in a **graphical description** are represented by **gate symbols** and interconnections by **lines** going from gate outputs to gate inputs. The gate symbols indicate the gate types and, if necessary, a unique identifier is assigned to each gate. Gate inputs and outputs can also be labeled by unique identifiers (e.g., a pin number if the assignment of gates to devices [chips] has already been made) and possibly by the corresponding input load factors, fanout factors and delays. The individual gate characteristics can be replaced by a definition of the entire gate family (as in Table 3.1).

On the other hand, the **tabular representation** consists of two lists: a list of gates and a list of connections (see Figure 4.4*b*). The list of gates specifies the gate types (gate identifier if necessary) and the identifiers of the gate inputs and outputs, whereas the list of connections describes each connection by a pair of identifiers corresponding to the source and the destination of the connection. The gate characteristics, such as load, fanout factors and delays, are given in an additional table representing the entire gate family (as in Table 3.1).

Representations based on a hardware description language (HDL) are text-based descriptions that use statements from a special language to convey the functionality and connectivity of the network. Basic gates may be described as operators or as modules (entities), including their functionality and timing characteristics. Connections are represented as **signals** (names), which are used as inputs to the expressions/modules (see Figure 4.4*c*).

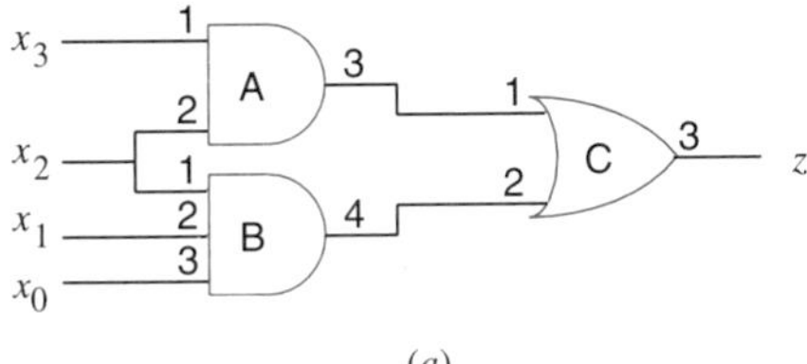

(a)

Gate	Type	Inputs	Output
A	AND2	A_1	A_3
		A_2	
B	AND3	B_1	B_4
		B_2	
		B_3	
C	OR2	C_1	C_3
		C_2	

Gates

From	To
x_3	A_1
x_2	A_2
x_2	B_1
x_1	B_2
x_0	B_3
A_3	C_1
B_4	C_2
C_3	z

Connections

(b)

```
A_3 <= x3 and x2;
B_4 <= x2 and x1 and x0;
C_3 <= A_3 or B_4;
z   <= C_3;
```

(c)

Figure 4.4 Network representation: (*a*) Graphical. (*b*) Tabular. (*c*) HDL-based.

EXAMPLE 4.1

Figure 4.4*a* is a graphical representation of a gate network. The corresponding tabular representation for gates and connections is shown in Figure 4.4*b*, whereas an equivalent HDL-based description is depicted in Figure 4.4*c*. ■

The graphical representation gives more insight into the structure of the network to the human user, but the HDL-based representation allows for better encapsulation of modules and more expressiveness; on the other hand, the tabular representation is easier to manipulate in a computer. Modern computer-aided design (CAD) tools use all these descriptions: the HDL-based form and the graphical form are used for entering the description into the computer, as well as for displaying the system to the human user/designer; the tabular form is used internally for analysis, simulation, and synthesis.

The **specification** of a gate network includes all characteristics needed to use the network as a module in a larger network (using the hierarchical approach). These characteristics are:

- the functional specification (in any of the forms discussed in Chapter 2);
- the input load factors of the network inputs;
- the fanout factors of the network outputs; and
- the propagation delays through the network.

In the next sections we present the **analysis** of gate networks. The objective of the analysis process is to obtain the network characteristics. On the other hand, the design process, described in Chapter 5, consists of deriving a network that satisfies a set of specified characteristics. Before presenting the analysis process, we discuss the use of different sets of gates in a network.

4.3 SETS OF GATES

Universal Set

A gate network is composed of different types of gates, such as AND, NOT, and NOR. A set of gates is said to be **universal** if any combinational system can be implemented using gates just from that set. One way of showing that a set G is universal consists of implementing all gates of a known universal set U using only gates from the set G. We now present several universal sets and discuss their advantages.

Set {AND, OR, NOT}

The set {AND, OR, NOT}, composed of AND, OR, and NOT gates, is universal. This is a consequence of the fact that any combinational system can be described by a set of switching expressions, and that there is a one-to-one correspondence between a switching expression and an AND-OR-NOT network. The network is obtained by assigning the corresponding gate to each operator in the expression, as depicted in Figure 4.5.

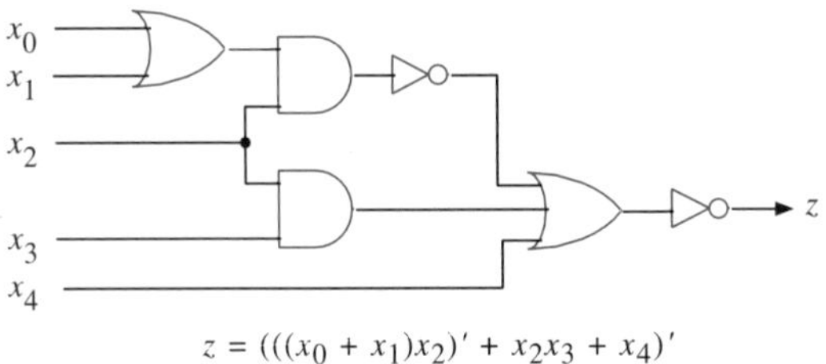

Figure 4.5 Correspondence between a switching expression and an AND-OR-NOT network.

Sets {AND, NOT} and {OR, NOT}

Having already one universal set, we can use it to show other universal sets. The set {AND, NOT}, a subset of the set {AND, OR, NOT}, is also universal. This is shown by the following correspondence:

{AND, OR, NOT}		{AND, NOT}
AND	→	AND
NOT	→	NOT
OR	→	see Figure 4.6

The network realization of the OR gate is a result of DeMorgan's rule, that is,

$$x_{n-1} + x_{n-2} + \cdots x_i + \cdots x_0 = (x'_{n-1}x'_{n-2} \ldots x'_i \ldots x'_0)'$$

As a result, all OR gates in an AND-OR-NOT network can be replaced by the structure depicted in Figure 4.6, resulting in a network with only AND and NOT gates. Thus, {AND, NOT} is a universal set: these two types of gates are sufficient to implement any combinational system.

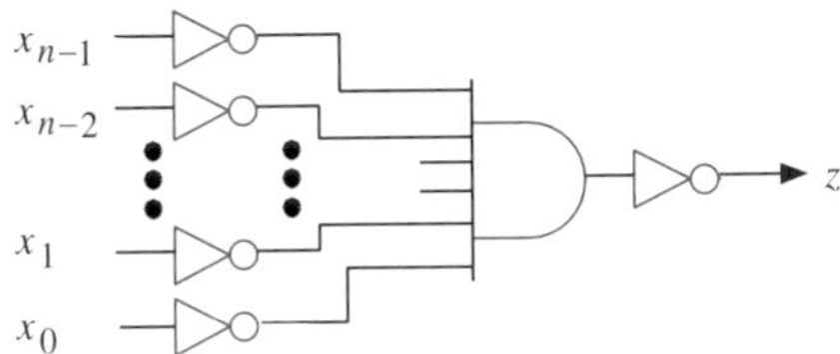

Figure 4.6 AND-NOT implementation of an OR gate.

The universality of the set {OR, NOT} is shown in a similar manner.

Sets {NAND} and {NOR}

As a follow-up to the discussion in the previous section, we now show two universal sets that have only one gate type: the sets {NAND} and {NOR}.

The set {NAND} is universal as long as we can implement the AND and NOT operators by networks of NAND gates. As depicted in Figure 4.7*a*, the NOT operator can be expressed as

$$x' = (xx)'$$

Consequently, by the definition of NAND, it follows that

$$\text{NOT}(x) = \text{NAND}(x, x)$$

The alternative implementation $\text{NOT}(x) = \text{NAND}(x, 1)$ can also be used; this requires the constant 1, but reduces the load on signal x.

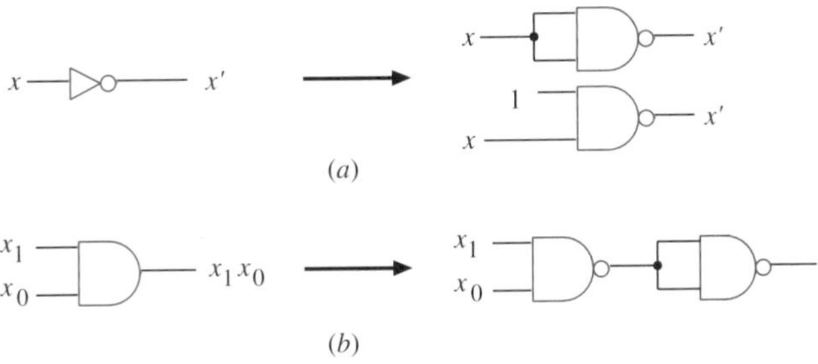

Figure 4.7 Implementations with NAND gates. (*a*) NOT. (*b*) AND.

For the two-input AND operator (see Figure 4.7*b*),

$$x_1x_0 = ((x_1x_0)')' = ((x_1x_0)'(x_1x_0)')'$$

which can be written as

$$\text{AND}(x_1, x_0) = \text{NAND}(\text{NAND}(x_1, x_0), \text{NAND}(x_1, x_0))$$

The verification of universality of the two-input NAND gate generalizes directly for an n-input NAND gate. The universality of the NOR gate is shown in a similar manner.

As apparent by DeMorgan's rule, there are two representations for the NAND and NOR gates. These two representations, shown in Figure 4.8, are used to simplify the analysis and design of networks using these gates; the use of both representations in the same network is known as **mixed-logic notation.**

Even though the implementation of a combinational system can be done using a single universal set of gates, networks with better characteristics (such as shorter delay and lower cost) might be obtained by using a larger set of gates. As shown in Chapter 3, the basic gates available in a family usually consist of NOT, NAND, NOR, AND, and OR. Moreover, for each gate type there are versions with several number of inputs. In addition, some families

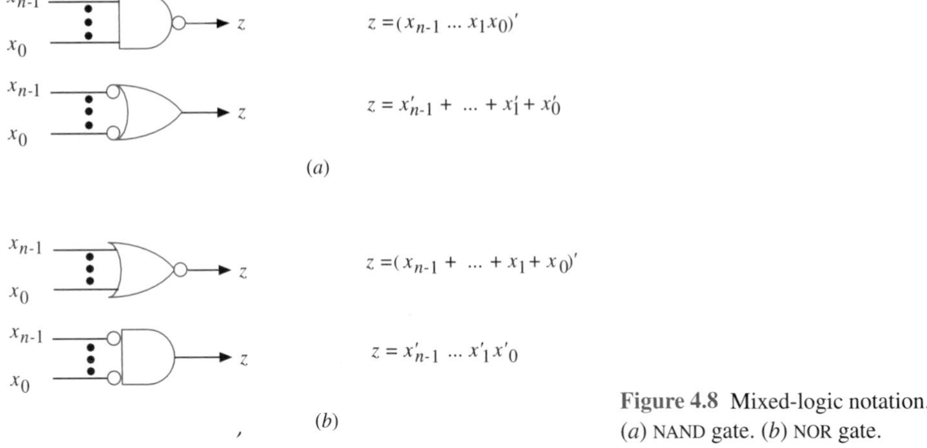

Figure 4.8 Mixed-logic notation. (*a*) NAND gate. (*b*) NOR gate.

provide more complex gates; typical complex gates for CMOS technology are XOR, XNOR, AND-NOR, and OR-NAND structures, with symbols shown in Figure 4.9. These structures are implemented effectively in this technology and are useful in a variety of systems.

4.4 ANALYSIS OF GATE NETWORKS

The **analysis** of a gate network produces a **specification** of the corresponding combinational system, which consists of two elements:

- a functional specification (functional analysis); and
- the characteristics of the network (input load factors, fanout factors, delays, size).

Functional Analysis

The **functional analysis** of a gate network produces its function, in one of the forms presented in Chapter 2. The analysis procedure consists of the following steps (some of these steps might be omitted in particular cases):

1. Obtain switching expressions for the network outputs in terms of the network inputs.
2. Obtain a tabular representation of the (binary) function. This is feasible only if the number of input variables is small.
3. Define high-level input and output variables, and use codes to relate these variables with the corresponding bit-vectors.
4. Obtain a high-level specification of the system.

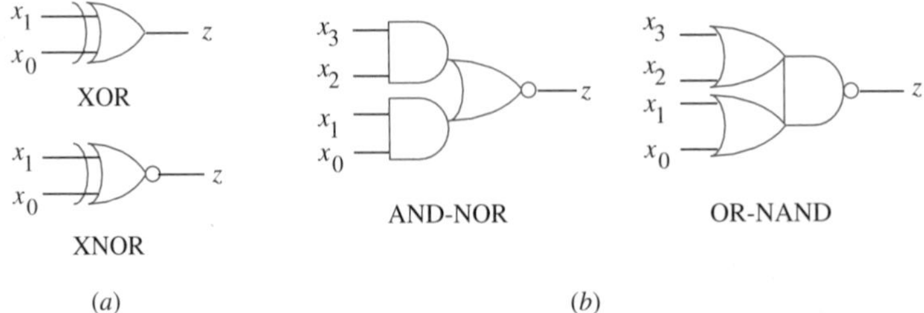

Figure 4.9 Additional gates in CMOS technology. (*a*) XOR and XNOR gates. (*b*) Complex gate structures: AND-NOR and OR-NAND.

Steps 3 and 4 require some apriori information about the type of system being analyzed and the codes used. This information is usually known either because the analysis is performed after a design has been made, so that the intended specification is available, or because of knowledge about the purpose of the combinational subsystem being analyzed, as part of a larger system. If this type of information is not known, obtaining a high-level specification is very difficult.

The process of obtaining the switching expressions (step 1) is performed as follows:

1. Assign identifiers (names) to each connection in the network.
2. Write the switching expressions for each gate output.
3. Substitute the internal identifiers until the **network expressions** are obtained (external outputs in terms of external inputs). This task can be carried out in two ways:
   - **forward analysis:** the substitutions are performed beginning with the gates nearest to the network inputs;
   - **backward analysis:** the substitutions proceed from the gates nearest to the network outputs.

Backward analysis might be more appropriate, especially for networks with several outputs, because it preserves the structure of each output.

EXAMPLE 4.2

Obtain switching expressions for the gate network shown in Figure 4.10.

First, the identifiers T_1, T_2, T_3, T_4, T_5, and T_6 are assigned to internal connections, as shown in Figure 4.10. Then, backward analysis is performed as follows:

$$\begin{aligned} z_0 &= T_2 + T_3 \\ &= x_0' x_1' x_2 + x_0 T_1 \\ &= x_0' x_1' x_2 + x_0(x_2' + x_3) \\ &= x_0' x_1' x_2 + x_0 x_2' + x_0 x_3 \end{aligned}$$

$$\begin{aligned} z_1 &= T_5 + T_6 \\ &= x_1 x_2 x_3 + T_4' \\ &= x_1 x_2 x_3 + (T_1 x_0' x_1)' \\ &= x_1 x_2 x_3 + T_1' + x_0 + x_1' \\ &= x_1 x_2 x_3 + x_2 x_3' + x_0 + x_1' \end{aligned}$$

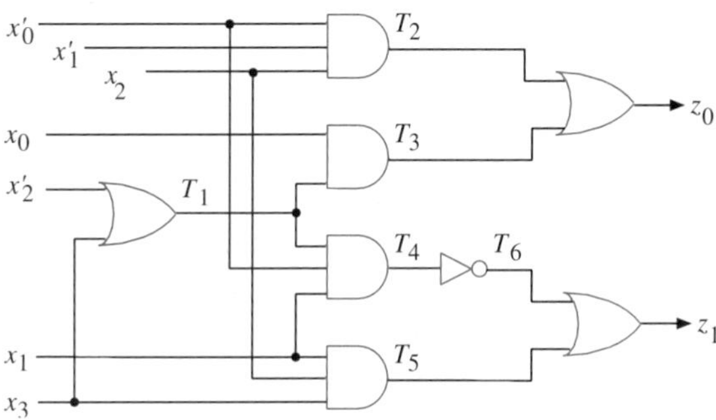

Figure 4.10 Gate network for analysis.

These expressions can be reduced to

$$z_0 = x_0'x_1'x_2 + x_0x_2' + x_0x_3 \quad \text{(no reduction possible)}$$
$$z_1 = x_0 + x_1' + x_2$$

■

The procedure used in this example (brute-force substitutions) is impractical when a network contains a large number of gates. A better alternative in those cases is a **hierarchical** approach, in which

- the network is decomposed into subnetworks (modules);
- each subnetwork is analyzed separately; and
- substitution is used to obtain the network function.

If possible, the subnetworks should be described at a high level before combining them. This procedure is illustrated in the following example. Note that the network considered is relatively simple in order to make it pedagogically suitable; therefore, the necessity of this hierarchical approach might not be fully appreciated from it.

EXAMPLE 4.3

Let us verify that the network shown in Figure 4.11 has the following functional specification.

Inputs: $x, y, w \in \{0, 1, \ldots, 7\}$
Output: $z \in \{0, 1, \ldots, 7\}$

Function: $$z = \begin{cases} (y+1) \bmod 8 & \textbf{if} \quad x \neq 0 \\ (w+1) \bmod 8 & \textbf{if} \quad x = 0 \end{cases}$$

In words, the network increments modulo-8 either y or w, depending whether $x \neq 0$ or $x = 0$; integers x, y, w, and z are represented by vectors $\underline{x}$, $\underline{y}$, $\underline{w}$, and $\underline{z}$, respectively, in the radix-2 number system.

We begin by identifying three subnetworks, as indicated by the dashed rectangles in the figure. Next, we analyze each subnetwork (module) separately.

We illustrate here a forward analysis. For subnetwork M_1, we have

$$t = x_2 + x_1 + x_0$$

Because we know that the vector $\underline{x}$ represents an integer in the radix-2 number system, from the definition of the OR function we can write

$$t = \begin{cases} 1 & \textbf{if} \quad x \neq 0 \\ 0 & \textbf{otherwise} \end{cases}$$

Subnetwork M_2 is composed of three identical parts, so that

$$v_i = y_i t + w_i t' \qquad (i = 0, 1, 2)$$

This can be written in vector form as

$$\underline{v} = \begin{cases} \underline{y} & \textbf{if} \quad t = 1 \\ \underline{w} & \textbf{if} \quad t = 0 \end{cases}$$

This subnetwork is called a **vector selector** because it selects between two vectors (in this case $\underline{y}$ and $\underline{w}$), depending on the value of a "select" variable (in this case t).

Again, because $\underline{y}$ and $\underline{w}$ represent integers, we can write

$$v = \begin{cases} y & \textbf{if} \quad t = 1 \\ w & \textbf{if} \quad t = 0 \end{cases}$$

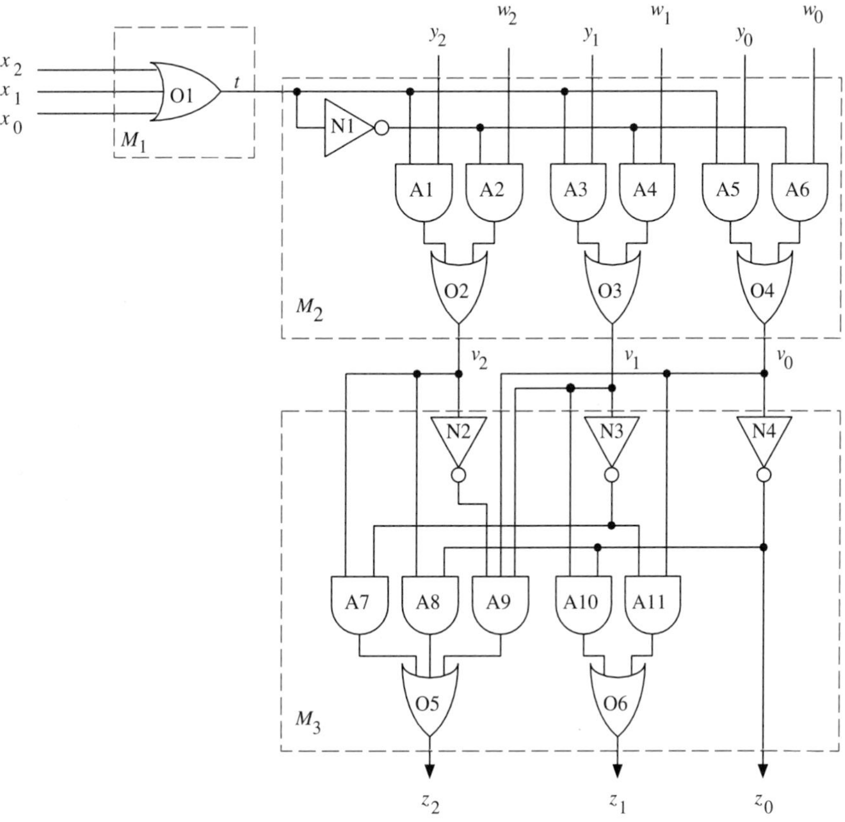

Figure 4.11 Network for hierarchical analysis.

Finally, for subnetwork M_3,

$$z_2 = v_2' v_1 v_0 + v_2 v_1' + v_2 v_0'$$

$$z_1 = v_1 v_0' + v_1' v_0$$

$$z_0 = v_0'$$

To obtain the high-level specification for this subnetwork, we first produce a table of the functions described by the corresponding expressions, as follows:

v_2	v_1	v_0	z_2	z_1	z_0
0	0	0	0	0	1
0	0	1	0	1	0
0	1	0	0	1	1
0	1	1	1	0	0
1	0	0	1	0	1
1	0	1	1	1	0
1	1	0	1	1	1
1	1	1	0	0	0

$\rightarrow$

v	z
0	1
1	2
2	3
3	4
4	5
5	6
6	7
7	0

From this table, we infer that

$$z = (v + 1) \bmod 8$$

Now we perform the second level of the analysis. Substituting the expressions for v and t, we get

$$z = \begin{cases} (y+1) \bmod 8 & \textbf{if} \quad x \neq 0 \\ (w+1) \bmod 8 & \textbf{if} \quad x = 0 \end{cases}$$

which corresponds to the specification that we wanted to check. ■

Analysis of Networks With NOT, NAND, and NOR Gates

Although the analysis process presented in the previous section is applicable to a network with any type of gates, networks containing NOT, NAND, and/or NOR gates are more difficult to analyze due to the complementation of subexpressions. We now present a way of using mixed-logic notation (see Figure 4.8) to eliminate these complementations.

First, let us consider the case in which the network consists only of NAND or NOR gates. For the analysis process, the two equivalent representations of NAND (or NOR) gates are used in such a way as to produce complements that can be canceled. As a result, the network is transformed into one with AND and OR gates, and complementation in the input variables. This technique is illustrated in the following examples.

EXAMPLE 4.4

Obtain a sum of products expression for the NAND network shown in Figure 4.12*a*, using mixed-logic transformations.

We first redraw the network using mixed-logic notation, as depicted in Figure 4.12*b*. Both networks are equivalent because we have just replaced some NAND gates by their equivalent representation. As already stated, the idea is to perform this transformation in a way that either removes a complementation or produces two complementations in the

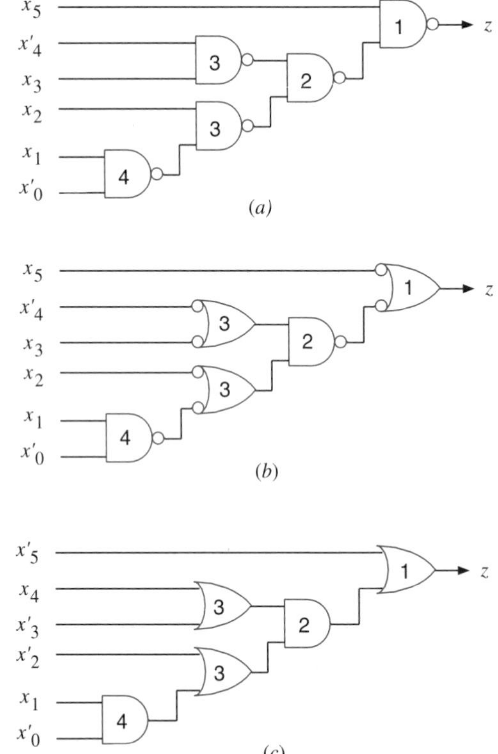

Figure 4.12 (*a*) NAND network. (*b*) Network redrawn in mixed-logic notation. (*c*) Equivalent network after canceling complementations.

connections so that they cancel each other. This objective is achieved by **transforming all gates in every other level** (starting from the output gate) to the OR-like form. That is, in the example, gates labeled 1 and 3 are transformed into the OR-like form. As a result, each network level contains only one representation of the corresponding gates.

The analysis of the network shown in Figure 4.12*c* leads to

$$\begin{aligned} z &= x_5' + (x_4 + x_3')(x_2' + x_1 x_0') \\ &= x_5' + x_4 x_2' + x_3' x_2' + x_4 x_1 x_0' + x_3' x_1 x_0' \end{aligned}$$

■

EXAMPLE 4.5

Obtain a sum of products expression for the NOR network shown in Figure 4.13*a*.

The network is first redrawn using mixed-logic notation, as shown in Figure 4.13*b*, where all gates in every other level (starting from the output gate) have been transformed into the AND-like form. Canceling complementations leads to

$$\begin{aligned} z &= [(x_2 + x_1')(x_2' + x_1) + x_0](x_2' + x_1' + x_0) \\ &= (x_2 x_1 + x_2' x_1' + x_0)(x_2' + x_1' + x_0) \\ &= x_2' x_1' + x_0 \end{aligned}$$

■

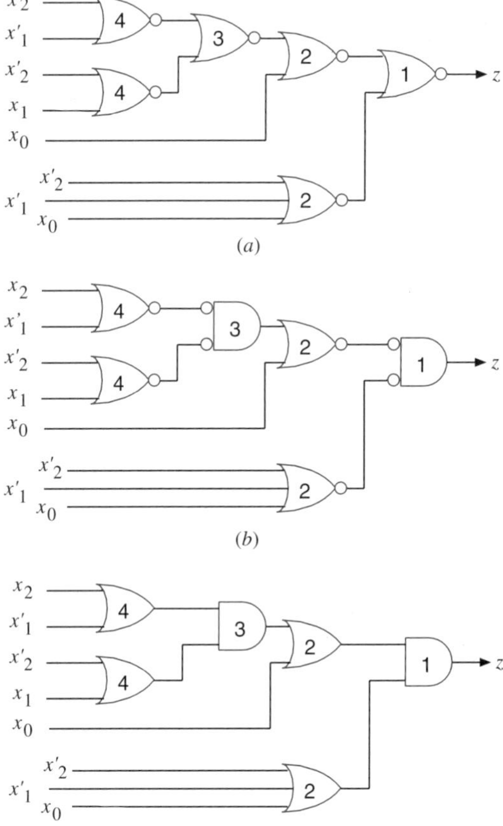

Figure 4.13 (*a*) NOR network. (*b*) Network redrawn in mixed-logic notation. (*c*) Equivalent network after canceling complementations.

If the network contains both NAND and NOR gates, then the analysis process consists of using the mixed-logic notation in such a way that the representation that places the complements at the gate inputs is used in every other level starting from the outputs of the network, whereas the representation that places the complement at the gate output is used for the other levels.

Note that this technique for NAND/NOR networks cannot be applied directly when the output of one gate is connected to the input of more than one gate, and such gates are in levels with different representations.

Analysis of Network Characteristics

We now show how to determine the characteristics of a network in terms of the characteristics of the gates. In the examples, we use the characteristics of the family of gates listed in Table 3.1, which is repeated as Table 4.1.

The network characteristics are determined as follows:

The load factor of a network input is the sum of all the input load factors of the gate inputs to which that network input is connected.

The fanout factor of a network output is the fanout factor of the corresponding gate output minus the sum of the input load factors of those gate inputs to which that gate output is connected.

The size of the network corresponds to the area it occupies on a chip. This area is composed of the area of the gates and the area of the interconnections (which includes some unused space). Consequently, determining the actual area requires laying out the corresponding circuit on a chip.

Because chip layout is outside the scope of this book, we measure the size of a network by the number of equivalent gates, as given in Table 4.1, and neglect the interconnections and unused space. This measure is acceptable for some realization technologies such as gate arrays. An even less accurate measure of size is the number of gates in the network, but this is still sufficient for some purposes.

The network (propagation) delay. Because the propagation delay corresponds to the time interval from the stabilization of an input to the stabilization of an output, the network delay is defined for each input-output pair. This delay is computed as the maximum delay obtained for all paths from the input to the output. The path(s) with maximum delay is (are) called the **critical path(s)**.

The delay of each path is obtained by adding the delays of all gates and connections in the path. Because gates have two different delays, that is, t_{pLH} and t_{pHL}, the network also has two delays, which we call T_{pLH} and T_{pHL}, respectively. The delays of the connections are obtained from a circuit realization of the network; as a first approximation, an average delay per connection can be added to each gate.

The determination of a particular network delay requires considering the correct transition, taking into account that gates such as NOT, NAND, and NOR invert the transition.

The number of levels of a network. The **level** of a gate in a network is the number of gates in the longest path going from an external input to the output of that gate. Thus, **the number of levels** of a network (N) is the maximum level of a gate. This number can be used as a first approximation of the network delay; if all gates have the same delay d, then the network delay is $T = Nd$.

The dynamic characteristics of the network are represented in a **timing diagram**. This is a graphical representation that shows the propagation of the signals as a function of time.

Table 4.1 Characteristics of a family of CMOS gates

Gate Type	Fan-in	Propagation Delays t_{pLH} (ns)	t_{pHL} (ns)	Load Factor I (standard loads)	Size (equivalent gates)
AND	2	$0.15 + 0.037L$	$0.16 + 0.017L$	1.0	2
AND	3	$0.20 + 0.038L$	$0.18 + 0.018L$	1.0	2
AND	4	$0.28 + 0.039L$	$0.21 + 0.019L$	1.0	3
OR	2	$0.12 + 0.037L$	$0.20 + 0.019L$	1.0	2
OR	3	$0.12 + 0.038L$	$0.34 + 0.022L$	1.0	2
OR	4	$0.13 + 0.038L$	$0.45 + 0.025L$	1.0	3
NOT	1	$0.02 + 0.038L$	$0.05 + 0.017L$	1.0	1
NAND	2	$0.05 + 0.038L$	$0.08 + 0.027L$	1.0	1
NAND	3	$0.07 + 0.038L$	$0.09 + 0.039L$	1.0	2
NAND	4	$0.10 + 0.037L$	$0.12 + 0.051L$	1.0	2
NAND	5	$0.21 + 0.038L$	$0.34 + 0.019L$	1.0	4
NAND	6	$0.24 + 0.037L$	$0.36 + 0.019L$	1.0	5
NAND	8	$0.24 + 0.038L$	$0.42 + 0.019L$	1.0	6
NOR	2	$0.06 + 0.075L$	$0.07 + 0.016L$	1.0	1
NOR	3	$0.16 + 0.111L$	$0.08 + 0.017L$	1.0	2
NOR	4	$0.23 + 0.149L$	$0.08 + 0.017L$	1.0	4
NOR	5	$0.38 + 0.038L$	$0.23 + 0.018L$	1.0	4
NOR	6	$0.46 + 0.037L$	$0.24 + 0.018L$	1.0	5
NOR	8	$0.54 + 0.038L$	$0.23 + 0.018L$	1.0	6
XOR	2*	$0.30 + 0.036L$	$0.30 + 0.021L$	1.1	3
		$0.16 + 0.036L$	$0.15 + 0.020L$	2.0	
XOR	3*	$0.50 + 0.038L$	$0.49 + 0.027L$	1.1	6
		$0.28 + 0.039L$	$0.27 + 0.027L$	2.4	
		$0.19 + 0.036L$	$0.17 + 0.025L$	2.1	
XNOR	2*	$0.30 + 0.036L$	$0.30 + 0.021L$	1.1	3
		$0.16 + 0.036L$	$0.15 + 0.020L$	2.0	
XNOR	3*	$0.50 + 0.038L$	$0.49 + 0.027L$	1.1	6
		$0.28 + 0.039L$	$0.27 + 0.027L$	2.3	
		$0.19 + 0.036L$	$0.17 + 0.025L$	1.3	
2-OR/NAND2	4	$0.17 + 0.075L$	$0.10 + 0.028L$	1.0	2
2-AND/NOR2	4	$0.17 + 0.075L$	$0.10 + 0.028L$	1.0	2

L: Load on the gate output.

*Different characteristics for each input.

EXAMPLE 4.6

Using the gate characteristics listed in Table 4.1, determine the characteristics of the network shown in Figure 4.14. For illustration, we consider an implementation without using complex gates (although using those gates would produce a smaller and faster network; see Exercise 6.5).

This network uses five types of gates: two-input AND, three-input AND, two-input OR, three-input OR, and NOT. Its characteristics are as follows:

Load factors. All network inputs have load factor 1 because each one is connected only to one gate input, and the input load factor of all gates is $I = 1$.

Fanout factors. As indicated in Chapter 3, a limitation of 12 standard loads exists to assure adequate signal rise and fall times, so we use $F = 12$ for all gates. In such a case, the fanout factors $F(z_2)$ and $F(z_1)$ are both 12, whereas $F(z_0) = 12 - 2 = 10$

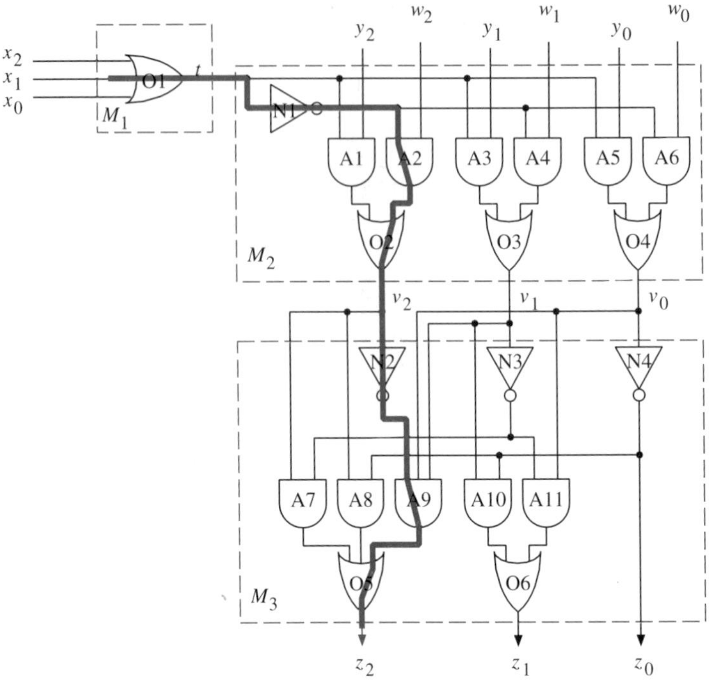

Figure 4.14 Network for hierarchical analysis.

(because the output of gate N_4 is also connected to two internal inputs, each with input load factor $I = 1$).

Network size. Because NOT has size 1 and all other gates have size 2, the size of the network is 38 (equivalent gates). Note that there are only 21 gates.

Number of levels. There are 7 levels in the network.

Network delay. A network delay is obtained for each input-output pair. We illustrate this delay just for pair (x_1, z_2). Because there are several paths from x_1 to z_2, it is necessary to consider them all and determine the maximum delay. Due to the regularity of the network (see Figure 4.14), we conclude that the maximum delay corresponds to the path

$$O_1 \rightarrow N_1 \rightarrow A_2 \rightarrow O_2 \rightarrow N_2 \rightarrow A_9 \rightarrow O_5$$

because it includes two NOT gates and three three-input gates. Note that the NOT gate inverts the slope of the transition (i.e., a high-to-low transition at the input produces a low-to-high transition at the output, and vice versa); this has to be taken into account when computing the corresponding network delays. Consequently, the network delays for this input-output pair are

$$\begin{aligned}T_{pLH}(x_1, z_2) &= t_{pLH}(O_1) + t_{pHL}(N_1) + t_{pHL}(A_2) + t_{pHL}(O_2)\\&\quad + t_{pLH}(N_2) + t_{pLH}(A_9) + t_{pLH}(O_5)\\T_{pHL}(x_1, z_2) &= t_{pHL}(O_1) + t_{pLH}(N_1) + t_{pLH}(A_2) + t_{pLH}(O_2)\\&\quad + t_{pHL}(N_2) + t_{pHL}(A_9) + t_{pHL}(O_5)\end{aligned}$$

Using the expressions from Table 4.1, we get the following table:

Gate	Identifier	Output load	t_{pLH} (ns)	t_{pHL} (ns)
OR3	O_1	4	0.27	0.43
NOT	N_1	3	0.13	0.10
AND2	A_2	1	0.19	0.18
OR2	O_2	3	0.23	0.26
NOT	N_2	1	0.06	0.07
AND3	A_9	1	0.24	0.20
OR3	O_5	L	$0.12 + 0.038L$	$0.34 + 0.022L$

Because the output load of the network is not specified, the network delay is obtained as a function of this output load (L). From the values in the table, it follows that

$$T_{pLH}(x_1, z_2) = 0.27 + 0.10 + 0.18 + 0.26 + 0.06 + 0.24 + 0.12 + 0.038L$$
$$= 1.23 + 0.038L \text{ (ns)}$$
$$T_{pHL}(x_1, z_2) = 0.43 + 0.13 + 0.19 + 0.23 + 0.07 + 0.20 + 0.34 + 0.022L$$
$$= 1.59 + 0.022L \text{ (ns)}$$

Figure 4.15 shows the corresponding timing diagram.

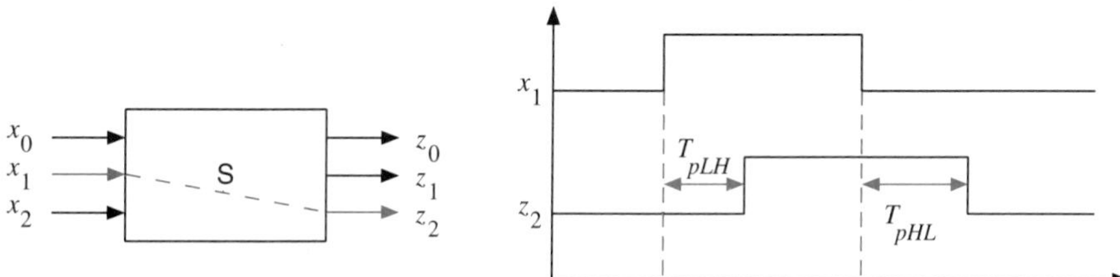

Figure 4.15 Timing diagram from network analysis.

■

4.5 DESCRIPTION OF GATE NETWORKS USING μVHDL

Gate networks can also be described using a hardware-description language. This has the advantage of providing an executable representation that can be used for simulation and verification. We now discuss this description using μVHDL, which has already been used in previous chapters for functional specification and for describing the characteristics of basic gates.

A network is described at the structural level, that is, by listing the gates comprising the network and their interconnection. The functionality and other characteristics of the gates are described at the behavioral level separately, as discussed in Chapter 3. Those descriptions become part of a structural description by declaring the entities used in the network.

Similarly to a behavioral description, a structural description consists of an `ENTITY` and an `ARCHITECTURE`. Only the architecture body reflects the structure of the system; the entity declaration does not contain any indication whether the architecture body is described in terms of behavior or structure. The overall format of a structural architecture body is as follows:

```
ARCHITECTURE arch_name OF entity_name IS
  signal_declarations;
BEGIN
  module_instantiation and net_list_declaration;
END arch_name;
```

The interconnections between the gates are defined in the **signal declarations** section by giving them names and their corresponding TYPE, whereas the gates used in the network and their connections are described in the body, as illustrated in the following example.

EXAMPLE 4.7

We now give the μVHDL description of the gate network depicted in Figure 4.16*a*. The description of the gates is similar to that given in Chapter 3 for the AND and XOR gates, including the GENERIC specifying the load and the ATTRIBUTE specifying the input factor and the fanout; we assume that descriptions for the gates listed in Table 4.1 are available in the library WORK, so we just use them here.

The entity declaration for this network is as follows:

```
USE WORK.ALL;
ENTITY gate_netw IS
  PORT(x,y    : IN  BIT;
       cin    : IN  BIT;
       z,cout: OUT BIT);
END gate_netw;
```

The architecture body lists the gates used in the network and their interconnections. Labeling the gates as depicted in Figure 4.16*a*, we obtain the following structural description:

```
ARCHITECTURE structural OF gate_netw IS
  SIGNAL s1, c1, c2, c3 : BIT;
BEGIN
  U1 : ENTITY xor_gate   GENERIC MAP (2.0)          -- L=2.0
                         PORT MAP (x, y, s1)  ;
  U2 : ENTITY xor_gate   GENERIC MAP (3.0)          -- L=3.0
                         PORT MAP (s1, cin, z);
  U3 : ENTITY and_gate   PORT MAP (x, y, c1)  ;   -- L=1.0
  U4 : ENTITY and_gate   PORT MAP (y, cin, c2);   -- L=1.0
  U5 : ENTITY and_gate   PORT MAP (x, cin, c3);   -- L=1.0
  U6 : ENTITY or_gate_3  GENERIC MAP (3.0)          -- L=3.0
                         PORT MAP (c1, c2, c3, cout);
END structural;
```

Each gate in the network is indicated in the module instantiation section by giving it a name (a label), specifying the type of gate, a PORT MAP statement indicating which signals are connected to the corresponding input and output ports, and a GENERIC MAP statement if the gate entity has generic parameters. For these purposes, let us assume that the load on each of the network outputs is 3.0. From Table 4.1, we note that the XOR gate has load

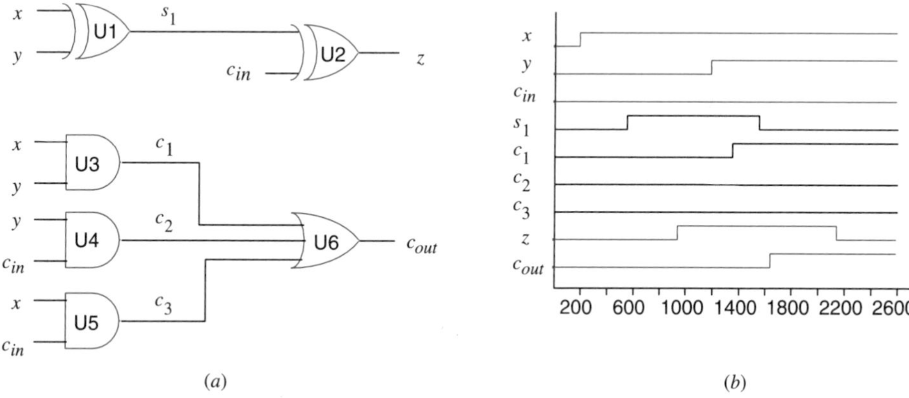

Figure 4.16 Gate network and timing diagram for Example 4.7.

factor 2.0 in one of the inputs; let us assume the topmost input to the XOR gate has this load factor. As a result, gate `U1` has a load of 2.0, and gates `U2,U6` (the network outputs) have load of 3.0.

Note that the structural μVHDL representation has no explicit description of the network timing characteristics; instead, such characteristics are derived from the time-behavior of the signals connected to the gates that compose the network. A timing diagram generated from this μVHDL description is depicted in Figure 4.16*b*. ■

In practice, the determination of the values used for the `GENERIC` parameters is done through a **back-annotation** process. That is, once the network is described, the description is inspected to determine, for example, the load on each gate output as the sum of the input load factors of all the inputs to which it is connected. These load factors are extracted from the `ATTRIBUTE` declarations. This process can be easily automated, and most modern CAD tools have such capabilities; the tool can then **annotate** the μVHDL description with the corresponding parameters. In the foregoing example, we have performed this task manually.

As stated in Chapter 3, the characteristics of a module are not included in the specification when the description is used for synthesis; in such cases, the characteristics are determined as part of the synthesis process.

4.6 FURTHER READINGS

See Further Readings in Chapter 5.

EXERCISES

Network construction and description

Exercise 4.1 Determine whether each of the AND-OR-NOT networks shown in Figure 4.17 is a valid gate network. If not, state all reasons.

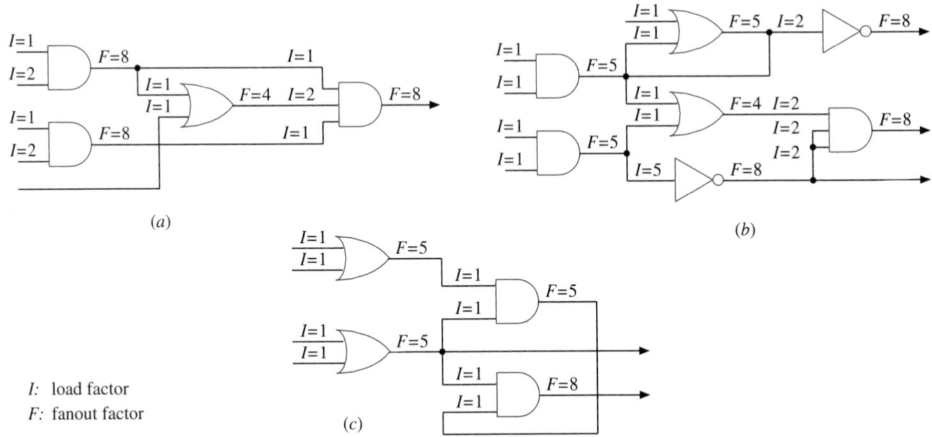

Figure 4.17 AND-OR-NOT networks for Exercise 4.1.

Exercise 4.2 Show that the network in Figure 4.18 is combinational even though there is a physical loop.

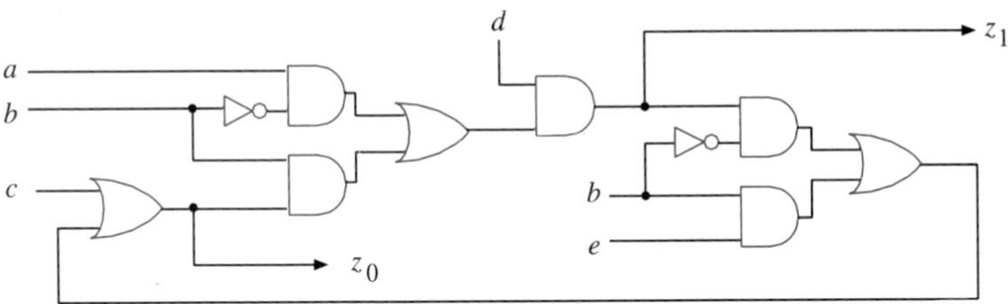

Figure 4.18 Network for Exercise 4.2.

Exercise 4.3 Give a tabular description of the network shown in Figure 4.19.

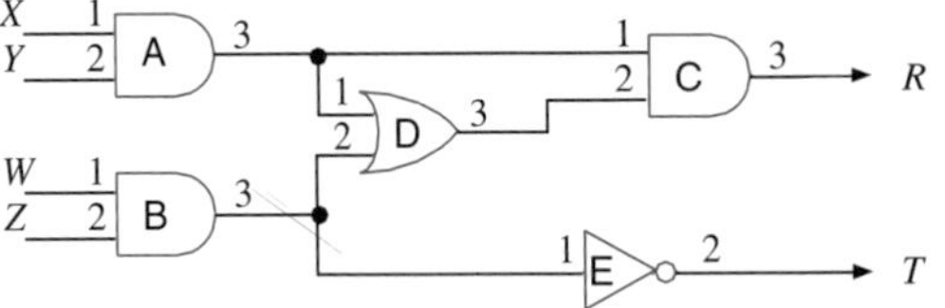

Figure 4.19 Network for Exercise 4.3.

Exercise 4.4 For the following tabular description of a network, give its graphical description and determine whether the network is valid. If not valid, make modifications in the description so that it is valid.

From	To
R	A_1
S	A_2
A	B_1
A_2	C_1
T	C_2
X	C_3
C	D_1
Y	D_2
B	E_1
D	E_2
E	Z

Gate	Type	Input	Output
A	AND2	A_1	A
		A_2	
B	NOT	B_1	B
C	AND3	C_1	C
		C_2	
		C_3	
D	OR2	D_1	D
		D_2	
E	OR2	E_1	E
		E_2	

Exercise 4.5 For the following tabular description of a network, give its graphical description and determine whether the network is valid. If not valid, make modifications in the description so that it becomes valid.

From	To
R	A_1
S	A_2
A	B_1
B	C_1
E	C_2
T	$D1$
A_2	E_1
D_1	E_2
D	B_2, C_2
C	Z

Gate	Type	Input	Output
A	AND2	A_1	A
		A_2	
B	AND2	B_1	B
		B_2	
C	AND2	C_1	C
		C_2	
D	NOT	D_1	D
E	OR2	E_1	E
		E_2	

Exercise 4.6 Determine whether the networks shown in Figures 4.17 and 4.20 are loop free.

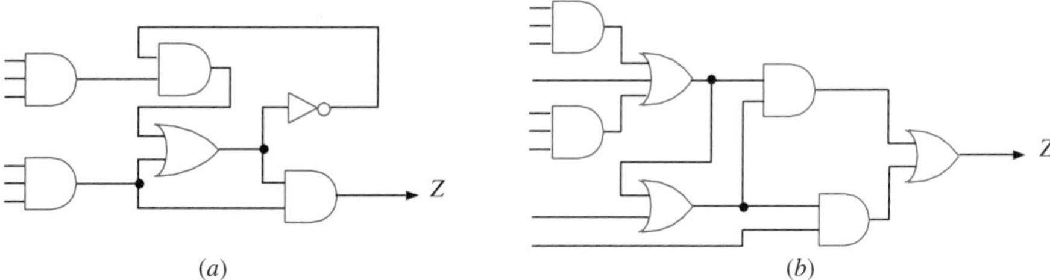

Figure 4.20 Networks for Exercise 4.6.

Universal set of gates

Exercise 4.7 Show that the operation (gate) represented by the switching expression $x'yz + xy' + y'z$ is universal. You can use the constants 0 and 1.

Exercise 4.8 Show that the set {XNOR, OR} is universal. You can use the constant 0 or 1 (only one of them).

Exercise 4.9 Show that the operation (gate) $*$ described by the following table is universal. You can use the constant 1.

*	0	1
0	0	1
1	0	0

Analysis of gate networks

Exercise 4.10 Analyze the NAND-NOR network shown in Figure 4.21. Obtain switching expressions for the outputs.

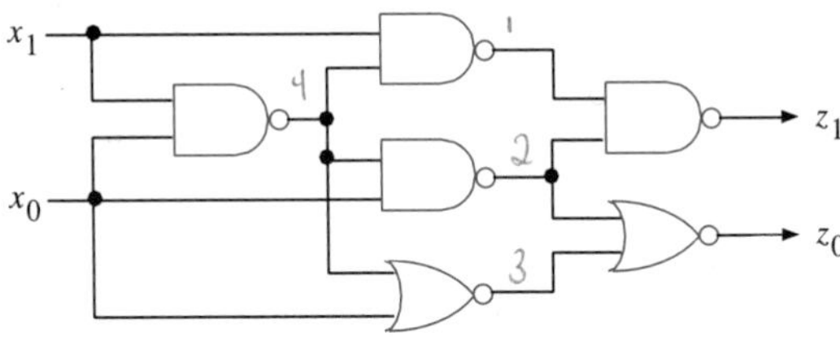

Figure 4.21 NAND-NOR network for Exercise 4.10.

Exercise 4.11 Analyze the NAND network shown in Figure 4.22. Obtain a reduced switching expression for the output. Give a high-level description in terms of the number of zeros in the input.

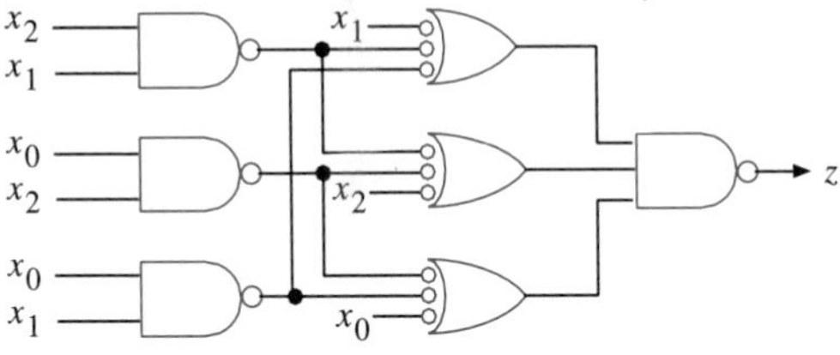

Figure 4.22 NAND network for Exercise 4.11.

Exercise 4.12 Analyze the NOR network shown in Figure 4.23. Obtain switching expressions for the outputs and give the truth table. Show that the network implements a code converter from Excess-3 to BCD.

Exercise 4.13 Analyze the network shown in Figure 4.24. Obtain:

a. Switching expressions for each of the outputs.
b. A high-level description assuming that the bit-vector $\underline{z} = (z_2, z_1, z_0)$ represents an integer in the radix-2 representation.
c. For the gate characteristics given in Table 4.1, determine (decompose the gates not available in the table):
   - the load factor of each input; and
   - the maximum delay of the network (consider the input-output pair that produces the maximum delay). Give this delay as a function of the output load.
d. Give a timing diagram showing the delays in the critical path.

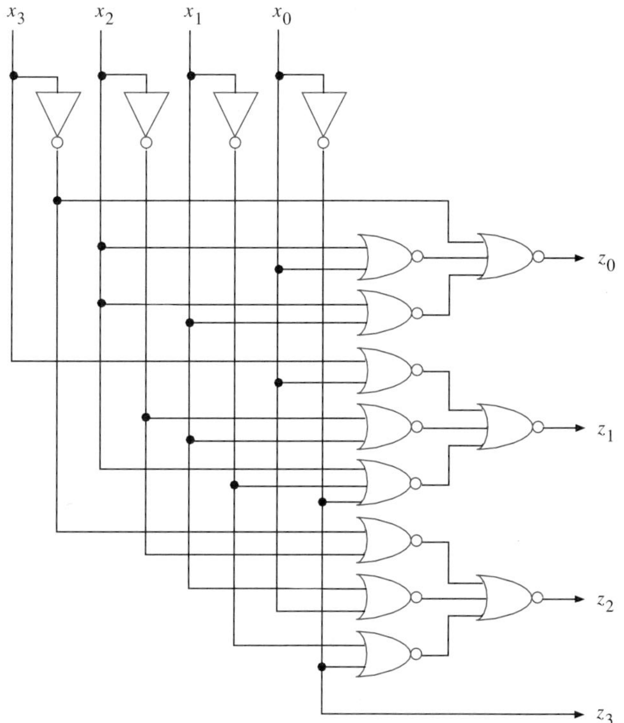

Figure 4.23 NOR network for Exercise 4.12.

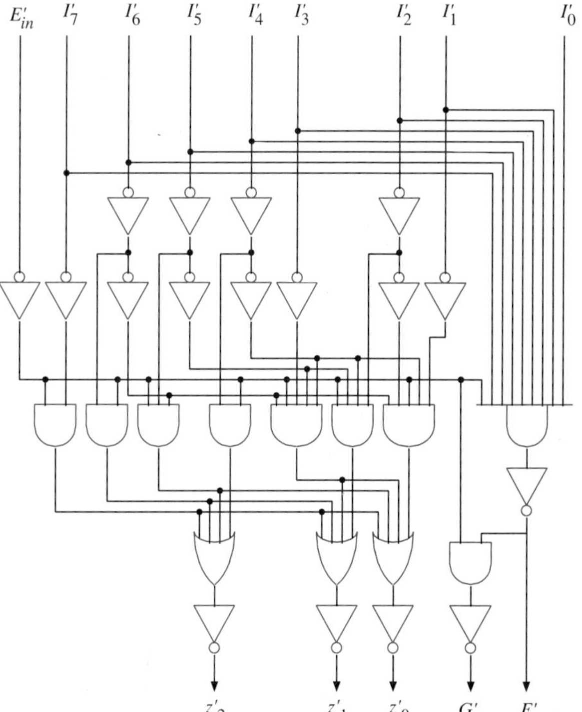

Figure 4.24 Network for Exercise 4.13.

Exercise 4.14 Analyze the network shown in Figure 4.25. Obtain:

a. Switching expressions for each of the outputs.
b. A high-level description assuming that the bit-vector $\underline{s} = (s_2, s_1, s_0)$ represents an integer in the radix-2 representation.
c. For the gate characteristics given in Table 4.1, determine (decompose the gates not available in the table):
   - the load factor of each input;
   - the load for each gate output; and
   - the delay of the network. Give this delay in terms of the load of the output.
d. Give a timing diagram showing the delays in the critical path.

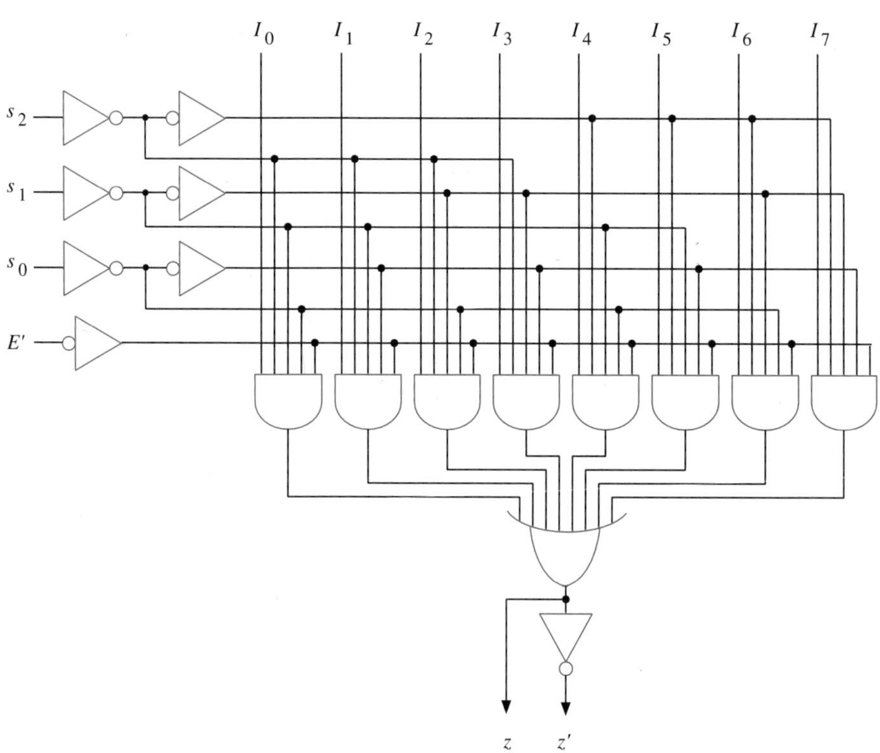

Figure 4.25 Network for Exercise 4.14.

Exercise 4.15 Analyze the network shown in Figure 4.26. Perform a two-level analysis, that is, define some modules in the network, analyze these modules and then analyze the network formed by the modules.

For each module obtain reduced switching expressions and then obtain switching expressions for the whole network. Obtain a high-level description.

Using the gate characteristics given in Table 4.1, determine the delay of the network.

Exercise 4.16 Analyze the network shown in Figure 4.27. Perform a two-level analysis, that is, define some modules in the network, analyze these modules, and then analyze the network formed by the modules.

If the vectors $\underline{A}$, $\underline{B}$, and $\underline{S}$ represent integers in a radix-2 representation, show that the network implements a four-bit adder.

Description using μVHDL

The networks of the exercises under the heading "Analysis of gate networks" can be described using μVHDL.

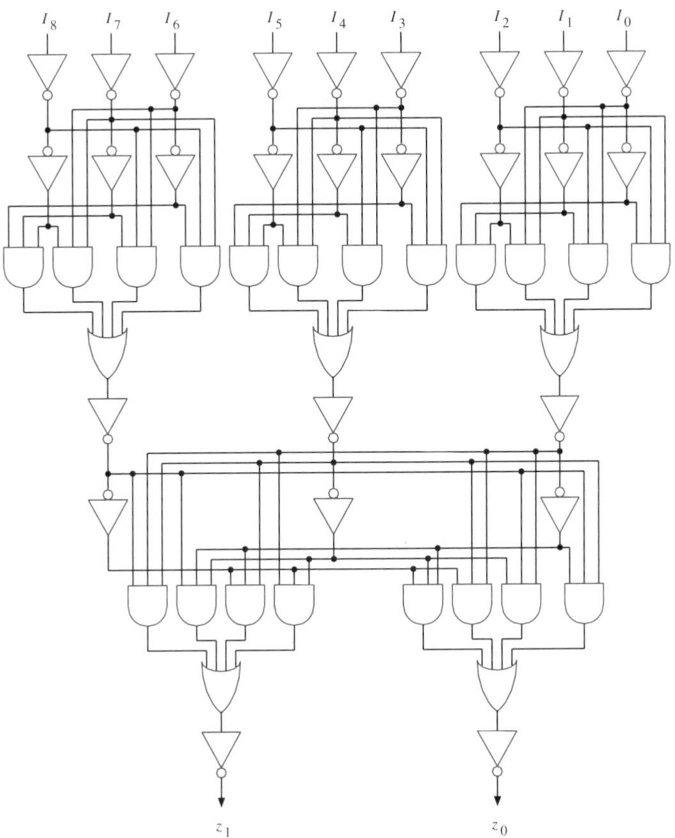

Figure 4.26 Network for Exercise 4.15.

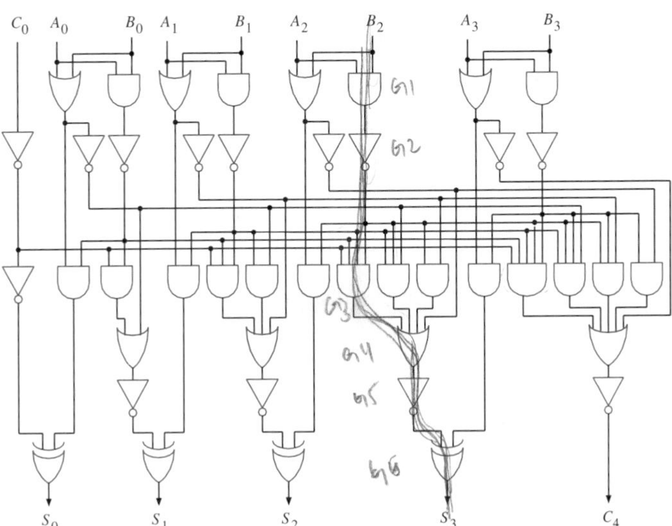

Figure 4.27 Network for Exercise 4.16.

Chapter 5

Design of Combinational Systems: Two-Level Gate Networks

In this chapter we present

- Design of two-level gate networks: AND-OR and OR-AND.
- Minimal two-level networks. Karnaugh maps. Minimization procedure and tools. Limitations of two-level networks.
- Design of two-level NAND-NAND and NOR-NOR networks.
- Programmable logic: PLAs and PALs.

The design of a gate network is the process of obtaining a network that implements a given functional specification and satisfies some additional constraints, such as delay and number of gates. In this chapter, we present direct methods for the design of simple networks. Complex networks require a hierarchical (modular) approach, which is discussed in later chapters.

We begin describing the design of two-level gate networks, for which there is a well-defined systematic procedure. In Chapter 6 we consider the more general case of multilevel networks, for which the design procedure is somewhat less systematic.

Any combinational system can be implemented by a network formed by one level of NOT gates, a second level of AND gates, and a third level of OR gates. This implementation results from the fact that any switching function can be represented by a sum of products (SP), and this expression is composed of the following elements:

1. Literals (uncomplemented and complemented variables). The level of NOT gates in the network is used to obtain the complemented variables whenever they are not available as external inputs.
2. Products, which are implemented by the level of AND gates.
3. Sum, implemented by one OR gate.

If the network has several outputs, one OR gate is used for each output; the output from NOT and AND gates can be shared as inputs to the OR gates.

In an analogous fashion, a network formed by one level of NOT gates, one level of OR gates, and one AND gate is obtained from a product of sums.

EXAMPLE 5.1

Consider the implementation of a modulo-64 incrementer whose high-level specification is

Input: $0 \leq x \leq 63$
Output: $0 \leq z \leq 63$

Function: $z = (x + 1) \bmod 64$

A binary specification is obtained by coding the variables x and z on bit-vectors $\underline{x}$ and $\underline{z}$, respectively. We use a radix-2 representation of integers, so that the bit vectors have six bits each. The table that describes this specification is somewhat large so we give the sum of products directly. This can be achieved by noting that z_i is 1 whenever x_i is 1 and at least one of the less significant bits of $\underline{x}$ is 0, or when $x_i = 0$ and all less significant bits of $\underline{x}$ are 1. This is illustrated by the following cases:

x	010101
z	010110

x	001111
z	010000

The specification is then

$$z_0 = \begin{cases} 1 & \textbf{if} \quad x_0 = 0 \\ 0 & \textbf{otherwise} \end{cases}$$

and for $i > 0$

$$z_i = \begin{cases} 1 & \textbf{if} \quad (x_i = 1 \textbf{ and } \text{there exists } j < i \text{ such that } x_j = 0) \\ & \quad \textbf{or} \quad (x_i = 0 \textbf{ and } x_j = 1 \text{ for all } j < i) \\ 0 & \textbf{otherwise} \end{cases}$$

The corresponding expressions are

$$\begin{aligned} z_5 &= x_5(x_4' + x_3' + x_2' + x_1' + x_0') + x_5'x_4x_3x_2x_1x_0 \\ &= x_5x_4' + x_5x_3' + x_5x_2' + x_5x_1' + x_5x_0' + x_5'x_4x_3x_2x_1x_0 \\ z_4 &= x_4x_3' + x_4x_2' + x_4x_1' + x_4x_0' + x_4'x_3x_2x_1x_0 \\ z_3 &= x_3x_2' + x_3x_1' + x_3x_0' + x_3'x_2x_1x_0 \\ z_2 &= x_2x_1' + x_2x_0' + x_2'x_1x_0 \\ z_1 &= x_1x_0' + x_1'x_0 \\ z_0 &= x_0' \end{aligned}$$

The resulting NOT-AND-OR network is shown in Figure 5.1. ■

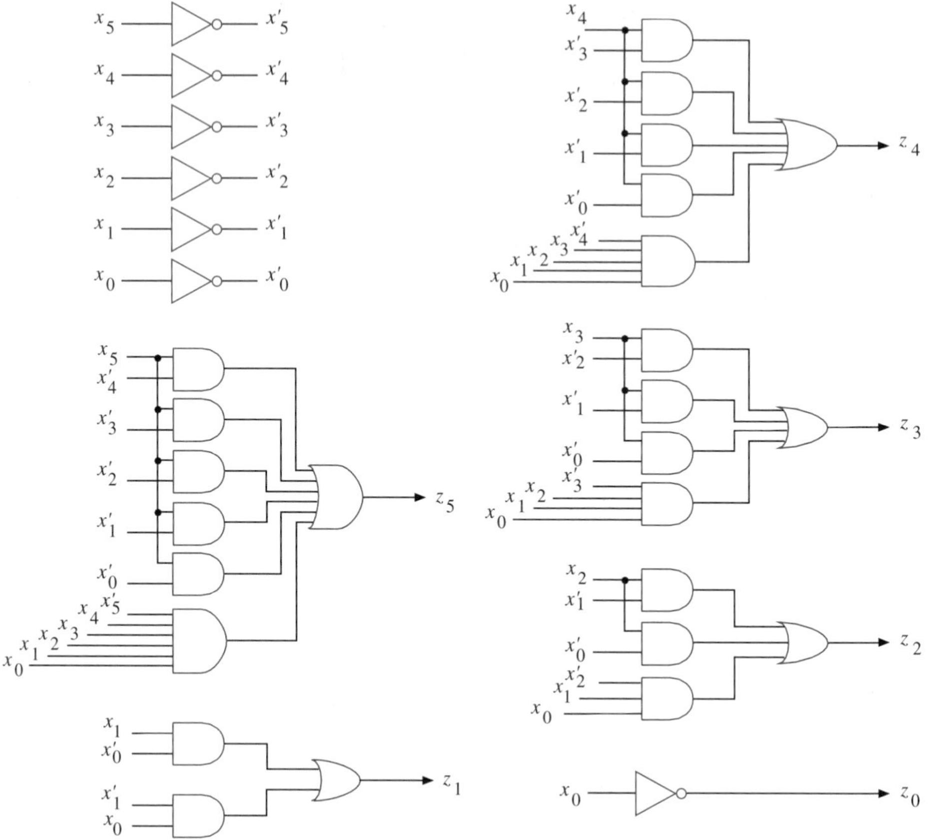

Figure 5.1 NOT-AND-OR modulo-64 incrementer network.

Uncomplemented and Complemented Inputs

If complemented and uncomplemented variables are available at the input of a network, the first level of NOT gates is not required and a **two-level network** results. In the rest of this section we assume complemented variables are available (this is particularly true for the implementation of some sequential systems, as discussed in Chapter 8).

Two-level networks are important because they have a small delay. Furthermore, there exists a systematic design procedure that minimizes the number of gates. On the other hand, these networks are not practical for functions of many variables, as discussed later.

Two types of two-level networks can be defined, as follows:

AND-OR network. This two-level network consists of a first level of AND gates and a second level of one OR gate per network output. It corresponds to sums of products (one sum of products per output). These networks are easily transformed into two-level NAND-NAND networks (as discussed later).

OR-AND network. This two-level network has a first level of OR gates and a second level of one AND gate per network output. It corresponds to products of sums. These networks are easily transformed into two-level NOR-NOR networks.

EXAMPLE 5.2

Figure 5.2*a* depicts the implementation as a two-level AND-OR network of the switching expression

$$E(x_2, x_1, x_0) = x_2'x_1'x_0 + x_2x_1 + x_1x_0'$$

whereas Figure 5.2*b* depicts the implementation as a two-level OR-AND network of the switching expression

$$E(x_2, x_1, x_0) = (x_2' + x_1)(x_1 + x_0')(x_2 + x_1' + x_0)$$

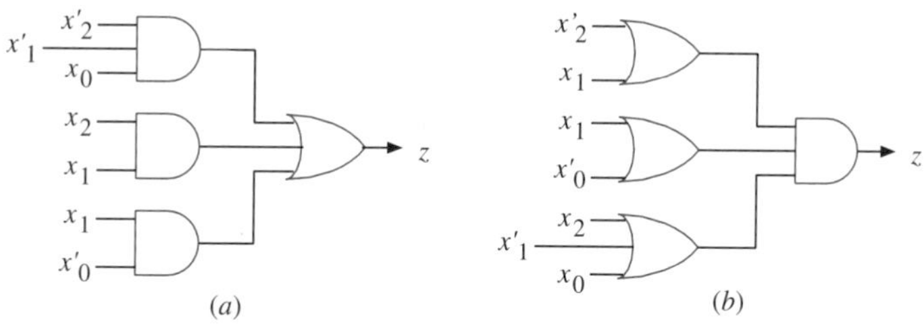

Figure 5.2 AND-OR and OR-AND networks. ■

5.1 MINIMAL TWO-LEVEL NETWORKS

The problem of selecting a suitable network to implement a switching function depends strongly on the technology to realize the network. We consider now a method of network selection applicable to the class of two-level AND-OR and OR-AND networks. Because a switching function can be realized by several two-level networks (different switching expressions), it is of interest to determine a network that satisfies some optimality criterion (minimal cost function). The method to be described produces networks with the following properties:

1. Inputs are available in uncomplemented and complemented form.
2. Gates have no limitations in the number of inputs.
3. Networks have only one output (single-output gate networks).
4. The cost minimization metric consists of minimizing the number of gates. If there is more than one network with the minimum number of gates, then the network with the minimum number of gate inputs is selected. That is, a **minimal network** has the minimum number of gates with the minimum number of inputs.

EXAMPLE 5.3

Networks *A* and *B* in Figure 5.3 both implement the function $f(x_2, x_1, x_0) = \textit{one-set}\,(3,6,7)$. Because network *A* consists of 4 gates and 12 gate inputs, whereas network *B* consists of 2 gates and 4 gate inputs, network *B* has lower cost than network *A*.

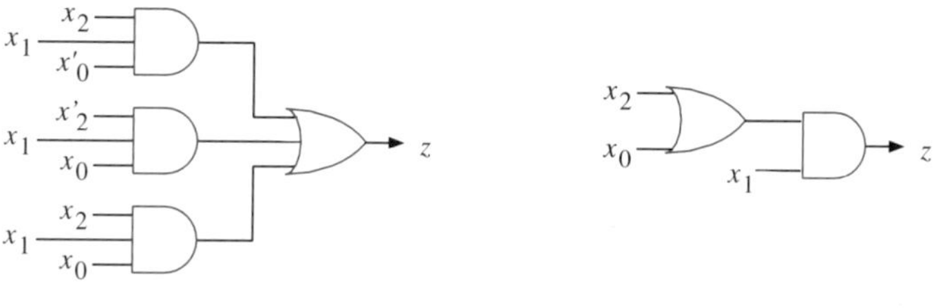

Figure 5.3 Networks with different cost to implement $f(x_2, x_1, x_0) = \textit{one-set}\,(3,6,7)$. ■

We now present a minimization procedure for gate networks under the previous assumptions. Later, we consider the practicality of the procedure due to the restrictions imposed by the aforementioned conditions.

Minimal Expressions

As we already know, there is a one-to-one correspondence among switching expressions and gate networks. Because a switching function can be represented by more than one switching expression, the minimization method consists of determining an expression that corresponds to a minimal network; such an expression is called a **minimal expression**. To correspond to a two-level network, the minimal expression has to be a sum of products or a product of sums. Based on the cost criterion given in the previous section, the **cost of an expression** is minimal if it has the minimum number of terms with the minimum number of literals.

EXAMPLE 5.4

The following expressions are equivalent, that is, they represent the same switching function. This can be verified by algebraic manipulation.

$$E_1(x_2, x_1, x_0) = x_2'x_1x_0' + x_1'x_0 + x_2x_0$$

$$E_2(x_2, x_1, x_0) = x_2x_1x_0 + x_2'x_1x_0' + x_2'x_1'x_0 + x_2x_1'x_0$$

Expression E_1 has lower cost than expression E_2 because it has only three terms and 7 literals (instead of four terms and 12 literals). ∎

To obtain a minimal expression for a two-level network, both a minimal sum of products and a minimal product of sums must be obtained and their costs compared. The procedure used to find a minimal expression is based on the systematic application of the following identities:

$$ab + ab' = a \quad \text{(for sum of products)}$$

$$(a + b)(a + b') = a \quad \text{(for product of sums)}$$

These identities allow reducing the number of terms in an expression as well as the size of their terms.

Obtaining minimal expressions is a nontrivial task in the general case, requiring use of computer-based tools as discussed later. The technique discussed first is most suitable for manual minimization of expressions of up to four variables. As an aid in this process, we use a graphical representation of switching functions. This representation, Karnaugh maps, is discussed next.

5.2 KARNAUGH MAPS

A **Karnaugh map** (K-map) is a two-dimensional array of cells used to represent a switching function. The n variables of the function are divided into two vectors $\underline{S}_1 = (x_{n-1}, \ldots, x_k)$ and $\underline{S}_2 = (x_{k-1}, \ldots, x_0)$; there is a row for each assignment of $\underline{S}_1$ (in total 2^{n-k} rows) and a column for each assignment of $\underline{S}_2$ (in total 2^k columns) and, consequently, one cell for each binary n-tuple. The rows and columns are labeled with the assignments of the corresponding vectors.

The rows and columns are labeled in such a way that the assignments for any set of 2^r adjacent rows (columns) differ only in r variables. That is, the assignments are the same for $n-k-r$ row variables and $k-r$ column variables. This is called the **adjacency condition.** Adjacency should also be satisfied across the borders of the map; that is, the map is a torus (a doughnut). This adjacency condition is needed for the simplification of expressions, as shown later.

Figure 5.4 shows K-maps for functions of one, two, three, and four variables. Because the adjacency condition can be satisfied only up to two variables in each dimension, two-dimensional K-maps are possible only for up to four variables. A row and column order that satisfies the adjacency condition is shown in Figure 5.4. Note that the order for the case of four rows (columns) does not correspond to the normal consecutive order 00,01,10,11, because this order does not satisfy the adjacency condition.

For simplicity, it is customary to label only the rows (columns) where a particular variable takes the value 1. For example, as shown in Figure 5.4, in the four-variable map the two center columns are labeled x_0 because for these two columns the variable x_0 has value 1. Moreover, it is also convenient to label each cell of the map with the integer whose binary representation is the assignment of that cell. For example, in the four-variable map the cell corresponding to $x_3x_2 = 11$ and $x_1x_0 = 01$ is labeled 13.

A function with more than four variables requires several four-variable K-maps. For instance, a five-variable K-map using two four-variable maps is labeled as indicated in

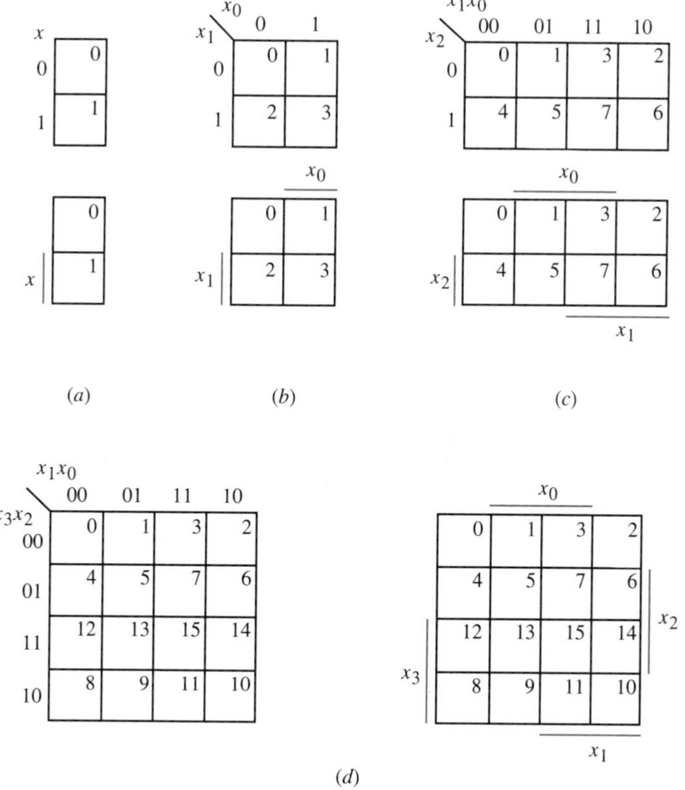

Figure 5.4 Karnaugh maps for (*a*) one, (*b*) two, (*c*) three, and (*d*) four variables.

$(x_4 = 0)$

0	1	3	2
4	5	7	6
12	13	15	14
8	9	11	10

$(x_4 = 1)$

16	17	19	18
20	21	23	22
28	29	31	30
24	25	27	26

Figure 5.5 Karnaugh map for five variables formed of two Karnaugh maps of four variables.

Figure 5.5. Notice the adjacency among corresponding cells of both four-variable maps. A function with six variables requires four four-variable maps.

Representation of Switching Functions

A switching function is represented in a K-map by inscribing in each cell the corresponding value of the function. Consequently, a cell can be a 0-cell, a 1-cell, or a dc-cell (don't care), depending on the value of the function for the corresponding assignment.

EXAMPLE 5.5

The following K-maps represent the given functions:

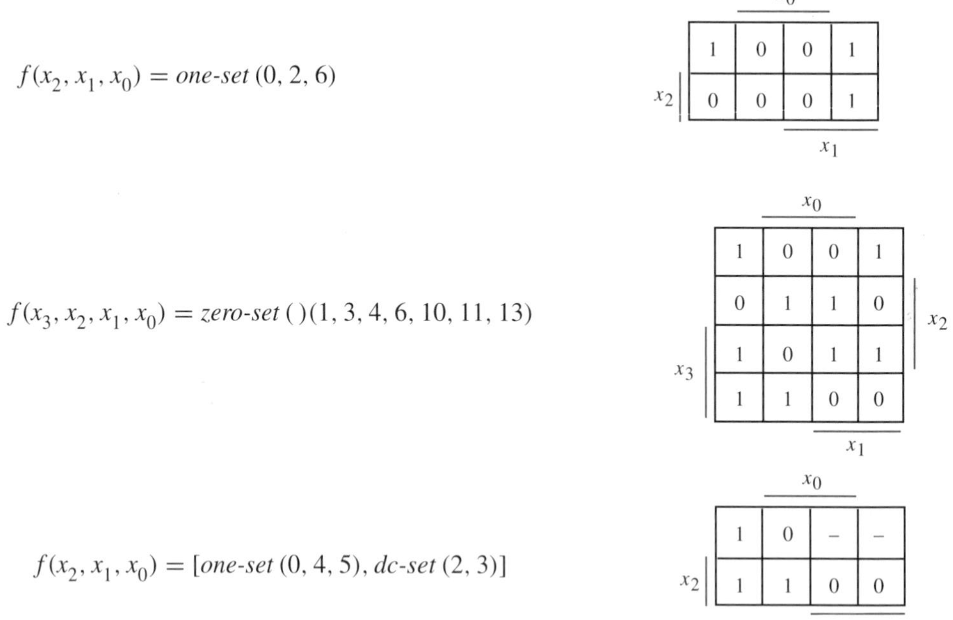

■

Rectangles of 1-cells and Sum of Products

A rectangle of 1-cells in a K-map corresponds to a product term, as follows:

1. Minterm m_j corresponds to the 1-cell with label j. For example, in a four-variable K-map, minterm $x_3'x_2'x_1x_0$ is represented by the 1-cell with label 3.
2. A product term of $n-1$ literals corresponds to a rectangle of two adjacent 1-cells. Such a product term is the sum of two minterms that differ only in the variable missing from the product term (one minterm has the variable uncomplemented, whereas the other has it complemented). Consequently, the corresponding 1-cells in the map are adjacent. For example, in a four-variable K-map the product term $x_3x_1'x_0$ is represented by the 1-cells 9 and 13, as illustrated in Figure 5.6*a*, because

$$\begin{aligned} x_3x_1'x_0 &= x_3x_1'x_0(x_2 + x_2') \\ &= x_3x_2x_1'x_0 + x_3x_2'x_1'x_0 \\ &= m_{13} + m_9 \end{aligned}$$

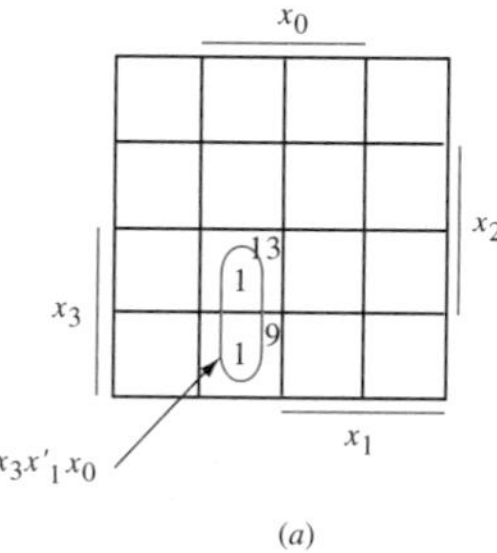

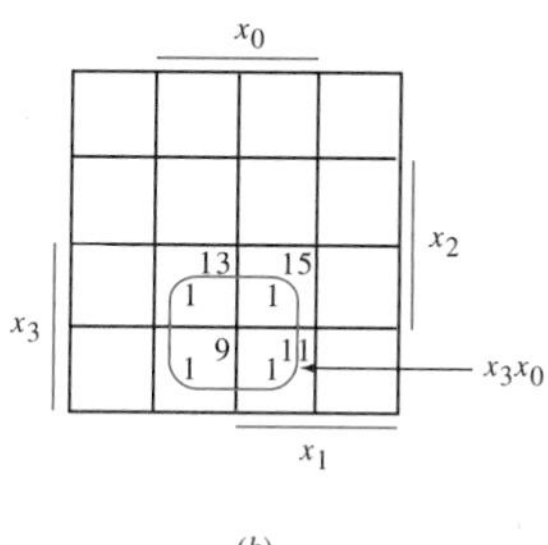

Figure 5.6 Representation of product terms. (*a*) $x_3x_1'x_0$. (*b*) x_3x_0.

3. A product term of $n-2$ literals corresponds to a rectangle of four adjacent 1-cells. The product term is equivalent to the sum of four minterms; $n-2$ literals coincide for the four minterms and they differ in the other two variables, so that all four combinations of uncomplemented and complemented variables appear.

   For example, in a four-variable K-map the product term x_3x_0 is represented by the 1-cells 9, 11, 13, and 15, as shown in Figure 5.6*b*. This is so because

$$\begin{aligned} x_3x_0 &= x_3x_0(x_1 + x_1')(x_2 + x_2') \\ &= x_3x_2'x_1'x_0 + x_3x_2'x_1x_0 + x_3x_2x_1'x_0 + x_3x_2x_1x_0 \\ &= m_9 + m_{11} + m_{13} + m_{15} \end{aligned}$$

4. As a generalization of the previous cases, a product term of $n-k$ literals corresponds to a rectangle of 2^k adjacent 1-cells. This is illustrated in Figures 5.7 and 5.8.

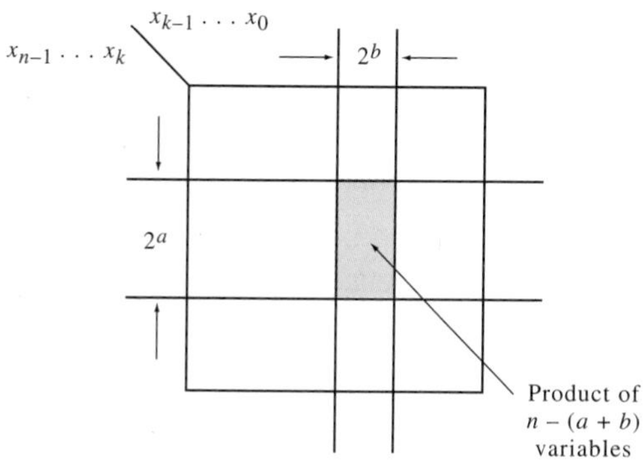

Figure 5.7 Representation of product of $n-(a+b)$ variables.

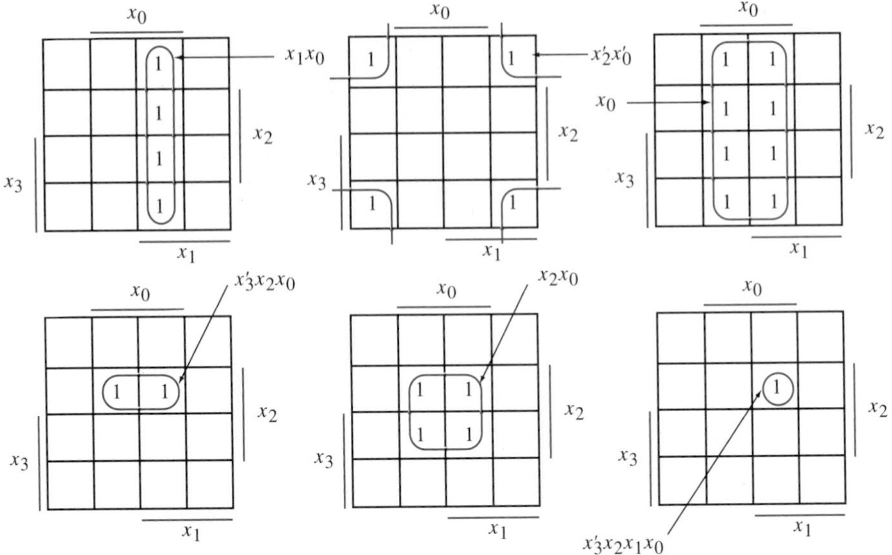

Figure 5.8 Product terms and rectangles of 1-cells.

Note that a rectangle corresponding to a product of p literals has 2^{n-p} 1-cells and, consequently, its dimensions are **powers of two.**

A **sum of products** is represented in a K-map by the union of the rectangles that represent each of the products. This is illustrated by the following example.

EXAMPLE 5.6

The following K-maps correspond to the given expressions:

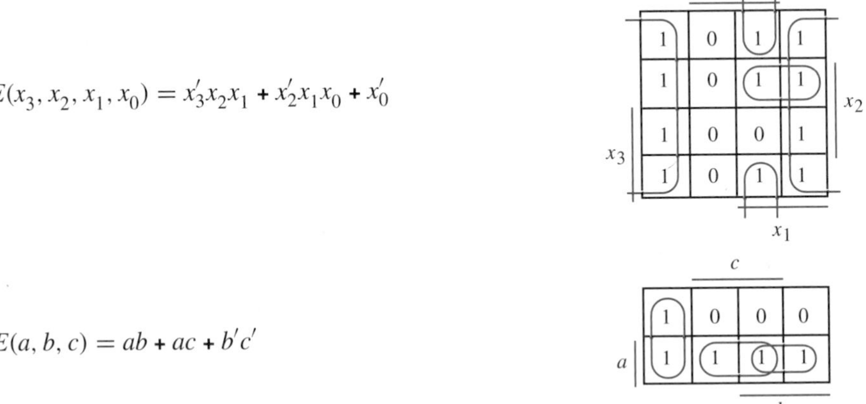

■

Rectangles of 0-cells and Product of Sums

Similar to the case of 1-cells, a rectangle of 0-cells in a K-map is related to a sum term. The 0-cell j corresponds to the maxterm M_j. According to the rules for the M-notation, defined in Section 2.5, the maxterm is obtained by including an uncomplemented variable if the corresponding bit of j is 0 and a complemented variable if the bit is 1. For example, in a four-variable map the 0-cell 13 corresponds to the maxterm $M_{13} = x_3' + x_2' + x_1 + x_0'$.

A rectangle of two adjacent 0-cells corresponds to a sum term of $n-1$ literals. For example, in a four-variable K-map the sum $(x_3 + x_2' + x_1')$ corresponds to the rectangle of 0-cells 6 and 7 because

$$(x_3 + x_2' + x_1') = (x_3 + x_2' + x_1' + x_0')(x_3 + x_2' + x_1' + x_0) = M_6 M_7$$

In general, a rectangle of $2^a \times 2^b$ 0-cells corresponds to a sum term of $n-(a+b)$ literals. The literals are those that have constant value for all cells in the rectangle; they appear uncomplemented if they have value 0 and complemented if they have value 1.

EXAMPLE 5.7

The following K-maps correspond to the given expressions:

$$E(x_2, x_1, x_0) = \prod M(1, 3, 4, 6, 7)$$

$$E(x_3, x_2, x_1, x_0) = (x_3 + x_2')(x_3' + x_1 + x_0')$$

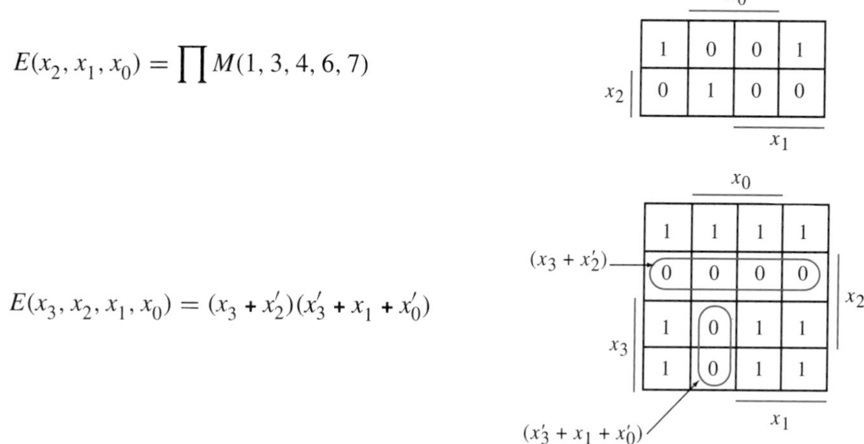

■

5.3 MINIMIZATION OF SUM OF PRODUCTS AND PRODUCT OF SUMS

We now consider a method to obtain minimal sum of products and product of sums expressions according to the cost function presented in Section 5.1.

5.3.1 Sum of Products

The procedure to obtain a minimal sum of products requires the following definitions:

Implicant. A product term p is an **implicant** of a function f if for any assignment for which p has value 1, the function has also value 1.

For example, the product term x_1x_0 is an implicant of the function $f(x_2, x_1, x_0) =$ *one-set* (0,1,3,6,7) because the product term has value 1 for assignments 011 and 111, and these are included in the one-set of the function (i.e., they correspond to the elements 3 and 7 of the one-set). On the other hand, the product term x_1x_0' is not an implicant of the function because the product has value 1 for assignment 010, corresponding to element 2, which is not part of the one-set.

Because an implicant is a product term, it is represented in a K-map by a rectangle of 1-cells. For instance, the rectangles A and B in Figure 5.9 correspond to two of the implicants of the function represented by the map. Moreover, the set of all implicants

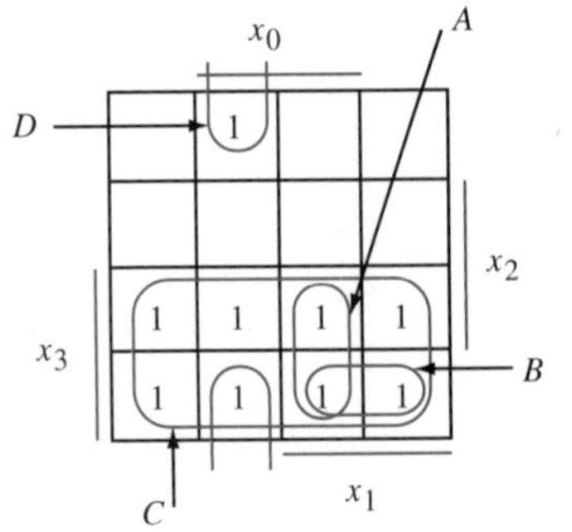

Figure 5.9 Implicant representation.

of a function corresponds to all rectangles formed by 1-cells in the map representing the function.

Note that any product term appearing in a sum of products that represents a function is an implicant of that function. This is so because the expression (and therefore the function it represents) has value 1 whenever the product term has value 1.

Prime Implicant. A **prime implicant** of a function is an implicant that is not covered by any other implicant of the same function. In the K-map representation, this means that the corresponding rectangle is not totally included in another rectangle of 1-cells.

For example, rectangles C and D in Figure 5.9 correspond to prime implicants of the function.

The K-map representation can be used to obtain all the prime implicants of a function. This is done by identifying all rectangles of 1-cells not included in other rectangles. Recall from page 119 that a rectangle of $2^a \times 2^b$ cells corresponds to a product of $n - (a + b)$ literals, and that the product is obtained by including those literals that have the same value in all the labels of the 1-cells in the rectangle; they are uncomplemented if the value is 1 and complemented if the value is 0.

EXAMPLE 5.8

For each of the following switching functions, find all the prime implicants:

(a) $f(x_2, x_1, x_0) = one\text{-}set\ (2, 4, 6)$

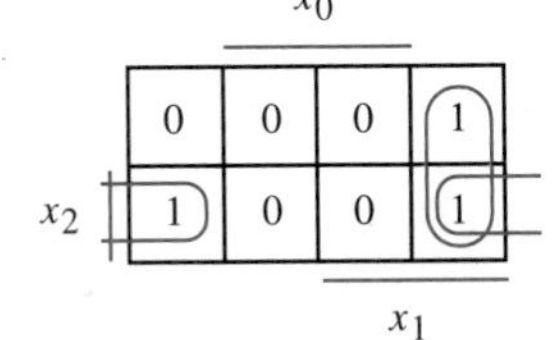

From the Karnaugh map we determine that the prime implicants are

$$x_2 x_0' \quad \text{and} \quad x_1 x_0'$$

(b) $f(x_2, x_1, x_0) = one\text{-}set\ (0, 1, 5, 7)$

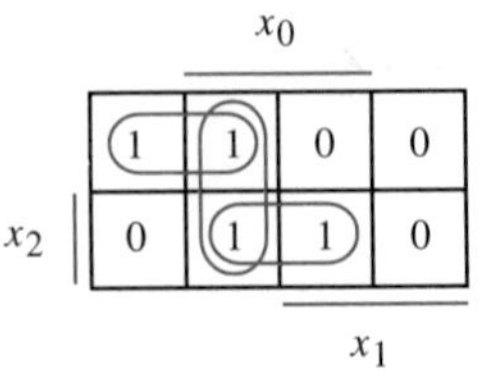

The Karnaugh map shows that the prime implicants are

$$x_2' x_1', \quad x_2 x_0, \quad \text{and} \quad x_1' x_0$$

(c) $f(x_3, x_2, x_1, x_0) = one\text{-}set\,(0, 3, 5, 7, 11, 12, 13, 15)$

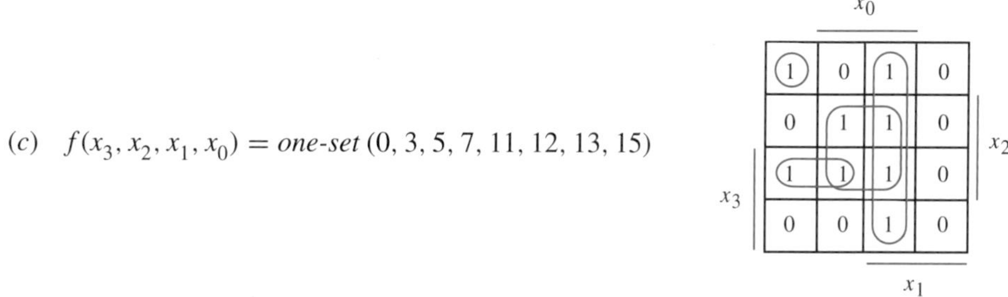

From the K-map, the prime implicants are

$$x_2x_0,\quad x_1x_0,\quad x_3x_2x_1',\quad \text{and}\quad x_3'x_2'x_1'x_0'$$

■

Minimal Sum of Products Consists of Prime Implicants

Prime implicants are important because **every minimal sum of products consists of a sum of prime implicants**. This is shown by contradiction. Consider a sum of products

$$E = p_1 + p_2 + \cdots + p + \cdots + p_n$$

which is not a sum of prime implicants, and let us show that E is not a minimal expression. From the assumption that E is not a sum of prime implicants, it follows that there exists in E a product term, say p, which is not a prime implicant. Because p is an implicant of the function represented by E (it appears in a sum of products), there exists a prime implicant q that covers p, as illustrated in Figure 5.10. If p is replaced by q in E, the resulting expression

$$p_1 + p_2 + \cdots + q + \cdots + p_n$$

is equivalent to E. This new expression has the same number of terms as E but fewer literals. Consequently, this expression has lower cost than E and therefore E is not minimal.

By applying this argument to every product term in E that is not a prime implicant, an expression consisting only of prime implicants and with fewer literals is obtained.

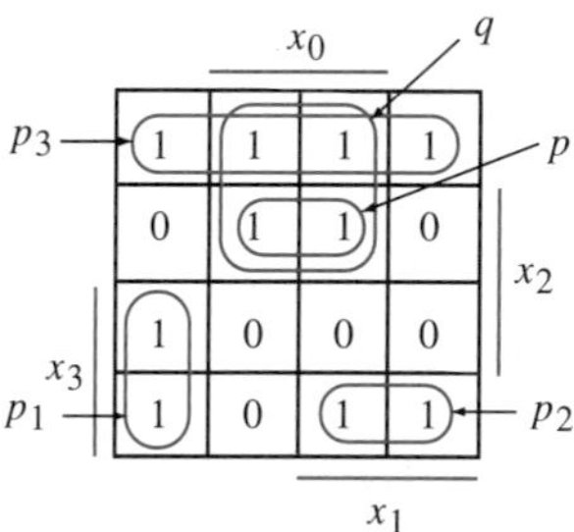

$p_1 + p_2 + p_3 + p = p_1 + p_2 + p_3 + q$

Figure 5.10 Minimal sum of products and prime implicants.

EXAMPLE 5.9

Consider the following expression

$$E(x_2, x_1, x_0) = x_2x_1'x_0' + x_2x_1x_0' + x_1x_0'$$

As illustrated in the following Karnaugh map, products $x_2x_1'x_0'$ and $x_2x_1x_0'$ are not prime implicants; x_2x_0' is a prime implicant that covers both of them. Consequently, $E(x_2, x_1, x_0)$ can be reduced to the sum of prime implicants $x_2x_0' + x_1x_0'$.

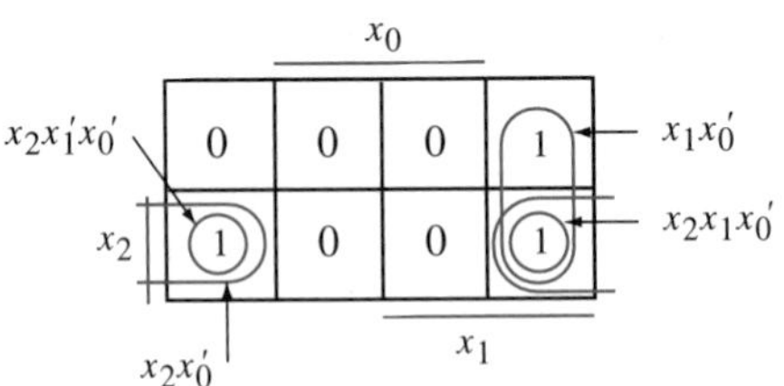

■

The foregoing statement does not imply that a minimal expression contains **all** prime implicants of a function. To determine which prime implicants should be included, prime implicants are divided into two classes: **essential** and **nonessential**.

Essential prime implicant. A prime implicant p_e of a function f is an **essential prime implicant** if there exists an assignment $\underline{a}$ such that $p_e(\underline{a}) = 1$ and $p(\underline{a}) = 0$ for any other prime implicant p.

This definition indicates that an essential prime implicant corresponds to a prime implicant whose rectangle contains cells that are not covered by any other prime implicant. In Example 5.8 (a) and (c), all prime implicants are essential, whereas in (b) only $x_2'x_1'$ and x_2x_0 are essential. In this latter case, the prime implicant $x_1'x_0$ is not essential because both 1-cells of the rectangle it represents are included in those of other prime implicants.

All Essential Prime Implicants are Included in a Minimal Sum of Products.

Because each essential prime implicant covers at least one 1-cell of the function f not covered by any other prime implicant, **all** essential prime implicants must be included in every minimal expression representing f (this fact originates the name essential). However, the set of all essential prime implicants of a function does not necessarily cover all 1-cells of the function. Consequently, to form a minimal expression, all essential and possibly some nonessential prime implicants are needed; the latter ones have to be selected so that the cost is minimum. This is illustrated in Example 5.10.

Procedure

The procedure for obtaining a minimal sum of products of a switching function is as follows:

1. Determine all prime implicants. For a small number of variables, this can be done using a K-map.
2. Obtain the essential prime implicants. They have to form part of any minimal sum of products.
3. If not all 1-cells in the K-map are covered by the essential prime implicants, then choose from the remaining prime implicants a set that covers all uncovered 1-cells and has minimum cost.

This selection of nonessential prime implicants is not unique and, therefore, there might be more than one minimal sum of products.

EXAMPLE 5.10 Find a minimal sum of products for the following cases:

(*a*) $E(x_3, x_2, x_1, x_0) = x_3'x_2' + x_3'x_2x_0 + x_1x_0$

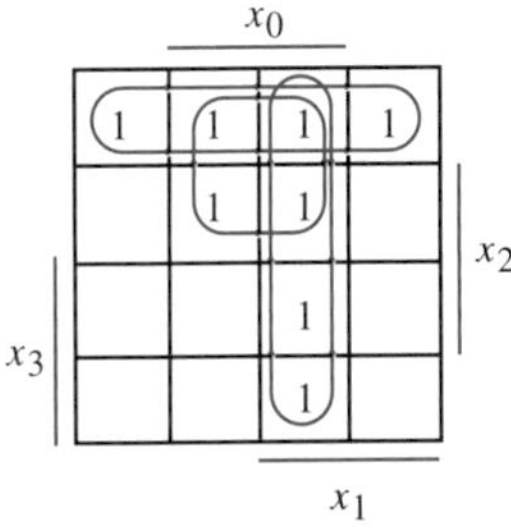

From the Karnaugh map we see that the prime implicants are $x_3'x_2'$, $x_3'x_0$, and x_1x_0. Because the prime implicants are all essential, the unique minimal sum of products is

$$x_3'x_2' + x_3'x_0 + x_1x_0$$

(*b*) $E(x_2, x_1, x_0) = \sum m(0, 3, 4, 6, 7)$

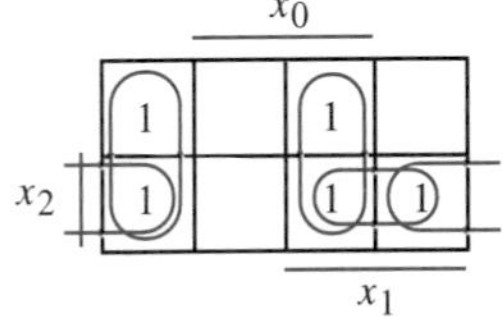

From the map, the prime implicants are $x_1'x_0'$, x_1x_0, x_2x_0', and x_2x_1. The essential prime implicants are $x_1'x_0'$ and x_1x_0. To cover all the 1-cells we have to include one of the terms x_2x_0' or x_2x_1. This leads to two minimal sums of products

$$x_1'x_0' + x_1x_0 + x_2x_0' \quad \text{and} \quad x_1'x_0' + x_1x_0 + x_2x_1$$

(*c*) $E(x_2, x_1, x_0) = \sum m(0, 1, 2, 5, 6, 7)$

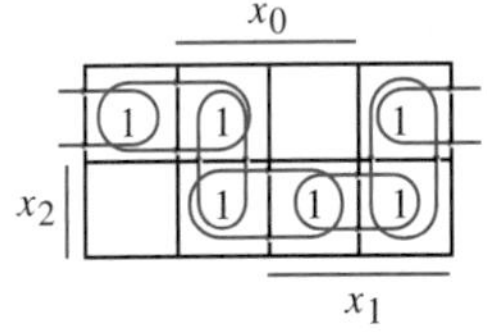

The K-map shows that the prime implicants are $x_2'x_1'$, $x_2'x_0'$, x_2x_0, x_2x_1, $x_1'x_0$, and x_1x_0'. None of them is essential. Two combinations cover all 1-cells, resulting in the minimal sums of products

$$x_2'x_1' + x_2x_0 + x_1x_0' \quad \text{and} \quad x_2'x_0' + x_1'x_0 + x_2x_1$$

■

Minimal Sum of Products for Incompletely Specified Functions

The "don't care" cells in the Karnaugh map of an incompletely specified function can be considered as 1-cells when forming the rectangles. This permits the selection of larger rectangles and, consequently, reduces the cost of the resulting expressions. Note that it is not necessary to cover all "don't care" cells; they are used only to maximize the size of 1-cell rectangles.

EXAMPLE 5.11

An incompletely specified function of four variables is represented by the following K-map:

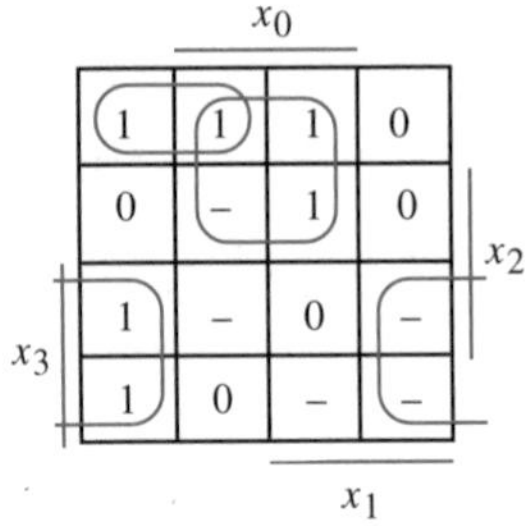

A minimal sum of products is

$$E(x_3, x_2, x_1, x_0) = x_3x_0' + x_3'x_0 + x_3'x_2'x_1' \qquad \blacksquare$$

5.3.2 Product of Sums

We now derive a procedure to obtain a minimal product of sums. Because the development of this procedure is analogous to the sum of products case, we proceed at a faster pace.

Implicate. A sum term s is an **implicate** of a function f if $f(\underline{a}) = 0$ whenever $s(\underline{a}) = 0$.

A sum term appearing in a product of sums representing a function is an implicate of that function.

An implicate of a function is represented in a K-map by a rectangle of 0-cells.

Prime implicate. A **prime implicate** is an implicate representing a rectangle of 0-cells that is not completely included in another rectangle of 0-cells.

Essential prime implicate. An **essential prime implicate** is a prime implicate that contains at least one 0-cell that is not included in any other prime implicate.

EXAMPLE 5.12

The prime implicates of the function

$$f(x_3, x_2, x_1, x_0) = \textit{zero-set}\,(7,13,15)$$

are obtained from the K-map

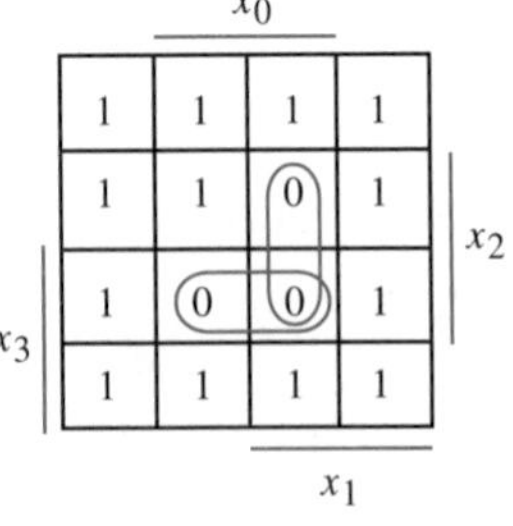

The prime implicates are

$$(x_3' + x_2' + x_0') \quad \text{and} \quad (x_2' + x_1' + x_0') \qquad \blacksquare$$

Procedure

As with sum of products, a minimal product of sums has to contain all essential prime implicates and, possibly, some other prime implicates. The procedure to obtain a minimal sum of products is similar to the one used for product of sums. It can be stated as follows:

1. Determine all prime implicates. For a small number of variables, this can be done using a K-map.
2. Determine the essential prime implicates. These essential prime implicates form part of all minimal products of sums.
3. From the set of nonessential prime implicates, select a set that includes all remaining 0-cells and has minimum cost.

EXAMPLE 5.13

Obtain a minimal product of sums for the function described by the following K-map:

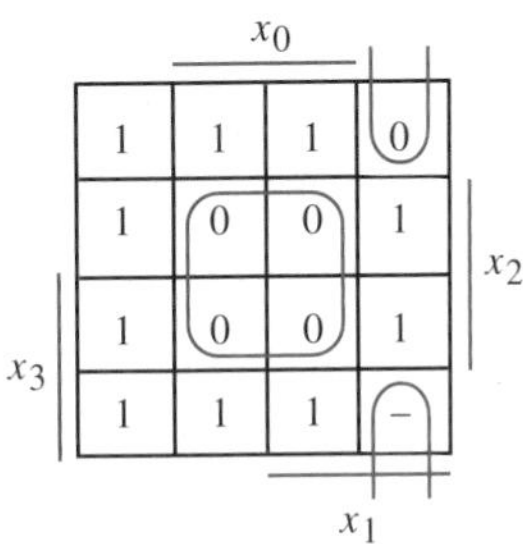

The prime implicates are

$$(x_0' + x_2') \quad \text{and} \quad (x_0 + x_2 + x_1')$$

Because both prime implicates are essential, the minimal product of sums is

$$(x_0' + x_2')(x_0 + x_2 + x_1')$$

Note that the "don't care" is used to obtain a larger rectangle. ■

5.3.3 Examples of Design of Minimal Two-level Gate Network

We now give two examples to illustrate the use of the minimization procedure in the design of single-output two-level networks.

EXAMPLE 5.14

Design a minimal gate network for a combinational system specified as follows:

Input: $x \in \{0, 1, 2, ..., 9\}$, coded in BCD as $\underline{x} = (x_3, x_2, x_1, x_0)$, $x_i \in \{0, 1\}$

Output: $z \in \{0, 1\}$

Function:
$$z = \begin{cases} 1 & \textbf{if} \quad x \in \{0, 2, 3, 5, 8\} \\ 0 & \textbf{otherwise} \end{cases}$$

Because the input is a decimal digit, the values {10,11,12,13,14,15} never appear and are considered "don't cares." The corresponding K-map of the function is

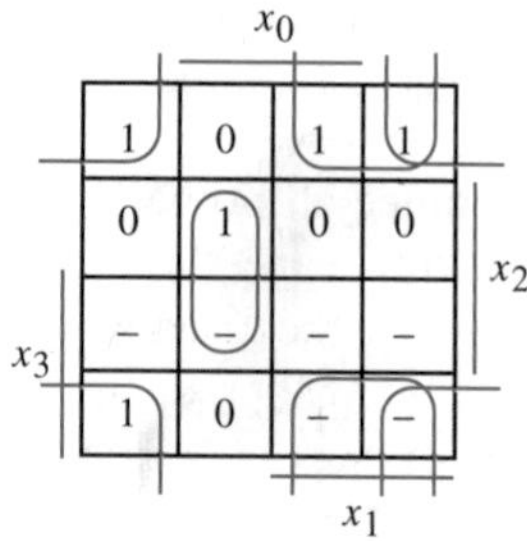

Using the procedure just described, the minimal sum of products is

$$z = x_2'x_1 + x_2'x_0' + x_2x_1'x_0$$

Similarly, the minimal product of sums is

$$z = (x_2' + x_1')(x_2' + x_0)(x_2 + x_1 + x_0')$$

In this case, both expressions have three terms with a total of seven literals, so that either one is the minimal expression. The corresponding AND-OR network is shown in Figure 5.11.

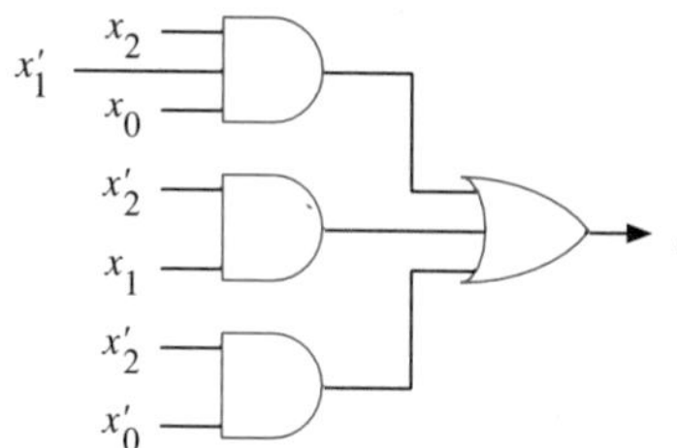

Figure 5.11 Minimal AND-OR network for Example 5.14. ■

EXAMPLE 5.15

Design a minimal network for the following combinational system:

Input: $x \in \{0, 1, 2, \ldots, 15\}$, represented in the binary code by the input vector $\underline{x} = (x_3, x_2, x_1, x_0)$

Output: $z \in \{0, 1\}$

Function: $z = \begin{cases} 1 & \textbf{if} \quad x \in \{0, 1, 3, 5, 7, 11, 12, 13, 14\} \\ 0 & \textbf{otherwise} \end{cases}$

The K-map for the function is

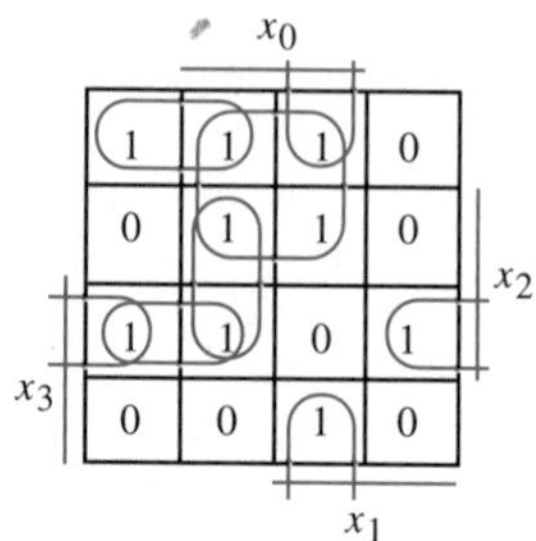

There are two minimal sums of products:

$$z = x_3'x_0 + x_3'x_2'x_1' + x_3x_2x_0' + x_2'x_1x_0 + x_2x_1'x_0$$
$$z = x_3'x_0 + x_3'x_2'x_1' + x_3x_2x_0' + x_2'x_1x_0 + x_3x_2x_1'$$

The minimal product of sums is unique:

$$z = (x_3' + x_2 + x_1)(x_3 + x_2' + x_0)(x_2 + x_1' + x_0)(x_3' + x_2' + x_1' + x_0')$$

The cost of the minimal product of sums is lower than that of the minimal sums of products. Consequently, the minimal two-level gate network is the OR-AND network shown in Figure 5.12.

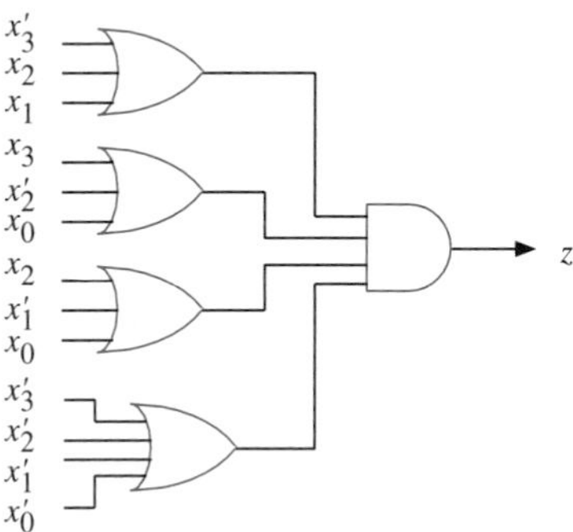

Figure 5.12 Minimal OR-AND network for Example 5.15. ■

5.3.4 Quine-McCluskey Tabular Method

We have discussed methods for obtaining minimal sum of products and minimal product of sums, using Karnaugh maps with up to four variables. The methods can be generalized to five variables by using two maps, and to six variables by using four maps. For more than six variables, or for cases in which it is desired to have a minimization by computer, there exist **tabular methods**. One of these is the **Quine-McCluskey** method, which consists of the following two parts:

a. determination of the prime implicants (or prime implicates) of the function; and
b. selection of a set of prime implicants (or prime implicates) that covers the given function and has the minimum cost.

We now illustrate the Quine-McCluskey method for the following four-input function:

$$f(x_3, x_2, x_1, x_0) = \textit{one-set}\,(0,1,3,5,7,11,12,13,14)$$

Two tables are constructed, as illustrated in Figure 5.13 for the function above. The first table, which provides the prime implicants by using the identity $xy + xy' = x$, is organized as follows:

- The first column corresponds to a list of minterms of the function, which are obtained directly from the one-set. The notation assigns a 1 to an uncomplemented variable, and a 0 to a complemented variable; for instance, minterm $x_3'x_2'x_1x_0$ is represented by 0011. The minterms are grouped according to the number of 1's in the binary representation.
- The second column shows the implicants with $n-1$ literals (three literals in the example). These implicants are obtained by pairing elements of the first column that differ only in the value of one variable (as these elements form rectangles of two

1-cells). Note that an element in the first column can be used in the formation of more than one pair. To produce the pairing, it is sufficient to examine adjacent groups.

The entry in the second column corresponding to a given pair lists the common values of the elements that form the pair, and a "–" for the variable whose value differs. For instance, the pair (0001,0011) results in 00–1. The elements from the first column that participate in forming pairs are marked with an N, which indicates that they are not prime implicants.

- The third column shows the implicants of $n-2$ literals (two literals in the example). This is obtained by forming pairs of elements from the second column. To form a pair, two elements must have their "–" in the same position, and the rest must differ only in one variable. For instance, (00–1,01–1) are paired to form the element 0 – – 1. As before, the elements from the second column that participate in forming the pairs are marked with an N, which indicates that they are not prime implicants.
- The process is continued in the same manner until no more elements can be paired.
- The prime implicants are all those elements that are not marked with an N.

The second step of the method consists of obtaining a **minimum cover,** that is, the minimum number of prime implicants that covers the one-set. A second table, called the **prime-implicant chart,** is constructed for these purposes, in which the rows correspond to the prime implicants obtained from the first table, and the columns to the elements of the one-set. For each row (prime implicant), we mark with "x" the entries corresponding to the one-set elements covered by the prime implicant. For instance, the prime implicant –101

Minterms		3-literal products		2-literal products	1-literal products
0000	N	000–		0 – – 1	
0001	N	00–1	N		
		0–01	N		
0011	N				
0101	N	0–11	N		
1100	N	–011			
		01–1	N		
0111	N	–101			
1011	N	110–			
1101	N	11–0			
1110	N				

Prime-implicant chart:

	0	1	3	5	7	11	12	13	14	
0 0 0 –	x	x								•
– 0 1 1			x			x				•
– 1 0 1				x				x		
1 1 0 –							x	x		
1 1 – 0							x		x	•
0 – – 1		x	x	x	x					•
										Essential prime implicants

Figure 5.13 Tabular minimization (Quine-McCluskey method).

covers minterms 0101 (5) and 1101 (13). Then, we identify the essential prime implicants as those that have an "x" in a column that has no other "x." In the example, this is the case for 000–, 0– –1, –011, and 11–0 (columns 0, 7, 11, and 14, respectively). These essential prime implicants are part of any cover, so the elements of the one-set that they cover are eliminated (as already covered). In the example, this corresponds to elements 0,1,3,5,7,11,12,14. Finally, the remaining one-set elements are covered with as few prime implicants as possible. In the example, the only remaining element is 13 which can be covered either by –101 or 110–.

The resulting minimal sums of products are

$$x_3'x_2'x_1' + x_2'x_1x_0 + x_2x_1'x_0 + x_3x_2x_0' + x_3'x_0$$

and

$$x_3'x_2'x_1' + x_2'x_1x_0 + x_3x_2x_1' + x_3x_2x_0' + x_3'x_0$$

The method is readily extended to the case with "don't cares." These "don't cares" are included in the first step (to obtain the prime implicants) but are not used in the second step (to obtain the minimum cover).

The Quine-McCluskey method is quite straightforward to program; however, for practical problems the number of prime implicants is usually very large so that obtaining a minimum cover is very time consuming. Moreover, this method is applicable only to single-output networks, whereas in practice it is necessary to consider the multiple-output case. This is discussed in Section 5.4.

5.4 DESIGN OF MULTIPLE-OUTPUT TWO-LEVEL GATE NETWORKS

Section 5.3 considered the derivation of minimal networks with one output. In practice, networks have several outputs so that it is necessary to extend the procedure to this more general case. Because the representation of a multiple-output network corresponds to several switching functions, a straightforward generalization is to use the single-output procedure separately for each output. We now illustrate this procedure with two examples and then comment on the fact that this does not produce a minimal network overall.

EXAMPLE 5.16

Design a minimal network that has three binary inputs and whose output represents the number of input variables having the value 1. That is,

Inputs: $(x_2, x_1, x_0),\ x_i \in \{0, 1\}$
Output: $z \in \{0, 1, 2, 3\}$

Function: $z = \sum_{i=0}^{2} x_i$

The input set contains all eight combinations of the three binary variables x_2, x_1, and x_0. We code the output as two binary variables (z_1, z_0) using the binary code. The design process is as follows:

1. The switching functions in tabular form are

x_2	x_1	x_0	z_1	z_0
0	0	0	0	0
0	0	1	0	1
0	1	0	0	1
0	1	1	1	0
1	0	0	0	1
1	0	1	1	0
1	1	0	1	0
1	1	1	1	1

2. The corresponding K-maps are

z_1 (x_0 over the middle two columns, x_1 over the right two columns):

	0	0	1	0
x_2	0	1	1	1

z_0 (x_0 over the middle two columns, x_1 over the right two columns):

	0	1	0	1
x_2	1	0	1	0

3. The minimal sum of product expressions are

$$z_1 = x_2x_1 + x_2x_0 + x_1x_0$$
$$z_0 = x_2'x_1'x_0 + x_2'x_1x_0' + x_2x_1'x_0' + x_2x_1x_0$$

The minimal product of sums expressions are

$$z_1 = (x_2 + x_0)(x_2 + x_1)(x_1 + x_0)$$
$$z_0 = (x_2 + x_1 + x_0)(x_2 + x_1' + x_0')(x_2' + x_1 + x_0')(x_2' + x_1' + x_0)$$

4. Both sets of expressions have the same cost. The AND-OR network is shown in Figure 5.14

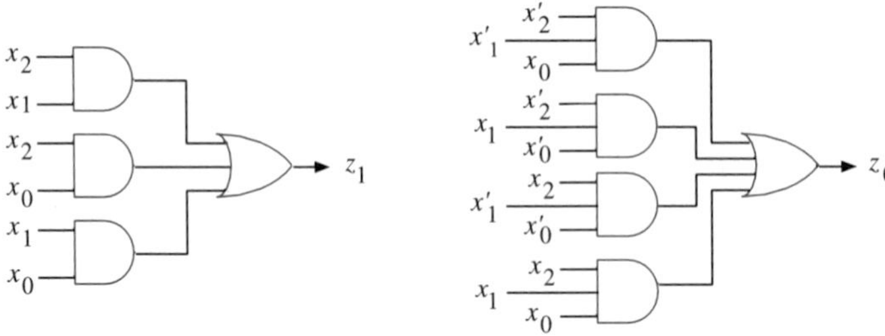

Figure 5.14 Minimal two-output AND-OR network for Example 5.16.

■

EXAMPLE 5.17

A digit code-converter converts the binary representation of a digit from one code to another. Table 5.1 gives the binary description of a code converter for decimal digits from the BCD code to the 2-out-of-5 code. The corresponding Karnaugh maps are as follows:

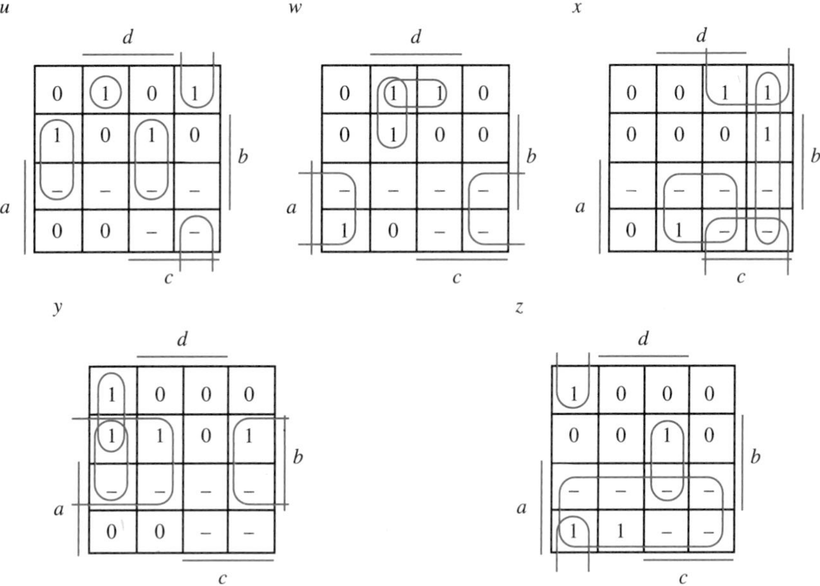

The following minimal sum of products are obtained from the K-maps:

$$u = bc'd' + bcd + b'cd' + a'b'c'd$$

$$w = ad' + a'c'd + a'b'd$$

$$x = ad + cd' + b'c$$

$$y = bc' + bd' + a'c'd'$$

$$z = a + bcd + b'c'd'$$

Table 5.1 BCD-to-"2-out-of-5" code conversion

BCD *abcd*	2-out-of-5 *uwxyz*	BCD *abcd*	2-out-of-5 *uwxyz*
0000	00011	0101	01010
0001	11000	0110	00110
0010	10100	0111	10001
0011	01100	1000	01001
0100	10010	1001	00101

We leave the derivation of the minimal products of sums and the comparison with the minimal sum of products to the reader. ■

As pointed out at the beginning of this section, the method of minimizing the network for each output separately does not necessarily produce the minimal overall network. This is because it might be possible to share first-level gates among outputs.

The methods to obtain a minimal two-level network for the multioutput case are beyond the scope of this text. Moreover, any such method becomes impractical for relatively large networks. Consequently, methods have been developed that achieve good designs, but not necessarily the minimal. Such methods are called heuristic methods. A popular program resulting from these efforts is ESPRESSO, which forms the basis for many commercial products. The methods used are still being refined, and better programs are being produced.

5.5 TWO-LEVEL NAND-NAND AND NOR-NOR NETWORKS

A two-level NAND network is a two-level network with only NAND gates. Such a network can be obtained from an AND-OR network by a simple transformation. Consider the following sum of products expression:

$$E = p_1 + p_2 + p_3 + \dots + p_n$$

where $p_1, p_2, \dots$ are product terms. By DeMorgan's rule we can write

$$E = (p_1' \cdot p_2' \cdot p_3' \cdots p_n')'$$

Using the NAND operator this expression can be stated as

$$E = \text{NAND}(\text{NAND}_1, \text{NAND}_2, \text{NAND}_3, \dots, \text{NAND}_n)$$

Consequently, the AND-OR network associated to the sum of products expression can be directly converted into a NAND network, as illustrated in Figure 5.15. The corresponding transformation consists of simply replacing the AND and OR gates by NAND gates. An additional transformation is necessary for input variables that are directly connected as inputs to the OR gate; these variables must be complemented, as shown in the figure.

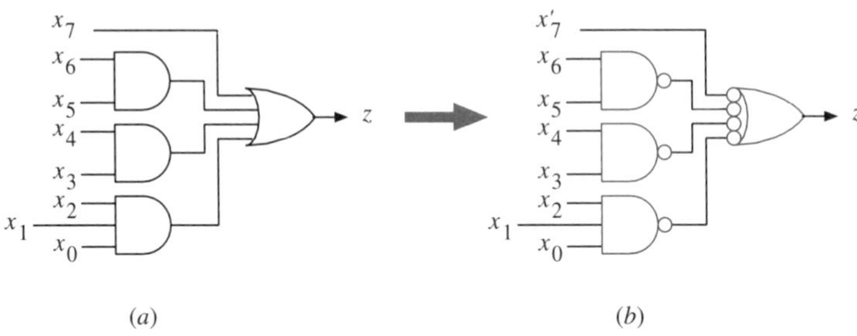

Figure 5.15 Transformation of an AND-OR network into a NAND network.

When we use the same cost metric as in Section 5.6 for AND-OR networks, a minimal NAND network is obtained by converting a minimal AND-OR network into its equivalent NAND form.

Similarly, a two-level NOR network is a two-level network with only NOR gates. Using a similar approach as for two-level NAND networks, the design of these networks is based on the transformation of a two-level OR-AND network into a NOR network by replacing each AND and OR gate by a NOR gate (and complementing inputs going directly to the AND gate).

EXAMPLE 5.18

Implement the following expression using only NOR gates:

$$z = x_5'(x_4 + x_3')(x_2 + x_1 + x_0)$$

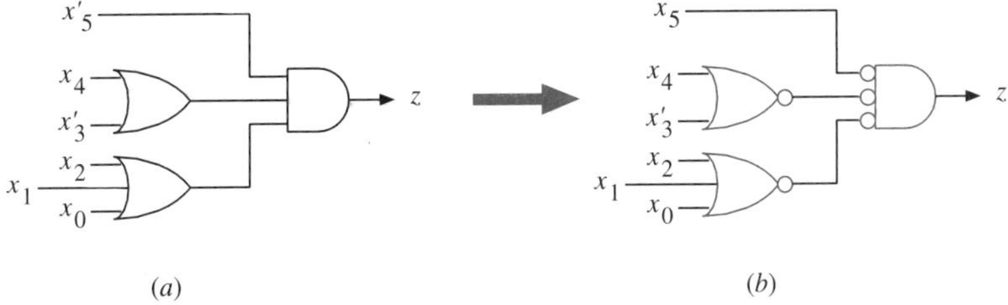

Figure 5.16 Transformation of OR-AND into a NOR network.

The OR-AND network is shown in Figure 5.16*a*; the corresponding NOR network is depicted in Figure 5.16*b*. ■

Because NAND and NOR gates in CMOS are simpler to implement than AND and OR gates, these transformations usually result in networks with better characteristics, such as size and delay.

5.6 LIMITATIONS OF TWO-LEVEL NETWORKS

We now comment on the limitations of two-level networks. We consider the relationship between the characteristics of networks discussed in Chapter 4 and practical design constraints, as well as other related issues:

1. The requirement of uncomplemented and complemented inputs to the network is satisfied in some instances, especially for the sequential networks discussed in Chapter 8. If this requirement is not satisfied, an additional level of NOT gates is needed.
2. Although there is a procedure to minimize the number of gates for a two-level implementation, for practical systems this number might be quite large, resulting in a large chip area.
3. Existing technologies have limitations in the number of gate inputs. This restriction makes a two-level network for functions with many literals and/or terms impossible. Moreover, even if the maximum number of gate inputs is acceptable, the delay of a gate is dependent on its number of inputs; consequently, a two-level implementation might not have the minimum delay.

   As an illustration of points 2 and 3, consider a modulo-2^{16} incrementer (16-bit incrementer). The specification is given in Example 5.1, and the two-level implementation is an extension of Figure 5.1. Consequently, output z_{15} would have 16 AND gates with up to 16 inputs and one OR gate of 16 inputs. Moreover, input x_{15} would be connected to 15 AND gates. Due to these factors, a two-level network is not practical.
4. The procedure is essentially limited to the single-output case. However, most combinational systems have several outputs. If the procedure is used separately for each output, the resulting implementation is not necessarily minimal. The technique has been extended to multiple-output networks, but it becomes more complex than for the single-output case. As a consequence, for a large number of inputs and outputs, it is necessary to resort to approximate methods that provide good but not necessarily optimal designs.
5. The cost criterion of minimizing the number of gates is not adequate for many MSI/LSI/VLSI designs, in which other considerations—such as regularity of the layout and regularity and minimization of the connections—might be of greater significance.

In spite of these limitations, the design of two-level networks is of special interest because of the two-level programmable modules discussed in Section 5.7 and because the minimal two-level description serves as an intermediate step for many tools for the design of multilevel networks.

5.7 PROGRAMMABLE MODULES: PLAS AND PALS

Ideally, a large number of gates should be packaged per chip, so that the implementation of a network may be achieved with fewer modules (fewer ICs), fewer off-chip wiring, and shorter delay. For economic reasons, chips should implement functions widely used in combinational networks. Consequently, modules that implement some frequently used combinational functions have been developed, as discussed in Chapters 9 and 10. However, these standard modules do not cover all possible functions; **programmable modules** can be used for those functions not covered. Programmable modules are characterized by having a standard (fixed) structure, and are customized (programmed) for a particular function either at the last stage of fabrication or when the module is incorporated into a system.

Programmable modules (**programmable logic devices** or PLDs) have become quite popular but, in spite of the advantages arising from their flexibility, they have not replaced fixed-function standard modules in all applications because they are somewhat more expensive and slower than a well-suited fixed-function module. Moreover, in the case of VLSI implementations, programmable modules occupy a larger area than the fixed-function counterparts.

We now describe two widely used programmable modules: PLAs and PALs. These modules implement two-level combinational networks. Multilevel combinational and sequential programmable devices are discussed in Chapter 12.

5.7.1 Programmable Logic Arrays

A n-input, k-output **programmable logic array** (PLA) is a combinational module that provides a NOT-AND-OR or NOT-OR-AND implementation of k switching functions $\underline{z} = (z_{k-1}, \ldots, z_0)$ of n variables $\underline{x} = (x_{n-1}, \ldots, x_0)$, in which the number of product terms is not more than r. These modules usually provide three-state outputs and a **module enable** input E to facilitate the design of multimodule PLA networks. When $E = 0$, all outputs of the module are in the high-impedance state.

A high-level description of a PLA is given as follows:

Inputs: $\underline{x} = (x_{n-1}, \ldots, x_0), \quad x_i \in \{0, 1\}$
$E \in \{0, 1\}$

Outputs: $\underline{z} = (z_{k-1}, \ldots, z_0), \quad z_i \in \{0, 1\}$

Function: NOT-AND-OR or NOT-OR-AND implementation of k switching functions, with maximum r terms in total

Following tradition, we describe the NOT-AND-OR type except when discussing a MOS implementation, in which case the NOT-OR-AND type is more appropriate. As shown in Figure 5.17, a PLA consists of n NOT gates, which provide the complement of the input variables, r AND gates, which generate the product terms, and k OR gates which produce the sums. The AND gates are organized in a regular structure called the AND array, whereas the OR gates are similarly organized in the OR array. This organization corresponds to a sum of

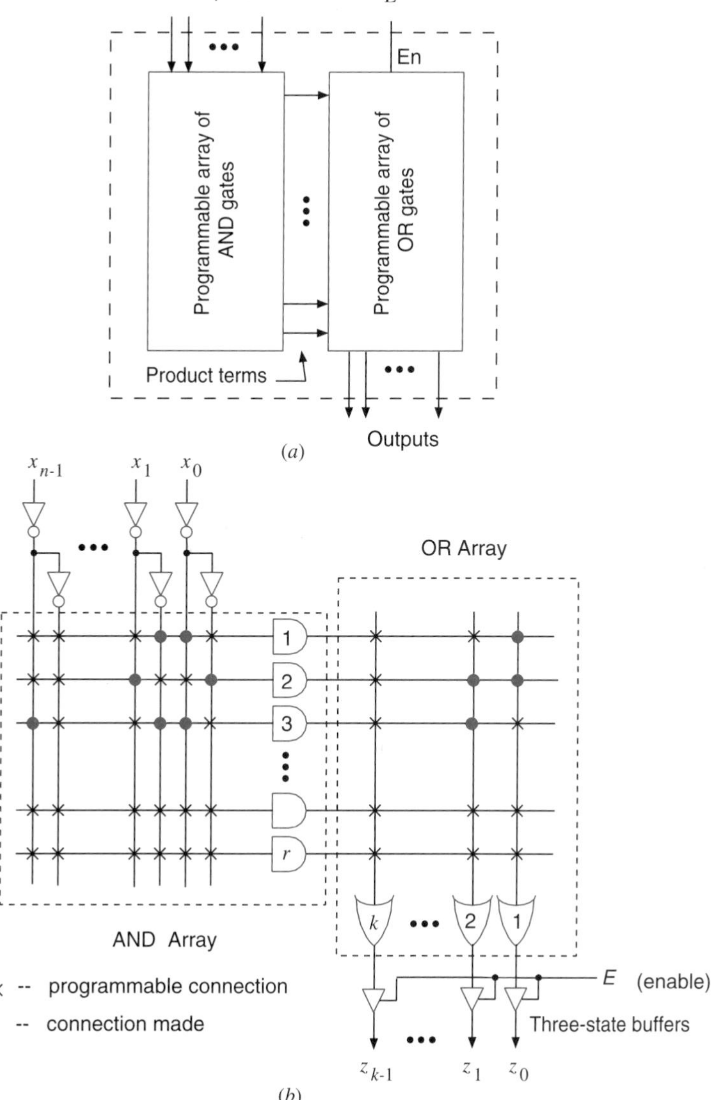

Figure 5.17 Programmable logic array (PLA). (*a*) Block diagram. (*b*) Logic diagram.

products implementation. In a similar manner, a PLA can be defined to implement a product of sums, in which case an OR array is followed by an AND array.

The connections from the module inputs (or their complements) to the AND gates are established in a way that implements the required product terms. That is, the functionality of this array is "customized" or "programmed" by selecting which input signals are connected to which AND gate without changing the structure of the array. Similarly, the connections between the outputs from the AND array and the inputs to the OR gates are also customized, as illustrated in Figure 5.17*b*. To simplify the diagram, just one horizontal line is drawn for all inputs to each AND gate; similarly, one vertical line represents all inputs to each OR gate. The big dots in the figure indicate those connections that have been made (programmed) for a particular set of functions; for example, AND gate 1 implements the product x_1x_0', and

AND gate 2 implements $x_1' x_0$, whereas AND gate 3 implements $x_{n-1}' x_1 x_0'$. The programmed outputs are $z_0 = x_1 x_0' + x_1' x_0 = x_1 \oplus x_0$ and $z_1 = x_1' x_0 + x_{n-1}' x_1 x_0'$.

Actual implementations of PLAs differ depending on the technology. Among other differences, the programming of a PLA (i.e., setting the connections to the AND and OR arrays) can be done

- during fabrication of the module (**mask-programmed** PLA); or
- in the field (**field-programmable** PLA or FPLA).

For technological reasons, a PLA may implement each function as a product of sums. Figure 5.18 shows a fragment of a pseudo-nMOS PLA with a NOR-NOR implementation; as discussed earlier in this chapter, this is equivalent to an OR-AND network.

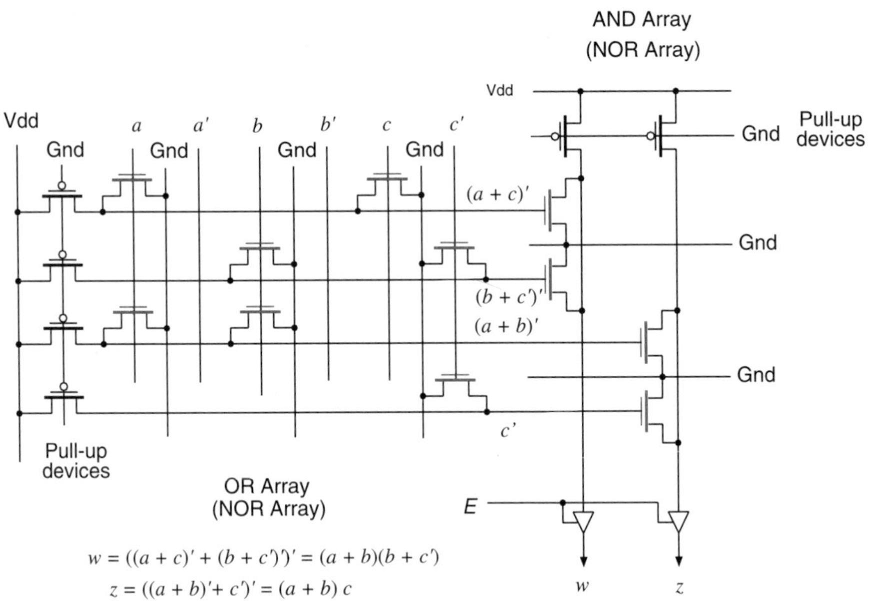

Figure 5.18 Example of PLA implementation at the circuit level: fragment of a MOS PLA.

Implementation of Switching Functions Using PLAs

The implementation of switching functions using a PLA consists of determining the corresponding sum of products (product of sums) expressions, and mapping such expressions onto the module, as illustrated in the following example. To reduce the number of product terms (AND gates), minimal expressions obtained as discussed earlier in this chapter are utilized. Moreover, design tools for two-level networks are appropriate.

EXAMPLE 5.19

A BCD-to-Gray converter has the following tabular description:

Inputs: $\underline{d} = (d_3, d_2, d_1, d_0),\ d_j \in \{0, 1\}$

Outputs: $\underline{g} = (g_3, g_2, g_1, g_0),\ g_j \in \{0, 1\}$

Function:

i	$d_3d_2d_1d_0$	$g_3g_2g_1g_0$
0	0000	0000
1	0001	0001
2	0010	0011
3	0011	0010
4	0100	0110
5	0101	0111
6	0110	0101
7	0111	0100
8	1000	1100
9	1001	1101

The corresponding minimal sum of products expressions are

$$g_3 = d_3$$
$$g_2 = d_3 + d_2$$
$$g_1 = d_2'd_1 + d_2d_1'$$
$$g_0 = d_1d_0' + d_1'd_0$$

These expressions lead to the PLA implementation depicted in Figure 5.19.

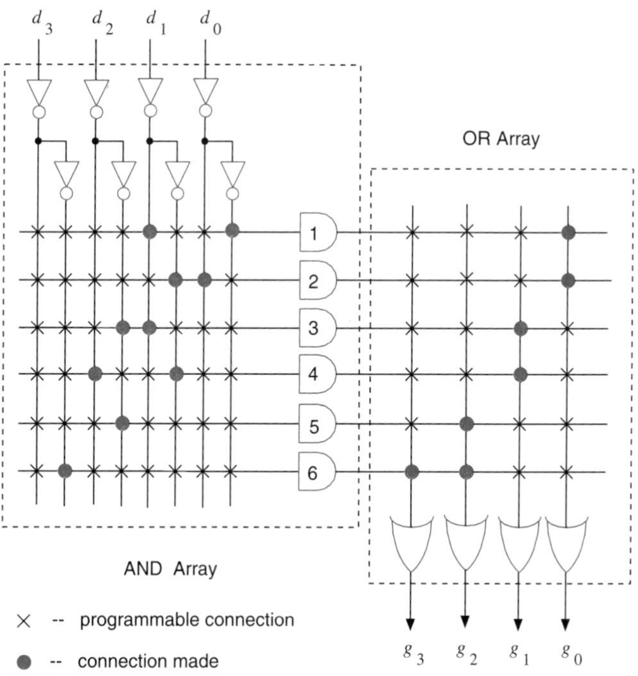

Figure 5.19 PLA implementation of BCD-to-Gray code converter.

■

5.7.2 Programmable Module with Fixed OR Array

A module called Programmable Array Logic (PAL) has been introduced for simplifying the implementation of PLAs.[1] In such a module, each OR gate is permanently connected to a subset of the AND gates. As in a PLA, the AND array is programmed to obtain the desired product terms (see Figure 5.20). PALs are faster than PLAs because there is only one programmed connection in a signal path. PALs can also accommodate more inputs and product terms than PLAs by not having two programmable arrays.

An example of a commercial PAL is shown in Figure 5.21. It consists of

1. Up to 16 inputs and up to 8 outputs. Six pins (IO2–IO8) are bidirectional, that is, they can be programmed to serve as input or output pins.
2. A fixed array of eight OR gates. Each OR gate is permanently connected to seven AND gates. The output of the OR gate is connected through a three-state programmable buffer with the corresponding chip pin. The buffer can be always disabled (in which case the output pin can serve as an input), always enabled, or enabled by a product term of the inputs. When the buffer is disabled, the corresponding pin can be used as input.
3. A programmable AND array of 64 rows and 32 columns. There are 64 AND gates. Each row allows programmed connection of up to 16 variables (complemented or uncomplemented) to an AND gate. The product terms cannot be shared by several outputs.

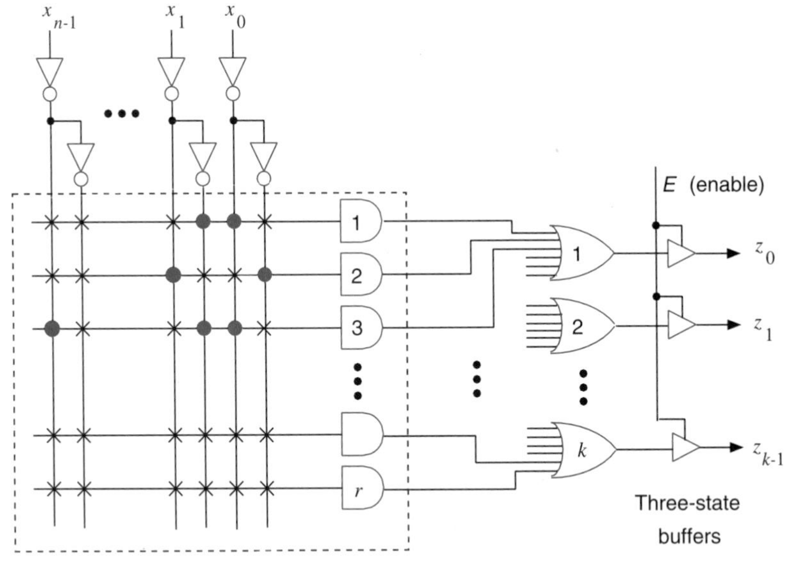

Figure 5.20 Logic diagram of a PAL.

[1] PAL is a trademark of Advanced Micro Devices (AMD), Sunnyvale, CA. Due to the widespread use of these devices, it is common to use the name PAL to denote the corresponding concept.

The description of PLAs and PALs is usually specified in a hardware description language such as ABEL. The simplification of expressions to be implemented can be done using ESPRESSO.

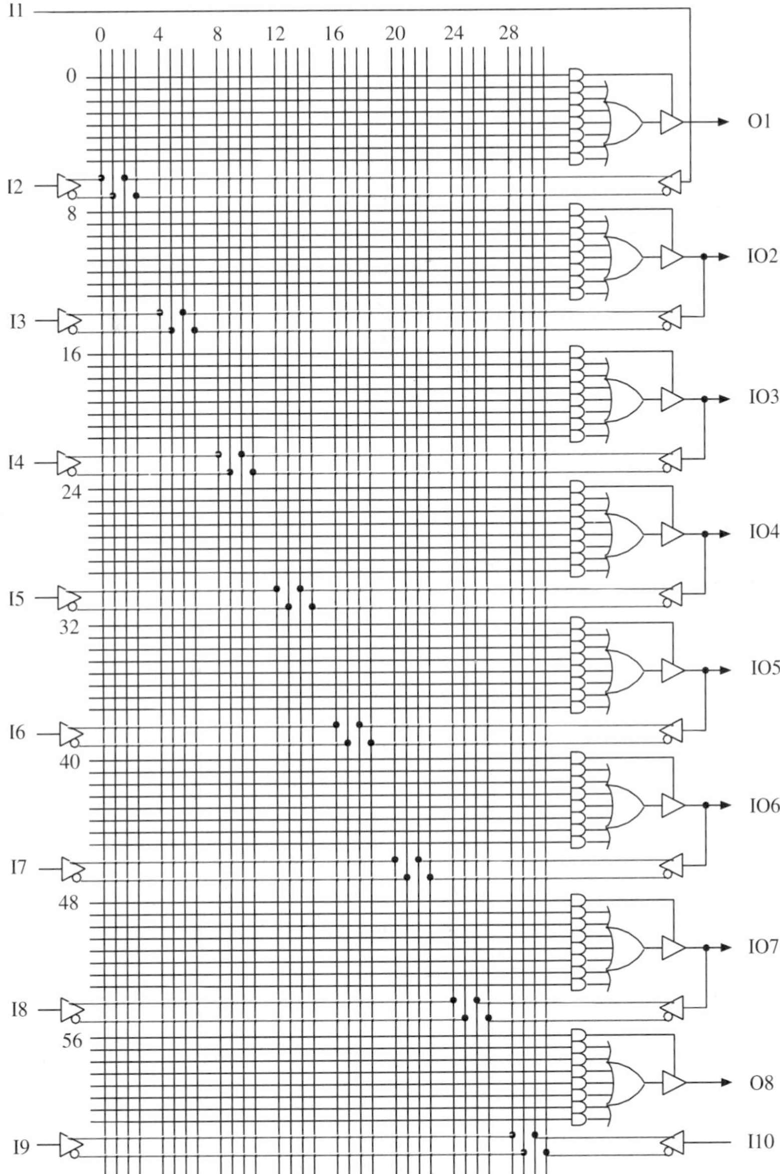

Figure 5.21 A 16-input, 8-output PAL.

5.8 FURTHER READINGS

Many traditional texts on switching theory and logic design have a substantial treatment of AND-OR gate networks and minimization techniques for two-level networks. Examples are *Logic Design Principles With Emphasis on Testable Semicustom Design* by E. J. McCluskey, Prentice-Hall, Englewood Cliffs, NJ, 1986, which discusses a tabular minimization method;

Introduction to Digital Logic Design by J. P. Hayes, Addison-Wesley, Reading, MA, 1993; *Digital Design Principles and Practices* by J. F. Wakerly, 2nd ed., Prentice-Hall, Englewood Cliffs, NJ, 1994; *Contemporary Logic Design* by R. H. Katz, The Benjamin/Cummings Publishing Company, Redwood City, CA, 1994; and *Synthesis and Optimization of Digital Circuits* by G. De Micheli, McGraw-Hill, New York, 1994.

A good survey of CAD tools for reduction of two-level networks and a description of ESPRESSO is given in *Logic Minimization Algorithms for VLSI Synthesis* by R. K. Brayton et al., Kluwer Academic Publishers, Norwell, MA, 1984.

Programmable logic devices, such as PLAs and PALs are discussed in many textbooks on digital design such as *Digital Design* by J. Wakerly, Prentice-Hall, Englewood Cliffs, 1994, *Contemporary Logic Design* by R. H. Katz, The Benjamin/Cummings Publishing Co., Redwood City, CA, 1994; and in books dedicated to programmable devices such as *Digital Systems Design with Programmable Logic* by M. Bolton, Addison-Wesley, Reading, MA, 1990; and *Digital Designing with Programmable Logic Devices* by J. W. Carter, Prentice-Hall, Englewood Cliffs, NJ, 1997.

To learn about specific programmable devices, design tools, and applications there is abundant literature provided by the manufacturers.

EXERCISES

Representation by K-maps

Exercise 5.1 Represent on K-maps the functions described by the following table:

xyz	f_1	f_0
000	0	–
001	1	0
010	1	1
011	0	1
100	0	–
101	1	0
110	0	1
111	0	0

Exercise 5.2 Represent on K-maps the functions described by the following expressions:

a. $E(x, y, z) = \sum m\,(1, 5, 7)$
b. $E(w, x, y, z) = w'x'y + y'z + xz'$

Exercise 5.3 Represent on K-maps the functions described by the following expressions:

a. $E(w, x, y, z) = \prod M(1, 3, 4, 7, 10, 13, 14, 15)$
b. $E(w, x, y, z) = \sum m\,(0, 4, 5, 9, 11, 14, 15)$, $dc(w, x, y, z) = \sum m\,(2, 8)$
c. $E(x, y, z) = \sum m\,(0, 1, 4, 6)$

Minimal two-level networks

Exercise 5.4 For $f(w, x, y, z) = one\text{-}set\,(0,1,2,3,5,7,8,10,11,15)$

a. Find all the prime implicants.
b. Indicate which of these prime implicants are essential.
c. Obtain a minimal sum of products for f. Is it unique?

Exercise 5.5 Show an example of a function of three variables x, y, and z, which has

a. More implicants than minterms.
b. Equal number of implicants and minterms.

Exercise 5.6 Using K-maps, find the minimal sum of products and product of sums that are equivalent to the following expressions:

a. $E(w, x, y, z) = \prod M(1, 3, 4, 7, 10, 13, 14, 15)$
b. $E(w, x, y, z) = \sum m(0, 4, 5, 9, 11, 14, 15), dc\,(w, x, y, z) = \sum m(2, 8)$
c. $E(x, y, z) = \sum m(0, 1, 4, 6)$

Exercise 5.7 For $f(w, x, y, z) = \textit{one-set}\ (1, 5, 7, 8, 9, 10, 14)$:

a. Find all the prime implicates of f.
b. Indicate which of these prime implicates are essential.
c. Obtain a minimal product of sums for f. Is it unique?

For Exercises 5.8 to 5.17 assume that both input forms (uncomplemented and complemented) are available. Perform the following steps:

a. Obtain minimal expressions (sum of products and product of sums). Determine one minimal expression for each output.
b. Map each expression into a gate network.

Exercise 5.8 A combinational system has four inputs a, b, c, d, and one output y. The output y is 1 if and only if the number represented by (a, b, c, d) in binary code is prime. Design a minimal two-level network to implement this system (0 and 1 are not prime).

Exercise 5.9 Repeat Exercise 5.8 using the Quine-McCluskey minimization method.

Exercise 5.10 Design a minimal two-level network that implements the five-input majority function, that is, the output is 1 whenever three or more inputs are 1. Use the Quine-McCluskey minimization method.

Exercise 5.11 Design a minimal two-level single-error detector for the 2-out-of-5 code. The input is a digit in the 2-out-of-5 code and the output is 0 if the number of 1s in the input is 2. Use the Quine-McCluskey minimization method.

Exercise 5.12 Design a minimal two-level network that implements the addition of two integers, in the range 0 to 3, and of an input carry. Minimize each five-variable expression separately using the Quine-McCluskey method.

Exercise 5.13 Design a two-level network that computes the residue mod 7 of an integer in the range 0 to 15. Minimize each output expression separately.

Exercise 5.14 Design a minimal two-level NAND network that computes the product of two integers, with input values from 0 to 3. Minimize each output expression separately.

Exercise 5.15 Design a two-level NOR network that performs a code conversion from the four-bit binary to the four-bit Gray code. Minimize each output expression separately using K-maps.

Exercise 5.16 Repeat Exercise 5.15 using the Quine-McCluskey minimization method.

Exercise 5.17 Design a two-level NAND or NOR network (not necessarily minimal) to determine whether an alphanumeric character coded in ASCII (see Chapter 2) belongs to the set {A,B,C,D,E}.

PLAs and PALs

Exercise 5.18 Using a PLA, implement a system that produces the square of a BCD digit. The output should be in the binary representation.

Exercise 5.19 Using a PLA, implement a system that converts from BCD to Excess-3.

Exercise 5.20 Using the PAL of Figure 5.21 implement a code converter from the Excess-3 to the 2-out-of-5 code.

Exercise 5.21 Using the PAL of Figure 5.21 implement a system that has as input a decimal digit represented in BCD and as output the input multiplied by three. The output is also in BCD (two digits).

Chapter 6

Design of Combinational Systems: Multilevel Gate Networks

In this chapter we present

- Design of multilevel networks. Transformations to satisfy constraints, such as number of gate inputs, network size, and network delay.
- Design of networks with XOR and XNOR gates.
- Design of networks with multiplexers (MUXes).

Based on the discussion in the previous chapter, it follows that there are cases in which the constraints and requirements of an implementation are better met by gate networks with more than two levels; these are called **multilevel networks**. The design of these networks is more complex than for two-level ones, for the following reasons:

- There is no standard form for these networks (in contrast to the AND-OR and OR-AND two-level networks). Consequently, a large variety of networks is possible.
- In practical cases, several requirements and constraints have to be met simultaneously. The most typical requirements are related to the size of the network, its delay, and the set of gates that can be used.
- Usually the system has several outputs and, to meet the requirements, it is not possible to consider each output separately.

Because of its complexity, the design of multilevel networks is usually done using CAD tools (called **logic synthesis** tools), except for very regular networks. These tools use an initial representation of the network and then transform this representation to satisfy the constraints. The particular representation and the corresponding transformations depend on the specific tool. Significant research and development is still being done in this area, and better tools are being produced. As an introduction to the ideas underlying these tools we now describe a design procedure that can be used manually for simple networks and illustrates the type of transformations involved. The procedure is as follows:

1. Obtain sum of products or product of sums for the functions of the system.
2. Transform the expressions (or the corresponding two-level networks) so that the requirements are met. This results in multilevel networks with AND, OR, and NOT gates. Some suitable transformations are discussed in the next section.
3. Transform the network resulting from step 2 into an equivalent one that uses gates from the set of gates available. We use the set of gates described in Table 4.1. Because the delay and size of NAND and NOR gates are smaller than those for AND and OR gates, we mainly replace the latter gates with the former. This transformation is done by introducing pairs of complementations in all lines connecting even levels to odd levels.

   The use of other gates, such as XOR and two-input multiplexers, is discussed in the last two sections of this chapter.

After this process is performed, it might be that the required network characteristics, such as delay and/or area, are not met. In such a case, a new design iteration must be attempted.

6.1 TYPICAL TRANSFORMATIONS TO MEET NETWORK REQUIREMENTS

We now identify the characteristics of switching expressions that correspond to the most important requirements of the network, and indicate expression transformations that modify these characteristics. It is important to emphasize that these requirements are interdependent, that is, the adaptation to one of them might disrupt another. This makes the design optimization difficult for systems which have many requirements.

The Size of the Network: Factoring

In the cost criterion used before, the size of the network has been approximated by the number of gates and the number of gate inputs. Because the number of gates corresponds to the number of operators in the switching expression, the number of gates can be reduced by **factoring** the expression. Moreover, subexpressions can be shared by several network outputs. This transformation is difficult to perform so that CAD tools rely on heuristic pattern matching techniques.

EXAMPLE 6.1

Obtain a multilevel gate network for a one-bit comparator, which is the component of an n-bit comparator, as shown in Figure 6.1. The specification is as follows:

Inputs: $x, y \in \{0, 1\}$
$c \in \{\text{GREATER, EQUAL, LESS}\}$

Output: $z \in \{\text{GREATER, EQUAL, LESS}\}$

Function:
$$z = \begin{cases} \text{GREATER} & \textbf{if } \; x > y \textbf{ or } (x = y \textbf{ and } c = \text{GREATER}) \\ \text{EQUAL} & \textbf{if } \; x = y \textbf{ and } c = \text{EQUAL} \\ \text{LESS} & \textbf{if } \; x < y \textbf{ or } (x = y \textbf{ and } c = \text{LESS}) \end{cases}$$

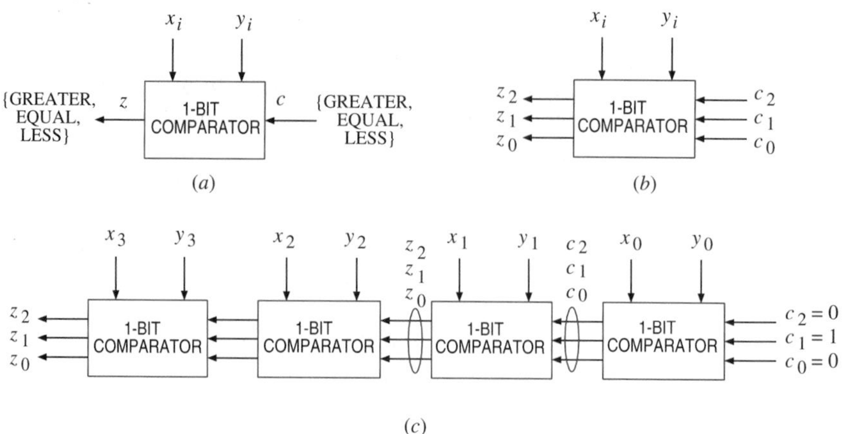

Figure 6.1 (*a*) One-bit comparator module (high-level). (*b*) One-bit comparator module (binary level). (*c*) Four-bit comparator.

The input c and the output z have to be coded onto binary variables. We select the following codes (the same for c and z):

c z	c_2 z_2	c_1 z_1	c_0 z_0
GREATER	1	0	0
EQUAL	0	1	0
LESS	0	0	1

Note that we use three binary variables for the encoding instead of the minimum two; this is done to simplify the gate network.

Next, we have to determine the switching functions that describe the system and the corresponding switching expressions. Using the foregoing codes, the tabular form of these functions is

	x, y			
$c_2c_1c_0$	00	01	10	11
100	100	001	100	100
010	010	001	100	010
001	001	001	100	001
		$z_2z_1z_0$		

The rows for the other values of c are "don't cares." From the corresponding Karnaugh maps, the following minimal two-level expressions are obtained:

$$z_2 = xy' + xc_2 + y'c_2$$

$$z_1 = (x' + y)(x + y')c_1$$

$$z_0 = x'y + x'c_0 + yc_0$$

Note that the expressions for z_2 and z_0 are sums of products, whereas that for z_1 is a product of sums. For the case in which both uncomplemented and complemented inputs are available, these expressions result in a two-level network with 7 AND and 4 OR gates (corresponding to 22 equivalent gates, for the gates described in Table 4.1) and 25 gate inputs. To reduce these numbers, variables c_2 and c_0 can be factored to share the subexpressions $(x + y')$ and $(x' + y)$, resulting in

$$t = (x + y')$$
$$w = (x' + y)$$
$$z_2 = xy' + tc_2$$
$$z_1 = twc_1$$
$$z_0 = x'y + wc_0$$

We use these expressions directly for the implementation of the gate network shown in Figure 6.2*a*, corresponding to a size of 18 equivalent gates (the tag above each gate indicates its equivalent size). Using NAND gates, we obtain the network depicted in Figure 6.2*b*, which can be reduced by eliminating repeated gates to the network of Figure 6.2*c*; the resulting network has a size of nine equivalent gates—half the size of the network with AND and OR gates.

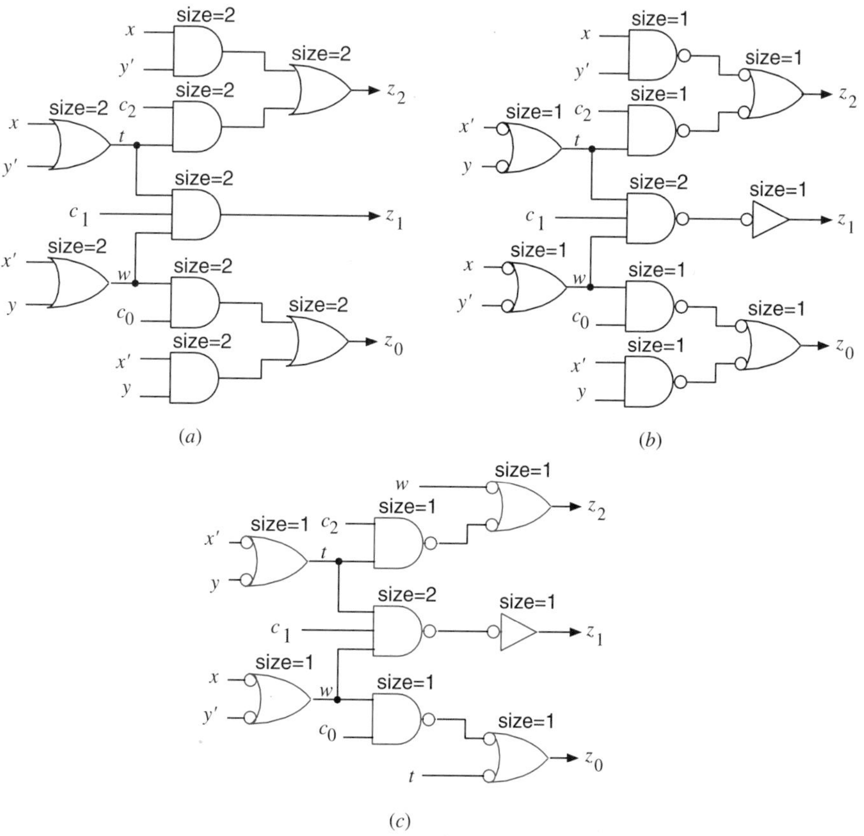

Figure 6.2 Network in Example 6.1. (*a*) With AND and OR gates. (*b*) With NAND gates. (*c*) After eliminating repeated NAND gates.

■

EXAMPLE 6.2

A two-level implementation of a modulo-64 incrementer (see Example 5.1) corresponds to the following expressions:

$$z_5 = x_5x_4' + x_5x_3' + x_5x_2' + x_5x_1' + x_5x_0' + x_5'x_4x_3x_2x_1x_0$$

$$z_4 = x_4x_3' + x_4x_2' + x_4x_1' + x_4x_0' + x_4'x_3x_2x_1x_0$$

$$z_3 = x_3x_2' + x_3x_1' + x_3x_0' + x_3'x_2x_1x_0$$

$$z_2 = x_2x_1' + x_2x_0' + x_2'x_1x_0$$

$$z_1 = x_1x_0' + x_1'x_0$$

$$z_0 = x_0'$$

The resulting network (shown in Figure 6.3) has 7 NOT gates, 20 AND gates, 5 OR gates, and 77 gate inputs.

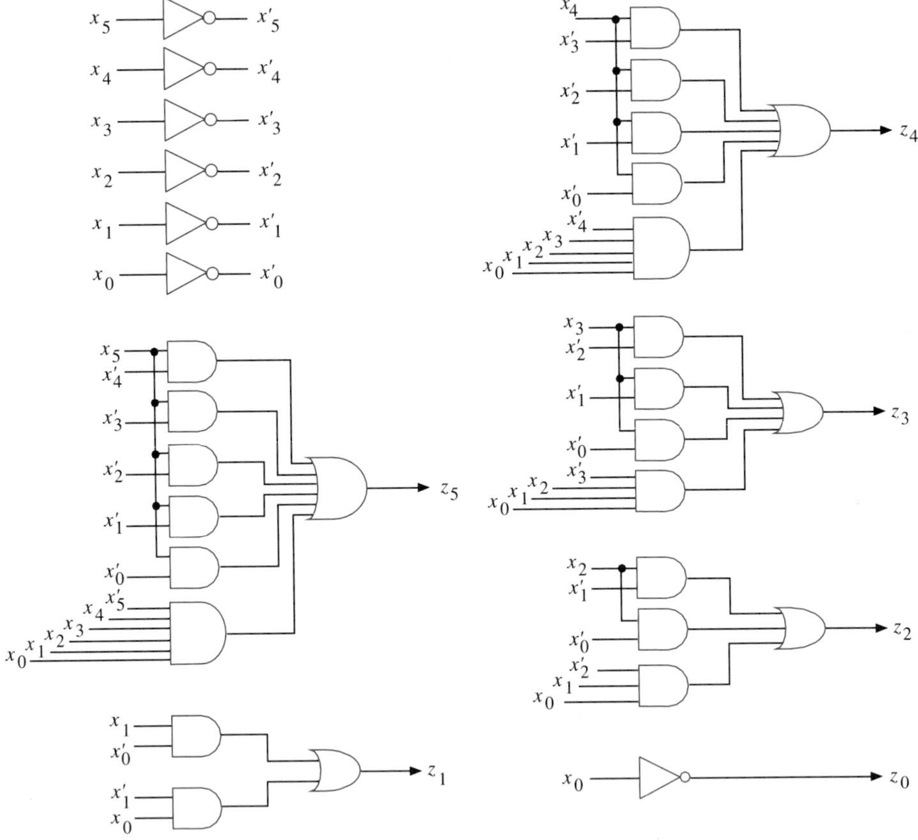

Figure 6.3 NOT-AND-OR network for modulo-64 incrementer network.

To reduce the number of gates and gate inputs, it is possible to factor the expressions as follows:

$$z_5 = x_5(x_4' + x_3' + x_2' + x_1' + x_0') + x_5'x_4x_3x_2x_1x_0$$

$$z_4 = x_4(x_3' + x_2' + x_1' + x_0') + x_4'x_3x_2x_1x_0$$

$$z_3 = x_3(x_2' + x_1' + x_0') + x_3'x_2x_1x_0$$

$$z_2 = x_2(x_1' + x_0') + x_2'x_1x_0$$

$$z_1 = x_1x_0' + x_1'x_0$$

$$z_0 = x_0'$$

This results in a network (Figure 6.4) with four levels (NOT-OR-AND-OR), 7 NOT, 10 AND and 9 OR gates, and 61 gate inputs.

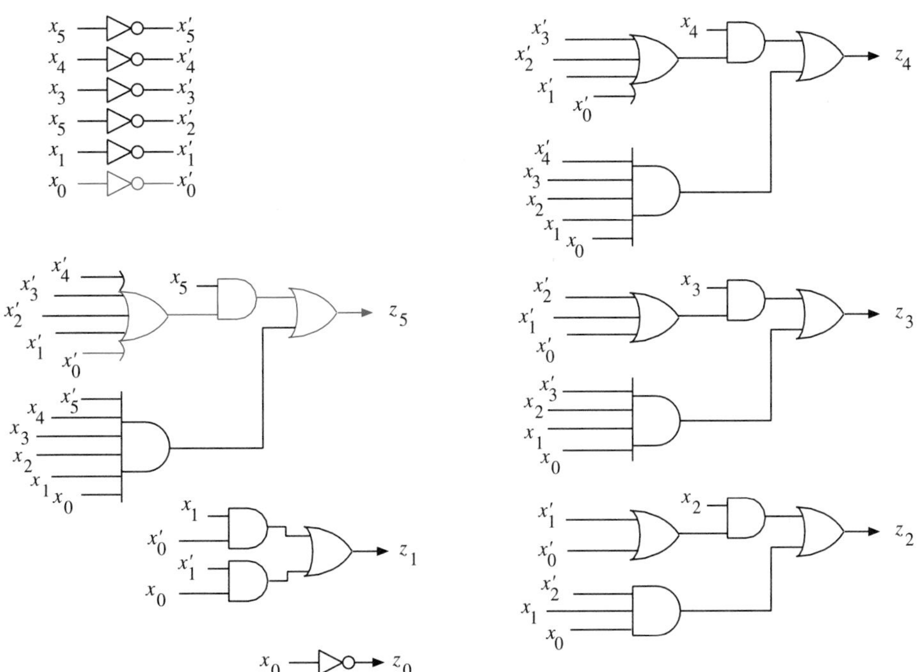

Figure 6.4 Four-level network for modulo-64 incrementer. ∎

The Number of Gate Inputs: Gate Decomposition

The number of inputs to a gate is equal to the number of literals in the corresponding term in the expression. Consequently, the number of inputs can be reduced by decomposing a multi-input gate into several smaller gates. Because AND and OR are associative, this decomposition is straightforward. For example,

$$a + b + c + d + e + f = (a + b + c) + (d + e + f)$$

In the logic diagram, this reduction consists of decomposing gates with a large number of inputs into networks of gates with fewer inputs.

EXAMPLE 6.3

Consider the implementation of Example 6.2 using gates with a maximum of three inputs. For these purposes, we decompose the sums and products with more than three literals ($x_4' + x_3' + x_2' + x_1' + x_0'$, $x_5'x_4x_3x_2x_1x_0$, $x_3' + x_2' + x_1' + x_0'$, and $x_4'x_3x_2x_1x_0$) by defining the following intermediate products and sums:

$$a_{43} = x_4x_3$$

$$a_{210} = x_2x_1x_0$$

$$r_{210} = x_2' + x_1' + x_0'$$

The resulting expressions are

$$z_5 = x_5(x_4' + x_3' + r_{210}) + x_5' a_{43} a_{210}$$

$$z_4 = x_4(x_3' + r_{210}) + x_4' x_3 a_{210}$$

$$z_3 = x_3 r_{210} + x_3' a_{210}$$

$$z_2 = x_2(x_1' + x_0') + x_2' x_1 x_0$$

$$z_1 = x_1 x_0' + x_1' x_0$$

$$z_0 = x_0'$$

This transformation increases the number of gates and the number of levels. However, the increase in the number of gates is reduced because some of the OR and AND gates are shared among several outputs. The resulting network is shown in Figure 6.5. As in earlier examples, this network can be transformed into an equivalent one which includes other gates, such as NAND and NOR gates, if those alternatives are more advantageous for a given technology. Performing this transformation results in a network with 6 NOT gates, 18 NAND and 3 NOR gates, and its size is 31 equivalent gates. The critical path goes from the inputs through r_{210} to z_5.

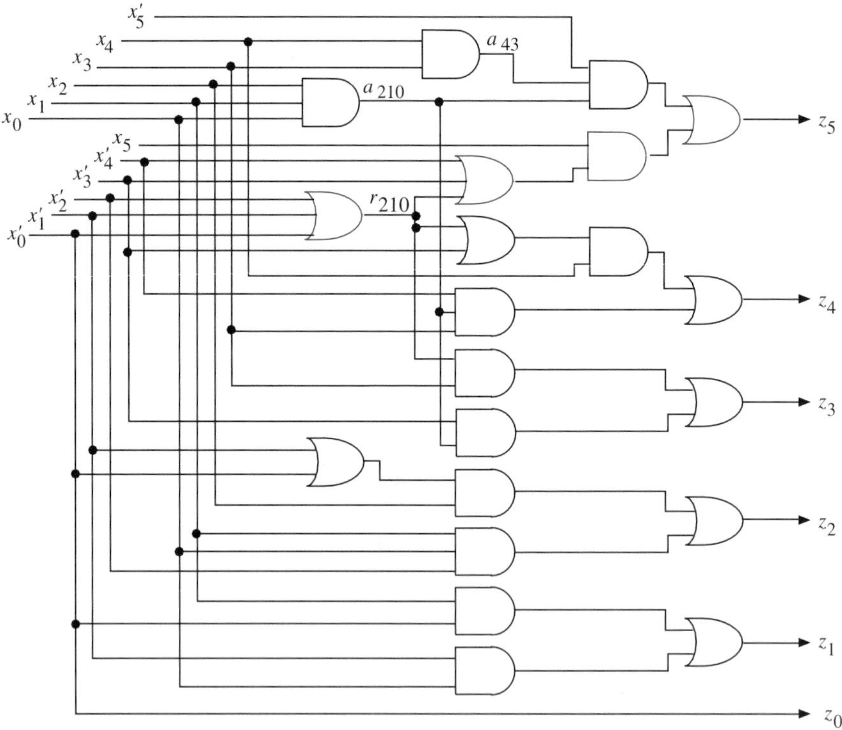

Figure 6.5 Reducing the number of gate inputs. ■

Note that the decomposition used to reduce the number of inputs to a gate cannot be done directly for NAND and NOR gates because the corresponding operators are not associative. However, the resulting network with AND and OR gates can be transformed to a NAND or NOR network by adding the complementation pairs, as discussed before.

The Output Load of a Gate: Buffering

The output load of a gate corresponds to the sum of the input load factors of the inputs connected to that output. The value of this load can be computed from the switching expressions but is simpler to obtain from a logic diagram.

Because the maximum output load is limited and high loads produce a large propagation delay, it is convenient to transform the network to reduce these loads. We now show an example of such a transformation.

EXAMPLE 6.4

The network in Figure 6.6a implements the set of expressions

$$z_i = w \cdot x \cdot y_i \qquad 0 \leq i \leq 63$$

As illustrated in the figure, the output load of the NAND gate producing $w \cdot x$ is $64I$, where I is the input load factor of the NOR gates in the second level. As indicated in Chapter 4, this load is not acceptable for the CMOS family listed in Table 4.1 (maximum 12). Moreover, even if it was acceptable, the resulting propagation delay would be high; for instance, the high-to-low propagation delay between x and any output (for a load of 5 at the output) is $(0.05 + 0.038 \times 64) + (0.07 + 0.016 \times 5) = 2.63$ ns.

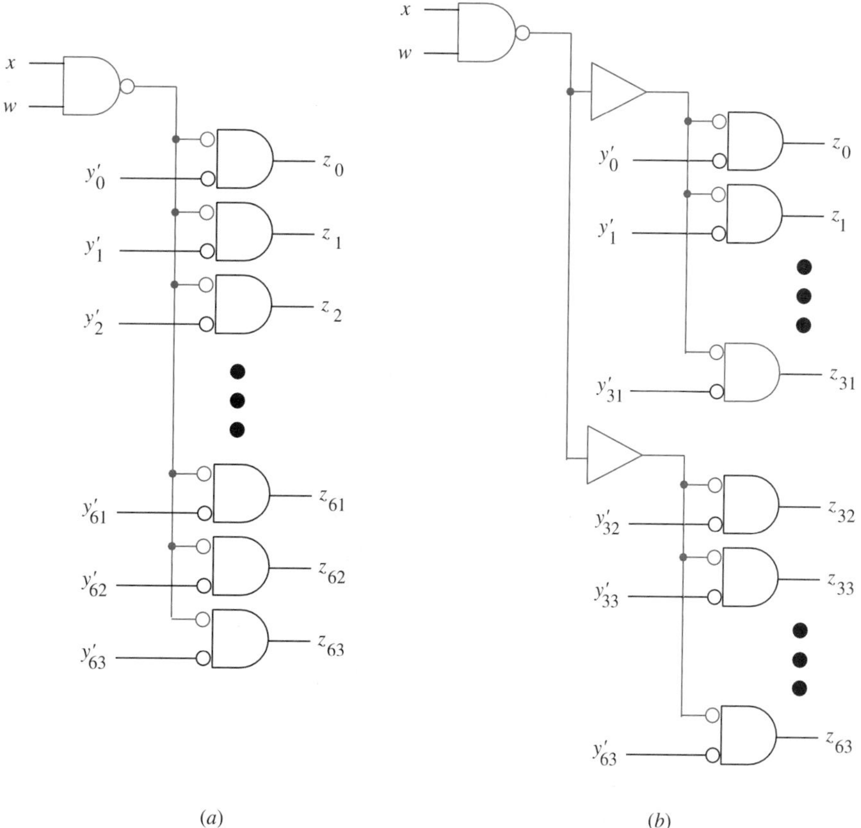

Figure 6.6 Reducing the output load.

Large output loads are usually handled by utilizing **buffers**. As indicated in Chapter 3, these are special gates with one input and one output that can drive a large load and have a reduced effect of load on delay. They usually come in two versions: noninverting (performing the identity function) and inverting (performing the NOT function). Table 6.1 gives the main parameters for two buffers from the same family described in Table 4.1. In our example, it is possible to reduce the delay by placing two buffers as shown in Figure 6.6*b*. Now the delay is $(0.05 + 0.038 \times 4) + (0.15 + 0.006 \times 32) + (0.07 + 0.016 \times 5) = 0.69$ ns.

Table 6.1 Characteristics of noninverting and inverting buffers.

Gate Type	Fanin	Propagation Delays		Load Factor	Size
		t_{pLH} (ns)	t_{pHL} (ns)	I (standard loads)	(equivalent gates)
Buffer (noninverting)	1	$0.15 + 0.006L$	$0.19 + 0.003L$	2.0	4
Inverting buffer	1	$0.04 + 0.006L$	$0.05 + 0.006L$	4.7	3

L: output load of the gate.

■

The Delay of Each Network Output: Critical Path Reduction

In a first approximation, it is possible to use the number of levels in a network as a measure of delay. Consequently, the technology-independent method for reducing the network delay consists of reducing the number of network levels. By this measure, the minimum-delay network is a two-level network. However, as discussed earlier, such a network might not be realizable due to large number of gate inputs and high load, so that the two-level network must be transformed. Moreover, the load on the gates and their number of inputs also has a significant effect on delay. Consequently, the transformations required to reduce the delay tend to reduce the number of levels, the number of gate inputs, and the load of the gates in the critical path.

6.2 ALTERNATIVE IMPLEMENTATIONS

In the following example we compare two alternative implementations of a combinational system.

EXAMPLE 6.5

A combinational system has as input an eight-bit binary vector $\underline{x}$ and as output a binary variable z. The output is 1 whenever the number of 1's in the vector $\underline{x}$ is even; this is called the **even-parity** function. That is,

Input: $\underline{x} = (x_7, x_6, \ldots, x_0), \quad x_i \in \{0, 1\}$
Output: $z \in \{0, 1\}$

Function:
$$z = \begin{cases} 1 & \textbf{if} \quad \sum_{i=0}^{7} x_i \text{ is even} \\ 0 & \textbf{otherwise} \end{cases}$$

Implementation 1: A Two-level Network.

The sum of minterms includes all minterms in which the number of uncomplemented variables is even. There are 128 of these minterms (half of the total number of minterms).

Moreover, these minterms are not adjacent (it is necessary to change two literals to get another of the minterms), so this expression cannot be reduced. Consequently, the AND-OR two-level implementation requires 128 AND gates and one OR gate. Each AND gate has 8 inputs and the OR gate has 128 inputs.

This implementation is not practical due to the large number of gates and their inputs.

Implementation 2.

In this case, let us assume that the maximum number of inputs to both AND and OR gates is limited to four, and that no three-state gates are available. To achieve a suitable network, one possibility consists of dividing the eight-bit vector $\underline{x}$ into two four-bit subvectors $\underline{x} = (x_l, x_r)$, computing the (even) parity P of each half, and then combining them. That is,

$$P(\underline{x}) = P(\underline{x}_l)P(\underline{x}_r) + P'(\underline{x}_l)P'(\underline{x}_r)$$

Each of the functions $P(\underline{x}_l)$ and $P(\underline{x}_r)$ requires eight four-input AND gates and one eight-input OR gate. Because the number of inputs to the OR gate is limited to four, the OR is decomposed into two levels of OR gates, as shown in Figure 6.7.

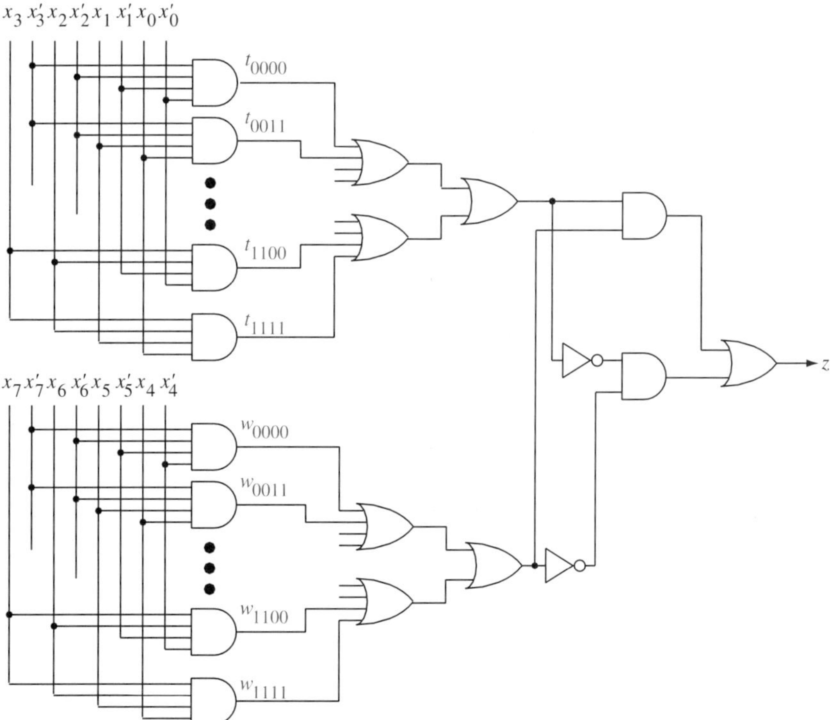

Figure 6.7 Network with gates with a maximum of four inputs.

The combination of the two parity functions requires two NOT gates, two two-input AND gates, and one two-input OR gate. This implementation satisfies the constraints; moreover, it uses fewer gates than the previous ones. However, it has six levels of gates. This implementation is suitable for a family of gates such as the one described in Table 4.1.

Table 6.2 summarizes the characteristics of the two implementations described here. Of course, there are many other possible implementations for this function, one of which is presented in the next section.

Table 6.2 Characteristics of alternative implementations for the function in Example 6.5

Implementation	Network input load	Gates Type	Fanin	Fanout	Number	No. levels
1	64	AND	8	1	128	2
		OR	128	—	1	
2	4	AND	4	1	16	6
		OR	4	1	4	
		OR	2	1	3	
		AND	2	1	2	
		NOT	1	1	2	

■

6.3 NETWORKS WITH XOR AND XNOR GATES

Up to now we have not used XOR gates in the designs. In some cases, the use of these gates reduces the size of the network and/or the delay. This results from the fact that the XOR gate has a smaller size and delay than an equivalent network of NAND gates (for the set of gates that we use, the size of XOR is three equivalent gates, whereas the corresponding network with NAND gates has a size of five equivalent gates).

We illustrate now two examples in which XOR gates produce a better network (in terms of size and delay).

EXAMPLE 6.6

An eight-input odd-parity checker is a combinational system whose output has value 1 only when an odd number of inputs has value 1. That is,

Input: $\underline{x} = (x_7, \ldots, x_0),\ x_i \in \{0, 1\}$
Output: $z \in \{0, 1\}$

Function: $$z = \begin{cases} 0 & \text{if number of 1's in } \underline{x} \text{ is even} \\ 1 & \text{if number of 1's in } \underline{x} \text{ is odd} \end{cases}$$

This function is the complement of that in Example 6.5, so the corresponding implementations can be compared.

An expression for this function using the XOR operator is

$$z = x_7 \oplus x_6 \oplus x_5 \oplus x_4 \oplus x_3 \oplus x_2 \oplus x_1 \oplus x_0$$

An implementation of this system using only two-input XOR gates is shown in Figure 6.8. The size of the network is 21 equivalent gates. Note that this implementation is an extension of that of Alternative 2 in the previous example, but now the four-bit parity functions are further decomposed into two-bit parity functions. If this approach were used with AND, OR, and NOT gates, the resulting network would have nine levels.

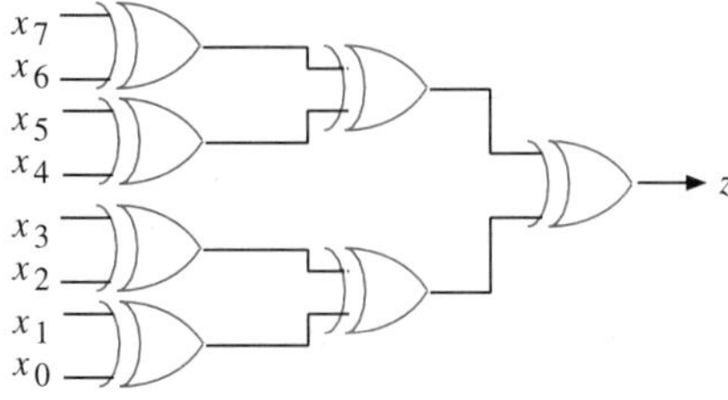

Figure 6.8 Odd-parity checker.

Note that, due to the associativity of the XOR operator, the transformation for reduction of number of gate inputs is similar to that for AND and OR gates. ■

EXAMPLE 6.7

An equality comparator compares two bit-vectors (which can represent integers, characters, or other sets) and produces a value 1 if they are equal. A 32-bit equality comparator is specified as follows:

Input: $\underline{x} = (x_{31}, \ldots, x_0), x_i \in \{0, 1\}$

$\underline{y} = (y_{31}, \ldots, y_0), y_i \in \{0, 1\}$

Output: $z \in \{0, 1\}$

Function: $$z = \begin{cases} 1 & \textbf{if} \quad x_i = y_i \ \textbf{for} \ 0 \leq i \leq 31 \\ 0 & \textbf{otherwise} \end{cases}$$

The equality of each bit is obtained by the equivalence (XNOR) function, and the overall equality by the AND function. That is,

$$z = \text{AND}(\text{XNOR}(x_{31}, y_{31}), \ldots, \text{XNOR}(x_i, y_i), \ldots, \text{XNOR}(x_0, y_0))$$

The direct implementation consists of 32 two-input XNOR gates and one 32-input AND gate; because it is not possible to implement directly a 32-input AND gate, this gate is decomposed into a tree of AND gates. Figure 6.9 illustrates a decomposition into two levels of 6-input gates.

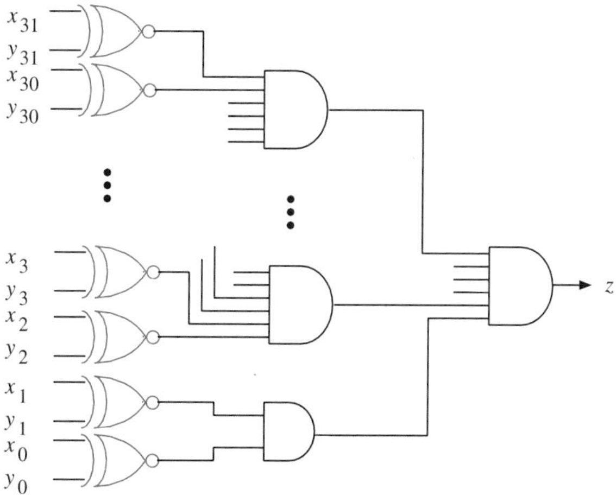

Figure 6.9 32-bit equality comparator. ■

It should be noted that, according to the definition given in Chapter 2, switching expressions contain only AND, OR, and NOT operators; however, it is also customary to call switching expressions those containing XOR operators.

6.4 NETWORKS WITH TWO-INPUT MULTIPLEXERS

A two-input **multiplexer** (MUX) is a module with two binary data inputs (x_1, x_0), one binary control input s, and one binary output z. This module implements the function represented by the following expression:

$$z = \text{MUX}(x_1, x_0, s) = x_1 s + x_0 s'$$

The logic symbol of a multiplexer is shown in Figure 6.10*a*; a circuit implementation is discussed in Chapter 3 (see Figure 3.8). A multiplexer is also called a **selector** because the output is either x_1 or x_0, depending on the value of the control variable (i.e., this value selects which of the inputs appears at the output). The extension to multiplexers with more than two data inputs is discussed in Chapter 9.

The multiplexer constitutes a universal set of gates, if the constants 0 and 1 are available. As indicated in Chapter 4, this can be shown by implementing with the multiplexer a known universal set. We select the set {NOT, AND}. Then,

$$\text{NOT}(x) = \text{MUX}(0, 1, x) = 0 \cdot x + 1 \cdot x' = x'$$

$$\text{AND}(x_1, x_0) = \text{MUX}(x_1, 0, x_0) = x_1x_0 + 0 \cdot x_0' = x_1x_0$$

Figure 6.10*b* shows the implementation of NOT and AND gates with 2-input multiplexers.

Because the multiplexer constitutes a universal set, any switching function can be implemented as a network of multiplexers. One possible type of network is a **tree of multiplexers**. The design of this type of network is based on the repeated application of **Shannon's decomposition**, which is as follows:[1]

$$f(x_{n-1}, x_{n-2}, \ldots, x_0) = f(x_{n-1}, x_{n-2}, \ldots, 1) \cdot x_0 + f(x_{n-1}, x_{n-2}, \ldots, 0) \cdot x_0'$$

This expression is correct because both sides have the same value for each possible assignment of x_0, that is, $x_0 = 1$ and $x_0 = 0$. Of course, the decomposition can be done with respect to any of the arguments. This decomposition results in the implementation shown in Figure 6.11*a*, which corresponds to the expression

$$z = f(x_{n-1}, x_{n-2}, \ldots, x_0) = \text{MUX}(f(x_{n-1}, x_{n-2}, \ldots, 1), f(x_{n-1}, x_{n-2}, \ldots, 0), x_0)$$

In this implementation, the (data) inputs to the MUX are functions of $n-1$ variables. The decomposition can be applied to each of these functions, using one of the remaining $n-1$ variables as the "control." Figure 6.11*b* shows the network after two applications of Shannon's decomposition. The process is continued until functions of just one variable are obtained. Each decomposition is implemented by a MUX, resulting in a tree of multiplexers.

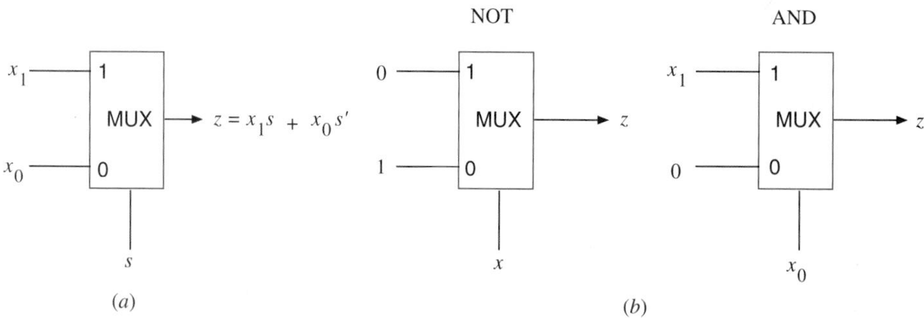

Figure 6.10 (*a*) Two-input multiplexer. (*b*) Implementation of NOT and AND gates.

[1]Note that we use the operations +, ·, and ′ on switching functions. These correspond to the OR, AND, and NOT functions, respectively. That is, equivalently we could write

$$f(x_{n-1}, x_{n-2}, \ldots, x_0) = \text{OR}(\text{AND}(f(x_{n-1}, x_{n-2}, \ldots, 1), x_0), \text{AND}(f(x_{n-1}, x_{n-2}, \ldots, 0), \text{NOT}(x_0)))$$

Note also that $f(x_{n-1}, x_{n-2}, \ldots, 1)$ denotes the function of $n-1$ variables, which is obtained from $f(x_{n-1}, x_{n-2}, \ldots, x_0)$ by assigning the value 1 to x_0.

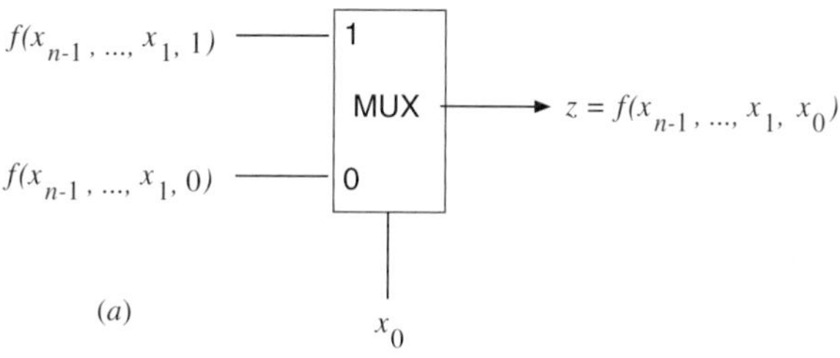

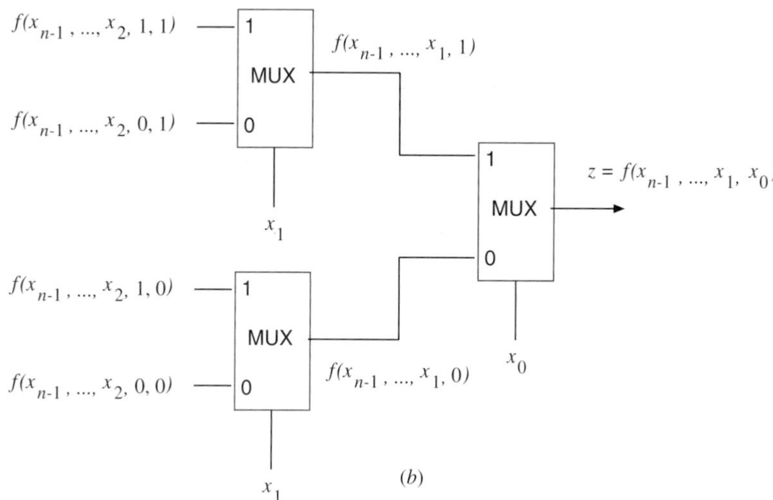

Figure 6.11 (*a*) Realization of Shannon's decomposition with multiplexer. (*b*) Repeated decomposition.

EXAMPLE 6.8

Consider the function $f(x_3, x_2, x_1, x_0)$ described by the expression

$$z = x_3(x_1 + x_2x_0)$$

Applying Shannon's decomposition with respect to x_0, we obtain

$$f(x_3, x_2, x_1, 0) = x_3x_1$$
$$f(x_3, x_2, x_1, 1) = x_3(x_1 + x_2)$$

so that

$$z = (x_3x_1)x_0' + x_3(x_1 + x_2)x_0$$

Figure 6.12*a* shows the corresponding multiplexer tree.

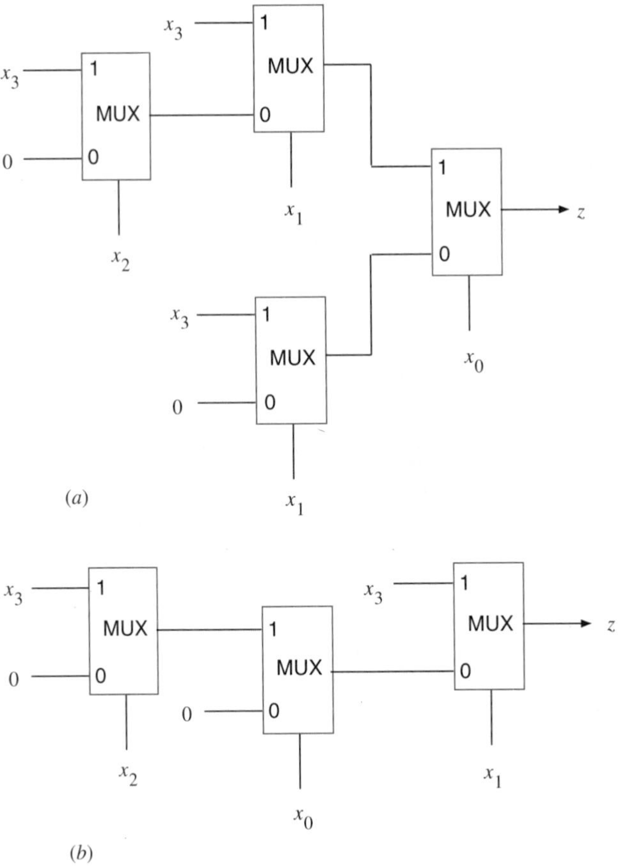

Figure 6.12 Network for Example 6.8. ■

In practical cases the tree might not be complete, as shown in Figure 6.12*a*. In this case, for instance, the function is independent of x_2 when $x_0 = 0$. Moreover, the order of the variables used in each subtree influences the number of multiplexers used, as depicted in Figure 6.12*b*. The implementation with the minimum number of multiplexers is hard to find; CAD tools use some heuristics for these purposes.

A multiplexer is a **programmable module** because it can implement different functions depending on the connections made to the inputs, as illustrated in Figure 6.10. Multiplexer type cells are used in some programmable gate arrays. These arrays, commonly called **Field Programmable Gate Arrays,** are the subject of Chapter 12. For example, the Act-1 Logic Block in an ACTEL FPGA includes a tree of three multiplexers and an OR gate. CAD tools are used to design networks of these cells.

6.5 FURTHER READINGS

Techniques for the design of gate networks with more than two levels are discussed, for example, in *Introduction to Digital Logic Design* by J. P. Hayes, Addison-Wesley, Reading, MA, 1993; *Synthesis and Optimization of Digital Circuits* by G. De Micheli, McGraw-Hill, New York, 1994, and in *Logic Synthesis* by S. Devadas, A. Ghosh, and K. Keutzer,

McGraw-Hill, New York, 1994. *Logic Design and Switching Theory* by S. Muroga, Wiley, New York, 1979 presents methods for the design of multilevel NAND-NOR networks.

A discussion on CAD tools for multilevel synthesis is given in "Synthesis of Multilevel Logic under Timing Constraints" by K. Bartlett et al., *IEEE Transactions on Computer-Aided Design of Integrated Circuits*, CAD-5(4):682–695, October 1986 and "MIS: A Multiple-Level Logic Optimization System" by R. Brayton et al., *IEEE Transactions on Computer-Aided Design of Integrated Circuits*, CAD-6(6):1062–1081, November 1987.

EXERCISES

Design of networks using gates from a family

Exercise 6.1 Design a single-error detector for the 2-out-of-5 code. The input is a digit in the 2-out-of-5 code, and the output is 0 if the number of ones in the input is 2. Use only gates from the set described in Table 4.1. Try to minimize the network delay.

Exercise 6.2 Design a network that implements addition of two integers, in the range 0 to 3, and of an input carry. Use only gates from the set described in Table 4.1. Reduce the number of gates by sharing subnetworks among the outputs.

Exercise 6.3 Design a gate network that has as input a decimal digit represented in BCD and as output the input multiplied by 3. The output is also in BCD (two digits).

Exercise 6.4 Design a gate network that compares two decimal digits coded in the Excess-3 code. A 2-bit output should encode the conditions greater, equal, and smaller.

Exercise 6.5 Consider the network of Example 4.6. Transform the network so that four 2-AND/NOR2 complex gates are used. Determine the characteristics of the network for the gates listed in Table 4.1.

Networks with XOR gates

Exercise 6.6 Design a magnitude comparator for two integers in the range [0,3] using only AND and XOR gates. The input are two 2-bit vectors and the output has three values: greater, equal, and smaller.

Exercise 6.7 Redesign the magnitude comparator shown in Figure 6.2 so that only XOR and NAND gates are used.

Exercise 6.8 Design a network using only XOR gates which performs the following function:

$$z_i = \begin{cases} x_i & \textbf{if} \quad c = 0 \\ x_i' & \textbf{if} \quad c = 1 \end{cases}$$

for $0 \leq i \leq 3$ where x_i's and c are the network inputs and z_i's are the network outputs. Such a network is called a **complementer**.

Networks with multiplexers

Exercise 6.9 Implement the following gates with 2-input multiplexers, assuming that complemented and uncomplemented variables are available: 2-input OR, 2-input NOR, 3-input NAND, XOR, and XNOR.

Exercise 6.10 Analyze the MUX network in Figure 6.13 and show that

$$z_1 = (a + b + c) \bmod 2$$

$$z_2 = 1 \textbf{ if } \text{two or more inputs have a value 1}$$

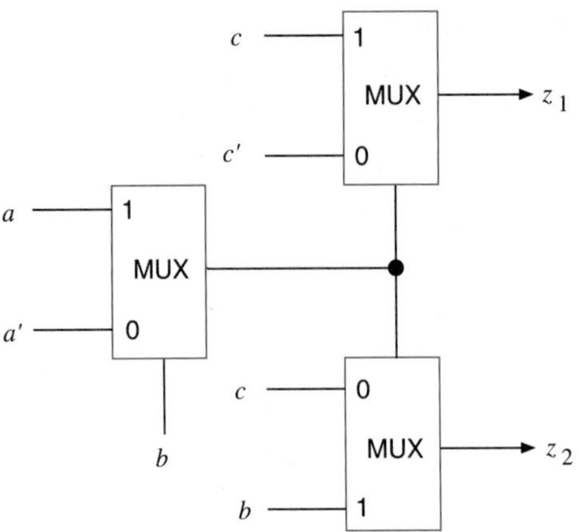

Figure 6.13 Network for Exercise 6.10.

Exercise 6.11 Show a tree of multiplexers implementing the expressions:

a. $E(a, b, c, d) = a'b + a'b'c' + bc'd + abd' + b'cd$
b. $E(a, b, c, d, e, f) = a \oplus b \oplus c \oplus d \oplus e \oplus f$

Exercise 6.12 Show an implementation of the equality comparator of two 2-bit vectors using a network of 2-input multiplexers.

Chapter 7

Specification of Sequential Systems

The main topics of this chapter are

- The definition of synchronous sequential systems.
- The state description and time behavior of sequential systems.
- Mealy and Moore machines.
- Finite-memory systems.
- The description of controllers as sequential systems.
- Equivalent systems and minimization of the number of states.
- Examples of specification of sequential systems.
- Specification of sequential systems in μVHDL.

We now address the specification of sequential systems. As we already know, a specification describes the function of a system in a way that is adequate for using the system as a component in a larger system, and for implementing the system as a network of simpler modules.

As described in Chapter 2, the specification of a combinational system consists of the input and output sets (both finite), and the input-output function; the function can be defined in different ways, such as a table, an expression (arithmetic, conditional, or logical), or a composition of simpler functions. Sequential systems, on the other hand, use two different types of descriptions: the **state description,** which consists of two functions on finite sets, and the **time behavior,** which corresponds to a function on time sequences. In this chapter we discuss and relate these two types of descriptions.

The sequential systems specified in this chapter have a significantly more complex behavior than the combinational systems specified in Chapter 2. However, they still are relatively simple compared to the complexity of, for example, a digital processor. The specification techniques presented here are suitable to describe rather simple systems, which are used as components in more complex ones. Those complex systems require the register-transfer level specification approach presented in later chapters of this book.

7.1 SYNCHRONOUS SEQUENTIAL SYSTEMS

A **sequential system** is a digital system in which the output at any given time depends not only on the input at that time but also on previous inputs. That is, the output at time t, denoted by $z(t)$, depends on the input time function in the interval $(0, t)$, denoted by $x(0, t)$ (see Figure 7.1). This can be expressed as

$$z(t) = F(x(0, t))$$

where $x(t)$ belongs to the input set I and $z(t)$ to the output set O, with both sets finite. The specification of the system by the function F is called its **time behavior**.

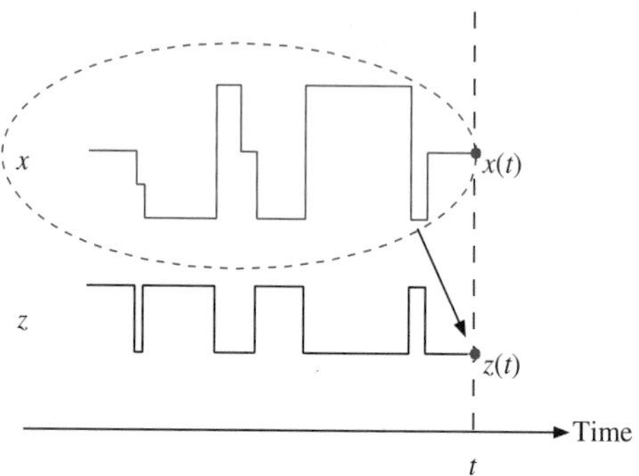

Figure 7.1 Input and output time functions.

7.1.1 Synchronous and Asynchronous Systems

According to the time instants at which the inputs and outputs are considered, sequential systems are classified into **synchronous** and **asynchronous** systems as follows:

Synchronous system. Inputs and outputs are considered at discrete time instants that are defined by **pulses** of a synchronizing signal called **clock** and denoted *CLK*. Figure 7.2*a* shows an ideal clock that has pulses of zero width (the implementation of real clocks is addressed in Chapter 8). Normally, the separation between consecutive pulses of the clock is constant; this period is called a **clock cycle** or simply a **cycle**. Moreover, the instants are labeled by consecutive natural numbers, that is, $t = 0$, $t = 1$, $t = 2$, etc.

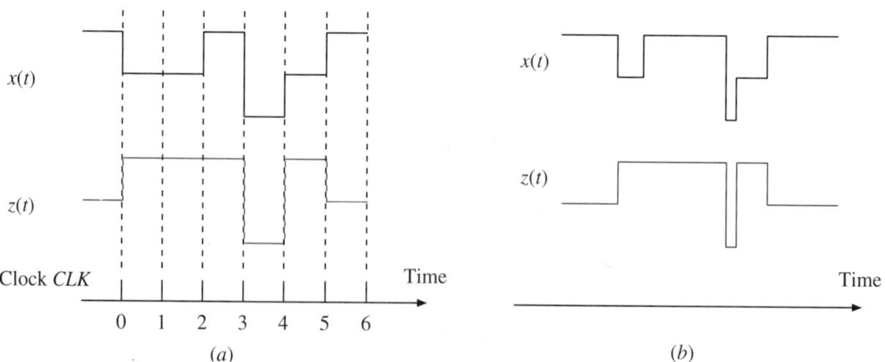

Figure 7.2 (*a*) Synchronous behavior. (*b*) Asynchronous behavior.

The input and output time functions for synchronous systems are called input and output **sequences**, respectively. We denote by $x(t_1, t_2)$ an input sequence from time t_1

to t_2; this sequence has length $t_2 - t_1 + 1$. Similarly, $z(t_1, t_2)$ is an output sequence. For example, the following is an input-output pair of length four:

$$x(2,5) = aabc$$

$$z(2,5) = 1021$$

Asynchronous system. The time variable is continuous (see Figure 7.2*b*) so that the input and output signals are defined at every value of t.

Asynchronous systems are more difficult to describe, analyze, and design than synchronous systems. Because most implementations used nowadays are synchronous, we limit our study to this case.

EXAMPLE 7.1

A serial adder is a sequential system in which the input at time i corresponds to digit i of both operands, and the output to digit i of the result, starting from the least-significant digit. For example, the input-output pair for a decimal serial adder with inputs 1638753 + 3652425 is

t	0	1	2	3	4	5	6
$x(t)$	3	5	7	8	3	6	1
$y(t)$	5	2	4	2	5	6	3
$z(t)$	8	7	1	1	9	2	5

■

7.1.2 State Description of Finite State Systems

From its definition, it follows that a sequential system must have the capability to capture the influence of all past inputs on present and future outputs. Consequently, it seems necessary to "memorize" the complete input sequence $x(0, t_1)$ to be able to determine the output at time $t \geq t_1$. However, in the systems studied here, the values of the input sequences can be grouped into a finite number of **classes** in such a way that all time functions having the same effect on the output at time $t \geq t_1$ are included in the same class. As a result, the determination of $z(t)$ does not need the whole input sequence $x(0, t)$ because it is sufficient to know the class to which the function belongs. The class is kept in an auxiliary variable s called the **state,** which is also a time function. Because the number of classes (i.e., the number of states of the system) is finite, the systems are called **finite state systems** or **finite state machines**.

EXAMPLE 7.2

Consider again the decimal serial adder described in Example 7.1. The determination of $z(t)$ requires knowing only $x(t)$, $y(t)$, and **the carry from previous digits** $c(t)$. That is, it is not necessary to know all previous input digits but only the value of the carry into digit t. Consequently, the carry $c(t)$ is the state, and this state has two values, that is, $c(t) = 0$ and $c(t) = 1$. ■

The state description of a sequential system uses three time variables: the input, the state, and the output. Moreover, as illustrated in Figure 7.3, there are two functions, as follows:

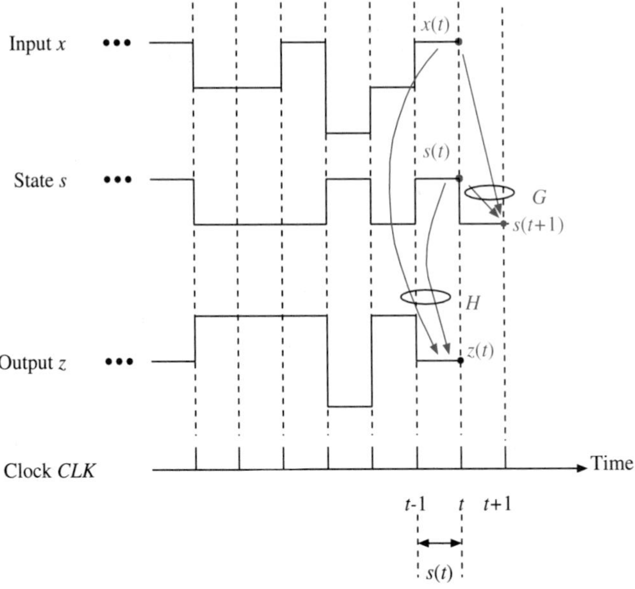

Figure 7.3 Output and state transition functions.

- The **state transition function**, or just **transition functions** which produces the next state (the state at time $t+1$) as a function of the present input $x(t)$ and present state $s(t)$.
- The **output function,** which produces the present output $z(t)$ as a function of the present input and present state.

Consequently, the complete state description of a finite state system consists of the input set I, the output set O, the state set S, the initial state $s(0)$, and the following two functions:

State transition function:	$s(t+1) = G(s(t), x(t))$
Output function:	$z(t) = H(s(t), x(t))$

Note that, since the system is synchronous, the next state is $s(t+1)$. States $s(t)$ and $s(t+1)$ are called the **present state** (*PS*) and **next state** (*NS*), respectively.

EXAMPLE 7.3

A complete state description of the decimal serial adder in Example 7.1 is

Input:	$x(t), y(t) \in \{0, 1, \ldots, 9\}$
Output:	$z(t) \in \{0, 1, \ldots, 9\}$
State:	$c(t) \in \{0, 1\}$ (the carry)
Initial state:	$c(0) = 0$

Functions: The transition and output functions are

$$c(t+1) = \begin{cases} 1 & \textbf{if} \quad x(t) + y(t) + c(t) \geq 10 \\ 0 & \textbf{otherwise} \end{cases}$$

$$z(t) = (x(t) + y(t) + c(t)) \bmod 10$$

Because the state also varies with time, the time behavior is now described as follows:

t	0	1	2	3	4	5	6	7
$x(t)$	3	5	7	8	3	6	1	
$y(t)$	5	2	4	2	5	6	3	
$c(t)$	0	0	0	1	1	0	1	0
$z(t)$	8	7	1	1	9	2	5	

■

EXAMPLE 7.4

Consider a system whose input has two values, called a and b, and whose output also has two values, 0 and 1. The output at time t is 1 if the number of b's in the input time function $x(0, t)$ is even, and 0 otherwise.

A time-behavior specification of this system is

Input: $x(t) \in \{a, b\}$
Output: $z(t) \in \{0, 1\}$

Function: $$z(t) = \begin{cases} 1 & \textbf{if} \quad x(0,t) \text{ contains an even number of } b\text{'s} \\ 0 & \textbf{otherwise} \end{cases}$$

Alternatively, the function can be expressed by the set of all input-output sequence pairs. As this is not practical, an illustration of the function can be given by a few of these pairs. One such pair is as follows:

t	0	1	2	3	4	5	6	7
x	a	b	b	a	b	a	b	a
z	1	0	1	1	0	0	1	1

This system does not need to memorize the whole input sequence to determine the output at time t and beyond; it is sufficient to know whether the number of b's in the sequence is even or odd. Thus, a state variable with two values (two states) can be used for this purpose. If we call the two values EVEN and ODD, the state description of the system is:

Input: $x(t) \in \{a, b\}$
Output: $z(t) \in \{0, 1\}$
State: $s(t) \in \{\text{EVEN}, \text{ODD}\}$
Initial state: $s(0) = \text{EVEN}$

Functions: The transition and output functions are shown in the **state table:**

PS	$x(t) = a$	$x(t) = b$
EVEN	EVEN, 1	ODD, 0
ODD	ODD, 0	EVEN, 1
	$NS,\ z(t)$	

The transition function is obtained by noticing that the state does not change if the input is an a, and changes when the input is a b. The initial state is EVEN because zero b's is an even number of b's. Note that we have used only one table to describe both functions; each entry corresponds to the pair (Next State, Output). ■

7.1.3 Mealy and Moore Machines

Sequential systems are classified according to the type of output function, as follows:

Mealy machine is a sequential system whose output at time t depends on the state and on the input at time t. That is,

$$z(t) = H(s(t), x(t))$$

This is precisely the type of system we have discussed until now.

Moore machine is a sequential system whose output at time t depends only on the state at time t. Its output function is

$$z(t) = H(s(t))$$

Note that the output of a Moore machine is not independent of the input sequence; instead, the influence of the input on the output is only through the state. Thus, the output can be associated directly with the state by means of an additional column in the table, as illustrated in the following example.

EXAMPLE 7.5

A Moore sequential system has the following state description:

Input: $x(t) \in \{a, b, c\}$
Output: $z(t) \in \{0, 1\}$
State: $s(t) \in \{S_0, S_1, S_2, S_3\}$
Initial state: $s(0) = S_0$

Functions: The transition and output functions are

PS	Input			
	a	b	c	
S_0	S_0	S_1	S_1	0
S_1	S_2	S_0	S_1	1
S_2	S_2	S_3	S_0	1
S_3	S_0	S_1	S_2	0
		NS		Output

■

From the definitions above, it follows that Moore machines are particular cases of Mealy machines. This might imply that to describe some time behaviors it is necessary to use a Mealy machine; however, it can be shown that every Mealy machine has a Moore machine that is equivalent to it, in the sense that it has the same time behavior. The proof of this fact, as well as a procedure to convert from one type of machine to the other, are outside the scope of this text.

7.2 REPRESENTATION OF THE STATE TRANSITION AND OUTPUT FUNCTIONS

The arguments and value of the state transition and output functions are variables with a finite number of discrete values. That is, they have the same form as those describing combinational systems and can be represented by tables, expressions, or maps. An additional graphical description is often used for sequential systems: the state diagram.

7.2.1 State Diagram

A **state diagram** is a directed graph used to represent the transition and output functions in a sequential system. Each state is represented by a node and each transition by an arc. An arc from node S_k to node S_j and labeled x/z specifies that, for a present state S_k and an input x, the next state is S_j and the output is z (see Figure 7.4*a*). A state diagram can be simplified by combining those arcs that produce the same transition, and indicating the various input/output pairs on the single arc (see Figure 7.4*b*). The node corresponding to the initial state is frequently labeled S_0, as illustrated in the following examples.

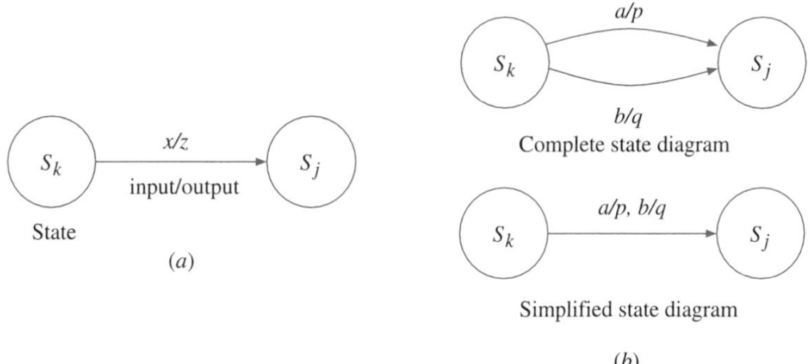

Figure 7.4 (*a*) State diagram representation. (*b*) Simplified state diagram notation.

EXAMPLE 7.6

A sequential system has the following state description:

Input:	$x(t) \in \{a, b\}$
Output:	$z(t) \in \{p, q\}$
State:	$s(t) \in \{S_0, S_1, S_2\}$
Initial state:	$s(0) = S_0$

Functions: The state transition and output functions are

$s(t)$	$x(t)$	
	a	b
S_0	S_1, p	S_2, q
S_1	S_1, p	S_0, p
S_2	S_1, p	S_2, p
	$s(t+1), z(t)$	

The state diagram, obtained directly from the foregoing table, is shown in Figure 7.5.

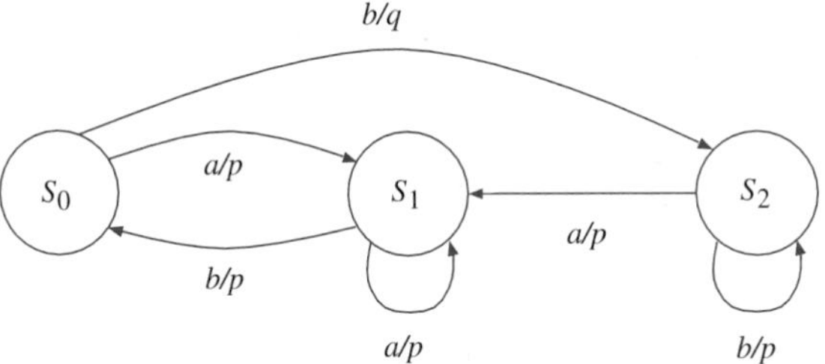

Figure 7.5 State diagram for Example 7.6. ■

In the case of a Moore machine, the output can be indicated inside each state instead of on the arcs. This is illustrated in Figures 7.6 and 7.7.

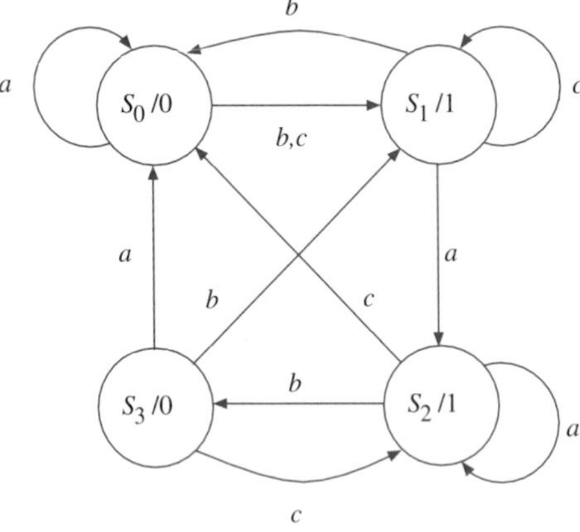

Figure 7.6 State diagram for Example 7.5.

EXAMPLE 7.7

A sequential system is specified by the following state description:

Input: $x(t) \in \{0, 1, 2, 3\}$
Output: $z(t) \in \{a, b\}$
State: $s(t) \in \{S_0, S_1\}$
Initial state: $s(0) = S_0$

Functions: The transition and output functions are

$$s(t+1) = \begin{cases} S_0 & \textbf{if} \quad (s(t) = S_0 \textbf{ and } [x(t) = 0 \textbf{ or } x(t) = 2]) \\ & \quad\quad \textbf{or } (s(t) = S_1 \textbf{ and } x(t) = 3) \\ S_1 & \textbf{otherwise} \end{cases}$$

$$z(t) = \begin{cases} a & \textbf{if} \quad s(t) = S_0 \\ b & \textbf{if} \quad s(t) = S_1 \end{cases}$$

The state diagram, obtained directly from these expressions, is shown in Figure 7.7.

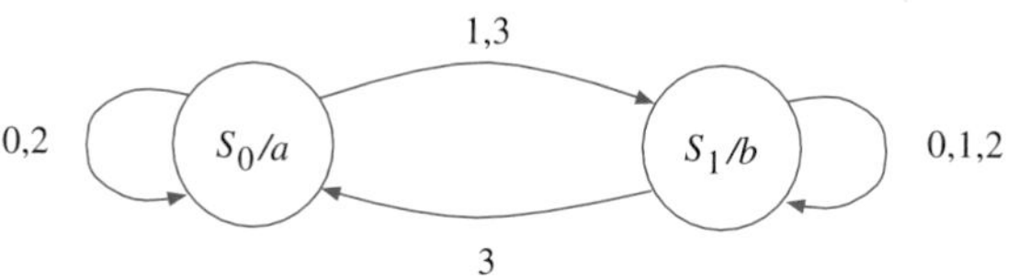

Figure 7.7 State diagram for Example 7.7. ■

7.2.2 State Names

The specification of a sequential system by means of a state description requires that each state is identified by a **state name**. In general, these names are arbitrary; no special names have to be used for the description by tables or diagrams. However, some descriptions by expressions are possible or are greatly simplified only if suitable names are used. A good example of this case is the use of **integers** as state names in order to use **arithmetic expressions** for the description.

EXAMPLE 7.8

A modulo-64 counter is a system whose input is a binary variable; the system counts (modulo-64) the number of 1's in the input sequence. The output corresponds to this count and, therefore, has 64 values corresponding to the integers 0 to 63. The state set also has 64 elements, which can be labeled with the integers 0 to 63.

A state specification of this system, using arithmetic expressions, is as follows:

Input: $x(t) \in \{0, 1\}$
Output: $z(t) \in \{0, 1, 2, \ldots, 63\}$
State: $s(t) \in \{0, 1, 2, \ldots, 63\}$
Initial state: $s(0) = 0$

Functions: The transition and output functions are

$$s(t+1) = [s(t) + x(t)] \bmod 64$$

$$z(t) = s(t)$$

Note that, if integers are not used for the state names, the description has to be given by a table or a state diagram, which would be impractical for a large number of states (e.g., a modulo-1000 counter). ■

In addition to selecting suitable state names, in some cases the description is simplified if the state is represented by a **vector** $\underline{s} = (s_{n-1}, \ldots, s_0)$ instead of by a single component. This is illustrated in the following example.

EXAMPLE 7.9

Consider a sequential system that records (counts) the occurrence of 55 different events (numbered from 1 to 55), which take place one at a time. When the count of event i becomes a multiple of 100 the output is $z(t) = i$, otherwise $z(t) = 0$.

The state corresponds to the count for each type of event. In this case, it is convenient to describe the state by a vector of 55 components, one per event, as $\underline{s} = (s_{55}, \ldots, s_1)$. The input consists of the event identifier e, wherein $e \in \{1, \ldots, 55\}$. That is,

Input: $e(t) \in \{1, 2, \ldots, 55\}$
Output: $z(t) \in \{0, 1, 2, \ldots, 55\}$
State: $\underline{s}(t) = (s_{55}, \ldots, s_1), \quad s_i \in \{0, 1, 2, \ldots, 99\}$
Initial state: $\underline{s}(0) = (0, 0, \ldots, 0)$

Functions: The transition and output functions are

$$s_i(t+1) = \begin{cases} [s_i(t) + 1] \bmod 100 & \textbf{if} \quad e(t) = i \\ s_i(t) & \textbf{otherwise} \end{cases} \qquad i = 1, 2, \ldots, 55$$

$$z(t) = \begin{cases} i & \textbf{if} \quad e(t) = i \textbf{ and } s_i(t) = 99 \\ 0 & \textbf{otherwise} \end{cases}$$

This kind of system would be quite difficult to describe without the use of state vectors. ■

7.3 TIME BEHAVIOR AND FINITE STATE MACHINES

We now discuss further the relationship among time behavior and state description.

7.3.1 Input-output Sequence Pairs from State Description

The time behavior of a sequential system is illustrated by pairs of input and output sequences. It is possible to obtain these pairs from the state description of a sequential system. This is achieved by following the evolution of the state when the input sequence is applied to a given initial state, and determining the corresponding outputs. This evolution of the state produces a **state sequence**, denoted by $s(t_1, t_2)$.

EXAMPLE 7.10

A state description of a sequential system is as follows:

Input: $x(t) \in \{a, b, c\}$
Output: $z(t) \in \{p, q\}$
State: $s(t) \in \{S_0, S_1, S_2, S_3\}$
Initial state: $s(0) = S_2$

Functions: The transition and output functions are

PS	x(t)			
	a	b	c	
S_0	S_0	S_1	S_1	p
S_1	S_2	S_0	S_1	q
S_2	S_2	S_3	S_0	q
S_3	S_0	S_1	S_2	p
		NS		$z(t)$

The state and output sequences for the input sequence $x(0, 3) = abca$ are obtained from the table as

t	0	1	2	3	4
x	a	b	c	a	
s	S_2	S_2	S_3	S_2	S_2
z	q	q	p	q	

■

7.3.2 State Description from Time Behavior

From the previous example, it is apparent that one can determine the time behavior of every finite state machine. On the other hand, not all time behaviors can be described by a finite state machine. As an example of a time behavior that cannot be described by a finite state machine, consider the following:

$$z(t) = \begin{cases} 1 & \textbf{if} \quad x(0,t) \text{ contains the same number of 0's and 1's} \\ 0 & \textbf{otherwise} \end{cases}$$

We could define the state at time t as the difference between the number of 1's and the number of 0's in $x(0, t)$, leading to the following state description:

$$s(t+1) = \begin{cases} s(t)+1 & \textbf{if} \quad x(t) = 1 \\ s(t)-1 & \textbf{otherwise} \end{cases}$$

$$z(t) = \begin{cases} 1 & \textbf{if} \quad s(t) = 0 \\ 0 & \textbf{otherwise} \end{cases}$$

So, why is this not a finite state machine? Because the value of the difference between the number of 1's and the number of 0's cannot be assured to be smaller than any integer, it is not possible to represent this difference by a state variable with a finite number of values. On the other hand, the system can be described by a finite state machine if the length of the input sequence is limited and the state is initialized whenever the maximum length is attained.

If a time behavior can be described by a finite state machine, then a procedure to obtain the state description is:

1. Determine the set of states by identifying the classes of input sequences that have to be discriminated. (This is quite dependent on the behavior of the systems, as illustrated in the examples that follow.)
2. Determine the transition function by considering how an input symbol produces a change from one class to another.
3. Determine the output function.

EXAMPLE 7.11

Obtain the state description of a sequential system having the following time behavior:

Input: $x(t) \in \{0, 1\}$
Output: $z(t) \in \{0, 1\}$

Function: $$z(t) = \begin{cases} 1 & \textbf{if} \quad x(t-3, t) = 1101 \\ 0 & \textbf{otherwise} \end{cases}$$

Note that this description of the time behavior requires the detection of overlapped patterns. For instance, an input-output sequence pair is

t	0	1	2	3	4	5	6	7	8
$x(t)$	0	0	1	1	0	1	1	0	1
$z(t)$	?	?	?	0	0	1	0	0	1

We now follow the steps in the procedure outlined above.

1. This system is a pattern detector. As such, it is necessary to discriminate the various subpatterns that form the pattern. We obtain the following four states:

State	indicates that
S_{init}	Initial state; also indicates that no subpattern has been detected.
$S1$	First symbol of pattern (1) has been detected.
$S11$	Subpattern 11 has been detected.
$S110$	Subpattern 110 has been detected.

2. The transition function is specified by the state diagram depicted in Figure 7.8. The transitions are obtained from the definition of the states. For example, if the present state is $S1$ and $x(t) = 1$, then the next state is $S11$ because $x(t-1, t) = 11$. On the other hand, if the state is $S1$ and $x(t) = 0$ the next state is S_{init} because no subpattern has been identified. Finally, due to the requirement of detecting overlapped patterns, the next state is $S1$ when the state is $S110$ and $x(t) = 1$ because this input is both the ending symbol of one instance of the pattern and might be the first symbol of the next instance.
3. The output is 1 only when the present state is $S110$ and $x(t) = 1$.

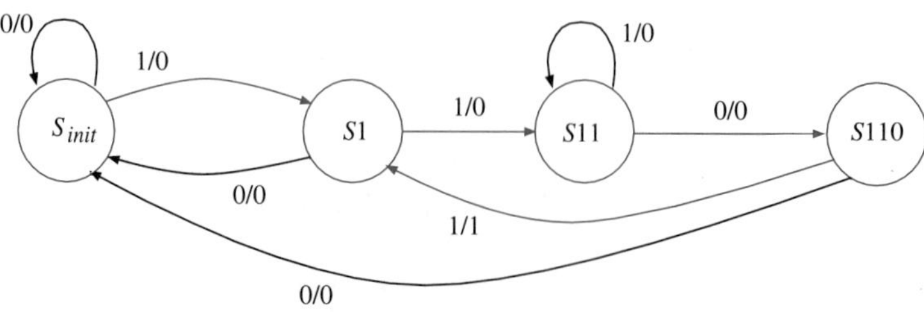

Figure 7.8 State diagram for Example 7.11.

■

7.4 FINITE MEMORY SEQUENTIAL SYSTEMS

A sequential system has **finite memory** of length m if $z(t)$ depends only on the last m input values, that is

$$z(t) = F(x(t - m + 1, t))$$

EXAMPLE 7.12

The time behavior of a sequential system is given by the following conditional expression:

$$z(t) = \begin{cases} p & \textbf{if} \quad x(t-3, t) = aaba \\ q & \textbf{otherwise} \end{cases}$$

This system has a finite memory of length four. ■

The time behavior of a sequential system with finite memory of length m can be described by the output produced at the end of each of the input sequences of length m. In Example 7.12, the set consists of 16 pairs; 2 of these pairs are $(aaaa, q)$ and $(aaba, p)$.

A finite-memory machine is a finite state system because the maximum number of states required corresponds to the number of different input sequences of length $m - 1$, and this number is I^{m-1}, where I is the number of elements in the input set. In Example 7.12, the maximum number of states required is 2^3 (assuming that the input set consists only of the symbols a and b). However, in a particular system just a small fraction of this number of states might be required.

On the other hand, not all finite state systems are finite memory. As an example, consider a system with a binary input x, a binary output z, and the following behavior:

$$z(t) = \begin{cases} 1 & \textbf{if} \quad \text{number of 1's in } x(0, t) \text{ is even} \\ 0 & \textbf{otherwise} \end{cases}$$

This certainly is a finite state system (only two states are required). However, the system is not a finite-memory one because it is not sufficient to know the last m inputs, for any fixed integer m, to determine the output.

7.5 CONTROLLERS

Up to now we have discussed sequential systems for which the primary description is the time behavior and the state description is secondary, providing a simpler description and/or a vehicle for implementation. However, there are sequential systems for which the state description is primary. We now consider a class of such systems called **controllers**.

A controller is a finite state system which, as the states are traversed, produces **control signals**. These control signals determine actions performed in another part of the system. Important examples of systems using a controller are the register-transfer level systems presented in later chapters. Because a controller is a finite state system, any of the previously discussed descriptions can be used.

Autonomous and Non-autonomous Controllers

In some controllers the state transitions follow a fixed sequence of states, independent of any input (except the clock); these are called **autonomous controllers.** Such systems may have a start signal, so that each time this signal has value 1 the system goes through the fixed sequence of states. This type of operation is illustrated by the state diagram shown in Figure 7.9*a* and the corresponding timing diagram in Figure 7.9*b*.

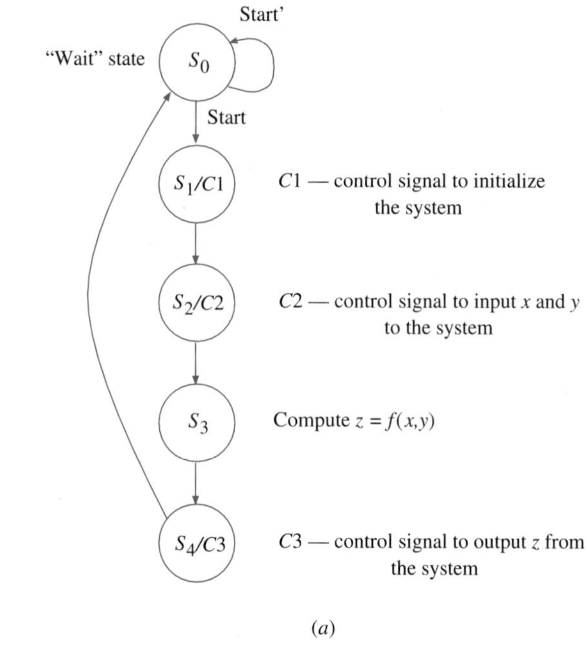

(a)

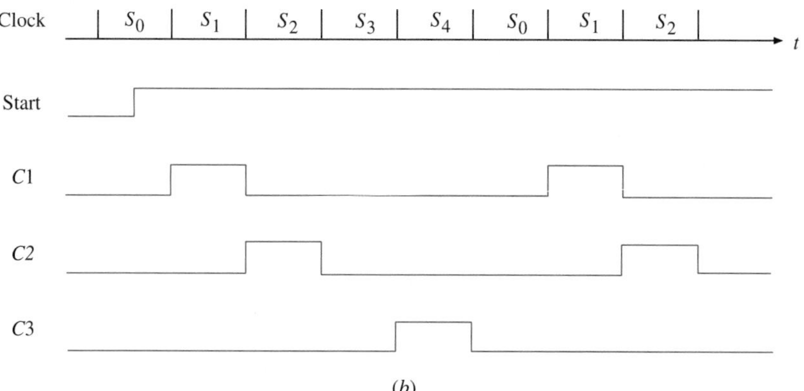

(b)

Figure 7.9 Autonomous controller. (*a*) State diagram. (*b*) Timing diagram.

In other controllers the transitions are determined by external inputs, in the same way as the sequential systems discussed before. This is illustrated in the state diagram depicted in Figure 7.10, which corresponds to the controller of a simple vending machine.

7.6 EQUIVALENT SEQUENTIAL SYSTEMS AND MINIMIZATION OF THE NUMBER OF STATES

Viewed from its external interface (inputs and outputs), a sequential system is characterized by its time behavior. In other words, from a functional point of view, a system can be replaced by another that has the same time behavior. This leads to the following definition of equivalent sequential systems:

Two sequential systems are **equivalent** if they have the same time behavior.

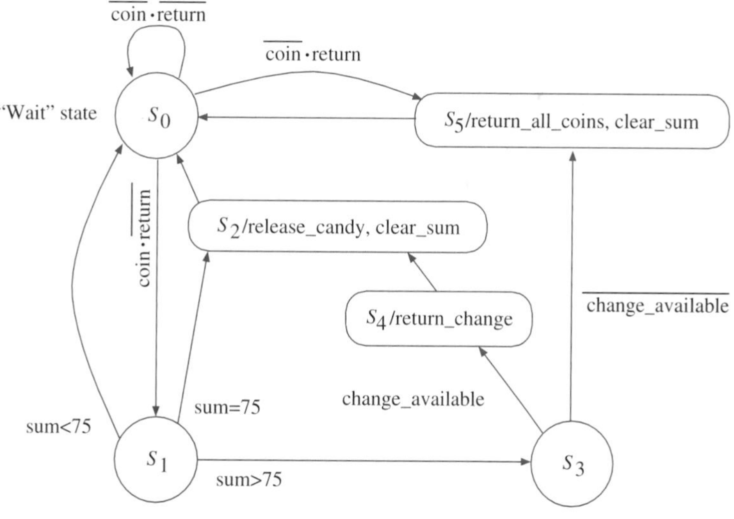

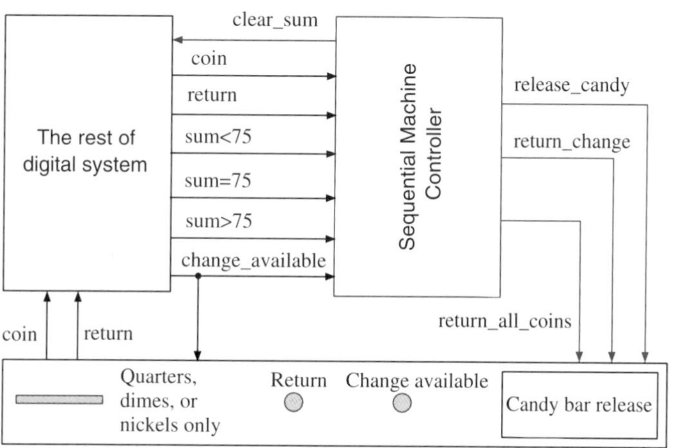

Note: coin · return = 0

Figure 7.10 A controller for a simple vending machine.

Because there can be several state descriptions for the same time behavior, it is convenient to identify the simplest description. In many instances, this corresponds to the description with the minimum number of states. Moreover, this description can lead to an effective implementation because it requires fewer devices to store the state and might reduce the complexity of the transition and output functions.

However, the description with the minimum number of states is not always the simplest nor does it always lead to the best implementation. In Section 7.8 we present some cases in which the use of a state vector produces simpler descriptions even if they have a significantly larger number of states; in addition, due to their regular structure, these vector descriptions result in implementations that are modular and have regular connections.

7.6.1 State Description with Redundant States

The first step in designing a sequential system consists of obtaining its state description, which is usually developed from the time behavior. This process might be quite difficult because the determination of the set of states requires some insight into the operation of the system. In many instances, it is simpler to obtain a "loose" state description having redundant states (more states than necessary), and then use a systematic procedure to reduce the number of states. We illustrate such a case in the following example.

EXAMPLE 7.13

Consider the determination of the state description of a sequential system having the following time behavior:

Input: $x(t) \in \{0, 1\}$
Output: $z(t) \in \{0, 1\}$

Function:
$$z(t) = \begin{cases} 1 & \textbf{if} \quad x(t-2, t) = 101 \\ 0 & \textbf{otherwise} \end{cases}$$

This system is a pattern detector with overlapped patterns (the last element of the pattern is also the first one), as illustrated by the following input-output pair:

t	0	1	2	3	4	5	6	7	8
x	0	0	1	0	1	0	1	0	0
z	0	0	0	0	1	0	1	0	0

A "loose" state description has seven states, as depicted by the state diagram in Figure 7.11*a*. This diagram is obtained by starting from an initial state and building a different sequence of states for each input sequence of length two (the states are labeled by the sequence). For example, if the input sequence is 01, the system will first go to state S_0 and then to state S_{01}. The transition produced by the third element of the input sequence triggers an output value 1 if the pattern has been detected. This is the case when the state is S_{10} and the input is $x(t) = 1$. Moreover, due to the overlapping of patterns, this third element takes the system to the state corresponding to the last two elements of the sequence. For instance, if the state is S_{01} and the input is $x(t) = 0$ the next state is S_{10} because for the next clock cycle $x(t-2, t-1) = 10$. Such a behavior is continued from there on.

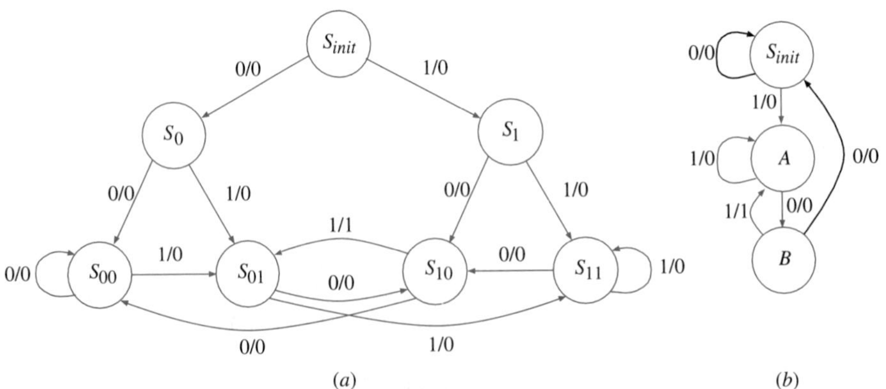

Figure 7.11 (*a*) State diagram with redundant states. (*b*) Reduced state diagram.

The state diagram in Figure 7.11*a* has redundant states; a reduced one is shown in Figure 7.11*b*. With some experience, it is possible to get this reduced description directly, as illustrated in Example 7.11. On the other hand, it is good to know that it is always possible to use a systematic procedure to reduce a "loose" description.

After studying the procedure given in the next subsection, the reader can verify that the two state descriptions shown in Figure 7.11 are indeed equivalent. ■

7.6.2 Equivalent Systems

We now describe a technique to transform a system into an equivalent one having the minimum number of states. The technique consists of the following two steps:

1. Find classes of equivalent states.
2. Describe the system using only one state per class.

We first define **state equivalence** and then give the procedure to identify classes of equivalent states.

Distinguishable States

Two states S_v and S_w of a sequential system are **distinguishable** if there exists at least one finite input sequence that generates different output sequences, depending whether the input sequence is applied to the system in state S_v or S_w. A sequence that distinguishes these states is called a **distinguishing sequence** of (S_v, S_w). If there exists a distinguishing sequence of length k for pair (S_v, S_w), then (S_v, S_w) are ***k*-distinguishable**. In mathematical notation, S_v and S_w are k-distinguishable if there exists an input sequence $x(t, t+k-1)$, such that

$$z(x(t, t+k-1), S_v) \neq z(x(t, t+k-1), S_w)$$

where $z(x(t_1, t_2), S)$ is the output sequence when the input sequence $x(t_1, t_2)$ is applied with S being the state at time t_1.

Equivalent States

- Two states that are not k-distinguishable are said to be ***k*-equivalent**. The partition of states into the k-equivalent classes is called P_k.
- Two states that are not distinguishable for any k are said to be **equivalent**. The partition into equivalent states is called P.

EXAMPLE 7.14

A sequential system has the following "loose" state description.

Input:	$x(t) \in \{a, b, c\}$
Output:	$z(t) \in \{0, 1\}$
State:	$s(t) \in \{A, B, C, D, E, F\}$
Initial state:	$s(0) = A$

Function: The transition and output functions are

PS	$x = a$	$x = b$	$x = c$
A	$E, 0$	$D, 1$	$B, 0$
B	$F, 0$	$D, 0$	$A, 1$
C	$E, 0$	$B, 1$	$D, 0$
D	$F, 0$	$B, 0$	$C, 1$
E	$C, 0$	$F, 1$	$F, 0$
F	$B, 0$	$C, 0$	$F, 1$
		NS, z	

For this system,

- A and B are 1-distinguishable, because $z(b, A) \neq z(b, B)$.
- A and C are 1-equivalent because

$$\begin{aligned} z(a, A) &= z(a, C) = 0 \\ z(b, A) &= z(b, C) = 1 \\ z(c, A) &= z(c, C) = 0 \end{aligned}$$

- A and C are also 2-equivalent because

$$\begin{aligned} z(aa, A) &= z(aa, C) = 00 \\ z(ab, A) &= z(ab, C) = 01 \\ z(ac, A) &= z(ac, C) = 00 \\ z(ba, A) &= z(ba, C) = 10 \\ z(bb, A) &= z(bb, C) = 10 \\ z(bc, A) &= z(bc, C) = 11 \\ z(ca, A) &= z(ca, C) = 00 \\ z(cb, A) &= z(cb, C) = 00 \\ z(cc, A) &= z(cc, C) = 01 \end{aligned}$$

■

7.6.3 Procedure to Minimize the Number of States

The classes of equivalent states are obtained in several steps, beginning from the classes of 1-equivalent states, following with the classes of 2-equivalent states, and so on. Consequently, the minimization procedure indicates how to obtain P_1, how to determine partition P_{i+1} from P_i, and when to stop.

Obtaining P_1

The classes of 1-equivalent states are obtained directly from the state table, as two states are 1-equivalent if they have the same row pattern in the output function of the state table. In Example 7.14, states A, C, and E are 1-equivalent because the row pattern for all three states is 010. Similarly, B, D, and F are 1-equivalent with row pattern 001. Therefore,

$$P_1 = (A, C, E)\ (B, D, F)$$

From P_i to P_{i+1}

The procedure is based on the following facts:

1. Partition P_{i+1} is a refinement of partition P_i. That is, to obtain P_{i+1} it is only possible to break down classes from P_i but not to recombine states that are in different classes of P_i. This is illustrated next:

	possible	not possible
P_i	$(A, B, C)\ (D)$	
P_{i+1}	$(A, C)\ (B)\ (D)$	$(A, D)\ (B)\ (C)$

We now give a proof of this. We have to prove that if S_v and S_w are $(i+1)$-equivalent, they are also i-equivalent.

Proof: Consider an arbitrary input sequence $x(t, t+i)$ (of length $i+1$). Then, because by hypothesis S_v and S_w are $(i+1)$-equivalent, the output sequences satisfy

$$z(x(t, t+i), S_v) = z(x(t, t+i), S_w)$$

For example, an input sequence of length four produces

$$z(abcd, S_v) = z(abcd, S_w) = 1234$$

Then, an arbitrary sequence of length i would also produce the same output sequence when applied from these two states, because the sequence of length i is a subsequence of a sequence of length $(i+1)$. In the example,

$$z(abc, S_v) = z(abc, S_w) = 123$$

Consequently, S_v and S_w are i-equivalent. ■

2. Two states are $(i+1)$-equivalent if and only if

   a. they are i-equivalent (this was already proved above), and
   b. for all $x \in I$, the corresponding successors are i-equivalent.
      (A successor of state S for input x is the next state when the system is in state S and the input x is applied. For instance, in Example 7.14, the successor of state B for input c is state A).

Proof: If S_v and S_w are i-equivalent, $i > 1$, then they are also 1-equivalent (the sequence of length 1 is a subsequence of a sequence of length i). Now, if S_v and S_w are 1-equivalent and their next states are i-equivalent, then S_v and S_w are $(i+1)$-equivalent. This is illustrated in Figure 7.12.

Conversely, as also illustrated in Figure 7.12, if for some input, say a, the next states are not i-equivalent, then there exists a distinguishable sequence of length i, say T, that produces different output sequences for each of the next states. Then,

$$z(aT, S_v) \neq z(aT, S_w)$$

where aT is the input sequence formed by a followed by T. Consequently, S_v and S_w are not $(i+1)$-equivalent. ■

In Example 7.14, states A and C are 2-equivalent because they are 1-equivalent and their successors are 1-equivalent (E for $x = a$, D and B for $x = b$, and B and D for $x = c$). On the other hand, B and F are not 2-equivalent because their successors for $x = b$ are D and C, which are not 1-equivalent.

When to Stop

The procedure stops when partition P_{i+1} is the same as partition P_i. In fact, if $P_{i+1} = P_i$ for some i, then $P_k = P_i$ for all $k > i$. (The proof by induction is left as an exercise.)

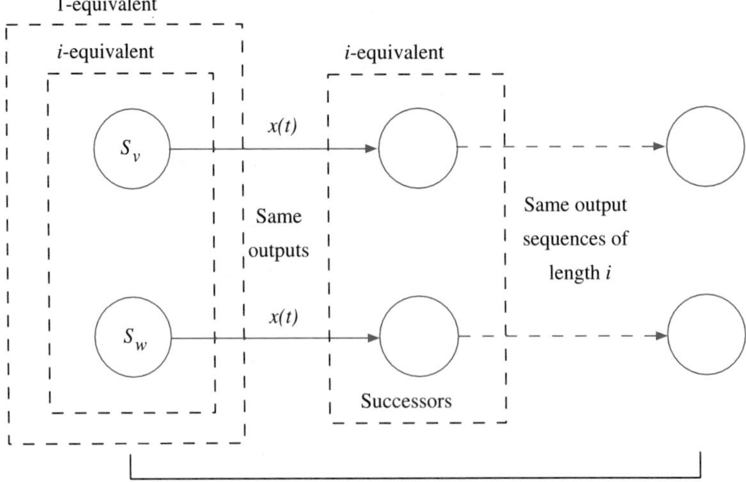

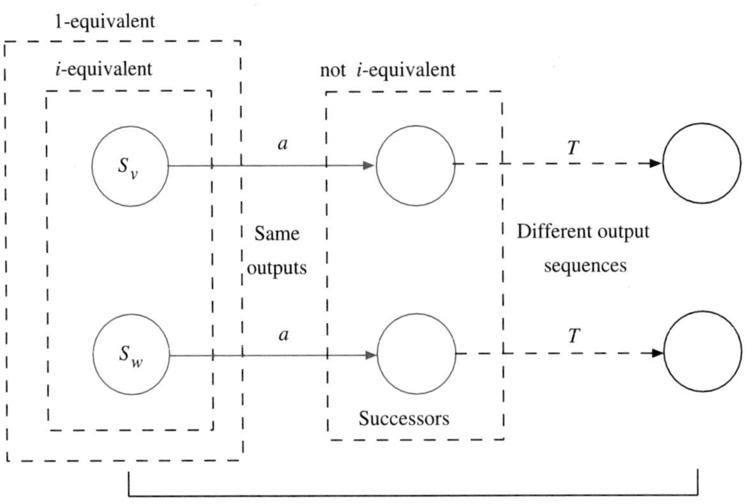

Figure 7.12 Illustration of $(i + 1)$-equivalence relation.

The process always terminates because, for a system with n states, there can be at most $n - 1$ different partitions. This is shown by noting that, because P_{i+1} is a refinement of P_i, if all partitions up to P_{n-1} are different then P_{n-1} has n classes with one state in each class.

Procedure

Consequently, the procedure to find the minimal set of states is as follows:

1. Obtain P_1 by grouping the states that have the same output under all input sequences of length 1 (directly from the state table).
2. Obtain P_{i+1} from P_i by grouping states that are i-equivalent and whose corresponding successors are also i-equivalent.
3. Terminate when $P_{i+1} = P_i$.
4. Write the reduced table.

EXAMPLE 7.15

We now apply the complete procedure to the system in Example 7.14. To obtain P_1, from the state table we extract the output function. That is,

PS	*x*(*t*)		
	a	*b*	*c*
A	0	1	0
B	0	0	1
C	0	1	0
D	0	0	1
E	0	1	0
F	0	0	1
		z	

States are 1-equivalent if they have the same "row pattern" in the output table above. The two row patterns are 010 and 001 so that partition P_1 is

$$P_1 = (A, C, E)\ \ (B, D, F)$$

To determine partition P_2, we analyze the next states of (A, C, E) and (B, D, F). From the state table we obtain that their next states are

PS	*x*(*t*)		
	a	*b*	*c*
A	*E*	*D*	*B*
C	*E*	*B*	*D*
E	*C*	*F*	*F*
		NS	

PS	*x*(*t*)		
	a	*b*	*c*
B	*F*	*D*	*A*
D	*F*	*B*	*C*
F	*B*	*C*	*F*
		NS	

The columns of these tables have to be considered now. In the case of (A, C, E), the three next-state values in each column are 1-equivalent so that states (A, C, E) are 2-equivalent. On the other hand, in the case of (B, D, F), (B, D) are 2-equivalent (because (B, D) and (A, C) are 1-equivalent) but (D, F) are not 2-equivalent ($((B, C)$ and (C, F) are not 1-equivalent). Therefore,

$$P_2 = (A, C, E)\ \ (B, D)\ \ (F)$$

A simpler way of determining this partition consists of numbering the classes of P_1 and writing the corresponding numbers for the successors under each state (instead of the state itself). Then, two states are in the same class of P_2 if their successor columns have the same numbers:

		1			2	
P_1	(*A*,	*C*,	*E*)	(*B*,	*D*,	*F*)
a	1	1	1	2	2	2
b	2	2	2	2	2	1
c	2	2	2	1	1	2

By identifying identical columns of successors, we get

$$P_2 = (A, C, E) \quad (B, D) \quad (F)$$

We apply the same process to obtain the next partition:

		1		2		3
P_2	$(A,$	$C,$	$E)$	$(B,$	$D)$	(F)
a	1	1	1	3	3	
b	2	2	3	2	2	
c	2	2	3	1	1	

By identifying identical columns of successors, we have

$$P_3 = (A, C) \quad (E) \quad (B, D) \quad (F)$$

Similarly, we determine $P_4 = (A, C)\ (E)\ (B, D)\ (F)$. Because $P_4 = P_3$ this is also the equivalence partition P.

Consequently, the minimal system has the following state transition and output functions:

PS	$x = a$	$x = b$	$x = c$
A	$E, 0$	$B, 1$	$B, 0$
B	$F, 0$	$B, 0$	$A, 1$
E	$A, 0$	$F, 1$	$F, 0$
F	$B, 0$	$A, 0$	$F, 1$
		NS, z	

■

The preceding procedure produces an equivalent state description with the minimum number of states. The procedure can be quite time consuming and its complexity depends on the number of states, so that it is convenient to begin with a relatively "tight" description whenever possible.

7.7 BINARY SPECIFICATION OF SEQUENTIAL SYSTEMS

The descriptions discussed in the previous sections are high-level ones. In a similar manner as for combinational systems, a binary description is obtained by coding the input, output, and state onto binary variables. The state coding is also called **state assignment**. Due to the binary representation, each arc in the state diagram of a binary description can be labeled with a switching expression; the corresponding transition is performed whenever the expression has value 1.

EXAMPLE 7.16

In Example 7.14, the system has three input values, two output values and four states (after minimization). Consequently, it is possible to use a two-bit vector for the input, one bit for the output, and a two-bit vector for the state. Possible codes are as follows:

Input code

$x(t)$	$x_1(t)x_0(t)$
a	00
b	01
c	10

Output code

$z(t)$	
0	0
1	1

State assignment

$s(t)$	$s_1(t)s_0(t)$
A	00
B	01
E	10
F	11

With these code s, the resulting binary specification is

$s_1(t)s_0(t)$	$x_1x_0 = 00$	$x_1x_0 = 01$	$x_1x_0 = 10$
00	10, 0	01, 1	01, 0
01	11, 0	01, 0	00, 1
10	00, 0	11, 1	11, 0
11	01, 0	00, 0	11, 1
	$s_1(t+1)s_0(t+1), z(t)$		

Note that the column $x_1x_0 = 11$ are "don't cares." The resulting switching functions (for $s_1(t+1)$, $s_0(t+1)$, and z) can be described by three switching expressions, using the procedures discussed in Chapter 2.

The state diagram in Figure 7.13 illustrates the use of switching expressions in labeling arcs.

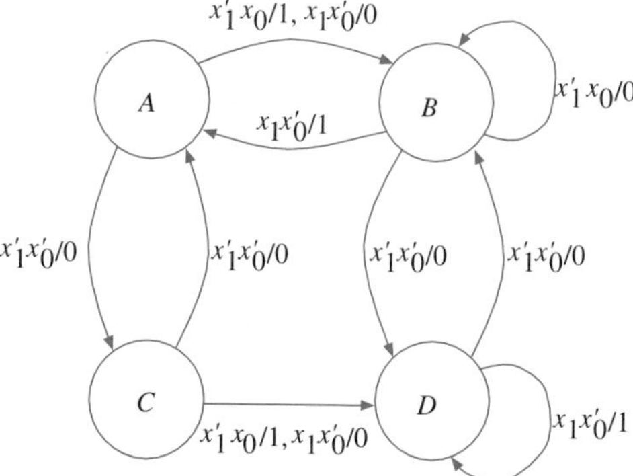

Figure 7.13 Switching expressions as arc labels. ■

7.8 SPECIFICATION OF DIFFERENT TYPES OF SEQUENTIAL SYSTEMS

We now present two examples of specification of sequential systems, in addition to those already given throughout this chapter. Additional systems are described in subsequent chapters.

Modulo-p Counter

A modulo-p counter is a sequential system whose input is a binary variable and whose output has integer values from the set $\{0, 1, \ldots, p-1\}$. Its time behavior is described as follows:

Input: $x(t) \in \{0, 1\}$
Output: $z(t) \in \{0, 1, 2, \ldots, p-1\}$

Function: $$z(t) = \left[\sum_{i=0}^{t-1} x(i)\right] \bmod p$$

A state description requires p states. Assigning the integers 0 to $p-1$ as the state labels, the following description is obtained:

Input: $x(t) \in \{0, 1\}$
Output: $z(t) \in \{0, 1, 2, \ldots, p-1\}$
State: $s(t) \in \{0, 1, 2, \ldots, p-1\}$
Initial state: $s(0) = 0$

Function: The transition and output functions are

$$s(t+1) = [s(t) + x(t)] \bmod p$$

$$z(t) = s(t)$$

Figure 7.14 shows the state diagram of a modulo-5 counter.

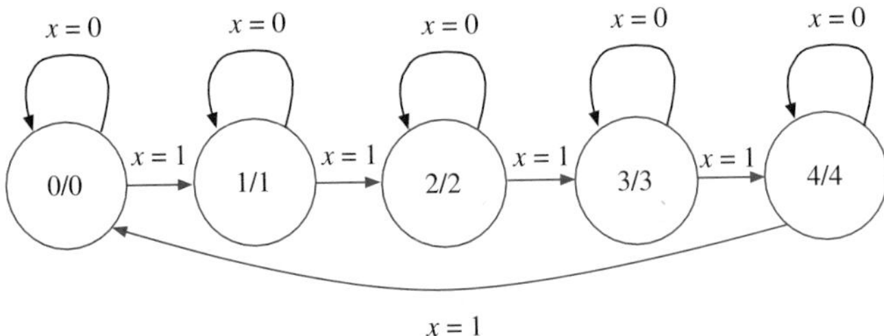

Figure 7.14 State diagram of a modulo-5 counter.

Pattern Recognizer

A pattern recognizer is a sequential system whose binary output at time t indicates whether the input subsequence ending at time t corresponds to the particular pattern recognized by the system. Consequently, a pattern recognizer is a finite-memory system as defined in Section 7.4.

A sequential system that recognizes the pattern $P = (p_0, p_1, \ldots, p_{m-1})$ has the following time-behavior description:

Input: $x(t) \in I$
Output: $z(t) \in \{0, 1\}$

Function: $$z(t) = \begin{cases} 1 & \textbf{if} \quad x(t-m+1, t) = P \\ 0 & \textbf{otherwise} \end{cases}$$

Note that this description implies the recognition of overlapped patterns.

There are two possible state descriptions for pattern recognizers: the first one uses a vector to represent the state, with as many elements as the length of the pattern; the second uses states that correspond to partial recognition of the pattern (see Example 7.11). Let us discuss both approaches.

To obtain a state description using a vector to represent the state, we define a state vector of $m-1$ components $\underline{s} = (s_{m-2}, \ldots, s_0)$. The corresponding state equations are

$$s_i(t+1) = s_{i-1}(t) \qquad 1 \le i \le m-2$$
$$s_0(t+1) = x(t)$$

That is, the last input symbol is stored as $s_0(t+1)$ and all previous state values are "shifted" to the left by one position. By substitution in the expression above, we get

$$\underline{s}(t) = (x(t-m+1), \ldots, x(t-1))$$

so that the state stores the last $m-1$ input symbols. As a result, the output is

$$z(t) = \begin{cases} 1 & \textbf{if} \quad (\underline{s}(t), x(t)) = P \\ 0 & \textbf{otherwise} \end{cases}$$

wherein $(\underline{s}(t), x(t))$ denotes the sequence formed by the concatenation of $\underline{s}(t)$ and $x(t)$.

EXAMPLE 7.17

Determine a state description of a sequential system that recognizes the pattern 0101011.

Because the pattern has length seven, the description requires a state vector of six elements (64 states), as follows:

Input:	$x(t) \in \{0, 1\}$
Output:	$z(t) \in \{0, 1\}$
State:	$s(t) = (s_5, s_4, s_3, s_2, s_1, s_0), \quad s_i \in \{0, 1\}$
Initial state:	$s(0) = (1, 1, 1, 1, 1, 1)$

Function: The transition and output functions are

$$s_i(t+1) = s_{i-1}(t) \quad \textbf{if} \quad 5 \ge i \ge 1$$
$$s_0(t+1) = x(t)$$

$$z(t) = \begin{cases} 1 & \textbf{if} \quad (\underline{s}(t), x(t)) = 0101011 \\ 0 & \textbf{otherwise} \end{cases}$$

Note that the initial state is (1, 1, 1, 1, 1, 1) because the pattern to recognize begins with 0 (if the initial state is (0, 0, 0, 0, 0, 0) then the pattern 101011 would be incorrectly recognized). A fragment of the state diagram is shown in Figure 7.15.

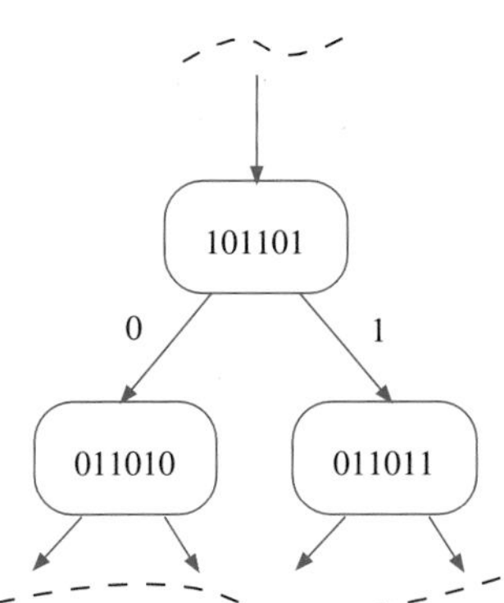

Figure 7.15 A fragment of the state diagram for Example 7.17. ∎

The state vector description has 2^{m-1} states; it is a general description for all pattern recognizers and produces a modular implementation. However, it does not result in the minimum number of states because a description with only m states is possible. In this second type of state description, the system begins in an initial state and goes through $m - 1$ states as the pattern is being recognized. Whenever an input does not belong to the pattern, the system returns to the state that corresponds to the subpattern already recognized.

EXAMPLE 7.18

For the pattern recognizer in Example 7.17, the second type of description requires seven states, labeled $S0$ to $S6$; the corresponding state diagram is shown in Figure 7.16. State Si represents the partial recognition of a subpattern consisting of the first i elements of P (this is indicated by the labels shown next to each state in the state diagram). As an example of a transition, the system is in state $S6$ when it has already recognized 010101; if $x(t) = 0$, the system returns to state $S5$ because the previous five input values were 01010 and therefore only two more symbols are required to recognize the pattern. The output is 1 in the transition from $S6$ to $S0$.

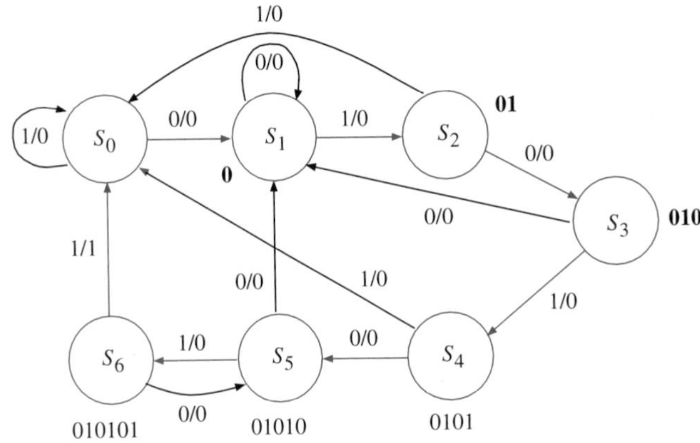

Figure 7.16 State diagram for Example 7.18.

■

7.9 SPECIFICATION OF SEQUENTIAL SYSTEMS IN μVHDL

We now address the μVHDL-based behavioral description of sequential systems, which is based on the state description.

The two components of a sequential system, that is, the state transition function and the output function, are described as separate `PROCESS`es. Because the output process must respond to changes in the state, and since the mechanism for activating a process is through signals, the state is described by a `SIGNAL` defined inside the `ARCHITECTURE` body. The possible states are listed as an enumerated type.

Consequently, the `PROCESS` describing the state transition function is activated whenever there is an event in the clock signal `clk`, which captures the synchronous nature of the systems considered in this book. On the other hand, the `PROCESS` describing the output function is activated whenever there is a state transition or an event in the input signals (if applicable). In other words, the state transition process can be regarded as having signal `clk` as input and a signal `state` as output, whereas the output process has the state signal and the inputs to the module as inputs, and the module output as its output.

These aspects of μVHDL-based behavioral descriptions are illustrated in the following example, which addresses the case of a sequential system whose output may change either when the state changes or when an input signal changes value (a Mealy machine).

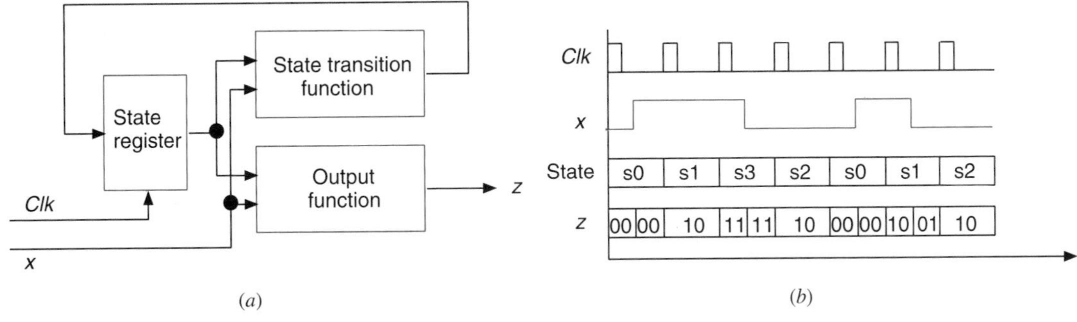

Figure 7.17 Simple sequential system for Example 7.19.

EXAMPLE 7.19

The simple sequential machine depicted in Figure 7.17*a* is described in μVHDL as follows:

```
ENTITY simple_seq IS
  PORT(x     : IN  BIT ;
       z     : OUT BIT_VECTOR(1 DOWNTO 0);
       clk   : IN  BIT);
END simple_seq;

ARCHITECTURE behavioral OF simple_seq IS
  TYPE   stateT is (S0, S1, S2, S3);
  SIGNAL state: stateT;               -- state
BEGIN
  PROCESS (clk)                       -- process triggered by clk
  BEGIN
    IF (clk'EVENT AND clk='1') THEN
      CASE state IS                     -- determine new state value
        WHEN S0 => IF (x = '0') THEN state <= S0;
                   ELSE              state <= S1;
                   END IF;
        WHEN S1 => IF (x = '0') THEN state <= S2;
                   ELSE              state <= S3;
                   END IF;
        WHEN S2 => IF (x = '0') THEN state <= S0;
                   ELSE              state <= S1;
                   END IF;
        WHEN S3 => IF (x = '0') THEN state <= S2;
                   ELSE              state <= S3;
                   END IF;
      END CASE;
    END IF;
  END PROCESS;

  PROCESS (state,x)          -- process tiggered by state or input
  BEGIN
    CASE state IS
      WHEN S0 => z <= "00";
      WHEN S1 => z <= x & NOT(x);
      WHEN S2 => z <= NOT(x) & x;
      WHEN S3 => z <= "11";
    END CASE;
  END PROCESS;
END behavioral;
```

According to this description, and as illustrated in Figure 7.17*b*, the process describing the state transitions is interpreted whenever there is a transition in the clock signal, and the state signal is modified. The attribute `EVENT`, of type `BOOLEAN`, is used to detect the direction of the transition in the signal; the attribute has the value `TRUE` if an event has occurred in the corresponding signal at the current time or `FALSE` otherwise.

Similarly, a transition in the state signal or in input signal `x` activates the process describing the output function, which generates the new output using the current value of state and input signals. ■

7.10 FURTHER READINGS

The material covered in this chapter is treated in depth in books on switching and automata theory. However, most of these books consider the representation of finite functions by tables, maps, diagrams, and switching expressions, but do not discuss the representation by high-level expressions. This characteristic drastically limits the complexity of the systems that can be described. Typical books of this class are *Switching and Automata Theory* by Z. Kohavi, McGraw-Hill, New York, NY, 1978; and *Logic Design Principles* by E. J. McCluskey, Prentice-Hall, Englewood Cliffs, NJ, 1986.

A detailed discussion of state reduction, including the case of incompletely specified systems, is given in *Theory and Design of Switching Circuits* by A. D. Friedman and P. R. Menon, Computer Science Press, Woodland Hills, CA, 1975; and *Switching and Automata Theory* by Z. Kohavi, McGraw-Hill, New York, 1978. These books also present a study of different types of sequential systems, such as finite-memory and linear systems.

For a treatment of asynchronous sequential systems, not discussed in this text, the reader may consult *Switching and Automata Theory* by Z. Kohavi, McGraw-Hill, New York, 1978; *Theory and Design of Switching Circuits* by A. D. Friedman and P. R. Menon, Computer Science Press, Woodland Hills, CA, 1975; and *Asynchronous Sequential Circuits* by S. H. Unger, Wiley-Interscience, New York, 1969.

EXERCISES

State description

Exercise 7.1 A sequential system has one input with values a, b, and c and one output with values p and q. The output is q whenever the input sequence has an even number of a's and an odd number of b's. Obtain a state description of the system.

Exercise 7.2 A sequential system has one decimal digit as input and a radix-5 digit as output. The value of the output at time t corresponds to the sum modulo-5 of the input digits from time 0 to t. Obtain a state description of the system. *Hint:* use arithmetic expressions for the state transition and output functions.

Exercise 7.3 Determine the state table corresponding to the state diagram shown in Figure 7.18.

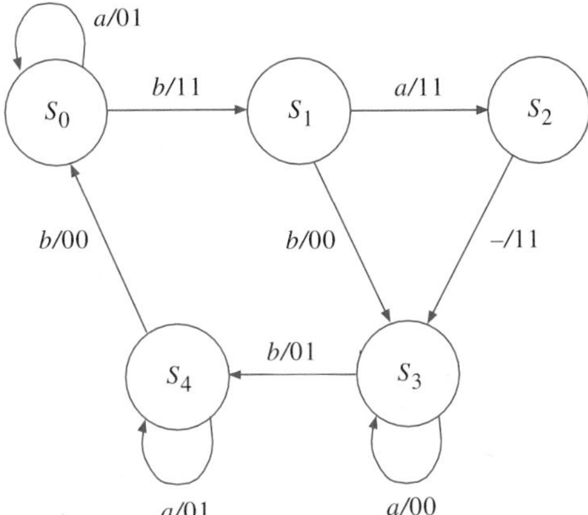

Figure 7.18 State diagram for Exercise 7.3.

Exercise 7.4 Determine the state diagram corresponding to the following state table.

	Input		
PS	$x = a$	$x = b$	$x = c$
A	$A, 0$	$B, 1$	$A, 0$
B	$B, 0$	$C, 1$	$A, 1$
C	$C, 0$	$D, 1$	$A, 1$
D	$D, 0$	$E, 1$	$A, 0$
E	$E, 0$	$A, 1$	$A, 1$
	NS, Output		

Exercise 7.5 Determine the state diagram for the sequential system described by the following expressions:

$$s(t+1) = \begin{cases} s(t) & \textbf{if} \quad x = a \\ (s(t)+1) \bmod 5 & \textbf{if} \quad x = b \\ 2 & \textbf{if} \quad x = c \end{cases}$$

$$z(t) = \begin{cases} 0 & \textbf{if} \quad s(t) \text{ is even} \\ 1 & \textbf{otherwise} \end{cases}$$

The system has five states labeled 0, 1, 2, 3, and 4.

Exercise 7.6 A sequential system is described by the following state table. Rename the states using integers from 0 to 6 so that A becomes 0, B becomes 1, C becomes 2, etc. Write arithmetic expressions that describe the transition and output functions. Describe in words the function of the system.

	Input		
PS	$x = 0$	$x = 1$	
A	A	B	1
B	B	C	0
C	C	D	1
D	D	E	0
E	E	F	1
F	F	G	0
G	G	A	1
	NS		Output

Exercise 7.7 A sequential system is described by the following expressions, where the state is a bit-vector of four components (s_3, s_2, s_1, s_0):

$$s_0(t+1) = s_3(t) \oplus x(t)$$

$$s_i(t+1) = s_{i-1}(t) \quad \text{for } 1 \leq i \leq 3$$

$$z(t) = s_3(t)$$

Obtain the corresponding state diagram.

Exercise 7.8 A sequential system is described by the following state table. Rename the states using a three-bit vector so that A becomes 000, B becomes 001, etc. Describe the system by vector expressions.

	Input		
PS	$x = 0$	$x = 1$	
A	A	E	0
B	E	A	0
C	B	F	0
D	F	B	1
E	C	G	0
F	G	C	0
G	D	H	0
H	H	D	1
	NS		Output

Exercise 7.9 Determine whether the sequential systems described by the following tables correspond to Moore or Mealy machines.

	Input	
PS	$x = 0$	$x = 1$
A	A, 0	B, 1
B	C, 1	C, 0
C	A, 0	B, 1
	NS, Output	

	Input	
PS	$x = 0$	$x = 1$
A	B, 0	C, 0
B	B, 1	C, 1
C	A, 1	B, 1
	NS, Output	

	Input		
PS	$x = 0$	$x = 1$	
A	*A*	*B*	0
B	*A*	*C*	1
C	*A*	*D*	1
D	*A*	*A*	0
	NS		Output

Exercise 7.10 For the sequential system specified by the state diagram shown in Figure 7.19, give a code for the input, output, and state, and describe the system by means of switching expressions.

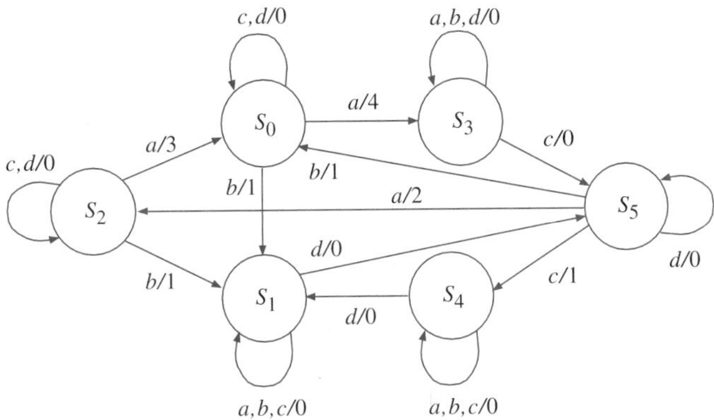

Figure 7.19 State diagram for Exercise 7.10.

Time behavior

Exercise 7.11 Describe the time behavior of a modulo-p counter assuming that any of the p states can be the initial state.

Exercise 7.12 For the system described by the state diagram shown in Figure 7.20, we want to describe the time behavior from $t_1 = 5$ to $t_2 = 16$, assuming that the initial state for $t_0 = 4$ is s_3. How many sequence pairs would be needed? Give three different sequence pairs.

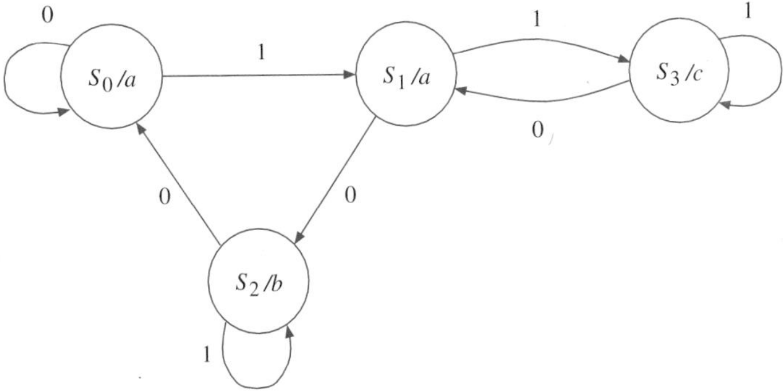

Figure 7.20 State diagram for Exercise 7.12.

Equivalent systems and reduction in the number of states

Exercise 7.13 Check that the two state diagrams given in Figure 7.11 represent equivalent systems.

Exercise 7.14 A sequential system has an input with values a, b, and c, and one binary output. The output at time t is 1 if $x(t-3,t) = abca$ and the number of a's in $x(0,t)$ is even. Obtain a "loose" state description and minimize the number of states.

Exercise 7.15 Determine the minimal state table that is equivalent to the following:

	Input	
PS	$x = 0$	$x = 1$
a	$f, 0$	$b, 0$
b	$d, 0$	$c, 0$
c	$f, 0$	$e, 0$
d	$g, 1$	$a, 0$
e	$d, 0$	$c, 0$
f	$f, 1$	$b, 1$
g	$g, 0$	$h, 1$
h	$g, 1$	$a, 0$
	NS, z	

Exercise 7.16 Reduce the number of states in the following state table and show the corresponding minimal table.

	Input	
PS	$x = 0$	$x = 1$
A	$F, 0$	$C, 0$
B	$H, 1$	$A, 1$
C	$H, 0$	$D, 1$
D	$B, 0$	$H, 0$
E	$G, 0$	$C, 0$
F	$C, 1$	$E, 1$
G	$H, 1$	$E, 1$
H	$C, 0$	$A, 1$
	NS, z	

Exercise 7.17 Determine the minimal state table equivalent to the following one:

	Input			
PS	$x = a$	$x = b$	$x = c$	$x = d$
A	$E, 1$	$C, 0$	$B, 1$	$E, 1$
B	$C, 0$	$F, 1$	$E, 1$	$B, 0$
C	$B, 1$	$A, 0$	$D, 1$	$F, 1$
D	$G, 0$	$F, 1$	$E, 1$	$B, 0$
E	$C, 0$	$F, 1$	$D, 1$	$E, 0$
F	$C, 1$	$F, 1$	$D, 0$	$H, 0$
G	$D, 1$	$A, 0$	$B, 1$	$F, 1$
H	$B, 1$	$C, 0$	$E, 1$	$F, 1$
		NS, z		

Exercise 7.18 Minimize the following state table:

	Input	
PS	$x = a$	$x = b$
N	S, f	Z, e
O	T, f	Y, e
P	Y, e	R, f
Q	W, f	V, e
R	W, f	Y, e
S	N, e	V, e
T	Z, e	Y, e
U	V, e	Q, f
V	P, e	N, f
W	X, e	P, e
X	W, f	N, e
Y	U, e	Z, f
Z	T, f	N, e
	NS, z	

Examples of systems

Exercise 7.19 A pattern recognizer has an input set $I = \{a, b, c, d\}$ and an output set $O = \{0, 1\}$. The output at time t is 1 whenever $x(t-3, t) = abca$. Give a state description and determine the output sequence when $x(0, 14) = aabcabcadaaabca$. Use a state vector approach and a minimum-number-of-states approach.

Exercise 7.20 Describe a procedure to obtain the state description with $m - 1$ states for a pattern recognizer of a pattern of length m.

Exercise 7.21 A sequential system has an input set $I = \{a, b, c, d\}$ and an output set $O = \{0, 1\}$. The output is 1 when the pattern *abca* has occurred an even number of times in $x(0, t)$. Give a state description of the system. Use a state vector approach and a minimum-number-of-states approach.

Exercise 7.22 A sequential system has a decimal digit as input and a radix-5 digit as output. The output counts modulo-5 the number of times the pattern 358 has occurred in $x(0, t)$. Give a state description of the system. *Hint:* Decompose the system into two: a pattern recognizer and a modulo-5 counter.

Exercise 7.23 A sequential system has a binary input and a three-valued output. The output is 0 if the pattern 0110 has not occurred in $x(0, t)$; it has value 1 if the pattern 0110 has occurred but the pattern 1001 has not; and it has value 2 if both 0110 and 1001 have occurred. Give a state description and show the output and the state sequence for the input sequence 0010111011001010. *Hint:* Decompose the system into two pattern recognizers. Note that the pattern is recognized in the sequence $x(0, t)$ and not $x(t-3, t)$.

Exercise 7.24 A pattern generator has two outputs. One output is the periodic pattern GO UCLA and the other produces the pattern RUN each time the input *start* has value 1. Describe the system by a state diagram.

Exercise 7.25 A sequential system is the controller for a stamp-vending machine. There is an input to reset the controller (put it in an initial state), one input whose value corresponds to the type of coin inserted, one input to select between three choices of stamps, and one input to request return of coins. Assume that the values of the three selections are 20 cents, 40 cents, and 50 cents, and that the machine should give change. The outputs are release stamp 1, release stamp 2, release stamp 3, return coins, give 5 cents change, and give 10 cents change.

Give a state diagram of the controller. Assume that coins can be inserted in any order.

Description of systems in μVHDL

Any of the systems in the exercises under the heading "Examples of systems" can be described using μVHDL.

Chapter 8

Sequential Networks

In this chapter we discuss:

- Canonical form of sequential networks: state register plus combinational network.
- Characteristics of binary cells: latches and edge-triggered cells. The D flip-flop.
- Timing parameters for cells and networks: setup time, hold time, and propagation delay. Example for a family of CMOS modules.
- Analysis and design of canonical networks.
- Other flip-flop modules: SR, JK, and T flip-flops. Tables, state diagrams, and characteristic equations.
- Analysis of flip-flop networks.
- Design of flip-flop networks. The excitation functions.
- Special state assignments: one flip-flop per state and shifting register.
- Specification of sequential networks in μVHDL.

In the same way as for combinational systems (see Chapter 4), the realization of a sequential system involves a circuit level and a logic level. The circuit level deals with the physical realization of elementary sequential modules. In contrast, the logic level consists of the realization of a sequential system by a collection of simpler networks, both combinational and sequential, leading to a **sequential network.** As in the case of combinational systems, the network concept can be used at several levels in a hierarchical manner (a module in a network can itself be realized as a network of simpler modules).

We begin studying the realization of synchronous sequential systems by showing a **canonical implementation,** which consists of a set of binary cells to store the state and combinational networks to realize the output and transition functions. Consequently, the only additional element required for the implementation is the binary cell. We show how this cell, called the **D flip-flop,** can be realized by a gate network in which the sequential operation is achieved by a loop in the network.

8.1 CANONICAL FORM OF SEQUENTIAL NETWORKS

A standard form for all sequential networks is the **canonical implementation** (also called **Huffman-Moore implementation**), which is based directly on the state description of a system:

State transition function	$s(t+1) = G(s(t), x(t))$
Output function	$z(t) = H(s(t), x(t))$

This implementation, whose components are organized as depicted in Figure 8.1*a*, consists of

- a **state register** to store the state; and
- a **combinational network** to implement the transition and output functions.

Because the system is synchronous, a **synchronizing signal** (called the **clock** CLK) determines the time instants at which the next state is loaded into the state register. At time t, the next state is loaded into the state register and remains stored there until time $t + 1$. The clock consists of periodic **clock pulses** (see Figure 8.1*b*), which in the ideal case have zero width. Actual clock pulses, whose nonzero width affects the operation of the sequential network, are discussed in Section 8.3.

In general, the description of a sequential system includes an initial state, being necessary to bring the system into such a state in order to have the desired input-output behavior. This initialization is accomplished by a special input **initialize**. For simplicity, in this book we usually do not indicate the initialization signal but assume that it is implemented as required.

From the discussion in Section 7.1.3, any sequential system is classified either as a Mealy or Moore machine. The canonical form of these systems differs slightly, as illustrated in Figure 8.2. In a Mealy machine, the networks for both the transition function and the output function have the external input $x(t)$ and the state $s(t)$ as inputs, whereas in a Moore machine the network implementing the output function has only $s(t)$ as input. It should be noted that the separation of the combinational network into two independent subnetworks is made only to illustrate the difference; in a practical implementation, this separation would not necessarily be made because both networks could share some modules.

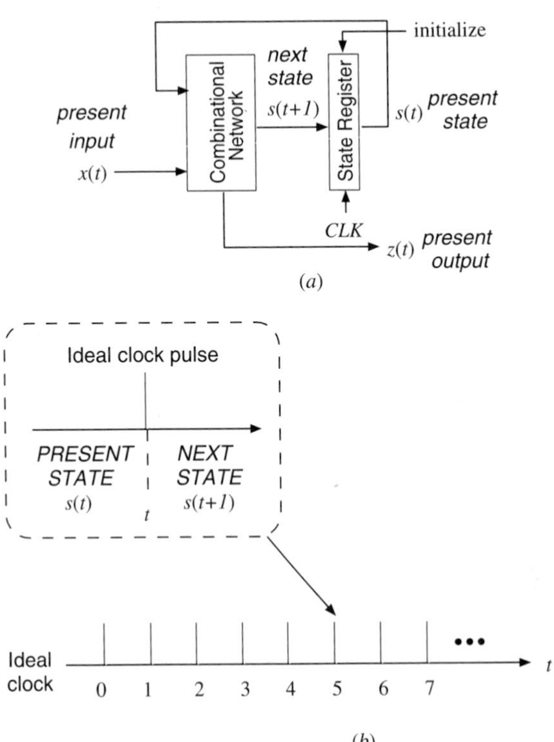

Figure 8.1 (*a*) Canonical implementation of sequential network. (*b*) Ideal clock signal and its interpretation.

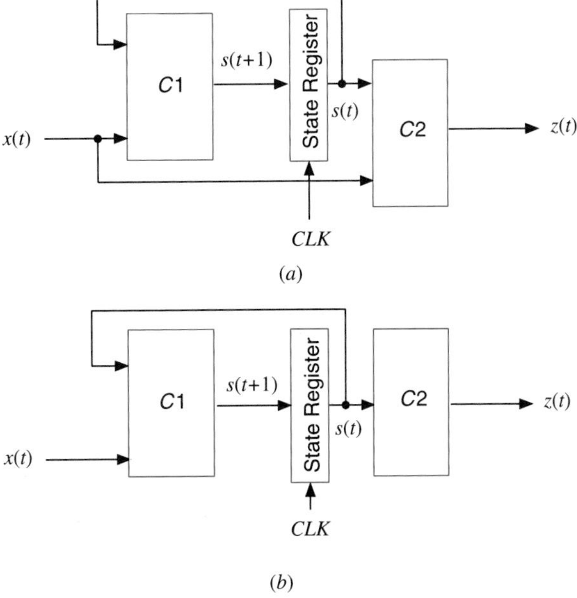

Figure 8.2 Canonical implementations. (*a*) Mealy machine. (*b*) Moore machine.

8.2 HIGH-LEVEL AND BINARY IMPLEMENTATIONS

The high-level description of the canonical form of a sequential system uses multivalued variables for input, state, and output. This compact and manageable description is used whenever the particular binary representation is not significant.

On the other hand, as we have discussed for combinational networks, the physical implementation of digital systems uses binary variables. Consequently, a high-level description must be converted into a binary description by introducing codes for the input, output, and state variables, so that the variables x, s, and z are represented by the bit-vectors $\underline{x}$, $\underline{s}$, and $\underline{z}$, respectively.

The canonical form of a binary system is illustrated in Figure 8.3. In this implementation, the state register consists of k **binary cells**, wherein k is the number of state variables. Each binary cell has a binary input (the next state), a binary output (the present state), and a

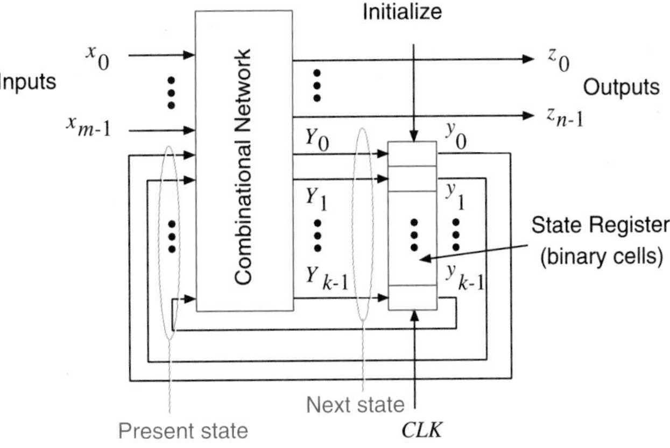

Figure 8.3 Canonical implementation with binary variables.

synchronizing input (the clock). As depicted in the figure, it is customary to denote the present-state vector (*PS*) by $\underline{y}$ and the next-state vector (*NS*) by $\underline{Y}$.

EXAMPLE 8.1

Figure 8.4 depicts the (binary) canonical form of a sequential system having the following description:

Input: $\underline{x}(t) = (x_1, x_0),\ \ x_i \in \{0, 1\}$
Output: $z(t) \in \{0, 1\}$
State: $\underline{y}(t) = (y_3, y_2, y_1, y_0),\ \ y_i(t) \in \{0, 1\}$
Initial state: $\underline{y}(0) = (0, 0, 0, 0)$

Function: The transition and output functions are

$$\begin{aligned} Y_3 &= y_2x_1'x_0 \\ Y_2 &= (y_1 + y_2)x_0' + y_3x_1 \\ Y_1 &= (y_0 + y_3)x_1'x_0 + (y_0 + y_1)x_1 \\ Y_0 &= (y_0 + y_3)x_0'y_1x_1'x_0 + y_2x_1 \end{aligned}$$

$$z = y_3 + y_2 + y_1 + y_0$$

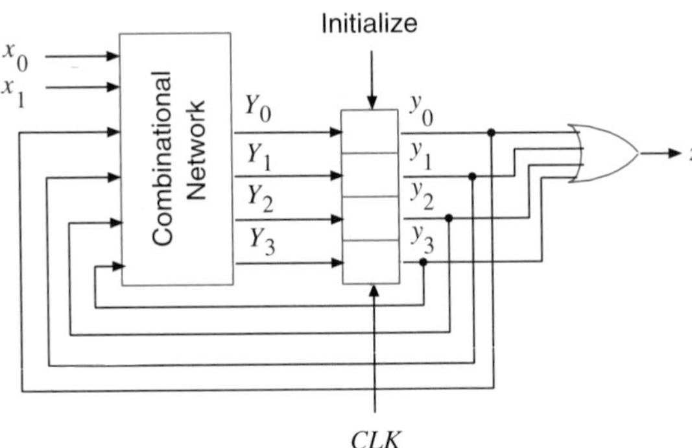

Figure 8.4 Canonical network for Example 8.1. ■

8.3 GATED LATCH AND D FLIP-FLOP

So far we have considered the ideal case in which the clock pulse has zero width, and the binary cells change state instantaneously. In practice, the clock pulse has a finite width and the cell has some timing characteristics that have to be taken into account for a satisfactory operation of a system. These characteristics also determine the speed of the resulting network.

The basic characteristics of the clock signal with respect to network timing, depicted in Figure 8.5, are

- the **clock period** T (or the **clock frequency** $f = 1/T$); and
- the **(clock) pulse width** t_w.

Let us now consider the characteristics required from binary cells so that they perform adequately in a synchronous sequential network. The most basic binary cell is called a (controlled) **gated latch;** it has one binary input signal D (for data), one binary output signal Q, and an enable input E, as shown in Figure 8.6*a*. The output of the cell corresponds to the state; this output follows the value of the input when $E = 1$ and does not change (is

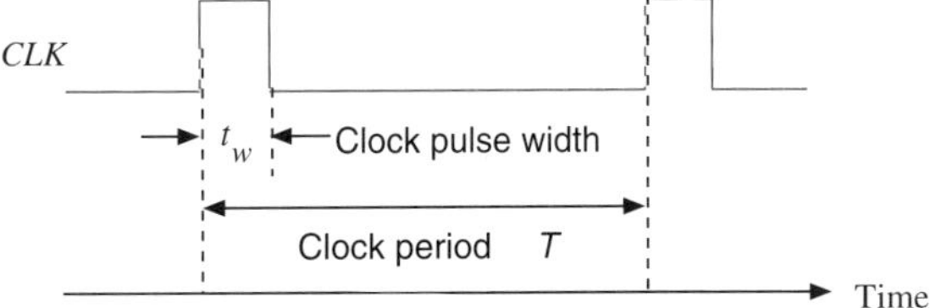

Figure 8.5 Clock pulse and clock period.

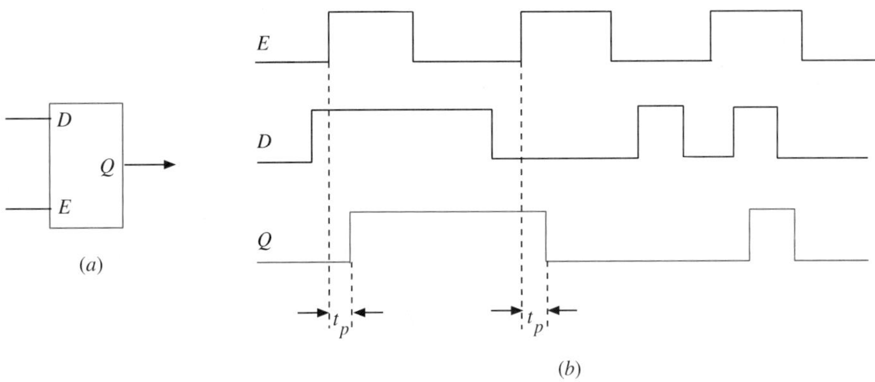

Figure 8.6 (*a*) Gated latch. (*b*) Timing behavior.

latched) when $E = 0$, so the cell is called **level-sensitive** (in contrast to the edge-sensitive cell discussed later)

The change of value of the output signal has a **propagation delay** t_p with respect to a change in the enable signal (see Figure 8.6*b*). That is,

$$Q(t + t_p) = D(t) \cdot E(t) + Q(t) \cdot E'(t)$$

Figures 8.7 and 8.8 show two alternative implementations of a gated latch. These implementations consist of a gate network that includes a loop that is responsible for storing the state. In the first implementation, the loop consists of two NOR gates. The operation, illustrated by the timing diagram in Figure 8.7*b* (wherein the arrows indicate "cause-effect" relations among signal changes), is as follows:

- When $E = 1$, signals b and d correspond to the value of D and D', respectively. Two situations can occur:

  - if $b = 1$ and $d = 0$, then $c = 0$ and $Q = 1$; and
  - if $b = 0$ and $d = 1$, then $Q = 0$ and $c = 1$.

  Consequently, in both cases $Q = D$.

- When $E = 0$, $b = d = 0$ and the loop is used to store the value of Q.

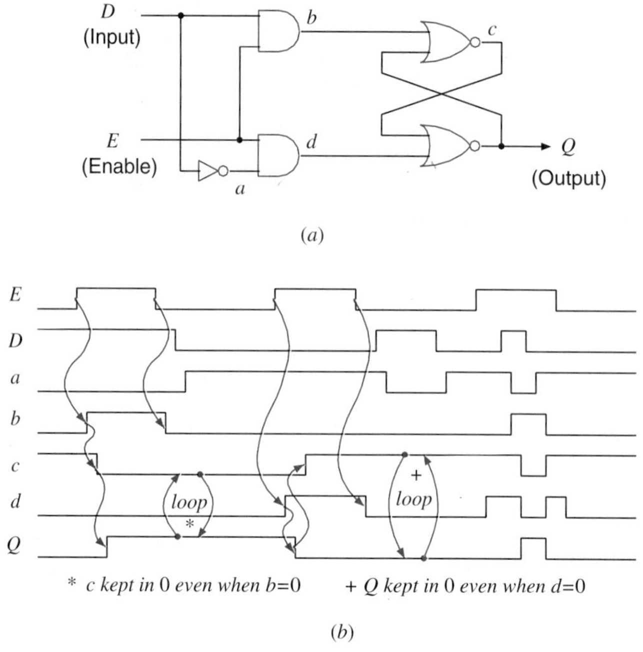

Figure 8.7 (*a*) Implementation of gated latch with NOR gates. (*b*) Timing diagram.

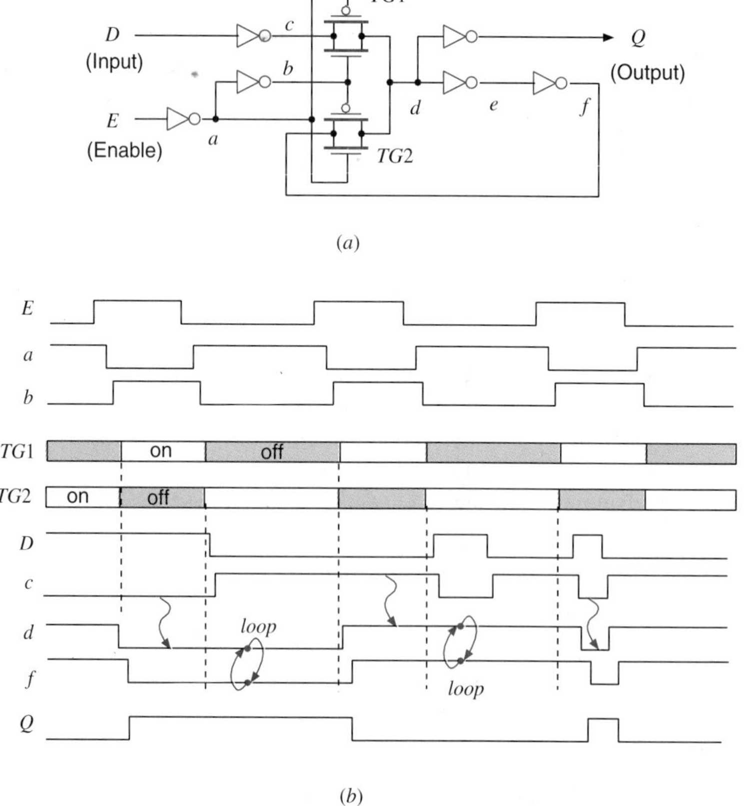

Figure 8.8 (*a*) Implementation of gated latch with transmission gates. (*b*) Timing diagram.

In the second implementation (see Figure 8.8), the operation is as follows:

- When $E = 1$, the upper transmission gate corresponds to a closed switch and the lower transmission gate corresponds to an open switch. Therefore, the value of the output Q is equal to the input D.
- When $E = 0$, the situation reverses so that the input is disconnected from the output and the two-inverter loop maintains the state.

In both implementations, the (noninverting) loop is the basis for the operation of the network as a sequential system.[1] In the second implementation, the inverters in the loop are needed to compensate for the voltage drop across the transmission gate.

Limitations of Gated Latch for Use in a Synchronous Network

The gated latch could be used in a synchronous sequential system by connecting the clock to input E, but this might not produce the desired behavior. To show this, consider the sequential system with state description

$$s(t + 1) = s(t) \oplus x(t)$$

whose implementation is depicted in Figure 8.9*a*.

If the clock pulse is narrow (smaller than the delay of the gated latch), the system operates correctly as indicated in the timing diagram depicted in Figure 8.9*b*. The state changes at

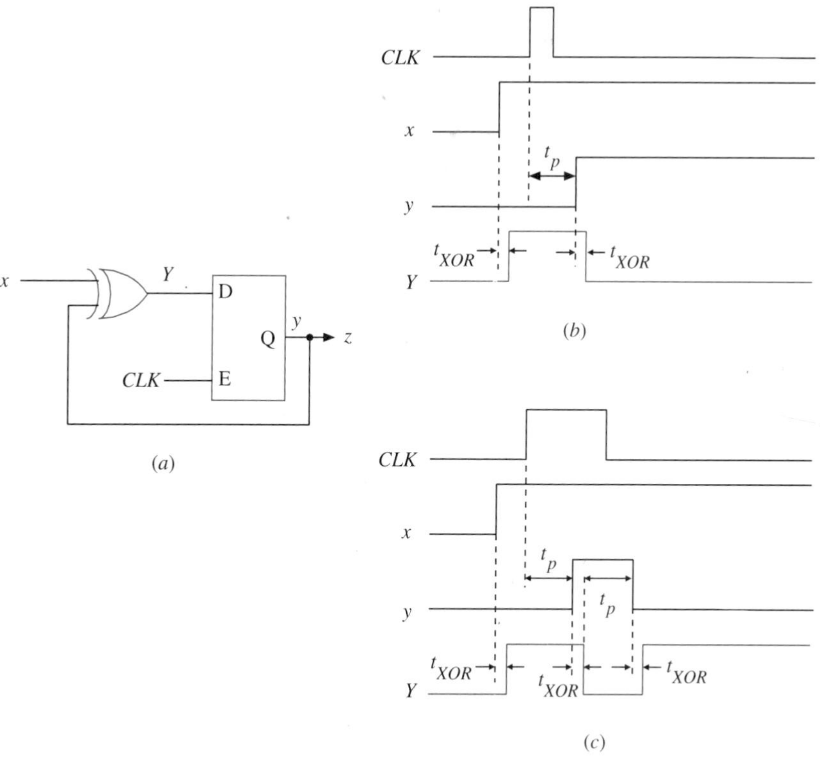

Figure 8.9 (*a*) Sequential network. (*b*) Correct timing behavior. (*c*) Incorrect timing behavior.

---

[1] An inverting loop produces an oscillator, in which the output changes periodically from 0 to 1 to 0, the period depending on the delay in the loop.

most once per clock pulse, and the system behavior corresponds to the state transition function described previously. On the other hand, if the width of the clock pulse is larger than the gated-latch delay, then the operation is as indicated in Figure 8.9*c*. The new value of the state is fed back to the gated-latch input while the clock signal is still 1, which produces another change of state. The behavior of the system **does not** correspond to the expected state transition function. If the clock pulse is even wider, then more than two state changes could occur. This behavior of multiple state changes per clock pulse is called a **race condition**, and must be avoided for correct operation.

EXAMPLE 8.2

If the minimum propagation delay of the XOR gate in Figure 8.9*a* is 1.5 ns and the minimum propagation delay of the latch is 1.2 ns, then the maximum width of the clock pulse to avoid races is 2.7 ns. ■

Consequently, the correct behavior of a synchronous sequential network depends on the relative values of the pulse width and the gated-latch delay. The desired values of these parameters conflict: small gated-latch delays are desirable for fast network operation, but very narrow clock pulses are not easily realizable. Moreover, the gated-latch delay and the clock width might have variations during the operation of the system. Thus, a gated latch as the binary cell of a synchronous sequential system does not lead to reliable operation, therefore other type of cells must be used.

Edge-triggered Cell

The solution to the above mentioned problem consists in using an **edge-triggered cell** (also called **edge-sensitive cell,** in contrast to the level-sensitive cell considered before). In this new cell, loading of a new state is caused (triggered) by the **transition (edge)** of the clock signal instead of by its value (level). As shown in Figure 8.10, two types of edge-triggered cells exist, depending on which edge produces the state change:

- **Leading-edge-triggered cell** (also called **positive-edge triggered).** The triggering transition is the first (rising) edge of the pulse, when the clock changes from 0 to 1.
- **Trailing-edge-triggered cell** (also called **negative-edge triggered).** The transition occurs at the second (falling) edge, when the clock changes from 1 to 0.

Because there is only one edge of each type per clock pulse, this type of operation assures that at most one change of state occurs per clock cycle. Figure 8.10 illustrates the convention used for designating both types of edge-triggered cells, and the timing diagram for the network depicted in Figure 8.9 when an edge-triggered cell is used.

Master-slave Implementation

Edge-triggered cells can be implemented with a **master-slave** structure, which consists of two gated latches as shown in Figure 8.11*a*.[2] The clock signal is connected to input E of the first latch (called the **master**) so that its output follows the input to the cell while the clock signal has value 1 and does not change when the clock has value 0. In contrast, the complement of the clock is connected to input E of the second latch (called the **slave**) so that its output follows its input (which corresponds to the output of the master cell)

[2]Some TTL-oriented texts make a distinction among a master-slave cell and an edge-triggered cell. However, as the behavior is the same and the master-slave implementation is used in CMOS, we do not make such a distinction.

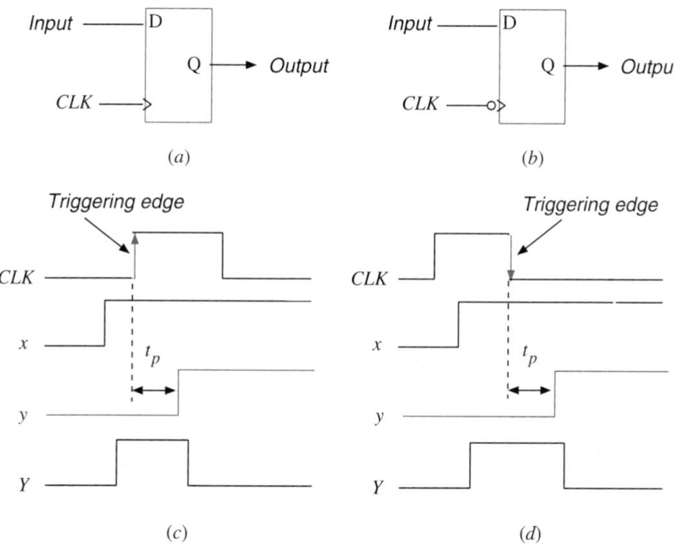

Figure 8.10 Edge-triggered cell. (*a*) Leading-edge-triggered cell. (*b*) Trailing-edge-triggered cell. (*c*) Leading-edge-triggered cell in network of Figure 8.9. (*d*) Trailing-edge-triggered cell in network of Figure 8.9.

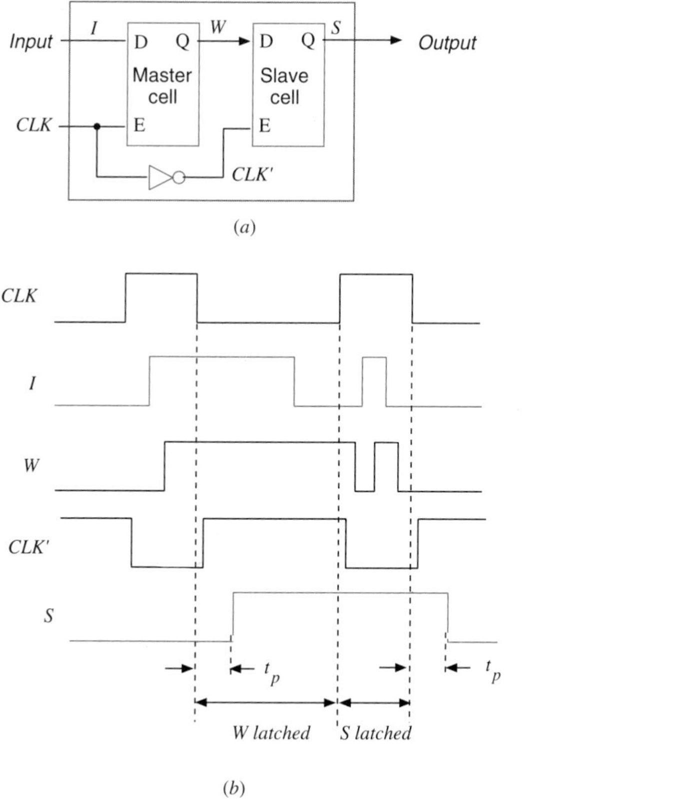

Figure 8.11 (*a*) Master-slave implementation of trailing-edge-triggered cell. (*b*) Master-slave state change process.

while the clock has value 0 and does not change when the clock has value 1. As shown in Figure 8.11*b*, the input to the master-slave cell is loaded into the master cell during the clock pulse and is transferred to the slave cell after the clock pulse has terminated. This assures that the change of state (output S) occurs when the clock changes from 1 to 0, so the cell is trailing-edge triggered.

As a follow-on to the discussion above, a leading-edge-triggered cell is obtained by connecting the complemented clock signal to the master cell and the uncomplemented clock signal to the slave cell.

D Flip-flop

The edge-triggered binary cell just presented is called a D **flip-flop**. As shown in Figure 8.12, the D flip-flop has one input called D (data) and two outputs corresponding to the state (Q) and its complement (Q'). The complement output is optional. When $Q = 1$ the flip-flop is said to be in the "one" or "set" state; similarly, when $Q = 0$ it is in the "zero" or "reset" state. An additional input, called CLK, receives the clock signal.

The transition function of a D flip-flop is

$PS = Q(t)$	$D(t)$	
	0	1
0	0	1
1	0	1
	$NS = Q(t+1)$	

That is, the next state $Q(t+1)$ corresponds to the value of the input $D(t)$. Thus, the D flip-flop is called a "delay" flip-flop. Equivalently, the transition function can be described by the **characteristic expression**

$$Q(t+1) = D(t)$$

or by the state diagram shown in Figure 8.12. Note that the binary cells of the state register in the canonical implementation (see Figure 8.3) precisely correspond to D flip-flops.

A D flip-flop may also have "asynchronous" inputs, usually labeled PR (preset) and CLR (clear), which are used to force the flip-flop into the 1 or 0 state, respectively, independent of other inputs and the clock. Preset and clear are used to initialize flip-flops at the beginning of the system operation. Because we are concerned with synchronous sequential systems, we will not include preset and clear inputs in logic diagrams and textual specifications.

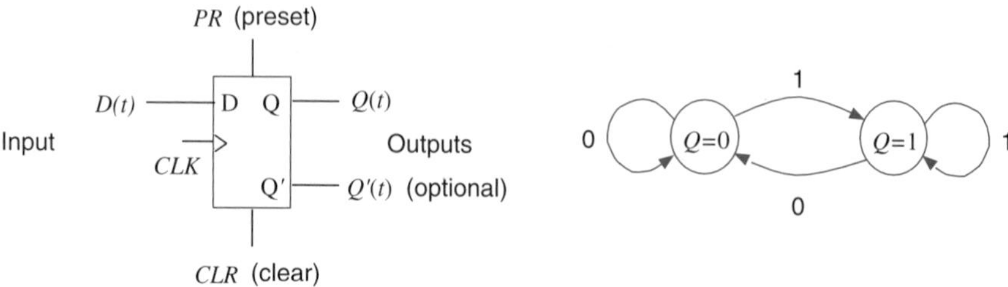

Figure 8.12 D flip-flop and its state diagram.

Timing Parameters of a Binary Cell

We now discuss some basic timing parameters of binary cells. More specifically, we consider a leading-edge-triggered cell in which the change of state is caused by the leading edge of the clock pulse. With respect to this synchronizing event, the following timing parameters are required for correct operation (see Figure 8.13):

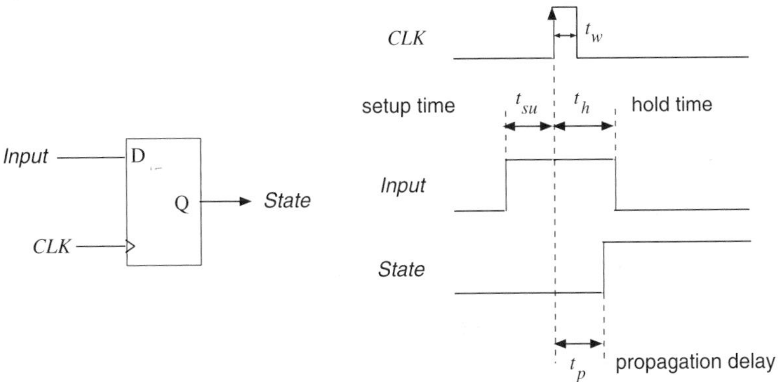

Figure 8.13 Time behavior of cell.

Set up time (t_{su}) is the minimum time interval from the stabilization of the cell input to the triggering edge of the clock.

Hold time (t_h) is the minimum time interval from the triggering edge of the clock to a subsequent change in the input to the cell.

Pulse width (t_w) is the minimum width of the synchronizing clock pulse.

Propagation delay (t_p) is the time interval from the triggering edge of the clock to the stabilization of the new state (cell output). When it is appropriate, we distinguish low-to-high (t_{pLH}) and high-to-low (t_{pHL}) propagation delays. As for gates, the propagation delay depends on the load connected to the cell output.

The characteristics of a CMOS D flip-flop (of the same family as the gates of Chapter 3) are shown in Table 8.1. In addition to the timing characteristics, the input load factor and the size of the module are given; these are defined in the same manner as for gates.

Table 8.1 Characteristics of a CMOS D flip-flop

Delays					Input load factor	Size
t_{pLH} (ns)	t_{pHL} (ns)	t_{su} (ns)	t_h (ns)	t_w (ns)	(standard loads)	(equivalent gates)
$0.49 + 0.038L$	$0.54 + 0.019L$	0.30	0.14	0.2	1	6

L: output load of the flip-flop. This flip-flop has only the uncomplemented output.

8.4 TIMING CHARACTERISTICS OF SEQUENTIAL NETWORKS

We now determine the timing parameters of a sequential network in the canonical implementation, in terms of the timing parameters of the binary cells and the delays of the associated combinational networks. For simplicity, we consider a Moore-type sequential network; the extension to a Mealy-type network is straightforward.

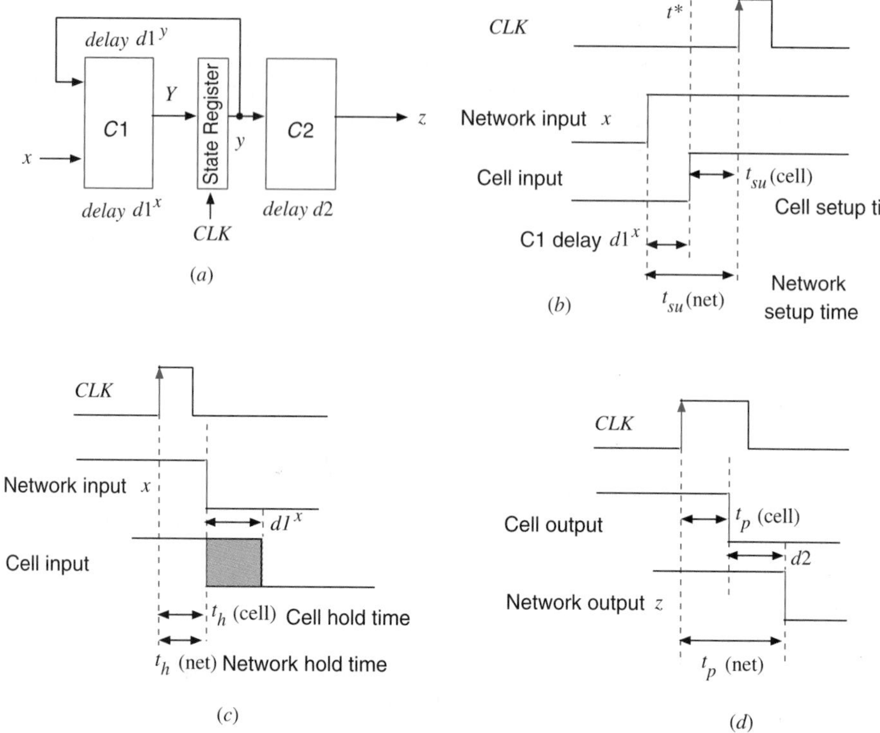

Figure 8.14 Timing factors in sequential networks. (*a*) The network. (*b*) Network setup time. (*c*) Network hold time. (*d*) Network propagation delay.

Figure 8.14 depicts a canonical network in which $d1^x$ and $d1^y$ are the delays of combinational network $C1$ with respect to input x and to the input from the state register y, respectively. Moreover, $d2$ is the delay of the output network $C2$. Then, the following relationships hold:

Network setup time. As illustrated in Figure 8.14*b*, the cell setup time restriction requires that the input to the cell be stable at t^*. Since the cell input corresponds to the output from network $C1$, which has a delay $d1^x$, the input x to the network must be stable that much earlier. That is,

$$t_{su}^x(net) = d1^x + t_{su}(cell)$$

Network hold time. Because the network input x changes a time interval $d1^x$ before the cell input Y, it would seem that the network hold time should be $t_h(cell) - d1^x$. However, $d1^x$ is the maximum delay between the stabilization of x and that of Y, but Y might begin to change earlier, as shown by the shaded interval in Figure 8.14*c*. Usually the minimum time for which the output of $C1$ remains stable after input x changes is not known, so we assume that this time is 0; therefore, the hold time of the network is conservatively made equal to the hold time of the cell. That is,

$$t_h(net) = t_h(cell)$$

Network propagation delay. Because network $C2$ has delay $d2$, the network output (see Figure 8.14*d*) stabilizes $d2$ time units after a change in the output of the cell. That is,

$$t_p(net) = t_p(cell) + d2$$

Maximum clock frequency. Another important timing parameter of a sequential system is the minimum clock period required for correct operation (or its inverse, the maximum clock frequency) because it determines the speed at which the system operates. The determination of this minimum period requires considering all the delays that occur in a clock cycle, as shown by the timing diagram in Figure 8.15*a*. In addition to those discussed earlier, these delays include:

- t_{in}, which is the time between the triggering edge of the clock and the stabilization of input x; and
- t_{out}, which is the time between the stabilization of output z and the next clock triggering edge.

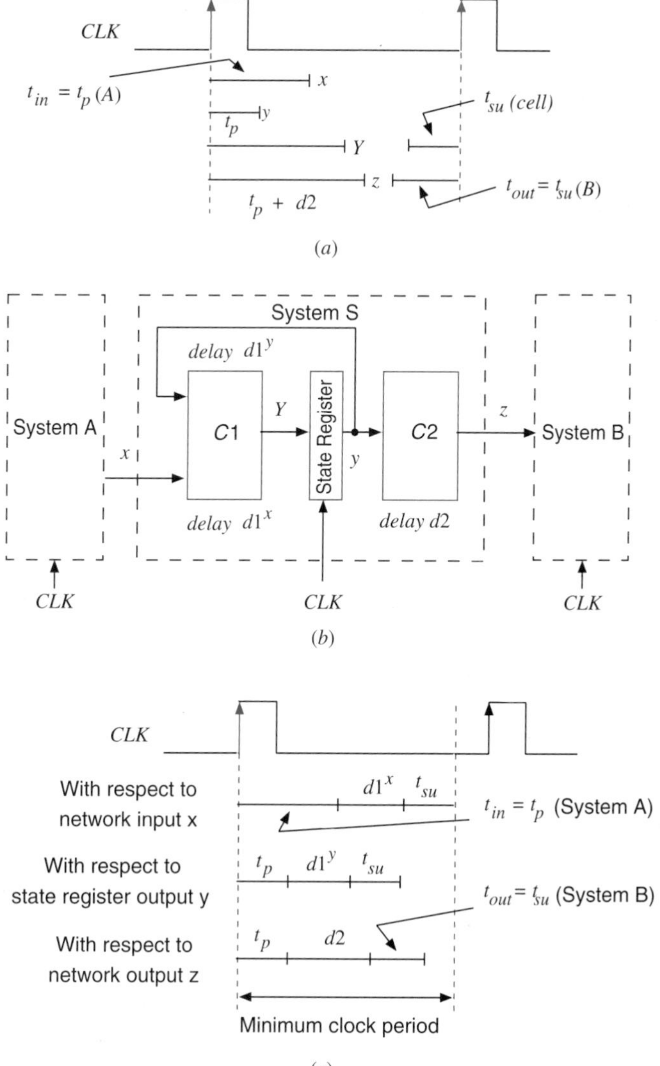

Figure 8.15 Maximum clock frequency. (*a*) Clock period and signal delays. (*b*) The network. (*c*) Minimum clock period.

In a completely synchronous system, input x is produced by the output of another sequential module (see Figure 8.15*b*), so that t_{in} is the propagation delay of the module producing x (i.e., $t_{in} = t_p(A)$). Similarly, output z is the input to another sequential module, so that $t_{out} = t_{su}(B)$ is the setup time of this module.

In terms of the parameters just defined, the minimum clock period $T_{min} = 1/f_{max}$ is (see Figure 8.15*c*)

$$T_{min} = \max[(t_{in} + t^x_{su}(net)), (t_p(cell) + t^y_{su}(net)), (t_p(net) + t_{out})]$$

The derivation of this expression assumes that $t_h(cell) \leq t_p(cell)$.

Substituting, we get the following expression in terms of the characteristics of the cell

$$\begin{aligned} T_{min} = \max[&(t_{in} + d1^x + t_{su}(cell)), \\ &(t_p(cell) + d1^y + t_{su}(cell)), \\ &(t_p(cell) + d2 + t_{out})] \end{aligned}$$

EXAMPLE 8.3

Determine the maximum clock frequency for a Moore canonical network in which the propagation delays of the input and output networks are $d1^x = d1^y = 2.5$ ns and $d2 = 3$ ns, respectively. The setup time of the register cells is $t_{su} = 0.3$ ns, and the propagation delay is $t_p = 1$ ns. The network input stabilizes no later than $t_{in} = 2$ ns after the triggering edge of the clock; the output needs to be stable for $t_{out} = 3$ ns before the next triggering edge.

The minimum clock period is

$$T_{min} = \max[(2 + 2.5 + 0.3),\ (1 + 2.5 + 0.3),\ (1 + 3 + 3)] = 7 \text{ ns}$$

and the maximum frequency is

$$f_{max} = \frac{1}{7 \times 10^{-9}} \approx 140 \text{ MHz}$$

■

Clock skew. For synchronous operation, all cells of a network should receive the triggering edge of the clock at the same time. As illustrated in Figure 8.16*b*, incorrect operation occurs if one cell receives the edge, changes state, and the change propagates to the input of another cell before that cell receives its triggering edge.

On the other hand, due to the delay produced by the lines that carry the clock and the buffers required to restore the clock shape, it is not possible to ensure that the triggering edge is received exactly at the same time by all cells. The time difference between the instants that the triggering edge is received by two cells is called the **clock skew** between these two cells. As indicated, clock skew between any pair of cells has to be limited for correct operation. This problem is aggravated for larger networks, in which the distance between cells is larger, and for high-speed systems, in which the propagation of signals is fast. Special clock distribution networks are used to limit clock skew.

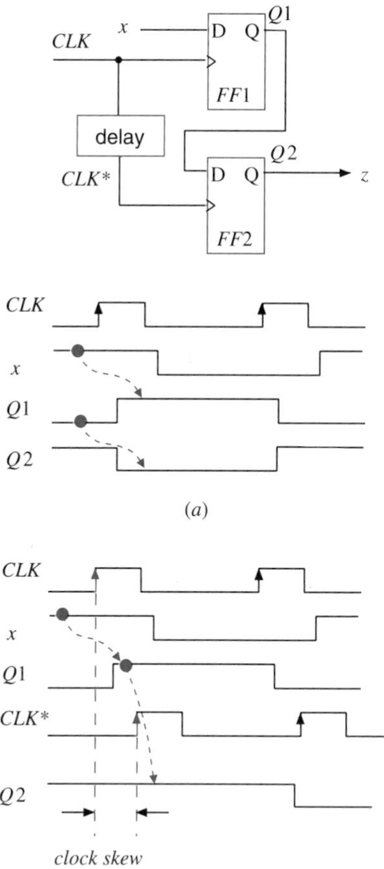

Figure 8.16 (*a*) Network behavior without clock skew. (*b*) Network behavior with inadmissible clock skew.

8.5 ANALYSIS OF CANONICAL SEQUENTIAL NETWORKS

Let us now focus our attention on the analysis of canonical sequential networks, that is, in determining a specification of the system implemented by a network. In this case, the functional analysis consists of the following steps:

1. Analyze the combinational network to determine the transition and output functions, using the procedures described in Chapter 4.
2. Determine a suitable high-level specification of the transition and output functions.
3. If desired (or required), determine a description of the time behavior of the system.

In addition, the analysis also produces other characteristics of the network, such as the input load factors and size (as discussed in Chapter 4), and the timing characteristics, as described in the previous section.

EXAMPLE 8.4

Analyze the synchronous sequential network depicted in Figure 8.17.

This network consists of a two-cell state register and combinational logic. Representing the present state by the vector (y_1, y_0) and the next state by the vector (Y_1, Y_0), the analysis of the combinational network produces the following expressions for the state-transition and output functions:

State transition $Y_0 = x'y_1' + xy_0'$

$Y_1 = xy_0'y_1' + x'y_0'y_1 + xy_0y_1 + x'y_0y_1'$

Output $z_0 = y_1'$

$z_1 = y_0$

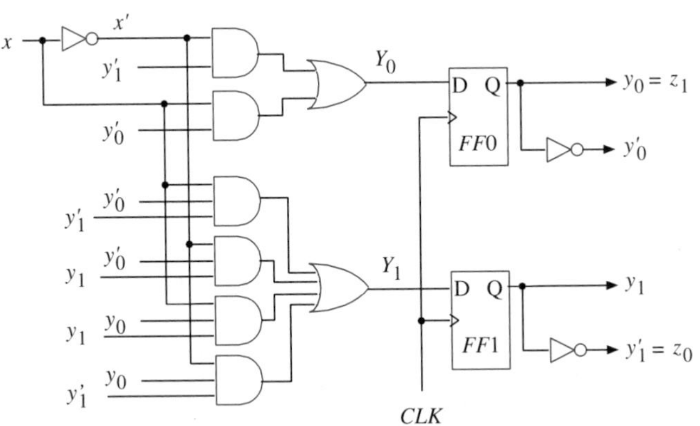

Figure 8.17 Sequential network in Example 8.4.

These functions are also described by the following table, obtained by evaluating the expressions for all combinations of y_1, y_0, and x:

PS	Input		
y_1y_0	$x = 0$	$x = 1$	
00	01	11	01
01	11	00	11
10	10	01	00
11	00	10	10
	Y_1Y_0		z_1z_0
	NS		Output

To obtain a high-level description, let us define the following codes:

x	x
0	*a*
1	*b*

z_1z_0	z
00	*c*
01	*d*
10	*e*
11	*f*

$y_1\,y_0$	s
00	S_0
01	S_1
10	S_2
11	S_3

Using these codes, and assuming that the initial state is S_2, the high-level specification of the system is

Input:	$x(t) \in \{a, b\}$
Output:	$z(t) \in \{c, d, e, f\}$
State:	$s(t) \in \{S_0, S_1, S_2, S_3\}$
Initial state:	$s(0) = S_2$

Functions: The state transition and output functions are

PS	$x(t) = a$	$x(t) = b$	
S_0	S_1	S_3	d
S_1	S_3	S_0	f
S_2	S_2	S_1	c
S_3	S_0	S_2	e
	NS		$z(t)$

The corresponding state diagram and a sequence of input-output pairs are shown in Figure 8.18.

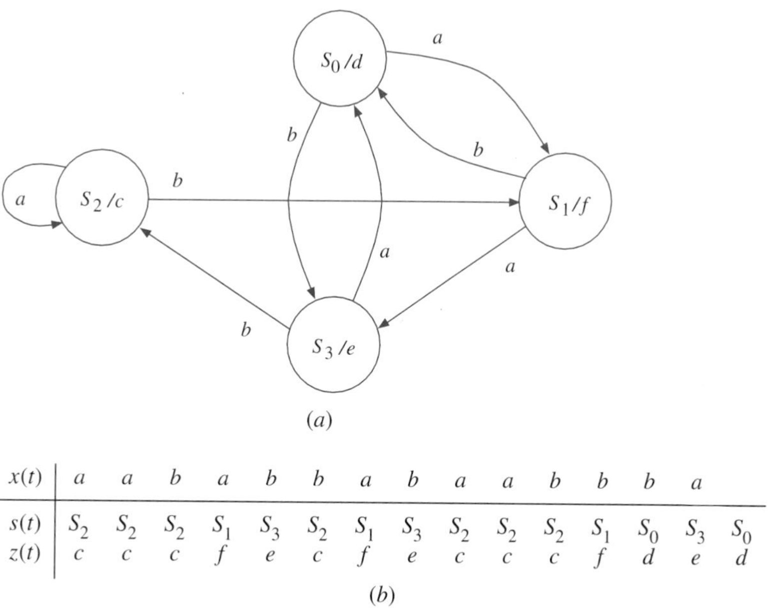

$x(t)$	a	a	b	a	b	b	a	b	a	a	b	b	b	a	
$s(t)$	S_2	S_2	S_2	S_1	S_3	S_2	S_1	S_3	S_2	S_2	S_2	S_1	S_0	S_3	S_0
$z(t)$	c	c	c	f	e	c	f	e	c	c	c	f	d	e	d

(b)

Figure 8.18 (*a*) State diagram for sequential network. (*b*) A sequence of input-output pairs.

For the gates and D flip-flops of the family described in Table 4.1 and Table 8.1, the following characteristics are obtained. We consider the case when x changes from 0 to 1 and z_0 changes from 1 to 0; the other cases are calculated in a similar manner. The critical path for the setup time is through gates NOT, AND3, and OR4.

$$\begin{aligned}
&\text{Input load factors:} & I_x &= 4\\
&\text{Setup time:} & t_{su}(net) &= t_{pHL}(\text{NOT}) + t_{pHL}(\text{AND3}) + t_{pHL}(\text{OR4}) + t_{su}\\
& & &= (0.05 + 0.017 \times 3) + (0.18 + 0.018) + (0.45 + 0.025) + 0.3\\
& & &= 1.07 \text{ ns}\\
&\text{Hold time:} & t_h(net) &= 0.14 \text{ ns}\\
&\text{Propagation delay:} & t_p(z_0) &= t_{pLH}(\text{FF}) + t_{pHL}(\text{NOT})\\
& & &= (0.49 + 0.038 \times 3) + (0.05 + 0.017 \times (L + 3))\\
& & &= 0.70 + 0.017L \text{ ns}\\
& & &\quad (\text{load of NOT is } L + 3, \text{ load of flip-flop is } 3)\\
&\text{Size:} & &= 6 \times 2 + 2 + 3 + 2 \times 6 + 3 \times 1\\
& & &= 32 \text{ equivalent gates}
\end{aligned}$$

■

8.6 DESIGN OF CANONICAL SEQUENTIAL NETWORKS

The design of a canonical sequential network, which requires the state description of the system, consists of the following steps:

1. Transform the transition and output functions into a form suitable for implementation. For example, if these functions are specified by means of a state diagram, transform them into high-level expressions or state tables.
2. Specify a state register to encode the required number of states.
3. Design the required combinational network. If the design is done at a high level, the high-level descriptions can be used directly. On the other hand, if the design is done at the binary level, then it is necessary to select codes for the input, output, and state, and transform the high-level description of the functions into descriptions by switching functions (tables, expressions, or maps). In either case, the design of the combinational network uses the methods described in Chapters 5 and 6.

This procedure is illustrated in the following example.

EXAMPLE 8.5

Design a binary-level sequential network to implement a system having the following specification:

Input:	$x(t) \in \{a, b, c\}$
Output:	$z(t) \in \{0, 1\}$
State:	$s(t) \in \{A, B, C, D\}$
Initial state:	$s(0) = A$

Functions: The state transition and output functions are

PS	Input		
	$x = a$	$x = b$	$x = c$
A	*C*,0	*B*,1	*B*,0
B	*D*,0	*B*,0	*A*,1
C	*A*,0	*D*,1	*D*,0
D	*B*,0	*A*,0	*D*,1
		NS, *z*	

In this case, the system is specified by a state table, so that step 1 in the foregoing procedure is not required. Because there are four states, we need a state register with two cells. Let us select the following codes for the input and the state (the output is already coded):

Input code

x	x_1	x_0
a	0	1
b	1	0
c	1	1

State code

s	y_1	y_0
A	0	0
B	1	0
C	0	1
D	1	1

With these codings, the corresponding state-transition and output functions are

PS	x_1x_0		
y_1y_0	01	10	11
00	01,0	10,1	10,0
10	11,0	10,0	00,1
01	00,0	11,1	11,0
11	10,0	00,0	11,1
		Y_1Y_0, z *NS*, output	

Note that the combination $x_1x_0 = 00$ never appears, so it is considered a "don't care" case. From this table, we obtain the Karnaugh maps shown below.

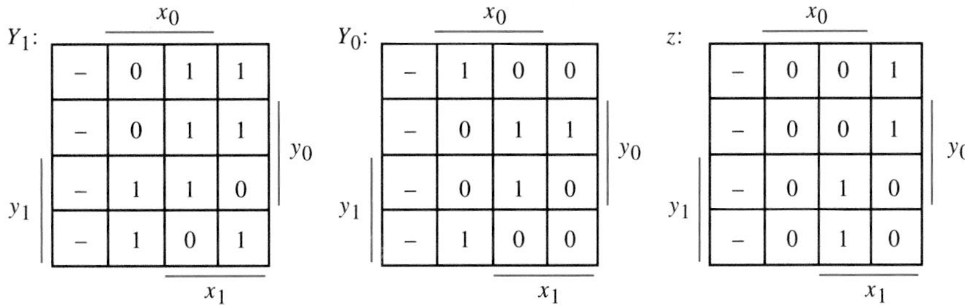

From these maps, we obtain the following sum of products expressions:

$$Y_1 = y_1'x_1 + y_1x_1' + y_0'x_0' + y_0x_1x_0$$
$$Y_0 = y_0'x_1' + y_1'y_0x_1 + y_0x_1x_0$$
$$z = y_1'x_0' + y_1x_1x_0$$

The sequential network, consisting of a two-level gate network and a two-cell state register, is shown in Figure 8.19.

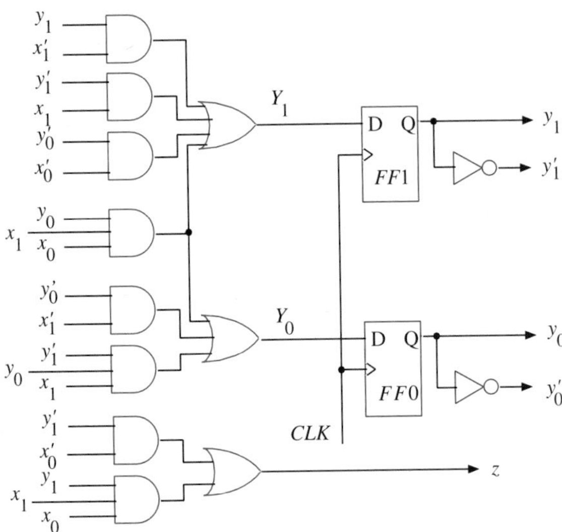

Figure 8.19 Sequential network in Example 8.5. ■

8.7 OTHER FLIP-FLOP MODULES: SR, JK, AND T

We now discuss the logical definitions of three other flip-flops. Implementations of these flip-flops are provided in some families, and can be used instead of D flip-flops to reduce the complexity of the combinational part of a sequential network.

SR (Set-reset) Flip-flop

The set-reset (SR) flip-flop has two inputs, as indicated in Figure 8.20. Its transition function is

$PS = Q(t)$	$S(t)R(t)$			
	00	01	10	11
0	0	0	1	–
1	1	0	1	–
	$NS = Q(t+1)$			

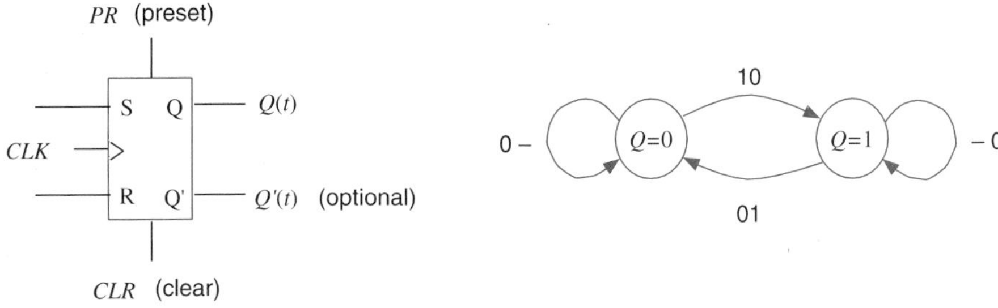

Figure 8.20 SR flip-flop and its state diagram.

In words, the flip-flop is **set** ($Q(t+1) = 1$) if $S(t) = 1$ and $R(t) = 0$; it is **reset** ($Q(t+1) = 0$) if $S(t) = 0$ and $R(t) = 1$; it **does not change** state when $S(t) = 0$ and $R(t) = 0$; and the combination $S(t) = 1, R(t) = 1$ is **not allowed**. The corresponding characteristic expression, obtained from a K-map, is

$$Q(t+1) = Q(t)R'(t) + S(t)$$

with the restriction that

$$R(t) \cdot S(t) = 0$$

The corresponding state diagram is also shown in Figure 8.20.

JK Flip-flop

The JK flip-flop, shown in Figure 8.21, is a variation of the set-reset flip-flop. The transition function is

$PS = Q(t)$	$J(t)K(t)$			
	00	01	10	11
0	0	0	1	1
1	1	0	1	0
	$NS = Q(t+1)$			

The operation is the same as for the SR flip-flop, except that the combination $J(t) = 1$, $K(t) = 1$ is allowed and produces a change of state. The characteristic expression is

$$Q(t+1) = Q(t)K'(t) + Q'(t)J(t)$$

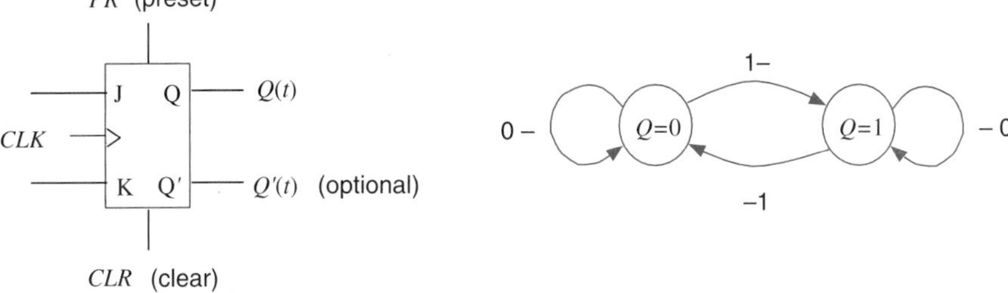

Figure 8.21 JK flip-flop and its state diagram.

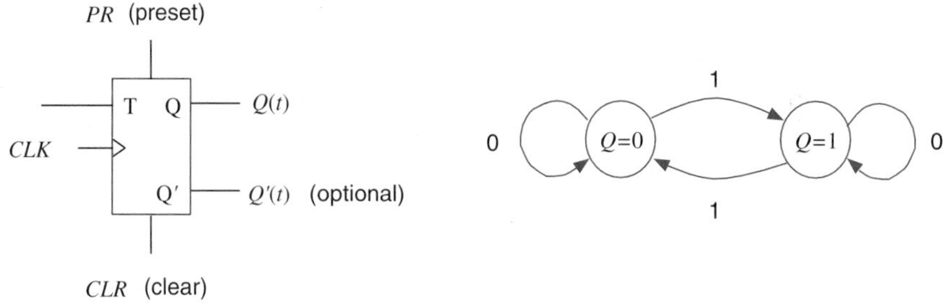

Figure 8.22 T flip-flop and its state diagram.

T (Toggle) Flip-flop

The T flip-flop, shown in Figure 8.22, has only one input called T. It remains in the same state if $T = 0$ and changes state if $T = 1$. The transition function is

$PS = Q(t)$	$T(t)$	
	0	1
0	0	1
1	1	0
	$NS = Q(t+1)$	

The characteristic expression is

$$Q(t+1) = Q(t) \oplus T(t)$$

One type of flip-flop can be implemented using another type and a combinational network. For example, Figure 8.23 illustrates the implementation of a T flip-flop using a JK flip-flop.

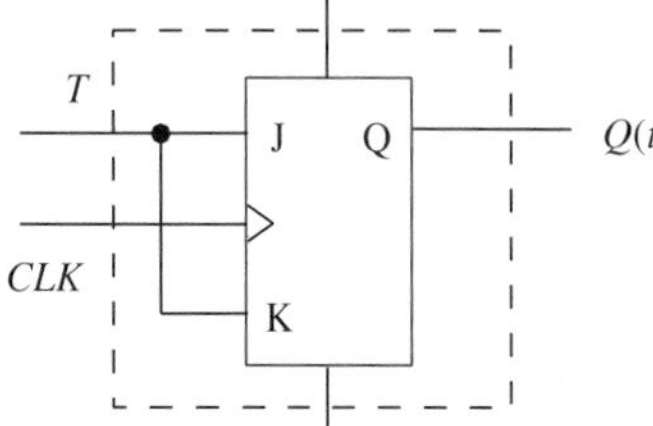

Figure 8.23 T flip-flop implemented with a JK flip-flop.

8.8 ANALYSIS OF NETWORKS WITH FLIP-FLOPS

The procedure to analyze synchronous sequential networks with flip-flops is a generalization of the procedure for canonical networks. The functional analysis is performed as follows:

1. Obtain the transition function of the network by the following two-step process:
   a. Determine the inputs to the flip-flops in terms of the present state and the inputs to the network. This requires the analysis of the corresponding combinational network.
   b. Use the transition function of the flip-flops to determine the next state.

This two-step process can be performed using tables, diagrams, or expressions.

2. Obtain the output function by analyzing the corresponding combinational network.
3. Determine a suitable high-level specification of the transition and output functions.

In addition to the functional analysis, other characteristics such as timing and size might be required. The process to determine the timing characteristics is similar to that for the canonical implementation. For the size of the network, it is necessary to add the size of all gates and flip-flops. The characteristics of flip-flops of the same family as the gates described in Chapter 3 are given in Table 8.2. Note that this family does not include SR nor T flip-flops.

Table 8.2 Characteristics of a family of CMOS flip-flops

Flip-flop type	Delays					Input load factor	Size
	t_{pLH} (ns)	t_{pHL} (ns)	t_{su} (ns)	t_h (ns)	t_w (ns)	(standard loads)	(equivalent gates)
D	$0.49 + 0.038L$	$0.54 + 0.019L$	0.30	0.14	0.20	1	6
JK	$0.45 + 0.038L$	$0.47 + 0.022L$	0.41	0.23	0.20	1	8

L: output load of the flip-flop. These flip-flops have only uncomplemented outputs

EXAMPLE 8.6

Analyze the network given in Figure 8.24.

The network has two T flip-flops, so that the state variables are Q_A and Q_B. The expressions for the flip-flop inputs are

$$T_A = x_1 Q_B$$
$$T_B = x_0 Q_A$$

Let us use expressions for the description. Because the characteristic expression for T flip-flops is $Q(t+1) = Q(t) \oplus T(t)$, the transition function is represented by

$$Q_A(t+1) = Q_A(t) \oplus x_1 Q_B(t)$$
$$Q_B(t+1) = Q_B(t) \oplus x_0 Q_A(t)$$

and the output expression is

$$z(t) = x_1(t) Q'_B(t)$$

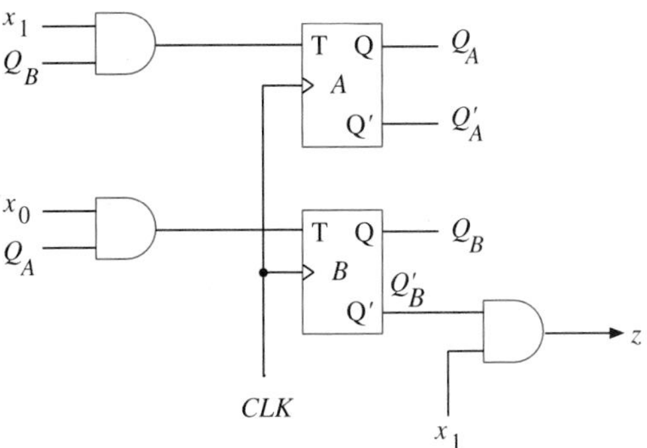

Figure 8.24 Sequential network for Example 8.6.

Using these expressions, we obtain the transition and output tables as follows:

PS	Input				Input			
Q_AQ_B	x_1x_0				x_1x_0			
	00	01	10	11	00	01	10	11
00	00	00	00	00	0	0	1	1
01	01	01	11	11	0	0	0	0
10	10	11	10	11	0	0	1	1
11	11	10	01	00	0	0	0	0
	Q_AQ_B				z			
	NS				Output			

Using the following state assignment and input code

Q_A	Q_B	s
0	0	S_0
0	1	S_1
1	0	S_2
1	1	S_3

x_1	x_0	x
0	0	a
0	1	b
1	0	c
1	1	d

the high-level specification of the system is

Input: $x(t) \in \{a, b, c, d\}$
Output: $z(t) \in \{0, 1\}$
State: $s(t) \in \{S_0, S_1, S_2, S_3\}$
Initial state: $s(0) = S_0$

Functions: The state transition and output functions are

PS	x				x			
	a	b	c	d	a	b	c	d
S_0	S_0	S_0	S_0	S_0	0	0	1	1
S_1	S_1	S_1	S_3	S_3	0	0	0	0
S_2	S_2	S_3	S_2	S_3	0	0	1	1
S_3	S_3	S_2	S_1	S_0	0	0	0	0
	NS				z			

■

EXAMPLE 8.7

Obtain a high-level description of the sequential network shown in Figure 8.25.

The network has two JK flip-flops (A and B) so that there are two state variables Q_A and Q_B. From an analysis of the combinational network, the flip-flop input functions are described by the following switching expressions:

$$J_A = x'Q_B' + xQ_A \qquad K_A = Q_B$$
$$J_B = Q_A \qquad K_B = x'Q_A'$$

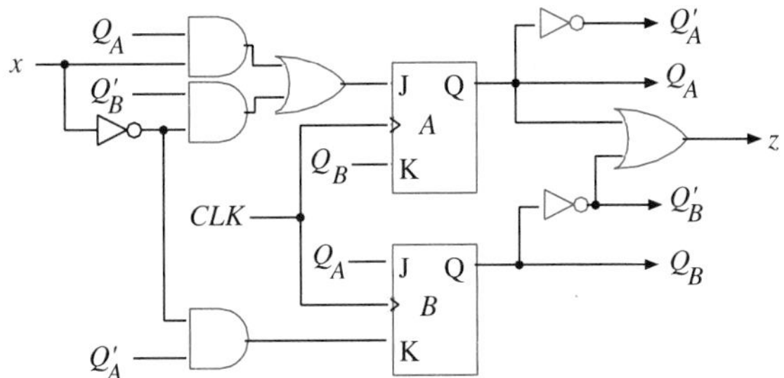

Figure 8.25 Sequential network for Example 8.7.

In addition, the output function is

$$z = Q_A + Q'_B$$

The transition function is obtained from the JK flip-flop characteristic expression:

$$\begin{aligned}
Q_A(t+1) &= Q_A K'_A + Q'_A J_A \\
&= Q_A Q'_B + Q'_A(x'Q'_B + xQ_A) \\
&= Q'_B(Q_A + x') \\
Q_B(t+1) &= Q_B K'_B + Q'_B J_B \\
&= Q_B(x + Q_A) + Q'_B Q_A \\
&= Q_B x + Q_A
\end{aligned}$$

resulting in the following table:

PS	*NS*		Output
	$x = 0$	$x = 1$	z
$Q_A Q_B$	$Q_A Q_B$	$Q_A Q_B$	
00	10	00	1
01	00	01	0
10	11	11	1
11	01	01	1

The output function, also shown in the table, is obtained directly as a function of the present state.

To obtain a high-level description, let us assign state symbols as follows:

Q_A	Q_B	S
0	0	S_0
0	1	S_1
1	0	S_2
1	1	S_3

The corresponding high-level specification is

Input:	$x(t) \in \{0, 1\}$
Output:	$z(t) \in \{0, 1\}$
State:	$s(t) \in \{S_0, S_1, S_2, S_3\}$
Initial state:	$s(0) = S_0$

Functions: The state-transition and output functions are

PS	Input $x = 0$	Input $x = 1$	
S_0	S_2	S_0	1
S_1	S_0	S_1	0
S_2	S_3	S_3	1
S_3	S_1	S_1	1
	NS		z

These functions are depicted in the state diagram shown in Figure 8.26.

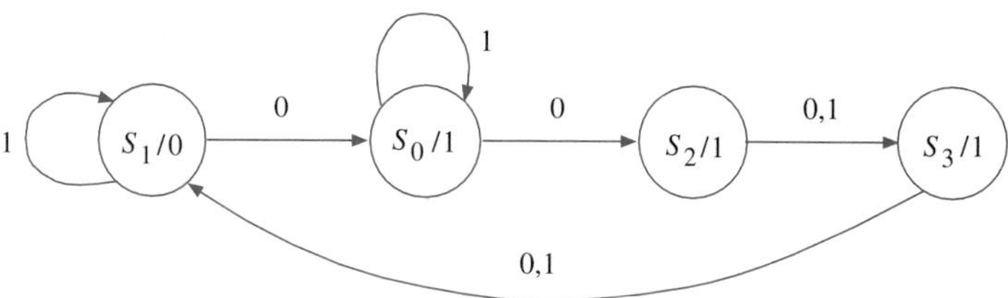

Figure 8.26 State diagram in Example 8.7.

Using the family of gates and flip-flops described in Table 4.1 and Table 8.2, the following characteristics are obtained. We consider the case in which x changes from 1 to 0 and z changes from 0 to 1; the analysis of the other cases is similar. The critical path for the setup time is through gates NOT, AND, and OR.

Input load factor: $I_x = 2$

Setup time:

$$\begin{aligned} t_{su}(net) &= t_{pLH}(\text{NOT}) + t_{pLH}(\text{AND}) + t_{pLH}(\text{OR}) + t_{su}(FF) \\ &= (0.02 + 0.038 \times 2) + (0.15 + 0.037) \\ &\quad +(0.12 + 0.037) + 0.41 \\ &= 0.85 \text{ ns} \end{aligned}$$

Hold time: $t_h(net) = 0.23$ ns

Propagation delay:

$$\begin{aligned} t_p(net) &= t_{pHL}(\text{FF}) + t_{pLH}(\text{NOT}) + t_{pLH}(\text{OR}) \\ &= (0.47 + 0.022 \times 2) + (0.02 + 0.038 \times 2) \\ &\quad +(0.12 + 0.037L) \\ &= 0.73 + 0.037L \text{ ns} \end{aligned}$$

Size:

$$\begin{aligned} &= 3 + 2 \times 5 + 8 \times 2 \\ &= 29 \text{ equivalent gates} \end{aligned}$$

■

8.9 DESIGN OF NETWORKS WITH FLIP-FLOPS

The procedure for the design of flip-flop networks is a generalization of the one used for the canonical implementation at the binary level. The main difference is that, while in the canonical case the input to each D flip-flop corresponds directly to the component of the next state, the input to other flip-flop types are designed to produce the desired transitions.

The input values required for particular transitions depend on the type of flip-flop. The corresponding function indicating the flip-flop inputs required for each transition is called the **excitation function** $E(Q(t), Q(t+1))$. We now describe how to obtain the excitation function for the SR flip-flop, and then give this function for the other flip-flops.

For the SR flip-flop, a transition from $Q(t) = 0$ to $Q(t+1) = 0$ requires $S(t) = 0$, $R(t) = 0$ (no change), or $S(t) = 0$, $R(t) = 1$ (reset). Consequently, this transition requires $S(t) = 0$ and $R(t) = dc$. Similarly,

from	to	inputs should be
$Q(t) = 0$	$Q(t+1) = 1$	$S(t) = 1, R(t) = 0$
$Q(t) = 1$	$Q(t+1) = 0$	$S(t) = 0, R(t) = 1$
$Q(t) = 1$	$Q(t+1) = 1$	$S(t) = dc, R(t) = 0$

Following a similar procedure, we obtain the excitation functions for the four types of flip-flops being considered:

D flip-flop

PS	*NS* 0	*NS* 1
0	0	1
1	0	1
	$D(t)$	

$D(t) = Q(t+1)$

SR flip-flop

PS	*NS* 0	*NS* 1
0	0–	10
1	01	–0
	$S(t)R(t)$	

JK flip-flop

PS	*NS* 0	*NS* 1
0	0–	1–
1	–1	–0
	$J(t)K(t)$	

T flip-flop

PS	*NS* 0	*NS* 1
0	0	1
1	1	0
	$T(t)$	

$T(t) = Q(t) \oplus Q(t+1)$

Note the expression for the *D* and *T* flip-flop. On the other hand, in order to exploit the "don't cares," it is not suitable to use expressions for the SR and JK flip-flops.

The procedure for the design of flip-flop networks consists of the following steps:

1. Obtain a binary description of the system. This step is performed by selecting codes for the input, output, and state, and transforming the state transition and output functions into the corresponding set of switching functions.

2. Select the type of flip-flop used to store the state vector. In most cases all flip-flops in a network are of the same type, but the procedure can also be applied to the case in which several types of flip-flops are used.
3. Use the state transition function of the system to determine the inputs to the flip-flops required to produce the desired transitions. For this step, use the excitation function of the flip-flop.
4. Design a combinational network to produce these flip-flop inputs in terms of the present state and the network inputs.

The following examples illustrate this procedure.

EXAMPLE 8.8

Using T flip-flops, design a modulo-5 counter whose specification is as follows:

Input: $x(t) \in \{0, 1\}$
Output: $z(t) \in \{0, 1, 2, 3, 4\}$
State: $s(t) \in \{S_0, S_1, S_2, S_3, S_4\}$
Initial state: $s(0) = S_0$

Functions: The system counts modulo-5 the number of 1's in the input sequence (i.e., it counts 0,1,2,3,4,0,1,2,3,4,0,...), as depicted in the state diagram shown in Figure 8.27.

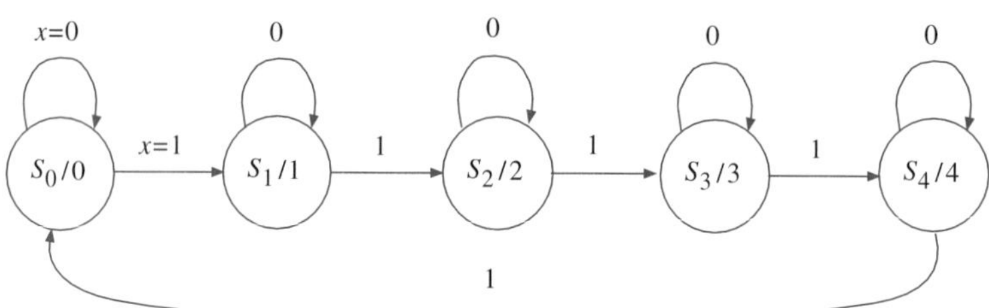

Figure 8.27 State diagram for Example 8.8.

We begin the design by coding the input, output, and state sets. Because the input is a binary variable, it is already coded. The output set requires at least three binary variables. One possibility is to code the values of z by their representations in a radix-2 number system, as follows:

z	z_2	z_1	z_0
0	0	0	0
1	0	0	1
2	0	1	0
3	0	1	1
4	1	0	0

Because there are five states, at least three binary variables are required to code the state. To simplify the output network, we use the same code for the state and the output vector, so that $(z_2, z_1, z_0) = (Q_2, Q_1, Q_0)$.

With these codes, the state transition table and the flip-flop input functions are

PS	Input		Input	
$Q_2\,Q_1\,Q_0$	$x = 0$	$x = 1$	$x = 0$	$x = 1$
000	000	001	000	001
001	001	010	000	011
010	010	011	000	001
011	011	100	000	111
100	100	000	000	100
	NS		$T_2\,T_1\,T_0$	

The functions for the flip-flop inputs T_2, T_1, and T_0 are obtained from the excitation function of a T flip-flop (i.e., $T = Q(t) \oplus Q(t+1)$) and the state transition table. For example, when $PS = (0, 0, 0)$ and $x(t) = 0$, then $Q_0(t) = 0$ and $Q_0(t+1) = 0$ so that $T_0(t) = 0$; similarly, when $PS = (0, 0, 0)$ and $x(t) = 1$ then $Q_0(t) = 0$ and $Q_0(t+1) = 1$ so that $T_0(t) = 1$. The corresponding switching functions are described by the following Karnaugh maps:

T_2: (x over the middle two columns; Q_0 over the right two columns; Q_1 beside the middle two rows; Q_2 beside the bottom two rows)

0	0	0	0
0	0	1	0
–	–	–	–
0	1	–	–

T_1:

0	0	1	0
0	0	1	0
–	–	–	–
0	0	–	–

T_0:

0	1	1	0
0	1	1	0
–	–	–	–
0	0	–	–

From these maps, we obtain the input expressions

$$T_2 = xQ_2 + xQ_1Q_0$$
$$T_1 = xQ_0$$
$$T_0 = xQ_2'$$

The resulting sequential network is shown in Figure 8.28.

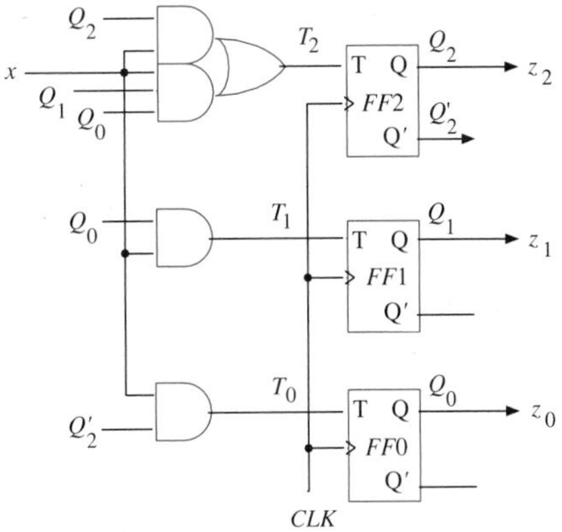

Figure 8.28 Sequential network in Example 8.8. ■

EXAMPLE 8.9

Using SR flip-flops, design a network for a system which has the following high-level description:

Input: $\underline{x}(t) = (x_1, x_0),\ x_i \in \{0, 1\}$
Output: $z(t) \in \{0, 1\}$
State: $s(t) \in \{a, b, c, d\}$
Initial state: $s(0) = a$

Functions: The transition and output functions are

PS	x_1x_0 01	10	11
a	$b, 0$	$c, 1$	$c, 0$
b	$a, 0$	$d, 1$	$d, 0$
c	$d, 0$	$c, 0$	$a, 1$
d	$c, 0$	$a, 0$	$d, 1$
		NS, z	

The input and output are already coded on binary variables. Note that the combination $(x_1, x_0) = (0, 0)$ is not present, so it is considered a "don't care" case. Two flip-flops are needed to store the state, and a possible state assignment is

State	Q_1Q_0
a	00
b	01
c	10
d	11

Consequently, the transition function becomes

PS Q_1Q_0	x_1x_0 01	10	11
00	01	10	10
01	00	11	11
10	11	10	00
11	10	00	11
		NS	

The required input functions are obtained from the transition function and the excitation function of the SR flip-flop. As a reminder, this excitation function is

$Q(t)$	$Q(t+1)$	S	R
0	0	0	–
0	1	1	0
1	0	0	1
1	1	–	0

Now we can obtain the flip-flop inputs and represent them in K-maps. As an illustration of the way the entries in the maps are generated, consider the case $Q_1(t) = 0$, $Q_0(t) = 1$, $x_1 = 0$, $x_0 = 1$. For this case the next state is $Q_1(t+1) = 0$, $Q_0(t+1) = 0$. From the excitation table we get $S_1 = 0$, $R_1 = dc$, $S_0 = 0$, and $R_0 = 1$, as shown in the corresponding K-map cell. Consequently, the input functions are:

S_1: (x_0 over columns 2–3; x_1 over columns 3–4; Q_0 beside rows 2–3; Q_1 beside rows 3–4)

–	0	1	1
–	0	1	1
–	–	–	0
–	–	0	–

R_1:

–	–	0	0
–	–	0	0
–	0	0	1
–	0	1	0

S_0:

–	1	0	0
–	0	–	–
–	0	–	0
–	1	0	0

R_0:

–	0	–	–
–	1	0	0
–	1	0	1
–	0	–	–

From the maps, we obtain the expressions for the flip-flop inputs as follows:

$$S_1 = x_1 Q_1'$$
$$R_1 = x_0' Q_1 Q_0 + x_1 x_0 Q_1 Q_0'$$
$$S_0 = x_1' Q_0'$$
$$R_0 = x_1' Q_0 + x_0' Q_1$$

The Karnaugh map for the output is

z: (x_0 over columns 2–3; x_1 over columns 3–4; Q_0 beside rows 2–3; Q_1 beside rows 3–4)

–	0	0	1
–	0	0	1
–	0	1	0
–	0	1	0

The output expression is

$$z = x_0' Q_1' + x_1 x_0 Q_1$$

The resulting sequential network is shown in Figure 8.29.

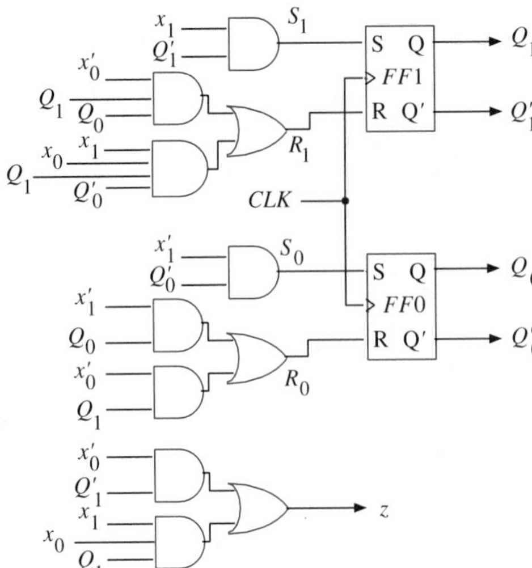

Figure 8.29 Sequential network in Example 8.9.

■

8.10 DESIGN USING SPECIAL STATE ASSIGNMENTS

The coding of states on binary variables (state assignment) affects the complexity of an implementation as well as the design process. We discuss two state assignment approaches that, when applicable, greatly simplify the design.

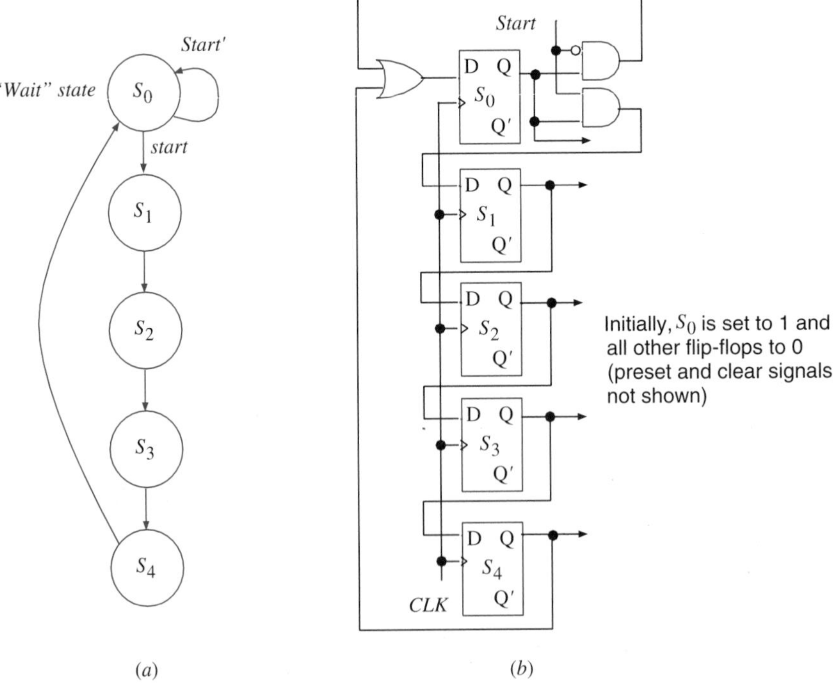

Figure 8.30 One flip-flop per state approach. (*a*) State diagram. (*b*) Implementation (outputs omitted).

One Flip-flop Per State

If the number of states is small, sequential networks with one flip-flop per state result in straightforward correspondence among state diagram and implementation. As an example, Figure 8.30 shows the state diagram and implementation of the autonomous controller presented in Section 7.5. Note that only one flip-flop is in state 1 at any time, whereas all others are in state 0; thus, this implementation is also called a **one-hot** approach. The system is initialized by setting to 1 the flip-flop corresponding to the initial state.

We now discuss the correspondence among the state diagram and the one flip-flop per state implementation. The simplest case is a state with one predecessor and one successor, as shown in Figure 8.31*a*; the corresponding implementation is given in Figure 8.31*a*′. In the more general case, a state has several predecessors and several successors, and a particular successor is chosen by input values. This situation is shown in Figure 8.31*b* and the corresponding implementation in Figure 8.31*b*′.

Figure 8.32 illustrates the one flip-flop per state implementation of a controller for the simple vending machine considered in Section 7.5.

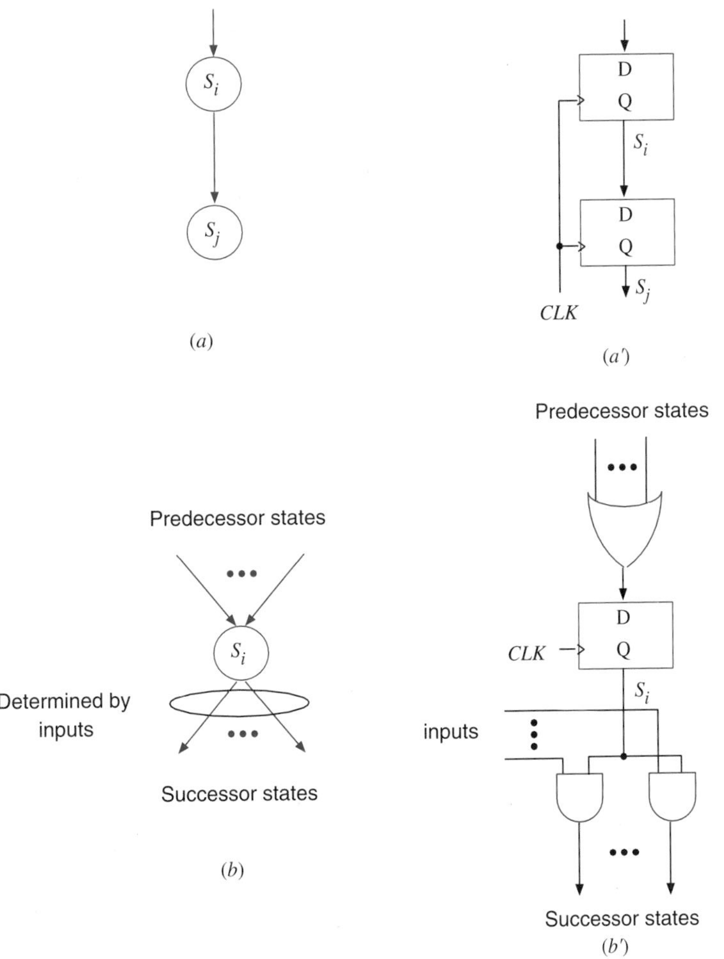

Figure 8.31 Primitives for the one flip-flop per state approach.

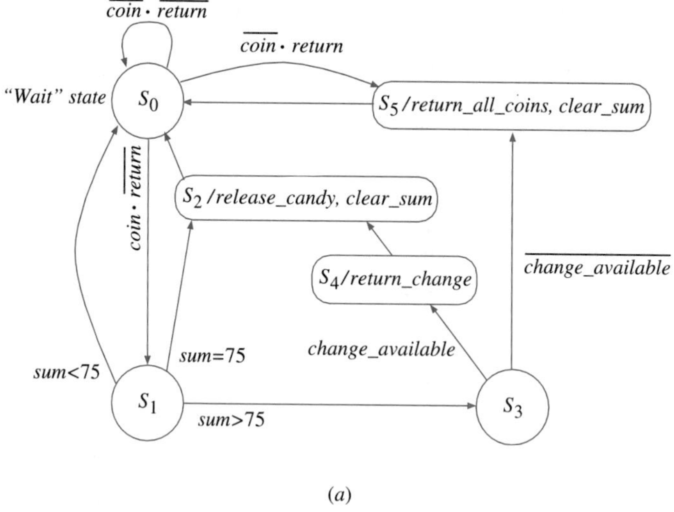

(*a*)

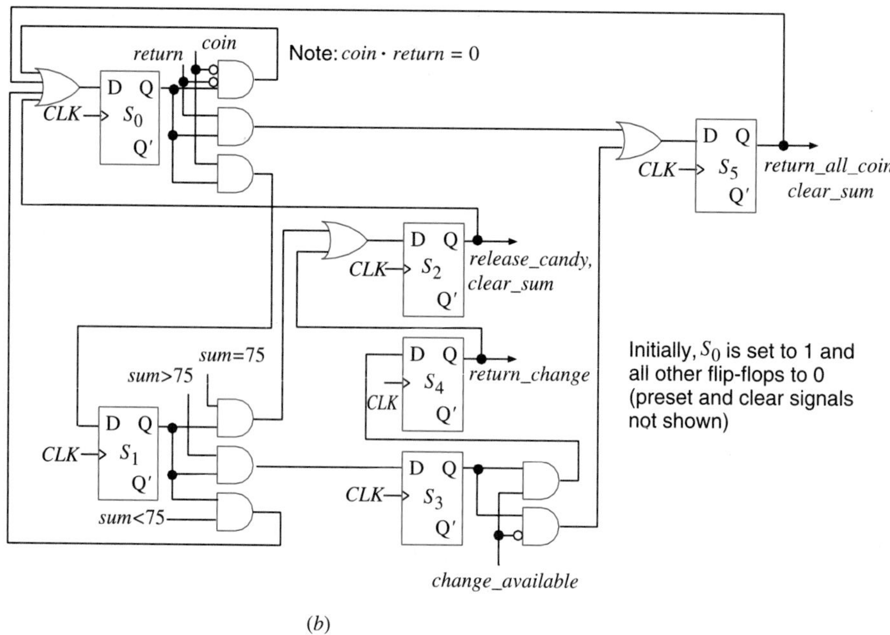

(*b*)

Figure 8.32 A one flip-flop per state implementation of a controller for vending machine. (*a*) State diagram. (*b*) Implementation.

Shifting State Register

Implementations with a shifting state register are especially suitable for finite memory sequential systems. As discussed in Section 7.8, the (not necessary minimum) state in such a system corresponds to the last $m - 1$ inputs. Consequently, these inputs can be stored in a register and **shifted** one position each clock cycle, as shown in Figure 8.33; note the implementation of the shift register with D flip-flops.

EXAMPLE 8.10

Obtain an implementation using D flip-flops of a sequential system having the following time behavior:

Input:	$x(t) \in \{0, 1\}$
Output:	$z(t) \in \{0, 1\}$

Function: $$z(t) = \begin{cases} 1 & \textbf{if} \quad x(t-3, t) = 1101 \\ 0 & \textbf{otherwise} \end{cases}$$

Figure 8.33 illustrates an implementation with a state register consisting of three D flip-flops, connected so that at time t they contain $x(t-3, t-1)$; that is, the last three inputs represent the state. The output $z(t)$ is obtained using a four-input AND gate connected to the state register and the external input. Initially, the flip-flops are cleared.

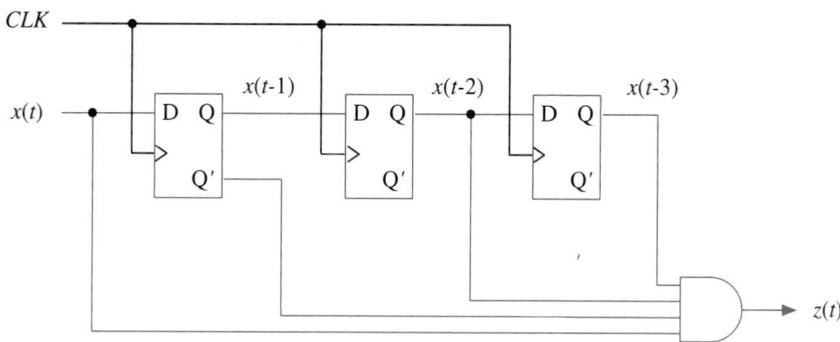

Figure 8.33 Implementation of pattern recognizer in Example 8.10.

■

8.11 DESCRIPTION OF FLIP-FLOPS AND SEQUENTIAL NETWORKS IN μVHDL

Let us now address the description of flip-flop modules and their characteristics in μVHDL, as well as the description of simple sequential networks using such modules. The description of the function of these basic sequential modules follows the definitions and examples given in Chapter 7 for sequential systems. However, because the functionality of flip-flops is quite simple, the corresponding behavioral descriptions are also quite simple.

The interpretation of the `PROCESS` describing the transition function of these modules is triggered by a transition of the clock signal, so the description must detect whether the clock transition is the appropriate one. For this purpose, an `IF` statement checking for the current value of the clock signal is sufficient: in the case of a leading-edge transition, the value of the clock must be 1, whereas in the case of a trailing-edge transition the value must be 0.

8.11.1 Description of Flip-flops

Let us first consider the description of the flip-flops in Table 8.2, but assuming constant delay (independent from the transition direction and from the load).

EXAMPLE 8.11

Flip-flops with constant delays are described as follows:

```
ENTITY Dff IS
  PORT(d   : IN  BIT;
       q   : OUT BIT;
       clk : IN  BIT);
END Dff;

ARCHITECTURE basic OF Dff IS
  SIGNAL ds: BIT;             -- flip-flop state
BEGIN
  PROCESS (clk)               -- transition function
    CONSTANT delay: TIME := 500 ps;
  BEGIN
    IF (clk'EVENT AND clk = '1') THEN
      ds <= d AFTER delay;
    END IF;
  END PROCESS;

  PROCESS (ds)               -- output function
  BEGIN
      q  <= ds;
  END PROCESS;
END basic;


ENTITY JKff IS
  PORT(j,k : IN  BIT;
       q   : OUT BIT;
       clk : IN  BIT);
END JKff;

ARCHITECTURE basic OF JKff IS
  SIGNAL jks: BIT;               -- flip-flop state
BEGIN
  PROCESS (clk)                  -- transition function
    CONSTANT delay: TIME := 450 ps;
    VARIABLE jk   : BIT_VECTOR(1 DOWNTO 0);
  BEGIN
    IF (clk'EVENT AND clk = '1') THEN
      jk:= j & k;
      CASE jk IS
        WHEN "00" => jks <= jks AFTER delay;
        WHEN "01" => jks <= '0' AFTER delay;
        WHEN "10" => jks <= '1' AFTER delay;
        WHEN "11" => jks <= not(jks) AFTER delay;
      END CASE;
    END IF;
  END PROCESS;

  PROCESS (jks)                  -- output function
  BEGIN
      q  <= jks;
  END PROCESS;
END basic;
```

These descriptions consist of two processes, one for the state transition function and the other for the output function. The process describing the state transition function contains an IF statement, which checks for a leading-edge transition in the clock signal, and the rest of the process gives the functionality of the transition function. In the case of the D flip-flop, such a functionality consists of latching the data at the d input, whereas in the case of the JK flip-flop the functionality is described by the body of the CASE statement. Because in both cases the flip-flop output corresponds to the state, the process describing the output function is just the assignment of the state to the output signal.

The state of the flip-flop is saved in SIGNAL ds and jks, respectively. The propagation delay of the cell is given with respect to the clock edge triggering the transition function; since the output corresponds to the state, there is no delay in the output function.

Figure 8.34 depicts a timing diagram for the operation of the JK flip-flop described above.

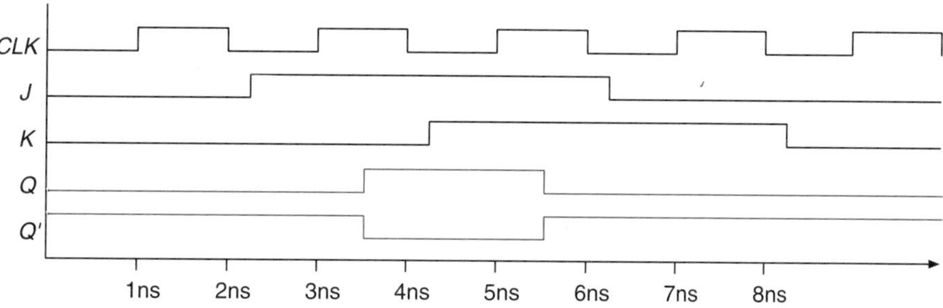

Figure 8.34 Timing diagram for JK flip-flop.

■

As in the case of basic gates, let us now show a refinement of the behavioral descriptions in the foregoing example by giving another architecture body for the D flip-flop, in which there are different delays depending on the type of output transition.

EXAMPLE 8.12

The following description corresponds to a D flip-flop whose transition delay depends on the type of output transition:

```
ARCHITECTURE delays OF Dff IS
  SIGNAL ds: BIT;   -- state
BEGIN
  PROCESS (clk)
    CONSTANT TpHL : TIME := 540 ps;
    CONSTANT TpLH : TIME := 490 ps;
    VARIABLE ds_d : BIT_VECTOR(1 DOWNTO 0);
  BEGIN
    IF (clk'EVENT AND clk = '1') THEN
      ds_d := ds & d;     -- previous state and current input
      CASE ds_d IS
        WHEN "00" | "11" => null;
        WHEN "10"        => ds <= d AFTER TpHL;
        WHEN "01"        => ds <= d AFTER TpLH;
      END CASE;
    END IF;
  END PROCESS;

  PROCESS (ds)
  BEGIN
      q <= ds;
  END PROCESS;
END delays;
```

In this case, the description uses a variable to momentarily capture the previous state. The propagation delay of the cell depends on the previous and new values of the state, as described by the entries in the CASE statement. ■

Also as in the case of basic combinational gates, the delay of a flip-flop can be dependent on the load imposed on the module; the corresponding μVHDL description is an extension of the one in the previous example, along the same lines as done for the case of basic gates in Chapter 3, using a GENERIC statement in the entity declaration defining the load. Similarly, aspects such as input load-factor, fanout factor, and the size of the flip-flop (in terms of equivalent gates) are described using ATTRIBUTE statements.

Flip-flop modules have additional timing parameters, that is, setup time, hold time, and clock pulse width. These parameters correspond to constraints that must be fulfilled to guarantee correct behavior. A complete description of a flip-flop module should include the detection of violations to these constraints. The statement ASSERT, and the signal attributes DELAYED, STABLE are used for these purposes:

- The attribute DELAYED(t), a signal of the same type of the original signal, provides the signal delayed by t time units; this attribute allows inspecting the value of a signal in the past (i.e., a version of the signal "shifted" in time).
- The attribute STABLE(t), a signal of type BOOLEAN, has the value TRUE if an event has not occurred on the signal for the past t time units.
- ASSERT is a reporting mechanism with an associated condition, which has the following structure:

```
ASSERT(condition)
  REPORT "report string"
  SEVERITY level;
```

  If the condition specified in the ASSERT is FALSE, then the text string that follows the clause REPORT is displayed together with the optional severity level specified in the clause SEVERITY; predefined severity levels are WARNING and FATAL. (In the case of FATAL, the simulation ends at that point.)

EXAMPLE 8.13

The following description uses μVHDL statements that allow reporting the violation of timing constraints:

```
ARCHITECTURE constraints OF Dff IS
  SIGNAL ds: BIT;  -- state
  CONSTANT Tsu  : TIME :=  300 ps;    -- setup time
  CONSTANT Th   : TIME :=  140 ps;    -- hold time
  CONSTANT Tw   : TIME :=  200 ps;    -- clock pulse width
BEGIN
  PROCESS (clk)              -- transition function
    CONSTANT Tp: TIME:= 500 ps;   -- delay
  BEGIN
    IF (clk'EVENT AND clk = '1') THEN
      ds <= d AFTER Tp;
    END IF;
  END PROCESS;
```

```
  PROCESS (ds)              -- output function
  BEGIN
    q <= ds;
  END PROCESS;

  ASSERT NOT (clk'EVENT AND clk='1' AND NOT d'STABLE(Tsu))
     REPORT "setup time violation";

  ASSERT NOT (clk'DELAYED(Th)'EVENT AND clk'DELAYED(Th)='1' AND
              NOT d'STABLE(Th))
     REPORT "hold time violation";

  ASSERT NOT (clk'EVENT AND clk='0' AND NOT clk'DELAYED(Tw)='1')
     REPORT "clock pulse width violation";

END constraints;
```

This description contains three concurrent ASSERT statements to verify the timing constraints: the first one detects setup time violations, the second one detects hold time violations, and the last one detects clock pulse width violations. So, for example, if input d changes at time 1250 ps, and the clock pulse is received at time 1500 ps, then the condition clk'DELAYED(Th)'EVENT AND clk'DELAYED(Th)='1' is true, the condition NOT d'STABLE(Th) is also true, then the assert condition is false and the timing violation is reported. ■

8.11.2 Description of Flip-flop Networks

Let us now address the description of flip-flop networks. Such networks are described at the structural level, that is, by listing the flip-flops and combinational modules comprising the network and their interconnection. The functionality and other characteristics of flip-flops and gates are described separately, as discussed in previous chapters. As we already know, those descriptions become part of a structural description by declaring the entities used in the network.

EXAMPLE 8.14

We now give the μVHDL description of the network depicted in Figure 8.35. The description of flip-flops and gates has already been discussed; we assume such descriptions are available in the library WORK, so we just use them here.

The entity declaration for this network is as follows:

```
USE WORK.ALL;
ENTITY seq_netw IS
  PORT(x1,x1p: IN  BIT;
       x0,x0p: IN  BIT;
       z     : OUT BIT;
       clk   : IN  BIT);
END seq_netw;
```

The architecture body lists the modules used in the network and their interconnections. Labeling the modules and signals as depicted in Figure 8.35, we obtain the structural description given in Figure 8.36.

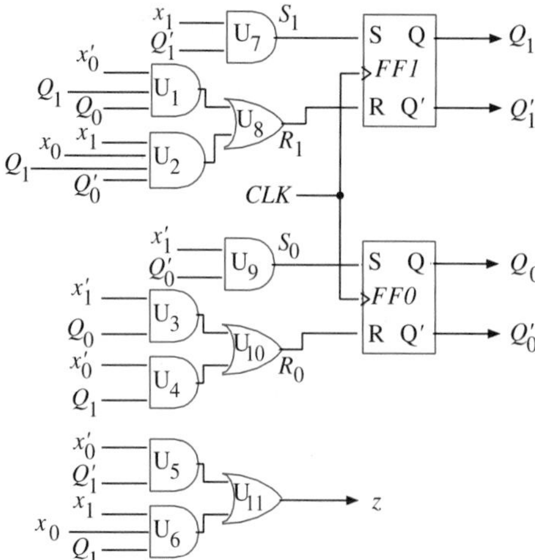

Figure 8.35 Sequential network in Example 8.14. ■

```
ARCHITECTURE structural OF seq_netw IS

  SIGNAL a1,a2,a3,a4,a5,a6: BIT;
  SIGNAL S0,R0,S1,R1      : BIT;
  SIGNAL Q0,Q0p,Q1,Q1p    : BIT;

BEGIN
  U1 : ENTITY and3 PORT MAP (x0p,Q1,Q0,a1);
  U2 : ENTITY and4 PORT MAP (x1,x0,Q1,Q0p,a2);
  U3 : ENTITY and2 PORT MAP (x1p,Q0,a3)  ;
  U4 : ENTITY and2 PORT MAP (x0p,Q1,a4)  ;
  U5 : ENTITY and2 PORT MAP (x0p,Q1p,a5) ;
  U6 : ENTITY and3 PORT MAP (x1,x0,Q1,a6);
  U7 : ENTITY and2 PORT MAP (x1,Q1p,S1)  ;
  U8 : ENTITY or2  PORT MAP (a1,a2,R1)   ;
  U9 : ENTITY and2 PORT MAP (x1p,Q0p,S0) ;
  U10: ENTITY or2  PORT MAP (a3,a4,R0)   ;
  U11: ENTITY or2  PORT MAP (a5,a6,z)    ;
  FF1: ENTITY SRff PORT MAP (S1,R1,Q1,Q1p,clk);
  FF0: ENTITY SRff PORT MAP (S0,R0,Q0,Q0p,clk);
END structural;
```

Figure 8.36 Structural description for network in Figure 8.35.

8.12 FURTHER READINGS

Textbooks such as *Switching and Automata Theory*, by Z. Kohavi, McGraw-Hill, New York, 1978; *Introduction to Switching Theory and Logical Design* by F. J. Hill and G. R. Peterson, Wiley, New York, 1981; *An Engineering Approach to Digital Design* by W. I. Fletcher, Prentice-Hall, Englewood Cliffs, NJ, 1980; *Logic Design Principles* by E. J. McCluskey, Prentice-Hall, Englewood Cliffs, NJ, 1986; *Introduction to Digital Logic Design* by J. P. Hayes, Addison-Wesley, Reading, MA, 1993; *Digital Design Principles and Practices* by J. F. Wakerly, 2nd ed., Prentice-Hall, Englewood Cliffs, NJ, 1994; and *Contemporary Logic Design* by R. H. Katz, The Benjamin/Cummings Publishing Company, Redwood City, CA, 1994, cover the analysis and synthesis of sequential networks at the binary level, specially using flip-flops as the primitive component.

For additional information on flip-flop characteristics, the reader can consult integrated circuits manuals such as the *LSI Logic Databook* published by LSI Logic Inc., Milpitas, CA and *TTL Data Book for Design Engineers* published by Texas Instruments, Dallas, TX.

EXERCISES

Timing in synchronous sequential networks

Exercise 8.1 This problem is related to the limitations in the use of a gated latch, as discussed in Section 8.3. Consider the sequential network shown in Figure 8.37, which consists of gated latches and a combinational network. For a clock pulse width of 5 ns and a latch propagation delay of 2 ns:

a. Determine the minimum delay of the combinational network in order to avoid races.
b. If the delay of the combinational network can decrease by 30% from the minimum value computed in (a) and the latch delay can decrease by 10%, determine the maximum clock pulse width that will guarantee no races.

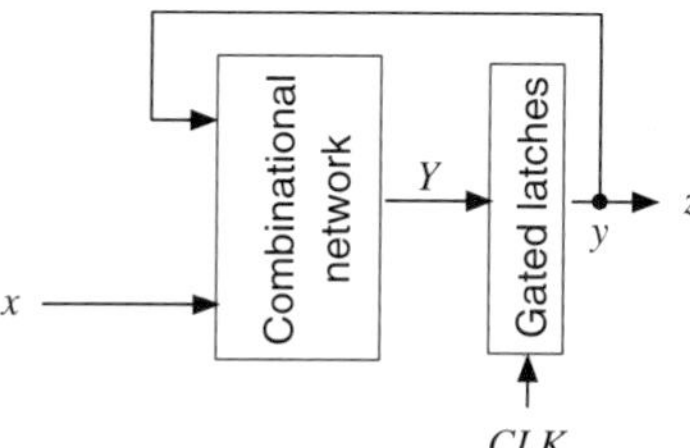

Figure 8.37 Network for Exercise 8.1.

Exercise 8.2 For the canonical sequential network shown in Figure 8.38, determine the timing factors (in terms of the timing factors of cells and gates) for $t_{in} = 2.0$ ns and $t_{out} = 2.5$ ns.

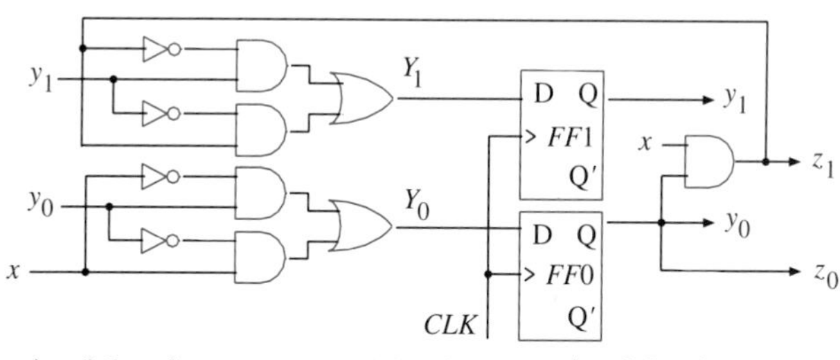

$t_p = 0.5$ ns for gates $t_{su} = 1.0$ ns for cells $t_h = 0.5$ ns for cells
$t_p = 3.0$ ns for cells

Figure 8.38 Network for Exercise 8.2.

Exercise 8.3 A generalization of the master-slave approach is depicted in Figure 8.39. The network consists of two registers, formed by gated latches, and two combinational networks. The network has a two-phase (nonoverlapping) clock, as shown in the figure, phase 1 being applied to one register and phase 2 to the other.

a. Show that this configuration does not have race problems.
b. How many states does the system have if each register has n cells?
c. Implement the system of Exercise 8.4 using this configuration and compare the two implementations.

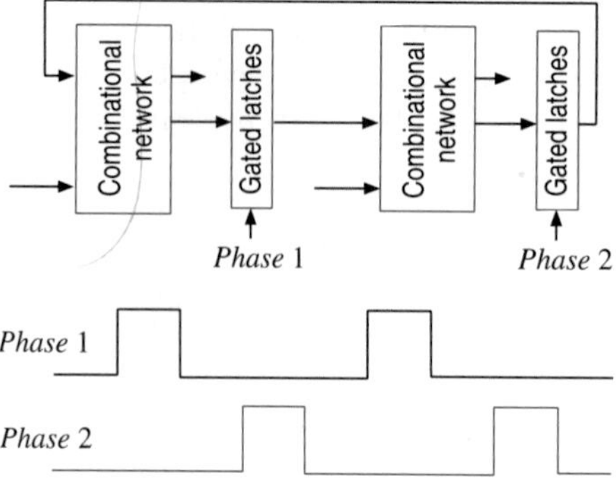

Figure 8.39 Network for Exercise 8.3.

Analysis and design of canonical sequential networks

Exercise 8.4 Analyze the pattern recognizer shown in Figure 8.40. Give a state diagram. Assuming that the initial state is 00, determine five input patterns that the system recognizes (produces output 1).

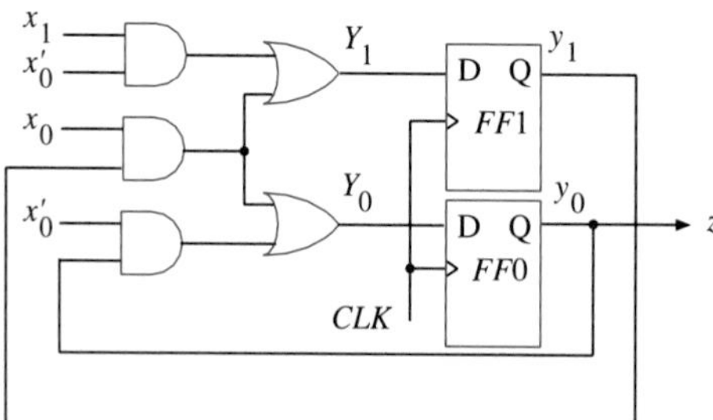

Figure 8.40 Network for Exercise 8.4.

Exercise 8.5 Obtain the canonical implementation of a pattern recognizer that recognizes the pattern 0101011.

Exercise 8.6 Obtain the canonical implementation of a pattern generator that generates the continuously repeated pattern *abcaba*.

Exercise 8.7 Design a canonical sequential network whose output is 1 whenever the input sequence consists of a 1 followed by a block of 0's of even length, followed by two 1's, followed by a block of 0's of odd length.

Exercise 8.8 Design a canonical sequential network that has the following state table:

PS	Input	
	$x = 0$	$x = 1$
A	B, a	F, b
B	C, a	A, c
C	D, a	B, b
D	E, b	C, c
E	F, b	D, b
F	A, c	E, c
	NS, *z*	

Exercise 8.9 Design a canonical sequential network whose input is a sequence of decimal digits in BCD and whose output is the minimum digit of the sequence. If some input does not correspond to a BCD digit, the output should be 1111.

Exercise 8.10 Implement a sequential (bit-serial) network for converting an n-bit representation of an integer from binary code to Gray code. Use the fact that $g_i = b_i \oplus b_{i+1}$, where b_i is the ith bit of the binary representation and g_i is the corresponding bit of the Gray code.

Exercise 8.11 Implement a sequential (bit-serial) binary adder/subtracter. A control input k indicates whether an addition ($k = 1$) or a subtraction ($k = 0$) is performed.

Exercise 8.12 Implement a sequential (bit-serial) binary magnitude comparator for 16-bit operands. Describe two implementations: one beginning with the most-significant bit and the other with the least-significant bit.

Exercise 8.13 A combination lock opens when the string of decimal digits (0,5,6,8) is entered serially at its input. The lock has two binary outputs z_1 and z_2. The correct combination produces $z_1 = 1$ and an incorrect combination produces $z_2 = 1$. The output has value 00 while the string is being entered. Implement this lock as a canonical sequential network.

Flip-flop modules

Exercise 8.14 Design a gate network to implement a JK flip-flop. Show a timing diagram for the following sequence of JK inputs: 00, 10, 01, 11, 00. The initial state of the flip-flop is 0.

Exercise 8.15 Design a gate network to implement a T flip-flop.

Analysis of networks with flip-flops

Exercise 8.16 Analyze the network shown in Figure 8.41. Give a state table and a state diagram.

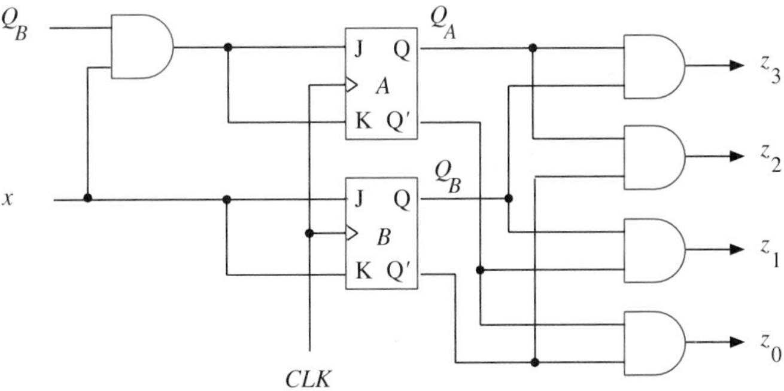

Figure 8.41 Network for Exercise 8.16.

Exercise 8.17 Analyze the network depicted in Figure 8.42. Give a timing diagram of its operation.

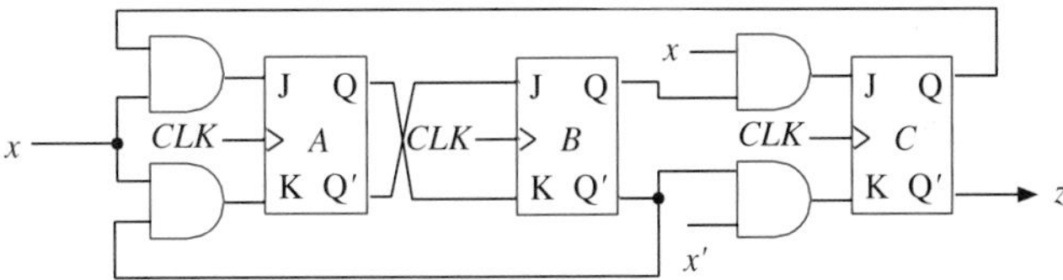

Figure 8.42 Network for Exercise 8.17.

Exercise 8.18 Analyze the network depicted in Figure 8.43. Give a state diagram and a high-level description.

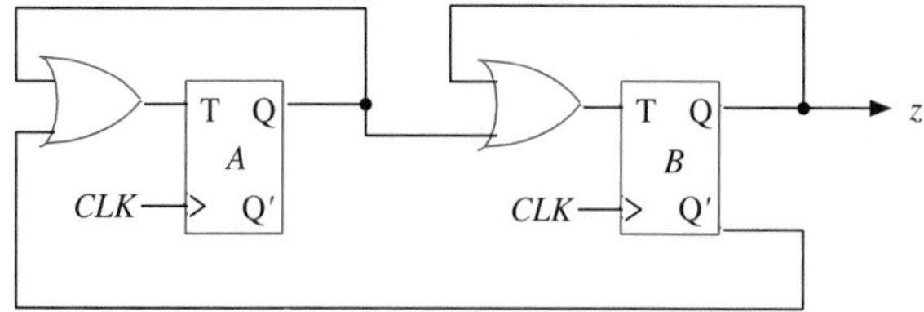

Figure 8.43 Network for Exercise 8.18.

Exercise 8.19 Analyze the network shown in Figure 8.44. Show that it produces a 1 at the output every six clock cycles.

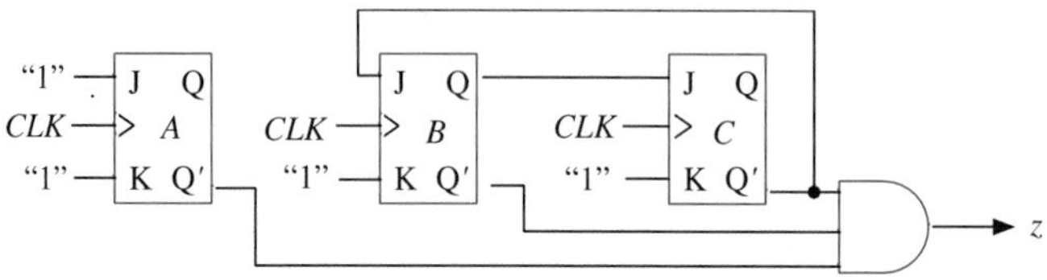

Figure 8.44 Network for Exercise 8.19.

Exercise 8.20 Analyze the network given in Figure 8.45. Show that it is a modulo-3 counter.

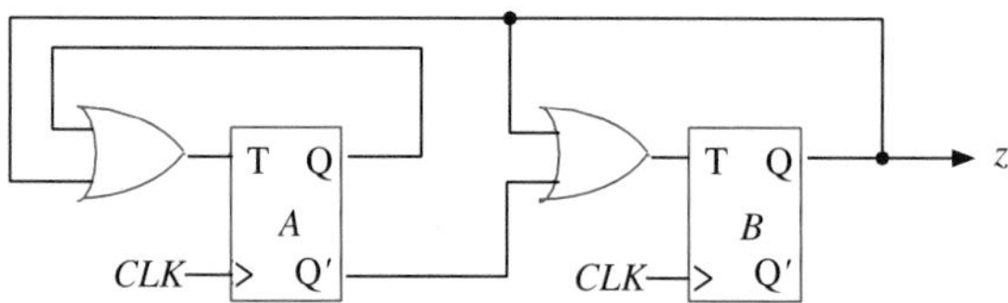

Figure 8.45 Network for Exercise 8.20.

Exercise 8.21 Analyze the network depicted in Figure 8.46. Show that it is a serial converter from BCD to Excess-3. Give a timing diagram.

Design of networks with flip-flops

Exercise 8.22 Using a D flip-flop, design networks that correspond to an SR flip-flop, a T flip-flop, and a JK flip-flop.

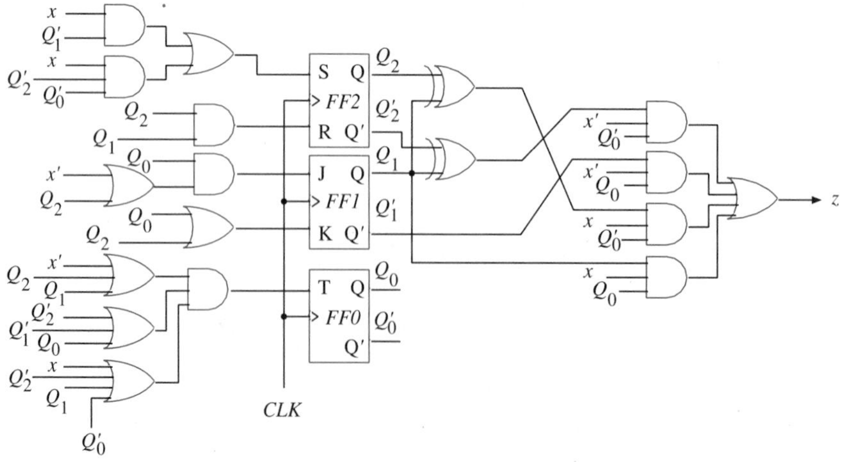

Figure 8.46 Network for Exercise 8.21.

Exercise 8.23 Design a sequential system with one binary input x and one binary output z. The output is 1 whenever two consecutive 1's followed by a 0 are observed, otherwise the output is 0. Use JK flip-flops.

Exercise 8.24 Design a sequential network that has one binary input x and one binary output z. The output at time t has value 1 whenever $x(t-3, t)$ has an odd number of 1's. Overlapping sequences are acceptable; for example, for the input sequence

$$x(t-7, t) = 01011111$$

the output sequence is

$$z(t-7, t) = ???01100$$

(the ?'s indicate that the output is not known because it depends on input values not given). Use D flip-flops.

Exercise 8.25 A sequential system has one binary input x and one binary output z. The output at time t has value 1 whenever $x(t-1, t) = 11$. Design a Mealy sequential network using JK flip-flops.

Exercise 8.26 Design a modulo-3 binary counter using SR flip-flops.

Exercise 8.27 Design a cyclic counter with the output sequence 0,1,3,7,6,4,0,1... (of period 6) using JK flip-flops. Compare the following two approaches in implementing the system:

a. Select a state assignment that is the same as the coding for the output, that is, $z(t) = s(t)$.
b. Select the state assignment for a modulo-6 binary counter and implement the required output function.

Exercise 8.28 An up/down counter counts up or down depending on the value of a binary control signal. Design a modulo-7 binary up/down counter using:

a. Three T flip-flops.
b. Three D flip-flops.
c. Two T flip-flops (for the two least-significant flip-flops) and one D flip-flop.

Exercise 8.29 Design a sequential system with one binary input x and one binary output z. The output at time t is 1 whenever $x(t-3, t) = 0101$ or 0110. Implement using JK flip-flops and NAND gates.

Exercise 8.30 Design the sequential system given in Example 8.8 using D flip-flops and compare the two implementations with respect to the number of gates required.

Exercise 8.31 Design the sequential system given in Example 8.9 using JK flip-flops and compare the two implementations with respect to the number of gates required.

Exercise 8.32 Design a modulo-3 binary counter using the "one flip-flop per state" approach. The output is in the binary code.

Exercise 8.33 Design a sequential network described by the following state/output table, using the "one flip-flop per state" approach.

PS	Input	
	$x = 0$	$x = 1$
A	B, a	F, b
B	C, a	A, c
C	D, a	B, b
D	E, b	C, c
E	F, b	D, b
F	A, c	E, c
	NS, z	

Exercise 8.34 Design a sequential network with a shifting state register. The network has one binary input x and one binary output z. The output is 1 whenever three consecutive 1's are followed by two 0's, otherwise the output is 0.

Descriptions in μVHDL

All the exercises corresponding to analysis and design can be done using μVHDL.

Chapter 9

Standard Combinational Modules

In this chapter, we present

- A set of widely used standard combinational modules.
- The specification of these standard modules.
- A gate network implementation for each of these standard modules.
- The main uses of these standard modules.
- The implementation of large modules as networks of smaller ones.

Complex digital systems are implemented as modular networks. Although fully custom-designed modules are used in special cases, most frequently the systems are built using **standard modules.** These standard modules (components) correspond to subfunctions that have been identified as useful for a large variety of applications, and have been made available as "off-the-shelf" and library components, that is, ready to use as part of a modular network. This approach is applicable at all levels of integration (MSI, LSI, VLSI).

The design of a system using standard modules consists of two steps:

- decompose the overall functionality of the system into subfunctions that can be mapped onto standard components; and
- interconnect the chosen standard components as a modular network.

If the decomposition still produces complex subfunctions, a new level of decomposition is applied until the mapping of subfunctions onto standard components becomes feasible.

In this chapter, we begin the study of standard modules by introducing a set of widely used combinational components, namely decoders, encoders, multiplexers, demultiplexers and shifters. We define the function of these modules, give high-level and binary-level descriptions, and indicate their basic use. We also describe how to construct networks of these standard modules. Other standard combinational and sequential modules are described in the following chapters.

9.1 BINARY DECODERS

An ***n*-input binary decoder** (see Figure 9.1) is a combinational system that has n binary inputs $\underline{x} = (x_{n-1}, \ldots, x_0)$ and 2^n binary outputs $\underline{y} = (y_{2^n-1}, \ldots, y_0)$. The input vector $\underline{x}$ can be considered as representing integers from 0 to $2^n - 1$ in the radix-2 representation.

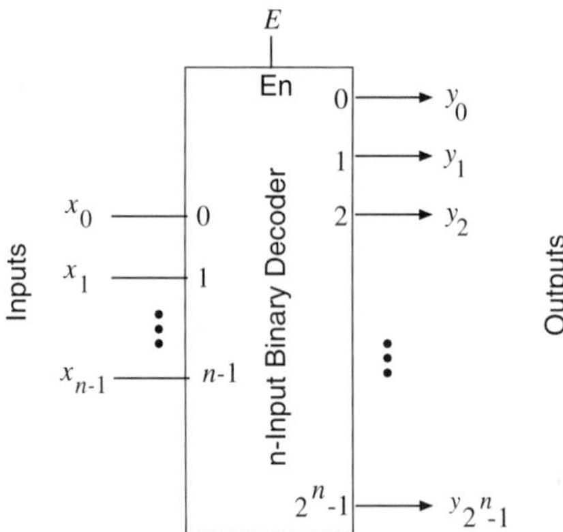

Figure 9.1 n-input binary decoder.

At any given time, at most one binary output—say y_i—is equal to 1 and all other outputs are equal to 0; $y_i = 1$ indicates that the input bit-vector represents the integer i. That is, the module can be regarded as a code converter from the binary code to the 1-out-of-2^n code.

An additional input, called **module enable** E, is used to facilitate the implementation of network of decoders; when $E = 0$, all outputs from the module are equal to 0 (or they are in the high-impedance state for three-state outputs).

A high-level description of an n-input binary decoder is

Inputs: $\underline{x} = (x_{n-1}, \ldots, x_0), \; x_j \in \{0, 1\}$
$E \in \{0, 1\}$

Outputs: $\underline{y} = (y_{2^n-1}, \ldots, y_0), \; y_i \in \{0, 1\}$

Function: $$y_i = \begin{cases} 1 & \textbf{if} \quad (x = i) \textbf{ and } (E = 1) \\ 0 & \textbf{otherwise} \end{cases}$$

where $x = \sum_{j=0}^{n-1} x_j 2^j$ and $i = 0, \ldots, 2^n - 1$

EXAMPLE 9.1

The function of a three-input binary decoder is described by the following table:

E	x_2	x_1	x_0	x	y_7	y_6	y_5	y_4	y_3	y_2	y_1	y_0
1	0	0	0	0	0	0	0	0	0	0	0	1
1	0	0	1	1	0	0	0	0	0	0	1	0
1	0	1	0	2	0	0	0	0	0	1	0	0
1	0	1	1	3	0	0	0	0	1	0	0	0
1	1	0	0	4	0	0	0	1	0	0	0	0
1	1	0	1	5	0	0	1	0	0	0	0	0
1	1	1	0	6	0	1	0	0	0	0	0	0
1	1	1	1	7	1	0	0	0	0	0	0	0
0	–	–	–	–	0	0	0	0	0	0	0	0

■

Each decoder output corresponds to a switching function having value 1 for exactly one assignment, so it can be represented by one minterm. Consequently, the binary specification is given by

Inputs: $\underline{x} = (x_{n-1}, \ldots, x_0),\ \ x_j \in \{0, 1\}$
$E \in \{0, 1\}$

Outputs: $\underline{y} = (y_{2^n-1}, \ldots, y_0),\ \ y_i \in \{0, 1\}$

Function: $y_i = E \cdot m_i(\underline{x})\ ,\ \ i = 0, \ldots, 2^n - 1$

where $m_i(\underline{x})$ is the ith minterm of the n variables $\underline{x}$

A gate network implementation consists of n NOT gates and 2^n AND gates with $n + 1$ inputs each.

EXAMPLE 9.2

The switching expressions describing a two-input binary decoder are

$$y_0 = x_1' x_0' E$$
$$y_1 = x_1' x_0 E$$
$$y_2 = x_1 x_0' E$$
$$y_3 = x_1 x_0 E$$

A gate network implementation of this binary decoder is shown in Figure 9.2.

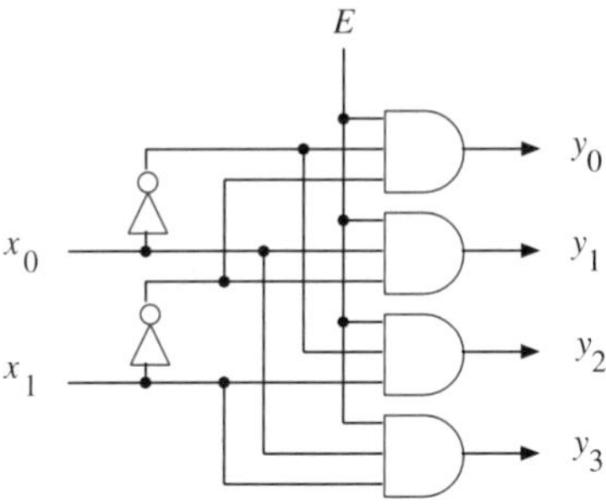

Figure 9.2 Gate network implementation of a two-input binary decoder. ■

As a shorthand notation, a decoder module is denoted by

$$\underline{y} = \text{DEC}(\underline{x}, E)$$

For example, for a three-input decoder,

$$\underline{y} = \text{DEC}((1, 1, 0), 1) = (0, 1, 0, 0, 0, 0, 0, 0)$$

Uses

A binary decoder is used whenever a set of values has been encoded using a binary code and they have to be separated, that is, **decoded**. Specifically, a set of 2^n elements can be encoded on n binary variables. Then, an n-bit decoder can be used to identify which element of the set has been encoded. Typical examples are decoding the operation code (opcode) in a computer instruction, or decoding the address (location) referenced when accessing a memory.

EXAMPLE 9.3

A computer instruction has an opcode field of four bits, so that up to 16 different operations can be specified. Part of the instruction execution process consists of determining the operation specified in the instruction. A binary decoder can be used for these purposes, as shown in Figure 9.3.

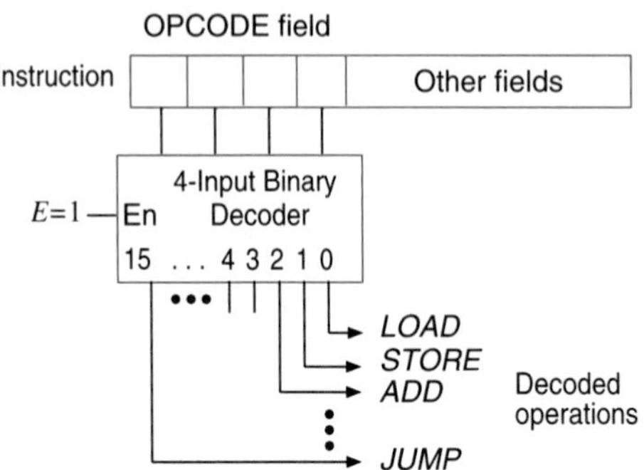

Figure 9.3 Operation decoding.

EXAMPLE 9.4

A 16K×1 memory module stores 16K[1] words of 1 bit each. This module has a 14-bit **address** used to specify one particular word input (see Figure 9.4), a 1-bit data input, a 1-bit data output, and one control input to specify a memory operation (read or write). The implementation of the module consists basically of two parts: an array of 16K binary cells, each storing one bit, and a binary decoder that selects one of the cells for a read or write operation. Due to its size, this decoder cannot be implemented with a gate network of the type shown in Figure 9.2; a network of decoders has to be used instead, as discussed later.

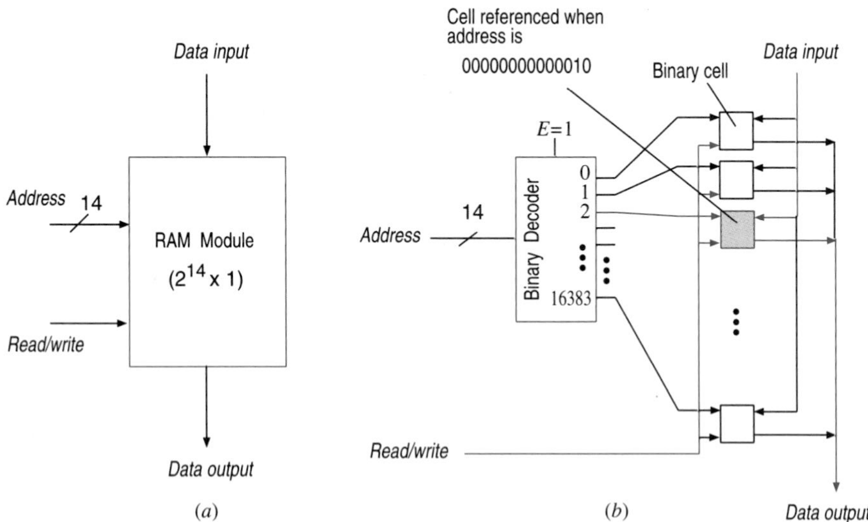

Figure 9.4 Random-access memory (RAM). (a) Module. (b) Addressing of binary cells.

[1]The notation 1K is used to denote $1024 = 2^{10}$, so that 16K denotes $16384 = 2^{14}$.

Decoders also exist for other input representations. For example, decimal decoders have ten outputs for codes such as BCD and Excess-3; their definition and implementation are similar to those of the binary decoder, so we do not discuss them further.

9.1.1 Binary Decoder and OR Gate as Universal Set

An n-input binary decoder and an OR gate can realize **any** switching function of n variables, so that these two components correspond to a universal set of combinational modules. This is a consequence of the definition of a binary decoder: because the ith decoder output corresponds to minterm $m_i(\underline{x})$, then the implementation of any sum of minterms is obtained by performing an OR with the outputs of the decoder that correspond to the minterms in the expression. Moreover, several functions of the same variables can be generated with one decoder and with one OR gate per function.

EXAMPLE 9.5

Consider the combinational system described by the following table:

$x_2\,x_1\,x_0$	z_2	z_1	z_0
000	0	1	0
001	1	0	0
010	0	0	1
011	0	1	0
100	0	0	1
101	1	0	1
110	0	0	0
111	1	0	0

This system can be implemented using a three-input binary decoder and OR gates, as shown in Figure 9.5 and described at the binary level as follows:

$$(y_7, \ldots, y_0) = \text{DEC}(x_2, x_1, x_0, 1)$$
$$z_2(x_2, x_1, x_0) = y_1 + y_5 + y_7$$
$$z_1(x_2, x_1, x_0) = y_0 + y_3$$
$$z_0(x_2, x_1, x_0) = y_2 + y_4 + y_5$$

■

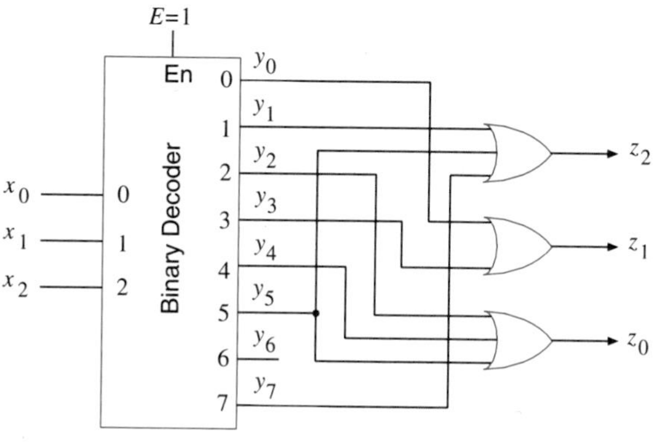

Figure 9.5 Network in Example 9.5.

9.1.2 Decoder Networks

Due to limitations in the maximum number of connections to a module and the number of gates in an implementation, standard modules implement decoders with a small number of inputs (i.e., four inputs). Larger decoders are often required, but it is impractical to implement them as one module, so decoder networks are used instead. We now discuss two approaches for the design of these networks: **coincident decoding** and **tree decoding.**

Coincident decoding

Let us consider the implementation of an eight-input binary decoder using standard four-input binary decoders. For these purposes, let us divide the eight-bit input vector $(x_7, x_6, \ldots, x_1, x_0)$ into two four-bit subvectors, as follows:

$$\underline{x} = (\underline{x}_{\text{left}}, \underline{x}_{\text{right}})$$

$$\underline{x}_{\text{left}} = (x_7, x_6, x_5, x_4)$$

$$\underline{x}_{\text{right}} = (x_3, x_2, x_1, x_0)$$

The coincident decoder is built as illustrated in Figure 9.6, where each subvector is decoded by one four-input decoder, producing the vectors $\underline{y} = (y_{15}, \ldots, y_0)$ and $\underline{w} = (w_{15}, \ldots, w_0)$. Then, every pair consisting of one output from each decoder is applied as input to one of 256 two-input AND gates. The outputs from these gates correspond to the outputs from the eight-input decoder. Outputs are labeled by noting that

$$x = 2^4 \times x_{\text{left}} + x_{\text{right}}$$

where x, x_{left}, and x_{right} are the integers represented by $\underline{x}$, $\underline{x}_{\text{left}}$, and $\underline{x}_{\text{right}}$, respectively. Consequently, z_i corresponds to the output from the AND gate with inputs y_s and w_t, where

$$i = 2^4 \times s + t$$

For example, output z_{36} is obtained from the AND gate whose inputs are y_2 and w_4 because $36 = 2^4 \times 2 + 4$.

The external (network) enable input E is connected to the enable input of one decoder module, whereas the enable input of the other module is set to 1. Consequently, if $E = 0$ then all outputs from one decoder module are 0, resulting in $z_i = 0$ for all i.

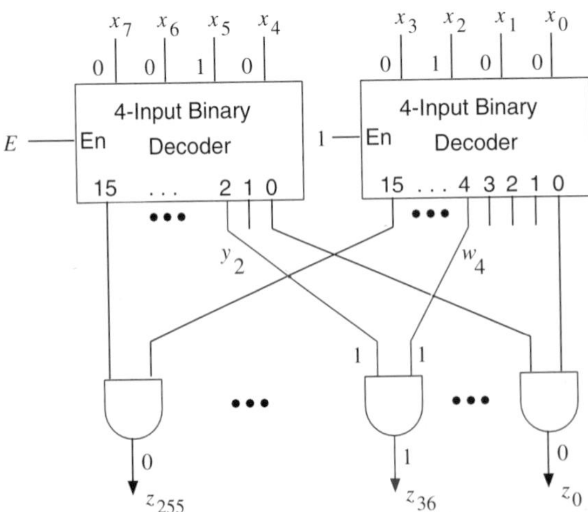

Figure 9.6 Eight-input coincident decoder.

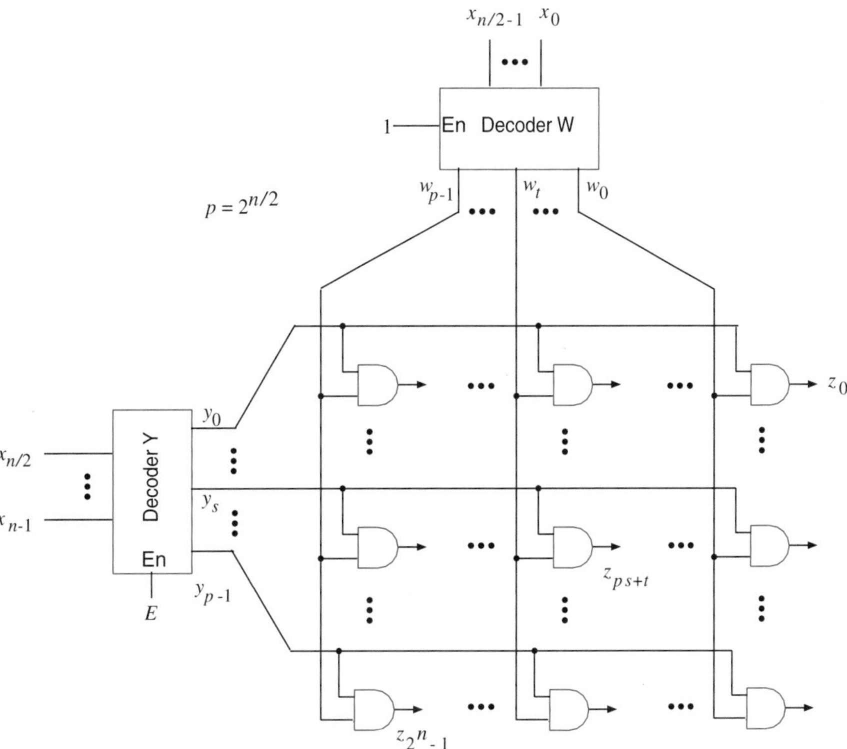

Figure 9.7 n-input coincident decoder.

As a generalization of this network, an n-input binary decoder is implemented by two $(n/2)$-input binary decoders and 2^n AND gates, as indicated in Figure 9.7. The input to decoder W is $\underline{x}_{\text{right}} = (x_{(n/2)-1}, \ldots, x_0)$, whereas the input to decoder Y is $\underline{x}_{\text{left}} = (x_{n-1}, \ldots, x_{n/2})$. The network enable input is connected to the enable of one of the decoders (e.g., Y).

A functional description that captures the network shown in Figure 9.7 is

$$\underline{y} = \text{DEC}(\underline{x}_{\text{left}}, E)$$

$$\underline{w} = \text{DEC}(\underline{x}_{\text{right}}, 1)$$

$$\underline{z} = (\text{AND}(y_{2^{n/2}-1}, w_{2^{n/2}-1}), \ldots, \text{AND}(y_s, w_t), \ldots, \text{AND}(y_0, w_0))$$

Tree decoding

Another approach to the implementation of large decoders is a **tree decoder network.** For this case, let us consider the implementation of a four-input binary decoder using standard two-input binary decoders. As in the coincident decoder, let us divide the four-bit input vector into two two-bit subvectors, as follows:

$$\underline{x} = (\underline{x}_{\text{left}}, \underline{x}_{\text{right}})$$

$$\underline{x}_{\text{left}} = (x_3, x_2)$$

$$\underline{x}_{\text{right}} = (x_1, x_0)$$

Based on this decomposition, we can build a two-level tree network that has one decoder in the first level and four decoders in the second level, as depicted in Figure 9.8. Subvector $\underline{x}_{\text{left}}$

is decoded in the first level, whereas $\underline{x}_{\text{right}}$ is decoded in the second level. The 16 network outputs are partitioned into four groups of four outputs each, where each group is produced by one decoder module. The operation is as follows:

- each output from decoding $\underline{x}_{\text{left}}$ enables one of the decoders in the second level; and
- the decoding of $\underline{x}_{\text{right}}$ produces the corresponding output from the enabled decoder.

For example, if $\underline{x} = (0, 1, 1, 0)$ then $\underline{x}_{\text{left}} = (0, 1)$ so that decoder DEC1 is enabled. Moreover, $\underline{x}_{\text{right}} = (1, 0)$, which produces a 1 at output 2 of decoder DEC1, that is, at output $4 \times 1 + 2 = 6$. Note the essential role of the decoder enable input in the operation of this network.

In general, an n-input decoder can be implemented by a two-level tree with one $(n/2)$-input decoder in the first level and $2^{n/2}$ $(n/2)$-input decoders in the second level, as depicted in Figure 9.9.

A functional description that captures the network shown in Figure 9.9 is

$$\underline{w} = \text{DEC}(\underline{x}_{\text{left}}, E)$$

$$\underline{z} = (\text{DEC}(\underline{x}_{\text{right}}, w_{2^{n/2}-1}), \ldots, \text{DEC}(\underline{x}_{\text{right}}, w_t), \ldots, \text{DEC}(\underline{x}_{\text{right}}, w_0))$$

The tree decoder network can be generalized to a multilevel tree. If $n = rk$, where k is the number of inputs to a decoder module, then k input variables are introduced at each level producing a tree of r levels. The number of decoder modules in such a case is

$$1 + 2^k + 2^{2k} + \cdots + 2^{(r-1)k} = (2^n - 1)/(2^k - 1)$$

For example, for $n = 12$ and $k = 4$, there are $r = 3$ levels and the number of modules is $(2^{12} - 1)/(2^4 - 1) = 273$.

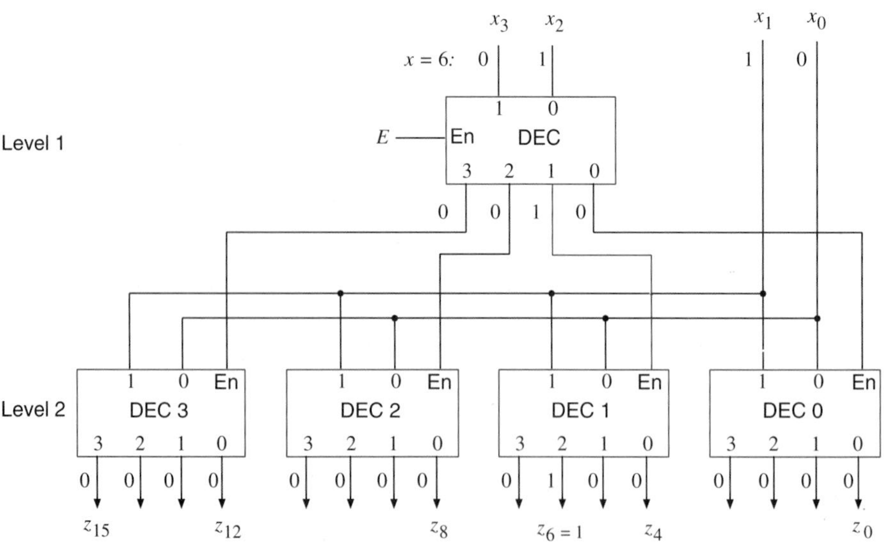

Figure 9.8 Four-input tree decoder.

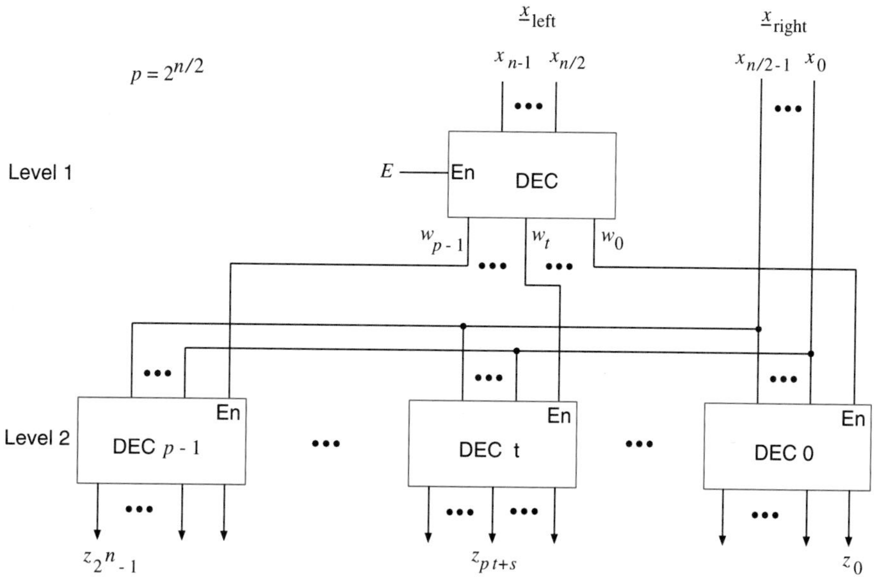

Figure 9.9 n-input two-level tree decoder.

Comparison of decoder networks

The following table compares the two decoder networks just presented. Each network implements a $2k$-input decoder using k-input decoder modules and two-input AND gates.

	Coincident	Tree
Decoder modules	2	$2^k + 1$
AND gates	2^{2k}	—
Load per network input	1 decoder input	2^k decoder inputs (max)
Load per decoder output	2^k AND inputs	1 enable input
Number of module inputs (related to number of connections)	$2k + 2 + 2^{2k+1}$	$1 + k + 2^k + k2^k$
Delay	$t_{\text{decoder}} + t_{\text{AND}}$	$2t_{\text{decoder}}$

EXAMPLE 9.6

A six-input decoder is implemented using coincident and tree decoder networks, as illustrated in Figure 9.10.

As shown in the following table, the coincident scheme requires two three-input decoders and 64 two-input AND gates. If the delay of decoders and AND gates are $2d$ and d,

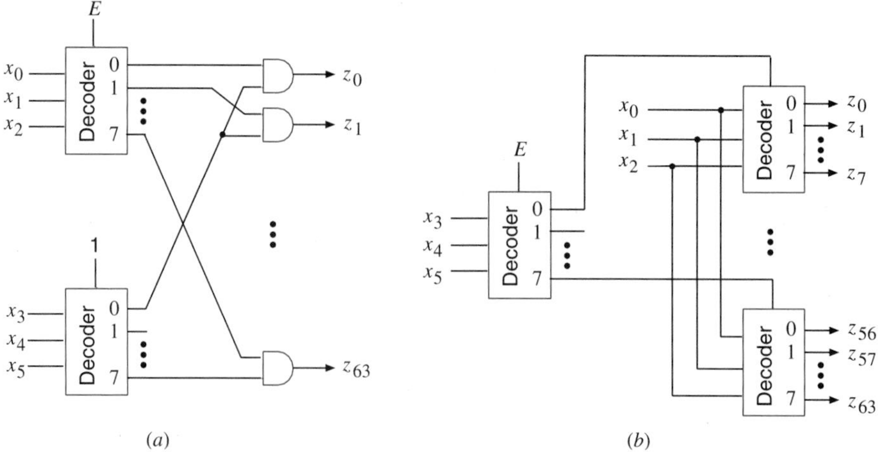

Figure 9.10 Implementation of six-input decoder. (*a*) Coincident decoder. (*b*) Tree decoder.

respectively, then the total delay is $3d$. On the other hand, the tree decoder requires nine decoder modules and its delay is equal to $4d$.

	Coincident	Tree
Decoder modules	2	9
AND gates	64	—
Load per network input	1 decoder input	8 decoder inputs (max)
Load per decoder output	8 AND inputs	1 enable input
Number of module inputs	136	36
Delay	$3d$	$4d$

■

As it can be inferred from the foregoing example, the tree decoder network is better than the coincident network in terms of the number of interconnections. Coincident decoding, on the other hand, allows a reduction in the complexity of the connections from the generation of the decoding function to its use in other parts of the network. This is illustrated by the implementation of the system shown in Figures 9.11*a* and 9.11*b*, which consists of a 12-input decoder and an array of 4096 storage cells; each cell is selected by one output from the decoder. In the case of the tree network, 4096 lines go from the decoder to the array as depicted in Figure 9.11*a*. On the other hand, in the case of the coincident network, the AND gates can be part of the array of cells so that just 128 lines are required (see Figure 9.11*b*).

9.2 BINARY ENCODERS

A **2^n-input binary encoder** (see Figure 9.12) is a combinational system that has 2^n binary inputs $\underline{x} = (x_{2^n-1}, \ldots, x_0)$ and n binary outputs $\underline{y} = (y_{n-1}, \ldots, y_0)$. This module performs the inverse function of a decoder: it converts from the 1-out-of-2^n code into a binary code. At any given time, at most one of the inputs—say x_i—may be equal to 1 and all other inputs must be equal to 0; the output bit-vector represents, in a binary code, the index of the input with the value 1 (i.e., i).

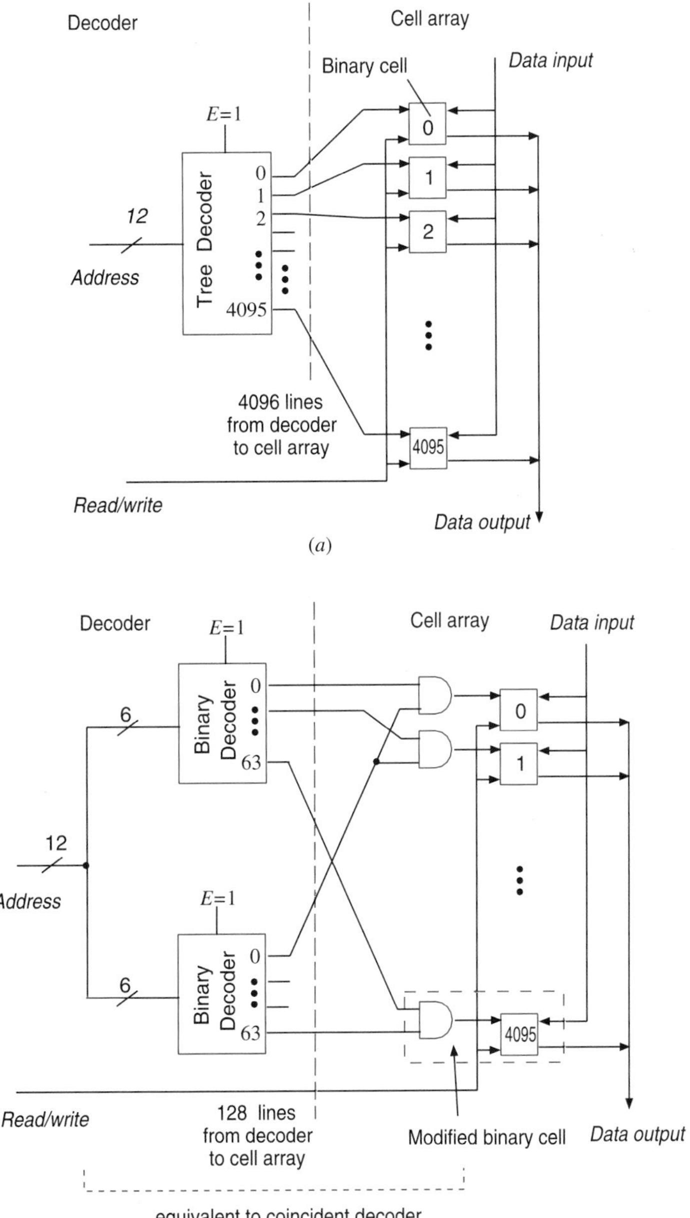

Figure 9.11 (*a*) System with tree decoder. (*b*) System with coincident decoder.

An additional input and an additional output, called **module enable *E*** and **module active *A*,** respectively, are used to facilitate the implementation of encoder networks. The enable input has the same functionality as in the case of decoders, whereas output A indicates whether the module is "active" (i.e., there is an input with value 1).

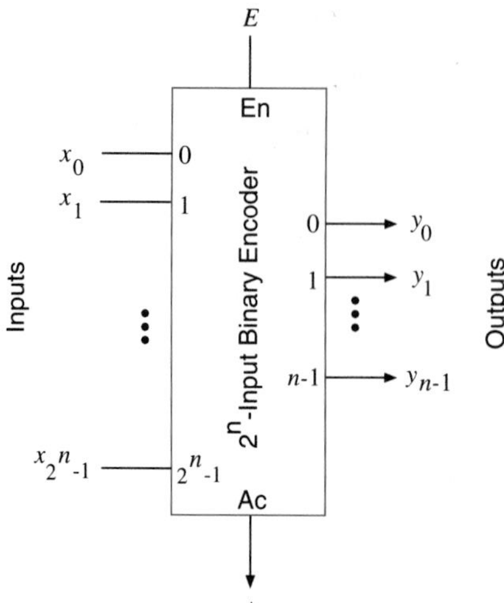

Figure 9.12 2^n-input binary encoder.

A high-level description of a binary encoder is

Inputs: $\underline{x} = (x_{2^n-1}, \ldots, x_0),\ \ x_i \in \{0, 1\}$, with at most one $x_i = 1$
$E \in \{0, 1\}$

Outputs: $\underline{y} = (y_{n-1}, \ldots, y_0),\ \ y_j \in \{0, 1\}$
$A \in \{0, 1\}$

Function:

$$y = \begin{cases} i & \textbf{if} \quad (x_i = 1) \textbf{ and } (E = 1) \\ 0 & \textbf{otherwise} \end{cases}$$

$$A = \begin{cases} 1 & \textbf{if} \quad (\text{some } x_i = 1) \textbf{ and } (E = 1) \\ 0 & \textbf{otherwise} \end{cases}$$

$$\text{where } y = \sum_{j=0}^{n-1} y_j 2^j \text{ and } i = 0, \ldots, 2^n - 1$$

EXAMPLE 9.7

The function of an eight-input binary encoder is given by the following table:

E	x_7	x_6	x_5	x_4	x_3	x_2	x_1	x_0	y	y_2	y_1	y_0	A
1	0	0	0	0	0	0	0	1	0	0	0	0	1
1	0	0	0	0	0	0	1	0	1	0	0	1	1
1	0	0	0	0	0	1	0	0	2	0	1	0	1
1	0	0	0	0	1	0	0	0	3	0	1	1	1
1	0	0	0	1	0	0	0	0	4	1	0	0	1
1	0	0	1	0	0	0	0	0	5	1	0	1	1
1	0	1	0	0	0	0	0	0	6	1	1	0	1
1	1	0	0	0	0	0	0	0	7	1	1	1	1
1	0	0	0	0	0	0	0	0	0	0	0	0	0
0	–	–	–	–	–	–	–	–	0	0	0	0	0

■

Notice that if $x_i = 1$, then y_j is 1 if the binary representation of i has a 1 in its jth bit. Consequently, the binary specification of an n-bit encoder is:

Inputs: $\underline{x} = (x_{2^n-1}, \ldots, x_0),\ \ x_i \in \{0, 1\}$, with, at most, one $x_i = 1$
$E \in \{0, 1\}$

Outputs: $\underline{y} = (y_{n-1}, \ldots, y_0),\ \ y_j \in \{0, 1\}$
$A \in \{0, 1\}$

Function: $y_j = E \cdot \sum(x_k),\ \ j = 0, \ldots, n-1$
$A = E \cdot \sum(x_i),\ \ i = 0, \ldots, 2^n - 1$

where x_k is included in the expression for y_j if the jth bit of the binary representation of k is 1.

EXAMPLE 9.8

The switching expressions describing an eight-input binary encoder are

$$y_0 = E \cdot (x_1 + x_3 + x_5 + x_7)$$
$$y_1 = E \cdot (x_2 + x_3 + x_6 + x_7)$$
$$y_2 = E \cdot (x_4 + x_5 + x_6 + x_7)$$
$$A = E \cdot (x_0 + x_1 + x_2 + x_3 + x_4 + x_5 + x_6 + x_7)$$

A gate-network implementation of this binary encoder is given in Figure 9.13.

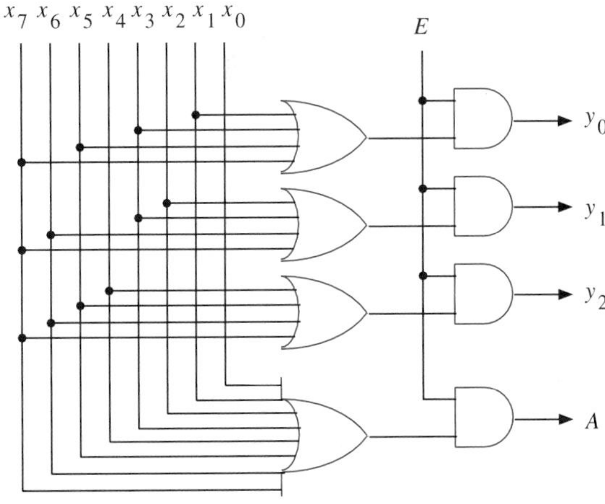

Figure 9.13 Implementation of an eight-input binary encoder. ■

Uses

A binary encoder is used whenever the occurrence of one of several disjoint events needs to be represented by an integer identifying the event.

EXAMPLE 9.9

A device determines the direction of the wind as being one of the following: {N, NE, E, SE, S, SW, W, NW}. As shown in Figure 9.14, the device has eight outputs specifying the wind direction in a 1-out-of-8 code. A binary encoder is used to encode this wind direction as a three-bit binary code.

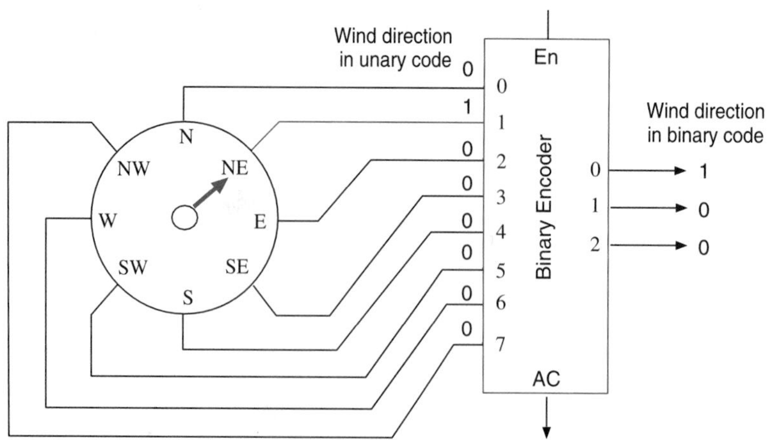

Figure 9.14 Wind direction encoder.

■

Encoders also exist for other output representations, such as BCD and Gray; their definition and implementation are similar to those of the binary encoder, so that we do not discuss them further.

As in the case of decoders, and for all other standard modules discussed later, limitations in the maximum number of connections to a module and number of gates in an implementation restrict the size of encoders that are available as standard modules (i.e., 16 inputs). Large encoders must be implemented as networks of standard encoders.

9.3 PRIORITY ENCODERS

The binary encoder discussed in the previous section has the limitation that, at any given time, at most one input x_i may have the value 1. In contrast, a **priority encoder** may have several inputs with the value 1. The output represents, in a binary code, the index of the **highest priority** input having the value 1. The priority is a fixed ordering implemented by the encoder; usually, x_{2^n-1} has the highest priority, whereas x_0 has the lowest.

A high-level description of a priority encoder is

Inputs: $\underline{x} = (x_{2^n-1}, \ldots, x_0), \quad x_i \in \{0, 1\}$
Outputs: $\underline{y} = (y_{n-1}, \ldots, y_0), \quad y_j \in \{0, 1\}$

Function:

$$y = \begin{cases} i & \textbf{if} \quad (x_i = 1) \ \textbf{and} \ (x_k = 0,\ k > i) \ \textbf{and} \ (E = 1) \\ 0 & \textbf{otherwise} \end{cases}$$

$$A = \begin{cases} 1 & \textbf{if} \quad (\text{some } x_i = 1) \ \textbf{and} \ (E = 1) \\ 0 & \textbf{otherwise} \end{cases}$$

$$\text{where } y = \sum_{j=0}^{n-1} y_j 2^j \text{ and } i, k \in \{0, 1, \ldots, 2^n - 1\}$$

EXAMPLE 9.10

The function of an eight-input priority encoder is given by the following table:

E	x_7	x_6	x_5	x_4	x_3	x_2	x_1	x_0	y_2	y_1	y_0	A
1	0	0	0	0	0	0	0	1	0	0	0	1
1	0	0	0	0	0	0	1	–	0	0	1	1
1	0	0	0	0	0	1	–	–	0	1	0	1
1	0	0	0	0	1	–	–	–	0	1	1	1
1	0	0	0	1	–	–	–	–	1	0	0	1
1	0	0	1	–	–	–	–	–	1	0	1	1
1	0	1	–	–	–	–	–	–	1	1	0	1
1	1	–	–	–	–	–	–	–	1	1	1	1
1	0	0	0	0	0	0	0	0	0	0	0	0
0	–	–	–	–	–	–	–	–	0	0	0	0

■

A priority encoder can be implemented by two subsystems, as indicated in Figure 9.15. The first is a **priority resolution subsystem,** which changes to 0 all inputs with value 1 except the highest priority one, and the second is a binary encoder as the one discussed in the previous section.

A high-level description of the priority resolution subsystem is

Inputs: $\underline{x} = (x_{2^n-1}, \ldots, x_0), \quad x_i \in \{0, 1\}$

Outputs: $\underline{z} = (z_{2^n-1}, \ldots, z_0), \quad z_i \in \{0, 1\}$

Function:
$$z_i = \begin{cases} 1 & \textbf{if} \quad (x_i = 1) \textbf{ and } (x_k = 0, \ \ k > i) \\ 0 & \textbf{otherwise} \end{cases}$$
with $i, k = 0, 1, \ldots, 2^n - 1$

The corresponding binary description of the function is given by the following set of switching expressions:

$$z_i = x'_{2^n-1}x'_{2^n-2} \ldots x'_{i+1}x_i \qquad i = 0, 1, \ldots, 2^n - 1$$

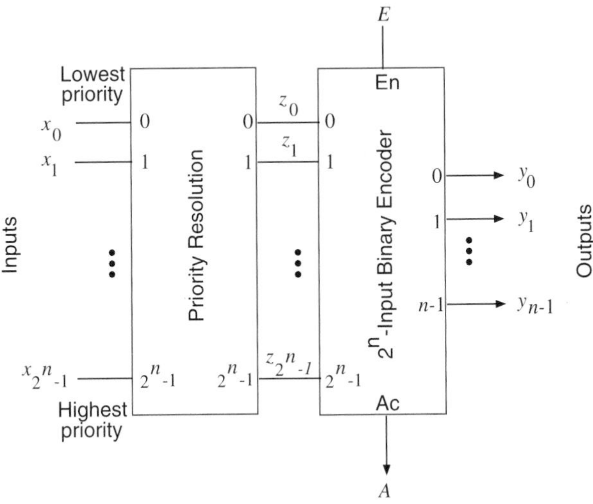

Figure 9.15 Priority encoder implementation.

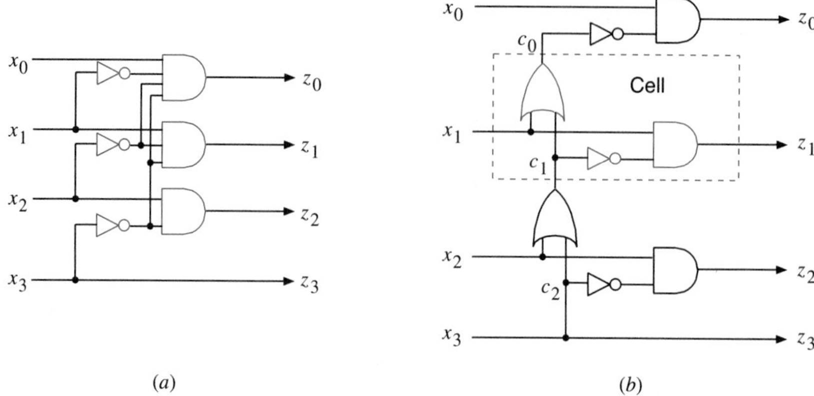

Figure 9.16 Four-bit priority resolution networks. (*a*) Parallel. (*b*) Iterative.

Figure 9.16*a* depicts a priority resolution network implemented with AND gates, in which output i requires a gate with $2^n - i$ inputs. Such an implementation is adequate for a small number of inputs but is impractical for larger modules due to the large gates required. Figure 9.16*b* shows an **iterative** implementation that is more suitable for a large number of inputs, although it has a large delay. This implementation is based on the replication of a cell described by the expressions

$$c_{i-1} = c_i + x_i$$

$$z_i = c_i' x_i$$

An analysis by substitution shows that these expressions implement the priority resolution.

Uses

A priority encoder is used to select, according to a predefined priority, one out of several events that can occur simultaneously; the selected event is represented by an integer. For example, the processor in a computer system receives requests for attention by means of interrupt signals. Several of these signals can be active at the same time, being necessary to select one of them for service; this is done according to preestablished priorities. As shown

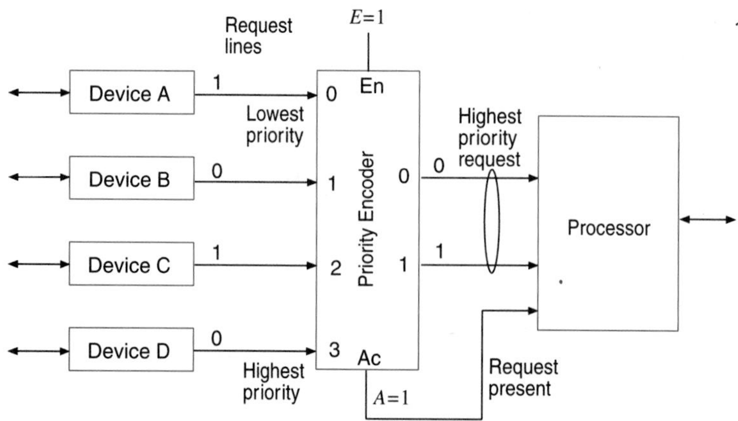

Figure 9.17 Resolving interrupt requests using a priority encoder.

in Figure 9.17, a priority encoder is used to identify the interrupting signal with the highest priority.

Another typical use of a priority encoder is to determine the position of the leftmost (or rightmost) bit set to 1 in a bit-vector. Sometimes this operation is followed by a shift of the bit-vector so that there are no leading (trailing) zeroes (see Figure 9.18).

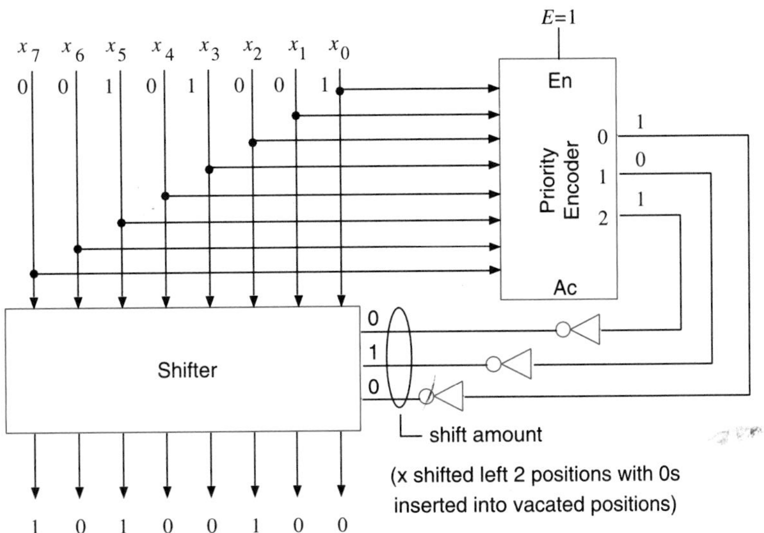

Figure 9.18 Detecting the leftmost 1 in a bit-vector and removing leading zeroes.

9.4 MULTIPLEXERS (SELECTORS)

A **2^n-input multiplexer** has 2^n binary (data) inputs $\underline{x} = (x_{2^n-1}, \ldots, x_0)$, n binary control (select) inputs $\underline{s} = (s_{n-1}, \ldots, s_0)$, a module enable input E, and one data output z (see Figure 9.19). The output of the multiplexer is equal to the data input selected by the

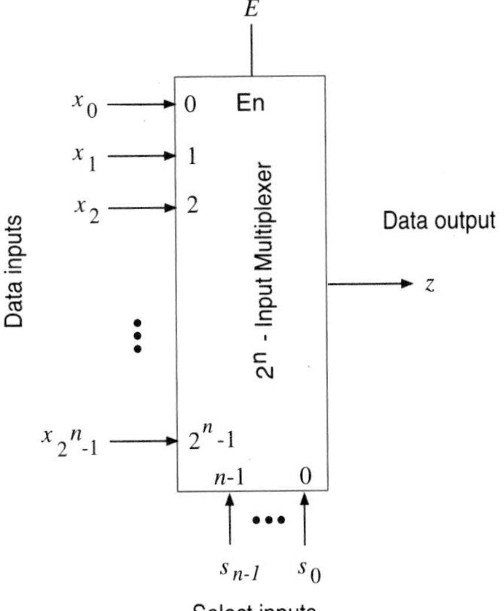

Figure 9.19 2^n-input multiplexer.

control input. Specifically, the values of the control variables $\underline{s}$ are interpreted as the binary representation of the integer s (in the range from 0 to $2^n - 1$) and the output is equal to x_s.

A high-level description of a multiplexer is

Inputs: $\underline{x} = (x_{2^n-1}, \ldots, x_0), \quad x_i \in \{0, 1\}$
$\underline{s} = (s_{n-1}, \ldots, s_0), \quad s_j \in \{0, 1\}$
$E \in \{0, 1\}$

Outputs: $z \in \{0, 1\}$

Function:
$$z = \begin{cases} x_s & \textbf{if} \quad E = 1 \\ 0 & \textbf{if} \quad E = 0 \end{cases}$$

$$\text{where } s = \sum_{j=0}^{n-1} s_j 2^j$$

Since the minterm $m_i(\underline{s})$ has value 1 only when $s = i$, a binary representation of the multiplexer function is given by the following switching expression:

$$z = E \cdot \left[\sum_{i=0}^{2^n-1} x_i \cdot m_i(\underline{s}) \right]$$

where $m_i(\underline{s})$ is the ith minterm of the n select inputs.

EXAMPLE 9.11

The function of a four-input multiplexer is described in tabular form as follows:

E	s_1	s_0	z
1	0	0	x_0
1	0	1	x_1
1	1	0	x_2
1	1	1	x_3
0	–	–	0

The corresponding switching expression is

$$\begin{aligned} z &= E \cdot (x_0 m_0(s_1, s_0) + x_1 m_1(s_1, s_0) + x_2 m_2(s_1, s_0) + x_3 m_3(s_1, s_0)) \\ &= E \cdot (x_0 s_1' s_0' + x_1 s_1' s_0 + x_2 s_1 s_0' + x_3 s_1 s_0) \end{aligned}$$

This switching expression results in the gate-network implementation illustrated in Figure 9.20. ∎

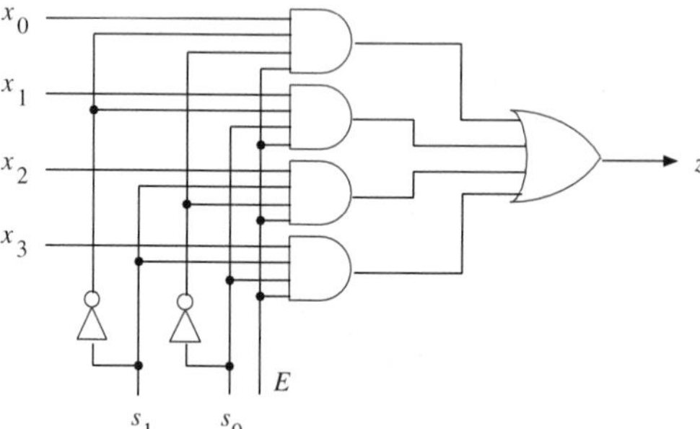

Figure 9.20 Gate implementation of four-input multiplexer.

A typical use of a multiplexer is selecting one of the bits of a bit-vector, and performing some action on the corresponding bit. Another typical use, depicted in Figure 9.21, is the placement of a multiplexer at the input of a functional unit that can operate with one of several operands; the multiplexer is used to select a particular operand.

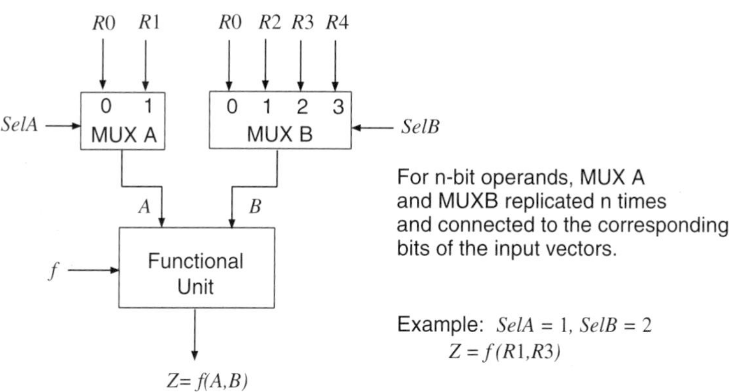

Figure 9.21 Multiplexer. Example of use.

9.4.1 Multiplexer as Universal Combinational Module

A 2^n-input multiplexer can be used to implement any switching function of n variables, as follows:

- connect the input variables $\underline{x}$ to the select inputs of the multiplexer $\underline{s}$; and
- set the data inputs to the multiplexer equal to the values of the function for the corresponding assignment of the select variables.

Figure 9.22*a* illustrates a case with $n = 3$. Because any function of n variables can be implemented with a 2^n-input multiplexer, this is a universal module.

The number of data inputs to the multiplexer can be reduced if, in addition to the constants 0 and 1, one variable or its complement is connected to the data inputs. In this way, a 2^n-input multiplexer can implement any function of $n + 1$ variables. To illustrate this approach, consider the function $f(x_2, x_1, x_0) = \textit{one-set}\,(1{,}2{,}4{,}6{,}7)$ shown in Figure 9.22*a*. To use variable x_2 as a data input, the corresponding sum of products expression is transformed as follows:

$$\begin{aligned}E(x_2, x_1, x_0) &= \sum m(1, 2, 4, 6, 7)\\ &= x_2'(x_1'x_0) + x_2'(x_1x_0') + x_2(x_1'x_0') + x_2(x_1x_0') + x_2(x_1x_0)\\ &= x_2'm_1(x_1, x_0) + x_2'm_2(x_1, x_0) + x_2m_0(x_1, x_0) + x_2m_2(x_1, x_0) + x_2m_3(x_1, x_0)\\ &= x_2m_0(x_1, x_0) + x_2'm_1(x_1, x_0) + 1 \cdot m_2(x_1, x_0) + x_2m_3(x_1, x_0)\end{aligned}$$

This decomposition can also be obtained from a K-map, as shown in Figure 9.22*b*. The corresponding implementation is given in Figure 9.22*c*.

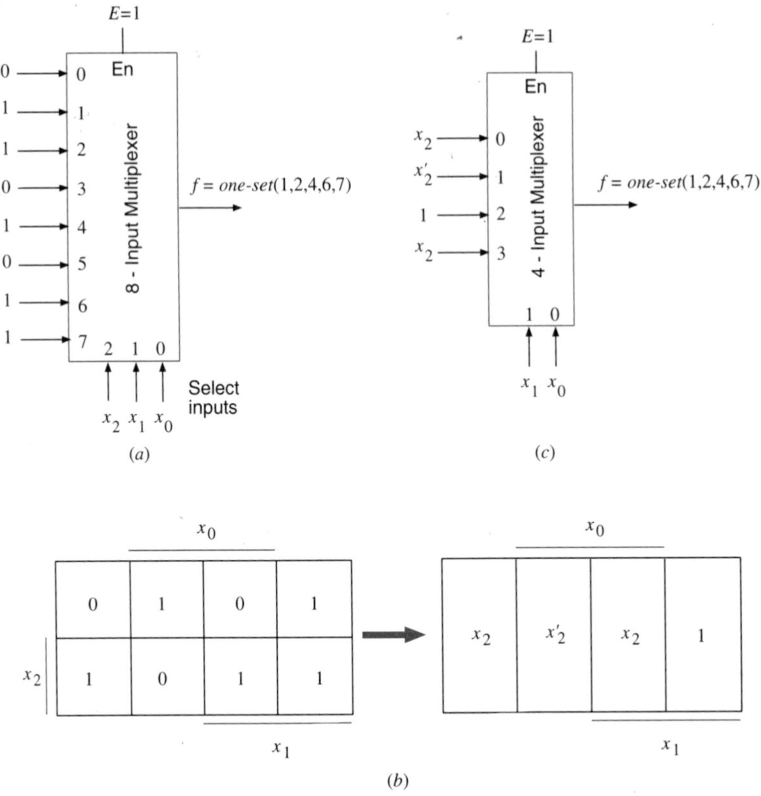

Figure 9.22 Implementation of $f(x_2, x_1, x_0) = \textit{one-set}\ (1,2,4,6,7)$. (*a*) Eight-input multiplexer. (*b*) K-map for four-input multiplexer implementation. (*c*) Four-input multiplexer.

EXAMPLE 9.12

Consider the implementation of a one-bit adder; its arithmetic function is described by

Inputs: $a, b, c_{in} \in \{0, 1\}$
Outputs: $z, c_{out} \in \{0, 1\}$

Function: $z = (a + b + c_{in}) \bmod 2$

$$c_{out} = \begin{cases} 1 & \textbf{if} \quad (a + b + c_{in}) \geq 2 \\ 0 & \textbf{otherwise} \end{cases}$$

This function is described by the following table:

a	b	c_{in}	z	c_{out}
0	0	0	0	0
0	0	1	1	0
0	1	0	1	0
0	1	1	0	1
1	0	0	1	0
1	0	1	0	1
1	1	0	0	1
1	1	1	1	1

This adder can be implemented using two four-input multiplexers, one for each output. We choose, among other possibilities, a and b as the control variables, and 0, 1, c_{in} and c'_{in} as the data inputs. For this choice, from the table we obtain the following switching expressions

$$\begin{aligned} z &= (a'b') \cdot c_{in} + (a'b) \cdot c'_{in} + (ab') \cdot c'_{in} + (ab) \cdot c_{in} \\ &= c_{in}m_0(a, b) + c'_{in}m_1(a, b) + c'_{in}m_2(a, b) + c_{in}m_3(a, b) \\ c_{out} &= 0 \cdot m_0(a, b) + c_{in}m_1(a, b) + c_{in}m_2(a, b) + 1 \cdot m_3(a, b) \end{aligned}$$

The corresponding K-maps and implementation are shown in Figure 9.23.

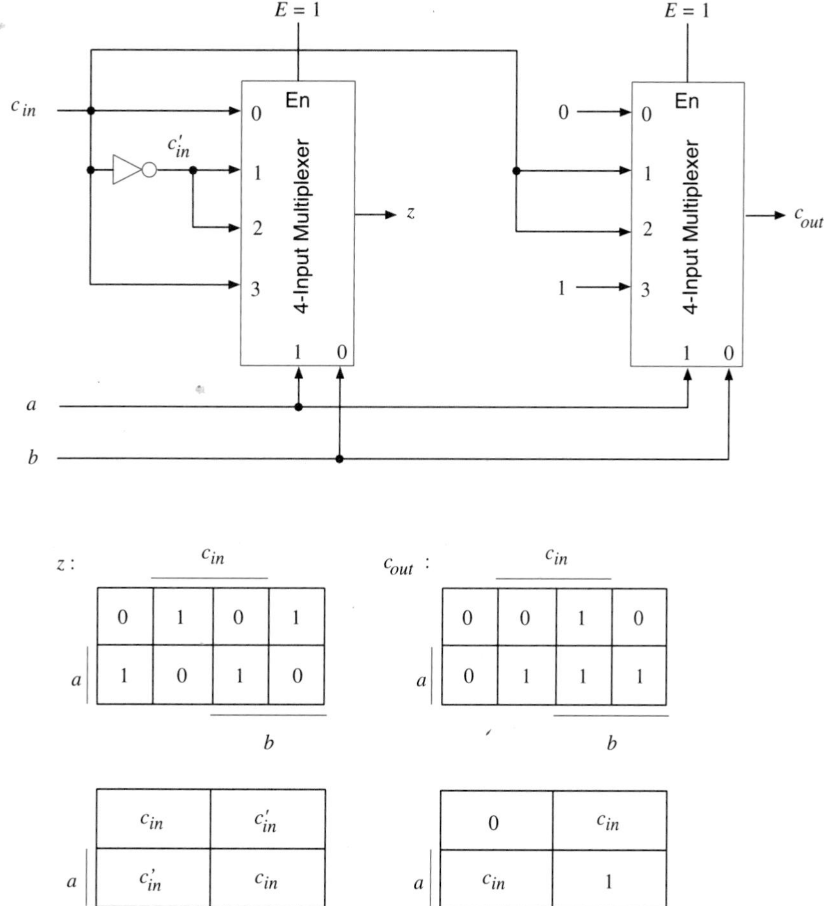

Figure 9.23 Implementation of one-bit adder with four-input multiplexers. ■

9.4.2 Multiplexer Trees

A large multiplexer can be implemented as a multilevel network of multiplexer modules with fewer inputs, called a **multiplexer tree.** To illustrate this case, let us consider the implementation of a 16-input multiplexer using a tree of 4-input multiplexer modules, as depicted in Figure 9.24.

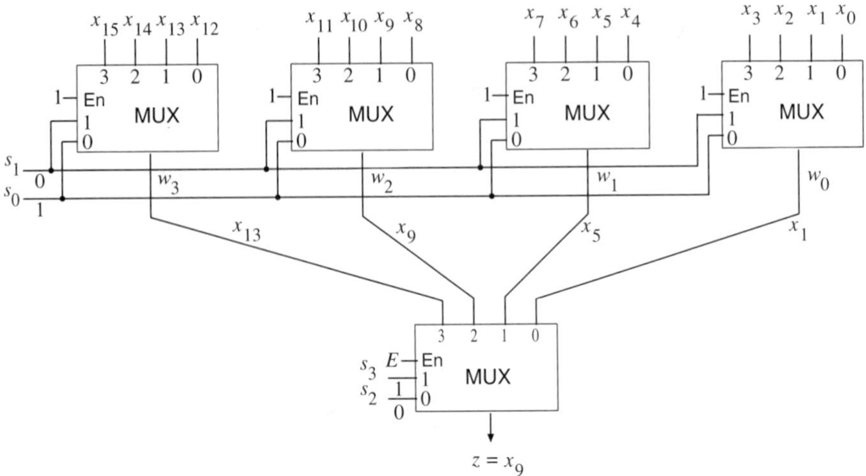

Figure 9.24 Tree implementation of a 16-input multiplexer.

The 16-input multiplexer network requires a select vector with four inputs, that is, $\underline{s} = (s_3, s_2, s_1, s_0)$. Let us divide this vector into two subvectors, as follows:

$$\underline{s}_{\text{left}} = (s_3, s_2)$$
$$\underline{s}_{\text{right}} = (s_1, s_0)$$

One of the subvectors (say $\underline{s}_{\text{right}}$, but either one can be used) is connected to the select inputs of all the modules at the first level of the tree; consequently, the input at the same position is selected in each of these modules. That is,

$$w_j = x_{(4j+s_{\text{right}})}, \quad 0 \leq j \leq 3$$

The other subvector ($\underline{s}_{\text{left}}$ in this case), is applied to the select inputs of the multiplexer module at the second level of the tree. This module selects one variable among the outputs from the modules at the first level, so that

$$z = w_{s_{\text{left}}}$$

By substitution, and taking into account that $s = 4s_{\text{left}} + s_{\text{right}}$, it follows that

$$z = x_{(4s_{\text{left}}+s_{\text{right}})} = x_s$$

For example, as shown in Figure 9.24, if $s = 9$, then $s_{\text{left}} = 2$ and $s_{\text{right}} = 1$. Consequently, the outputs from the multiplexers at the first level are x_1, x_5, x_9, and x_{13}. From these, x_9 is selected by the multiplexer in the second level.

9.5 DEMULTIPLEXERS (DISTRIBUTORS)

A **2^n-output demultiplexer** is a combinational system with n control (select) inputs $\underline{s} = (s_{n-1}, \ldots, s_0)$, one data input x, and 2^n data outputs $\underline{y} = (y_{2^n-1}, \ldots, y_0)$ (see Figure 9.25). This module performs the inverse function of a multiplexer: it routes the input data to the output selected by the select variables; all other outputs are zero. An additional **enable** input E is used to facilitate the implementation of networks of demultiplexer modules.

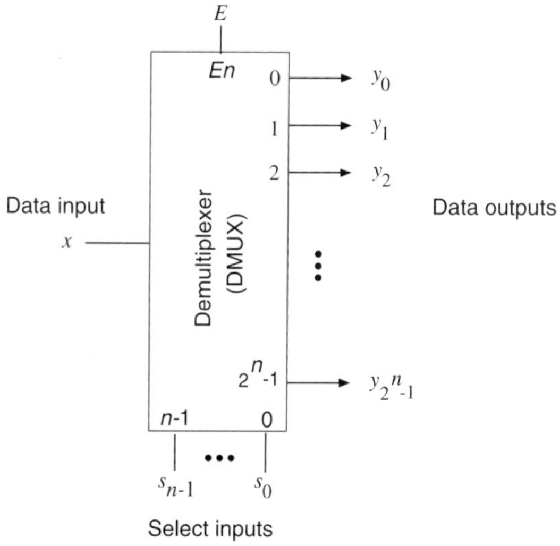

Data input
x

Demultiplexer (DMUX)

E — En

0 → y_0
1 → y_1
2 → y_2
⋮
2^n-1 → y_{2^n-1}

Data outputs

n-1 … 0
s_{n-1} … s_0
Select inputs

Figure 9.25 A 2^n-output demultiplexer.

A high-level description of a demultiplexer is

Inputs: $x, E \in \{0, 1\}$

$\underline{s} = (s_{n-1}, \ldots, s_0)\ ,\quad s_j \in \{0, 1\}$

Outputs: $\underline{y} = (y_{2^n-1}, \ldots, y_0)\ ,\quad y_i \in \{0, 1\}$

Function:
$$y_i = \begin{cases} x & \textbf{if} \quad (i = s) \ \textbf{and} \ (E = 1) \\ 0 & \textbf{otherwise} \end{cases}$$

$$\text{where } s = \sum_{j=0}^{n-1} s_j 2^j \text{ and } 0 \leq i \leq 2^n - 1$$

EXAMPLE 9.13

The input-output function of a four-output demultiplexer is shown in the following table:

E	s_1	s_0	s	y_3	y_2	y_1	y_0
1	0	0	0	0	0	0	x
1	0	1	1	0	0	x	0
1	1	0	2	0	x	0	0
1	1	1	3	x	0	0	0
0	–	–	–	0	0	0	0

■

At the binary level, a demultiplexer is described by the following switching expressions:

$$y_i = E \cdot x \cdot m_i(\underline{s}), \quad 0 \leq i \leq 2^n - 1$$

A gate network implementation for a four-output module is shown in Figure 9.26. Note the similarity with the implementation of the two-input decoder shown in Figure 9.2. What is the difference?

The basic use of a demultiplexer is for transmitting the input data to one out of several outputs, under control of the select inputs. This is required, for example, when the output of a functional unit has to be distributed to one of several other units (see Figure 9.27), or when data are transmitted by a common channel and have to be distributed at the destination.

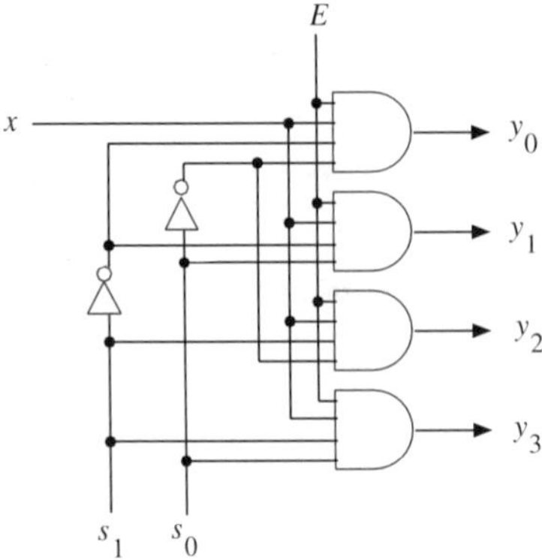

Figure 9.26 Gate network implementation of a 4-output demultiplexer.

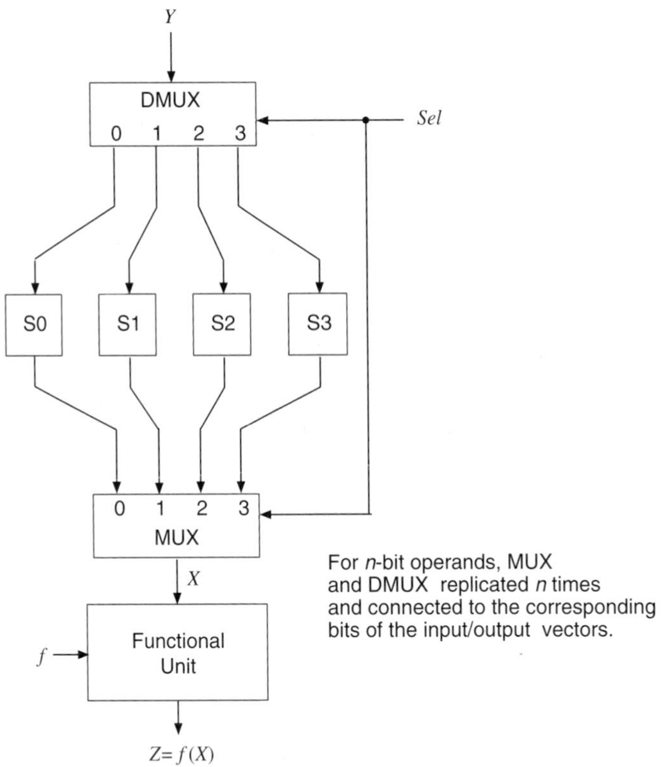

Figure 9.27 Example of a demultiplexer use.

9.6 SHIFTERS

Simple shifter

A **simple shifter** (see Figure 9.28) is a combinational system having an $(n+2)$-bit data input $\underline{x} = (x_n, x_{n-1}, \ldots, x_0, x_{-1})$, an n-bit data output $\underline{y} = (y_{n-1}, \ldots, y_0)$, and two one-bit control inputs: d (for the shifting direction) and s (for shift or no shift). This system shifts the input data by one bit, either to the left or to the right depending on the value of d, or delivers the input data unchanged. An additional enable input E is used to facilitate the implementation of networks of shifter modules.

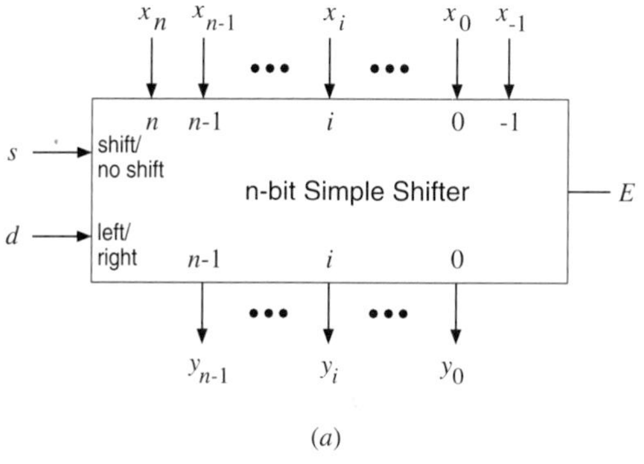

(*a*)

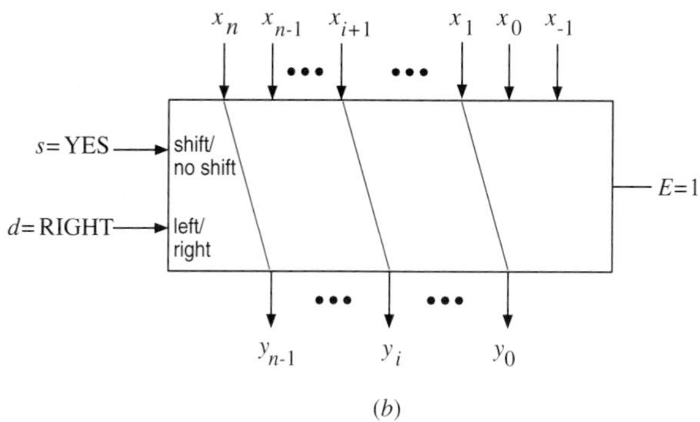

(*b*)

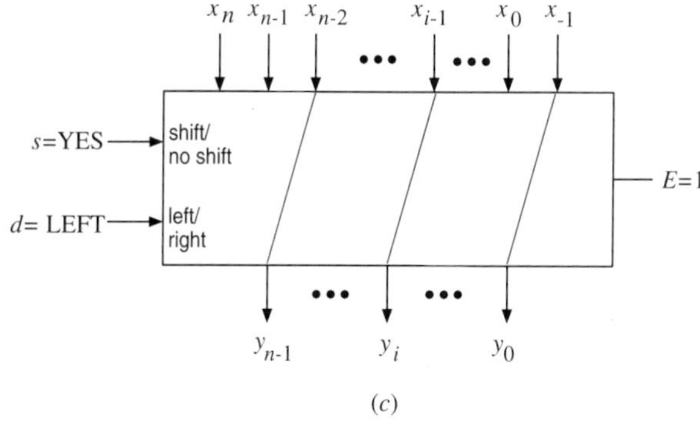

(*c*)

Figure 9.28 *n*-bit simple shifter. (*a*) Block diagram. (*b*) Right shift (*c*) Left shift.

A high-level description of a simple shifter is

Inputs: $\underline{x} = (x_n, x_{n-1}, \ldots, x_0, x_{-1}),\ x_j \in \{0, 1\}$
$d \in \{\text{RIGHT, LEFT}\}$
$s \in \{\text{YES, NO}\}$
$E \in \{0, 1\}$

Outputs: $\underline{y} = (y_{n-1}, \ldots, y_0),\ y_j \in \{0, 1\}$

Function:

$$y_i = \begin{cases} x_{i-1} & \textbf{if} \quad (d = \text{LEFT}) \textbf{ and } (s = \text{YES}) \textbf{ and } (E = 1) \\ x_{i+1} & \textbf{if} \quad (d = \text{RIGHT}) \textbf{ and } (s = \text{YES}) \textbf{ and } (E = 1) \\ x_i & \textbf{if} \quad (s = \text{NO}) \textbf{ and } (E = 1) \\ 0 & \textbf{if} \quad (E = 0) \end{cases}$$

for $0 \leq i \leq n - 1$

Note that $y_0 = x_{-1}$ in the left shift, whereas $y_{n-1} = x_n$ in the right shift. Depending on the values of these inputs, some special shift cases are as follows:

$$x_{-1} = \begin{cases} 0 & \text{left shift with 0 insert} \\ 1 & \text{left shift with 1 insert} \\ x_{n-1} & \text{left rotate} \end{cases}$$

$$x_n = \begin{cases} 0 & \text{right shift with 0 insert} \\ 1 & \text{right shift with 1 insert} \\ x_0 & \text{right rotate} \end{cases}$$

EXAMPLE 9.14

The operation of a four-input shifter is as follows:

	Control		Data					
	s	d	x_4	x_3	x_2	x_1	x_0	x_{-1}
			1	0	0	1	1	0
No shift	NO	–		0	0	1	1	
Right shift	YES	RIGHT		1	0	0	1	
Left shift	YES	LEFT		0	1	1	0	
				y_3	y_2	y_1	y_0	

■

Figure 9.29 illustrates a gate-based implementation and a multiplexer-based implementation of a simple shifter. For these implementations, the coding of the control variables is

s	
0	NO
1	YES

d	
0	RIGHT
1	LEFT

p-shifter

A ***p*-shifter** is a generalization of the simple shifter, in which a $(n + 2p)$-bit data input $\underline{x} = (x_{n+p-1}, \ldots, x_n, x_{n-1}, \ldots, x_0, x_{-1}, \ldots, x_{-p})$ is shifted $0, 1, \ldots, p$ positions, either to the left or to the right. The **shift distance,** that is, the number of positions shifted, is specified by a control input s; the shift direction is specified by input d. The subvectors $(x_{n+p-1}, \ldots, x_n)$ and $(x_{-1}, \ldots, x_{-p})$ provide the additional bits required for the shifts (see Figure 9.30). An additional enable input E is used to facilitate the implementation of networks of shifter modules.

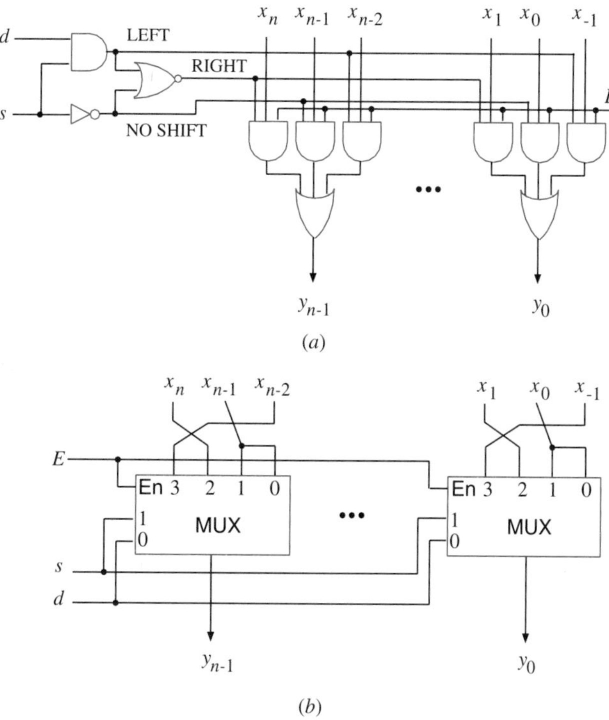

Figure 9.29 Implementation of a simple shifter. (*a*) With gates. (*b*) With multiplexers.

A high-level description of a *p*-shifter is

Inputs: $\underline{x} = (x_{n+p-1}, \ldots, x_n, x_{n-1}, \ldots, x_0, x_{-1}, \ldots, x_{-p}),\ x_j \in \{0, 1\}$
$s \in \{0, 1, \ldots, p\}$
$d \in \{\text{LEFT}, \text{RIGHT}\}$
$E \in \{0, 1\}$

Outputs: $\underline{y} = (y_{n-1}, \ldots, y_0),\ y_j \in \{0, 1\}$

Function:

$$y_i = \begin{cases} x_{i-s} & \textbf{if} \quad (d = \text{LEFT}) \textbf{ and } (E = 1) \\ x_{i+s} & \textbf{if} \quad (d = \text{RIGHT}) \textbf{ and } (E = 1) \\ 0 & \textbf{if} \quad (E = 0) \end{cases}$$
$$0 \le i \le n-1$$

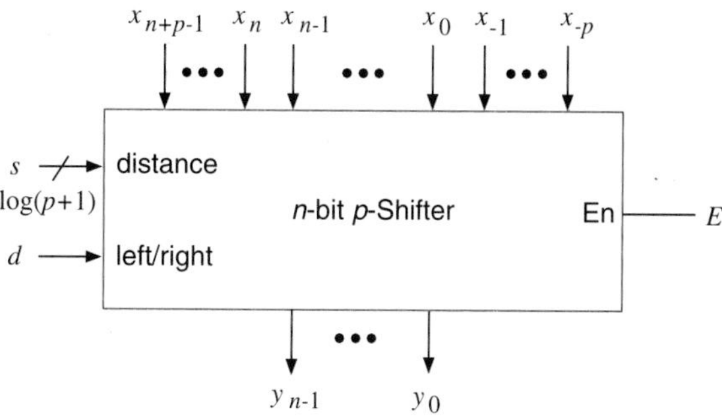

Figure 9.30 An *n*-bit *p*-shifter.

Barrel shifter

A p-shifter can be implemented by means of a **barrel shifter**. This implementation is based on the fact that any shift distance s can be obtained by a sequence of shift distances, each of them being either 0 or a power of 2. This results from the binary representation of the distance s by the bit-vector $\underline{s}$, such that

$$s = \sum_{j=0}^{r-1} s_j 2^j, \quad 0 \leq s \leq p$$

where $p = 2^r - 1$. Therefore, a network of r stages, in which the jth stage shifts a distance of 0 or 2^j, implements a $(2^r - 1)$-shifter (see Figure 9.31). Each stage is implemented by $n + 2p$ three-input multiplexers, which are controlled by the corresponding s_j bit and the direction bit d. The delay of a barrel shifter is proportional to the number of stages, that is, $r = \log_2(p + 1)$.

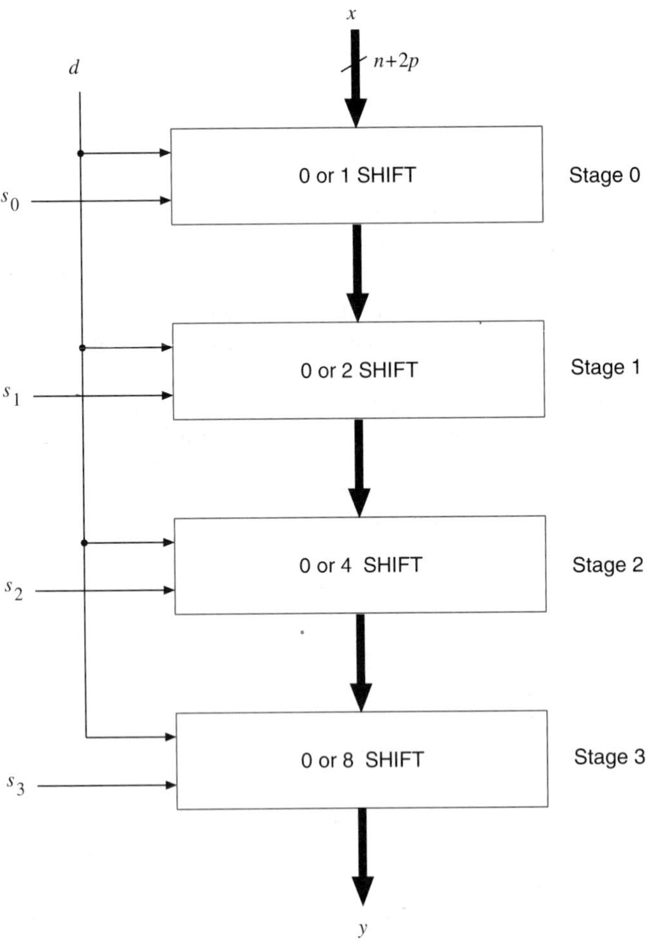

Figure 9.31 Barrel shifter for $p = 15$.

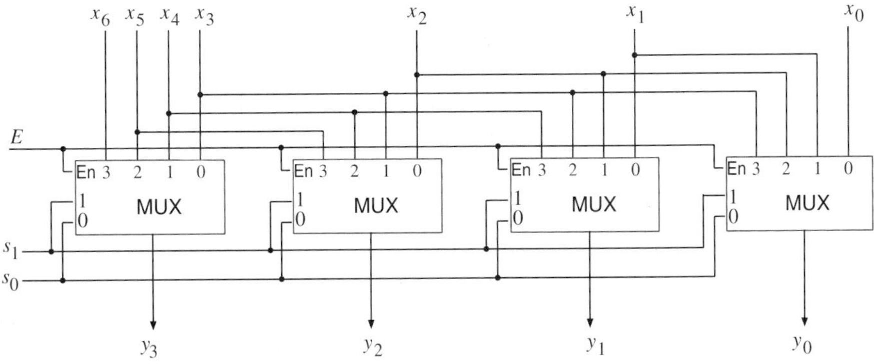

Figure 9.32 Multiplexer implementation of a four-bit right 3-shifter.

Unidirectional shifters

A **unidirectional shifter** is a simplification of a bidirectional shifter in which the data input vector is shifted in only one direction (either left or right). Figure 9.32 depicts a four-bit right 3-shifter implemented using multiplexers. Note that a left 3-shifter can be implemented using this right shifter just by reversing the order of the elements in the input vector.

Uses

Typical uses of shifters include

- Alignment of a bit-vector. For example, floating-point addition requires the exponents to be equal before adding the mantissas; adjusting the value with the smaller exponent implies shifting the corresponding mantissa to the right.
- Removal of the leading (or trailing) bits of a vector. For example, in arithmetic operations that require normalization of an operand, the leading zeros are eliminated by shifting.
- Performing multiplication or division by a power of two.
- Extracting a subvector from a bit-vector, using a shifter instead of a selector.

Large shifters are implemented by networks of shifter modules. The design of networks of unidirectional p-shifters is considered in Exercise 9.21.

9.7 IMPLEMENTATION OF MODULES

The modules we present in this chapter, as well as those of Chapters 10 through 12, are implemented either as individual chips or as part of more complex chips. Although their functionality has been used since the early digital systems, they became known as standard modules when they were integrated, first into separate cards and then into separate chips. Each manufacturer of digital circuits developed a family of these modules, the most popular being the 74-series. Modules of this series are available as single chips and as "macros" in most libraries of cells for the design of VLSI chips. The availability of these chips and macros allows a designer to use them freely in the design of complex systems.

The implementation of the standard modules in terms of gates and transistors depends on the technology and on characteristics such as delay and area. The chip manufacturers and the designers of cell libraries perform implementations optimized for their particular technology and compatible with the characteristics of other modules and cells. As a consequence, the networks of gates we show in this and successive chapters are conceptual and might not be optimal for a particular library.

9.8 FURTHER READINGS

A classical text covering the design with modules discussed in this chapter is *Digital Design with Standard MSI and LSI* by T. R. Blakeslee, 2nd Ed., Wiley, New York, 1979. Another example of a textbook covering in detail this subject is *Digital Systems and Hardware/Firmware Algorithms* by M. Ercegovac and T. Lang, Wiley, New York, 1985. The 74-series of modules is discussed in detail in *Digital Design: Principles and Practices* by J. F. Wakerly, Englewood Cliffs, Prentice-Hall, NJ, 1994. Additional details about implementation and use can be found in numerous literature available from manufacturers of integrated circuits.

EXERCISES

Decoders and encoders

Exercise 9.1 Implement 10-output (decimal) decoders using NAND gates for

a. 2-out-of-5 code;
b. 4-bit Gray code;
c. 2-4-2-1 code.

The corresponding codes are defined in Chapter 2.

Exercise 9.2 Implement a BCD decoder using one Excess-3 decoder, one two-input binary decoder, one two-input NOR gate, and one inverter. Make sure that the Excess-3 decoder is disabled when the input is out of range for that code.

Exercise 9.3 Implement the odd and even parity functions of four variables using a four-input decoder and OR gates.

Exercise 9.4 The coincident decoding approach can be extended to the case in which the input vector is divided into more than two subvectors. If $n = rk$, where k is the number of inputs to a decoder module, then the coincident scheme consists of r decoders and 2^n r-input AND gates. Design a coincident decoder for $n = 12$ and $k = 4$.

Exercise 9.5 Answer the following questions:

a. How many 4-input decoders are needed to implement a 20-input decoder using tree decoding? How many levels will there be?
b. How many 4-input decoders are needed to implement a 20-input decoder if coincident decoding is used? (See Exercise 9.4.) How many AND gates will be needed?

Exercise 9.6 Using AND and OR gates, implement a 10-input encoder for

a. 2-out-of-5 code;
b. Gray code;
c. Excess-3 code.

These codes are defined in Chapter 2.

Exercise 9.7 Analyze the network depicted in Figure 9.33 and show that it implements a priority encoder. Give a high-level specification. Note that in this implementation, inputs and outputs are complemented with respect to the normal description of the priority encoder. That is, the output

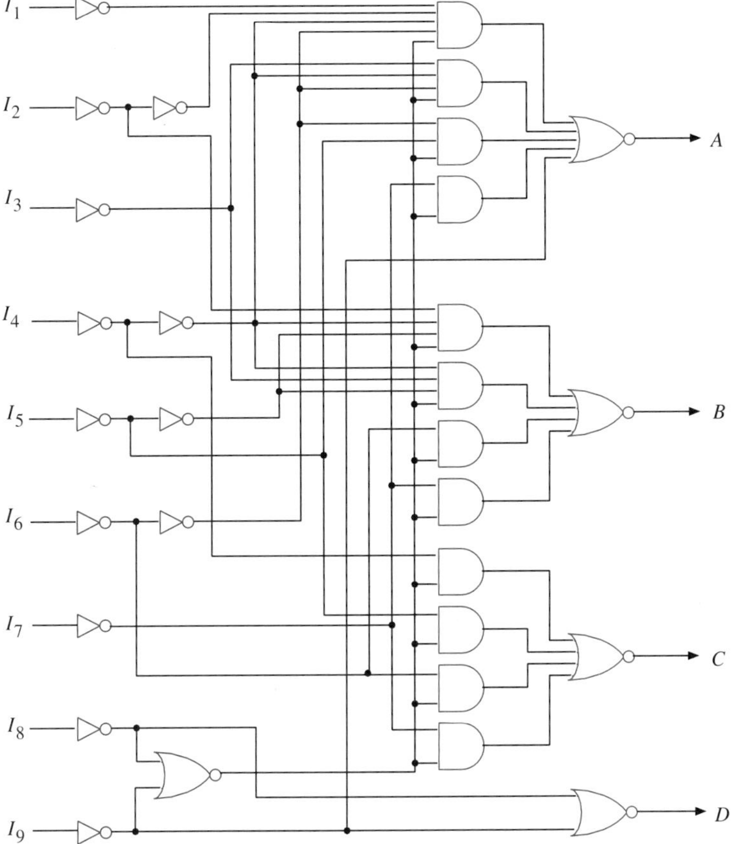

Figure 9.33 Network for Exercise 9.7.

encodes the highest priority input with value 0, and the encoding is the binary representation of the corresponding integer with each bit complemented.

Exercise 9.8 Specify and implement code converters for

a. BCD to seven-segment code (the seven-segment code can be inferred from Figure 9.34);
b. four-bit binary to four-bit Gray code;
c. BCD to 2-out-of-5 code.

Perform two implementations for each: a decoder plus OR gates, and a decoder plus an encoder.

Exercise 9.9 Using a three-input binary decoder and an eight-input binary encoder, implement a code converter from the three-bit Gray code into the three-bit binary code.

Exercise 9.10 Specify a cyclic priority encoder that has eight data inputs and three binary control inputs. The control inputs determine which of the data inputs is highest priority. The priority diminishes cyclically. For example, if input 5 is highest priority, then the order is 5,4,3,2,1,0,7,6.

Design a network that implements this function and consists of a priority encoder, a three-bit binary adder (see Section 10.1), and a shifter.

Exercise 9.11 Design a combinational network that has a three-bit input $\underline{x}$ representing the digits 0 to 7, and a three-bit output $\underline{y}$ representing the same set of integers. The function of the system is $y = (3x) \bmod 8$. Use a decoder and an encoder.

Exercise 9.12 Analyze the network shown in Figure 9.35 and show that it implements a 64-input binary encoder.

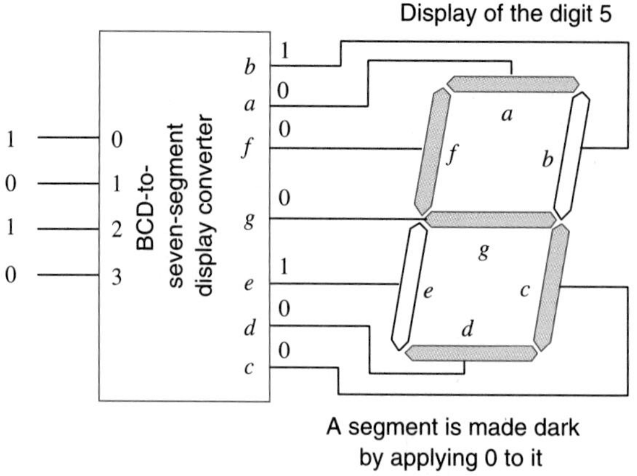

Figure 9.34 BCD to seven-segment decoder and display for Exercise 9.8.

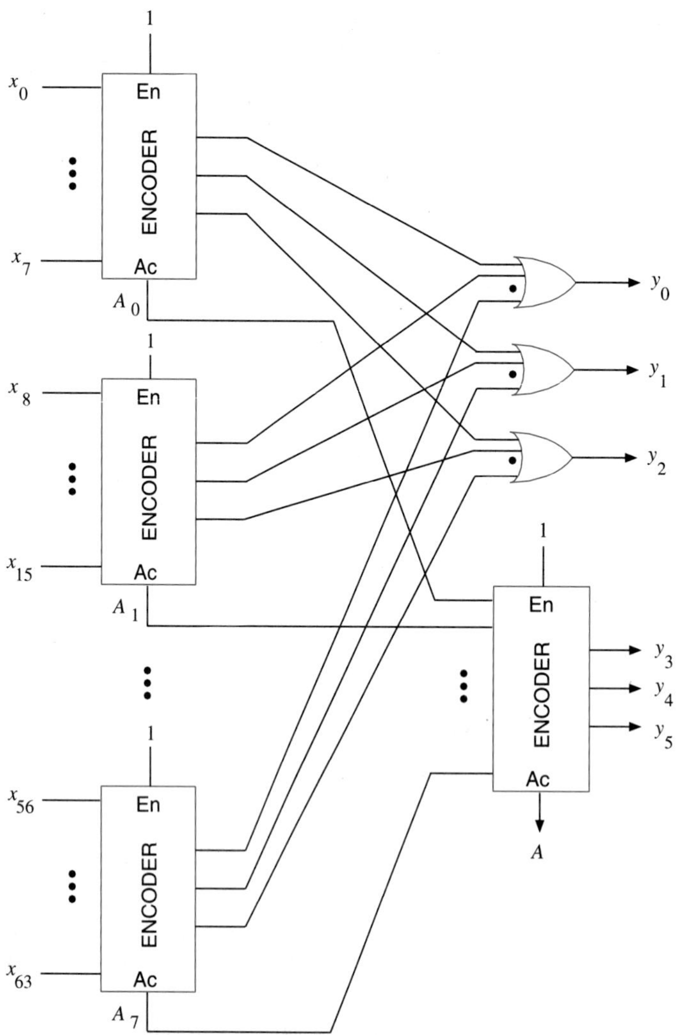

Figure 9.35 Implementation of a 64-input encoder.

Multiplexers and Demultiplexers

Exercise 9.13 How many 4-input multiplexers are needed to implement a 256-input multiplexer? How many levels will there be?

Exercise 9.14 In general, a 2^n-input multiplexer can be implemented by a two-level tree network of $2^{n/2}$-input multiplexer modules, as shown in Figure 9.36. This scheme can be generalized to the case in which there are r levels; assuming that $n = rk$, determine how many modules are needed.

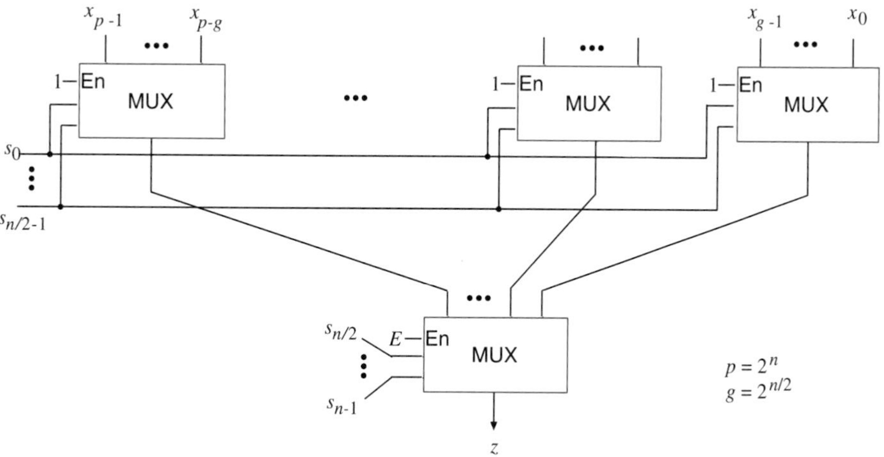

Figure 9.36 Network for Exercise 9.14.

Exercise 9.15 Implement the function $f(a, b, c, d) = one\text{-}set\,(1,3,4,9,14,15)$ using

a. an eight-input multiplexer;
b. a four-input multiplexer and NOR gates (use inputs a and b as select inputs to the multiplexer, the NOR gates for functions $f(0, 0, c, d)$, $f(0, 1, c, d)$, $f(1, 0, c, d)$ and $f(1, 1, c, d)$, and connect the outputs of these networks to the corresponding data input of the multiplexer).

Exercise 9.16 Implement an eight-input multiplexer using a three-input decoder and NAND gates.

Shifters

Exercise 9.17 Implement

a. an eight-bit simple shifter using multiplexers;
b. an eight-bit bidirectional 3-shifter using multiplexers.

Exercise 9.18 Implement a left 3-shifter using a right 3-shifter.

Exercise 9.19 Design a 32-bit 3-shifter using four 8-bit 3-shifters to implement

a. a left shifter;
b. a bidirectional shifter.

Exercise 9.20 Analyze the network shown in Figure 9.37. Can it be used for shifting? Rotation? Bidirectional shifting? How many positions?

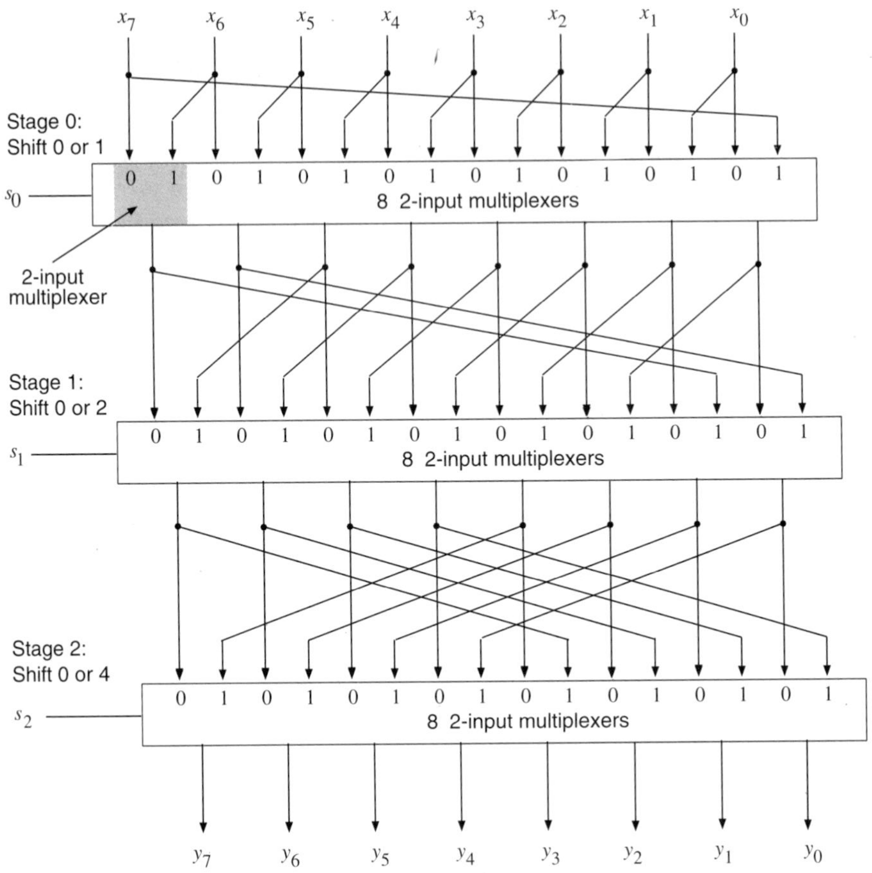

Figure 9.37 Network for Exercise 9.20.

Exercise 9.21

a. Design a 12-bit right 3-shifter using 4-bit right 3-shifter modules.
b. Show how to implement large shifters as networks of standard k-bit/p-shifter modules; for simplicity, consider only the case of a unidirectional right-shifter. How many k-bit/p-shifter modules are needed to implement an n-bit unidirectional p-shifter?

Networks of modules

Exercise 9.22 Analyze the network shown in Figure 9.38 and design a gate network using AND, OR, XOR, and NOR gates that implements the same function. (*Hint:* $z = 1$ if the inputs to the decoder and the multiplexer are identical. Implement an equality comparator using XOR gates and one NOR.)

Exercise 9.23 Show that the network in Figure 9.39 can be used to connect x_j to y_j. This network is used for bit-serial communications.

Exercise 9.24 Analyze the sequential system shown in Figure 9.40. Give a high-level description of its function. (*Hint:* Reduce the number of states and draw a state diagram). Is this a reasonable implementation for this function? If not, obtain a better canonical implementation.

Exercise 9.25 Analyze the controller depicted in Figure 9.41. Give a state diagram.

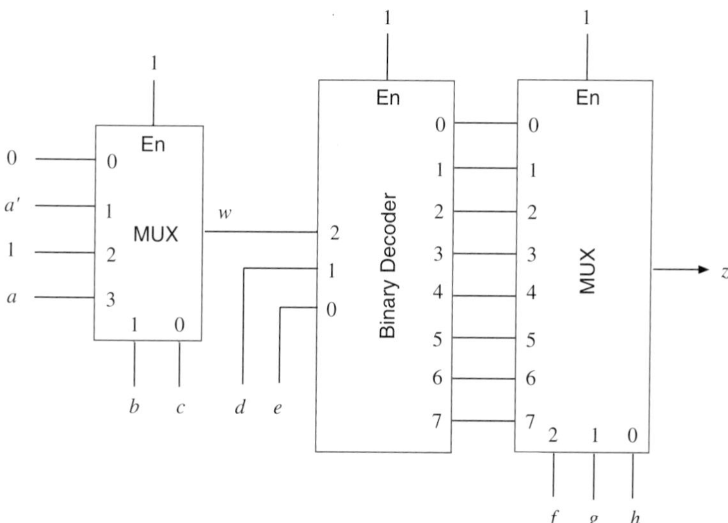

Figure 9.38 Network for Exercise 9.22.

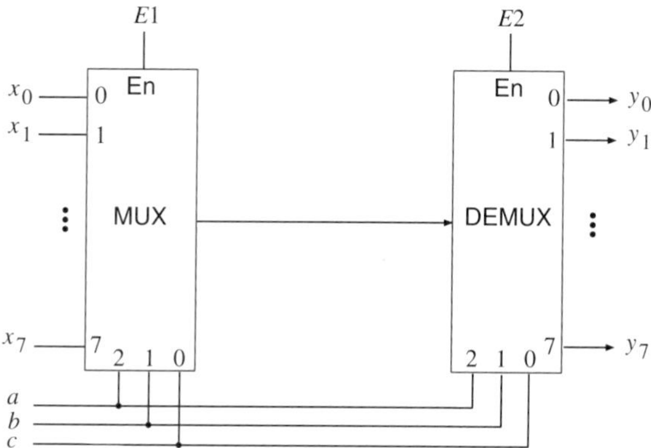

Figure 9.39 Network for Exercise 9.24.

Exercise 9.26 Two digital systems use unconventional codes to represent integers between 0 and 15 as follows:

- System A represents integer n as $p = 3n \bmod 16$, and p is represented by the vector $\underline{p}$ in binary code. For example, for $n = 3$, $p = 9 \bmod 16 = 9 = (1001)$ and for $n = 13$, $p = 39 \bmod 16 = 7 = (0111)$.
- System B represents integer m as $q = 7m \bmod 16$, where the code of q is binary. For example, for $m = 6$, $q = 42 \bmod 16 = 10 = (1010)$.

To link systems A and B, a combinational system is needed to convert an integer between 0 and 15 in the A code to the corresponding B code. Design such a system using

a. one 8-input multiplexer and one 2-input XOR gate;
b. one 4-input decoder and one 16-input encoder.

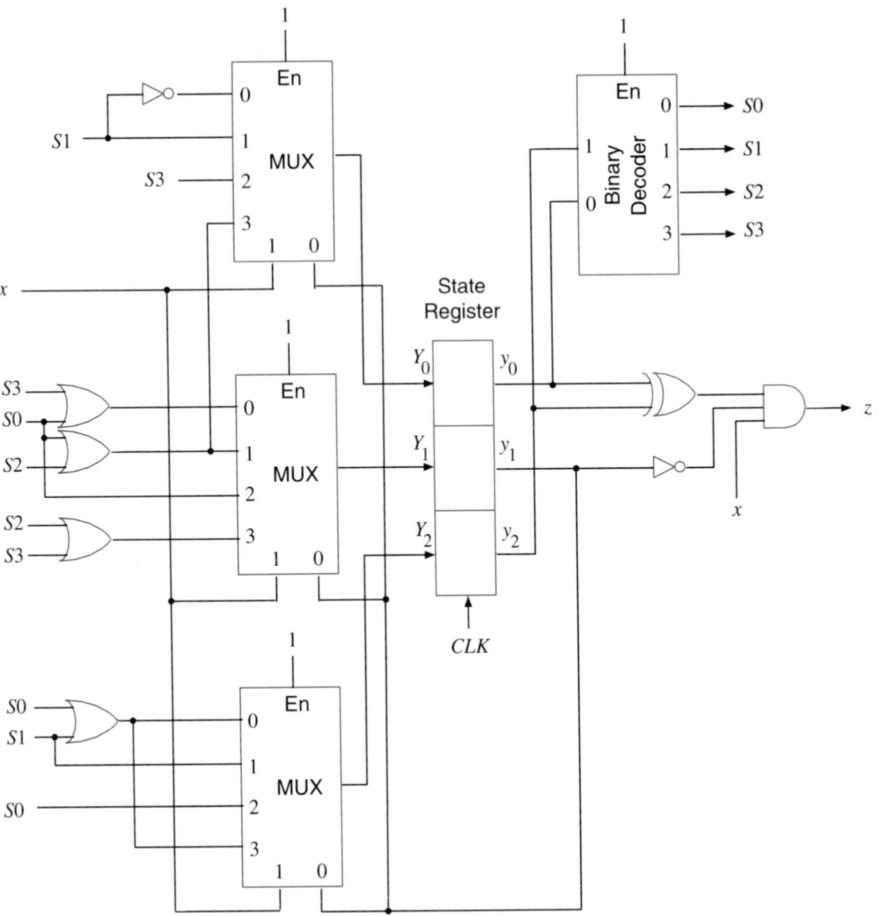

Figure 9.40 Network for Exercise 9.24.

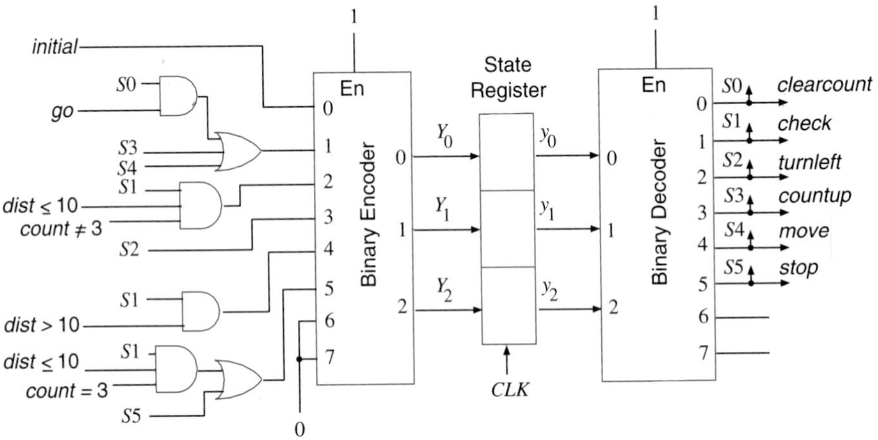

Figure 9.41 Network for Exercise 9.25.

Chapter 10

Arithmetic Combinational Modules and Networks

In this chapter we describe:

- The specification of adder modules for positive integers.
- Half-adder and full-adder modules.
- Carry-ripple and carry-lookahead adder modules.
- Networks of adder modules.
- The representation of signed integers: sign-and-magnitude, two's-complement, and ones'-complement systems.
- Addition and subtraction of signed integers in two's complement.
- Arithmetic-logic units (ALU).
- Comparator modules and networks.
- Multiplication of positive integers.

We now address another important set of combinational modules, that is, those used for the implementation of basic arithmetic operations on integer values. As with all other modules, these are useful for the implementation of more complex (in this case, arithmetic) systems. The inputs to these arithmetic modules consist of bit-vectors that represent integer values, whereas outputs can represent either integers or specify the results from relational operators, such as equal or greater.

Performing arithmetic operations on integers represented by bit-vectors requires the specification of a number system that defines this representation. We begin with adder modules, which perform addition of positive integers in the conventional radix-2 number system, in which the bit-vector $\underline{x} = (x_{n-1}, \ldots, x_0)$ represents the integer x such that

$$x = \sum_{i=0}^{n-1} x_i \times 2^i$$

This allows the representation of integers in the range 0 to $2^n - 1$.

Later in this chapter we discuss the representation of signed integers, and extend the basic addition of positive integers to addition and subtraction of signed integers. We also describe the following auxiliary arithmetic operations:

- change of sign, that is, $z = -x$;
- subtraction; and
- detection of result conditions: sign, zero value, and overflow.

Finally, we present arithmetic-logic units and a basic implementation of the multiplication operation.

10.1 ADDER MODULES FOR POSITIVE INTEGERS

An ***n*-bit binary adder** module (see Figure 10.1) is a combinational system that has two n-bit inputs $\underline{x} = (x_{n-1}, \ldots, x_0)$ and $\underline{y} = (y_{n-1}, \ldots, y_0)$ representing the operands x and y, respectively, and an n-bit output $\underline{z} = (z_{n-1}, \ldots, z_0)$ representing the result z (the sum). The module performs binary addition of the input operands.

Additional input and output signals, called **carry-in** c_{in} and **carry-out** c_{out}, respectively, are used to facilitate the implementation of larger adders. The module adds the carry-in value to the input vectors, and sets the carry-out signal to 1 whenever the result exceeds the maximum value representable with n bits (i.e., a result larger than $2^n - 1$). The arithmetic expression relating inputs and outputs is

$$x + y + c_{\text{in}} = 2^n c_{\text{out}} + z$$

A high-level specification of the n-bit binary adder is

$$\begin{array}{ll}
\text{Inputs:} & \underline{x} = (x_{n-1}, \ldots, x_0), \quad x_j \in \{0, 1\} \\
 & \underline{y} = (y_{n-1}, \ldots, y_0), \quad y_j \in \{0, 1\} \\
 & c_{\text{in}} \in \{0, 1\} \\
\text{Outputs:} & \underline{z} = (z_{n-1}, \ldots, z_0), \quad z_j \in \{0, 1\} \\
 & c_{\text{out}} \in \{0, 1\}
\end{array}$$

$$\text{Functions:} \quad z = (x + y + c_{\text{in}}) \bmod 2^n$$

$$c_{\text{out}} = \begin{cases} 1 & \textbf{if} \quad (x + y + c_{\text{in}}) \geq 2^n \\ 0 & \textbf{otherwise} \end{cases}$$

For example, for $n = 5$,

x	y	c_{in}	z	c_{out}
12	14	1	$(12 + 14 + 1) \bmod 32 = 27$	0 because $(12 + 14 + 1) < 32$
19	14	1	$(19 + 14 + 1) \bmod 32 = 2$	1 because $(19 + 14 + 1) > 32$

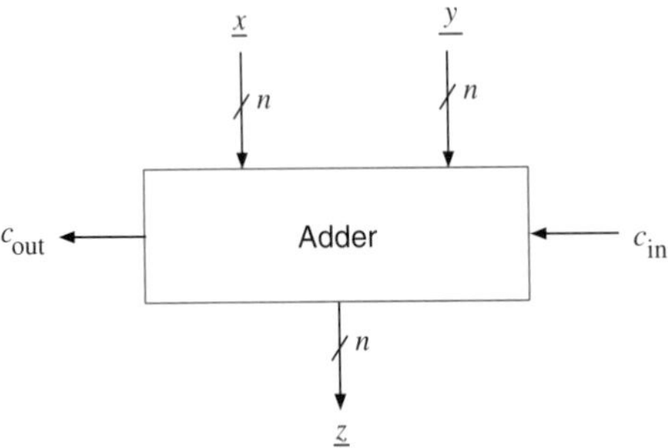

Figure 10.1 Adder module.

Carry-ripple Adder Implementation

Adder modules can be implemented in several ways, which differ in structure, cost, and speed (delay). As with any combinational system, a potential implementation of an n-bit adder is a two-level gate network; however, even for a moderate number of bits, such an implementation requires a large number of gates with a large number of inputs. Consequently, other implementations are necessary. Let us first study the one requiring the least number of gates, which is known as carry-ripple adder.

A **carry-ripple adder** module is a multilevel network formed by the connection of 1-bit adders, called **full-adders** (FA), as illustrated in Figure 10.2. This implementation corresponds to an iterative network of full-adder modules. The FA modules perform addition of a pair of input bits and a carry input, producing a sum bit and a carry output. That is, the inputs to full-adder i are bits x_i and y_i from the corresponding input vectors, and a **carry input** c_i coming from full-adder $i-1$. As output, full-adder i produces the sum bit z_i and the **carry-out** bit c_{i+1} (which is connected as carry input to full-adder $i+1$).

A high-level specification of a full-adder is

Inputs: $x_i, y_i, c_i \in \{0, 1\}$
Outputs: $z_i, c_{i+1} \in \{0, 1\}$

Function: $z_i = (x_i + y_i + c_i) \bmod 2$

$$c_{i+1} = \begin{cases} 1 & \textbf{if} \quad (x_i + y_i + c_i) \geq 2 \\ 0 & \textbf{otherwise} \end{cases}$$

Delay of Carry-ripple Adder

Let us address the delay of the carry-ripple adder (the functional analysis of this module is left as an exercise). The critical path begins in c_{in}, traverses all modules, and terminates either in z_{n-1} or c_{out}. Consequently, the worst-case propagation delay is approximately[1]

$$t_p(net) = (n-1)t_c + \max(t_z, t_c)$$

wherein

$$t_c = \text{Delay}(c_i \rightarrow c_{i+1})$$
$$t_z = \text{Delay}(c_i \rightarrow z_i)$$

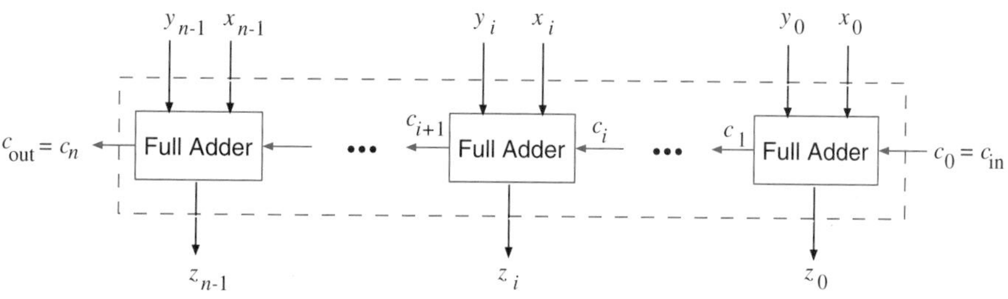

Figure 10.2 Carry-ripple adder module.

[1]A more precise expression is given after showing the implementation of a full-adder.

As is apparent from the expression, the worst-case delay is proportional to n. Consequently, the delay of the carry-ripple adder module is high for large n. Note that the most critical component of the full-adder delay is t_c.

Implementations of Full-adder

Let us now consider implementations of the full-adder. From the high-level description, we obtain the following table:

x_i	y_i	c_i	c_{i+1}	z_i
0	0	0	0	0
0	0	1	0	1
0	1	0	0	1
0	1	1	1	0
1	0	0	0	1
1	0	1	1	0
1	1	0	1	0
1	1	1	1	1

A multiplexer-based implementation using this table was given in Chapter 9. Minimal sum of products expressions for these functions are

$$z_i = x_i y_i' c_i' + x_i' y_i c_i' + x_i' y_i' c_i + x_i y_i c_i$$

$$c_{i+1} = x_i y_i + x_i c_i + y_i c_i$$

These expressions are the basis for the two-level implementation shown in Figure 10.3*a*.
An alternative implementation is based on the following reasoning:

- The addition mod 2 indicates that the sum bit has value 1 whenever the number of 1's in the inputs (including the carry-in) is odd, that is,

$$z_i = x_i \oplus y_i \oplus c_i$$

- The carry-out is 1 when $x_i + y_i = 2$ (i.e., $x_i y_i = 1$) or when $x_i + y_i = 1$ and $c_i = 1$ (which corresponds to $(x_i \oplus y_i)c_i = 1$), so that

$$c_{i+1} = x_i y_i + (x_i \oplus y_i)c_i$$

By defining the intermediate variables

Propagate	$p_i = x_i \oplus y_i$
Generate	$g_i = x_i \cdot y_i$

the previous expressions become

$$z_i = p_i \oplus c_i$$

$$c_{i+1} = g_i + p_i \cdot c_i$$

These expressions are the basis for the implementation shown in Figure 10.3*b*. The sub-module producing p_i and g_i is called a **half-adder** because it performs the addition of two

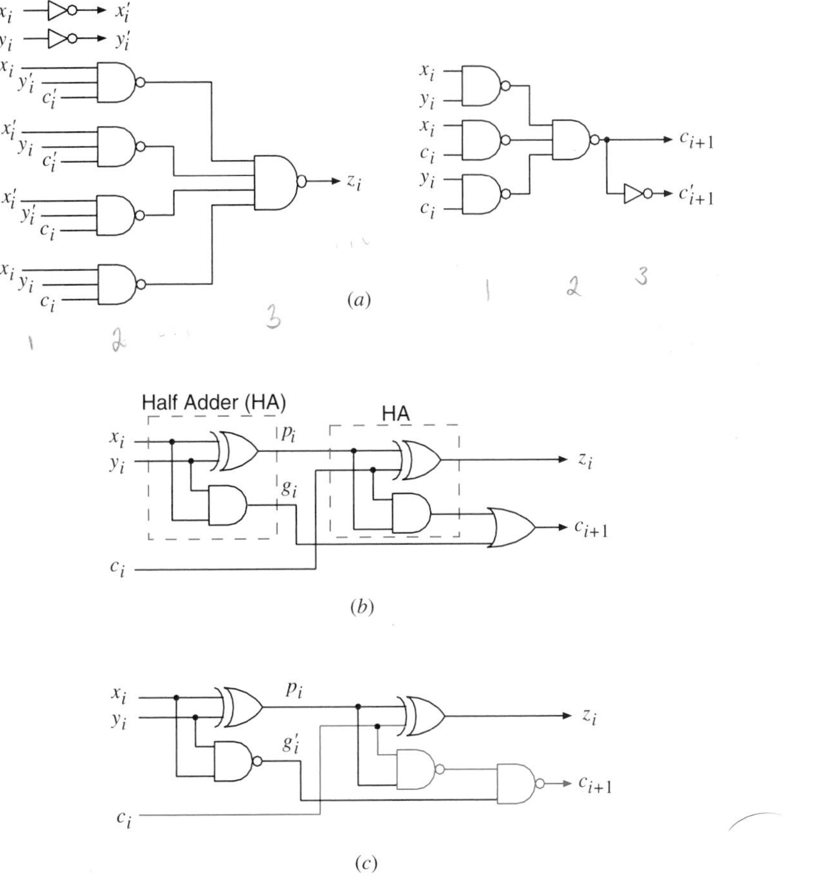

Figure 10.3 Implementations of full-adder module. (*a*) Two-level gate network. (*b*) Multilevel implementation with XOR, AND, and OR gates. (*c*) Multilevel implementation with XOR and NAND gates.

bits (instead of three for a full-adder), the sum bit is p_i and the carry bit is g_i, as shown in the following table:

x_i	y_i	g_i	p_i
0	0	0	0
0	1	0	1
1	0	0	1
1	1	1	0

The implementation of a full-adder using two half-adders and an OR gate requires fewer gates than the two-level network; moreover, the carry delay (from carry-in to carry-out), which is critical for the delay of the carry-ripple adder module, is smaller because it corresponds to the delay of two two-input gates.

Because NAND has shorter propagation delays than AND (OR) gates, the implementation shown in Figure 10.3*c* is preferable. Incorporating this implementation in the structure depicted in Figure 10.2, the worst-case propagation delay of the carry-ripple adder is

$$t_p = t_{\text{XOR}} + 2(n-1)t_{\text{NAND}} + \max(2t_{\text{NAND}}, t_{\text{XOR}})$$

The first t_{XOR} corresponds to p_0. Note that the delay of p_i for $i > 0$ is not in the critical path because all p_i's are computed simultaneously.

Most families of standard cells include a full-adder module. For instance, in the family we are using as example in this book, the full-adder module has the characteristics listed in Table 10.1.

Table 10.1 Characteristics of full-adder in family of CMOS gates

Input	Input load factor (standard loads)
c_i	1.3
x_i	1.1
y_i	1.3

Size: 7 (equivalent gates)

From	To	Propagation delays t_{pLH} (ns)	t_{pHL} (ns)
c_i	z_i	$0.43 + 0.03L$	$0.49 + 0.02L$
x_i	z_i	$0.68 + 0.04L$	$0.74 + 0.02L$
y_i	z_i	$0.68 + 0.04L$	$0.74 + 0.02L$
c_i	c_{i+1}	$0.36 + 0.04L$	$0.40 + 0.02L$
x_i	c_{i+1}	$0.73 + 0.04L$	$0.71 + 0.02L$
y_i	c_{i+1}	$0.37 + 0.04L$	$0.64 + 0.02L$

L: load on the gate output.

Carry-lookahead Adder Implementation

A faster alternative to the carry-ripple adder can be obtained at the cost of more gates with a larger number of inputs. Reducing the delay of the adder module requires "breaking" the carry-propagation path. For these purposes, a good compromise among speed and cost is obtained by performing addition as a two-step process, as follows:

- first, determine the values of all carries into the full-adder modules;
- then, simultaneously compute all result bits.

This approach, which is illustrated in Figure 10.4, leads to a **carry-lookahead adder** module. The name is derived from the way the module is constructed: the first step is

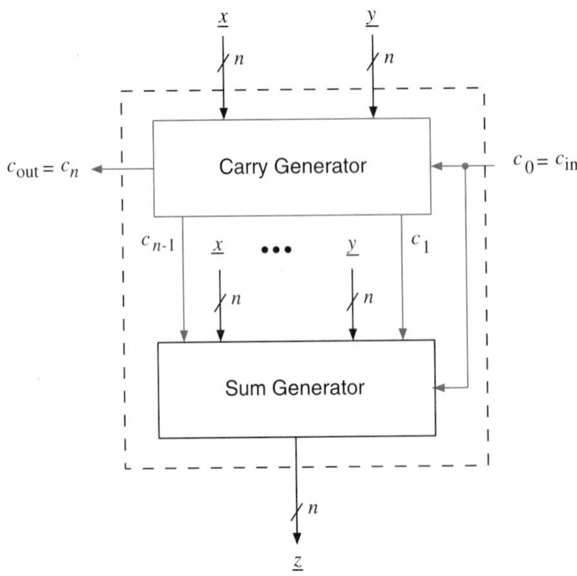

Figure 10.4 Carry-lookahead adder module.

implemented by a **carry-lookahead generator**, which determines the values of all intermediate carries before the corresponding sum bits are computed; the second step uses these precomputed carries to determine the value of the sum bits.

The computation of intermediate carries by a two-level network still requires a large fan-in and large number of gates. To reduce these requirements, we use the intermediate variables p_i and g_i introduced in the implementation of the full-adder. As shown in page 280, the computation of carries is specified by the following switching expression:

$$c_{i+1} = g_i + p_i \cdot c_i$$

where $g_i = x_i y_i$ and $p_i = x_i \oplus y_i$. This expression indicates that the carry-out from a full-adder has value 1 whenever a carry is generated in that cell ($g_i = 1$), or when a carry coming into the full-adder is propagated by it ($p_i = 1$). By substitution, we obtain

$$\begin{aligned}
c_1 &= g_0 + p_0 c_0 \\
c_2 &= g_1 + p_1 c_1 \\
&= g_1 + g_0 p_1 + p_0 p_1 c_0 \\
c_3 &= g_2 + p_2 c_2 \\
&= g_2 + g_1 p_2 + g_0 p_1 p_2 + p_0 p_1 p_2 c_0 \\
c_4 &= g_3 + p_3 c_3 \\
&= g_3 + g_2 p_3 + g_1 p_2 p_3 + g_0 p_1 p_2 p_3 + p_0 p_1 p_2 p_3 c_0
\end{aligned}$$

A gate network corresponding to the expressions above is shown in Figure 10.5*a* (the outputs *P* and *G* will be explained shortly). Moreover, $z_i = x_i \oplus y_i \oplus c_i = p_i \oplus c_i$ so that the complete four-bit carry-lookahead module is implemented as shown in Figure 10.5*b*.

EXAMPLE 10.1

The following tables show examples of the determination of the values of $\underline{p} = (p_3, p_2, p_1, p_0)$, $\underline{g} = (g_3, g_2, g_1, g_0)$, $\underline{c} = (c_4, \ldots, c_1)$ and $\underline{z} = (z_3, z_2, z_1, z_0)$.

- $c_{in} = c_0 = 0$

i	4	3	2	1	0
x_i		0	1	1	0
y_i		0	0	1	1
p_i		0	1	0	1
g_i		0	0	1	0
c_i	0	1	1	0	0
z_i		1	0	0	1

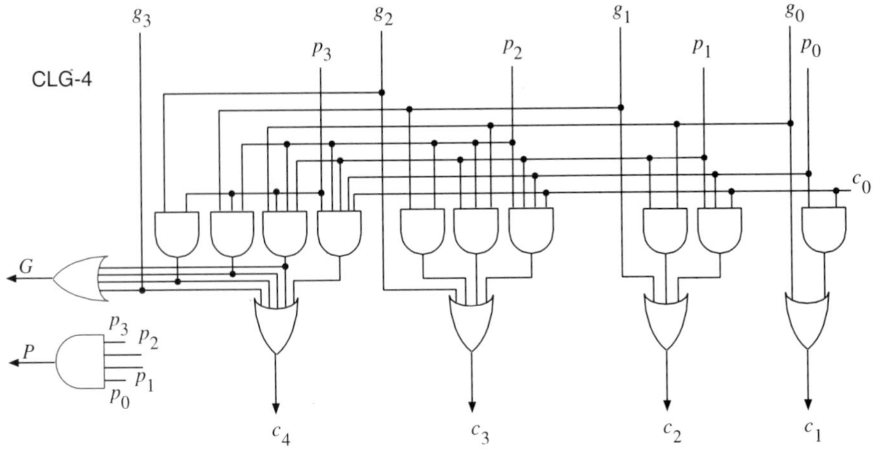

(a)

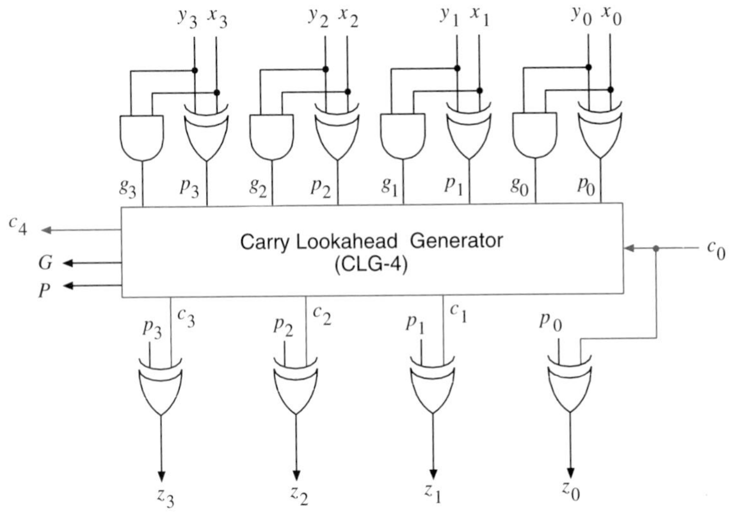

(b)

Figure 10.5 Carry-lookahead adder. (*a*) Four-bit carry-lookahead generator with P and G outputs (CLG-4). (*b*) Four-bit module (CLA-4).

- $c_{in} = c_0 = 1$

i	4	3	2	1	0
x_i		0	1	0	1
y_i		1	0	1	0
p_i		1	1	1	1
g_i		0	0	0	0
c_i	1	1	1	1	1
z_i		0	0	0	0

■

The carry expressions can be generalized if we interpret them as follows: c_3 is 1 if a carry is generated in FA_2, or if a carry is generated in FA_1 and propagated through FA_2, or if a carry is generated in FA_0 and propagated through FA_1 and FA_2, or if a carry comes in and is propagated through FA_0, FA_1, and FA_2. The generalization is then

$$c_{i+1} = g_i + g_{i-1} \cdot p_i + g_{i-2} \cdot p_{i-1} \cdot p_i + \cdots + g_{i-k} \cdot \prod_{j=0}^{k-1} p_{i-j} + \cdots + \prod_{j=0}^{i} p_j \cdot c_0$$

That is, a carry comes out from full-adder FA_i if such a carry is either generated in FA_i, or is generated in FA_{i-1} and propagated through FA_i, or is generated in FA_{i-2} and propagated through FA_{i-1} and FA_i, and so on.

Module Propagate and Generate Signals

To facilitate the construction of larger adders, the carry-lookahead adder module has two additional outputs as shown in Figure 10.5*a*:

- P, which indicates that the value of the carry input to the module is propagated by the module; and
- G, which indicates that the value $c_{out} = 1$ is generated by the module, regardless of the value of the corresponding carry input.

From these definitions we obtain

$$c_{out} = G + P \cdot c_{in}$$

A high-level specification of these additional outputs is

$$P = \begin{cases} 1 & \textbf{if} \quad x + y = 2^n - 1 \\ 0 & \textbf{otherwise} \end{cases}$$

$$G = \begin{cases} 1 & \textbf{if} \quad x + y \geq 2^n \\ 0 & \textbf{otherwise} \end{cases} \tag{10.1}$$

Note that P and G do not depend on the input carry to the module.

To obtain a switching expression for P, observe that $x + y = 2^n - 1$ implies that for all bits the sum of x_i plus y_i is equal to 1. Consequently, $p_i = x_i \oplus y_i = 1$ for all i and

$$P = \prod p_i \qquad i = 0, \ldots, n-1$$

Similarly, for G, if $x + y \geq 2^n$, then there exists some j for which $x_j = y_j = 1$ $(g_j = 1)$ and $p_k = x_k \oplus y_k = 1$, for all $k > j$. An example of this for $n = 8$ and $j = 3$ is

i	7	6	5	4	3	2	1	0
x_i	1	0	0	1	1	–	–	–
y_i	0	1	1	0	1	–	–	–

The corresponding expression is then

$$G = g_{n-1} + g_{n-2}p_{n-1} + g_{n-3}p_{n-1}p_{n-2} + \cdots + g_0 p_{n-1}p_{n-2} \ldots p_1$$

Figure 10.5*a* shows a two-level gate network CLG-4 that produces, besides carries, the module propagate P and module generate G signals for $n = 4$.

The propagation delay of a carry-lookahead adder module is:

$$t_p(x_0 \rightarrow c_4) = t_{\text{XOR}} + t_{\text{CLG-4}}$$

$$t_p(c_0 \rightarrow c_4) = t_{\text{CLG-4}}$$

$$t_p(x_0 \rightarrow P, G) = t_{\text{XOR}} + t_{\text{CLG-4}}$$

$$t_p(x_0 \rightarrow z_3) = t_{\text{XOR}} + t_{\text{CLG-4}} + t_{\text{XOR}}$$

This implementation is faster than the carry-ripple adder module discussed in the previous section. However, the number of input and output bits for this implementation is limited by the number and fan-in of gates and by the number of external connections; moreover, an exact analysis of propagation delay requires considering the delays of specific gates taking into account their fanout (see Exercise 10.2).

10.2 NETWORKS OF ADDER MODULES

As discussed earlier for other modules, the number of bits in operands and result of adder modules are limited because of the limitations in the number of module inputs and outputs, and the number of gates and gate inputs. Larger bit-vectors require the utilization of **adder networks** composed of adder modules.

Networks of adder modules are implemented with the same approaches used for the modules themselves, that is, iterative (or carry-ripple) and lookahead structures. These networks result from an extension of the corresponding two types of modules, as discussed next.

Iterative (Carry-ripple) Adder Network

Let us consider the implementation of a 16-bit adder, using standard 4-bit adder modules. For these purposes, the input and output bit-vectors are decomposed into 4-bit subvectors. For instance, for bit-vector $\underline{x}$ the decomposition is as follows:

$$\underline{x} = (\underline{x}^{(3)}, \underline{x}^{(2)}, \underline{x}^{(1)}, \underline{x}^{(0)})$$

$$\underline{x}^{(3)} = (x_{15}, x_{14}, x_{13}, x_{12})$$

$$\underline{x}^{(2)} = (x_{11}, x_{10}, x_9, x_8)$$

$$\underline{x}^{(1)} = (x_7, x_6, x_5, x_4)$$

$$\underline{x}^{(0)} = (x_3, x_2, x_1, x_0)$$

Because bit-vectors correspond to the radix-2 representation of integers, then

$$x = 2^{12}x^{(3)} + 2^8 x^{(2)} + 2^4 x^{(1)} + x^{(0)}$$

where $x^{(i)}$ stands for the integer value represented by $\underline{x}^{(i)}$. The same type of decomposition is applied to bit-vectors $\underline{y}$ and $\underline{z}$.

Based on this decomposition, we can build a network with four four-bit adder modules, as depicted in Figure 10.6. Each pair of corresponding subvectors is used as input to one of the adder modules, and each of these modules produces one of the output subvectors. The modules are interconnected in a carry-ripple (iterative) manner: the carry output from one module is used as the carry input to the left neighbor module. Note that the modules forming the iterative structure can be either carry-ripple or carry-lookahead type.

The iterative structure can be extended to any number of modules. However, as we have indicated earlier, the delay of this network is proportional to the number of modules.

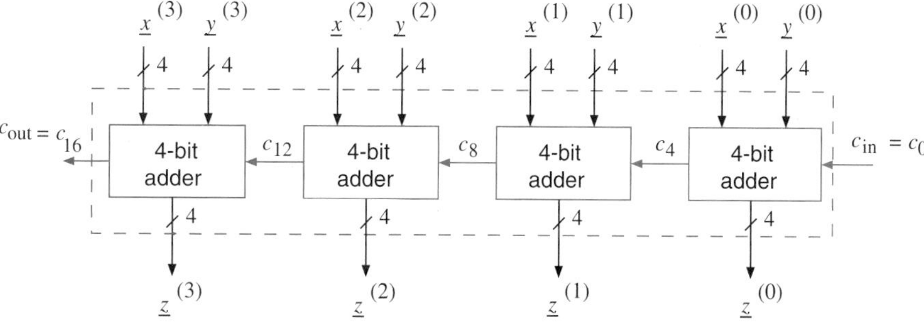

Figure 10.6 16-bit carry-ripple adder network using 4-bit adder modules.

Carry-lookahead Adder Network

Another approach to the implementation of large adders is the carry-lookahead adder network. This approach operates in the same way as in the case of carry-lookahead adder modules. That is, all carries going into the adder modules are computed simultaneously before computing the result bits, and all result bits are computed simultaneously using the intermediate carries obtained from the previous stage. The resulting network uses two levels of lookahead: one inside the modules, and the other between the modules.

For this case, let us consider the implementation of a 32-bit adder using 4-bit carry-lookahead adder modules (CLA-4). Consequently, eight CLA-4 modules are needed, as shown in Figure 10.7. The carries into these modules are computed using carry-lookahead generator modules (CLGs). To be consistent with the size of the adder modules, each carry-lookahead generator module produces four carries, so that two CLG-4 modules are needed, as shown in Figure 10.7.

The first CLG-4 module produces c_4, c_8, c_{12}, and c_{16}, as follows:

$$c_4 = G_0 + P_0c_0$$

$$c_8 = G_1 + P_1G_0 + P_1P_0c_0$$

$$c_{12} = G_2 + P_2G_1 + P_2P_1G_0 + P_2P_1P_0c_0$$

$$c_{16} = G_3 + P_3G_2 + P_3P_2G_1 + P_3P_2P_1G_0 + P_3P_2P_1P_0c_0$$

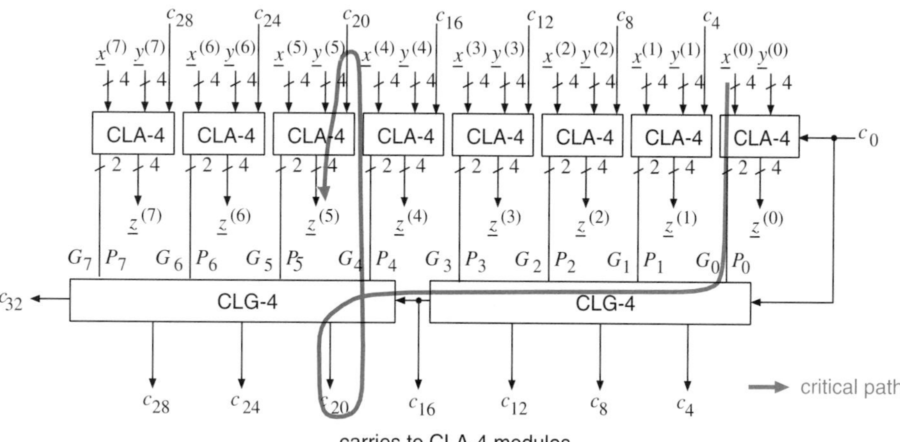

Figure 10.7 32-bit carry-lookahead adder using CLA-4 and CLG-4 modules.

where P_i and G_i are the module propagate and generate signals defined on page 285. Note that these expressions have the same form as in the carry-lookahead generator of the adder module.

The second CLG-4 module produces carries c_{20}, c_{24}, c_{28}, and c_{32}. The corresponding expressions are analogous to those of the first module. Note that the input carry to the second CLG-4 module is c_{16}, which is produced by the first module.

The inputs to the CLG modules are produced by CLA modules; each of these modules receives four-bit inputs, produces outputs P_i and G_i, and implements switching expressions such as these ones (as discussed in the previous section):

$$P_0 = p_3 \cdot p_2 \cdot p_1 \cdot p_0$$

$$G_0 = g_3 + g_2 p_3 + g_1 p_3 p_2 + g_0 p_3 p_2 p_1$$

where $p_i = x_i \oplus y_i$ and $g_i = x_i \cdot y_i$, as in the carry-lookahead adder module.

The propagation delay of this network is obtained by following the critical path in Figure 10.7, that is,

$$t_p(net) = t_{PG} + 2t_{\text{CLG-4}} + t_{\text{ADD}}$$

where t_{PG} is the delay of the CLA-4 module in producing P and G outputs, $t_{\text{CLG-4}}$ is the delay of the carry-lookahead generator module, and t_{ADD} is the delay of the sum outputs from the adder module. Note that t_{ADD} corresponds to the delay in generating the internal carries, which is done using the lookahead-generator inside the adder module, plus the generation of the sum.

This lookahead scheme is frequently used for fast adders; additional levels of lookahead can be used to further reduce the delay in large adders. A comparison among the two implementations discussed—ripple and lookahead adder networks—is left as an exercise.

10.3 REPRESENTATION OF SIGNED INTEGERS AND BASIC OPERATIONS

We consider now the representation of signed integers (positive and negative) and the implementation of the corresponding addition and subtraction operations.

10.3.1 Representation and Sign Detection

In Chapter 2 we described the representation of positive integers. We now extend the discussion to the representation of signed integers—positive and negative. Two representations are by far the most common: the sign-and-magnitude representation and the two's-complement representation. We also discuss the less used ones'-complement representation, and consider the implementation of sign detection.

Sign-and-magnitude (SM) System

A signed integer x is represented in the SM system by the pair (x_s, x_m), where x_s is the **sign** and x_m is the **magnitude**. The usual convention is that $x_s = 0$ corresponds to positive and $x_s = 1$ to negative.

In a binary representation with n bits, one bit is used for the sign and $n - 1$ bits for the magnitude. Consequently, the range of signed integers is

$$-(2^{n-1} - 1) \leq x \leq 2^{n-1} - 1$$

Note that zero has two representations: $x_s = 0, x_m = 0$ (positive zero) and $x_s = 1, x_m = 0$ (negative zero).

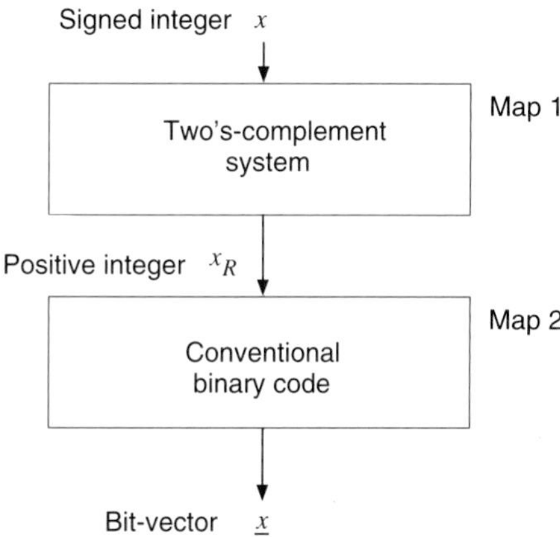

Figure 10.8 Signed integer represented by positive integer.

Because there is a specific bit to represent the sign, the sign detection operation is straightforward. However, due to the negative 0, the relation $x \geq 0$ requires checking for negative 0, that is,

$$x \geq 0 \quad \textbf{if} \ (x_s = 0) \ \textbf{or} \ (x_m = 0)$$

Two's-complement System

In the two's-complement system, no separation is made between the representation of the sign and the representation of the magnitude, but the whole signed integer is represented by a positive integer. Consequently, this representation involves an additional mapping as indicated in Figure 10.8. The signed integer x is represented by a positive integer x_R, which in turn is represented by the bit-vector $\underline{x}$. Map 1 defines the mapping between x and x_R, whereas Map 2 defines the representation of x_R by a bit-vector.

Let us first consider Map 2. The positive integer x_R is represented by the n-bit vector $\underline{x} = (x_{n-1}, x_{n-2}, \ldots, x_0)$ in the binary number system, so that

$$x_R = \sum_{i=0}^{n-1} x_i 2^i \qquad 0 \leq x_R \leq 2^n - 1$$

Then, for the two's complement system, Map 1 is defined by

$$x_R = x \bmod 2^n$$

By the definition of the mod function, for $|x| < 2^n$ this is equivalent to

$$x_R = \begin{cases} x & \textbf{if} \quad x \geq 0 \\ 2^n - |x| & \textbf{if} \quad x < 0 \end{cases}$$

Consequently, as illustrated in Table 10.2, the mapping divides the range of the representation into two regions: the region for positive integers (called **true forms** because no transformation is performed between x and x_R), and the negative region (called **complement forms** because the representation is obtained by subtracting $|x|$ from 2^n). The circular description given for $n = 4$ in Figure 10.9 shows the relationship among this representation and the mod function.

In order to have an unambiguous representation, the region for $x > 0$ should not overlap with the region for $x < 0$. This requires that

$$|x| \leq 2^{n-1} - 1$$

Table 10.2 Mapping in the two's-complement system

x	x_R	$\underline{x}$	
0	0	00...000	
1	1	00...001	
2	2	00...010	
–	–	–	True forms
–	–	–	(positive)
–	–	–	$x_R = x$
$2^{n-1} - 1$	$2^{n-1} - 1$	01...111	
-2^{n-1}	2^{n-1}	10...000	
$-(2^{n-1} - 1)$	$2^{n-1} + 1$	10...001	
–	–	–	
–	–	–	Complement forms
–	–	–	(negative)
-2	$2^n - 2$	11...110	$x_R = 2^n - \lvert x \rvert$
-1	$2^n - 1$	11...111	

However, this range does not include $x_R = 2^{n-1}$. Three choices are possible for this value: it can be used to represent the positive integer $x = 2^{n-1}$ or the negative integer $x = -2^{n-1}$ or it can be left unused. As shown in Table 10.2, the usual choice is the representation of the negative integer because it simplifies the detection of sign and overflow in the addition operation, as discussed later.

EXAMPLE 10.2

The following table presents the mappings for $-4 \leq x \leq 3$ in the two's-complement system. In this case $2^n = 8$ and x_R is represented by the three-bit vector $\underline{x} = (x_2, x_1, x_0)$.

x	x_R	$\underline{x}$	x	x_R	$\underline{x}$
3	3	011	-1	7	111
2	2	010	-2	6	110
1	1	001	-3	5	101
0	0	000	-4	4	100

■

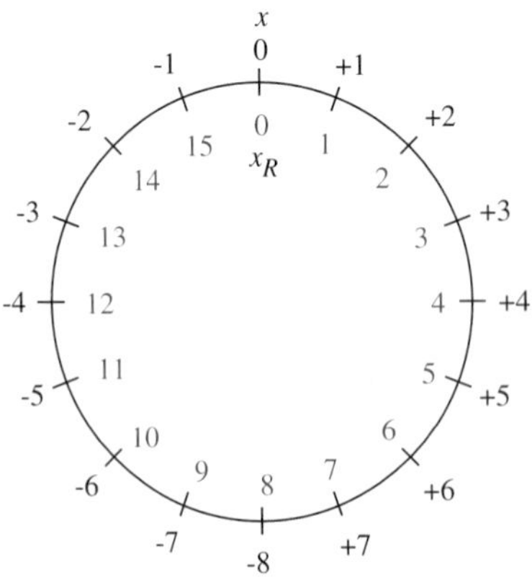

Figure 10.9 Two's complement representation for $n = 4$.

To obtain the signed integer x given the representation x_R, the converse mapping is

$$x = \begin{cases} x_R & \textbf{if} \quad x_R \le 2^{n-1} - 1 \ (x \ge 0) \\ x_R - 2^n & \textbf{if} \quad x_R \ge 2^{n-1} \quad\quad (x < 0) \end{cases}$$

This converse mapping can also be expressed in terms of the bits of x_R. For this, let us consider the two cases of the mapping, as follows:

i. $x = x_R$. Because $x_R < 2^{n-1}$, bit x_{n-1} is 0. Consequently,

$$x = x_R = 0 \times 2^{n-1} + \sum_{i=0}^{n-2} x_i 2^i$$

ii. $x = x_R - 2^n$. Because $x_R \ge 2^{n-1}$ bit x_{n-1} is 1. This results in

$$x = x_R - 2^n = (1 \times 2^{n-1} + \sum_{i=0}^{n-2} x_i 2^i) - 2^n = -1 \times 2^{n-1} + \sum_{i=0}^{n-2} x_i 2^i$$

Combining both cases we get

$$x = -x_{n-1} 2^{n-1} + \sum_{i=0}^{n-2} x_i 2^i$$

Two eight-bit examples are

$\underline{x}$	x
01000101	$0 + 69 = 69$
11000101	$-128 + 69 = -58$

The implementation of sign detection is obtained directly from the converse mapping, so that the sign is obtained from the most-significant bit of $\underline{x}$ as follows:

$$x \ge 0 \quad \textbf{if} \quad x_{n-1} = 0$$
$$x < 0 \quad \textbf{if} \quad x_{n-1} = 1$$

Ones'-complement System

The ones'-complement representation system belongs to the same class as the two's-complement system, namely, the true-and-complement systems. The representation for the generic element of this class is described by

$$x_R = x \bmod C$$

where C is the complementation constant.

For the two's-complement system $C = 2^n$, whereas for the ones'-complement system $C = 2^n - 1$. This representation is illustrated in Table 10.3. As shown there,

- the ones'-complement system is symmetrical, and the range is
$$-(2^{n-1} - 1) \le x \le 2^{n-1} - 1$$
- there are two representations for zero: $x_R = 0$ and $x_R = 2^n - 1$;
- the sign is also detected by the most-significant bit but, as in the sign-and-magnitude system, the relation $x \ge 0$ is implemented as

$$x \ge 0 \quad \textbf{if} \quad (x_{n-1} = 0) \ \textbf{or} \ (x_R = 2^n - 1)$$

Table 10.3 Mapping in the ones'-complement system

x	x_R	$\underline{x}$	
0	0	00. . . 000	
1	1	00. . . 001	
2	2	00. . . 010	
–	–	–	True forms
–	–	–	(positive)
–	–	–	$x_R = x$
$2^{n-1} - 1$	$2^{n-1} - 1$	01. . . 111	
$-(2^{n-1} - 1)$	2^{n-1}	10. . . 000	
–	–	–	
–	–	–	Complement forms
-2	$2^n - 3$	11. . . 101	(negative)
-1	$2^n - 2$	11. . . 110	$x_R = 2^n - 1 - \|x\|$
0	$2^n - 1$	11. . . 111	

10.3.2 Addition and Subtraction of Signed Integers

We now describe the operations of addition and subtraction of signed integers. Specifically, let x and y be signed integers represented by vectors $\underline{x}$ and $\underline{y}$, respectively. The addition operation ADD produces the bit-vector $\underline{z}$ representing the signed integer $z = x + y$. That is,

$$\underline{z} = \text{ADD}(\underline{x}, \underline{y})$$

For the difference $d = x - y$, as $d = x + (-y)$, it is sufficient to combine the ADD operation and the change-of-sign CS operation. That is,

$$\underline{d} = \text{ADD}(\underline{x}, \text{CS}(\underline{y}))$$

If the range of integers represented by $\underline{z}$ is the same as that of $\underline{x}$ and $\underline{y}$ (i.e., it has the same number of bits), the result of addition or subtraction might not be representable by $\underline{z}$. In such a case, an **overflow** signal $v = 1$ indicates this situation.

The complexity of implementing operations ADD and CS depends on the representation system used for the signed integers. We now consider these implementations for the two's-complement system, which is most often used in practice, and leave the sign-and-magnitude and ones'-complement cases as exercises.

Addition in the Two's-complement System

In the two's-complement system, $z = x + y$ is obtained by computing

$$z_R = (x_R + y_R) \bmod 2^n$$

We now show that this expression produces the correct result if there is no overflow, that is, if $-2^{n-1} \leq (x + y) \leq 2^{n-1} - 1$. Let us consider

$$(x_R + y_R) \bmod 2^n$$

and show that it corresponds to z_R, the representation of the sum z. By definition of the representation,

$$x_R = x \bmod 2^n$$

$$y_R = y \bmod 2^n$$

so that

$$(x_R + y_R) \bmod 2^n = (x \bmod 2^n + y \bmod 2^n) \bmod 2^n$$

However, this can be simplified because $(a \bmod 2^n + b \bmod 2^n) \bmod 2^n = (a+b) \bmod 2^n$; consequently,

$$(x_R + y_R) \bmod 2^n = (x + y) \bmod 2^n = z \bmod 2^n$$

and by definition

$$z \bmod 2^n = z_R$$

This means that, to perform the addition of two signed integers represented in the two's-complement system, we add the (positive) representations and obtain the residue (mod) of the sum with respect to 2^n. This operation is done regardless of the relative magnitudes of the operands and their signs (this is in contrast with the sign-and-magnitude case; see Exercise 10.14). Examples of addition for $2^n = 64$ and $-32 \le x, y, z \le 31$ are

Signed operands		Representation		Two's-complement addition	Signed result
x	y	x_R	y_R	$(x_R + y_R) \bmod 64 = z_R$	z
13	9	13	9	22 mod 64 = 22	22
13	−9	13	55	68 mod 64 = 4	4
−13	9	51	9	60 mod 64 = 60	−4
−13	−9	51	55	106 mod 64 = 42	−22

Consequently, the two's-complement addition operation consists of two steps:

- the addition of the positive representations; and
- the mod operation.

The first step is performed by an adder for positive operands as discussed in Sections 10.1 and 10.2; we now consider the mod operation. Let $w_R = x_R + y_R$; as $x_R, y_R < 2^n$, then $w_R < 2 \times 2^n$. Therefore, for this case the mod operation corresponds to:

$$z_R = w_R \bmod 2^n = \begin{cases} w_R & \textbf{if} \quad w_R < 2^n \\ w_R - 2^n & \textbf{if} \quad 2^n \le w_R < 2 \times 2^n \end{cases}$$

Consequently, this operation consists of determining if $w_R \ge 2^n$ and, if so, subtracting 2^n from it.

Because $w_R < 2 \times 2^n$, the representation of w_R in the radix-2 number system is a bit-vector $\underline{w} = (w_n, w_{n-1}, \ldots, w_0)$ of $n+1$ bits. The determination whether $w_R \ge 2^n$ can be accomplished by just checking the most significant bit of $\underline{w}$, so that

$$w_R = \begin{cases} < 2^n & \textbf{if} \quad w_n = 0 \\ \ge 2^n & \textbf{if} \quad w_n = 1 \end{cases}$$

In the first case, $w_R \bmod 2^n = w_R$ and its representation is $(w_{n-1}, \ldots, w_0)$. In the second case, it is necessary to subtract 2^n from w_R; this is simple to do because the representation of 2^n is a 1 followed by n 0's. Consequently,

$$w_R \bmod 2^n \Leftrightarrow (1, w_{n-1}, \ldots, w_0) - (1, 0, \ldots, 0) = (w_{n-1}, \ldots, w_0)$$

That is, in both cases, the mod operation is performed by discarding the most significant bit of the $\underline{w}$ bit-vector. This bit corresponds to the carry-out from the addition of x_R and y_R to produce w_R.

In summary, in the two's-complement system, the result of adding signed integers corresponds to the output of the adder, discarding the carry-out. We describe this as follows:

$$\underline{z} = \text{ADD}(\underline{x}, \underline{y}, 0)$$

where ADD is the addition of positive integers and the third operand corresponds to the carry-in. The two's-complement adder module is shown in Figure 10.10.

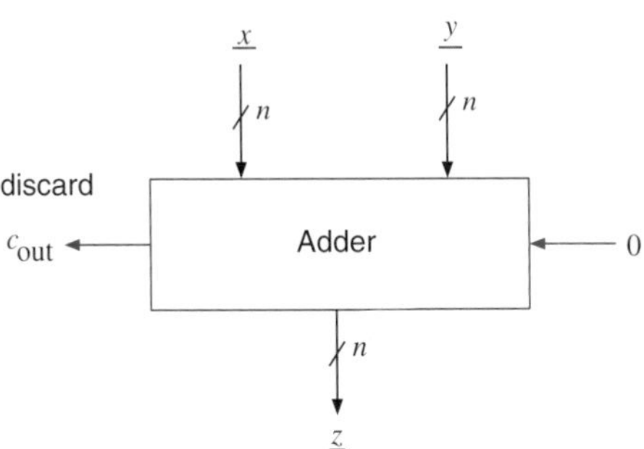

Figure 10.10 Two's-complement adder module.

EXAMPLE 10.3

Two examples of addition of signed integers in the two's-complement number system are:

	Bit-level computation	Positive representation	Signed values
$n = 4$	$\underline{x} =$ 1011 $\underline{y} =$ 0101	$x_R = 11$ $y_R = 5$	$x = -5$ $y = 5$
	$\underline{w} =$ 10000	$w_R = 16$	
	$\underline{z} =$ 0000	$z_R = 0$	$z = 0$
$n = 8$	$\underline{x} =$ 11011010 $\underline{y} =$ 11110001	$x_R = 218$ $y_R = 241$	$x = -38$ $y = -15$
	$\underline{w} =$ 111001011	$w_R = 459$	
	$\underline{z} =$ 11001011	$z_R = 203$	$z = -53$

■

Change of Sign in the Two's-complement System

The change of sign operation consists of obtaining z_R from x_R such that $z = -x$. The operation on the representation, also called complementation, is

$$z_R = (2^n - x_R) \bmod 2^n$$

To show the correctness of the operation, consider the three cases $x = 0$, $x \geq 0$, and $x < 0$. For the case $x \neq 0$, $x_R > 0$ so that $(2^n - x_R) \bmod 2^n = 2^n - x_R$. Consequently, in those cases we drop the mod 2^n.

$x = 0$: $-x = 0$, then $z_R = x_R = 0$. This verifies the above expression for the change of sign since $(2^n - 0) \bmod 2^n = 0$.

$x > 0$: $-x$ is negative, then $z_R = 2^n - |z| = 2^n - x$. Moreover, x is positive so that $x_R = x$. Substituting we get $z_R = 2^n - x_R$.

$x < 0$: $-x$ is positive, then $z_R = z = -x$. Moreover, x is negative so that

$$x_R = 2^n - |x| = 2^n + x.$$

Again, substituting we get $z_R = 2^n - x_R$.

Consequently, the change of sign operation consists of subtracting x_R from 2^n. The direct implementation requires a complete subtraction, which is complex; a simpler implementation is obtained by noting that $2^n = (2^n - 1) + 1$, so that

$$z_R = (2^n - 1 - x_R) + 1$$

Because the representation of $2^n - 1$ is $(1, 1, \ldots, 1)$, we obtain $2^n - 1 - x_R$ by complementing each bit of $\underline{x}$. For example, for $n = 6$

$$\begin{aligned} x_R &= 17 = 010001 \\ 63 - x_R &= 111111 - 010001 = 101110 = 46 \end{aligned}$$

Consequently, the change of sign operation consists of two steps:

- complement each bit to obtain $\underline{x}'$; and
- add 1.

The addition of 1 can be accomplished by setting carry-in $c_0 = 1$. The corresponding description is

$$\underline{z} = \text{ADD}(\underline{x}', \underline{0}, 1)$$

EXAMPLE 10.4

For $n = 4$ and $x = -3$, the following table describes the change of sign operation in the two's-complement system:

$\underline{x}$	1101	$x = -3$
$\underline{x}'$	0010	
$\underline{0}$	0000	
c_0	1	
$\underline{z}$	0011	$z = 3$

■

Subtraction in the Two's-complement System

As we already indicated, subtraction is performed by combining change of sign and addition because $z = x - y = x + (-y)$. In terms of the addition and change of sign operations already described, we get

$$z_R = (x_R + (2^n - 1 - y_R) + 1) \bmod 2^n$$

The two additions in this expression can be combined into a single one by setting to 1 the carry-in into the adder; the corresponding description is

$$\underline{z} = \text{ADD}(\underline{x}, \underline{y}', 1)$$

EXAMPLE 10.5

The following table describes subtraction in the two's complement system:

$\underline{x}$			01100000
$\underline{y}$	00110001	$\underline{y}'$	11001110
			1
$\underline{z}$			00101111

■

Summary

A summary of the implementation of addition, change of sign, and subtraction operations for the two's-complement system is as follows:

Operation	Two's-complement system
$z = x + y$	$\underline{z} = \text{ADD}(\underline{x}, \underline{y}, 0)$
$z = -x$	$\underline{z} = \text{ADD}(\underline{x}', 0, 1)$
$z = x - y$	$\underline{z} = \text{ADD}(\underline{x}, \underline{y}', 1)$

Overflow Detection in the Two's-complement System

An **overflow** exists whenever the result of addition or subtraction is out of the range of the representable integers; in such a case the result is incorrect, so it is necessary to detect this situation.

We consider the case of addition; the situation is similar for subtraction if the sign of y is changed. In the addition operation, an overflow can occur only when the operands are of the same sign; when the signs are different, the result cannot be more positive or more negative than both operands. In the case of operands with the same sign, an overflow occurs if the addition produces a result of the opposite sign (see Figure 10.11). Consequently, in the two's-complement system, overflow occurs ($v = 1$) if

$$v = x'_{n-1}y'_{n-1}z_{n-1} + x_{n-1}y_{n-1}z'_{n-1}$$

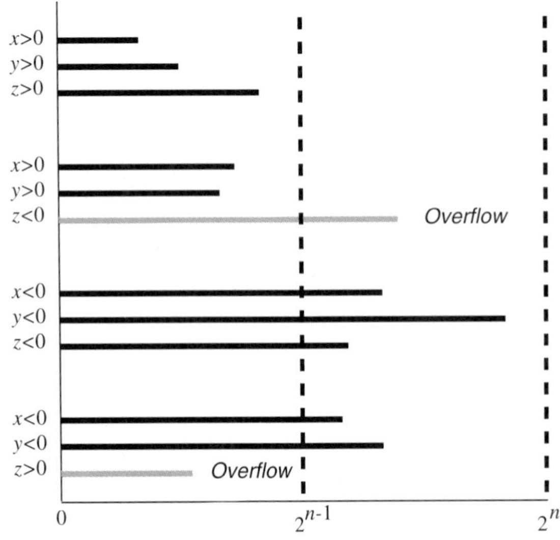

Figure 10.11 Overflow in two's-complement system.

Another way of detecting overflow in the two's-complement system consists of checking the two most-significant carries of the addition (see Exercise 10.15), as follows:

$$v = c_n \oplus c_{n-1}$$

Two's-complement Arithmetic Unit

We now describe a combinational implementation of a two's-complement arithmetic unit for basic operations on signed integers. The high-level specification of this unit is as follows:

Inputs:
$\underline{x} = (x_{n-1}, \ldots, x_0),\ x_j \in \{0, 1\}$
$\underline{y} = (y_{n-1}, \ldots, y_0),\ y_j \in \{0, 1\}$
$c_{in} \in \{0, 1\}$
$F = (f_2, f_1, f_0)$

Outputs:
$\underline{z} = (z_{n-1}, \ldots, z_0),\ z_j \in \{0, 1\}$
$c_{out}, sgn, zero, ovf \in \{0, 1\}$

Functions:

F	Operation		
001	ADD	add	$z = x + y$
011	SUB	subtract	$z = x - y$
101	ADDC	add with carry	$z = x + y + c_{in}$
110	CS	change sign	$z = -x$
010	INC	increment	$z = x + 1$

$sgn = 1$ **if** $z < 0$, 0 **otherwise** (the sign)
$zero = 1$ **if** $z = 0$, 0 **otherwise**
$ovf = 1$ **if** z overflows, 0 **otherwise**

The operation to be performed is specified by the operation code in bit-vector $F = (f_2, f_1, f_0)$. The code used simplifies the implementation of the control signals. The four binary outputs ovf (overflow), sgn (sign), $zero$ (zero), and c_{out} (carry-out) indicate for every operation the corresponding condition of the result; signal c_{out} is useful for multiple precision operations.

An implementation is shown in Figure 10.12; it consists of two complementer modules, a multiplexer, an adder, a combinational logic module, and some gates. Table 10.4 shows the binary-level operations, and the values of control signals to the multiplexer and the complementers for each operation. The complement operation $\underline{a} = \text{COMPL}(\underline{b}, K)$ is defined as

$$a_i = \begin{cases} b_i & \textbf{if} \quad K = 0 \\ b_i' & \textbf{if} \quad K = 1 \end{cases}$$

where K is the control signal into the complementer. Switching expressions for the control signals and carry are obtained from Table 10.4, as follows:

$$K_x = f_2 f_1$$

$$K_y = f_1$$

$$K_{MX} = f_0$$

$$c_0 = f_1 + f_2 f_0 c_{in}$$

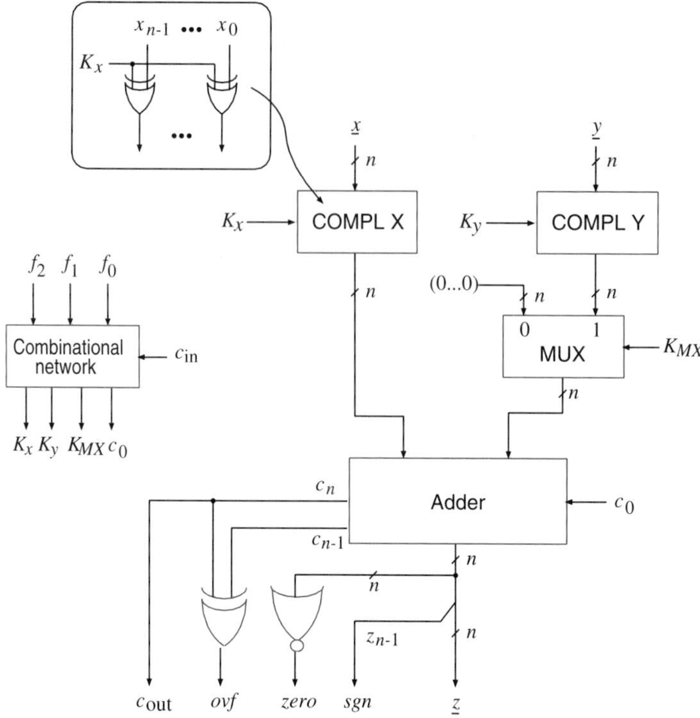

Figure 10.12 Implementation of two's-complement arithmetic unit.

Table 10.4 Control of two's-complement arithmetic operations

Operation	Op-code		Control Signals		
	$f_2 f_1 f_0$	$\underline{z}$	K_x	K_y	K_{MX}
ADD	001	ADD($\underline{x}$, $\underline{y}$, 0)	0	0	1
SUB	011	ADD($\underline{x}$, $\underline{y}'$, 1)	0	1	1
ADDC	101	ADD($\underline{x}$, $\underline{y}$, c_{in})	0	0	1
CS	110	ADD($\underline{x}'$, $\underline{0}$, 1)	1	dc	0
INC	010	ADD($\underline{x}$, $\underline{0}$, 1)	0	dc	0

dc = don't care.

10.4 ALU MODULES AND NETWORKS

An **arithmetic-logic unit** is a module capable of realizing a set of arithmetic and logic functions. To achieve this objective, an ALU has **data input/output vectors** as well as **control inputs;** these control inputs are used to select the specific function performed at a given time.

There are two reasons behind building arithmetic-logic units as standard modules:

1. A general arithmetic module makes it possible to use the same module in many different applications; consequently, it reduces the number of different modules required.
2. ALU modules can be effectively used in systems (processors), in which the specific operation to be performed by the unit is selected dynamically by the control unit of the processor. This type of application is discussed in Chapter 15.

Figure 10.13 shows the block diagram of a four-bit ALU module that has two four-bit data inputs, one four-bit data output, a carry-in input, P and G outputs, and one control input (coded on three bits). The outputs P and G are an extension of their definition for the adder module. The operations performed by this ALU are described in Figure 10.13. (The SUB and EXSUB functions are used to perform subtraction in two's-complement representation.) Note that the module does not have a carry-out signal; consequently it cannot be used directly in an iterative (carry-ripple) network. However, the carry-out signal can be implemented as

$$c_{\text{out}} = G + P \cdot c_{\text{in}}$$

Because the carry does not go through the module when propagated by it, the adder network is called a **carry-skip network;** its analysis is left as an exercise.

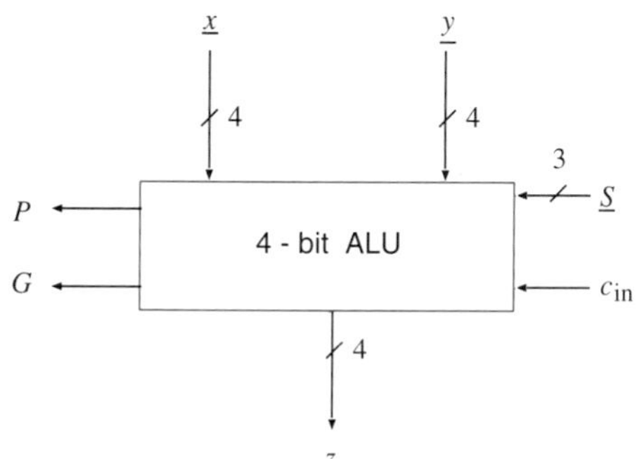

Control (S)	Function
ZERO	$z = 0$
ADD	$z = (x + y + c_{\text{in}}) \bmod 16$
SUB	$z = (x + y' + c_{\text{in}}) \bmod 16$
EXSUB	$z = (x' + y + c_{\text{in}}) \bmod 16$
AND	$\underline{z} = \underline{x} \cdot \underline{y}$
OR	$\underline{z} = \underline{x} + \underline{y}$
XOR	$\underline{z} = \underline{x} \oplus \underline{y}$
ONE	$\underline{z} = 1111$

Figure 10.13 Block diagram and operations in a four-bit ALU.

This ALU module can be used to construct larger ALUs (with more bits). Figure 10.14 illustrates a 16-bit ALU composed of four ALU modules. A carry-lookahead approach is used for addition and subtraction; this requires the use of a carry-generation module, as described in the section on adder networks.

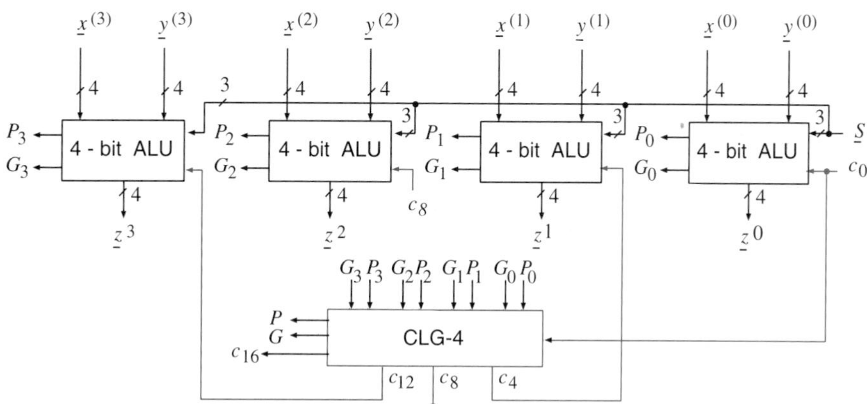

Figure 10.14 16-bit ALU.

10.5 COMPARATOR MODULES

An **n-bit comparator** is a combinational system having two n-bit input vectors $\underline{x} = (x_{n-1}, \ldots, x_0)$ and $\underline{y} = (y_{n-1}, \ldots, y_0)$, representing positive integers x and y, and one output z indicating the relationship among the magnitudes of the two inputs (see Figure 10.15*a*). The output can take values from the set {G,E,S} (greater, equal, and smaller, respectively). An additional input c_{in}, with values {G,E,S}, is used to facilitate the implementation of networks of comparators.

A high-level description of an n-bit comparator is

Inputs: $\underline{x} = (x_{n-1}, \ldots, x_0), \quad x_j \in \{0, 1\}$
$\underline{y} = (y_{n-1}, \ldots, y_0), \quad y_j \in \{0, 1\}$
$c_{\text{in}} \in \{\text{G,E,S}\}$

Output: $z \in \{\text{G,E,S}\}$

Function:
$$z = \begin{cases} \text{G} & \textbf{if} \quad (x > y) \textbf{ or } (x = y \textbf{ and } c_{\text{in}} = \text{G}) \\ \text{E} & \textbf{if} \quad (x = y) \textbf{ and } (c_{\text{in}} = \text{E}) \\ \text{S} & \textbf{if} \quad (x < y) \textbf{ or } (x = y \textbf{ and } c_{\text{in}} = \text{S}) \end{cases}$$

Let us now consider a gate network for a four-bit comparator module. Signals c_{in} and z are implemented as bit-vectors with three bits; each of these bits represents one of the possible values {G,E,S} as follows:

$$\underline{c_{\text{in}}} = (c_{\text{in}}^G, c_{\text{in}}^E, c_{\text{in}}^S), \quad c_{\text{in}}^G, c_{\text{in}}^E, c_{\text{in}}^S \in \{0, 1\}$$

$$\underline{z} = (z^G, z^E, z^S), \quad z^G, z^E, z^S \in \{0, 1\}$$

A binary-level description of the module, whose corresponding network is shown in Figure 10.15, is

$$S_i = x_i' y_i$$
$$E_i = (x_i \oplus y_i)', \quad i = 0, \ldots, 3$$
$$G_i = x_i y_i'$$

$$z^G = G_3 + E_3G_2 + E_3E_2G_1 + E_3E_2E_1G_0 + E_3E_2E_1E_0c_{\text{in}}^G$$
$$z^E = E_3E_2E_1E_0c_{\text{in}}^E$$
$$z^S = S_3 + E_3S_2 + E_3E_2S_1 + E_3E_2E_1S_0 + E_3E_2E_1E_0c_{\text{in}}^S$$

Iterative Comparator Network

Let us consider the implementation of a 16-bit comparator using standard 4-bit comparator modules. For these purposes, the input bit-vectors are decomposed into 4-bit subvectors (similarly to the case of iterative adders). Based on this decomposition, we can build a network with four 4-bit comparators, as depicted in Figure 10.16. Each pair of corresponding subvectors is used as input to one of the comparator modules, and the modules are interconnected in an iterative manner: the output from one module serves as carry-out and is connected as the carry input to the neighbor module to the left.

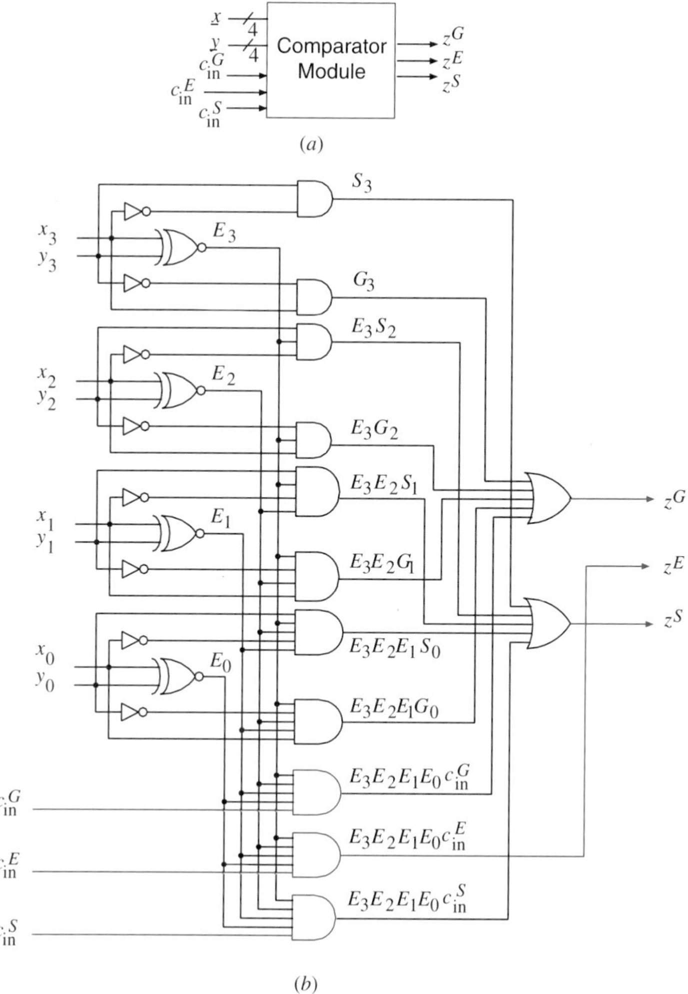

Figure 10.15 Four-bit comparator module. (*a*) Block diagram. (*b*) Gate-network implementation.

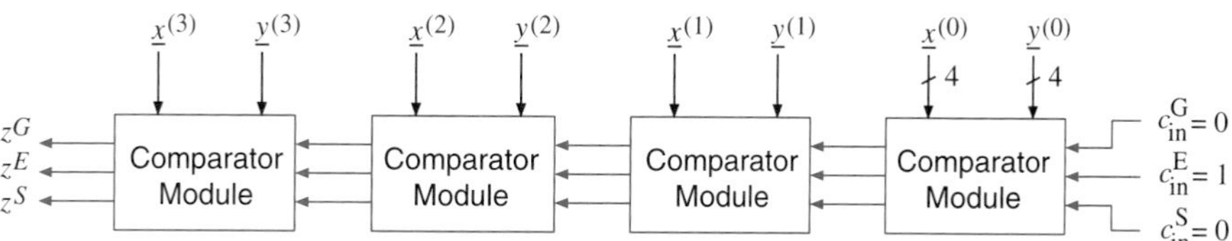

Figure 10.16 16-bit iterative comparator network.

The iterative structure shown in Figure 10.16 can be extended to any number of modules; however, the increase in delay is similar to the iterative (carry-ripple) adder. The analysis of this network is left as an exercise.

Tree Comparator Network

A faster alternative implementation of a comparator for large integers is a tree network. For example, let us consider again the implementation of a 16-bit comparator using standard

4-bit comparator modules, this time interconnected in a tree network as depicted in Figure 10.17. Each module compares two bit-vectors of four bits; consequently, the first level of the tree has four modules, whereas the second level has only one module. The outputs from the first level are connected as inputs to the second level. That is, all z^G outputs from the first level form the vector $\underline{g}$, which is connected as vector $\underline{x}$ at the second level. Similarly, vector $\underline{s}$ corresponds to vector $\underline{y}$ at the second level.

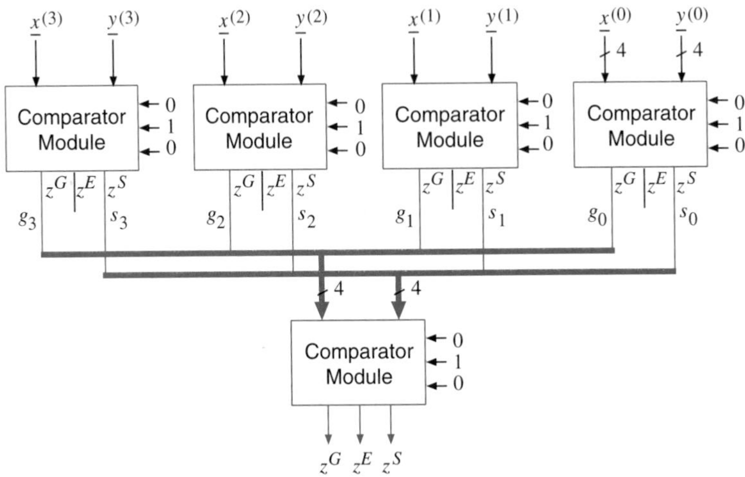

Figure 10.17 16-bit tree comparator network.

The analysis of this network is as follows. From the definition of the basic comparator module, the output of the tree network is

$$z^G = \begin{cases} 1 \textbf{ if } g > s \\ 0 \textbf{ otherwise} \end{cases}$$

$$z^E = \begin{cases} 1 \textbf{ if } g = s \\ 0 \textbf{ otherwise} \end{cases}$$

$$z^S = \begin{cases} 1 \textbf{ if } g < s \\ 0 \textbf{ otherwise} \end{cases}$$

where g and s are the integers represented by the vectors $\underline{g}$ and $\underline{s}$, respectively.

Now note that, because $\underline{g}$ and $\underline{s}$ are outputs from the first level comparator modules, it is not possible that both g_i and s_i are 1. Consequently, $g > s$ means that the most significant 1 of vector $\underline{g}$ is more significant than the most significant 1 of s, so $x > y$. Similarly, $g < s$ implies $x < y$. The case $g = s$ occurs only when $g = s = 0$ and corresponds to $x = y$. Consequently, the network implements the comparison function.

10.6 MULTIPLIERS

We now describe a combinational multiplier for positive integers; such a multiplier is used, for example, in floating-point processors and in many signal processing applications. (We present just a basic implementation; optimizations to obtain faster operation are out of the scope of this text.)

An $n \times m$ bits multiplier has two integer inputs, $0 \leq x \leq 2^n - 1$ (the multiplicand) and $0 \leq y \leq 2^m - 1$ (the multiplier), and produces the integer $0 \leq z \leq (2^n - 1)(2^m - 1)$ (the product). The high-level description is

Inputs:	$x \in \{0, 1, 2, \ldots, 2^n - 1\}$
	$y \in \{0, 1, 2, \ldots, 2^m - 1\}$
Output:	$z \in \{0, 1, 2, \ldots, (2^n - 1)(2^m - 1)\}$
Function:	$z = x \times y$

The integers are represented in the radix-2 number system by bit-vectors $\underline{x}$, $\underline{y}$, and $\underline{z}$, respectively, so that the function can be written as

$$z = x(\sum_{i=0}^{m-1} y_i 2^i) = \sum_{i=0}^{m-1} x y_i 2^i$$

That is, the multiplication is performed by adding the integers $xy_i 2^i$. Because y_i is either 0 or 1, we get

$$xy_i = \begin{cases} 0 & \text{if } y_i = 0 \\ x & \text{if } y_i = 1 \end{cases}$$

which is implemented by the AND gates shown in Figure 10.18*a*.

The multiplication by 2^i corresponds to a shift-left of i positions with insertion of 0s, which is implemented by aligning the operands being added as shown below for the 6×4 bit case:

$$\begin{array}{ccccccccccccc}
 & & & & & x_7y_0 & x_6y_0 & x_5y_0 & x_4y_0 & x_3y_0 & x_2y_0 & x_1y_0 & x_0y_0 \\
 & & & & x_7y_1 & x_6y_1 & x_5y_1 & x_4y_1 & x_3y_1 & x_2y_1 & x_1y_1 & x_0y_1 & \\
 & & & x_7y_2 & x_6y_2 & x_5y_2 & x_4y_2 & x_3y_2 & x_2y_2 & x_1y_2 & x_0y_2 & & \\
 & & x_7y_3 & x_6y_3 & x_5y_3 & x_4y_3 & x_3y_3 & x_2y_3 & x_1y_3 & x_0y_3 & & & \\
 & x_7y_4 & x_6y_4 & x_5y_4 & x_4y_4 & x_3y_4 & x_2y_4 & x_1y_4 & x_0y_4 & & & & \\
x_7y_5 & x_6y_5 & x_5y_5 & x_4y_5 & x_3y_5 & x_2y_5 & x_1y_5 & x_0y_5 & & & & &
\end{array}$$

Finally, the summation is done using $m - 1$ n-bit adders. Consequently, the implementation of the $n \times m$ multiplier consists of

- m arrays of n AND gates; and
- $m - 1$ n-bit adders.

The implementation of an 8×6 bit multiplier, using carry-ripple adders, is shown in Figure 10.18.

The delay of the multiplier (i.e., the critical path) consists of the sum of the following delays:

- the delay of the buffer required to connect signal y_0 to the n AND gates;
- the delay of the AND gate; and
- the delay of the adders.

If the adders are carry-ripple adders, formed of full adders with delays t_s and t_c for the sum and carry, respectively, the critical path through the adders is (see the path marked on Figure 10.18*b*)

$$t_{\text{adders}} = t_c(n - 1) + t_s + (t_c + t_s)(m - 2)$$

If $t_s = t_c$, we get

$$t_{\text{adders}} = (n + 2(m - 2))t_s = (n + 2m - 4)t_s$$

For the 8×6 case, this results in $t_{\text{adders}} = (8 + 12 - 4)t_s = 16t_s$.

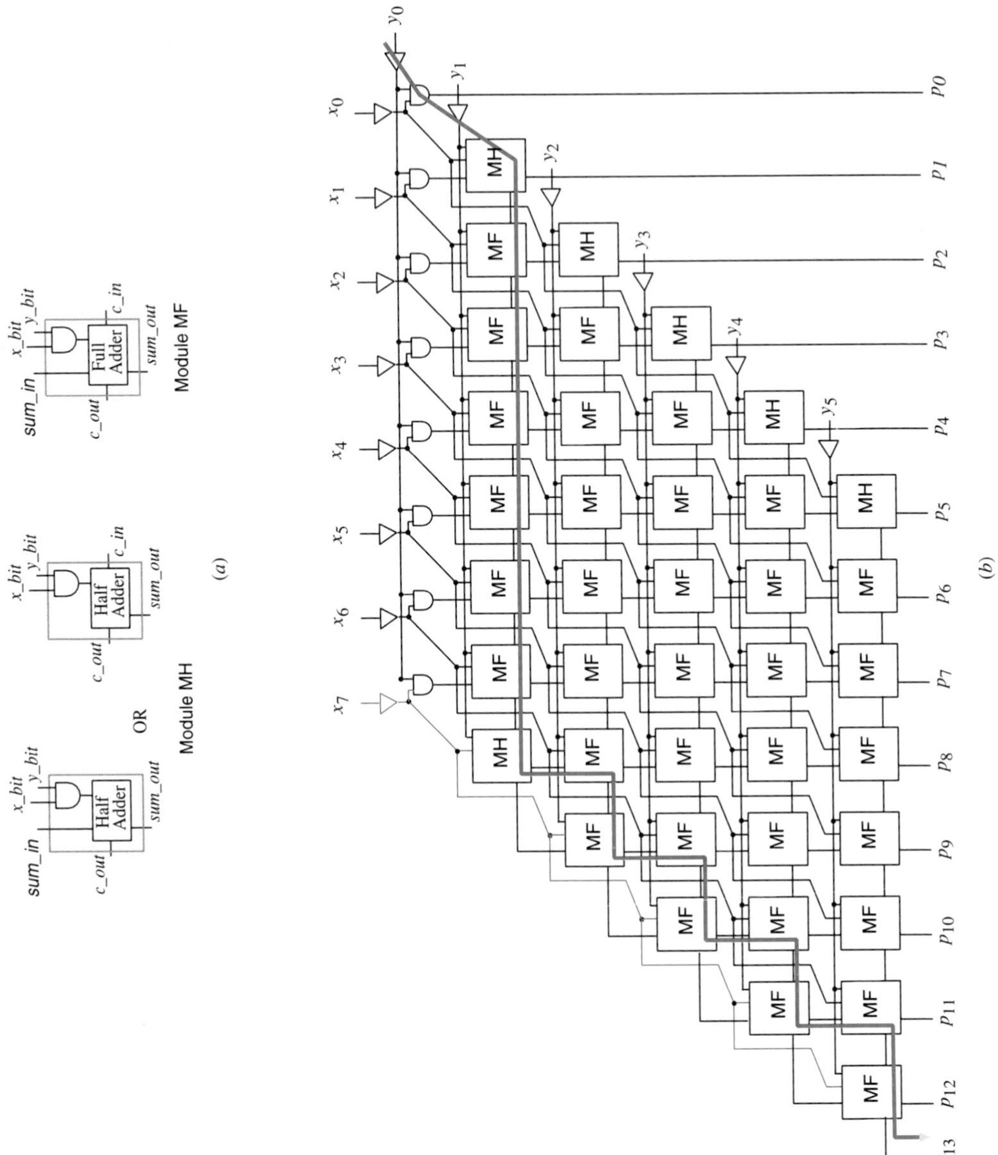

Figure 10.18 Implementation of an 8 × 6 multiplier. (*a*) Primitive modules. (*b*) Network.

10.7 EXAMPLE OF NETWORKS WITH STANDARD ARITHMETIC MODULES

We now illustrate the use of several standard combinational modules for the implementation of an arithmetic combinational system.

EXAMPLE 10.6

The inputs to an arithmetic combinational system are the bit-vector $\underline{e} = (e_3, e_2, e_1, e_0)$, indicating the occurrence of one or more of four independent events, and four pairs of integers $(a[3], b[3])$, $(a[2], b[2])$, $(a[1], b[1])$, $(a[0], b[0])$. The outputs are four integers $c[3], c[2], c[1], c[0]$, an integer d and a single-bit f. The system selects the highest-priority event, say e_j, according to a fixed-priority scheme that makes e_3 highest priority and e_0

lowest, adds the corresponding $a[j]$ and $b[j]$ inputs, and produces the corresponding output $c[j]$. Moreover, output d gives the index ($d = j$) of the selected event, and output $f = 1$ when at least one event occurred.

The high-level specification of the system is

Inputs: $a[3], a[2], a[1], a[0] \in \{0, \ldots, 2^{16} - 1\}$
$b[3], b[2], b[1], b[0] \in \{0, \ldots, 2^{16} - 1\}$
$\underline{e} = (e_3, e_2, e_1, e_0)$, $e_i \in \{0, 1\}$

Outputs: $c[3], c[2], c[1], c[0] \in \{0, \ldots, 2^{17} - 1\}$
$d \in \{0, 1, 2, 3\}$
$f \in \{0, 1\}$

Function:

$$f = \begin{cases} 1 & \textbf{if} \quad \text{at least one } e_j = 1 \\ 0 & \textbf{otherwise} \end{cases} \quad , j = 0, 1, 2, 3$$

$$d = \begin{cases} i & \textbf{if} \quad e_i = 1 \text{ and } e_j = 0 \text{ for all } j > i \\ 0 & \textbf{otherwise} \end{cases}$$

$$c[i] = \begin{cases} a[i] + b[i] & \textbf{if} \quad e_i = 1 \text{ and } e_j = 0 \text{ for all } j > i \\ 0 & \textbf{otherwise} \end{cases}$$

A modular implementation, shown in Figure 10.19, consists of the following modules:

- a PRIORITY ENCODER to determine the highest-priority event;
- an ADDER;
- two SELECTORS (multiplexers) to select the corresponding inputs to the adder;
- a DISTRIBUTOR (demultiplexer) to send the output of the adder to the corresponding system output; and
- an OR gate to determine whether at least one event has occurred.

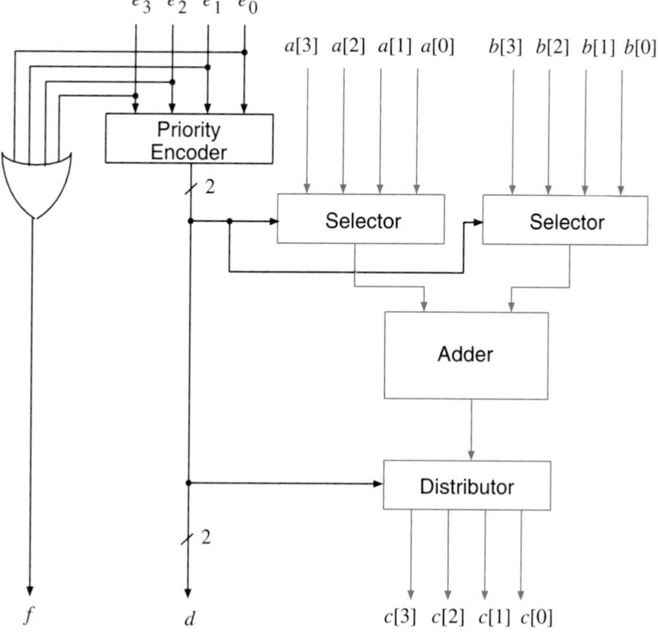

Figure 10.19 Network in Example 10.6.

■

10.8 FURTHER READINGS

There are several books dealing with the various aspects of the specification and implementation of arithmetic processors, such as *Computer Arithmetic* by K. Hwang, Wiley, New York, 1978; *Introduction to Arithmetic for Digital Systems* by S. Wasser and M. J. Flynn, Holt, Rinehart and Winston, New York, 1982; *Computer Number Systems & Arithmetic* by N. R. Scott, Prentice Hall, Englewood Cliffs, NJ, 1985; *Computer Arithmetic Algorithms* by I. Koren, Prentice Hall, Englewood Cliffs, NJ, 1993; and *Digital Systems and Hardware/Firmware Algorithms* by M. Ercegovac and T. Lang, Wiley, New York, 1985.

EXERCISES

Adder modules

Exercise 10.1 Compare the three implementations of a full-adder given in Figure 10.3 in terms of delay and number of equivalent gates. Use the gate characteristics given in Chapters 3 and 4.

Exercise 10.2 Compare the carry-ripple and carry-lookahead implementations of a 4-bit adder module in terms of delay and number of equivalent gates. Use the gate characteristics given in Chapters 3 and 4.

Exercise 10.3 Design a BCD to Excess-3 converter using a four-bit binary adder.

Exercise 10.4 Design a one-digit decimal adder in the BCD code. Use four-bit binary adder modules and NAND gates.

Exercise 10.5 Design a one-digit decimal adder in the Excess-3 code. Use two four-bit binary adders and one inverter.

Exercise 10.6 Determine the function implemented by the network shown in Figure 10.20, and design an equivalent network that uses fewer modules.

Exercise 10.7 Consider the implementation of a 2-bit adder as a two-level NAND-NAND network. Determine

- a. how many NAND gates are needed;
- b. the maximum number of inputs to the gates;
- c. the input load factors of the network.

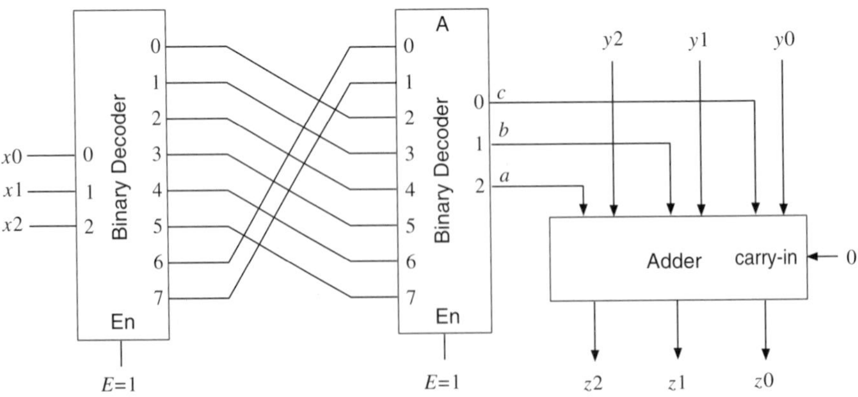

Figure 10.20 Network for Exercise 10.6.

Exercise 10.8 Applying the transformations discussed in Chapter 6, implement a six-bit carry-lookahead adder module using gates with a maximum of four inputs. Determine how many gates are required and the number of levels of the network.

Adder networks

Exercise 10.9 Consider a 64-bit adder. Draw the logic diagram of the network for the following implementations:

a. A carry-ripple adder using 4-bit carry-lookahead adder modules.
b. A carry-lookahead adder using 4-bit carry-lookahead adder modules (CLA-4) and 4-bit carry-lookahead generator modules (CLG-4).

Compare the two implementations in terms of number of modules and delay. Use the characteristics of the family of gates given in Chapters 3 and 4.

Signed integers: representation and addition/subtraction

Exercise 10.10 Complete the following table

	Signed integer (in decimal)	Representation (in decimal)	Bit-vector
a	−37		
b		205	
c			11011
d	9		

for

a. Two's complement, $n = 7$ bits
b. Ones' complement, $n = 8$ bits
c. Two's complement, $n = 5$ bits
d. Two's complement, $n = 8$ bits

Exercise 10.11 The representation of integers can be generalized to representation of **fixed-point** numbers. That is, the binary point, which for integers is assumed to be to the right of the least-significant digit, can be placed between any two digits. For the bit-vector $\underline{x} = (x_6, x_5, \ldots, x_0)$ and a binary point between bits x_4 and x_3, determine the most positive number x_{max} and the most negative number x_{min}; show their corresponding bit-vector representation in

a. The sign-and-magnitude system.
b. The two's-complement system.
c. The ones'-complement system.

Exercise 10.12 For the following pairs of 8-bit vectors $\underline{x}$ and $\underline{y}$ representing integers in the two's-complement system, obtain the eight-bit vectors $\underline{z}$ and $\underline{d}$ representing $z = x + y$ and $d = x - y$, respectively. Perform the operation directly on the bit-vectors using the two's-complement arithmetic unit (Figure 10.12) presented in this chapter. That is, show the values of control signals, c_0, and the bit-vectors at the output of the complementer and at the output of the adder, as well as the conditions ovf, $zero$, and $sign$.

Verify that you have obtained the correct result.

$\underline{x}$	$\underline{y}$
01010011	00100111
01010011	01000001
10101010	10100000
10101010	11110001
10110110	00110011
10110110	01100111

Exercise 10.13

a. Show that in the ones'-complement representation, where $C = 2^n - 1$, the addition of two signed integers represented by n-bit vectors can be performed by the following two steps:

- Add the representations with an n-bit adder.
- If the carry-out of the adder is 1, add 1 to the result of the addition and discard the carry-out. Remember that, in the ones'-complement system, $2^n - 1$ is also a representation of 0.

b. Show that the second step of the operation can be implemented by connecting signal c_{out} to the adder input c_{in}, as shown in Figure 10.21. This is a combinational network with a loop, so it is necessary to verify that the operation is combinational.

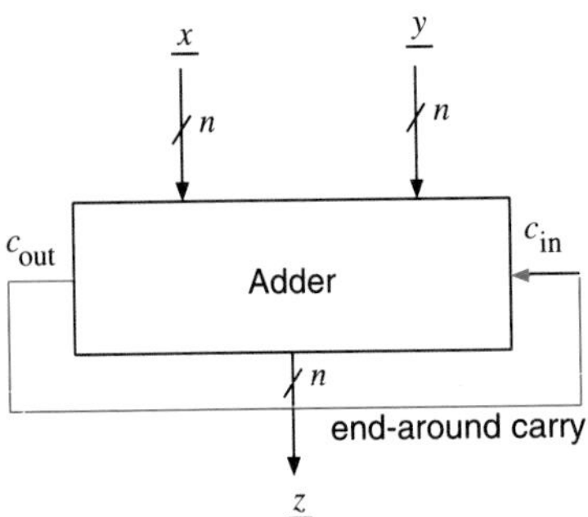

Figure 10.21 Ones'-complement adder (Exercise 10.13).

Exercise 10.14 Develop two implementations for addition of signed integers represented in the sign-and-magnitude form for $n = 8$ (including the sign bit):

a. Using one subtractor of magnitudes (to determine which of the operands has a larger magnitude) and one adder/subtractor (which has a control signal to determine whether to add or subtract). In addition, you can use two-input multiplexers and gates.
b. Converting first the operands to two's-complement representation, performing the addition in two's-complement, and then converting the result to sign-and-magnitude.

Compare the cost of these implementations with the cost of an eight-bit two's-complement adder.

Exercise 10.15 Prove that, in the two's-complement system, overflow can be detected by checking the two most significant carries. That is,

$$v = c_n \oplus c_{n-1}$$

Does this method work in the ones'-complement system? Explain.

Exercise 10.16 **Range extension** is performed when it is necessary to represent the value x by a bit-vector of m bits, given its representation by a bit-vector of $n < m$ bits. That is, $z = x$ and

$$\underline{z} = (z_{m-1}, z_{m-2}, \ldots, z_0), \quad \underline{x} = (x_{n-1}, x_{n-2}, \ldots, x_0)$$

In the two's-complement system, the range extension operation is implemented by

$$z_i = \begin{cases} x_{n-1} & \textbf{for } i = m-1, \ldots, n \\ x_i & \textbf{for } n-1, \ldots, 0 \end{cases}$$

Prove the correctness of this implementation.

ALU modules

Exercise 10.17 Design a four-bit ALU that performs one arithmetic operation (ADD) and one logic operation (NAND).

Comparator modules

Exercise 10.18 Analyze the implementation of the four-bit comparator module depicted in Figure 10.15.

Exercise 10.19 Design an iterative binary comparator in which the internal variable (carry) goes in the direction from most-significant to least-significant bit.

Exercise 10.20 Design a network that sorts two nonnegative integers a and b. Each integer is represented by four bits. You may use only the following modules: 4×2-input multiplexer and four-bit comparator. Indicate all inputs on the modules being used.

Exercise 10.21 Design a 32-bit tree comparator using 4-bit modules.

Exercise 10.22 For the network shown in Figure 10.22, determine the values of the outputs. Note the connection between the carry-out and carry-in in the adder.

Multipliers

Exercise 10.23 Determine the values at the outputs of all modules of the 8×6 multiplier shown in Figure 10.18, for $\underline{x} = 10110011$ and $\underline{y} = 111001$.

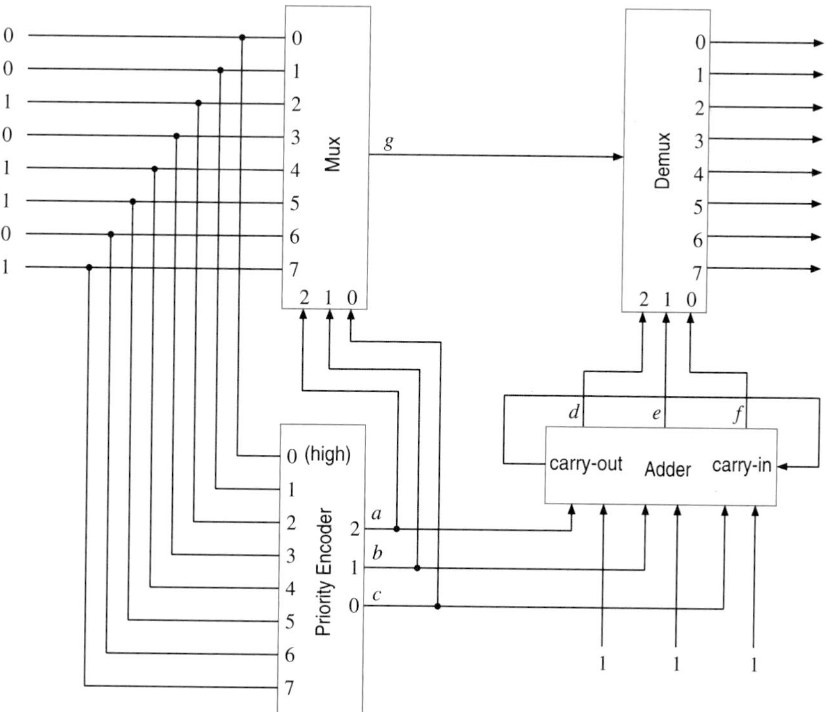

Figure 10.22 Network for Exercise 10.22.

Exercise 10.24 Design a 8×4 binary multiplier using AND gates and four-bit adder modules. Use the AND gates to produce the partial products and the adders to add them. Determine the worst-case multiplier delay in terms of the module delays.

Chapter 11

Standard Sequential Modules

In this chapter, we present

- A set of widely used standard sequential modules.
- The specification of these standard modules.
- An implementation with flip-flops and gates for each of these standard modules.
- The main uses of these standard modules.
- The implementation of large modules as networks of smaller ones.
- Multimodule sequential systems.

We now study a set of standard sequential modules, namely registers, shift registers, and counters; we discuss their specification and characteristics, and show how these modules are interconnected to form modular networks. In this chapter, the systems implemented as modular sequential networks correspond to rather simple ones. More complex sequential systems require a register-transfer level approach for their specification, analysis, and design; such an approach is discussed in Chapters 12 through 15.

11.1 REGISTERS

An n-bit **register** is a collection of n binary cells used to store a bit-vector. This standard module is an extension of the state register used in the canonical implementation of sequential networks, obtained by adding **control inputs** LD (LOAD) and CLR (CLEAR), as depicted in Figure 11.1. The data input and data output are the n-bit vectors $\underline{x}$ and $\underline{z}$, respectively. The output of the register corresponds to its state, and CLK is the synchronizing clock.

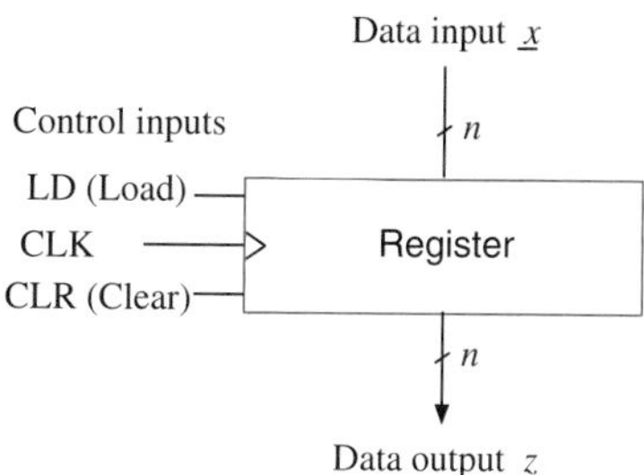

Figure 11.1 n-bit register module.

A description of an n-bit register module is

Inputs: $\underline{x} = (x_{n-1}, \ldots, x_0), \quad x_i \in \{0, 1\}$
LD, CLR $\in \{0, 1\}$

Outputs: $\underline{z} = (z_{n-1}, \ldots, z_0), \quad z_i \in \{0, 1\}$

State: $\underline{s} = (s_{n-1}, \ldots, s_0), \quad s_i \in \{0, 1\}$

Function: The state transition and output functions are

$$\underline{s}(t+1) = \begin{cases} \underline{x}(t) & \textbf{if} \quad \text{LD}(t) = 1 \textbf{ and } \text{CLR}(t) = 0 \\ \underline{s}(t) & \textbf{if} \quad \text{LD}(t) = 0 \textbf{ and } \text{CLR}(t) = 0 \\ (0 \ldots 0) & \textbf{if} \quad \text{CLR}(t) = 1 \end{cases}$$

$$\underline{z}(t) = \underline{s}(t)$$

The control input CLR is asynchronous; that is, its effect on the output takes place immediately rather than when the clock signal is received. This control input forces the value $(00\ldots0)$ into the register; it is commonly used for initialization purposes at the beginning of the operation of the system, to guarantee that the register contains a predefined value. The CLR input should not be used during the synchronous operation.

An implementation of a register using D flip-flops and multiplexers is given in Figure 11.2. Note that, when there is no change in state, the current state (output) of the register is used as input. A diagram describing the time-behavior of a register is shown in Figure 11.3.

Uses of Registers

Register modules are used primarily for storing the state in the implementation of sequential systems. With respect to the use of individual binary cells or flip-flops, the use of a register might result in a simplification of the combinational network required for the transition function due to the availability of the load signal: when the state does not change, it is sufficient to make the load input equal to 0. This feature is illustrated in the following example.

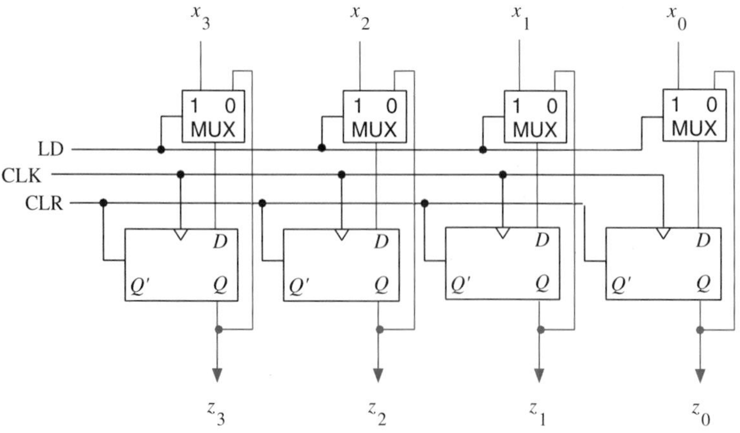

Figure 11.2 Implementation of a four-bit register.

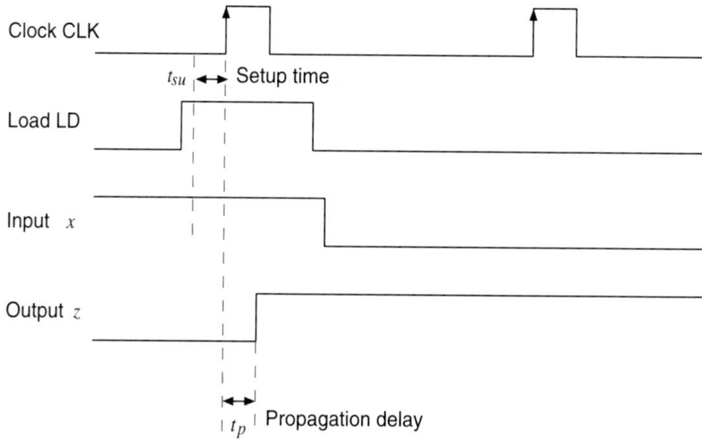

Figure 11.3 Time-behavior of a register.

EXAMPLE 11.1

A sequential system has the following specification:

Input: $x \in \{0, 1\}$
Output: (z_1, z_0), $z_i \in \{0, 1\}$
State: (s_1, s_0), $s_i \in \{0, 1\}$
Initial state: $(s_1, s_0) = (0, 0)$

Function: The transition and output functions are

PS	Input	
	$x = 0$	$x = 1$
00	00	01
01	01	11
11	11	10
10	10	00
	NS	

$z(t) = s(t)$

Using the procedure described in Chapter 8, the combinational network for the canonical implementation depicted in Figure 11.4*a* is given by

$$Y_1 = y_1x' + y_0x$$
$$Y_0 = y_0x' + y_1'x$$

In contrast, this system is implemented using a two-bit register module[1] as shown in Figure 11.4*b*, in which

$$Y_1 = y_0$$
$$Y_0 = y_1'$$
$$\text{LD} = x$$

[1]This smaller than usual register is used for illustration purposes only.

Note that input x is applied to the LD input; as a result, whenever $x = 0$ the register contents remain unchanged, whereas $x = 1$ loads a new value into the register. Consequently, the combinational logic only generates the state transitions required for $x = 1$.

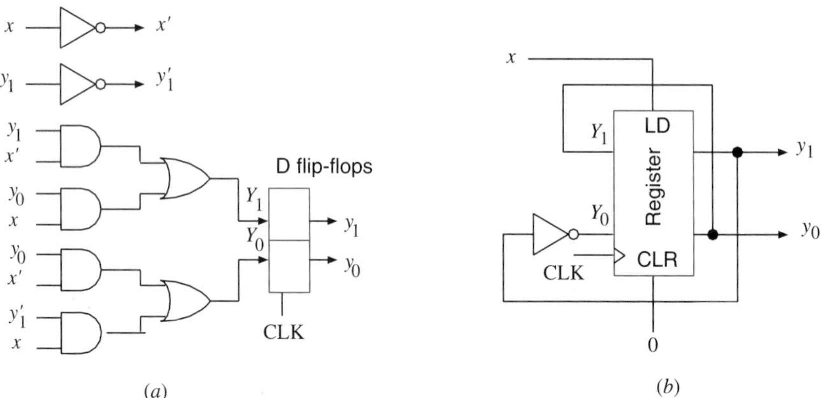

Figure 11.4 Networks for Example 11.1. (*a*) Network with state cells. (*b*) Network with standard register module. ■

11.2 SHIFT REGISTERS

An n-bit **shift register** (see Figure 11.5) is a register capable of transferring data among adjacent binary cells; these transfers can be bidirectional or unidirectional (either to the left or to the right). We discuss the general bidirectional case with parallel input and output, and then describe variations.

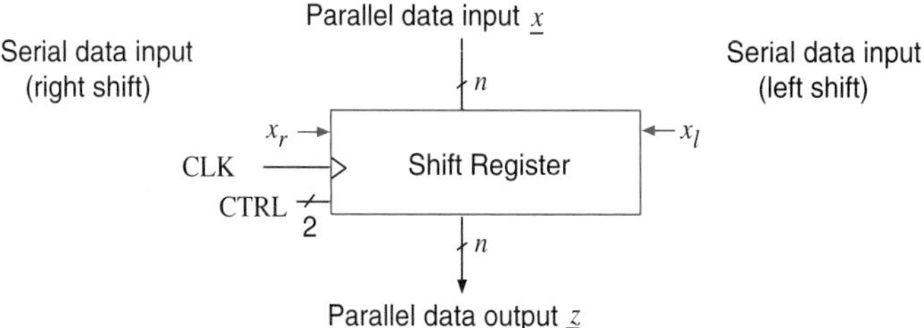

Figure 11.5 Shift register.

Parallel-in/parallel-out Bidirectional Shift Registers

An n-bit **parallel-in/parallel-out bidirectional shift register** (see Figure 11.6) has an n-bit **parallel** data input $\underline{x} = (x_{n-1}, \ldots, x_0)$, an n-bit **parallel** data output $\underline{z} = (z_{n-1}, \ldots, z_0)$,

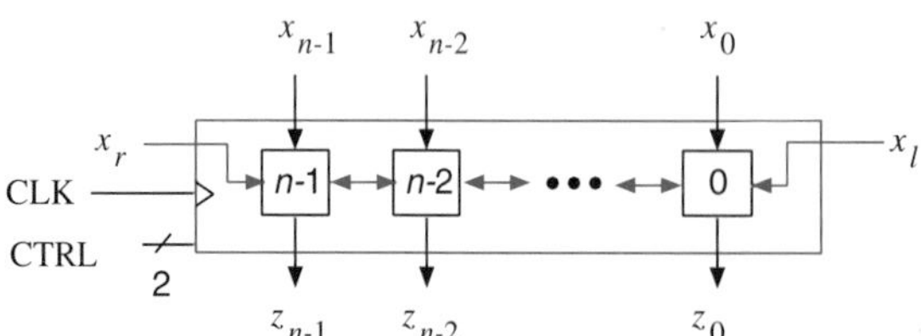

Figure 11.6 Parallel-in/parallel-out bidirectional shift register.

one-bit **serial** data inputs (left and right) x_l and x_r, respectively, and a control input CTRL to determine the operation of the shift register, as specified next.

A description of a bidirectional parallel shift register is

Inputs: $\underline{x} = (x_{n-1}, \ldots, x_0),\ x_i \in \{0, 1\}$
$x_l, x_r \in \{0, 1\}$
$\text{CTRL} \in \{\text{LOAD, LEFT, RIGHT, NONE}\}$

State: $\underline{s} = (s_{n-1}, \ldots, s_o),\ s_i \in \{0, 1\}$

Output: $\underline{z} = (z_{n-1}, \ldots, z_0),\ z_i \in \{0, 1\}$

Functions: The state transition and output functions are

$$\underline{s}(t+1) = \begin{cases} \underline{s}(t) & \textbf{if} \quad \text{CTRL} = \text{NONE} \\ \underline{x}(t) & \textbf{if} \quad \text{CTRL} = \text{LOAD} \\ (s_{n-2}, \ldots, s_0, x_l) & \textbf{if} \quad \text{CTRL} = \text{LEFT} \\ (x_r, s_{n-1}, \ldots, s_1) & \textbf{if} \quad \text{CTRL} = \text{RIGHT} \end{cases}$$

$$\underline{z}(t) = \underline{s}(t)$$

For a present state value $\underline{s}(t) = 0101$ and a data input $\underline{x}(t) = 1110$, the following table illustrates the output for all possible operations of a four-bit parallel bidirectional shift register:

Control	Serial Input	$s(t+1) = z(t+1)$
NONE		0101
LOAD		1110
LEFT	$x_l = 0$	1010
LEFT	$x_l = 1$	1011
RIGHT	$x_r = 0$	0010
RIGHT	$x_r = 1$	1010

A shift register can be implemented by a register and a shifter; it can also be implemented using individual flip-flops and multiplexers, as illustrated in Figure 11.7 for a four-bit parallel shift register. In this case, the coding of the control variable is

CTRL	c_1	c_0
NONE	0	0
LEFT	0	1
RIGHT	1	0
LOAD	1	1

Other Types of Shift Registers

There are variations in the shift register module with respect to the type of input and output and the shift capabilities. We now give several examples.

Serial-in/serial-out unidirectional shift register. This module has one binary data input x, one control input CTRL, and one binary data output z, as depicted in Figure 11.8a for the case of data transfers to the right.

This module can be used to serially store a bit-vector and read it serially later, and also to provide a delay of n clock periods. The latter function is obtained when the

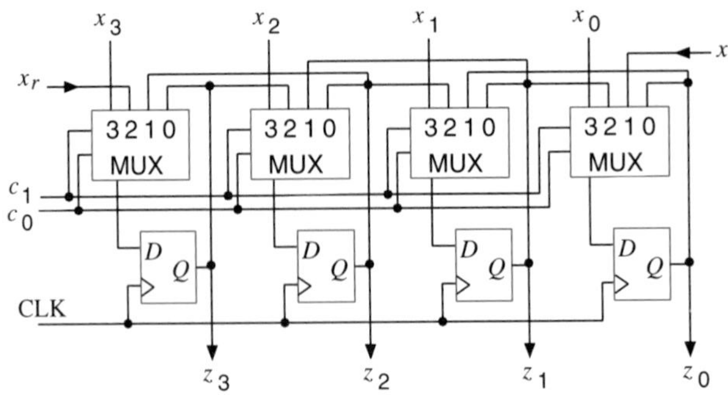

Figure 11.7 Implementation of a four-bit bidirectional shift register using D flip-flops.

operation is a right shift each clock period, so that the output of the shift register becomes

$$z(t) = x(t - n)$$

Parallel-in/serial-out unidirectional shift register. This module has one n-bit data input vector $\underline{x} = (x_{n-1}, \ldots, x_0)$, one control input CTRL, and one binary data output z, as shown in Figure 11.8*b*.

Serial-in/parallel-out unidirectional shift register. This is a register with one binary data input x, one control input CTRL, and one n-bit data output vector $\underline{z} = (z_{n-1}, \ldots, z_0)$, as depicted in Figure 11.8*c* for the case of a right shift register.

Uses of Shift Registers

Serial interconnection of systems. Parallel-in/serial-out and serial-in/parallel-out shift registers are often used to interconnect subsystems (see Figure 11.9), to keep the interconnection cost low. An n-bit data vector is sent from system A in bit-serial manner, using an n-bit parallel-in/serial-out shift register. The serial data are received by system B using an n-bit serial-in/parallel-out shift register. As a result, the rate of data transfer as well as the interconnection cost are n times lower than in the case of a parallel interconnection.

Bit-serial operations. Shift registers are used to provide operands and collect the result for bit-serial operators, such as adders, complementers, and comparators.

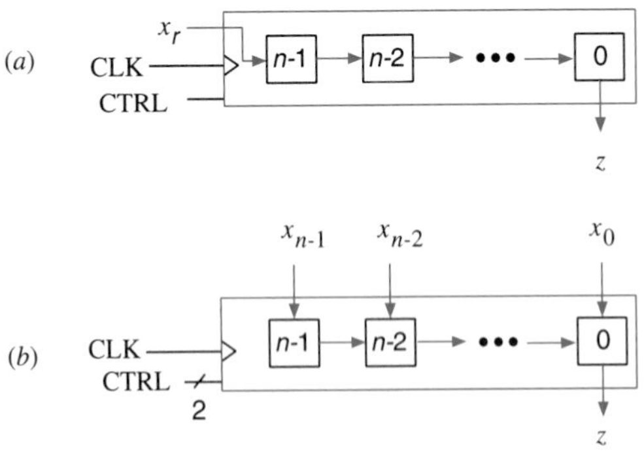

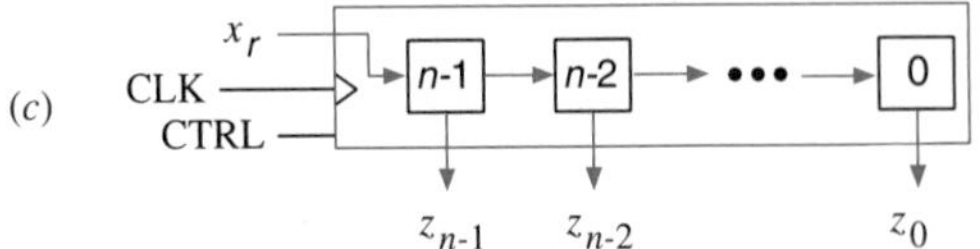

Figure 11.8 Common unidirectional shift registers. (*a*) Serial-in/serial-out. (*b*) Parallel-in/serial-out. (*c*) Serial-in/parallel-out.

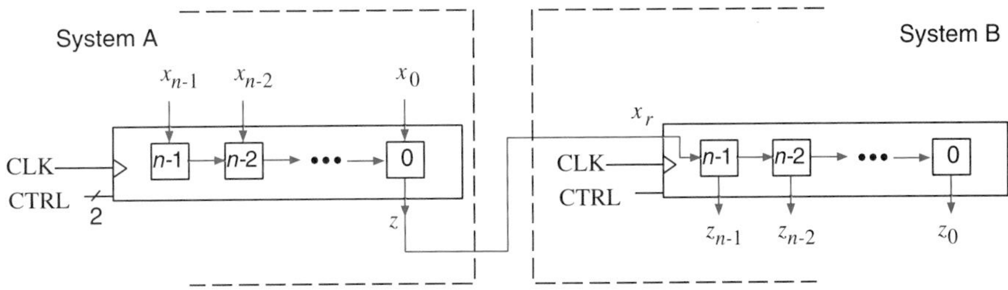

Figure 11.9 Serial interconnection of systems using shift registers.

For example, as shown in Figure 11.10, a 32-bit adder can be implemented by two 32-bit parallel-in/serial-out shift registers, one 32-bit serial-in/parallel-out shift register, and a 1-bit serial adder (this adder is formed by a full-adder and one flip-flop to store the carry-out). Operands are loaded in parallel in the operand registers, shifted least-significant bit first into the adder which produces the result, and shifted into the serial-in/parallel-out register. The operation takes 33 cycles (1 to load the operands and 32 to perform the addition); its completion is signaled by a counter (described in the next section).

State register. A serial-in shift register can also be used as the state register in a sequential network. In this case, the next state is obtained by shifting the register one position to the right and inserting the input x into the leftmost position. The network state transition function is

$$s_{n-1}(t+1) = x(t)$$
$$s_i(t+1) = s_{i+1}(t) \quad \textbf{for } i = n-2, \ldots, 0$$

The resulting network implements a **finite-memory** sequential system (as defined in Section 7.4) because the state corresponds to the last n inputs.

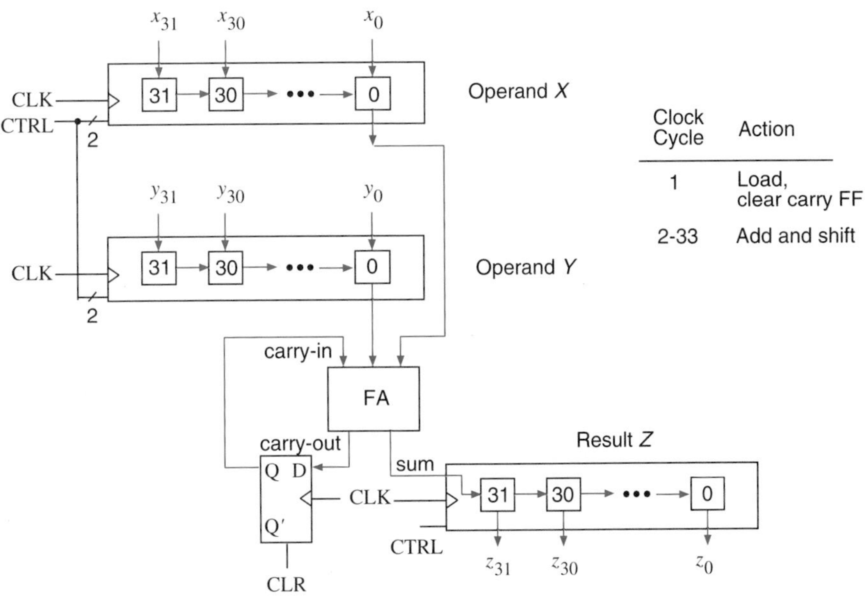

Figure 11.10 Bit-serial adder.

We now show two examples which differ in the type of output from the register: serial or parallel.

EXAMPLE 11.2

A sequential system has one input and one output. The function of the system is such that $z(t) = 1$ whenever $x(t) \cdot x(t-8) = 1$.

A state vector of eight bits is required; the state description is

$$s_7(t+1) = x(t)$$
$$s_i(t+1) = s_{i+1}(t) \quad \textbf{for } i = 6, \ldots, 0$$
$$z(t) = x(t)s_0(t)$$

The implementation of this system is illustrated in Figure 11.11; it consists of a shift register that delays the data input so that $x(t-8)$ can be ANDed with $x(t)$.

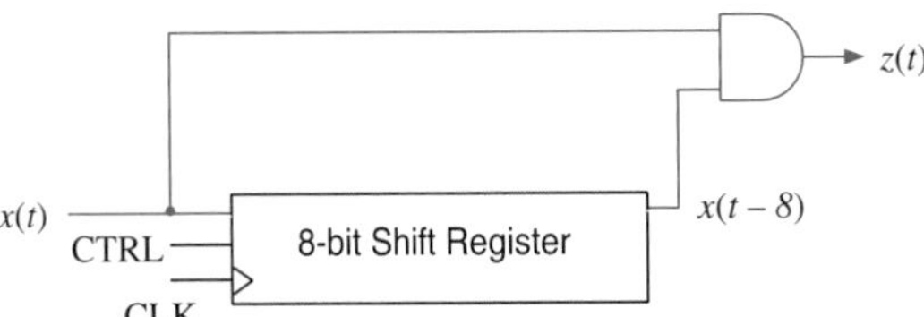

Figure 11.11 Implementation of network in Example 11.2. ■

In a more general case than the foregoing example, the whole state is used as input to the combinational network, resulting in a **pattern recognizer**. This requires a parallel output, as illustrated in the following example.

EXAMPLE 11.3

A sequential system has one binary input and one binary output. The output is 1 whenever the last nine inputs correspond to the sequence $x(t-8, t) = 011101101$.

The state description requires a state vector of eight bits, which correspond to the last eight inputs. Consequently, the state transition function is the same as in the previous example. The output function is

$$z(t) = \begin{cases} 1 & \textbf{if} \quad \underline{s}(t) = 01101110 \textbf{ and } x(t) = 1 \\ 0 & \textbf{otherwise} \end{cases}$$

The implementation of this system follows the previous example, and is shown in Figure 11.12. The input data are brought into and shifted by the register, so that the last eight inputs are available to the combinational network.

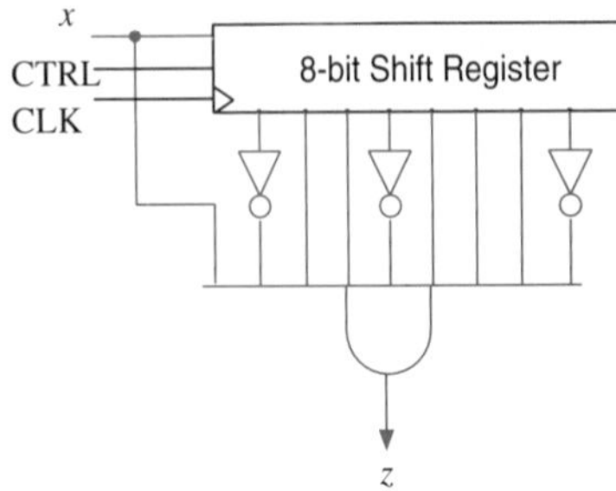

Figure 11.12 Implementation of network in Example 11.3. ■

Networks of Shift Registers

A larger shift register can be implemented as a network of shift-register modules. For instance, Figure 11.13 illustrates the case of 32-bit serial-input/serial-output shift register made of 8-bit shift registers. Note that connections are required between the serial output and the serial input of successive modules.

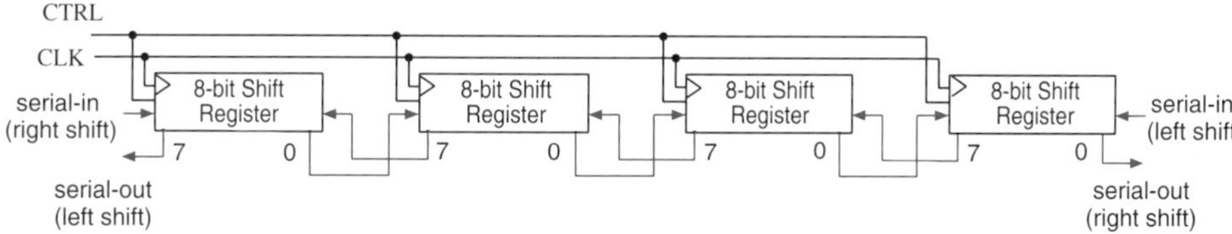

Figure 11.13 Network of serial-input/serial-output shift register modules.

11.3 COUNTERS

A **modulo-p counter** is a sequential system with one binary input x and p states; its state diagram is depicted in Figure 11.14. If the states are labeled with the integers $0, 1, \ldots, p-1$, the state transition function is described by the arithmetic expression

$$s(t+1) = (s(t) + x) \bmod p$$

Usually, the output of the module corresponds to the state. An additional binary output called **terminal count** TC is used to facilitate the implementation of networks of counters and of some specific counter applications. This output has value 1 when the counter is in state $p-1$ and the input is 1.

A high-level description of a modulo-p counter is

Input: $x \in \{0, 1\}$

Outputs: $z \in \{0, 1, \ldots, p-1\}$

$\text{TC} \in \{0, 1\}$

State: $s \in \{0, 1, \ldots, p-1\}$

Function: The state transition and output functions are

$$\begin{aligned} s(t+1) &= (s(t) + x) \bmod p \\ z(t) &= s(t) \end{aligned}$$

$$\text{TC}(t) = \begin{cases} 1 & \textbf{if} \quad s(t) = p-1 \ \textbf{and} \ x(t) = 1 \\ 0 & \textbf{otherwise} \end{cases}$$

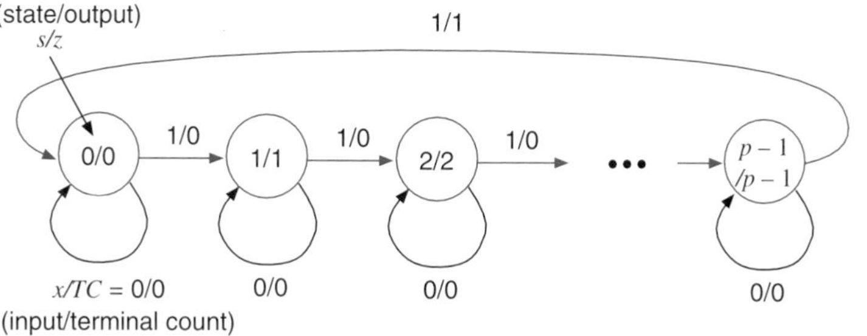

Figure 11.14 State diagram of a modulo-p counter.

Counter modules can count up or count down. In an **upward** counter, state i is followed by state $(i+1) \bmod p$, whereas in a **downward** counter state i is followed by state $(i-1) \bmod p$. **Up/down** counters count both ways, the direction being determined by a control input.

There are different types of counters, depending on the number of states and on the code used to represent the output (and state). We now describe some of the most typical ones; the corresponding output codes are illustrated in Table 11.1.

Binary counter: 2^k states and output coded on k binary variables. The code corresponds to the binary representation of the integers $\{0, \ldots, 2^k - 1\}$.

Decimal counter: Ten states. The output is coded on binary variables using a decimal code (e.g., BCD, Excess-3).

Gray-code counter: 2^k states. The output is coded on k binary variables; the coding is such that two consecutive states differ only in one bit.

Ring counter: this module produces the output in a 1-out-of-p code. That is, the output is the p-bit vector $(z_{p-1}, \ldots, z_0)$ such that

$$z_i = \begin{cases} 1 & \textbf{if} \quad s(t) = i \\ 0 & \textbf{otherwise} \end{cases}$$

This module is called **ring counter** because it can be implemented by a shift register of p bits, in which the leftmost output is connected to the rightmost input (see Figure 11.15*a*). This implementation has a very simple combinational network at the expense of more binary cells. This counter has the advantage that the output is decoded (only one binary output has value 1 for each state).

Twisted-tail ring counter: this is a modified ring counter that has twice as many states with the same number of binary variables. Thus, a modulo-p twisted-tail ring counter uses only $p/2$ binary variables. As shown in Table 11.1, the code of this counter is such that for the first half, state i is represented by a vector having the i least-significant bits equal to 1 and, for the second half, state $p - i$ has the i most-significant bits equal to 1. This module is called twisted-tail ring counter because it can be implemented using a shift register in which the **complement** of the leftmost output is connected to the rightmost input (see Figure 11.15*b*). Note that in this case the output is not decoded. However, the decoding function is simple.

Table 11.1 Output codes for modulo-8 and decimal counters

State	Binary	BCD	Excess-3	Gray	Ring	Twisted Tail
0	000	0000	0011	000	00000001	0000
1	001	0001	0100	001	00000010	0001
2	010	0010	0101	011	00000100	0011
3	011	0011	0110	010	00001000	0111
4	100	0100	0111	110	00010000	1111
5	101	0101	1000	111	00100000	1110
6	110	0110	1001	101	01000000	1100
7	111	0111	1010	100	10000000	1000
8		1000	1011			
9		1001	1100			

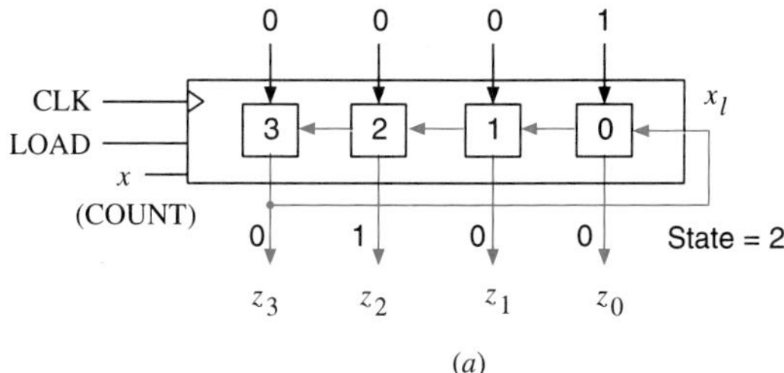

(a)

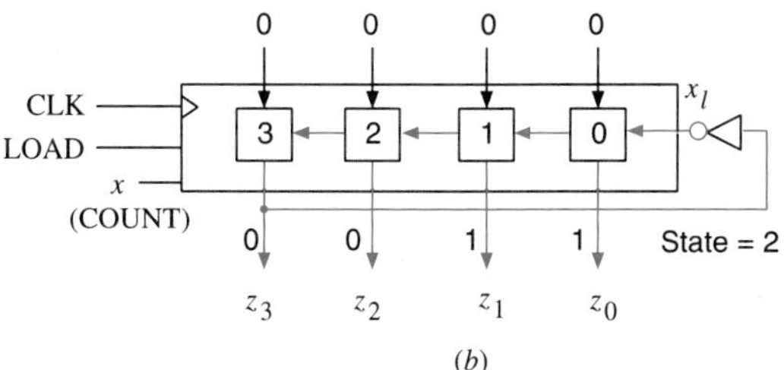

(b)

Figure 11.15 (a) Modulo-4 ring counter. (b) Modulo-8 twisted-tail counter.

Binary Counter with Parallel Input

A counter module can be extended with a control input that allows setting the state synchronously. This "state loading," controlled by input LOAD (LD), is useful for many applications of the counter module, as discussed later. In addition, an (asynchronous) control input CLEAR (CLR) is used to initialize the counter to the state 0. An illustration of a modulo-16 binary counter of this type is given in Figure 11.16. A high-level description is

Inputs: $\underline{I} = (I_3, \ldots, I_0), I_j \in \{0, 1\}, I \in \{0, 1..., 15\}$
CLR, LD, CNT $\in \{0, 1\}$

State: $\underline{s} = (s_3, \ldots, s_0), s_j \in \{0, 1\}, s \in \{0, 1, ..., 15\}$

Output: $\underline{s} = (s_3, \ldots, s_0), s_j \in \{0, 1\}, s \in \{0, 1, ..., 15\}$
TC $\in \{0, 1\}$

Function: The state-transition and output functions are

$$s(t+1) = \begin{cases} 0 & \textbf{if } \text{CLR} = 1 \\ I & \textbf{if } \text{LD} = 1 \\ (s(t)+1) \bmod 16 & \textbf{if } \text{CNT} = 1 \textbf{ and } \text{LD} = 0 \\ s(t) & \textbf{otherwise} \end{cases}$$

$$\text{TC} = \begin{cases} 1 & \textbf{if } s(t) = 15 \textbf{ and } \text{CNT} = 1 \\ 0 & \textbf{otherwise} \end{cases}$$

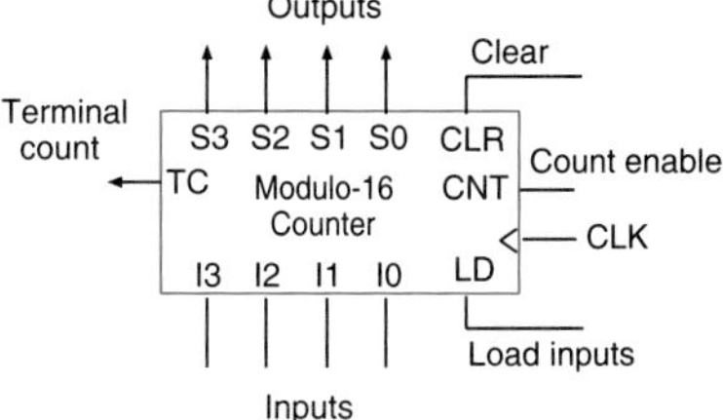

Figure 11.16 A modulo-16 binary counter with parallel input.

As in the case of registers, the control input CLR is asynchronous so that its effect on the output takes place immediately (not synchronized by CLK); the CLR input should not be used during synchronous operation. Note that, when LD $= 1$ the operation is LOAD even if CNT $= 1$.

We now describe the use of this counter to produce several counting applications.

Modulo-k Counter ($1 \leq k \leq 16$)

A modulo-k counter, with $1 \leq k \leq 16$, can be implemented with a modulo-16 counter as indicated in the state diagram depicted in Figure 11.17*a*.

This type of operation is achieved by using the input LD to force the transition from state $k-1$ to state 0, whereas normal counting is used for the other transitions. Therefore, the input signals to the modulo-16 counter become

$$\text{CNT} = x$$

$$\text{LD} = \begin{cases} 1 & \textbf{if} \quad (s = k-1) \ \textbf{and} \ (x = 1) \\ 0 & \textbf{otherwise} \end{cases}$$

$$I = 0$$

In this case, the output TC is not taken from the module; instead

$$\text{TC} = \text{LD}$$

An example of a modulo-12 counter and its time behavior are shown in Figure 11.17*b*.

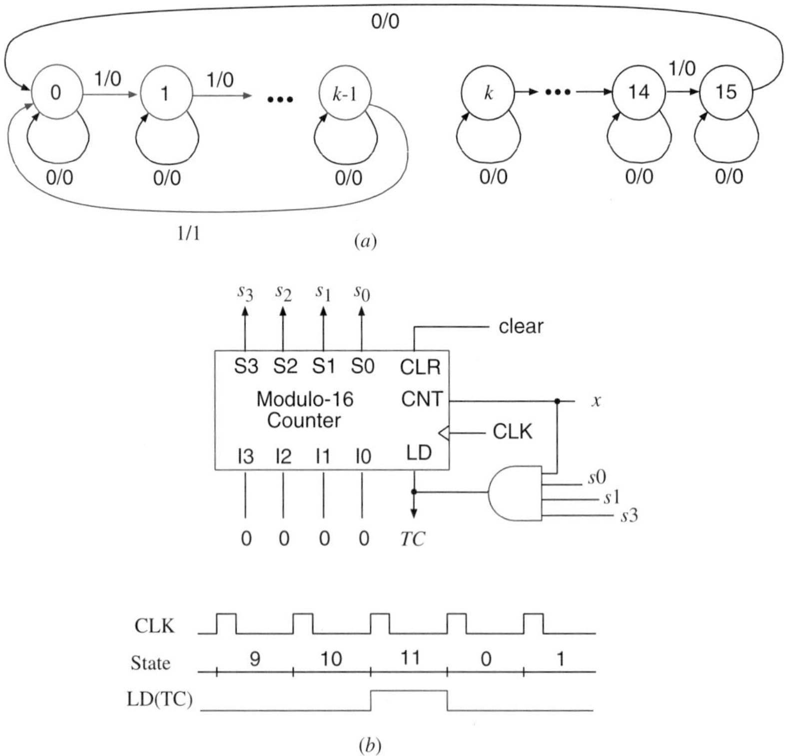

Figure 11.17 (*a*) State diagram of modulo-k counter ($1 \leq k \leq 16$). (*b*) Modulo-12 counter and its time behavior ($x = 1$).

a-to-b Counter ($0 \le a, b \le 15$)

An a-to-b counter, with $0 \le a, b \le 15$, is a counter that traverses states a through b, as depicted in the state diagram shown in Figure 11.18a. The transition from state b to state a is achieved by loading the value a after reaching state b, whereas normal counting is used for the other transitions. This is accomplished by setting the inputs to the standard counter module as follows:

$$\text{CNT} = x$$

$$\text{LD} = \begin{cases} 1 & \textbf{if} \quad (s = b) \ \textbf{and} \ (x = 1) \\ 0 & \textbf{otherwise} \end{cases}$$

$$I = a$$

The implementation of a 1-to-12 counter is given in Figure 11.18b. Note that the expression for LD can be simplified. For example, for the 1-to-12 counter, $\text{LD} = s_3 \cdot s_2 \cdot x$.

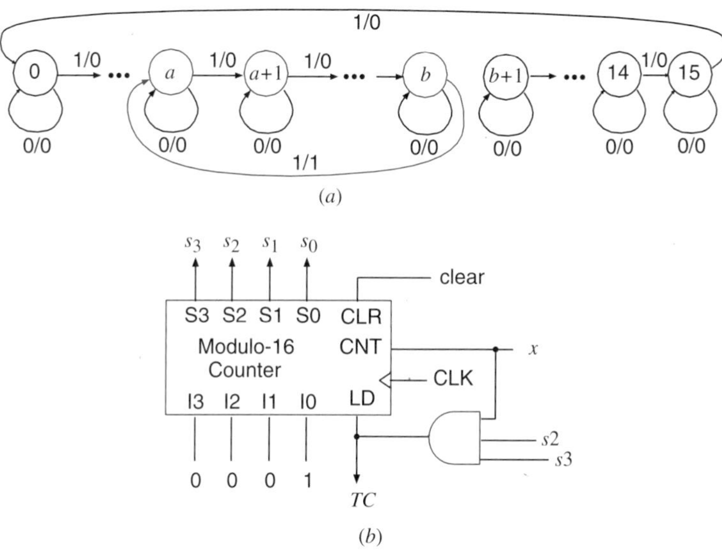

Figure 11.18 (a) State diagram of a-to-b counter; (b) 1-to-12 counter.

Modulo-k Frequency Divider ($1 \le k \le 16$)

A modulo-k frequency divider is a counter having just one binary output z that is set to 1 at every kth occurrence of the event $x = 1$. That is, this counter divides by k the number of 1's in the x sequence.

This type of operation is accomplished by taking the output from TC and loading the state $16 - k$ when $\text{TC} = 1$. That is,

$$\text{CNT} = x$$

$$\text{LD} = \begin{cases} 1 & \textbf{if} \ \text{TC} = 1 \\ 0 & \textbf{otherwise} \end{cases}$$

$$I = 16 - k$$

$$z = \text{TC}$$

As shown in the state diagram of Figure 11.19*a*, this counter cycles through states $16 - k$ to 15 and produces an output 1 when in state 15 and $x = 1$.

The implementation of a modulo-9 frequency divider and a portion of its time behavior are depicted in Figure 11.19*b*.

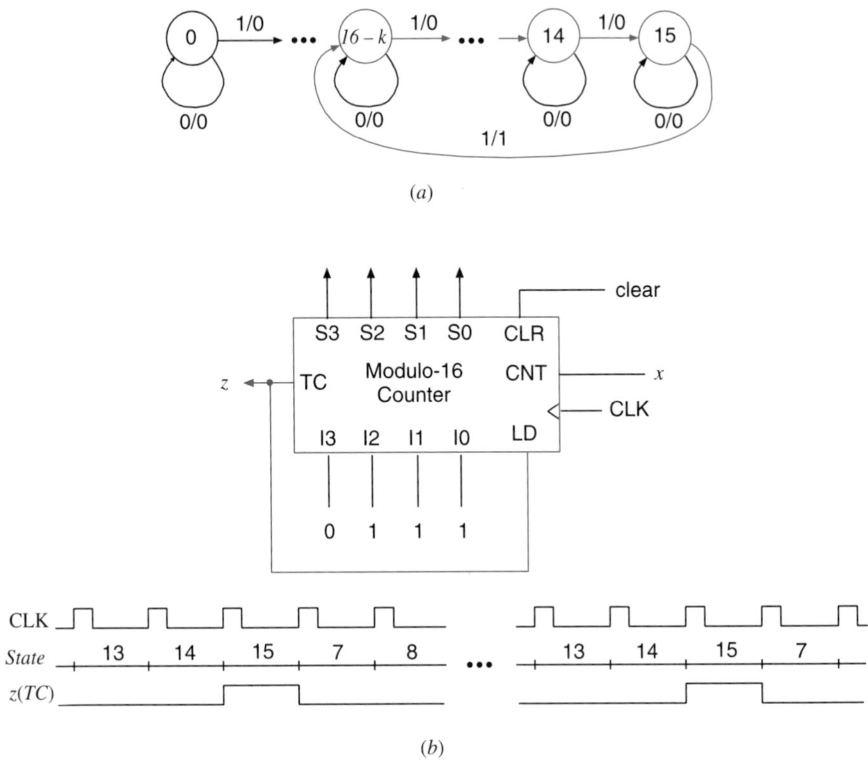

Figure 11.19 (*a*) State diagram of a modulo-*k* frequency divider. (*b*) Modulo-9 frequency divider and its time behavior ($x = 1$).

Uses of Counters

The most typical uses of counters are

- to count the number of times that a certain event takes place; the occurrence of event to be counted is represented by the input signal to the counter (Figure 11.20*a*);
- to control a fixed sequence of actions in a digital system (Figure 11.20*b*);
- to generate timing signals (Figure 11.21*a*); and
- to generate clocks of different frequencies (Figure 11.21*b*).

In addition, as shown in Figure 11.22, a counter module can be used as the state register in the implementation of a sequential system. This approach might reduce the number of modules required for the combinational network in those cases when the state transition function includes traversing states successively. In general, if the state is represented by an integer, then the state transition function can be divided into three cases:

Counting	$s(t+1) = (s(t)+1) \bmod p$
No change	$s(t+1) = s(t)$
Arbitrary	$s(t+1) \neq (s(t)+1) \bmod p$ **and** $s(t+1) \neq s(t)$

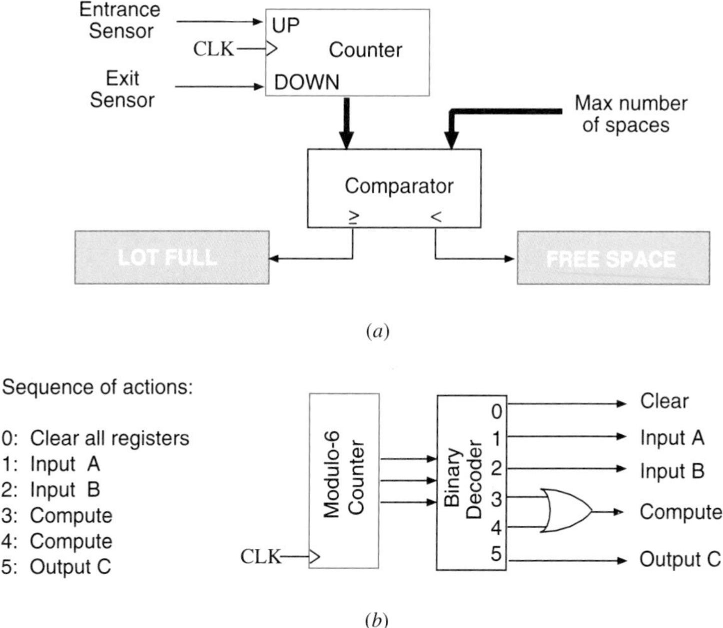

Figure 11.20 (*a*) Example of event counter. (*b*) Example of a controller.

The counting capability of a counter can be used in the first case. The case of arbitrary transitions is implemented by loading the next state into the counter, whereas the case of no changes requires neither counting nor loading. Consequently, the two binary functions COUNT and LOAD as well as the parallel input to the counter module I are used to implement the transition function, as follows:

$$\text{CNT} = \begin{cases} 1 & \textbf{if} \quad s(t+1) = (s(t)+1) \bmod p \ \textbf{and} \ x = 1 \\ 0 & \textbf{otherwise} \end{cases}$$

$$\text{LD} = \begin{cases} 1 & \textbf{if} \quad s(t+1) \neq s(t) \ \textbf{and} \ s(t+1) \neq (s(t)+1) \bmod p \ \textbf{and} \ x = 1 \\ 0 & \textbf{otherwise} \end{cases}$$

$$I = \begin{cases} s(t+1) & \textbf{if} \quad \text{LD} = 1 \\ - & \textbf{otherwise} \end{cases}$$

In reality, the decomposition of the transition function into the three cases indicated earlier is not as rigid as implied by the previous discussion, because there is a choice among counting and loading when $s(t+1) = (s(t)+1) \bmod p$. A similar choice exists for the case $s(t+1) = s(t)$: either loading or no change. Consequently, alternative designs are possible and the decision should be made so as to reduce the total complexity of the combinational network.

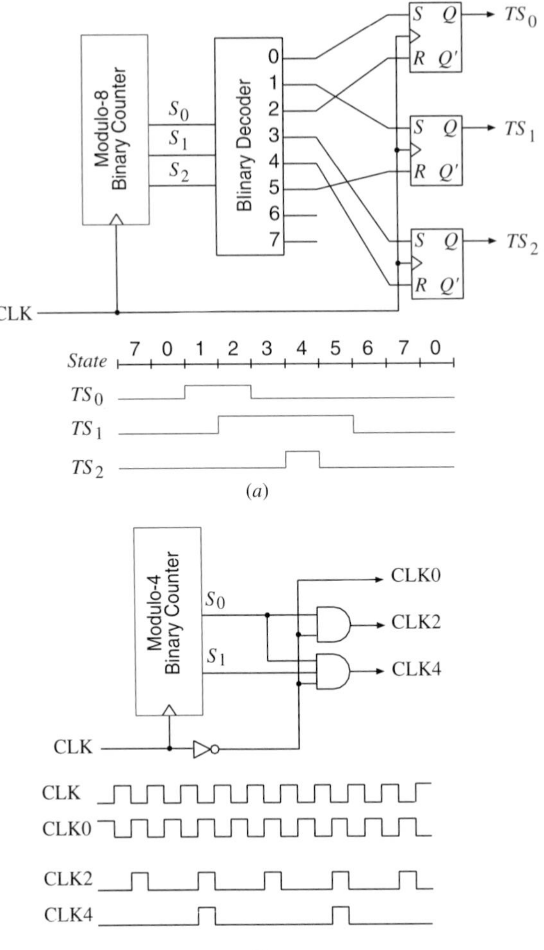

Figure 11.21 Examples of networks for generating (*a*) timing signals and (*b*) clocks with different frequencies.

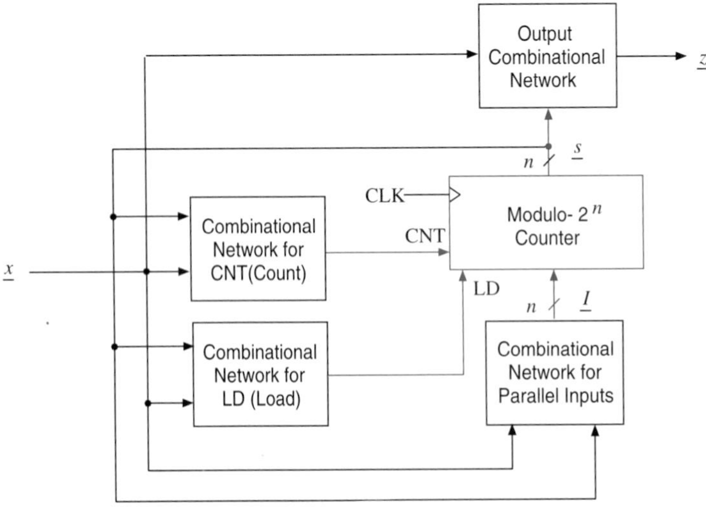

Figure 11.22 Implementation of sequential system with counter and combinational networks.

EXAMPLE 11.4

A sequential system has three binary inputs a, b, and c, and one binary output z. The transition and the output functions are specified by the state diagram depicted in Figure 11.23.

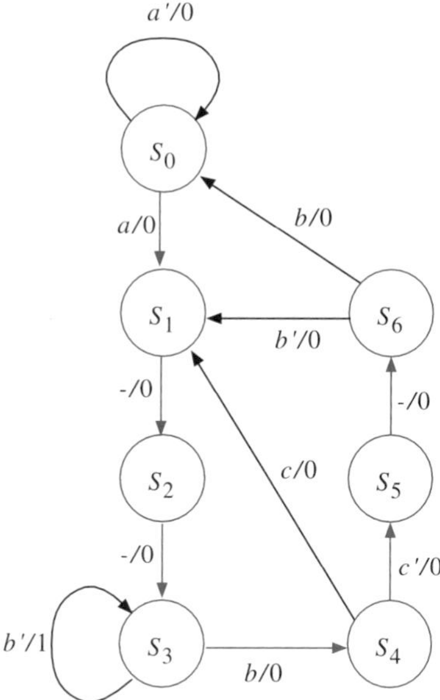

Figure 11.23 State diagram for Example 11.4.

The implementation of this system using a standard modulo-16 counter is illustrated in Figure 11.24. The functions CNT, LD, and $\underline{I} = (I_3, I_2, I_1, I_0)$, obtained directly from the state diagram, are

$$\text{CNT} = S_0 a + S_1 + S_2 + S_3 b + S_4 c' + S_5$$

$$\text{LD} = \text{CNT}'$$

$$(I_3, I_2, I_1, I_0) = \begin{cases} (0,0,0,0) & \textbf{if} \quad S_0 a' + S_6 b \\ (0,0,0,1) & \textbf{if} \quad S_4 c + S_6 b' \\ (0,0,1,1) & \textbf{if} \quad S_3 b' \end{cases}$$

where S_i indicates that the state is i. Note that we have chosen to load when no change of state occurs; this simplifies the implementation of signal LD. The expressions for the parallel inputs can be simplified as follows: $S_0 a' + S_6 b = S_0 + S_6 b$ because a parallel load happens in state S_0 only if $a' = 1$. Similarly, $S_4 c + S_6 b'$ can be simplified to $S_4 + S_6 b'$, and $S_3 b'$ to S_3. Note that in S_6 we load 0000 if $b = 1$ and 0001 if $b = 0$ so that the input b cannot be ignored. From the simplified equations, we obtain the K-maps shown in Figure 11.25 (don't cares are used when LD $= 0$).

From the K-maps the switching expressions for the parallel inputs are

$$I_3 = 0$$

$$I_2 = 0$$

$$I_1 = Q_0$$

$$I_0 = Q_0 + Q_2 Q_1' + Q_2 b'$$

The output z is

$$z = Q_1 Q_0 b'$$

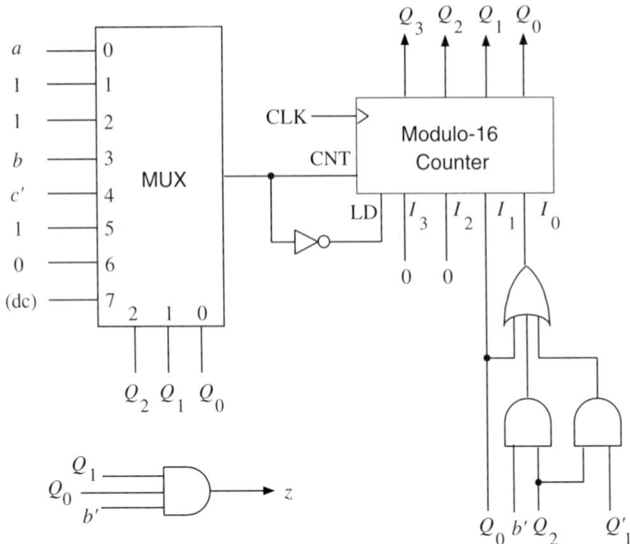

Figure 11.24 Sequential network for Example 11.4.

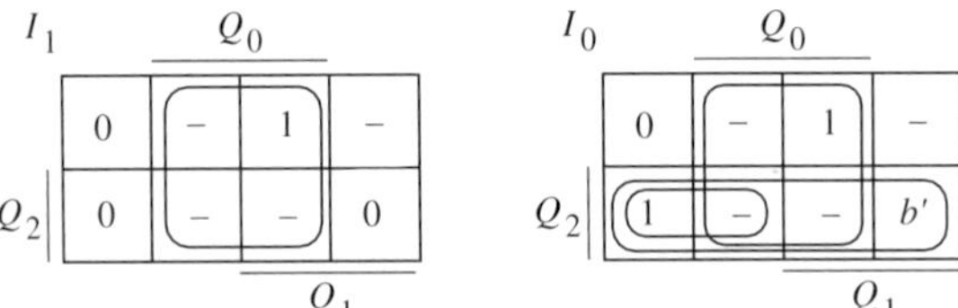

Figure 11.25 K-maps for parallel inputs (Example 11.4). ■

Networks of Counters

We now discuss two approaches to the implementation of a large counter by a network of counter modules.

Cascade Counters

A modulo-p^k counter can be implemented by a **cascade** of k modulo-p counters. The terminal count output (TC) from one modulo-p counter is connected to the CNT input of the next module, as illustrated in Figure 11.26.

The analysis of this network is as follows. The terminal-count output is

$$\text{TC} = \begin{cases} 1 & \textbf{if} \quad (s = p - 1) \ \textbf{and} \ (\text{CNT} = 1) \\ 0 & \textbf{otherwise} \end{cases}$$

so that for the ith module

$$\text{CNT}^i = \begin{cases} 1 & \textbf{if} \quad (s^j = p - 1) \ \textbf{and} \ (x = 1) \quad (\text{ for all } j < i) \\ 0 & \textbf{otherwise} \end{cases}$$

where s^j is the state of counter j.

That is, the ith counter counts when all less-significant counters are in state $(p - 1)$; consequently, a modulo-p^k counter is obtained.

Let us consider the worst-case delay and the maximum clock frequency at which this cascade counter can operate. This worst-case situation occurs when $x = 1$ always (counting the number of clock cycles) and module $k - 1$ counts. For this to happen, modules 0 to

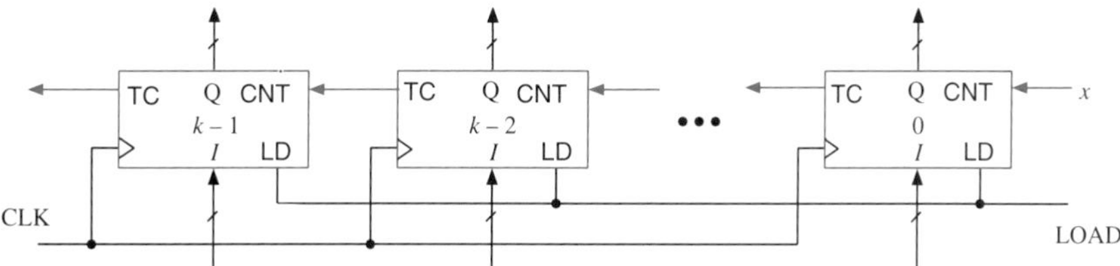

Figure 11.26 Cascade implementation of a modulo-p^k counter.

$k-2$ must be in state $p-1$; in this situation, $\text{TC}^{(0)}$ is generated, it propagates through modules 1 to $k-2$, and produces $\text{CNT}^{(k-1)} = 1$ so that module $k-1$ counts. Therefore, the worst-case delay is

$$T_{\text{worst-case}} = (k-1)t_{tc} + t_{su} + t_p$$

where t_{tc} is the terminal-count delay of the module, t_{su} is the module setup time, and t_p is the time required to change the state. This delay determines the maximum clock frequency possible, that is,

$$f_{max} = 1/T_{\text{worst-case}}$$

Therefore, the maximum frequency at which the counter can operate decreases with k, the number of modules.

EXAMPLE 11.5

Consider a modulo-16 counter with the following timing characteristics:

$t_{su} = 4.5$ ns (including the delay of the gates used to produce the inputs to the cells)
$t_p = 2$ ns
$t_{tc} = 3.5$ ns

The minimum clock period for a counter with one module is $T = 6.5$ ns, whereas this minimum period increases to 31 ns for a counter with eight modules. The corresponding maximum clock frequencies are 153 MHz and 32 MHz, respectively. ■

The speed of the cascade counter can be improved by introducing an additional input called CEF (Count Enable First). Now, the module counts if both CEF = 1 and CNT = 1, that is,

$$s(t+1) = \begin{cases} (s(t)+1) \bmod p & \textbf{if } \text{CEF} = 1 \textbf{ and } \text{CNT} = 1 \\ s(t) & \textbf{otherwise} \end{cases}$$

However, the generation of the TC signal is not influenced by CEF, that is,

$$\text{TC} = \begin{cases} 1 & \textbf{if } (s(t) = p-1) \textbf{ and } (\text{CNT} = 1) \\ 0 & \textbf{otherwise} \end{cases}$$

As indicated in Figure 11.27, the cascade connection of counter modules uses the terminal-count output of the least-significant module as the CEF inputs to all other modules. Moreover, the CEF input to the first module and the CNT input to the second module are set to 1. The operation is as follows:

- modules 0 and 1 count as in the system of Figure 11.26.
- module 2 counts whenever $\text{CEF}^{(2)} = 1$ and $\text{CNT}^{(2)} = 1$. This requires that module 0 be in state $(p-1)$, to produce $\text{CEF}^{(2)} = \text{TC}^{(0)} = 1$, and that module 1 be also in state $p-1$, to produce $\text{CNT}^{(2)} = \text{TC}^{(1)} = 1$.

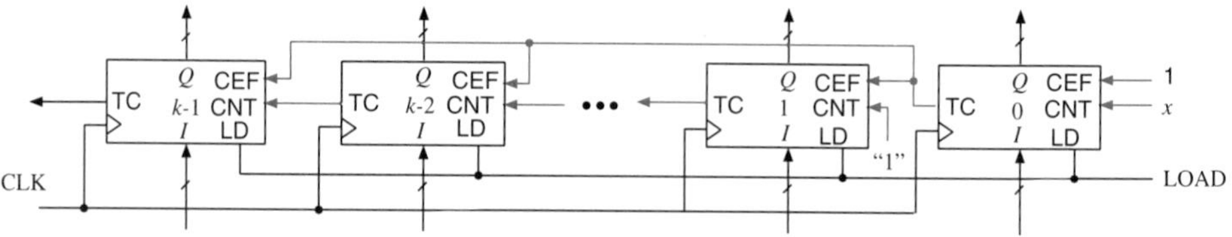

Figure 11.27 A faster version of a cascade counter.

Similarly, module i counts whenever $\text{CEF}^{(i)} = 1$ and $\text{CNT}^{(i)} = 1$. This requires that module 0 be in state $p-1$, to produce $\text{CEF}^{(i)} = \text{TC}^{(0)} = 1$, and all modules from 1 to $i-1$ be also in state $p-1$, to produce $\text{CNT}^{(i)} = \text{TC}^{(i-1)} = 1$. Consequently, the network is a modulo-p^k counter.

Let us now consider the worst-case delay. As in the cascaded counter considered earlier, this delay occurs when the most-significant module changes state. Now the TC signal has to propagate through modules $1, 2, \ldots, k-2$ to get to module $k-1$, that is, it has to propagate through $k-2$ modules. Consequently, the worst-case delay is

$$T_{\text{worst-case}} = (k-2)t_{tc} + t_{su} + t_p$$

It can be seen from this expression that the delay is reduced a little. However, the effect on the minimal clock period is much more significant because now the propagation of signal TC can span several clock cycles. To see this effect, let us determine the state when the signal begins to propagate and the state at which it has to arrive to module $k-1$ to make it count. Because $\text{CNT}^1 = 1$, the signal is generated in module 1 when its state becomes $p-1$ and then propagates through the other modules (also in state $p-1$). Consequently, as shown in Figure 11.28*b*, the signal is generated when the counter changes from state

$$(r, p-1, \ldots, p-1, p-2, p-1)$$

to state

$$(r, p-1, \ldots, p-1, p-1, 0)$$

On the other hand, the signal has to be available at module $k-1$ (and all the intermediate modules) when the counter is in state

$$(r, p-1, \ldots, p-1, p-1, p-1)$$

so that the state can change to

$$(r+1, 0, \ldots, 0, 0, 0)$$

That is, p clock cycles occur between the time of generation of the signal and its use. Consequently, if T is the clock period,

$$pT \geq (k-2)t_{tc} + t_{su} + t_p$$

That is, the clock period can be roughly p times smaller than that of the counter of Figure 11.26. On the other hand, the first two modules behave as in Figure 11.26. Therefore,

$$T \geq t_{tc} + t_{su} + t_p$$

Combining the previous two expressions, we get

$$T \geq \max\,(t_{tc} + t_{su} + t_p,\ [(k-2)t_{tc} + t_{su} + t_p]/p)$$

For the counter of Example 11.5 with eight modules, $T \geq \max\,(10, 1.7) = 10$; this results in a reduction of the minimum clock period from 31 to 10 ns.

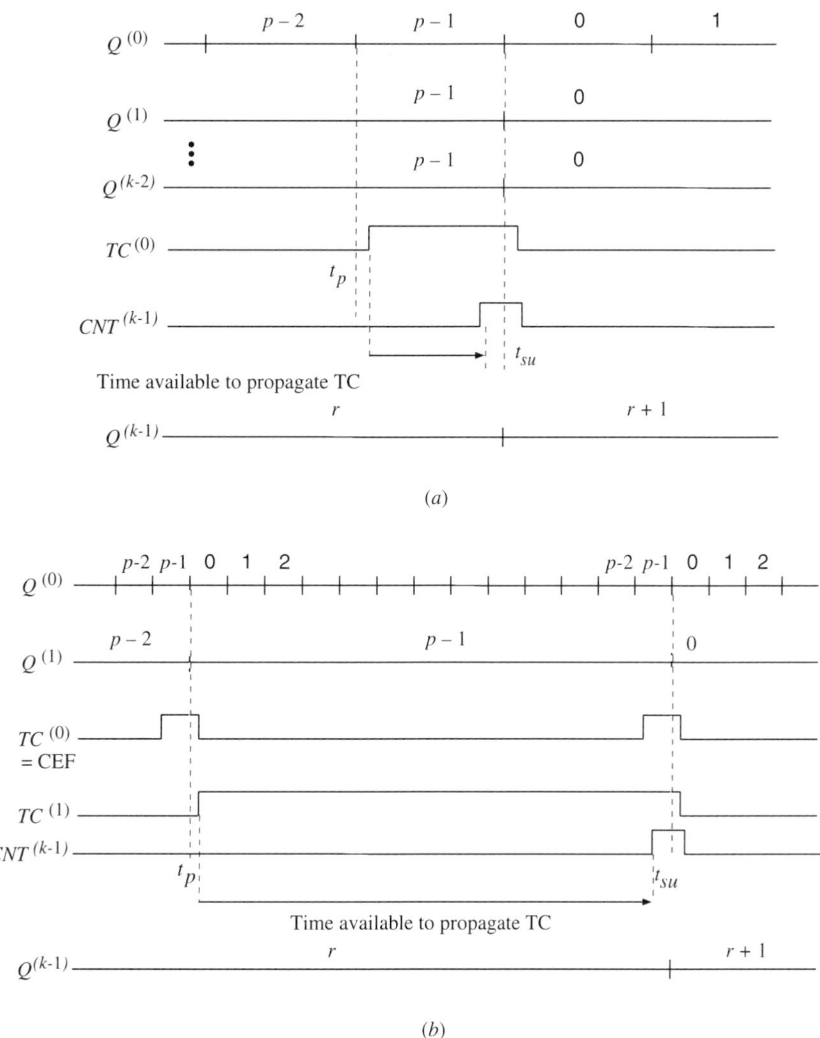

Figure 11.28 Timing relations in cascade counter. (*a*) Without *CEF*. (*b*) With *CEF*.

Parallel Counters

Another possibility of implementing a large counter consists of several counters in **parallel**. An example of such a counter is shown in Figure 11.29. It consists of three counter modules: one modulo-7, one modulo-8, and one modulo-9, which all receive the count signal. These modules count independently, and the overall count is the digit-vector formed by the three outputs. The order of these three digits is not significant, so we arbitrarily make the leftmost digit to be the output of the modulo-7 counter, the middle digit the output of the modulo-8 counter, and the rightmost digit the output of the modulo-9 counter. Consequently, beginning with state 000, the first part of the count sequence is

$$000, 111, 222, 333, 444, 555, 666, 077, 108, 210, 321, 432, \ldots$$

Because the moduli of the counters are relatively prime, all $7 \times 8 \times 9$ states are traversed before returning to the initial state, resulting in a modulo-504 counter. In general, a

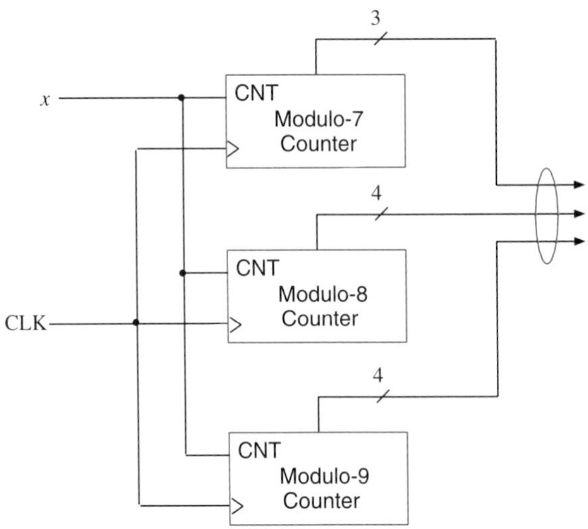

Figure 11.29 Parallel implementation of modulo-$(7 \times 8 \times 9)$ counter.

modulo-P counter with $P = p_1 \times p_2 \times \cdots \times p_k$, where the p_i's are relatively prime, can be implemented by a parallel connection of k counters, the ith counter being modulo-p_i.

This counter is faster than the cascaded version because the terminal count does not have to propagate through the other modules. However, the unconventional code might make this unsuitable for some applications. For a cost comparison with conventional counters, see Exercise 11.25.

11.4 MULTIMODULE SYSTEMS

When the sequential system is complex, several interacting subsystems might be required for its implementation. Given a description such as a state table or a state diagram, a possible approach for these cases would be to partition the description into subsystems. However, this general approach is rather difficult. An alternative, which works quite well in practical cases, is to perform a functional decomposition at the high level and then implement each subsystem separately. We illustrate this approach by two simple examples.

EXAMPLE 11.6

Consider a block pattern recognizer. For this system the input sequence is divided into blocks of k symbols and the pattern P is checked in each block.

As shown in Figure 11.30*a*, this system can be implemented by a modulo-k counter and a pattern recognizer.

The output of the counter is

$$TC(t) = \begin{cases} 1 & \textbf{if} \quad t \bmod k = k-1 \ \textbf{and} \ \text{CHECK} = 1 \\ 0 & \textbf{otherwise} \end{cases}$$

indicating the end of the block. The output of the pattern recognizer $p(t) = 1$ indicates that the pattern P is recognized. The output of the system is $z(t) = p(t) \cdot TC(t)$. Signal INITIALIZE clears the counter and sets the pattern recognizer to its initial state. The input sequence is checked for the pattern P when CHECK = 1. This time behavior is illustrated in the following table for $k = 3$, $x(t) \in \{0, 1, 2, \ldots, 9\}$ and $P = (374)$:

t	0	1	2	3	4	5	6	7	8	9	10	11
x	5	3	7	4	1	0	3	7	4	3	7	4
TC	0	0	1	0	0	1	0	0	1	0	0	1
p	0	0	0	1	0	0	0	0	1	0	0	1
z	0	0	0	0	0	0	0	0	1	0	0	1

The design of each of the subsystems follows the approach presented previously.

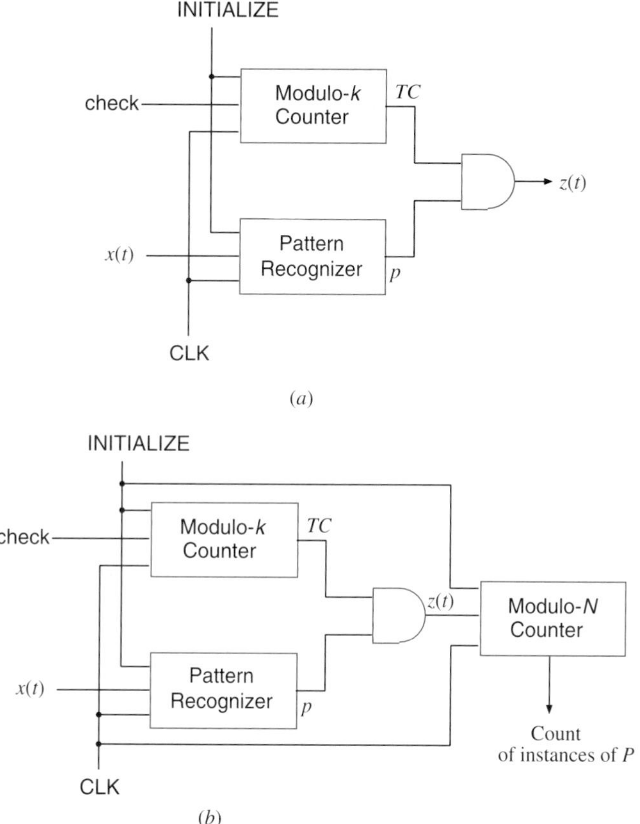

Figure 11.30 Block pattern recognizer ■

EXAMPLE 11.7

Extend the system in the previous example by adding the capability of counting the number of instances of the pattern P. The implementation, shown in Figure 11.30*b*, incorporates another counter to obtain this number of instances. Of course, because the counter is finite, the maximum count is limited. ■

11.5 FURTHER READINGS

Standard sequential modules implemented as MSI/LSI ICs are discussed in many texts. Examples of in-depth discussions can be found in *Digital Design with Standard MSI and LSI* by

T. R. Blakeslee (2nd ed.), Wiley, New York, 1979; *Digital Systems and Hardware/Firmware Algorithms* by M. Ercegovac and T. Lang, Wiley, 1985, and *Digital Design: Principles & Practices* by J. F. Wakerly, Prentice-Hall, Englewood Cliffs, NJ, 1994. Manufacturers' and trade literature are good sources of information about implementation and use of modules in modern technologies.

EXERCISES

Registers and shift registers

Exercise 11.1 Implement a four-bit register using SR flip-flops.

Exercise 11.2 Implement a serial-in/parallel-out bidirectional shift register using a parallel-in/parallel-out right shift register.

Exercise 11.3 Design a bit-serial arithmetic unit that performs addition and subtraction for 16-bit operands and result in the two's complement system.

Exercise 11.4 Design a pattern recognizer that recognizes the sequences 0101 and 0110. Use a serial-in/parallel-out shift register and gates.

Exercise 11.5 The network depicted in Figure 11.31 performs bit-serial BCD addition. The serial binary adder contains a full adder and a carry-out flip-flop. Signals K_1, K_2, and K_3 are produced by a modulo-4 counter, which is initialized to 0, so that K_i has value 1 when the counter is in state i.

a. If the shift register is initialized to 0000, and the flip-flop is reset, determine the 12-cycle output sequence z for the 8-cycle input sequences $x = 01101001$ (corresponding to the value 69) and $y = 00010110$ (corresponding to 16).
b. Show that the network performs bit-serial BCD addition. For this, consider what happens during the four cycles in which one digit of x and of y go through the first adder and during the four cycles to traverse the second adder.

Exercise 11.6 Design a 32-bit bit-serial magnitude comparator. Show the registers for the operands, the bit-serial operator, and the counter for control of completion. Perform two designs, as follows:

a. the operands are input to the operator least-significant bit first;
b. the operands are input most-significant bit first.

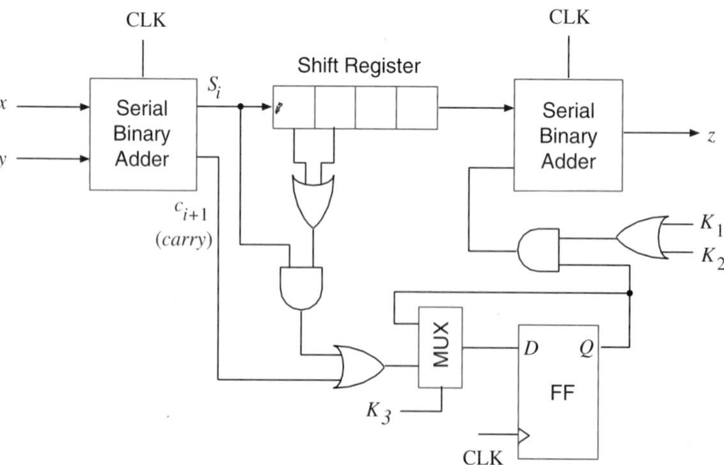

Figure 11.31 Network for Exercise 11.5.

Exercise 11.7 Design a 32-bit serial change-of-sign unit for an integer represented in the two's complement system. Use the same register for operand and result. Include a counter to control the completion of the operation. Perform two designs, as follows:

a. produce one bit of the result per cycle;
b. produce two bits per cycle.

Exercise 11.8 A variable-length shift register is a serial-in/serial-out shift register with a variable number of bits. It is used to provide variable number of cycles of delay from input to output. The length is specified by a control variable.

Design a variable-length shift register with lengths from one to eight bits, using an eight-bit serial-in/parallel-out shift register and combinational modules.

Counter modules

Exercise 11.9 Design a programmable modulo-m ($m < 16$) frequency divider. The inputs are m and the count input x; the output is 1 every mth occurence of the event $x = 1$. Use a modulo-16 binary counter with parallel input and combinational modules.

Exercise 11.10 Design a BCD counter using a four-bit register, a four-bit binary adder module, and one two-input AND gate.

Exercise 11.11 Using a modulo-16 binary counter with parallel inputs, implement

a. a 4-to-11 counter;
b. a modulo-13 counter; and
c. a counter with the following periodical sequence: 0,1,2,3,4,5,8,9,10,11,14,15

Exercise 11.12 Design the counters of Exercise 11.10 using the following modules:

a. T flip-flops and NAND gates; and
b. a register, an adder, and gates.

Exercise 11.13 Design a modulo-11 up/down counter using a modulo-16 binary counter and gates.

Exercise 11.14 Design a counter with the following counting sequence of 21 cycles period length: 5,6,. . . ,24,25. Use a modulo-16 counter with parallel inputs, one flip-flop, and NAND gates.

Exercise 11.15 A 50%-duty-cycle frequency divider has an output that is 1 for half of its period, as depicted in Figure 11.32*a*.

Analyze the 50%-duty-cycle frequency dividers shown in Figure 11.32*b*, which use a modulo-16 binary counter. Determine the modulo of operation and give timing diagrams for the outputs.

Exercise 11.16 Design a pattern recognizer that outputs a 1 whenever the input sequence $x(t_1, t)$ consists of a block of 0's of even length, followed by two 1's, followed by a block of 0's of odd length. Use a modulo-8 binary counter with parallel input, an 8-input multiplexer, and gates.

Exercise 11.17 For the sequential system shown in Figure 11.33, obtain $z(t)$ as a function of t, assuming that the output is an integer represented in the binary system. Determine the value of $z(10)$ if the initial state is $z(0) = 0$ and COUNT $= 0$.

Exercise 11.18 Implement the controller whose state diagram is given in Figure 11.34, using a modulo-16 counter with parallel input, an eight-input multiplexer, and gates. Compare three designs with different choices of counting and loading.

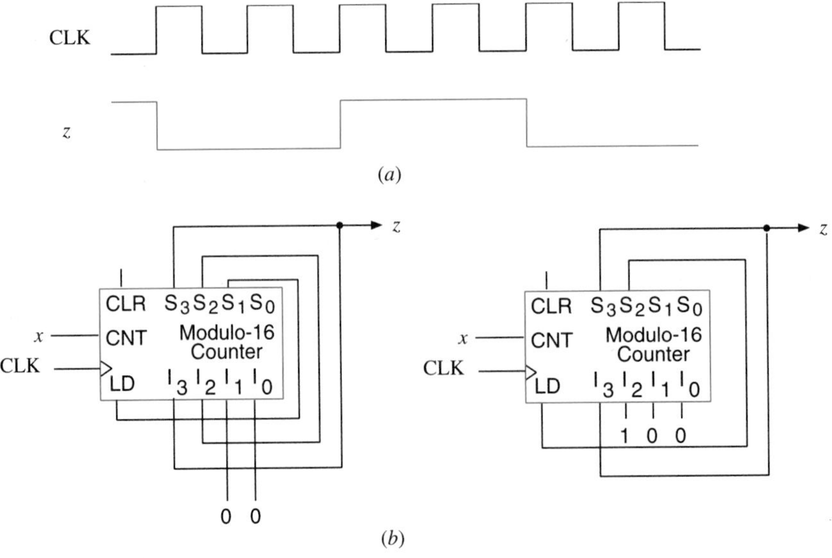

Figure 11.32 Frequency dividers for Exercise 11.15.

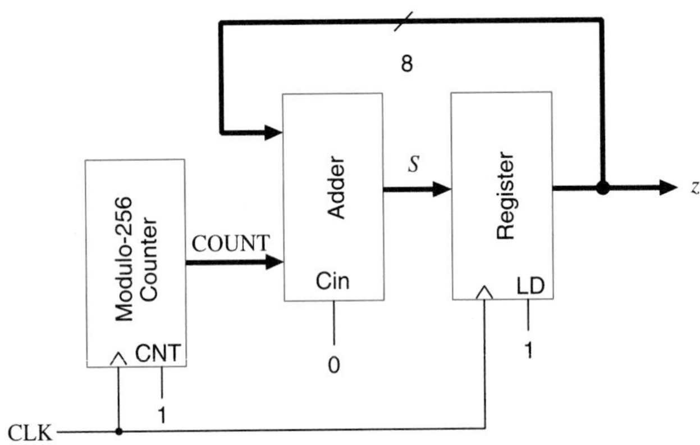

Figure 11.33 Network for Exercise 11.17.

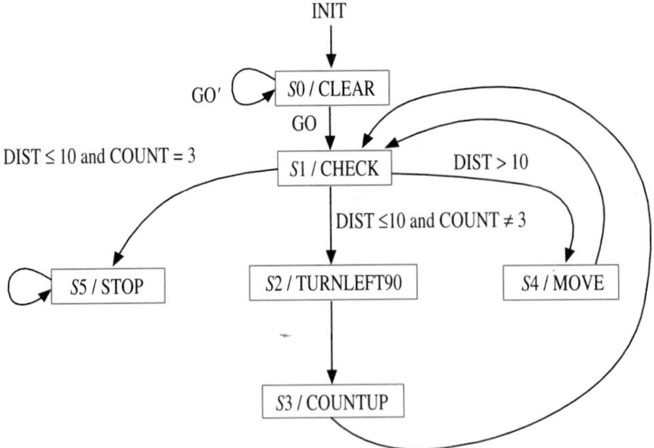

Figure 11.34 State diagram for Exercise 11.18.

Exercise 11.19 Using a modulo-16 up/down counter, design a sequential network that has the following state equations:

$$s(t+1) = \begin{cases} s(t) & \textbf{if} \quad x = 0 \\ (s(t)+1) \bmod 10 & \textbf{if} \quad x = 1 \\ (s(t)-1) \bmod 8 & \textbf{if} \quad x = 2 \end{cases}$$

$$z(t) = s(t)$$

Exercise 11.20 Using a modulo-16 counter, design a sequential network that has the following behavior:

$$z(t) = \begin{cases} 0 & \textbf{if} \quad (x(t-3,t) = 0110) \textbf{ and } \text{the number of 1's in } x(0,t) \text{ is even} \\ 1 & \textbf{if} \quad \text{the number of 1's in } x(0,t) \text{ is odd} \\ 2 \text{ or } 3 & \textbf{otherwise} \end{cases}$$

Exercise 11.21 Analyze the counter shown in Figure 11.35. It is composed of one four-bit serial-in/parallel-out (right) shift register and one NAND gate. The leftmost flip-flop is of JK type. Determine whether the counter is self-starting, that is, whether it reaches the counting sequence from any initial state.

Exercise 11.22 Show that the network depicted in Figure 11.36 is a self-starting counter; that is, from any initial state the module reaches a state in the counting sequence after a few cycles. In this shift-register module, a shift occurs whenever SHIFT=1 (independent of the value of LOAD) and a load occurs only when SHIFT=0 and LOAD=1.

Networks of counters

Exercise 11.23 Using two modulo-16 binary counters, implement cascade and parallel counters for

a. a modulo-23 counter;
b. an 11-to-29 counter; and
c. a frequency divider by 27.

To obtain these systems, implement a counter with modulo equal to or larger than the one required, and then adjust in a similar manner as is done in Section 11.3 when using the modulo-16 module. For example, for the parallel implementation of a modulo-23 counter, implement first a modulo-24 counter (as a modulo-3 and a modulo-8 counter).

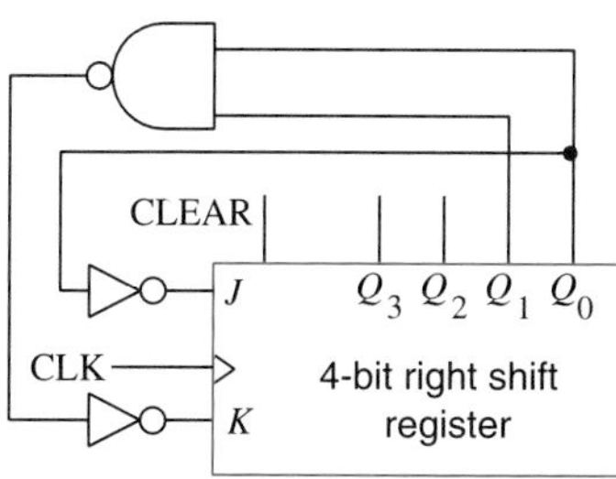

Figure 11.35 Network for Exercise 11.21.

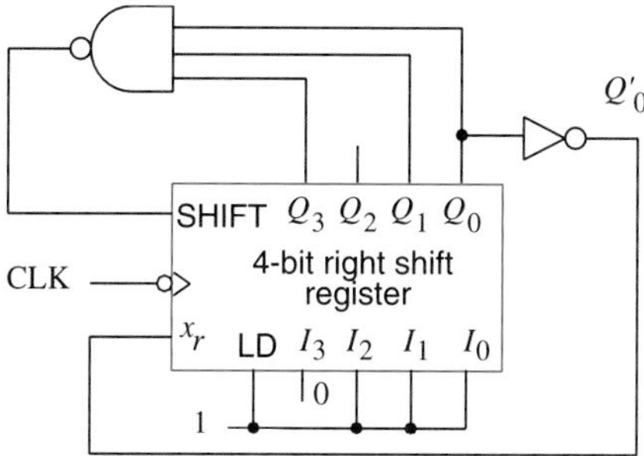

Figure 11.36 Network for Exercise 11.22.

Exercise 11.24 Using two modulo-16 counters and gates, design a counter with the following counting period: 0, 1, ..., 15, 1, 2, ..., 15, 2, 3, ..., 15, 3, 4, ..., 15, ..., 13, 14, 15, 14, 15.

Exercise 11.25 An autonomous counter counts the number of clocks (i.e., its input is always 1). Analyze the autonomous modulo-24 counter shown in Figure 11.37 and compare its cost (number of flip-flops, gates, and connections) and delay with respect to the following alternatives:

a. binary modulo-24 counter using T flip-flops and gates; and
b. twisted-tail modulo-24 counter using D flip-flops and gates.

Exercise 11.26

a. Design a modulo-40 frequency divider consisting of the parallel connection of a modulo-5 and modulo-8 frequency divider.
b. Determine the counting sequence of a parallel counter formed by a modulo-10 and a modulo-4 counter.

Multimodule systems

Exercise 11.27 Design a sequential lock. There are three push buttons A, B, and C, which provide binary inputs. The output z is 1 (lock open) if A is pressed five times, followed by pressing C three times followed by B four times. The lock controller is initialized when $z = 1$ or by pressing the reset button R. There are also three lights: the green one indicates that the controller is ready to accept the input sequence, the yellow indicates input in progress, and the red indicates a wrong input sequence.

Exercise 11.28 Design a controller that repeats n (< 32) times the sequence of four control signals shown bellow. The repetition count n is provided in the binary code as input to the controller.

t	0	1	2	3	4	5
c_0	0	1	1	1	1	0
c_1	1	1	0	0	0	0
c_2	0	0	1	1	1	0
c_3	0	0	0	0	1	1

Exercise 11.29 Design a multimodule sequential system that detects when $x(t-7, t-4) < x(t-3, t)$, where four-bit input sequences are interpreted as positive integers. Use appropriate standard modules.

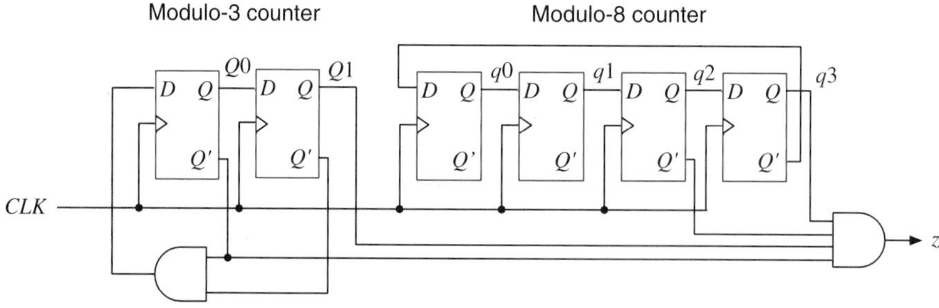

Figure 11.37 Network for Exercise 11.25.

Chapter 12

Programmable Modules

In this chapter we present:

- The specification of programmable combinational and sequential modules (PSA, ROM, PGA).
- The way the modules are programmed.
- Examples of uses of these modules.

The last chapters have discussed modules that realize specific functions, and the implementation of systems using those modules. The resulting implementations are characterized by being "rigid" in the sense that any changes in the specification (i.e., the functionality) of the system requires a redesign. An alternative to get flexibility in an implementation consists of using **programmable modules.** These modules have a standard (fixed) structure and are customized for a particular function either at the last stages of fabrication, or when the module is incorporated as part of a system, or when the system is activated (powered up). In Chapter 5 we already described two programmable combinational modules: PLAs and PALs. As mentioned there, programmable modules have become quite popular but, in spite of the advantages arising from their flexibility, they have not replaced fixed-function standard modules in all applications because they are somewhat more expensive and slower than a well-suited fixed-function module; moreover, in the case of VLSI implementations, programmable modules occupy a larger area than the fixed-function counterparts.

In this chapter, we present other types of combinational and sequential programmable modules; we describe their specification, their implementation, and how they are used in networks for the implementation of more complex digital systems. The programmable modules discussed are Programmable Sequential Arrays (PSA), Read-Only Memories (ROM), and Programmable Gate Arrays (PGA). We also give an overview of the advantages and limitations of programmable modules.

12.1 PROGRAMMABLE SEQUENTIAL ARRAYS

An n-input, 2^p-state, k-output **programmable sequential array** (PSA) is a module that provides a canonical implementation of a sequential system with 2^p states. A high-level description of this module is

Inputs:	$\underline{x} = (x_{n-1}, \ldots, x_0), \quad x_i \in \{0, 1\}$
	$E \in \{0, 1\}$
Outputs:	$\underline{z} = (z_{k-1}, \ldots, z_0), \quad z_i \in \{0, 1\}$
State:	$\underline{s} = (s_{p-1}, \ldots, s_0), \quad s_i \in \{0, 1\}$
Function:	NOT-AND-OR or NOT-OR-AND implementation of a sequential system with $k + p$ switching functions, with maximum r terms total

As depicted in Figure 12.1, a PSA consists of a PLA with $(n + p)$ inputs and $(k + p)$ outputs, and a register with p binary cells. The PSA module is an extension of the PLA module used for combinational systems: the register is used for storing the state, whereas the AND and the OR arrays are used for implementing the state transition and output functions.

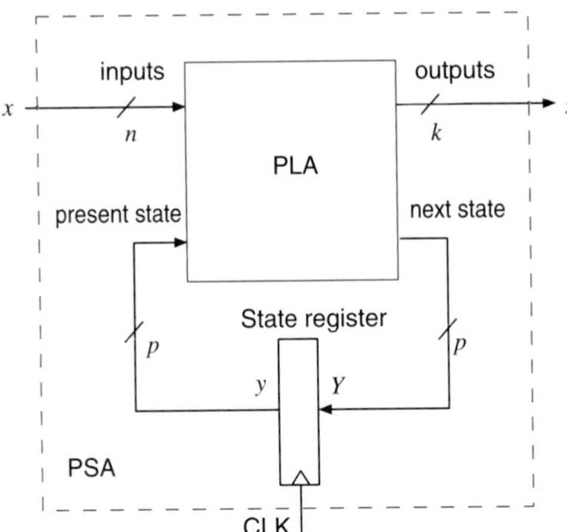

Figure 12.1 Programmable sequential array (PSA).

Implementation of Sequential Systems Using PSAs

The implementation of a sequential system using a PSA follows the procedures described in Chapter 8, as illustrated by the following example.

EXAMPLE 12.1

A sequence generator has one binary input x and a number in the set $\{0, 1, 3, 6, 7, 10, 14\}$ as output. The system generates one of two predefined sequences selected by x, as defined by the following high-level specification:

Inputs:	$x \in \{0, 1\}$
Outputs:	$z \in \{0, 1, 3, 6, 7, 10, 14\}$

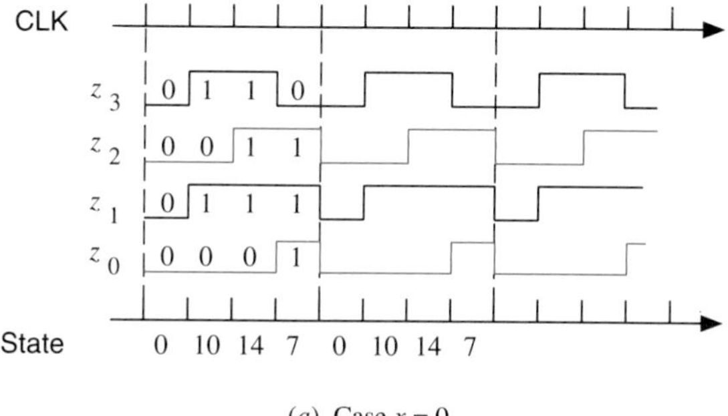

(a) Case $x = 0$

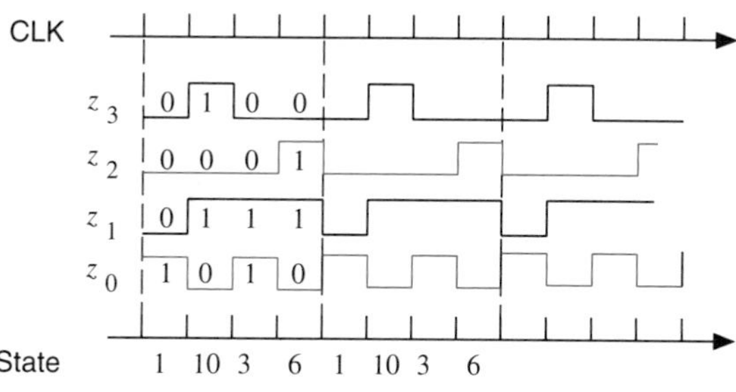

(b) Case $x = 1$

Figure 12.2 Timing sequences in Example 12.1.

Time behavior: The output sequence is described as follows:

$x = 0 : z = 0 \rightarrow 10 \rightarrow 14 \rightarrow 7 \rightarrow 0 \cdots$
$x = 1 : z = 1 \rightarrow 10 \rightarrow 3 \rightarrow 6 \rightarrow 1 \cdots$

The output sequence changes only at the end of each four-cycle period, but x can change in any clock cycle.

In words, each output sequence consists of four values, with a period of four clock cycles. The corresponding time behavior is shown in Figure 12.2.

This sequence generator is implemented using a PSA module with a five-bit state register. Four bits of the state are labeled with the corresponding output value; for simplicity, we use the radix-2 representation of the output integer as the label for those four bits. Thus, the binary specification of the output sequence is

$$x = 0 : z = 0000 \rightarrow 1010 \rightarrow 1110 \rightarrow 0111 \rightarrow 0000 \cdots$$

$$x = 1 : z = 0001 \rightarrow 1010 \rightarrow 0011 \rightarrow 0110 \rightarrow 0001 \cdots$$

In addition, input x is used as the fifth state bit, which we call k (sequence control); this bit is updated at the end of each sequence (every four clock cycles), as follows:

$$k(t+1) = \begin{cases} x(t) & \textbf{if} \quad s(t) = 3 \textbf{ or } 14 \\ k(t) & \textbf{otherwise} \end{cases}$$

Consequently, the state is $\underline{s} = (s_4, s_3, s_2, s_1, s_0) = (k, y_3, y_2, y_1, y_0)$. The system is initialized to $k = 0$ and $y = 0$. The corresponding transition function, in which y represents the present state (y_3, y_2, y_1, y_0) and Y corresponds to the next state (Y_3, Y_2, Y_1, Y_0), is

y	$k = 0$	$k = 1$	
0	10	–	k
1	–	10	k
3	–	6	x
6	0	1	k
7	0	1	k
10	14	3	k
14	7	–	x
	Y		K

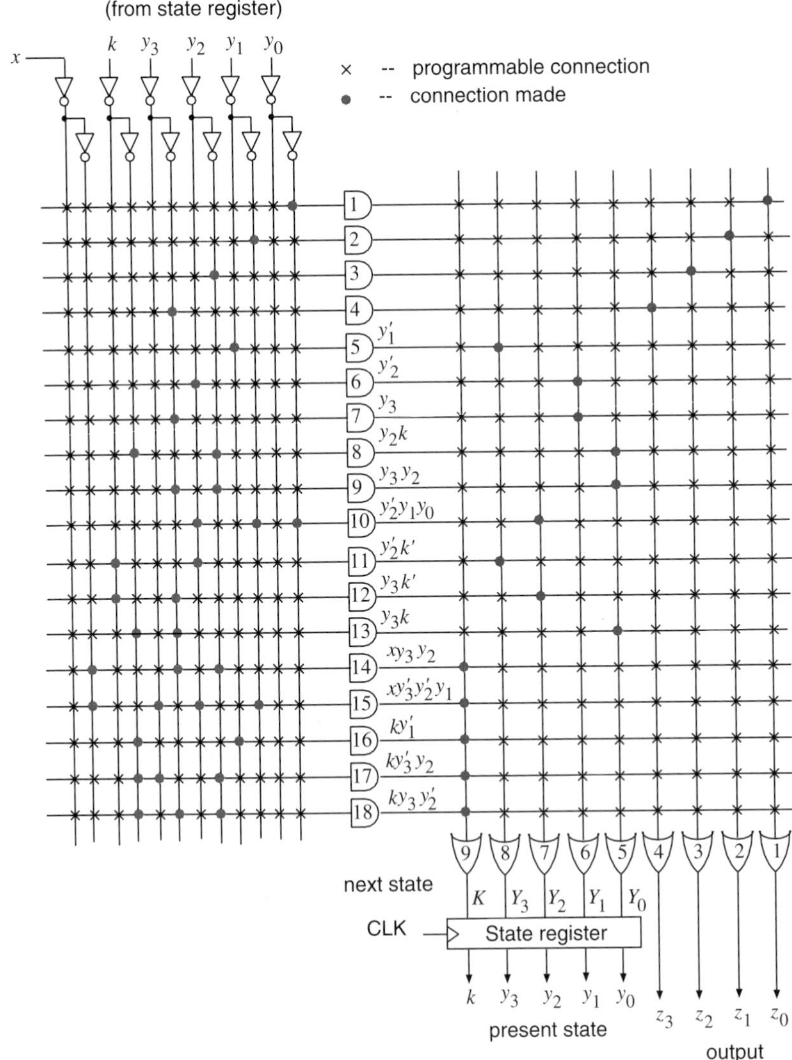

Figure 12.3 PSA implementation in Example 12.1.

States corresponding to $y \in \{2, 4, 5, 8, 9, 11, 12, 13, 15\}$ are don't care states. The corresponding minimal switching expressions are

$$K = xy_3y_2 + xy'_3y'_2y_1 + ky'_1 + ky'_3y_2 + ky_3y'_2$$
$$Y_3 = y'_1 + y'_2k'$$
$$Y_2 = y'_2y_1y_0 + y_3k'$$
$$Y_1 = y_3 + y'_2$$
$$Y_0 = y_3k + y_2k + y_3y_2$$

The implementation using a PSA module is shown in Figure 12.3. ■

From Example 12.1, it follows that all systems described in Chapter 8 can be implemented using PSA modules, subject to restrictions in the size of these modules.

12.2 READ-ONLY MEMORIES

A $2^n \times k$ **read-only memory ROM** (see Figure 12.4) is an array of 2^n rows that contains vectors of k bits holding constant (predefined) values. The n input variables $\underline{x} = (x_{n-1}, \ldots, x_0)$ correspond to the **memory address**, which is used to select one particular row of this array; the selected row is made to appear at the output $\underline{z} = (z_{k-1}, \ldots, z_0)$. In other words, a read-only memory corresponds to a tabular representation of a combinational system in which the input bit-vector is used to identify which row in the array is accessed. The contents of the rows are frequently referred to as **words**. These modules usually provide three-state outputs and a module-enable input E to facilitate the design of multimodule ROM networks. A high-level specification of a ROM is

Inputs: $\underline{x} = (x_{n-1}, \ldots, x_0), \quad x_i \in \{0, 1\}$
$E \in \{0, 1\}$
Outputs: $\underline{z} = (z_{k-1}, \ldots, z_0), \quad z_i \in \{0, 1\}$

Function: $\underline{z} = \text{ROM}(\underline{x})$
where ROM is a $2^n \times k$ table

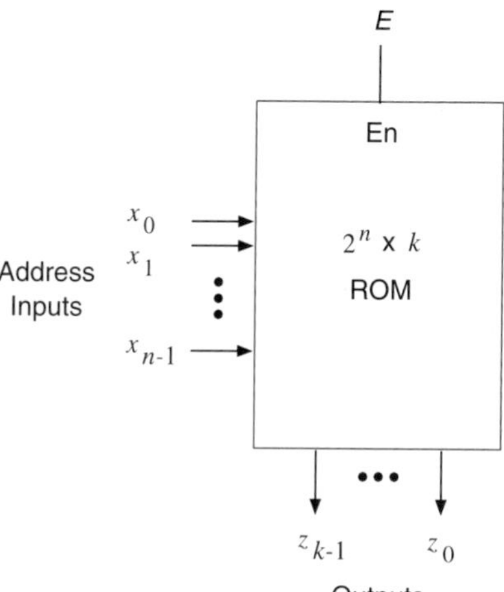

Figure 12.4 Read-only memory (ROM).

EXAMPLE 12.2 Given the 8 × 4 ROM with the contents shown as follows, for input $\underline{x} = (0, 1, 0)$, the output is $\underline{z} = (0, 1, 1, 1)$.

Address $\underline{x}$	Contents $\underline{z}$
000	1011
001	1101
010	**0111**
011	1000
100	0000
101	1111
110	1111
111	1011

■

Figure 12.5 depicts an implementation of a 4 × 4 ROM module. It consists of a decoder and a NOR array. Note that this implementation is similar to that of a PLA in which the first NOR array is replaced by a decoder, so that the programmability is restricted to the second NOR array. Because the decoder implements all minterms of the variables, the ROM does not have the limitation in the number of product terms that is inherent to the PLA. On the other hand, the decoder occupies more area than the restricted AND array of the PLA.

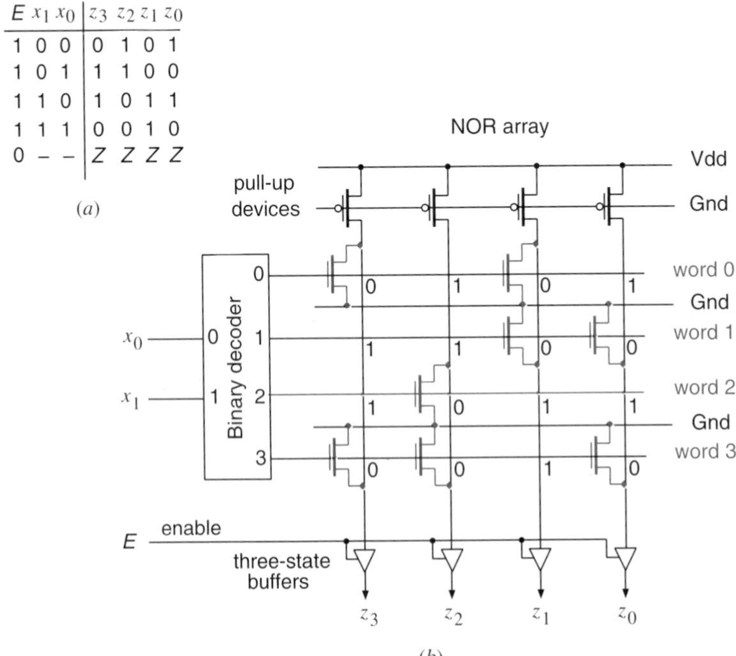

E	x_1	x_0	z_3	z_2	z_1	z_0
1	0	0	0	1	0	1
1	0	1	1	1	0	0
1	1	0	1	0	1	1
1	1	1	0	0	1	0
0	–	–	Z	Z	Z	Z

(*a*)

(*b*)

Figure 12.5 MOS implementation of a 4 × 4 read-only memory. (*a*) The function. (*b*) The circuit.

EXAMPLE 12.3

Figure 12.6 implements a four-bit adder using a 512 × 5 ROM module.

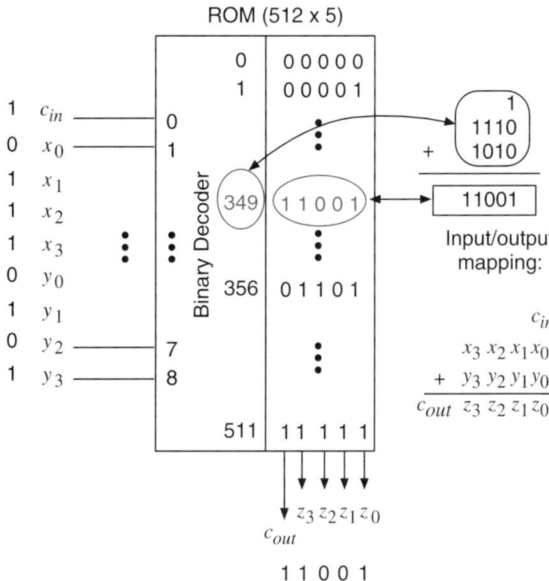

Figure 12.6 ROM-based implementation of a four-bit adder.

■

The ROM-based approach to the implementation of switching functions may seem very wasteful at first, because the whole truth table is stored in the array. Consider, for example, the implementation of an OR function of eight variables, and compare an OR gate implementation with the ROM-based implementation. Based on the structure depicted in Figure 12.5, one can infer that the ROM-based approach requires more transistors and a larger area. Consequently, a ROM is used only for relatively complex and ad hoc functions that would require several standard modules, but not for simple switching functions.

Implementation of Sequential Systems Using ROMs

A ROM can be used to implement the combinational part of a sequential system, that is, to store the transition and output functions in a canonical implementation. This is illustrated by the following example.

EXAMPLE 12.4

Consider a sequential system described by the following tabular representation (the combination $x_1x_0 = 00$ never appears, so it is considered a don't care case):

Inputs: $\underline{x} = (x_1, x_0), \quad x_i \in \{0, 1\}$
Outputs: $z \in \{0, 1\}$
State: $\underline{y} = (y_1, y_0), \quad y_i \in \{0, 1\}$

Function: The transition and output function are

PS	$x_1 x_0$		
$y_1 y_0$	01	10	11
00	01,0	10,1	10,0
01	00,0	11,1	11,0
10	11,0	10,0	00,1
11	10,0	00,0	11,1
	$Y_1 Y_0$, z *NS*, output		

A ROM-based implementation of this system is shown in Figure 12.7*a*. It consists of a 16×3 ROM and a two-bit state register S. This register contains the two most-significant bits of the ROM address. The inputs x_1 and x_0 determine the two least-significant address bits. A word in the ROM stores the next state and the output, as shown in Figure 12.7*b*.

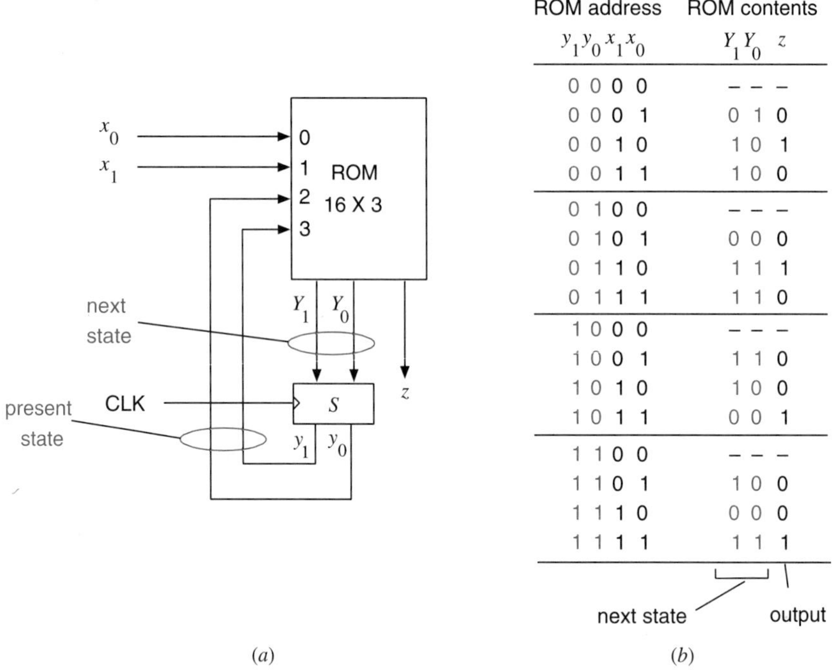

ROM address $y_1 y_0 x_1 x_0$	ROM contents $Y_1 Y_0$ z
0 0 0 0	– – –
0 0 0 1	0 1 0
0 0 1 0	1 0 1
0 0 1 1	1 0 0
0 1 0 0	– – –
0 1 0 1	0 0 0
0 1 1 0	1 1 1
0 1 1 1	1 1 0
1 0 0 0	– – –
1 0 0 1	1 1 0
1 0 1 0	1 0 0
1 0 1 1	0 0 1
1 1 0 0	– – –
1 1 0 1	1 0 0
1 1 1 0	0 0 0
1 1 1 1	1 1 1
	next state, output

(b)

Figure 12.7 ROM-based implementation of a sequential system. (*a*) Network. (*b*) ROM contents. ■

In general, for a sequential system with n binary inputs, k binary state variables, and m binary outputs, a ROM of 2^{n+k} words of $k + m$ bits is sufficient. A particular system may be implemented with fewer ROM words (techniques for reducing ROM requirements are beyond the scope of this text).

Types of ROM Modules

ROM modules can be classified according to the way that their contents (the values of the constant bit-vectors) are set, as follows:

Mask-programmed ROM: the contents are set when the module is fabricated and cannot be changed. Creating the mask that defines the contents is expensive, so that this type of ROM is justified only when a large number of modules is produced.

Field-programmable ROM: the contents are set in the field before the module is used; once set, they cannot be changed. These modules are usually called PROMs. The programming process requires a special device known as a PROM burner.

Erasable ROM: the contents are set in the field before the module is used, but they can be erased by exposing the module to ultraviolet light and reprogrammed electrically. This requires the module to be removed from the system where it is being used. The module can be repeatedly erased and reprogrammed. Such a module is called an EPROM.

Electrically erasable ROM, also known as **flash-memory** or EEPROM: the contents are set in the field before the module is used, but they can be erased and reprogrammed by electric signals. These changes can be performed in the system where the module is being used, and the changes are done to one word at a time. Special power and timing capabilities are required for changing the contents (compared to the requirements to access such contents).

Mask-programmed ROMs have a higher design cost, due to extra steps in chip fabrication, and do not exhibit field modifiability. On the other hand, field-programmable and erasable ROMs require a larger silicon area for the same capacity and, therefore, are more costly to build. Consequently, the decision to use one or the other depends on the production volume and the modification requirements. Modifiable modules have additional inputs to control the process of writing into the memory.

12.3 NETWORKS OF PROGRAMMABLE MODULES

As with all other modules, the size of the system that can be implemented with a programmable module is limited by the number of inputs and outputs in the module. In the case of PLAs and PSAs, there is an additional limitation arising from the number of product terms and the size of the state register. As with previous modules, networks of modules are used for the cases where the desired function cannot be implemented with a single module; we now describe the design of such networks.

Consider for example the implementation of two functions with five variables, using standard 8×2 ROM modules (this example is used only to illustrate the process; standard ROM modules have a larger number of inputs and outputs). The functions are

$$f_1(x_4, x_3, x_2, x_1, x_0) = \textit{one-set}\,(0,3,11,12,16,23,27)$$

$$f_0(x_4, x_3, x_2, x_1, x_0) = \textit{one-set}\,(5,7,19,21,31)$$

Because the ROM modules have three inputs and there are five input variables, the input vector $\underline{x}$ is partitioned into two subvectors, one containing three variables and the other having the rest. One such partition is

$$\underline{x} = (\underline{x}^{(0)}, \underline{x}^{(1)})$$

$$\underline{x}^{(0)} = (x_4, x_3)$$

$$\underline{x}^{(1)} = (x_2, x_1, x_0)$$

Based on this decomposition, we can build a network with four 8×2 ROM modules, as depicted in Figure 12.8. This network is designed as follows:

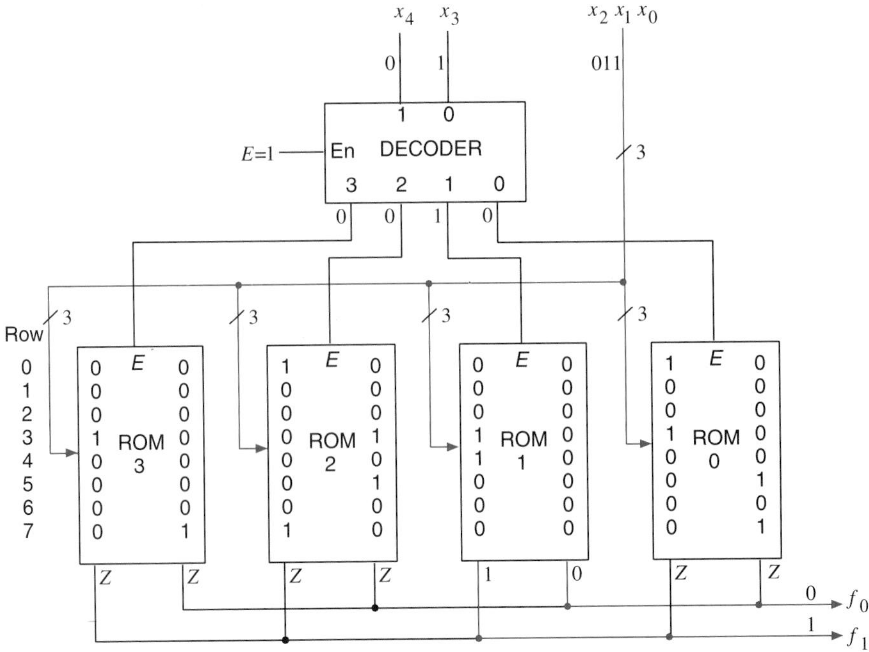

Figure 12.8 ROM-based network for the implementation of two functions.

- The functions are decomposed into "sections." Each section is implemented by one ROM module with inputs (x_2, x_1, x_0).
- A particular section (ROM module) is selected by the values of variables (x_4, x_3) by means of a decoder whose outputs are connected to the enable inputs to the ROMs.
- The corresponding outputs from the modules are connected with OR gates (wired connections in Figure 12.8 because the ROM modules have three-state outputs).

For instance, if the input vector $\underline{x} = 01011$, the decoder produces a 1 in its output number 1 (as $x_4 = 0, x_3 = 1$); this output enables ROM 1. The output from this module is 10 because $x_2 = 0, x_1 = 1, x_0 = 1$. The three-state connections produce the output $f_1 = 1, f_0 = 0$.

In general, as shown in Figure 12.9*a*, the implementation of a function of n variables $f(x_{n-1}, \ldots, x_0)$ using ROMs with k inputs consists of 2^{n-k} modules and a decoder with $n - k$ inputs. Module i stores the ith section of the function, and the decoder enables the ROM module that corresponds to the assignment of $(x_{n-1}, \ldots, x_k)$.

An alternative implementation is shown in Figure 12.9*b*; here, the decoder is replaced by a multiplexer that selects among the outputs of the ROM modules.

Because the number of ROM modules required in these networks is 2^{n-k}, this approach is acceptable only for small values of $(n - k)$. On the other hand, if the number of functions to be implemented is larger than the number of outputs from a module, then several modules have to be used. Figure 12.10 illustrates the case where 12 functions are required and each module has only four outputs.

Although the process above has been illustrated with ROM modules, it is exactly the same for PLAs. However, in the PLA case there is also the limitation in the number of product terms per module, so that more PLAs are required when sections of the function have more terms than what is available in one module. This is illustrated in Exercise 12.8.

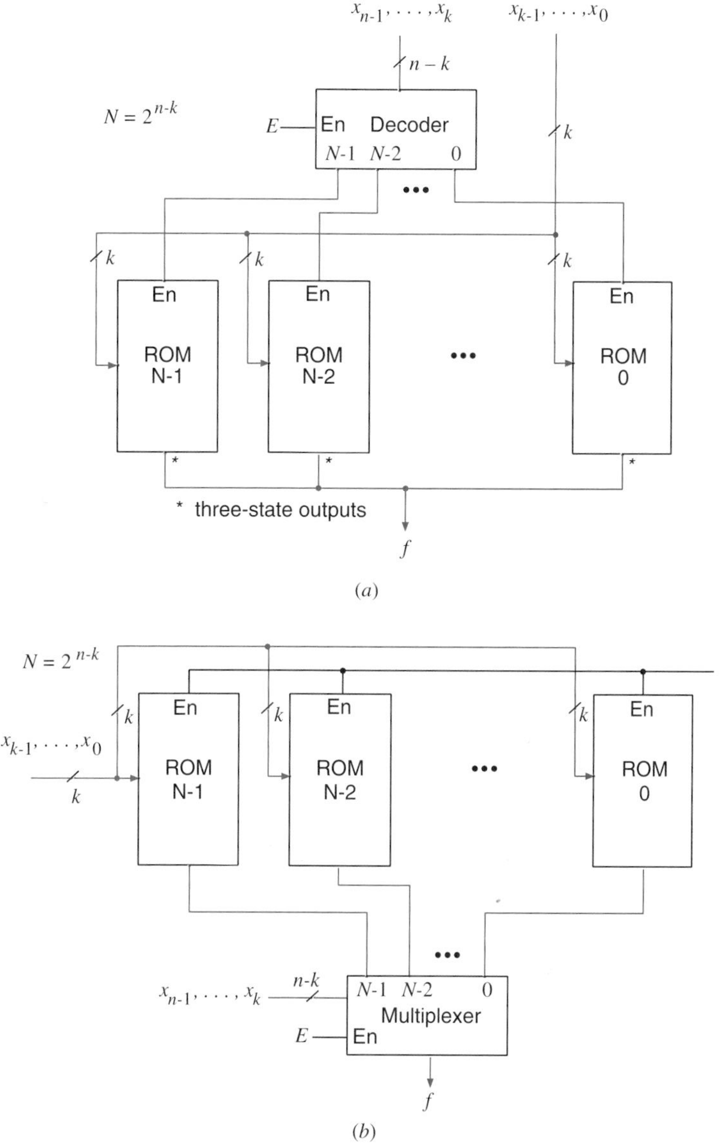

Figure 12.9 Implementations of functions with n variables. (*a*) ROMs and decoder. (*b*) ROMs and multiplexer.

12.4 ADVANTAGES AND DISADVANTAGES OF PROGRAMMABLE MODULES

We now summarize the advantages and disadvantages of using programmable modules such as ROMs, PLAs, PALs, and PSAs.

For an MSI/LSI implementation, these programmable modules are advantageous for the following reasons.

1. The cost of an integrated circuit depends more on the number of pins than on the number of gates included in the chip (up to a number of gates that is increasing rapidly with improvements in technology). Consequently, a chip containing a programmable

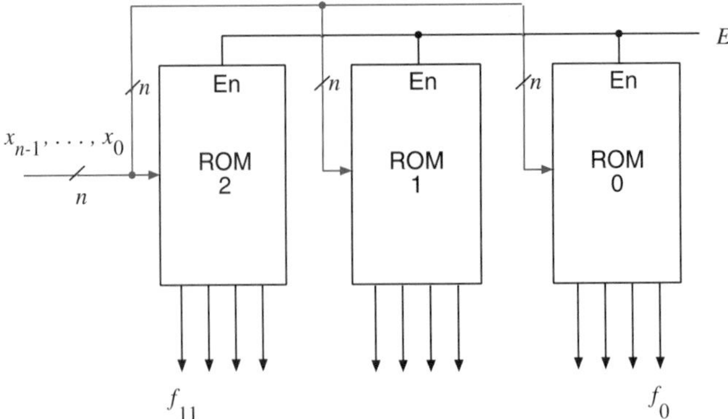

Figure 12.10 ROM-based implementation of large number of switching functions.

module is not more expensive than another standard module with the same number of pins.

2. The cost of an integrated circuit is very dependent on the number of chips of the same kind produced. Programmable modules are used in many applications, so they can be mass produced and customized for the particular application at the last stage of production or in the field.
3. The cost of an integrated circuit depends significantly on the cost of designing the chip. Programmable modules have a relatively low design cost due to their regularity.
4. The cost of a system depends heavily on the number of chips used. Due to the complex functions they can realize, programmable modules reduce considerably the number of chips required.
5. A field-programmable module allows for easier modification of the functions it implements than other approaches.

In VLSI designs, the use of programmable modules results in a low design cost because of their regularity and because they can be easily adapted from modules in a library.

On the other hand, the disadvantage of using programmable modules is that they might produce a slower network and require a larger silicon area than other approaches.

The main differences among PLAs and ROMs are as follows.

1. The PLA results in a more compact implementation because, instead of storing the whole table of the functions, it implements reduced sum of products (product of sums) expressions. This difference is due to having a decoder for ROM and an AND array for PLA. If the number of products (sums) required is significantly smaller than the maximum 2^n, then this reduction in size can be large.
2. The PLA implementation is limited to a set of functions that can be represented by a set of sums of products (products of sums) with no more than r products (sums). No such a limitation exists for the ROM.
3. PLAs are more difficult to program than ROMs. This results from the fact that, to achieve the compactness that is possible with a PLA, it is necessary to design a two-level AND-OR (OR-AND) network that has a small number of AND (OR) gates.

12.5 FIELD-PROGRAMMABLE GATE ARRAYS

A **field-programmable gate array** (FPGA) is a VLSI module that can be programmed to implement a digital system consisting of tens of thousands of gates. In contrast to PLA/PSA modules that implement two-level combinational and canonical sequential networks, FPGAs allow the realization of multilevel networks and complex systems on a single chip.

A FPGA module consists of an array of three kinds of programmable (configurable) elements:

- **logic blocks,** either combinational and/or sequential;
- **interconnection points** (switches); and
- **input/output blocks.**

In addition, there are wires grouped in horizontal and vertical **channels.** Figure 12.11 illustrates the organization of an FPGA module at the chip level.

Each logic module can be programmed to implement several switching functions of a few variables, and to control the use of the flip-flops in the module. Logic modules used in FPGAs are implemented either as a look-up table (LUT) or a multiplexer. A LUT of k inputs can be programmed as a truth table of a switching function of up to k variables. A 2^n-input multiplexer, as discussed in Chapter 9, can be used to implement any switching function of n variables. The interconnect points and input/output blocks can be programmed to achieve the desired connections.

There are three basic approaches in providing programmability of FPGAs:

- On-chip control latches (memory cells) that are set with bit patterns to define the chip configuration. This type is called SRAM-FPGA because the set of control latches can be considered as a static random access memory, as defined in Chapter 14. These FPGAs are volatile, that is, the programming information is not preserved after the chip is powered down.
- Antifuse-programmed devices that are programmed electrically to provide connections that define the chip configuration. The programming is done by permanently closing some of the antifuse switches. Thus, unlike SRAM-FPGAs, these devices cannot be

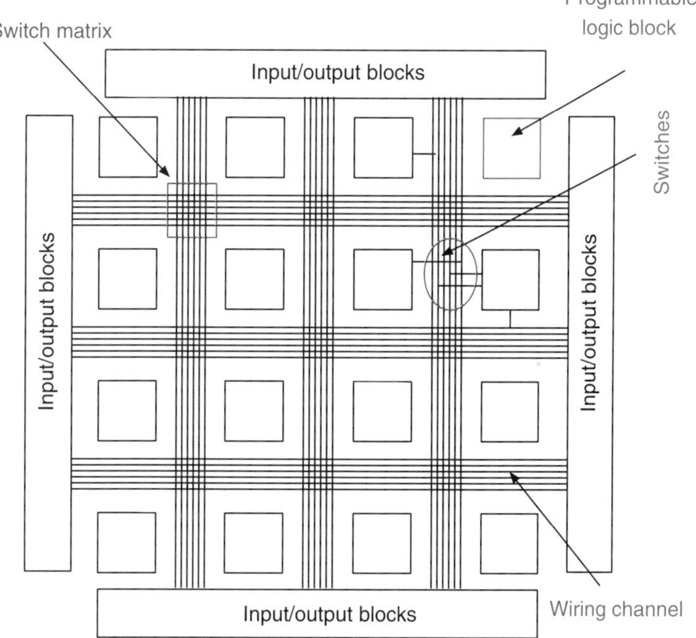

Figure 12.11 Organization of an FPGA chip.

reprogrammed (like mask-programmed ROMs and PLAs). However, these nonvolatile FPGAs are faster than the SRAM-type devices. One important advantage of antifuses is their very small size, allowing a large number of interconnections on a chip.
- Using several electrically programmable devices (EPROMs and EEPROMs) and a shared interconnect mechanism on a single chip. In contrast to SRAM-based FPGAs, EPROM and EEPROM technologies do not require external permanent memory to preserve chip configuration. On the other hand, they require more complex chip fabrication process and use larger cells.

We discuss only the SRAM-type of FPGAs, due to their high reprogrammability.

SRAM-FPGAS

In SRAM-FPGAs, each programmable element is controlled by a memory cell. Memory cells are loaded during the programming phase with binary values that represent the desired values of control signals that define the chip configuration. These signals remain constant until another configuration is loaded. That is, the bit pattern stored in the on-chip volatile reconfiguration memory defines the structure and behavior of the chip—the chip "personality." This approach, although requiring an external nonvolatile memory for storage of configuration patterns, offers dynamic flexibility. That is, the same FPGA module can be used for different purposes. For example, FPGA modules on a board can be initially configured to perform testing of components on the board; after testing, the FPGAs can be reprogrammed to perform functions as required by the board application. Loading a configuration pattern into an FPGA typically takes several milliseconds.

The following are typical elements of a SRAM-FPGA:

- Programmable switch: a SRAM cell attached to the gate of a transistor acts as a switch (see Figure 12.12*a*) that is used to provide connections between logic/storage blocks' inputs/outputs and interconnecting lines.
- Programmable multiplexer: this consists of a 2^k-input multiplexer controlled by k SRAM cells, as illustrated in Figure 12.12*b* for $k = 2$.
- Look-up table: an array of 2^k SRAM cells (k-input look-up table) implements a k-variable switching function (see Figure 12.12*c*).
- Flip-flop: to provide for operation as a sequential system.

As an example of a SRAM-controlled FPGA, let us consider a module consisting of an array of 10×10 programmable (configurable) logic blocks (CLBs), connected using a programmable interconnect made of horizontal and vertical wires organized as depicted in Figure 12.11.[1] A CLB (see Figure 12.13) contains one lookup table (LUT), several SRAM-controlled multiplexers, and a storage element that can behave either as an edge-sensitive D flip-flop or a level-sensitive D latch.

The LUT provides several options in generating functions, as illustrated in Figure 12.14.[2] Moreover, CLB outputs X and Y can come from either of the LUT outputs or from the flip-flop.

The programmable interconnect consists of metal segments and programmable switching points that are used to provide the desired routing of signals between CLBs as well as I/O blocks. There are three types of programmable interconnect resources (see Figure 12.15):

[1] This module corresponds to the Xilinx XC2000 family of FPGA chips made by Xilinx, Inc., San Jose, CA.

[2] The configurations in Figure 12.14 are not obtained directly from Figure 12.13.

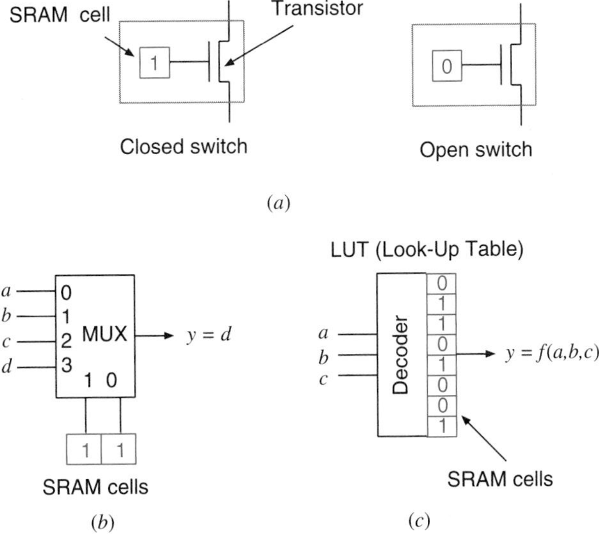

Figure 12.12 SRAM-FPGA programmable components. (*a*) Switch. (*b*) 4-input multiplexer. (*c*) Look-up table (LUT).

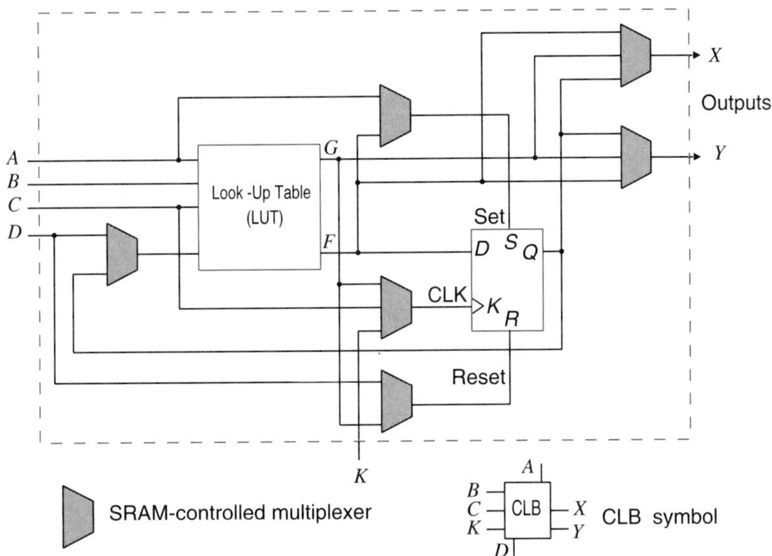

Figure 12.13 A programmable (configurable) logic block (CLB), partial view (courtesy of Xilinx, Inc.© Xilinx, Inc. 1992. All rights reserved).

1. Direct interconnections between horizontally and vertically adjacent CLBs. These provide fast signal paths when source and destination modules are adjacent.
2. General-purpose interconnects consist of vertical and horizontal wiring segments between switch matrices. The segments are connected by configuring switch matrices in a desired pattern. The signal delay depends on the placement of source/destination modules.
3. Long vertical and horizontal lines span the whole CLB array, providing means for transmitting signals to a large number of destinations whose delay is critical (e.g., clock signal).

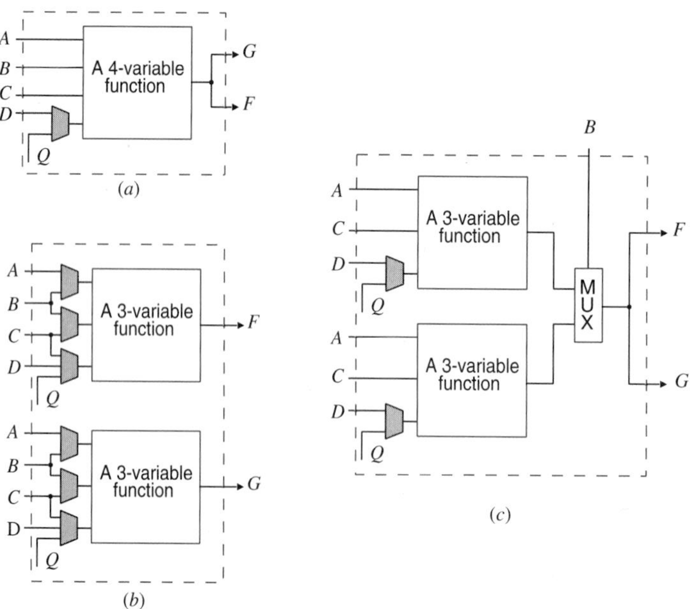

Figure 12.14 SRAM-FPGA options in generating functions. (*a*) One four-variable function. (*b*) Two three-variable functions. (*c*) Selection between two functions of three variables (courtesy of Xilinx, Inc.© Xilinx, Inc. 1992. All rights reserved).

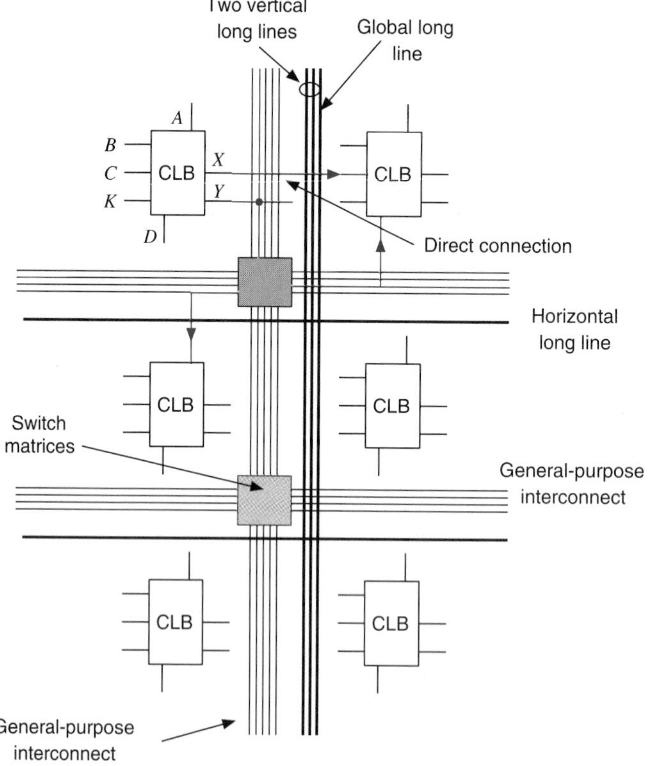

Figure 12.15 Programmable interconnect (courtesy of Xilinx, Inc.© Xilinx, Inc. 1992. All rights reserved).

The delays in FPGA networks are dependent on layout, that is, on the placement of the CLBs and routing of the signals. The actual delays in a design are determined with the help of simulation tools.

EXAMPLE 12.5

Design a one-digit BCD adder using a SRAM-FPGA module of type XC2000. The high-level specification of the system is:

Inputs:	$\underline{x} = (x_3, x_2, x_1, x_0)$,	$x_j \in \{0, 1\}$,	$x \in \{0, \ldots, 9\}$
	$\underline{y} = (y_3, y_2, y_1, y_0)$,	$y_j \in \{0, 1\}$,	$y \in \{0, \ldots, 9\}$
	$c_{in} \in \{0, 1\}$		
Outputs:	$\underline{s} = (s_3, s_2, s_1, s_0)$,	$s_j \in \{0, 1\}$,	$s \in \{0, \ldots, 9\}$
	$c_{out} \in \{0, 1\}$		

Function: $x + y + c_{in} = 10c_{out} + s$

The system has nine inputs and five outputs, so mapping into the FPGA requires decomposition into several CLBs. Many decompositions are possible. We rely on a scheme that uses two binary adders and a special module, as shown in Figure 12.16. Note that the second adder is actually a four-bit adder that adds either 0 or 6, depending on the value of t generated by the special module.

The basic idea behind this implementation is performing a modulo-16 addition, and then a correction whenever the output of this addition is not correct. The first adder produces

$$v = (x + y + c_{in}) \bmod 16$$

$$u = \begin{cases} 1 & \textbf{if} \quad (x + y + c_{in}) \geq 16 \\ 0 & \textbf{otherwise} \end{cases}$$

whereas the special module produces

$$t = \begin{cases} 1 & \textbf{if} \quad u = 1 \ \textbf{or} \ v \geq 10 \\ 0 & \textbf{otherwise} \end{cases}$$

On the other hand, the function of the system requires

$$s = (x + y + c_{in}) \bmod 10$$

$$c_{out} = \begin{cases} 1 & \textbf{if} \quad (x + y + c_{in}) \geq 10 \\ 0 & \textbf{otherwise} \end{cases}$$

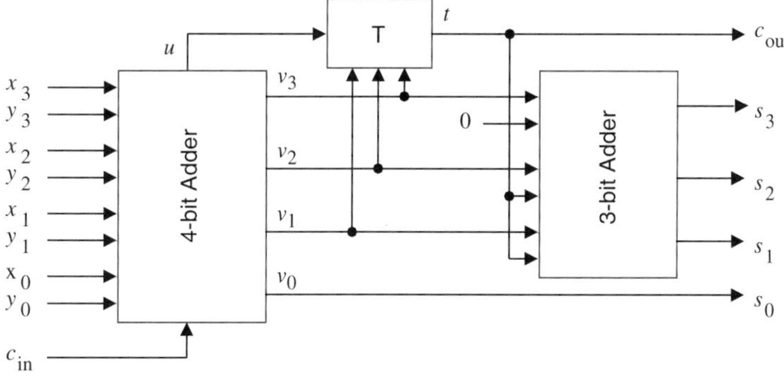

Figure 12.16 Implementation of a BCD adder module.

To obtain these outputs we consider three cases:

Case 1. If $(x + y + c_{in}) \leq 9$ then

$$s = v$$

$$c_{out} = 0$$

so the second adder should add 0 and $c_{out} = 0$. This is accomplished because $t = 0$.

Case 2. If $10 \leq (x + y + c_{in}) \leq 15$, the first adder produces

$$v = x + y + c_{in}$$

$$u = 0$$

Getting the correct s requires subtracting 10 from v and making $c_{out} = 1$. That is,

$$\begin{aligned} s &= v - 10 \\ &= x + y + c_{in} + 6 - 16 \\ &= (x + y + c_{in} + 6) \bmod 16 \\ c_{out} &= 1 \end{aligned}$$

which is achieved by the second adder because $t = 1$.

Case 3. If $(x + y + c_{in}) \geq 16$, the first adder produces

$$v = (x + y + c_{in} - 16)$$

$$u = 1$$

Then,

$$\begin{aligned} s &= x + y + c_{in} - 10 \\ &= v + 6 \\ c_{out} &= 1 \end{aligned}$$

The second adder should again add 6 and make $c_{out} = 1$, which happens because $t = 1$.

The condition $u = 1$ or $v \geq 10$ corresponds to the switching expression

$$t = u + v_3 v_2 + v_3 v_1$$

The three-bit adder with one operand equal to $(0, t, t)$ can be simplified to the following expressions (whose derivation is left as an exercise):

$$\begin{aligned} s_3 &= v_3 \oplus t(v_2 + v_1) \\ s_2 &= v_2 \oplus t v_1' \\ s_1 &= v_1 \oplus t \end{aligned}$$

Moreover,

$$s_0 = v_0$$

$$c_{out} = t$$

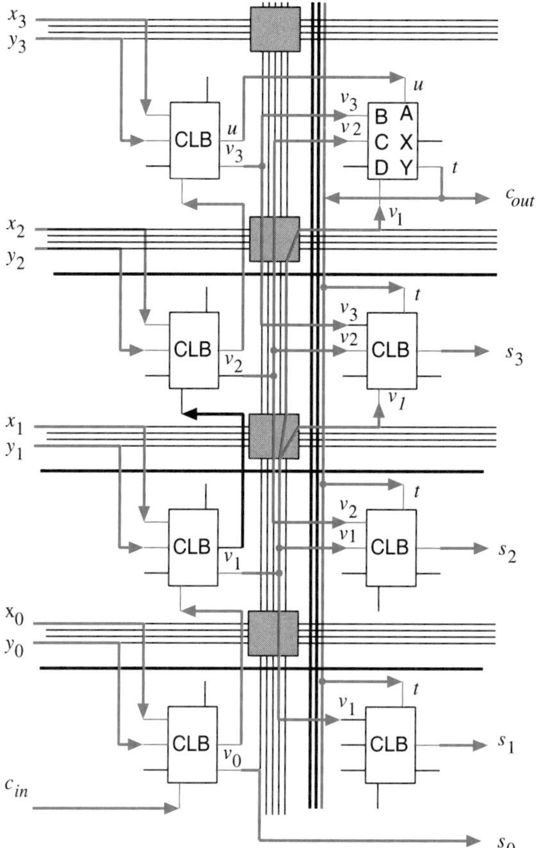

Figure 12.17 FPGA implementation of BCD adder module.

We now map this design onto the FPGA by implementing the four-bit adder as a carry-ripple adder (first column in Figure 12.17). In the second column, the upper module implements t, whereas the next three modules implement the simplified three-bit adder. ■

The design of a system based on FPGAs involves intensive use of CAD tools and module libraries. The basic design steps are:

Design entry, which can be a schematic entry or a behavioral description in a hardware description language such as VHDL.

Implementation, which involves partitioning the design into submodules that can be mapped onto CLBs, placement of submodules onto chips, and routing of signals to connect the submodules. These are nontrivial tasks, so specialized tools are needed to obtain good designs.

Design verification, which uses in-circuit testing, simulation, and timing analysis (again, with appropriate tools).

In practice, these three steps are repeated to achieve desired circuit delay and complexity features.

12.6 FURTHER READINGS

Programmable logic devices, such as PLAs, ROMs, and FPGAs are discussed in many textbooks on digital design such as *Digital Design* by J. Wakerly, Prentice-Hall, Englewood Cliffs, NJ, 1994, and *Contemporary Logic Design* by R. H. Katz, The Benjamin/Cummings Publishing Co., Redwood City, CA, 1994, and in books dedicated to programmable devices such as *Digital Systems Design with Programmable Logic* by M. Bolton, Addison-Wesley Publishing Co., Reading, MA, 1990; *PLD: Digital System Design Using Programmable Logic Devices* by P. K. Lala, Prentice-Hall, Englewood Cliffs, NJ, 1990; *Digital Designing with Programmable Logic Devices* by J. H. Carter, Prentice-Hall, Englewood Cliffs, NJ, 1997; and *Digital Design Using Field Programmable Gate Arrays* by P. K. Chan and S. Mourad, Prentice-Hall, Englewood Cliffs, NJ, 1994.

The use of VHDL is covered in *VHDL for Programmable Logic* by K. Skahill, Addison-Wesley Publishing Co., Reading, MA, 1996.

To learn about specific programmable devices, design tools, and applications, there is abundant literature provided by the manufacturers. Examples of data books on programmable devices are *Configurable Logic Databook*, Atmel, San Jose, CA, 1998; *Xilinx Data Book*, Xilinx Inc., San Jose, CA, 1998; *FPGA Data Book and Design Guide*, Actel, San Jose, CA, 1996; and *Data Book*, Altera, San Jose, CA, 1997.

EXERCISES

PSA modules

Exercise 12.1 Using a PSA, implement the controller specified by the state diagram shown in Figure 12.21.

Exercise 12.2 Design a modulo-11 counter using a PSA.

ROM modules

Exercise 12.3 Determine the minimum size of a ROM to implement a system that produces the square of a BCD digit. The output should be in the binary representation.

Exercise 12.4 Using a ROM, implement a system that converts from BCD to Excess-3.

Exercise 12.5 Using a ROM module, implement a three-input four-bit adder producing the sum $s = a + b + c$, with $a, b, c \in \{0, 1, \ldots, 15\}$ represented in the binary code. Just indicate the contents of row 3 of the ROM.

Exercise 12.6 Using a ROM module, design a one-digit decimal adder in the Excess-3 code.

Exercise 12.7

a. Implement the following switching functions using one decoder and ROM modules with eight four-bit words:

$$f_0(a, b, c, d, e) = \textit{one-set}\,(1,4,5,14,16,22,26,30)$$

$$f_1(a, b, c, d, e) = \textit{one-set}\,(0,3,11,23,29)$$

$$f_2(a, b, c, d, e) = \textit{one-set}\,(0,9,13,17,20,21,25,30)$$

$$f_3(a, b, c, d, e) = \textit{one-set}\,(6,8,12,19,24)$$

b. Repeat the exercise using ROM modules and a multiplexer. Compare the two implementations with respect to delay and number of interconnections.

Exercise 12.8 Using 12-input, 4-output, 128-term ($12 \times 4 \times 128$) PLA modules, implement a system with the following input and output vectors:

Inputs:	$\underline{x} = (x_{13}, \ldots, x_0)$,	$x_j \in \{0, 1\}$
Outputs:	$\underline{z} = (z_3, z_2, z_1, z_0)$,	$z_j \in \{0, 1\}$

A design tool for two-level networks produces a network with 283 product terms. Assume that the PLA modules have the three-state capability.

Exercise 12.9 Determine a ROM- and a PLA-based implementation for the following system:

Inputs: $\underline{a} = (a_2, a_1, a_0)$, $a_j \in \{0, 1\}$

$\underline{b} = (b_2, b_1, b_0)$, $b_j \in \{0, 1\}$

Outputs: $\underline{z} = (z_1, z_0)$, $z_j \in \{0, 1\}$

Function:
$$z = \begin{cases} 1 & \textbf{if} \quad a = (b-1) \bmod 8 \\ 2 & \textbf{if} \quad a = b \\ 0 & \textbf{otherwise} \end{cases}$$

where a, b, z are the integers represented by the corresponding vectors in a radix-2 number system. Note that $-1 \bmod 8$ is defined as 7.

Exercise 12.10 Design a BCD counter using a four-bit register, a ROM module, an adder module, and one two-input AND gate.

Exercise 12.11 Determine the size of the state register and ROM required to implement:

a. Any Moore sequential system with 512 states, three inputs, and two outputs.
b. Same as (a) for a Mealy system.
c. A Moore sequential system with 512 states, three inputs, and two outputs, with the restriction that a state transition depends only on one input. Indicate what additional modules are required in this case.
d. Same as (c) for a Mealy system
e. Same as (c) with the restriction that, for each state, the output depends only on two inputs.

Exercise 12.12 Analyze the network depicted in Figure 12.18. Give a state diagram of the sequential system.

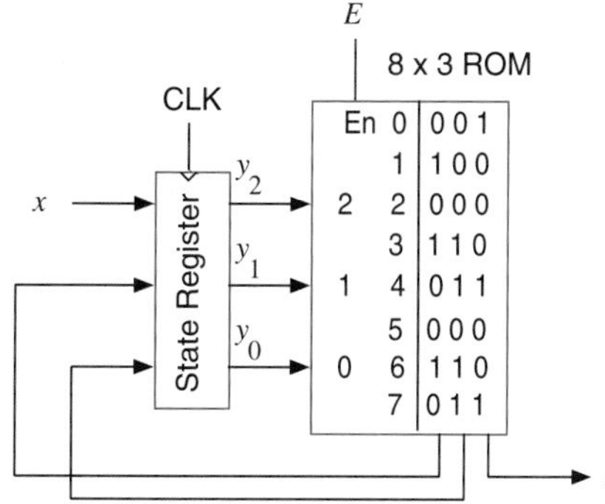

Figure 12.18 Network for Exercise 12.12.

Exercise 12.13 Implement the sequential system described by the state diagram shown in Figure 12.19. Use a register, a ROM, and a multiplexer.

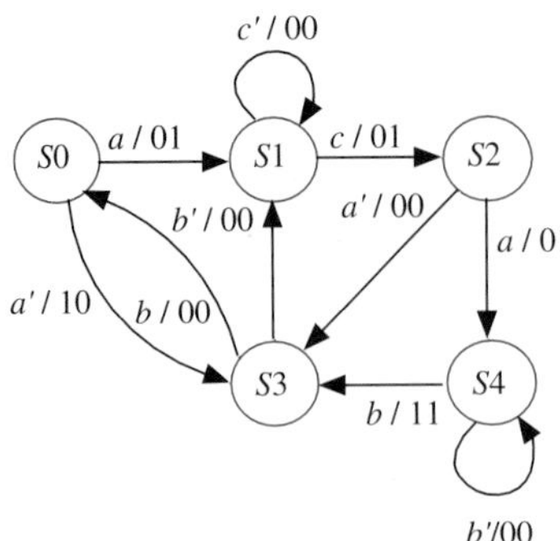

Figure 12.19 State diagram for Exercise 12.13.

Exercise 12.14 Consider a system that generates timing sequences as illustrated in Figure 12.20*a*. The system has the following specification:

Input:	$s \in \{0, 1, \ldots, 15\}$ control input
Output:	T_1, T_2, T_3 timing patterns
Function:	T_j, $(j = 1, 2, 3)$ is a timing pattern with a period of eight clock cycles. A sequence consists of three patterns and is selected from a set of 16 sequences by the input s. The input s is loaded into a four-bit register S in the seventh of the eight clock cycles and used during the eighth cycle to determine the next sequence.

An example of the sequence for $s = 5$ is depicted in Figure 12.20*b*.

a. Assuming that a ROM word contains the next state (three bits), the outputs T_1, T_2, T_3 and one bit L to control the loading of register S, determine the size of the ROM.
b. Show a diagram of the system. The address of the ROM is such that its four most-significant bits are contained in register S and its three least-significant bits in the state register C. The outputs are obtained directly from the ROM (no register for the outputs).
c. Show the contents of the ROM for $s = 5$.

Exercise 12.15 Implement the controller described by the state diagram shown in Figure 12.21 using a register, a ROM, and a multiplexer (if necessary).

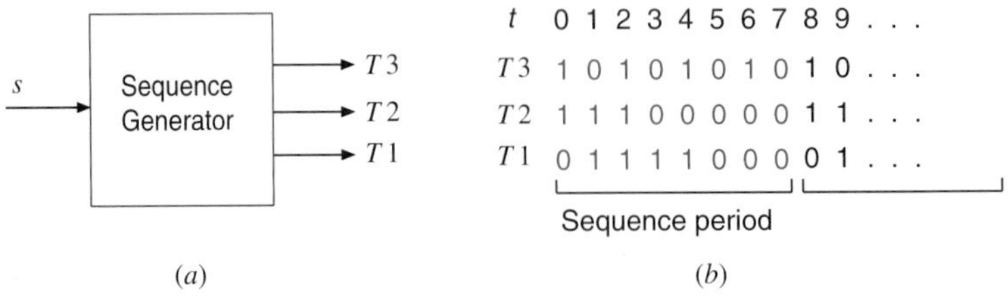

Figure 12.20 Timing generator. (*a*) Block diagram. (*b*) Timing sequence for $s = 5$.

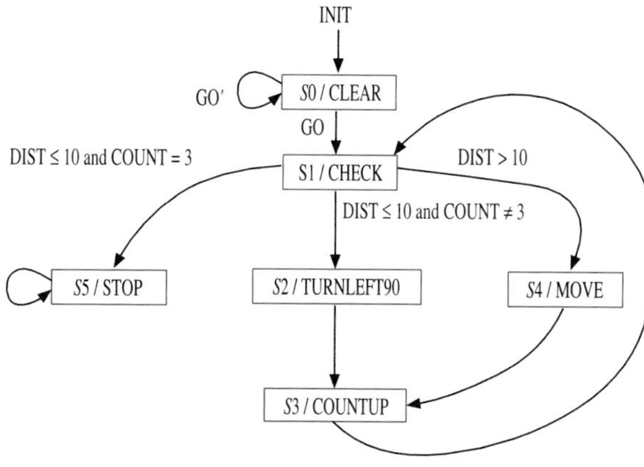

Figure 12.21 State diagram for Exercises 12.1 and 12.15.

Exercise 12.16 Implement a two-digit decimal counter using a register and a ROM.

Exercise 12.17 The high-level specification of a system is as follows:

Inputs: $X = (x_2, x_1, x_0)$, $Y = (y_2, y_1, y_0)$
where $x_2, y_2 \in \{0, 1, 2, 3, 4\}$, $x_1, y_1 \in \{0, 1, 2\}$, $x_0, y_0 \in \{0, 1\}$

Outputs: $Z = (z_2, z_1, z_0)$
where $z_2 \in \{0, 1, 2, 3, 4\}$, $z_1 \in \{0, 1, 2\}$, $z_0 \in \{0, 1\}$

Function:
$$z_2 = (x_2 \times y_2) \bmod 5$$
$$z_1 = (x_1 \times y_1) \bmod 3$$
$$z_0 = (x_0 \times y_0) \bmod 2$$

where $\times$ denotes integer multiplication.

This system corresponds to a multiplier in the (5,3,2) residue number system. In this system, an integer $0 \leq w \leq 29$ is represented by the three-digit vector (w_2, w_1, w_0) such that $w_2 = w \bmod 5$, $w_1 = w \bmod 3$, and $w_0 = w \bmod 2$.

In a binary implementation, a digit-vector is represented by a bit-vector of six bits: three bits for w_2, two bits for w_1, and one bit for w_0. Therefore, the implementation has 12 binary inputs and 6 binary outputs.

Show ROM- and PLA-based implementations for this system.

FPGA modules

Exercise 12.18 Determine the number of configurable logic blocks (CLBs) needed to implement the following networks, using the Xilinx XC2000 FPGA module.

a. 8-to-1 multiplexer.
b. 4-bit right/left shift register with parallel load.
c. Modulo-9 counter with parallel load and terminal count.
d. 8-bit two's complement adder.
e. 4 × 2 multiplier (positive integers).

Chapter 13

Register-Transfer Level (RTL) Systems

In this chapter we discuss:

- Execution graphs.
- A classification of execution graphs according to their sequencing structure.
- The organization of systems in terms of functional and control units.
- The notion of RTL description.
- The division of a system into data and control subsystems.
- The μVHDL specification of RTL systems.
- The concepts of register transfer, register-transfer group, and register-transfer sequence.
- The analysis of RTL systems.
- The design process for RTL systems, and the design of a serial-parallel multiplier.

In previous chapters we have studied methods for the analysis and design of combinational and synchronous sequential systems. In the case of sequential systems, these methods rely on the description of the system by means of state functions that are represented by tables, diagrams, or expressions. Such an approach is useful when the system is relatively simple, that is, the system has a small number of inputs, outputs, and states, or simple expressions adequately capture the functions.

We now describe an approach to specify, analyze, and design systems that are too complex to use the methods presented earlier. For example, the processor in a contemporary digital computer might have 2^5 (32) registers with 32 bits each; this results in a sequential system with 2^{37} states, which is clearly unmanageable by the previous methods.

13.1 EXECUTION GRAPHS

The **Register-Transfer Level (RTL)** approach described in this and the following chapters is characterized by

1. A digital system is viewed as divided into a **data subsystem** (also called the "data-path") and a **control subsystem**;
2. The **state** of the data subsystem consists of the contents of a set of registers.

3. The function of the system is performed as a **sequence of register transfers** (in one or more clock cycles).
4. A **register transfer** is a transformation performed on a datum while the datum is transferred from one register to another.
5. The sequence of register transfers is controlled by the control subsystem (a sequential system).

A sequence of register transfers is representable by an **execution graph**. We now consider an example to illustrate the concept of execution graph, introduce a classification, and indicate the form of execution graphs that is suitable for RTL systems.

EXAMPLE 13.1

Consider the evaluation of a polynomial of degree seven, that is

$$P_7(x) = \sum_{i=0}^{7} p_i x^i$$

The direct evaluation of this expression requires the calculation of x^i. Alternatively, the expression can be transformed to utilize only multiplications and additions. Two possible transformations are

$$P_7(x) = ((((((p_7 x + p_6)x + p_5)x + p_4)x + p_3)x + p_2)x + p_1)x + p_0$$

$$P_7(x) = (x^2)(x^2)[x^2(p_7 x + p_6) + (p_5 x + p_4)] + x^2(p_3 x + p_2) + (p_1 x + p_0)$$

To capture better the order of the operations, these expressions can be described by the **execution graphs** depicted in Figures 13.1 and 13.2, respectively. In these graphs, operations are represented by nodes and precedences by arcs. A node executes when all its predecessors have finished. The graphs in Figure 13.1 correspond to the first expression, whereas the graphs in Figure 13.2 to the second.

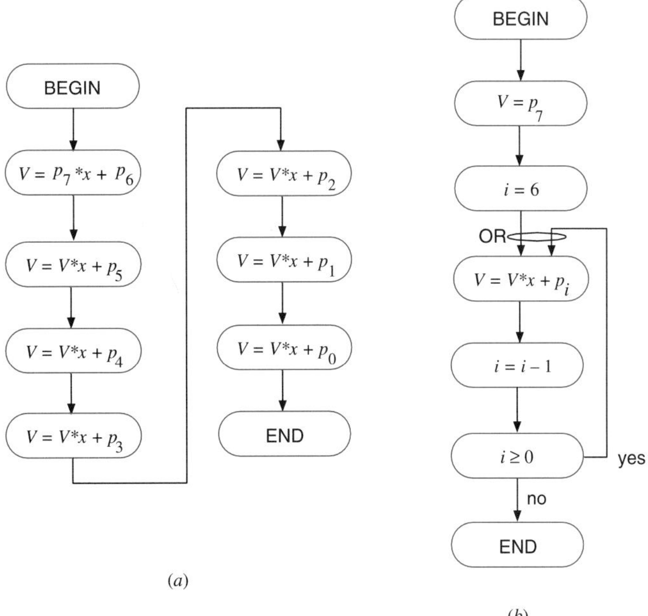

Figure 13.1 Sequential execution graphs for polynomial evaluation. (*a*) Unfolded. (*b*) Loop.

Graphs in Figure 13.1 are **sequential** execution graphs because only one node can be active at a time. Figure 13.1*a* depicts a straight-line (unfolded) graph, whereas Figure 13.1*b* uses a loop. In contrast, the graph in Figure 13.2*a* is a **concurrent** execution graph because more than one node can be active at a time.

The precedences in the graph in Figure 13.2*a* are such that each of the nodes $F = A * A$, $G = B * A + C$, and $H = D * C + E$ can initiate its corresponding operation at different times (when the corresponding set of predecessor nodes finish). A simpler execution graph is obtained if nodes are put together as groups of nodes, and the precedences are between groups as shown in Figure 13.2*b*. In this case, a group of nodes can begin execution when the preceding group has finished. This type of execution graph is called **group sequential**.

Because all graphs in Figures 13.1 and 13.2 describe the evaluation of the same function, these graphs are said to be **equivalent**.

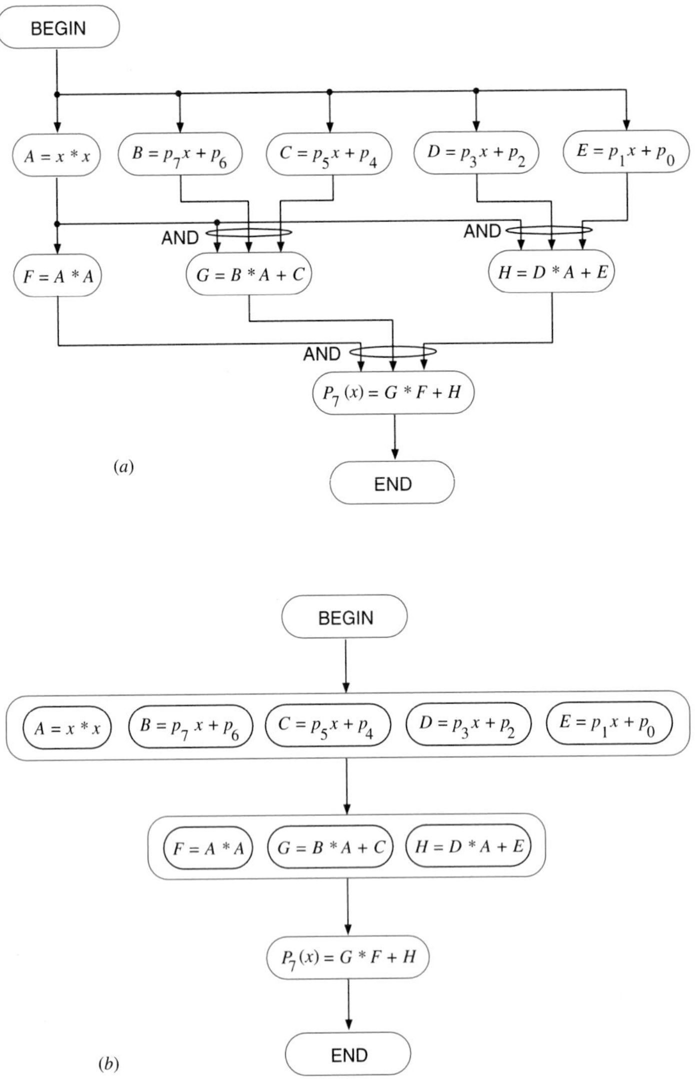

Figure 13.2 Concurrent execution graphs for polynomial evaluation. (*a*) Concurrent. (*b*) Group-sequential.

Any concurrent execution graph can be converted into an equivalent sequential one by introducing additional precedences that order (schedule) the initiation of some nodes, as depicted in the following example.

EXAMPLE 13.2

The concurrent execution graph depicted in Figure 13.2*a* is converted into a sequential one by adding precedences to the graph, as illustrated in Figure 13.3.

Note that the resulting sequential execution graph has nine multiplications and seven additions, whereas the graph in Figure 13.1*a* has only seven multiplications and seven additions.

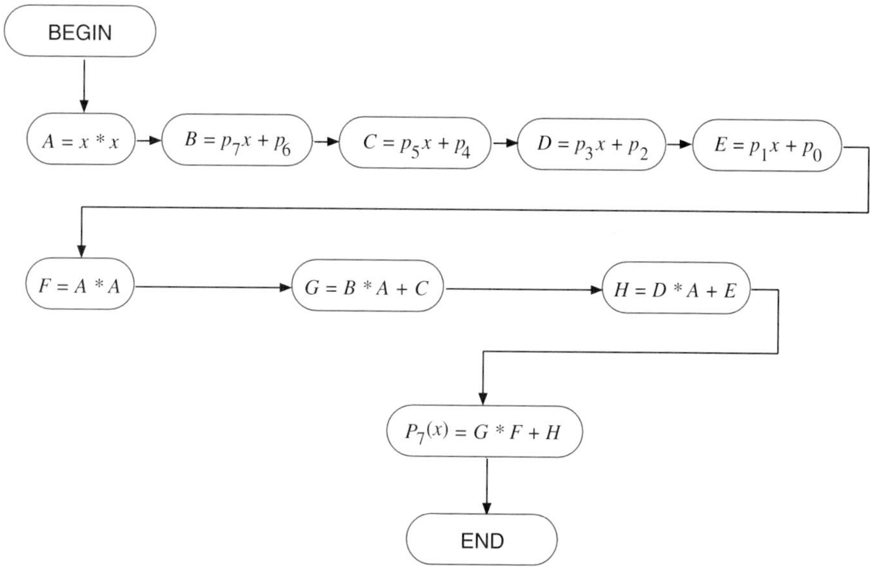

Figure 13.3 Transformation of a concurrent execution graph into a sequential one.

■

Sequential and group-sequential execution graphs have the following advantages over concurrent ones:

- they are usually simpler to develop because it is easier to keep track of the data transformations being performed;
- networks that implement them are simpler because the state of execution is determined by the single operation or group of operations in progress;
- the control of the sequencing is simple because these graphs have only two types of sequencing structures:

  1. a single arc goes from one node to its unique successor; or
  2. a node has several output arcs, but the sequencing follows one of these arcs depending on a condition (this is called a **conditional branch**).

  In contrast, several output arcs from a node can be active simultaneously in concurrent execution graphs.
- the sequencing can be controlled by a sequential machine in which each node or group of nodes corresponds to one state of the controller.

Given that sequential and group-sequential execution graphs are simpler to develop, represent, and execute, many systems implement only these types of graphs. On the other hand, concurrent execution graphs result in potentially faster implementations.

13.2 ORGANIZATION OF SYSTEMS

A system implementing an execution graph must perform two functions:

- data transformations; and
- control of the data transformations and their sequencing.

To perform these functions, the system contains **data-transformation units** (also called **functional units** or **operators**) and **control units.** We now consider the organization of these units in a system.

With respect to the functional units, the following types of structures can be identified:

Nonsharing system. This is the most direct structure, obtained by having one functional unit for each node in the execution graph. The connections among these units correspond to the arcs of the execution graph. The design of this structure is straightforward, but the resulting number of modules might be too large and they might not be used efficiently. Moreover, the interconnection between the modules might be too complex.

Sharing system. This structure relies on sharing functional modules, that is, on using modules that perform the operations in several nodes of the graph, but at different instants. Nodes are scheduled (ordered) so that they can be performed on the shared units without conflicts.

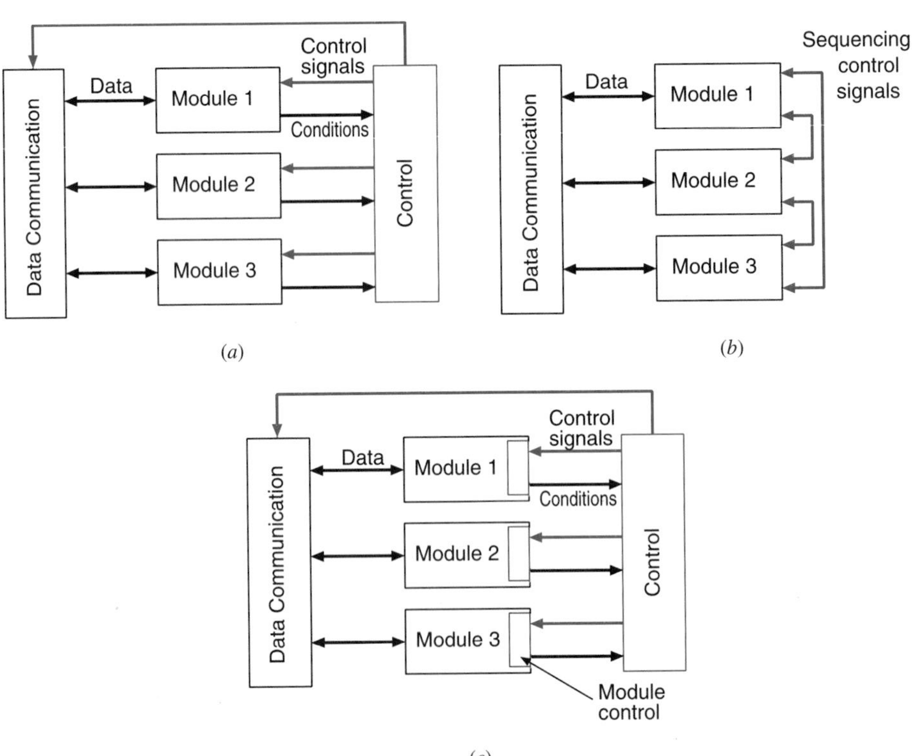

Figure 13.4 Control structures. (*a*) Centralized. (*b*) Decentralized. (*c*) Semicentralized.

Unimodule system. This structure corresponds to the extreme of sharing, in which just one module is used to perform all nodes.

Similarly, the control of the system can also be classified according to its structure, as follows (see Figure 13.4):

Centralized control. A single unit controls the entire system (controls the execution of the entire execution graph). The control unit generates control signals and receives conditions.

Decentralized control. Each module in the system contains mechanisms to control its own operation and sequencing. There are connections between the modules to coordinate the control of the whole system.

Semicentralized control. The control of the operation of each module is decentralized but the sequencing control is centralized.

EXAMPLE 13.3

Figure 13.5 illustrates a system with nonsharing functional units and decentralized control, obtained from the direct mapping of the execution graph in Figure 13.2*a* in Example 13.1. Each box is a module containing

- an operator (adder and/or multiplier);
- storage for operands, results, and any intermediate variable required by the execution of the operation; and
- a controller to control the execution of the operation.

The modules are connected by **data paths** for the communication of data, and **control paths** for the transmission of sequencing control signals. A module begins its operation when the control signals at its inputs are present. When its operation finishes, a module signals the next module to begin. The schedule of control signals in the network of modules corresponds to the execution graph. The number of modules required is 16. From these, a maximum of five can operate simultaneously: first, the five multipliers at the first level, and then the four adders at the second level and the leftmost multiplier at the third level. ■

EXAMPLE 13.4

In Example 13.3, a maximum of five modules can be used at a time. Consequently, it is possible to reduce the number of modules and still obtain the same execution time. Figure 13.6 shows a system with five modules, each containing one adder, one multiplier, storage, and control. Each module has two sets of inputs and outputs, and is used at most twice in executing the computation. A module performs the following operations:

$$\textbf{if} \quad c1 = 1 \quad \textbf{then} \quad O_1 = I_{11} \times I_{12} + I_{13}$$
$$\textbf{if} \quad c2 = 1 \quad \textbf{then} \quad O_2 = I_{21} \times I_{22} + I_{23}$$

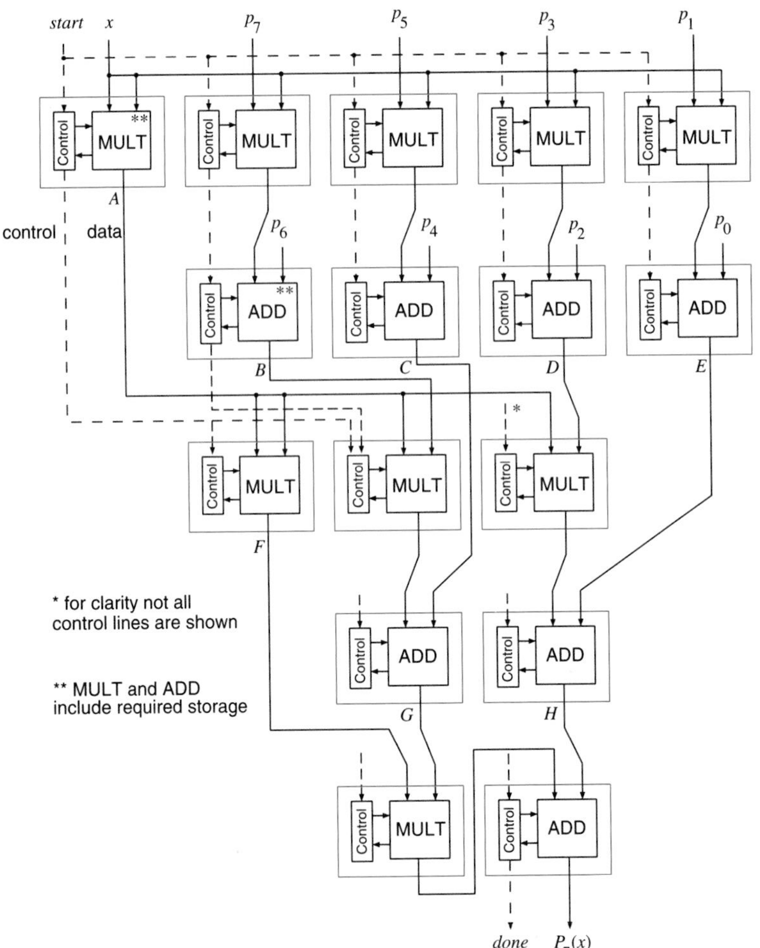

Figure 13.5 Nonsharing data/decentralized control implementation for $P_7(x)$.

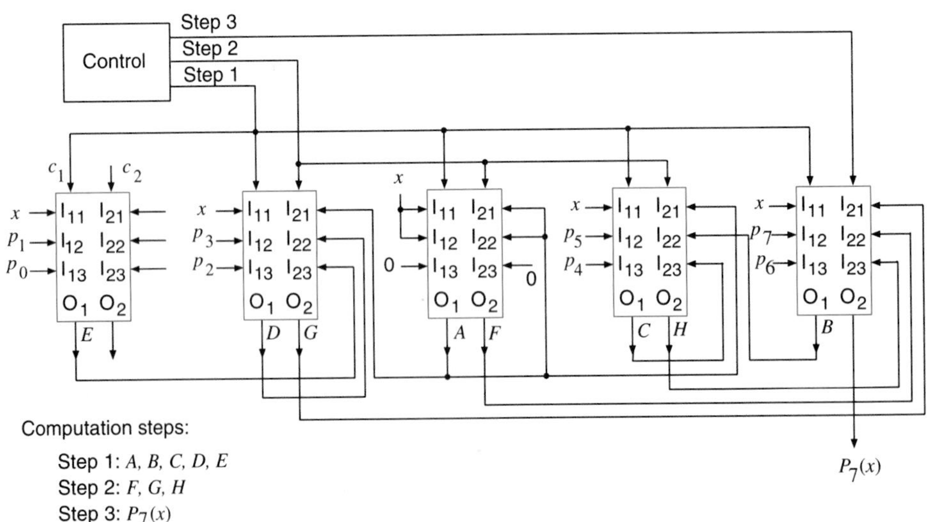

Figure 13.6 Sharing data subsystem for $P_7(x)$.

The operation performed is determined by the arrival of the corresponding control signal; only one of the two operations is activated at a given time.

The control is centralized. Moreover, the sequencing is done according to the group-sequential execution graph depicted in Figure 13.2*b*. ■

EXAMPLE 13.5

Figure 13.7 depicts a unimodule system whose single module M performs the operation $z \leftarrow a \times b + c$. This structure also contains a register array R, which is used to store operands and any intermediate results; the register array allows reading two values and writing one simultaneously. The connections between the modules allows the transfer of two operands from R to M and one result back from M to R. Because there is only a single data module, the controller is centralized.

Because only one data module is available, the corresponding execution graph corresponds to the one depicted in Figure 13.1*a*. This system requires transferring the operands from the register array into the input registers to the operator before performing each operation, thus leading to a sequence as follows:

1. $a \leftarrow p_7,\ b \leftarrow x$
2. $c \leftarrow p_6$
3. $z \leftarrow p_7 x + p_6$
4. $T \leftarrow z$
5. $a \leftarrow T,\ c \leftarrow p_5$
6. $z \leftarrow Tx + p_5$

   and so on.

The resulting implementation is less expensive but slower than those in the previous examples. Note that, in this case, the organization is useful for any sequential execution graph that has operations of the type $a * b + c$; only the control part has to be changed from one graph to another. As a consequence, the execution graph does not include features that might make a particular computation more efficient; for instance, the case at hand would benefit from the possibility of transferring directly from z to a, without going through the register array.

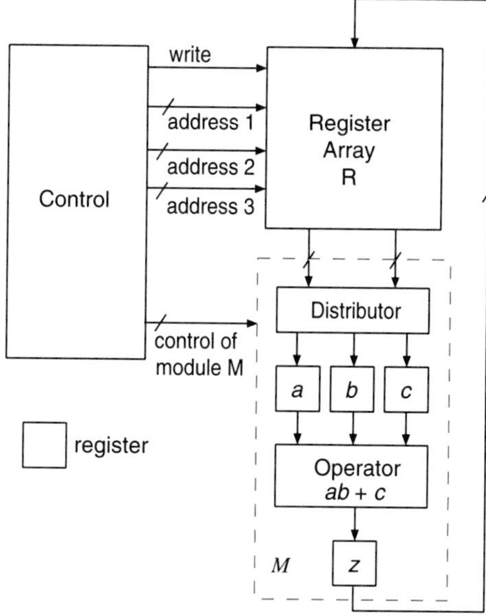

Figure 13.7 Unimodule data subsystem for $P_7(x)$. ■

Due to their simplicity and frequent use, in the rest of the book we focus on the implementation of sequential and group-sequential execution graphs, in systems with centralized control. The corresponding execution graphs are described in terms of register-transfer sequences, thereby leading to **register-transfer level systems** (RTL systems).

The organization of RTL systems consist of two subsystems, as follows (see Figure 13.8):

- the **data subsystem,** which implements data storage, data movement and data transfers; and
- the **control subsystem,** which controls the operations in the data subsystem and their sequencing.

The control subsystem generates sequences of **control signals** (**control sequences**), which dictate the subcomputations performed in the data subsystem. In turn, the data subsystem generates **conditions**, which are used by the control subsystem to generate data-dependent sequencing and control signals.

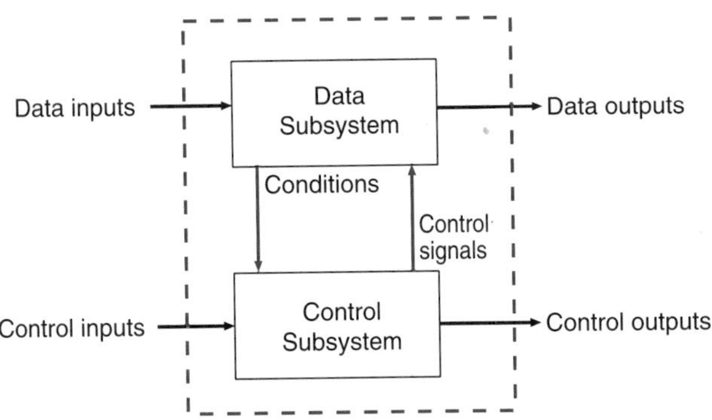

Figure 13.8 Structure of a RTL system.

13.3 SPECIFICATION OF RTL SYSTEMS USING μVHDL

The specification approach for RTL systems presented here relies on the language μVHDL used earlier for the description of simpler digital systems; this language is also used in the next chapter to describe the implementations.

EXAMPLE 13.6

Consider a system that performs the following computation without using a two-operand adder:

Inputs: $x, y \in \{-128, \ldots, 127\}$

Output: $z \in \{-256, \ldots, 508\}$

Function: $z = \begin{cases} 4\lceil (x + |y|)/2 \rceil & \textbf{if} \quad x < |y| \\ 4x & \textbf{otherwise} \end{cases}$

A specification for this computation is based on the expression

$$a = (x + |y|)/2 = x + (|y| - x)/2$$

so that, for $x < |y|$, this can be performed by initializing a to x and then incrementing a and decrementing $|y|$ while $a < |y|$. The resulting execution graph is given in Figure 13.9a.

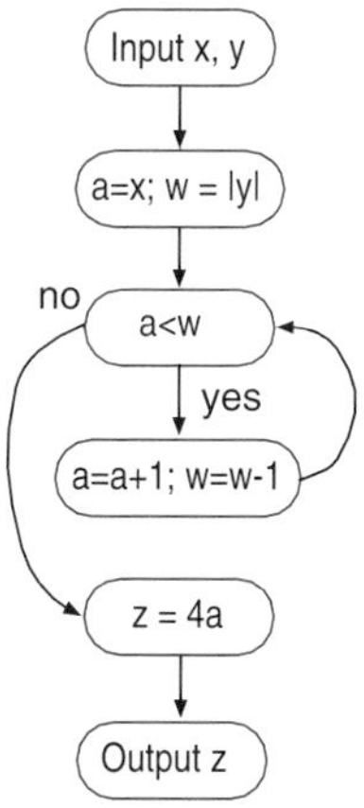

(a)

```
-- This is a high-level description; it is not intended
-- for synthesis. (The WHILE statement might not be
-- supported by a synthesis tool)

  PACKAGE inc_dec_pkg IS
    SUBTYPE SignDataT IS INTEGER RANGE -128 TO 127;
    SUBTYPE PosDataT  IS INTEGER RANGE    0 TO 128;
    SUBTYPE DataoutT  IS INTEGER RANGE -256 TO 508;
  END inc_dec_pkg;

  USE WORK.inc_dec_pkg.ALL;
  ENTITY inc_dec IS
    PORT(x_in,y_in: IN  SignDataT;
         z_out    : OUT DataoutT;
         clk      : IN  BIT);
  END inc_dec;

  ARCHITECTURE high_level OF inc_dec IS
  BEGIN
    PROCESS (clk)
      VARIABLE a : SignDataT;
      VARIABLE w : PosDataT;
    BEGIN
      IF (clk'EVENT AND clk = '1') THEN
        a:= x_in;                -- initialize variables
        w:= ABS(y_in);           -- compute abs(y_in)
        WHILE (a < w) LOOP
          a:= a+1;               -- if x < y compute
          w:= w-1;               -- by incr. x and decr. y
        END LOOP;
        z_out <= (a * 4);
      END IF;
    END PROCESS;
  END high_level;
```

(b)

Figure 13.9 System in Example 13.6. (*a*) Execution graph. (*b*) High-level description.

Figure 13.9*b* gives a μVHDL high-level specification of the corresponding system. This system responds to a leading-edge transition in the clock signal, at which point the process is executed with the values available at the inputs. Note that this description uses `VARIABLES` to represent the operands used, because values are assigned and used in the same invocation of the `PROCESS`. (It should be noted that a high-level description such as this one might not be amenable for synthesis of the module; for example, a synthesis system might require that loops have static bounds, so that `WHILE` loops might not be acceptable.) ■

Procedure to Obtain a Specification

As illustrated in the previous example, the procedure used to obtain the specification of a RTL system is as follows:

1. Draw an execution graph for the computation.
2. Write the μVHDL description of the system, based on the execution graph.

We now present an additional example illustrating this procedure.

EXAMPLE 13.7

Consider a system that computes an approximation z to the reciprocal of $1/2 \leq x < 1$. That is, obtain z such that $z - 1/x < \varepsilon$, where ε is the given approximation error.

A suitable RTL sequence is derived from the Newton-Raphson recurrence, which iteratively computes z_{i+1} in terms of z_i (wherein i denotes the iteration number) by the expression

$$z_{i+1} = z_i(2 - xz_i)$$

The initial value is $z_0 = 1$, and the process terminates when $x \times z_k - 1 < 0.5 \times \varepsilon$ which, since $x \geq 1/2$, corresponds to $z_k - 1/x < \varepsilon$. The number of iterations depends on the value of ε and on the closeness of the reciprocal to the initial value z_0. This computation sequence is characterized by a quadratic convergence because

$$|xz_k - 1| = (xz_{k-1} - 1)^2$$

The corresponding execution graph is given in Figure 13.10*a*, and a high-level specification of the system in Figure 13.10*b*. As in the previous example, this system responds to a leading-edge transition of the clock signal, at which moment the process is executed with the values present at the input signals. (Also as in the previous example, this high-level description might not be suitable for synthesis, due to the use of floating-point (`REAL`) types.) ■

13.4 IMPLEMENTATION OF RTL SYSTEMS

As already stated, RTL systems are organized as two interconnected subsystems: the data subsystem and the control subsystem. This organization is illustrated by the system depicted in Figure 13.11. The data subsystem carries out the operations specified in the execution graph, whereas the control subsystem controls the sequence.

At the binary level, the implementation of an RTL system has the following characteristics:

- The data elements in the data subsystem correspond to data input signals, data output signals, intermediate values, and data conditions. The control subsystem has control input signals, and produces control output signals and data subsystem control signals. All these elements are represented by bits, bit-vectors, and arrays of bit-vectors.

- The operation of the system is synchronized by a clock signal. In each clock cycle, the activity in the data subsystem consists of one or more register transfers. From the implementation's perspective, a register transfer corresponds to the synchronous loading of a register with a bit-vector; this bit-vector is obtained either from another register or from the output of an operator whose inputs come from registers.

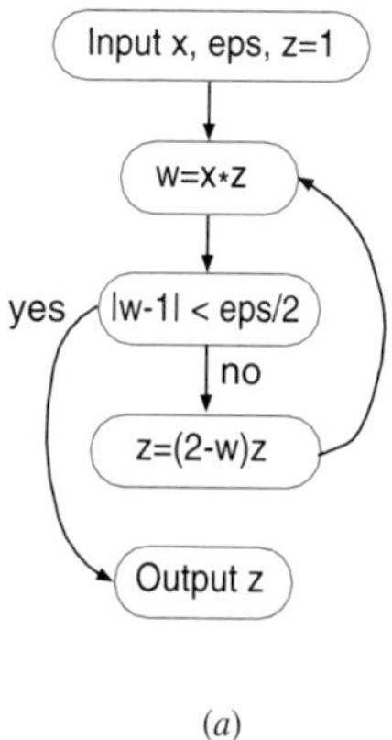

(*a*)

```
-- This is a high-level description; it is not intended
-- for synthesis. (The WHILE statement and REAL TYPE might
-- not be supported by a synthesis tool)

  PACKAGE recip_pkg IS
    SUBTYPE DatainT  IS REAL RANGE 0.5 TO 1.0;
    SUBTYPE DataoutT IS REAL RANGE 1.0 TO 2.0;
    SUBTYPE EpsT     IS REAL RANGE 0.0 TO 0.1;
  END recip_pkg;

  USE WORK.recip_pkg.ALL;
  ENTITY reciprocal IS
    PORT(x_in   : IN  DatainT ;
         eps_in: IN  EpsT    ;
         z_out : OUT DataoutT;
         clk   : IN  BIT     );
  END reciprocal;

  ARCHITECTURE high_level OF reciprocal IS
  BEGIN
    PROCESS (clk)
      VARIABLE x,w: DatainT ;
      VARIABLE z  : DataoutT;
    BEGIN
      IF (clk'EVENT AND clk = '1') THEN
        z := 1.0; x := x_in;
        w := x * z;
        WHILE (ABS(w - 1.0) > eps_in/2.0) LOOP
          z := (2.0 - w) * z;
          w := x * z;
        END LOOP;
        z_out <= z;
      END IF;
    END PROCESS;
  END high_level;
```

(*b*)

Figure 13.10 System in Example 13.7. (*a*) Execution graph. (*b*) High-level specification.

For example, the transfer R_Z:= ADD(R_X,R_Y,1) in Figure 13.11 has R_Z as destination register; the output of operator ADD is the source, whose operands are registers R_X and R_Y, and the carry-in c_0.

- A register transfer requires controlling the data subsystem so that the desired connectivity between the registers and operators involved is achieved. For the register transfer above, the controls are compl_x=0, cmpl_y=0, s_mux2=1, c_0=1, and ld_Z=1.
- Operators are limited to those realizable by hardware, such as the complementers (CMPL) and adder (ADD) shown in Figure 13.11; these operators are implemented as combinational networks
- Several register transfers can be performed in one clock cycle. These register transfers form a **register-transfer group** (RT-group), which corresponds to the transfers required for a group node in a group-sequential execution graph.

  An RT-group requires that the component register transfers do not conflict in the use of resources in the data subsystem. For instance, the data subsystem shown in Figure 13.11 does not allow performing the transfers R_Z:=ADD(R_X,R_Y,0) and R_Y:=ADD(R_X,0,0) in the same cycle, because both use the same ADD operator with different values of the inputs.
- The execution graph is implemented by a sequence of RT-groups, also known as a **register-transfer sequence** (RTL sequence).
- The clock cycle time is determined by the longest path from a source register to a destination register, including the transformations to the data in the path.
- The control subsystem is implemented as a sequential machine whose state transitions correspond to the sequencing of the group-sequential execution graph. The inputs to the control subsystem are control inputs to the system and conditions generated by the data subsystem; the outputs from the control subsystem are control signals directing the activities in the data subsystem, and control outputs from the system. Thus, the activities in the control subsystem are:

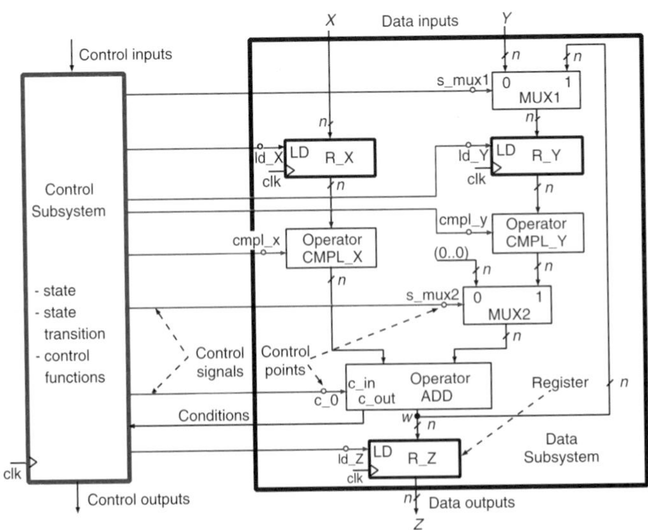

Figure 13.11 RTL system.

- state transitions; and
- generation of control signals and control outputs.

EXAMPLE 13.8

Figure 13.12 describes the registers transfers into R_Z,R_X and R_Y, which are possible in the data subsystem depicted in Figure 13.11. The values of the control signals are also indicated. Groups can be formed by compatible transfers, that is, only one transfer into each register is allowed per group, and the transfers into y and z must use the same instance of w.

A possible register-transfer sequence, in which each line corresponds to a register-transfer group, is:

```
(R_X=X;         R_Y=Y)        -- ld_X=1;  ld_Y=1;
(R_X=X;         R_Z=R_Y-r_X)  -- ld_X=1;  ld_Z=1; smux_2=1; cmpl_x=1; c_0=1;
(R_Y=R_X-R_Y;R_Z=R_X-R_Y)     -- ld_Y=1;  ld_Z=1; smux_1=1; cmpl_y=1; smux_2=1; c_0=1;
```

■

```
ENTITY data_sub IS
  PORT(X,Y               : IN  BIT_VECTOR;
       ld_X, ld_Y, ld_Z: IN  BIT;
       s_mux1, s_smux2 : IN  BIT;
       cmpl_x, cmpl_y  : IN  BIT;
       c_0, clk        : IN  BIT;
       Z               : OUT BIT_VECTOR;
       c_out           : OUT BIT);
END data_sub;

ARCHITECTURE behavioral OF data_sub IS
  SIGNAL R_X,R_Y,R_Z: BIT_VECTOR(n-1 DOWNTO 0);
BEGIN
  PROCESS (clk)
    VARIABLE zero_n: BIT_VECTOR(n-1 DOWNTO 0):= (OTHERS => '0');
    VARIABLE w     : BIT_VECTOR(n-1 DOWNTO 0);
    VARIABLE selec : BIT_VECTOR( 2 DOWNTO 0);
  BEGIN
  selec:= cmpl_x & cmpl_y & smux_2;
  CASE selec IS
    WHEN "000" => w := add(R_X,zero_n,c_0);
    WHEN "001" => w := add(R_X,R_Y,c_0)    ;
    WHEN "010" => w := add(R_X,zero_n,c_0);
    WHEN "011" => w := add(R_X,cmpl(R_Y),c_0)    ;
    WHEN "100" => w := add(cmpl(R_X),zero_n,c_0);
    WHEN "101" => w := add(cmpl(R_X),R_Y,c_0)    ;
    WHEN "110" => w := add(cmpl(R_X),zero_n,c_0);
    WHEN "111" => w := add(cmpl(R_X),cmpl(R_Y),c_0);
  END CASE;
  IF (clk'EVENT AND clk = '1') THEN
    IF (ld_X = '1') THEN R_X <= X; END IF;               -- R_X
    IF (ld_Z = '1') THEN R_Z <= w; END IF;               -- R_Z
    IF (ld_Y = '1') THEN
      IF (smux_1 = '0') THEN R_Y <= Y;                   -- R_Y
      ELSE                   R_Y <= w;
      END IF;
    END IF;
  END IF;
  END PROCESS;
END behavioral;
```

Figure 13.12 Register transfers in Figure 13.11.

13.5 ANALYSIS OF RTL SYSTEMS

We now describe the analysis of RTL systems, and illustrate it by means of an example. As we already know, the objective of the analysis process is obtaining a description of the system from an implementation.

A generalized μVHDL description resulting from analyzing a RTL system is depicted in Figure 13.13. As in the case of simple sequential systems, the description of the control subsystem consists of two PROCESS statements: one for the transition function and the other for the output function. The state register is represented by a SIGNAL. The data subsystem is described by a separate PROCESS, where data registers are represented by SIGNALs. The PROCESSes describing the state transition function and the data subsystem are activated by a clock edge (leading edge, by default); consequently, all register transfers are performed simultaneously.

The analysis process consists of the following steps:

1. Determine the inputs and outputs to/from the system. In the μVHDL description, this corresponds to determining the ENTITY declaration.
2. Partition the system into a data subsystem and a control subsystem. This is done by identifying the control signals and conditions; these correspond to the interface signals among the two subsystems.
3. Analyze the control subsystem. A suitable representation of its specification is a state diagram and the corresponding μVHDL description; the procedure for this analysis was presented in Chapter 7.
4. For the set of values of the control signals for each state, determine the register transfers that occur in the data subsystem, and the generation of control outputs (if any).
5. Write the corresponding register-transfer sequence. In the μVHDL description, this is represented by the behavioral architecture.

Once the register-transfer sequence is obtained, the final goal of the functional analysis is the derivation of a high-level description of the function of the system; for example, "the system sorts the elements of an array" or "obtains the maximum value among the elements of an array." However, this is quite difficult at best and not possible in many instances. Even when the function that the system should perform is known beforehand, the verification that the system actually computes the right function is difficult. Consequently, in many cases this verification is performed by simulation of the register-transfer sequence.

The analysis usually also produces other characteristics of the system, such as the number of clock cycles required and the cycle time. The cycle time is equal to the critical path (the slowest register transfer), which is composed of the time to obtain the control signals plus the time to perform the data transfer, including the delay to load the register.

EXAMPLE 13.9

Consider the system depicted in Figure 13.14, wherein the data operators are defined as follows:

$$\text{MULTF}(m, rec) = m \times rec$$

$$\text{SUB2F}(w) = 2 - w$$

$$\text{SUB1F}(w) = 1 - w$$

$$\text{COMP}(b, eps) = \begin{cases} 1 & \textbf{if} \quad b > eps \\ 0 & \textbf{otherwise} \end{cases}$$

```
ENTITY rtl_system IS
  GENERIC (n: NATURAL:=8);  -- bit-vectors width
  PORT(data_in : IN  BIT_VECTOR ; -- input data
       data_out: OUT BIT_VECTOR ; -- output data
       ctrl_in : IN  BIT_VECTOR ; -- input controls
       ctrl_out: OUT BIT_VECTOR ; -- output controls
       clk     : IN  BIT);
END rtl_system;

ARCHITECTURE general OF rtl_system IS
  TYPE stateT IS (S0,S1,...,Sk);
  SIGNAL state: stateT:= S0;                      -- state register
  SIGNAL reg_A,...  : BIT_VECTOR(n-1 DOWNTO 0); -- data registers

  CONSTANT c1: NATURAL:= ...;      --length of controls bit-vector
  CONSTANT c2: NATURAL:= ...;      --length of conditions bit-vector
  SIGNAL data_ctrls : BIT_VECTOR(c1-1 DOWNTO 0);  -- controls
  SIGNAL data_conds : BIT_VECTOR(c2-1 DOWNTO 0);  -- conditions
BEGIN
  PROCESS(clk)                      -- data subsystem  -----------------+
  BEGIN                             --                                  |
    IF (clk = '1') THEN             --                                  |
      CASE data_ctrls IS            --                                  |
        WHEN ... => ...;            -- register transfer group 0        |
        WHEN ... => ...;            --                                  |
        WHEN ... => ...;            -- register transfer group k        |
        WHEN OTHERS => NULL;        --                                  |
      END CASE;                     --                                  |
    END IF;                         --                                  |
  END PROCESS;                      -- --------------------------------+

  PROCESS (clk)                     -- control subsystem, --------------+
  BEGIN                             --   transition function            |
    IF (clk = '1') THEN             --   transitions might depend on    |
      CASE state IS                 --   data conditions, described by  |
        WHEN S0 => state <= ...;    --   IF statements in each state    |
        WHEN ....              ;    --                                  |
        WHEN Sk => state <= ...;    --                                  |
      END CASE;                     --                                  |
    END IF;                         --                                  |
  END PROCESS;                      --                                  |
                                    --                                  |
  PROCESS (state,ctrl_in)           -- control subsystem,               |
  BEGIN                             --      output function             |
    CASE state IS                   --                                  |
        WHEN S0 => data_ctrls <= ...; ctrl_out <= ...;                  |
        WHEN ....                   --                                  |
        WHEN Sk => data_ctrls <= ...; ctrl_out <= ...;                  |
    END CASE;                       --                                  |
  END PROCESS;                      -- --------------------------------+
END general;
```

Figure 13.13 Generalized description of RTL systems.

All quantities are positive and represented in a conventional radix-2 number system with n fractional bits and one integer bit when needed, as indicated in the figure; for instance, y is represented by $n+1$ bits, so that $0 \leq y < 2$. Because the multiplication produces more

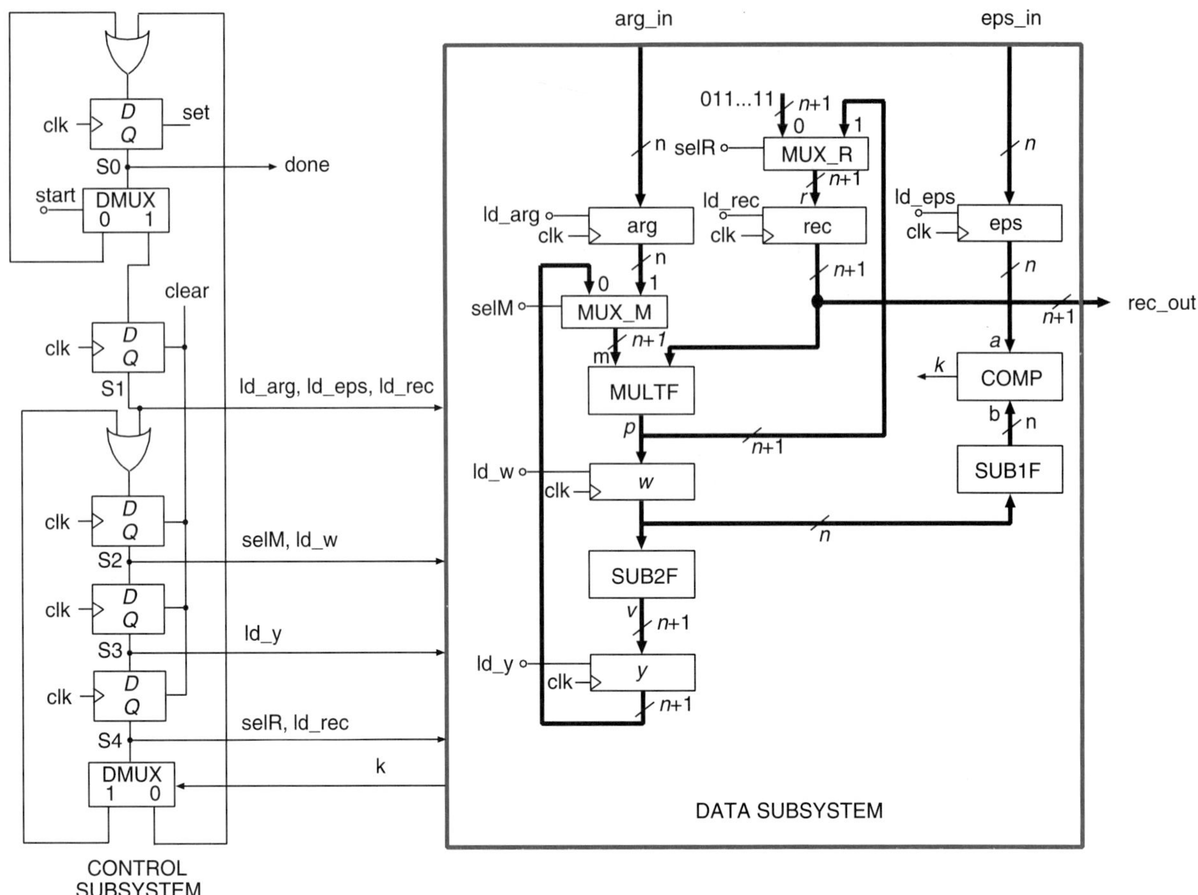

Figure 13.14 RTL system for Example 13.9.

than n fractional bits, the corresponding value is truncated to n bits. (In Figure 13.14, the signals coming out from the registers are labeled with the corresponding register name.)

To analyze this system, we follow the steps indicated in the procedure:

1. The inputs are `start`,`arg_in`,`eps_in`, and `clk`; the outputs are `rec_out` and `done`. Consequently, the `ENTITY` declaration for this system is as depicted in Figure 13.15. (For simplicity, we ignore inputs `set` and `clear`, whose only function is defining the initial state.)

```
LIBRARY ieee;
USE ieee.std_logic_1164.all;
USE ieee.std_logic_arith.all;

ENTITY example IS
  GENERIC(n: NATURAL:= 16);   -- bit-vectors length
  PORT(start          : IN  BIT      ;
       arg_in,eps_in: IN  UNSIGNED(n-1 DOWNTO 0);
       rec_out        : OUT UNSIGNED(n   DOWNTO 0);
       done           : OUT BIT      ;
       clk            : IN  BIT     );
END example;
```

Figure 13.15 Entity declaration for system in Example 13.9.

2. Figure 13.14 already shows the system partitioned into data and control subsystems. From this figure, we directly obtain the μVHDL description given in Figure 13.16. We assume that the functionality of the operators is defined in the package RecipPkg.
3. The analysis of the control subsystem produces the state diagram shown in Figure 13.17.
4. From the control signals per state, we obtain the following register transfers (in the data subsystem), control outputs, and conditions:

```
S0: done <= '1';
S1: done <= '0'; arg <= arg_in; rec <= "01...1"; eps <= eps_in;
S2: w    <= MULTF(arg,rec);
S3: y    <= SUB2F(w)
S4: rec  <= MULTF(y,rec);
    k    <= COMP(eps,SUB1F(w));
```

Note that condition k is generated by a combinational network and is not stored in a register; consequently, it is generated in all states. In the list above, we include it only in the state in which it is used.

5. We now determine a higher-level behavioral description. For this purpose, we describe the state transitions and operations per state as a CASE statement, using the state diagram and the register transfers above as the basis for the description. We also replace the operator names by the corresponding arithmetic or logic function, leading to the description given in Figure 13.18.

From the state diagram, it follows that the main part of the computation sequence is the loop traversing states S2,S3,S4; applying substitution, the following arithmetic expression corresponding to the function of the system can be obtained:

```
WHILE (1-arg * rec >  eps) LOOP
  rec := (2-arg * rec) * rec;
END WHILE;
```

This corresponds to the Newton-Raphson procedure for approximating the reciprocal of arg_in, as described in Example 13.7. Because the output has n fractional bits and one integer bit, then rec ≤ 2 so that arg $\geq 1/2$. Moreover, because arg has no integer bits, $1/2 \leq$ arg < 1 and $1 <$ rec ≤ 2. The widths of the other data paths are consistent with these ranges.

```
USE WORK.RecipPkg.ALL;

ARCHITECTURE direct OF example IS
  TYPE   stateT is (s0, s1, s2, s3, s4);
  SIGNAL state    : stateT:= s0;
  SIGNAL arg,eps,w: UNSIGNED(n-1 DOWNTO 0);  -- n-bit registers
  SIGNAL rec,y    : UNSIGNED(n   DOWNTO 0);  -- n+1 bit register
  SIGNAL k        : BIT                   ;  -- condition
  SIGNAL ld_arg,ld_rec,ld_eps,ld_w,ld_y,selR,selM: BIT;  -- controls
BEGIN
  PROCESS (clk)                              -- data subsystem ---------+
    VARIABLE b: UNSIGNED(n-1 DOWNTO 0);      -- internal data elements  |
    VARIABLE r,m,p,v: UNSIGNED(n DOWNTO 0);  --                         |
  BEGIN                                      -- combinational modules   |
    IF (selR = '0') THEN r:= (OTHERS=>'1'); r(n):= '0';               --|
                    ELSE r:= p; END IF;                               --|
    IF (selM = '0') THEN m:= y; ELSE m:='0' & arg; END IF;            --|
    p:= multf(m,rec); b:= sub1f(w); v:= sub2f(w); k <= compf(eps,b);  --|
                                               -- register modules      |
    IF (clk'EVENT AND clk = '1') THEN                                 --|
       IF (ld_arg = '1') THEN arg <= arg_in; END IF;                  --|
       IF (ld_rec = '1') THEN rec <= r;      END IF;                  --|
       IF (ld_eps = '1') THEN eps <= eps_in; END IF;                  --|
       IF (ld_w   = '1')  THEN w   <= p(n-1 DOWNTO 0); END IF;        --|
       IF (ld_y   = '1')  THEN y   <= v;      END IF;                 --|
    END IF;                                                           --|
    rec_out <= rec;                                                   --|
    END PROCESS;                               -- --------------------+
                                               -- control subsystem --+
    PROCESS (clk)                              -- transition function |
    BEGIN                                                             --|
    IF (clk'EVENT AND clk = '1') THEN                                 --|
      CASE state IS                                                   --|
        WHEN s0 => IF (start = '1') THEN state <= s1;                 --|
                   ELSE                 state <= s0; END IF;          --|
        WHEN s1 => state  <= s2;                                      --|
        WHEN s2 => state  <= s3;                                      --|
        WHEN s3 => state  <= s4;                                      --|
        WHEN s4 => IF (k = '1') THEN state <= s2;                     --|
                   ELSE              state <= s0; END IF;             --|
      END CASE;                                                       --|
    END IF;                                                           --|
    END PROCESS;                               -- --------------------+
    PROCESS (state)                            -- output function   --+
    BEGIN                                                             --|
    CASE state IS                                                     --|
      WHEN s0 => done   <= '1'; ld_rec <= '0';                        --|
      WHEN s1 => ld_arg <= '1'; ld_eps <= '1';                        --|
                 selR   <= '0'; ld_rec <= '1'; done   <= '0';         --|
      WHEN s2 => selM   <= '1'; ld_w   <= '1';                        --|
                 ld_arg <= '0'; ld_eps <= '0'; ld_rec <= '0';         --|
      WHEN s3 => ld_y   <= '1'; ld_w   <= '0';                        --|
      WHEN s4 => selM   <= '0'; selR   <= '1'; ld_rec <= '1';         --|
    END CASE;                                                         --|
  END PROCESS;                                 -- --------------------+
END direct;
```

Figure 13.16 Architecture body for system in Example 13.9.

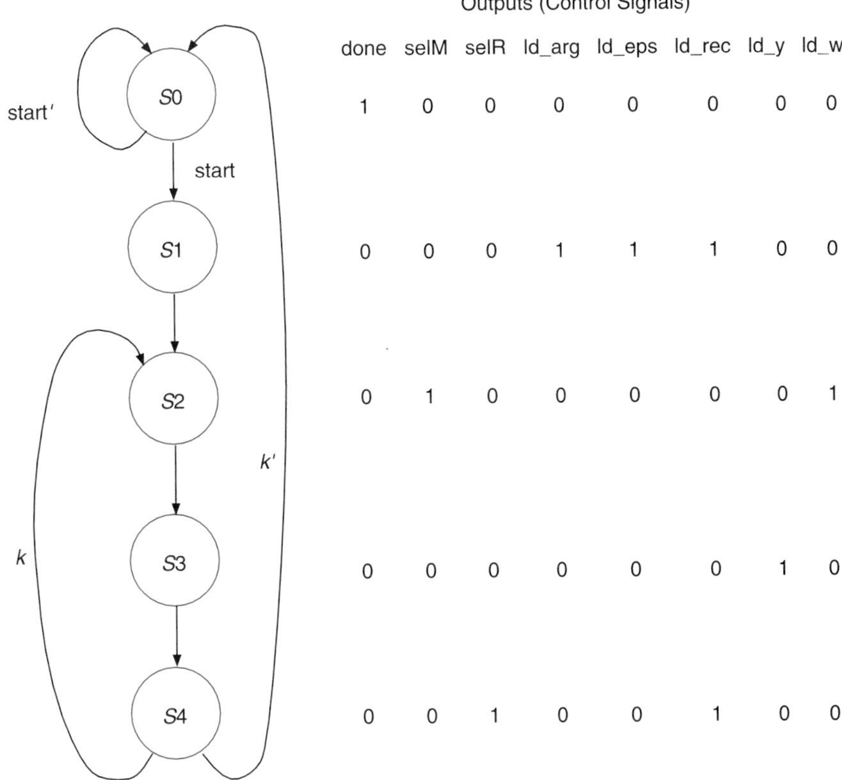

Figure 13.17 State diagram of system in Example 13.9.

The execution time is measured as the number of clock cycles from the cycle in which `start` is 1 to the cycle in which done becomes 1. As indicated in Example 13.7, the number of clock cycles required depends on how close the reciprocal is to the initial value (in this case 1).

The cycle time is determined by the longest of all register transfers. Because multiplication is the most complex operation, this time is

$$t_c = t_{mux} + t_{mult} + t_{reg}$$ ■

Note that the analysis of the data subsystem in the example above has been performed for the specific control subsystem. On the other hand, analyzing the data subsystem separately leads to additional register transfers which could be active for other control subsystems, leading to different computation sequences. The set of all possible register transfers with the given data subsystem is listed in Figure 13.19. As discussed before, RT groups are constructed in such a way that there are no conflicts in the use of shared resources.

13.6 DESIGN OF RTL SYSTEMS

Let us address now the design of RTL systems. The corresponding procedure begins with an execution graph that can be obtained for instance from the corresponding μVHDL behavioral description of the system. Then, we proceed as follows:

1. Design the data subsystem:

```
-- This is a high-level description
-- (The arithmetic and logic operators are assumed to operate
-- on fractional values represented by bit-vectors)

 ARCHITECTURE behavioral OF example IS
   TYPE   stateT IS (S0,S1,S2,S3,S4);
   SIGNAL state     : stateT:= S0;
   SIGNAL arg,eps,w : UNSIGNED(n-1 DOWNTO 0);
   SIGNAL rec,y     : UNSIGNED(n DOWNTO 0)   ;
 BEGIN
   PROCESS (clk)
   BEGIN
     IF (clk'EVENT AND clk = '1') THEN
       CASE state IS
         WHEN S0 => done <= '1';
                    IF (start = '1') THEN state <= S1;
                    ELSE                  state <= S0; END IF;
         WHEN S1 => arg   <= arg_in;
                    rec <= (OTHERS => '1'); rec(n) <= '0';
                    eps   <= eps_in;        done   <= '0';
                    state <= S2;
         WHEN S2 => w     <= arg * rec;
                    state <= S3   ;
         WHEN S3 => y     <= 2 - w;
                    state <= S4 ;
         WHEN S4 => rec   <= y * rec;
                    IF (1-w > eps) THEN state <= S2;
                    ELSE                state <= S0; END IF;
       END CASE;
     END IF;
   END PROCESS;
 END behavioral;
```

Figure 13.18 High-level description for system in Example 13.9.

```
IF (ld_arg = '1') THEN  arg <= arg_in;      END IF;
IF (ld_eps = '1') THEN  eps <= eps_in;      END IF;
IF (ld_w   = '1') AND (selM = '0') THEN w <= MULTF(y,rec)  ; END IF;
IF (ld_w   = '1') AND (selM = '1') THEN w <= MULTF(arg,rec); END IF;
IF (ld_y   = '1') THEN  y   <= SUB2F(w);      END IF;
IF (ld_rec = '1') AND (selR = '0') THEN rec <= '1'         ; END IF;
IF (ld_rec = '1') AND (selR = '1') AND (selM = '0') THEN
                                        rec <= MULTF(y,rec); END IF;
IF (ld_rec = '1') AND (selR = '1') AND (selM = '1') THEN
                                        rec <= MULTF(y,arg); END IF;
```

Figure 13.19 Register transfers possible in data subsystem of Example 13.9.

a. Determine the operators (functional units) required by the operations in the execution graph. A functional unit can be specialized for only one operation type (say, addition) or for several types.

   Two operations in the graph can be assigned to the same functional unit if such operations form part of different RT groups.

b. Determine the registers required to store operands, results, and intermediate variables.

Two variables can be assigned to the same register if they are active at disjoint time intervals.

c. Connect the components by datapaths (wires and multiplexers) as required by the transfers in the sequence.

d. Determine the control signals and conditions required by the sequence.

e. Describe the structure of the data section by a logic diagram, a net list, or a μVHDL structural description. Moreover, describe the behavior of the data subsystem by the transfers that occur for each control signal. A generalized description is given in Figure 13.20*a*.

2. Describe the interface between the subsystems. The control signals and the conditions are the connections between the two subsystems. This can be described by a logic diagram or by a μVHDL structural description. A generalized structural description is shown in Figure 13.21.

```
ARCHITECTURE generalized OF
          data_subsystem IS
BEGIN
  PROCESS (clk)
    SIGNAL reg_A,...: BIT_VECTOR;
  BEGIN
    IF (clk = '1') THEN
      IF (ctl0 = '1') THEN ... END IF;
      IF (ctl1 = '1') THEN ... END IF;
      .....
      IF (ctlj = '1') THEN ... END IF;
    END IF;
  END PROCESS;
END generalized;
```

(*a*)

```
ARCHITECTURE generalized OF
              control_subsystem IS
BEGIN
  PROCESS (clk)
    TYPE stateT is (s0, s1, sk);
    SIGNAL state: stateT:= s0;
  BEGIN
    IF (clk = '1') THEN
      CASE state IS
        WHEN s0 => ....;
        WHEN s1 => ....;
        WHEN sk => ....;
      END CASE;
    END IF;
  END PROCESS;
END generalized;
```

(*b*)

Figure 13.20 Generalized behavioral description of RTL systems. (*a*) Data subsystem. (*b*) Control subsystem.

```
ENTITY group_seq_system IS
  PORT    (data_in : IN  BIT_VECTOR; -- input data
           data_out: OUT BIT_VECTOR; -- output data
           ctrl_in : IN  BIT_VECTOR; -- input conditions
           ctrl_out: OUT BIT_VECTOR; -- output conditions
           clk     : IN  BIT       );
END group_seq_system;

ARCHITECTURE generalized OF group_seq_system IS
  SIGNAL controls : BIT_VECTOR; -- control signals to data subsystem
  SIGNAL conds    : BIT_VECTOR; -- condition signals from data subsystem
BEGIN
  U1: ENTITY data_subsystem
             PORT MAP (data_in,data_out,controls,conds,clk);
  U2: ENTITY control_subsystem
             PORT MAP (ctrl_in,ctrl_out,conds,controls,clk);
END generalized;
```

Figure 13.21 Generalized structural description of a RTL system.

3. Design the control subsystem:

   a. Determine the register-transfer sequence for the corresponding data section.
   b. Assign one state to each `RT-group` and determine the state-transition and output functions. These can be described by a state diagram or in μVHDL, as shown in Figure 13.20*b*.
   c. Implement the corresponding sequential system, as presented in Chapters 8 and 11.

13.7 DESIGN OF A MULTIPLIER FOR POSITIVE INTEGERS

Let us consider the design of a RTL system that computes the product of two positive integers. That is, the operands are x and y in the range 0 to $2^n - 1$, and the result is $z = x \times y$, in the range 0 to $(2^n - 1)(2^n - 1) = 2^{2n} - 2^{n+1} + 1$. A high-level description of this module is

Inputs:	$x, y \in \{0, 1, \ldots, 2^n - 1\}$
Output:	$z \in \{0, 1, \ldots, 2^{2n} - 2^{n+1} + 1\}$
Function:	$z = x \times y$

There are several alternatives for performing this computation; we first describe and implement the **radix-2 serial-parallel algorithm,** and then comment on other alternatives. In this case, operands are represented in the radix-2 number system by the n-bit vectors $\underline{x} = (x_{n-1}, \ldots, x_0)$ and $\underline{y} = (y_{n-1}, \ldots, y_0)$, and the result by the $2n$-bit vector $\underline{z} = (z_{2n-1}, \ldots, z_0)$. The computation sequence consists of n iterations of the following recurrence

$$z[i+1] = \left(\frac{1}{2}\right)\left(z[i] + (x \times 2^n) \times y_i\right)$$

with the initial condition $z[0] = 0$ and the result being $z = z[n]$. The corresponding execution graph is shown in Figure 13.22.

The operations in one iteration of the recurrence are

- Multiplication of x by 2^n. In a binary representation, multiplication by 2^n corresponds to shifting left by n bits and inserting 0s. Consequently, this operation results just in "aligning" the bits in x with the n most-significant bits of $z[i]$. (Note that this operation is not dependent on the index i so it could be performed outside the iteration.)
- Multiplication of $(x \times 2^n)$ by y_i, the i-th bit of $\underline{y}$. Because the value of y_i is either 0 or 1, this product has either value 0 or $x \times 2^n$.
- Addition of $z[i]$ and $(x \times 2^n) \times y_i$.

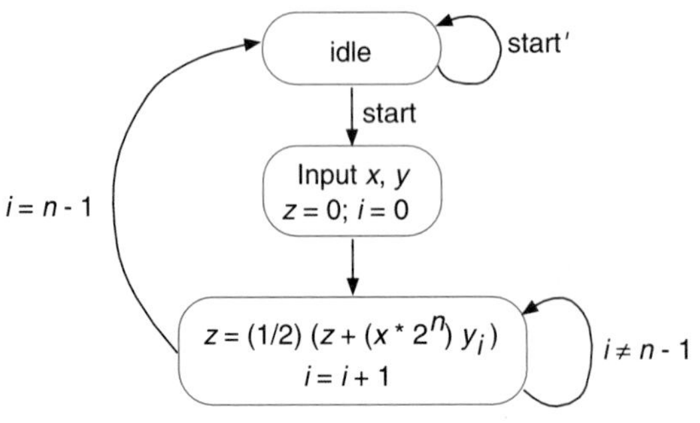

Figure 13.22 Execution graph of serial-parallel multiplier.

- Multiplication of the sum by $\frac{1}{2}$. Because operands are represented in the binary system, this operation is performed by a one-bit right shift.

Due to the operations involved, this algorithm is also called a **radix-2 add-and-shift multiplication**. Moreover, because one bit of $\underline{y}$ is used in each iteration (i.e., the bits are used serially) and all bits of $\underline{x}$ are used (i.e., $\underline{x}$ is used in parallel), this is a **serial-parallel** algorithm.

EXAMPLE 13.10

The operation of the serial-parallel multiplier for the following eight-bit operands is detailed below:

$$x = 188, \quad \underline{x} = 10111100$$

$$y = 203, \quad \underline{y} = 11001011$$

$z[0]$	=	00000000 00000000
$(x \times 2^8) \times y_0$	=	10111100 00000000
$z[0] + (x \times 2^8) \times y_0$	=	010111100 00000000
$z[1]$	=	01011110 00000000
$(x \times 2^8) \times y_1$	=	10111100 00000000
$z[1] + (x \times 2^8) \times y_1$	=	100011010 00000000
$z[2]$	=	10001101 00000000
$(x \times 2^8) \times y_2$	=	00000000 00000000
$z[2] + (x \times 2^8) \times y_2$	=	010001101 00000000
$z[3]$	=	01000110 10000000
$(x \times 2^8) \times y_3$	=	10111100 00000000
$z[3] + (x \times 2^8) \times y_3$	=	100000010 10000000
$z[4]$	=	10000001 01000000
$(x \times 2^8) \times y_4$	=	00000000 00000000
$z[4] + (x \times 2^8) \times y_4$	=	010000001 01000000
$z[5]$	=	01000000 10100000
$(x \times 2^8) \times y_5$	=	00000000 00000000
$z[5] + (x \times 2^8) \times y_5$	=	001000000 10100000
$z[6]$	=	00100000 01010000
$(x \times 2^8) \times y_6$	=	10111100 00000000
$z[6] + (x \times 2^8) \times y_6$	=	011011100 01010000
$z[7]$	=	01101110 00101000
$(x \times 2^8) \times y_7$	=	10111100 00000000
$z[7] + (x \times 2^8) \times y_7$	=	100101010 00101000
$z[8]$	=	10010101 00010100

The result is $z = z[8] = 1001010100010100 = 38164$. ■

Figure 13.23 shows the μVHDL specification of this multiplier, in which we have already identified the state and operations per state, and have also added control inputs and outputs (in this description, $n = 16$).

Implementation

Let us now develop an implementation of the serial-parallel multiplier. As indicated earlier, we begin with the design of the data subsystem and then give the top-level structural description.

Data Subsystem

The behavioral specification of the multiplier contains the composite operation $\left(\frac{1}{2}\right)\left(z[i] + (x \times 2^n) \times y_i\right)$. These dependent operations are simple, so the entire expression can be computed in one cycle. Consequently, the iteration is implemented by a single group in the execution graph. Such an implementation consists of the following components and connections (see Figure 13.25):

- An n-bit register `x` to store x and a $2n$-bit register `z` to store z. Register `z` has a `clear` signal because z is also loaded with the value 0.
- An n-bit register `y` to store y. Because the value of y is used one bit a time, register `y` is better implemented as a right-shift register with parallel input and serial output. The shifting capability is used to generate y_i by shifting the register at each iteration and obtaining y_i from the rightmost bit.
- A module to generate $x \times 2^n$. Because 2^n is a power of two, this corresponds to a n-bit left-shift which can be implemented by connecting the bits of `x` to the corresponding inputs to the adder (i.e., aligned with the n most significant bits of `z`).
- A module to generate $(x \times 2^n) \times y_i$. Because y_i has value 0 or 1, this module can be implemented as n 2-input AND gates that produce either 0 or $x \times 2^n$.
- A module to perform addition. The two $2n$-bit operands are aligned as follows (for $n = 8$):

$(x \times 2^8) \times y_i$	`x x x x x x x x 0 0 0 0 0 0 0 0`
$z[i]$	`z z z z z z z z z z z z z z z z`

  Due to the zeros introduced by the multiplication $x \times 2^n$, the adder needs only n bits; its inputs are the output from the AND gates and the most significant half of `z`.
- A module to perform multiplication by 1/2 and load the result in `z`. This is accomplished by loading `z` with the vector formed by the concatenation of the carry and sum outputs from the adder with the leftmost $n - 1$ bits from `z`.

Controlling these components requires the following control signals:

`ldX,ldY,ldZ`	for loading `x,y,z`, respectively
`shY`	for right-shifting `y`
`clrZ`	for loading 0 into `z`

Note that no condition signals are generated by this data subsystem.

The components, connections and control signals listed above lead to the behavioral description of the data subsystem depicted in Figure 13.24, which indicates the register transfers that occur for the various combinations of control signals. Figure 13.25 gives a structural description of this subsystem, which explicitly indicates all the modules and connections.

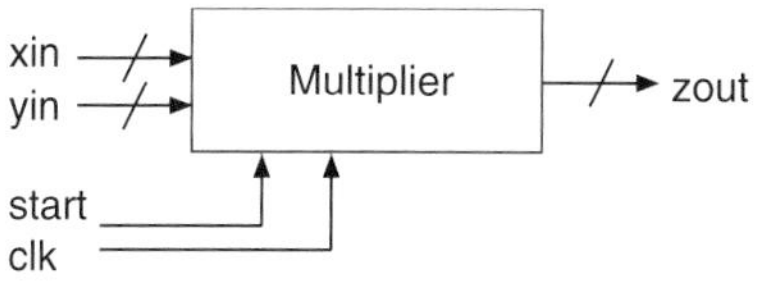

```
LIBRARY ieee;
USE ieee.std_logic_1164.all;
USE ieee.std_logic_arith.all;

ENTITY multiplier IS
  GENERIC(n : NATURAL:= 16);        -- number of bits in operands
  PORT   (strt   : IN  BIT ;
          xin,yin: IN  UNSIGNED(n-1 DOWNTO 0);
          clk    : IN  BIT ;
          zout   : OUT UNSIGNED(2*n-1 DOWNTO 0);
          done   : OUT BIT);
END multiplier;

ARCHITECTURE behavioral OF multiplier IS
  TYPE   stateT IS (idle,setup,active)    ;
  SIGNAL state  : stateT := idle          ;
  SIGNAL x,y    : UNSIGNED(n-1 DOWNTO 0)  ; -- operand registers
  SIGNAL z      : UNSIGNED(2*n-1 DOWNTO 0);
  SIGNAL count  : NATURAL RANGE 0 TO n-1  ;
BEGIN
  PROCESS (clk)
    VARIABLE zero_2n : UNSIGNED(2*n-1 DOWNTO 0); -- constant zero
    VARIABLE scale   : UNSIGNED(n-1 DOWNTO 0)  ; -- aligning vector
    VARIABLE add_out : UNSIGNED(2*n DOWNTO 0)  ;
  BEGIN
    zero_2n:= (OTHERS => '0');
    scale  := (OTHERS => '0');
    IF (clk'EVENT AND clk = '1') THEN
      CASE state IS
         WHEN idle   => done <= '1';
                        IF (strt = '1') THEN state <= setup;
                        ELSE                 state <= idle;
                        END IF;
         WHEN setup  => x <= xin; y <= yin; z <= zero_2n; count <= 0;
                        zout <= zero_2n;  done <= '0';
                        state <= active;
         WHEN active => IF (y(count) = '0') THEN
                           add_out := '0' & z;
                        ELSE
                           add_out := ('0' & z) + ('0' & x & scale);
                        END IF;
                        z    <= add_out(2*n DOWNTO 1);
                        zout <= add_out(2*n DOWNTO 1);
                        IF (count /= (n-1)) THEN
                          state <= active;
                          count <= count+1;
                        ELSE
                          state <= idle;
                          done  <= '1' ;
                        END IF;
      END CASE;
    END IF;
  END PROCESS;
END behavioral;
```

Figure 13.23 Specification of serial-parallel multiplier.

```
LIBRARY ieee;
USE ieee.std_logic_1164.all;
USE ieee.std_logic_arith.all;

ENTITY multdata_bhv IS
  GENERIC(n : NATURAL :=  16);    -- number of bits
  PORT   (xin,yin      : IN  UNSIGNED(n-1 DOWNTO 0);    -- data inputs
          ldX,ldY,ldZ  : IN  BIT;                       -- control signals
          shY,clrZ     : IN  BIT;                       -- control signals
          zout         : OUT UNSIGNED(2*n-1 DOWNTO 0);  -- data output
          clk          : IN BIT);
END multdata_bhv;

ARCHITECTURE behavioral OF multdata_bhv IS
    SIGNAL x,y : UNSIGNED(n-1 DOWNTO 0)   ; -- registers
    SIGNAL z   : UNSIGNED(2*n-1 DOWNTO 0);
BEGIN
  PROCESS(clk)
    VARIABLE zero_2n : UNSIGNED(2*n-1 DOWNTO 0); -- vector constant 0
    VARIABLE scale   : UNSIGNED(n-1 DOWNTO 0)  ; -- aligning vector
    VARIABLE add_out : UNSIGNED(2*n DOWNTO 0)  ;
  BEGIN
    zero_2n:= (OTHERS => '0');
    scale  := (OTHERS => '0');
    IF (clk'EVENT AND clk = '1') THEN
      IF (ldX = '1') THEN x <= xin; END IF;
      IF (ldY = '1') THEN y <= yin; END IF;
      IF (y(0) = '0') THEN
             add_out := '0' & z;
      ELSE
             add_out := ('0' & z) + ('0' & x & scale);
      END IF;
      IF (ldZ = '1') THEN z <= add_out(2*n DOWNTO 1);
                       zout <= add_out(2*n DOWNTO 1);
      END IF;
      IF (clrZ= '1') THEN z <= zero_2n;  END IF;
      IF (shY = '1') THEN y <= '0' & y(n-1 DOWNTO 1); END IF;
    END IF;
  END PROCESS;
END behavioral;
```

Figure 13.24 Behavioral description of multiplier data subsystem.

Structural Description of the Multiplier

Having determined the signals between its two subsystems, we can now give the structural description of the multiplier in terms of these subsystems. This description appears in Figure 13.26, in which we have repeated the `ENTITY` declaration for convenience.

Control Subsystem

From the execution graph, the states in the control subsystem are `idle`, `setup`, and `active/count=i, for i= 0 to n-1`. The transition function is shown in the state diagram depicted in Figure 13.27. Each state generates control signals; the corresponding values of these signals are obtained from the behavioral description of the system and the description of the data subsystem. These signals are also shown in the state diagram. The corresponding μVHDL description is depicted in Figure 13.28.

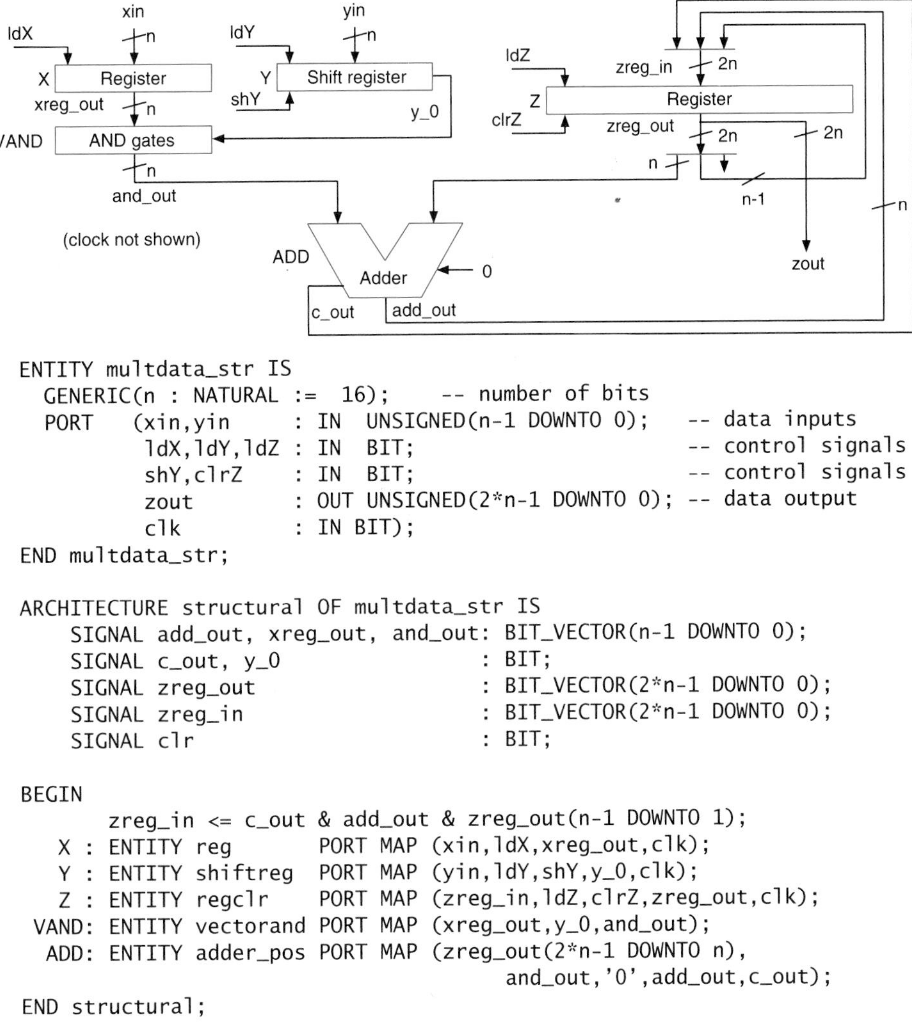


```
ENTITY multdata_str IS
  GENERIC(n : NATURAL :=  16);    -- number of bits
  PORT    (xin,yin      : IN  UNSIGNED(n-1 DOWNTO 0);     -- data inputs
           ldX,ldY,ldZ  : IN  BIT;                         -- control signals
           shY,clrZ     : IN  BIT;                         -- control signals
           zout         : OUT UNSIGNED(2*n-1 DOWNTO 0);  -- data output
           clk          : IN BIT);
END multdata_str;

ARCHITECTURE structural OF multdata_str IS
    SIGNAL add_out, xreg_out, and_out: BIT_VECTOR(n-1 DOWNTO 0);
    SIGNAL c_out, y_0                : BIT;
    SIGNAL zreg_out                  : BIT_VECTOR(2*n-1 DOWNTO 0);
    SIGNAL zreg_in                   : BIT_VECTOR(2*n-1 DOWNTO 0);
    SIGNAL clr                       : BIT;

BEGIN
       zreg_in <= c_out & add_out & zreg_out(n-1 DOWNTO 1);
   X : ENTITY reg        PORT MAP (xin,ldX,xreg_out,clk);
   Y : ENTITY shiftreg   PORT MAP (yin,ldY,shY,y_0,clk);
   Z : ENTITY regclr     PORT MAP (zreg_in,ldZ,clrZ,zreg_out,clk);
 VAND: ENTITY vectorand  PORT MAP (xreg_out,y_0,and_out);
  ADD: ENTITY adder_pos  PORT MAP (zreg_out(2*n-1 DOWNTO n),
                                   and_out,'0',add_out,c_out);
END structural;
```

Figure 13.25 Structural description of data subsystem.

Design of Components

The next level in the implementation corresponds to the design of the modules in the data and control subsystems. Because the modules used correspond to standard modules discussed in previous chapters, we omit this level.

Cycle Time and Multiplication Time

The minimum clock period for this system is determined by the critical path in the data subsystem. This path is the sum of the following delays:

- t_r : the delay of the registers to produce stable outputs. This includes the setup delay and the propagation delay.
- t_{buf} : the delay of the buffer required by the load on y_0.
- t_{and} : the delay of the AND gates.
- t_{add} : the delay of the adder.

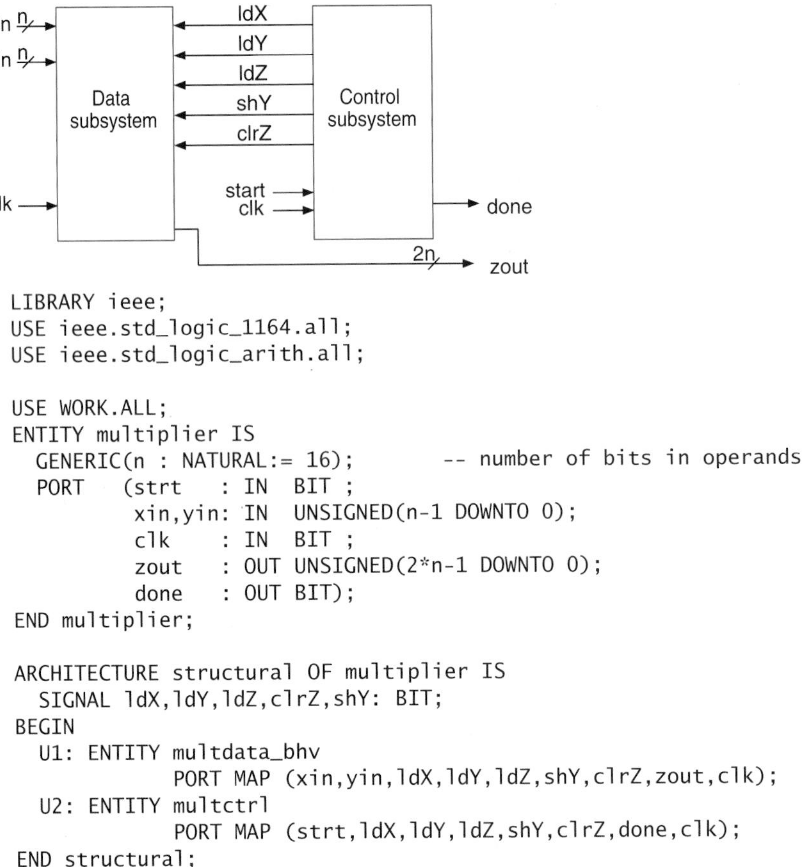


```
LIBRARY ieee;
USE ieee.std_logic_1164.all;
USE ieee.std_logic_arith.all;

USE WORK.ALL;
ENTITY multiplier IS
  GENERIC(n : NATURAL:= 16);        -- number of bits in operands
  PORT   (strt   : IN  BIT ;
          xin,yin: IN  UNSIGNED(n-1 DOWNTO 0);
          clk    : IN  BIT ;
          zout   : OUT UNSIGNED(2*n-1 DOWNTO 0);
          done   : OUT BIT);
END multiplier;

ARCHITECTURE structural OF multiplier IS
  SIGNAL ldX,ldY,ldZ,clrZ,shY: BIT;
BEGIN
  U1: ENTITY multdata_bhv
             PORT MAP (xin,yin,ldX,ldY,ldZ,shY,clrZ,zout,clk);
  U2: ENTITY multctrl
             PORT MAP (strt,ldX,ldY,ldZ,shY,clrZ,done,clk);
END structural;
```

Figure 13.26 Structural description of the serial-parallel multiplier.

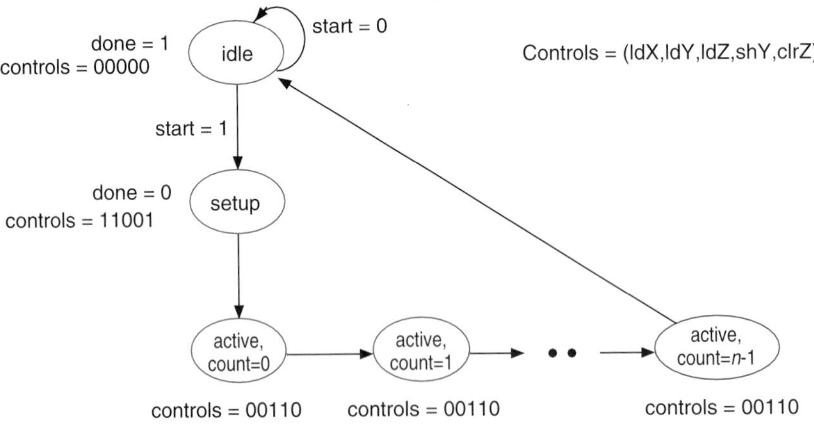

Figure 13.27 State diagram for multiplier control subsystem.

The execution time is equal to $n + 2$ cycles: one cycle in the idle state, one cycle in the setup state, and n cycles for the iterations.

```
ENTITY multctrl IS
  GENERIC(n: NATURAL :=   16);    -- number of bits
  PORT   (strt        : IN  BIT; -- control input
          ldX,ldY,ldZ: OUT BIT; -- control signals
          shY, clrZ   : OUT BIT; -- control signals
          done        : OUT BIT; -- control output
          clk         : IN  BIT);
END multctrl;

ARCHITECTURE behavioral OF multctrl IS
  TYPE   stateT IS (idle,setup,active);
  SIGNAL state   : stateT:= idle;
  SIGNAL count   : NATURAL RANGE 0 TO n-1;
BEGIN
  PROCESS (clk)                          -- transition function
  BEGIN
    IF (clk'EVENT AND clk = '1') THEN
      CASE state IS
        WHEN idle   => IF (strt = '1') THEN state <= setup;
                       ELSE                 state <= idle ;
                       END IF;
        WHEN setup  => state <= active; count <= 0;
        WHEN active => IF (count = n-1) THEN
                        count <= 0; state <= idle;
                       ELSE
                        count <= count+1; state <= active;
                       END IF;
      END CASE;
    END IF;
  END PROCESS;

  PROCESS (state,count)                  -- output function
    VARIABLE controls: Bit_Vector(5 DOWNTO 0);
                                         -- code = (done,ldX,ldY,ldZ,shY,clrZ)
  BEGIN
    CASE state IS
      WHEN idle   => controls := "100000";
      WHEN setup  => controls := "011001";
      WHEN active => controls := "000110";
    END CASE;
    done <= controls(5);
    ldX <= controls(4); ldY <= controls(3); ldZ <= controls(2);
    shY <= controls(1); clrZ<= controls(0);
  END PROCESS;
END behavioral;
```

Figure 13.28 Behavioral description of multiplier control subsystem.

Other Multiplication Algorithms

There are several algorithms for performing multiplication of positive integers, which differ in the number of steps needed to perform the operation and the resources required in an implementation. In particular,

- in a **serial algorithm**, at each step one bit of $\underline{x}$ is multiplied by one bit of $\underline{y}$ and this product is added to the previous partial product; if the addition is also done serially (one bit per cycle), this algorithm requires n^2 cycles. The basic hardware needed is an

AND gate for the multiplication, a one-bit adder (with flip-flop for the carry) and the corresponding shift registers.

- in a **serial-parallel algorithm**, at each step one bit of $\underline{y}$ (serial) is multiplied by all bits of $\underline{x}$ (parallel), and accumulated with the previous partial product; this is the algorithm used by the unit designed in this chapter. The operation is performed in n cycles and requires n AND gates, an n-bit adder, and registers.
- in a **parallel** algorithm, all bits of $\underline{x}$ are multiplied by all bits of $\underline{y}$ (the whole multiplication is done in one step). This is equivalent to unfolding the recurrence of the serial-parallel algorithm and, therefore, requires n^2 AND gates and n n-bit adders. Because addition is associative, these adders can be organized as a tree, which reduces the depth of the network and, consequently, the delay.

It is also possible to implement an intermediate scheme between the radix-2 serial-parallel and the parallel algorithms. This can be achieved by performing a multiplication of $n \times r$ bits per cycle, so that the whole multiplication is done in n/r cycles.

13.8 FURTHER READINGS

The classification of the sequencing approaches and the structure of the system to execute them is commonly discussed in texts on computer architecture. Register-transfer approaches in the description and design of digital systems are treated at various levels in textbooks on digital design. A general discussion, for example, is given in *Digital Systems and Hardware/Firmware Algorithms* by M. Ercegovac and T. Lang, Wiley, New York, 1985. Other texts containing related material are *Structure and Interpretation of Computer Programs* by H. Abelson and G. Sussman, MIT Press, Cambridge, MA, 1984, *The Art of Digital Design* by F. P. Prosser and D. E. Winkel, Prentice-Hall, Englewood Cliffs, NJ, 1987, *Computation Structures* by S. A. Ward and R. H. Halstead, Jr., McGraw-Hill, New York, 1990, *Introduction to Digital Logic Design* by J. P. Hayes, Addison Wesley, Reading, MA, 1993, and *Contemporary Logic Design* by R. H. Katz, The Benjamin Cummings Pub. Co., Redwood City, CA, 1994. The use of VHDL in specification and design of systems at the register-transfer level is discussed in, for example, *The Designer's Guide to VHDL* by P. J. Ashenden, Morgan Kaufmann Publishers, Inc., San Francisco, CA, 1996; *VHDL Analysis and Modeling of Digital Systems* by Z. Navabi, McGraw-Hill, New York, 1993; and *Structured Logic Design with VHDL* by J. P. Armstrong and F. G. Gray, Prentice-Hall, Englewood Cliffs, NJ, 1993.

EXERCISES

Computations

Exercise 13.1 Convert the concurrent execution graph shown in Figure 13.29 into the following:

a. An equivalent sequential execution graph. If T is the execution time of a node, determine the execution time for the concurrent and for the sequential cases.
b. An equivalent group-sequential graph with a maximum of two operations per group.

Exercise 13.2 For Example 13.6, give the sequence of values for variables `x` and `y` and signal `z`, for `x_in=5` and `y_in=-9`.

Exercise 13.3 Determine the number of iterations required by the computation sequence in Example 13.7, for $a = 2/3$ and $\varepsilon = 10^{-5}$.

Exercise 13.4 What happens if you apply the sequence given in Example 13.7 to obtain the reciprocal of $a = 1/3$? Modify the sequence so that the reciprocal can be computed by prescaling the argument.

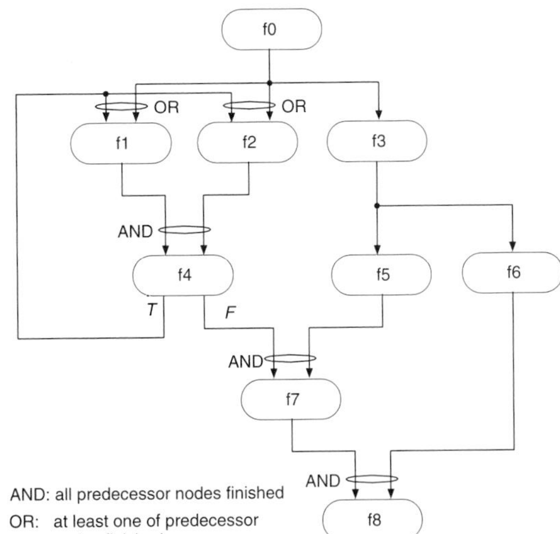

Figure 13.29 Execution graph for Exercise 13.1.

Exercise 13.5 Give an execution graph and develop a μVHDL description of a system similar to that of Example 13.7 to compute an approximation to $a^{1/2}$. The corresponding recurrence is $z_i = (1/2)(z_i + a/z_i)$. Assume that you have a division unit, and the multiplication by (1/2) is performed by shifting the data.

Exercise 13.6

a. Give a concurrent execution graph for computing 6!, using as primitive operation the multiplication of two operands. If the time for a multiplication is T, determine the execution time of your sequence. Generalize for n!.
b. Give a sequential execution graph for the computation in (a). Compare the execution times.

Exercise 13.7 Give a sequential execution graph for obtaining the maximum of n positive integers. Develop the μVHDL description of a system for this computation.

Organization of systems

Exercise 13.8 Describe two organizations of a system to evaluate a polynomial of degree 9, similar to those of Examples 13.3 and 13.4.

Analysis and design

Exercise 13.9 Show the implementation of the following μVHDL statements.

a.
```
IF (a < b) THEN a <= b; b <= a;
ELSE a <= c;
END IF;
```
b.
```
IF (c = '1') OR ((count-1) mod (2**16) = 1) THEN
temp <= count;
END IF;
```
c.
```
IF ((c OR d) = '1') THEN
IF (c = '1') THEN c <= a;
ELSE c <= b;
END IF;
ELSE
d <= a + b;
END IF;
```

Exercise 13.10 Show the state diagram for the following computation sequences:

a.

```
  SIGNAL state: NATURAL RANGE 1 TO 4:= 1;
PROCESS (clk)
BEGIN
  CASE state IS
    WHEN 1 => IF (start = '1') THEN state <= 2; END IF;
    WHEN 2 => IF (c = '1')     THEN A <= A + B;
              ELSE                  A <= A - B; N <= N - 1;
              END IF;
              state <= 3;
    WHEN 3 => A <= 2A; B <= M(N);
              IF (N /= 0) THEN state <= 2;
              ELSE             state <= 4;
              END IF;
    WHEN 4 => D <= A; E <= A-B; state <= 1;
  END CASE;
END PROCESS;
```

b.

```
  SIGNAL state : NATURAL RANGE 0 TO 5:= 0;
PROCESS (clk)
BEGIN
  CASE state IS
     WHEN 0 => IF (start = '1') THEN state <= 1; END IF;
     WHEN 1 => M <= X; SC <= n-1; MP <= Y; P  <= 0;
               state <:= 2;
     WHEN 2 => SC <= DEC(SC);
               IF (MP_0 = '0') THEN state <= 4;
               ELSE                 state <= 3;
               END IF;
     WHEN 3 => P <= ADD (P,M,0); state <= 4;
     WHEN 4 => rshift(P,MP);
               IF NOT(end) THEN state <= 2;
               ELSE             state <= 5;
               END IF;
     WHEN 5 => IF (MP_0 = '1') THEN
                 P <= ADD(P,COMPL(M),1);
               END IF;
               state <= 0;
  END CASE;
END PROCESS;
```

c.

```
  SIGNAL state: NATURAL RANGE 0 TO 6:= 0;
PROCESS (clk)
BEGIN
  CASE state IS
     WHEN 0 => IF (start = '1') THEN state <= 1; END IF;
     WHEN 1 => D <= X; (R,Q) <= Y; SC <= n-1; state <= 2;
     WHEN 2 => (R,Q) <- SL(R,Q); state <= 3;
     WHEN 3 => R <= ADD(R,COMPL(D),1); state <= 4;
     WHEN 4 => SC <= DEC(SC); (R,Q) <= SL(R,Q); state<= 5;
     WHEN 5 => IF (R_n = '1') THEN
                 R  <= ADD (R,D,0);
               ELSE
                 R <= ADD(R,COMPL(D),1);
               END IF;
               Q_0 <= NOT(R_n);
               IF NOT(done) THEN state <= 4;
               ELSE              state <= 6;
               END IF;
```

```
        WHEN 6 => IF (R_n = '1') THEN R <= ADD(R,D,0); END IF;
                  Q_0 <= 0; state <= 0;
      END CASE;
    END PROCESS;
```

Exercise 13.11 Determine the values of X after executing the following computation sequence for $N = 5$ and for $N = 7$.

```
  SIGNAL state: NATURAL RANGE 0 TO 2:= 0;
PROCESS (clk)
BEGIN
  CASE state IS
    WHEN 0 => X <= N; I <= "11"; state <= 1;
    WHEN 1 => IF (odd(X)) THEN X <= 5X+1;
              ELSE             X <= X/2;
              END IF;
              I <= I - 1; state <= 2;
    WHEN 2 => IF (I > 0) THEN state <= 1; END IF;
  END CASE;
END PROCESS;
```

Exercise 13.12 For each of the systems in Figure 13.30, give a μVHDL statement that describes its operation.

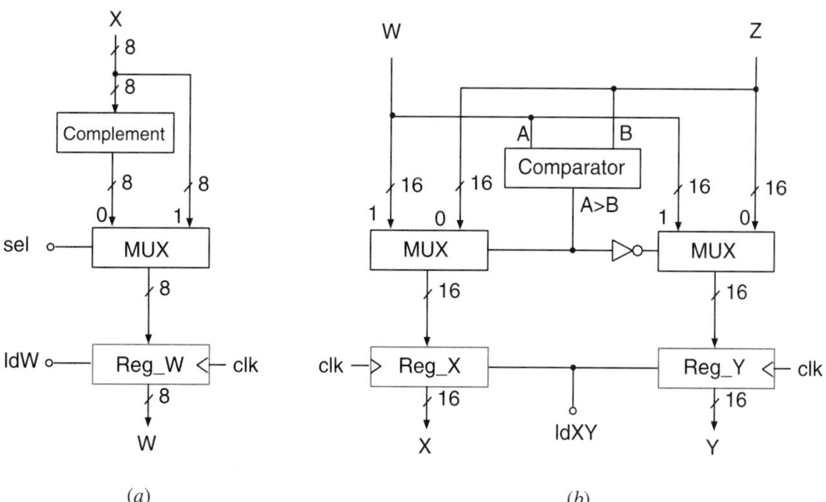

Figure 13.30 Systems for Exercise 13.12.

Exercise 13.13 For the system in Figure 13.31, give a computation sequence that describes its operation.

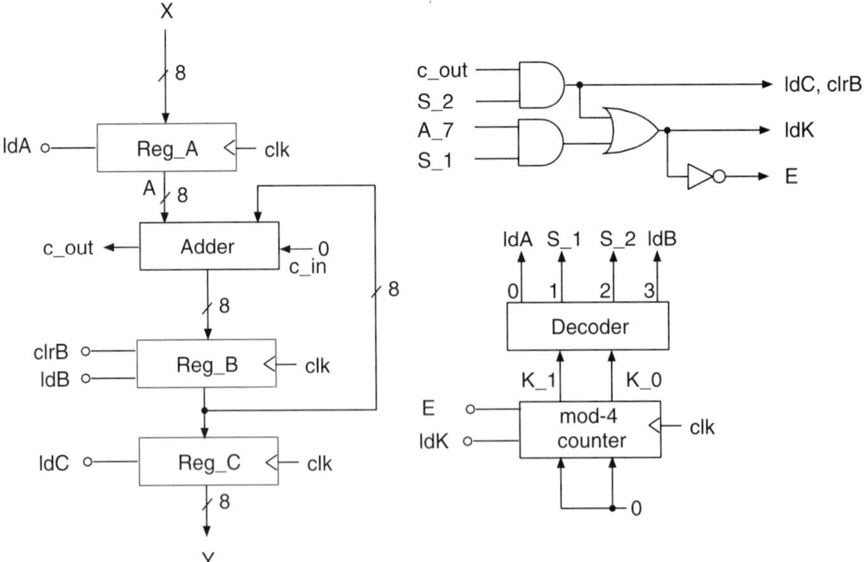

Figure 13.31 System for Exercise 13.13.

Multiplier

Exercise 13.14 Design a 32 × 32 serial-parallel multiplier module, with operands and result represented in the two's complement system. As in the example in the text, give a specification and an implementation. Show the operation of the system (contents of the registers after each cycle) for the 8 × 8 case with operand values $x = -125$, $y = -37$.

These might be hepful hints (see Chapter 10) for more details:

- If number a is represented in the two's complement system by the vector $(a_{n-1}, a_{n-2}, \ldots, a_0)$, then $a = -a_{n-1}2^{n-1} + \sum_{i=0}^{n-2} a_i 2^i$. Consequently, to take into account that the multiplier y is in 2's complement form, the last iteration requires subtracting instead of adding.
- For the addition, just use a two's complement adder.
- For the multiplication by 1/2, use the following algorithm: if b is represented in the two's complement system by $(b_{2n-1}, b_{2n-2}, \ldots, b_1, 0)$ (note the 0 for the least-significant bit), then $(1/2)b$ is represented by $(b_{2n-1}, b_{2n-1}, b_{2n-2}, \ldots, b_1)$ (note the shifting to the right one position with duplication of b_{2n-1}).

Exercise 13.15 Design a 32 × 32 serial-parallel multiplier for positive integers using a radix-4 algorithm. That is, the computation sequence consists of 16 iterations of the following recurrence:

$$z[i+1] = \frac{1}{4}(z[i] + (x \times 2^n) \times v_i)$$

where $v_i = 2y_{2i+1} + y_{2i}$. That is, the multiplier is considered as an integer in radix-4 representation, so that the binary representation is divided into groups of two bits and each group corresponds to a radix-4 digit. This results in a faster multiplication than the radix-2 case because fewer iterations are required.

As in the example in the text, give a specification and an implementation. Show an example of the operation (give contents of registers at the end of each cycle) for an 8 × 8 case with operand values $x = 135$, $y = 115$.

The following hints might be useful:

- The sequence requires the multiplication of $x \times 2^n$ by v_i, where $0 \leq v_i \leq 3$. The four possibilities are as follows:
  - if $v_i = 0$ then $x \times 2^n \times v_i = 0$;

   - if $v_i = 1$ then $x \times 2^n \times v_i = x \times 2^n$;
   - if $v_i = 2$ then $x \times 2^n \times v_i = 2(x \times 2^n)$; this is obtained by shifting $x \times 2^n$ one position to the left;
   - if $v_i = 3$ then $x \times 2^n \times v_i = 2(x \times 2^n) + x \times 2^n$; this addition is done before the iterations (an additional cycle), using the same adder that performs the iterations, and the result is stored in a register of $n + 2 = 34$ bits.

- The selection among the four values of $x \times 2^n \times v_i$ is done with a four-input multiplexer, in which the select inputs are the two least-significant bits of Y (which initially contains y and is shifted right by two positions each iteration).
- Due to the $n + 2$ bits of $3x \times 2^n$, the adder also has to have $n + 2$ bits.

Exercise 13.16 This exercise considers the design of a faster radix-2 serial-parallel multiplier. Because the main delay in an iteration is the addition, the idea is to reduce the delay of the addition by saving the carries instead of propagating them; the resulting adder is called a **carry-save adder.** This adder is implemented by n full adders, as shown in Figure 13.32. Note that both $z[i]$ and $z[i+1]$ are represented by two vectors: a sum vector and a carry vector.

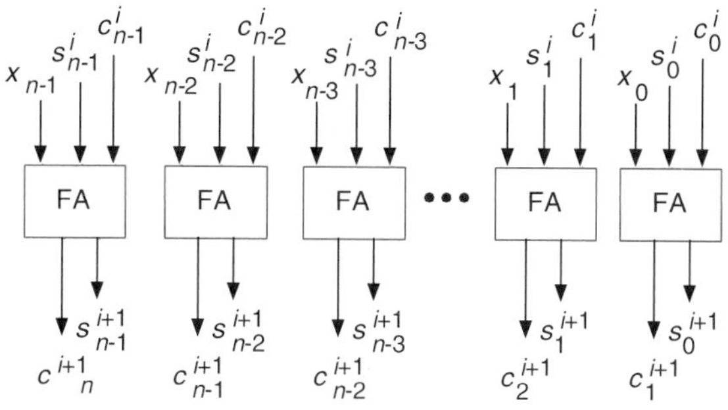

Figure 13.32 Carry-save adder for Exercise 13.16.

Because the result has to be delivered in conventional representation, the carry-save representation has to be converted at the end. This is done by adding the carry and the sum vectors. The adder for this addition can be obtained by reconfiguring the n full adders to have a carry-ripple adder, or another faster adder can be included.

Draw a diagram of the data section of the multiplier for the case in which the full adders are reconfigured as a carry-ripple adder.

If the cycle time is determined by the time of one iteration, the final addition using the carry-ripple adder takes several cycles. Estimate the cycle time and the number of cycles required for the final addition.

Modify the control section of the multiplier given in the text to include this final addition.

Compare the execution times of a 32×32 multiplier as given in the text and a 32×32 multiplier using the carry-save adder approach.

Chapter **14**

Data and Control Subsystems

In this chapter we discuss

- The components and organization of the data subsystem.
- The design of the data subsystem.
- The implementation of the control subsystem as a sequential machine.
- The specification and implementation of a microprogrammed controller.

We now address the organization of the data and control subsystems in a RTL system. In particular, we consider the components of the data subsystem and present a design example using some of these components. In addition, we discuss alternative implementations for the control subsystem, including the concept of a microprogrammed controller.

14.1 DATA SUBSYSTEM

As stated earlier, the data subsystem is the part of a RTL system in which data is stored, moved and transformed. This subsystem consists of (see the example depicted in Figure 14.1):

1. **storage modules,** such as registers or arrays of registers;
2. **functional modules** (operators);
3. **datapaths**, composed of switches and wires connecting storage and functional modules;[1]
4. **control points**, which are points where control signals are connected to the modules; and
5. **condition points**, which are points corresponding to output signals used by the control subsystem.

As depicted in Figure 14.1, the implementation of the data subsystem in a RTL system makes use of modules that are extensions to the modules presented in earlier chapters (the extensions being related to the ability to generate results in the form of bit-vectors instead of single bits, as in the case of the multiplexers), as well as other more complex storage modules (such as the register array). The operation performed by a module, either

[1]Some textbooks use the term **datapath** to refer to the entire data subsystem.

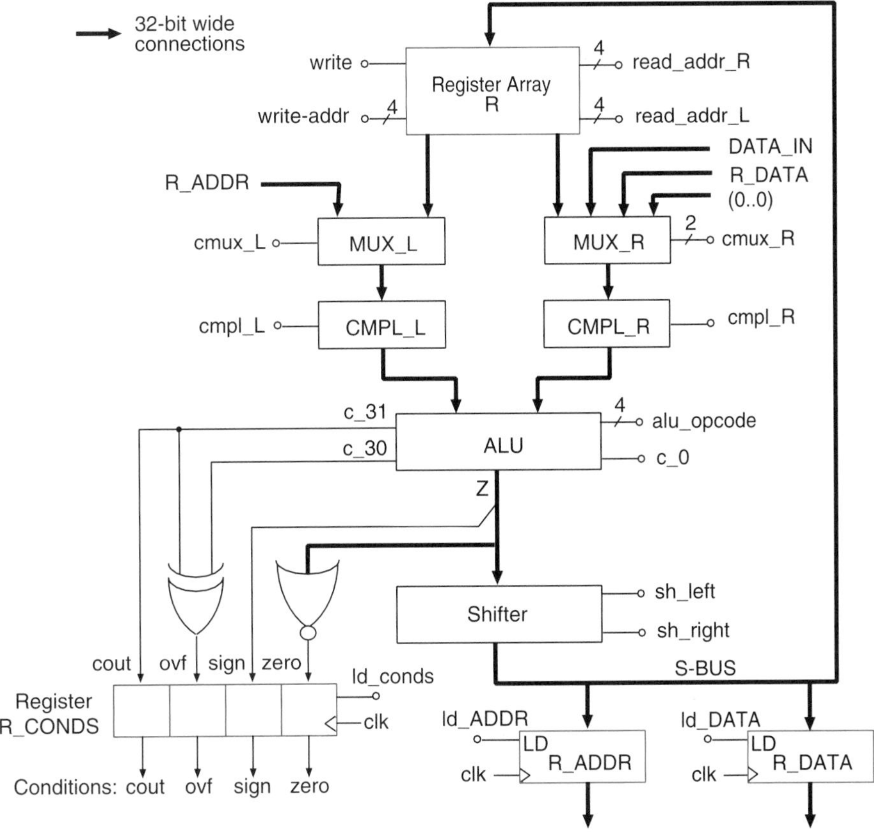

Figure 14.1 Example of a data subsystem.

storage or functional, is dictated by the control signals generated by the control subsystem and present at the control points. Let us now briefly review the characteristics of these modules.

14.1.1 Storage Modules

Storage modules provide storage for data and conditions. The basic storage module is a register; a data subsystem usually contains several of them. These registers can be organized as

- **individual** (separate) registers, with separate connections and controls;
- **arrays** of registers, sharing connections and controls; or
- **combination** of individual registers and arrays of registers.

Individual registers allow for more concurrency in the operation of a system than arrays of registers. Each individual register is accessed through separate datapaths and control signals, so that multiple accesses can be performed simultaneously but requiring many interconnections and controls. As a result, only a small number of individual registers is included in a typical data subsystem. For instance, the system in Example 13.9 uses five individual registers.

On the other hand, some datapaths are shared in an array of registers so that only one operation involving a shared datapath can be performed at a time; this imposes limitations on the concurrency achievable in the data subsystem but reduces the number of datapaths. For instance, the system in Figure 14.1 uses one array of registers with two output datapaths.

An array of registers is characterized by the number of registers, the register access method, and the type of operations that can be performed. Two of the most commonly used types of register arrays are **register file** and **random-access memory** (RAM), which we describe next.

Register File

A register file (see Figure 14.2) is an array of registers capable of performing multiple read and write operations simultaneously on different registers. The inputs to a register file are addresses specifying the registers to operate, control signals indicating the operation to perform, and data inputs providing the data for write operations. The outputs provide the data for read operations. In a register file containing 2^k registers, registers are labeled with the integers 0 to $2^k - 1$ so that an address is a k-bit vector representing the integer.

Figure 14.2 depicts a register file capable of two read and one write operations, whose description uses the data types defined in the IEEE library. Note that there is a write control signal (Wr) but no read controls; that is, read operations are performed as soon as an address is applied to the corresponding address input (i.e., combinational behavior). This difference is due to the fact that a write operation modifies the state of the registers, whereas a read does not.

As in the case of simpler standard modules, the μVHDL description of this register array specifies a delay in read operations (operations which produce an output).

Register files capable of performing two read and one write operations are frequently used in data subsystems that have an ALU that requires two operands and produces one result per cycle, as is the case in the processor of a computer system.

Register-file modules usually have a rather small number of registers, typically in the range from 8 to 32, and their delay is rather small (comparable to the delay of an ALU, for instance).

Random-access Memory

A random-access memory module, known as RAM (see Figure 14.3), is a register array in which only one operation (either read or write) on one register can be performed at a time. Consequently, a single address input is shared among read and write operations, so that the access control is simpler than in the case of register files. A register in a RAM of 2^k registers is identified by a k-bit address representing an integer $0 \leq i \leq 2^k - 1$. Two control signals are shown in Figure 14.3 (Rd, Wr), though some implementations have only one (as in the register file case).

RAM modules have more registers and exhibit larger delay than register files. In some cases, the delay of a RAM is substantially larger than the delay of other modules in a system, so RAM modules are not driven by the same clock signal used in the rest of the system. Instead, such RAM modules use the write control signal also as the clock signal, and do not have a separate clock input.

A random-access memory is normally used for storing large data sets, such as in the main memory of a computer system. As discussed in Chapter 15, the memory subsystem of a computer is implemented as a hierarchy of random-access memories, which go from a fast cache memory (say $8192 = 8$ K bytes) included in the processor chip, to slower memory of many megabytes connected to the processor via the memory bus.

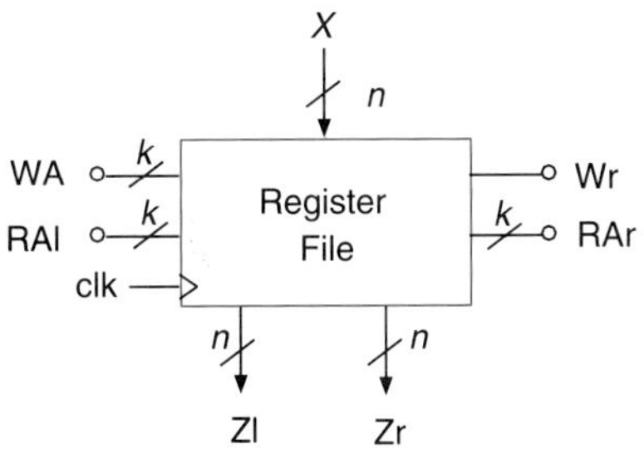

```
LIBRARY ieee;
USE ieee.std_logic_1164.all;
USE ieee.std_logic_arith.all;

ENTITY regfile IS
  GENERIC(n: NATURAL:=16;          -- word width
          p: NATURAL:= 8;          -- register file size
          k: NATURAL:= 3;          -- bits in address vector
         Td: TIME:=5 ns);          -- read address to output
  PORT(X     : IN  UNSIGNED(n-1 DOWNTO 0);     -- input
       WA    : IN  UNSIGNED(k-1 DOWNTO 0);     -- write address
       RAl   : IN  UNSIGNED(k-1 DOWNTO 0);     -- read address (left)
       RAr   : IN  UNSIGNED(k-1 DOWNTO 0);     -- read address (right)
       Zl,Zr: OUT UNSIGNED(n-1 DOWNTO 0);      -- output (left,right)
       Wr    : IN  BIT;                -- write control signal
       clk   : IN  BIT);               -- clock
END regfile;

ARCHITECTURE behavioral OF regfile IS
  SUBTYPE  WordT    IS UNSIGNED(n-1 DOWNTO 0);
  TYPE     StorageT IS ARRAY(0 TO p-1) OF WordT;
  SIGNAL   RF: StorageT;           -- reg. file contents
BEGIN
  PROCESS (clk)                    -- state transition
  BEGIN
    IF (clk'EVENT AND clk = '1') AND (Wr = '1') THEN
      RF(CONV_INTEGER(WA)) <= X;    -- write operation
    END IF;
  END PROCESS;

  PROCESS (RAI,RAr,RF)
  BEGIN                            -- output function
    Zl <= RF(CONV_INTEGER(RAl)) AFTER Td;
    Zr <= RF(CONV_INTEGER(RAr)) AFTER Td;
  END PROCESS;
END behavioral;
```

Figure 14.2 Description of a register file.

Other Storage Modules

The storage component of a data subsystem can be implemented using the modules described in this section plus suitable controls. However, there are some structures that are encountered frequently so that modules with their functionality are provided; as in previous cases, the use of these modules reduces the number of components and eliminates the need of repeated design. Two such modules, namely FIFO (First In First Out) and LIFO (Last In First Out), are described in the exercises at the end of this chapter.

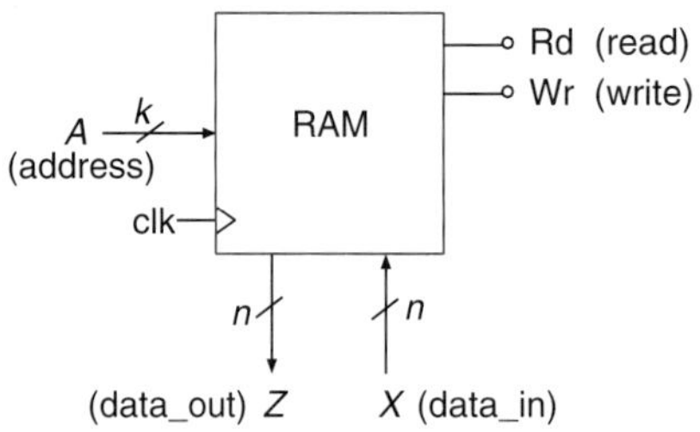

```
LIBRARY ieee;
USE ieee.std_logic_1164.all;
USE ieee.std_logic_arith.all;

ENTITY ram IS
  GENERIC(n: NATURAL:= 16;        -- RAM word width
          p: NATURAL:=256;        -- RAM size
          k: NATURAL:=  8;        -- bits in address vector
         Td: TIME:=40 ns);        -- RAM read delay
  PORT(X     : IN  UNSIGNED(n-1 DOWNTO 0);   -- input bit-vector
       A     : IN  UNSIGNED(k-1 DOWNTO 0);   -- address bit-vector
       Z     : OUT UNSIGNED(n-1 DOWNTO 0);   -- output bit-vector
       Rd,Wr: IN  BIT;                      -- control signals
       Clk   : IN  BIT);                    -- clock signal
END ram;

ARCHITECTURE behavioral OF ram IS
  SUBTYPE  WordT    IS UNSIGNED(n-1 DOWNTO 0);
  TYPE     StorageT IS ARRAY(0 TO p-1) OF WordT;
  SIGNAL   Memory: StorageT;              -- RAM state
BEGIN
  PROCESS (Clk)                   -- state transition
  BEGIN
    IF (Clk'EVENT AND Clk = '1') AND (Wr = '1') THEN
      Memory(CONV_INTEGER(A)) <= X;  -- write operation
    END IF;
  END PROCESS;

  PROCESS (Rd,Memory)             -- output function
  BEGIN
    IF (Rd = '1') THEN            -- read operation
        Z <= Memory(CONV_INTEGER(A)) AFTER Td;
    END IF;
  END PROCESS;
END behavioral;
```

Figure 14.3 Description of a RAM module.

14.1.2 Functional Modules

Functional modules (operators) perform transformations on bit-vectors. As depicted in Figure 14.4, an operator is specified by the names of input and output vectors, and the name of the function performed by the operator. Often operators can perform several operations as specified by operation-selection inputs. As with storage components, a data subsystem might have several operators.

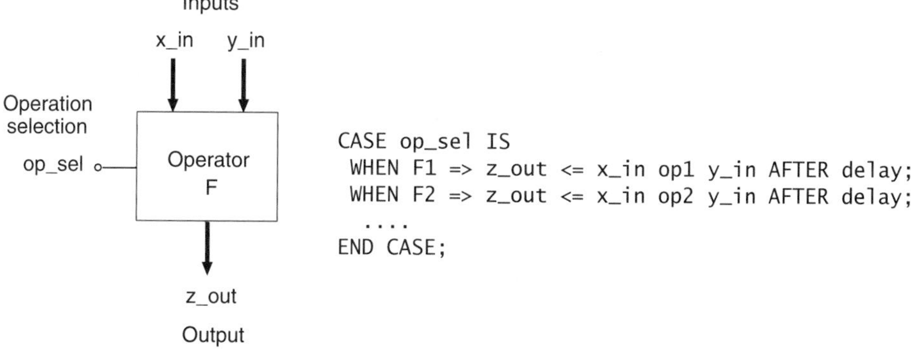

Figure 14.4 Functional module (operator).

14.1.3 Datapaths

Datapaths provide connections between components in the system. They consist of

- direct connections, also called **wires, links**, or **lines**; and
- **switches** to enable the connections.

Datapaths are classified according to different features, as follows:

- The **width** of a datapath is the number of bits that can be transmitted simultaneously (see Figure 14.5). A datapath is **parallel** when several bits are transmitted simultaneously, and **serial** when bits are transmitted one at a time. Parallel datapaths can transfer more data per unit of time but are more costly.

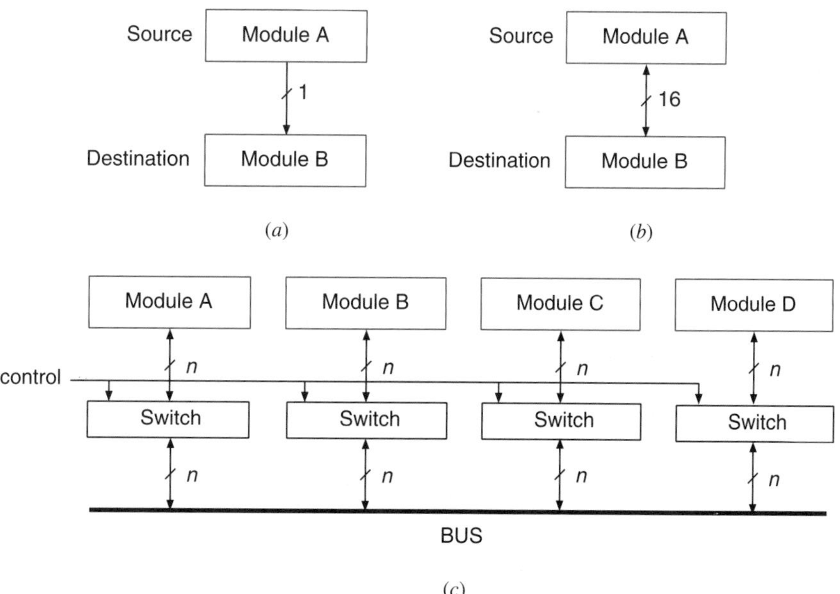

Figure 14.5 Examples of datapaths. (*a*) Unidirectional dedicated datapath (serial). (*b*) Bidirectional dedicated datapath (parallel). (*c*) Shared datapath (bus).

- A datapath is **unidirectional** if the source and destination ends are fixed and cannot be interchanged (Figure 14.5*a*); otherwise, a datapath is **bidirectional** (Figure 14.5*b*). Bidirectional datapaths reduce the number of connections, but the transmissions are limited to one at a time.
- A datapath is **dedicated** if it connects a unique **source** and **destination**. A **shared** datapath, also called **bus** (see Figure 14.5*c*), provides for transmission between several sources and destinations with the restriction that only one transmission can occur at a time.
- A datapath between two components can be **direct** if a connection exists between the components, or **indirect** if there is no direct connection, but the transmission of data can be accomplished by passing through other components.

Switches are required to enable paths in a shared datapath; these switches are implemented by three-state gates or by selectors (multiplexers) (see Figures 14.6 and 14.7). These modules are bit-vector extensions to the single-bit three-state gates and multiplexer discussed in Chapters 3 and 9.

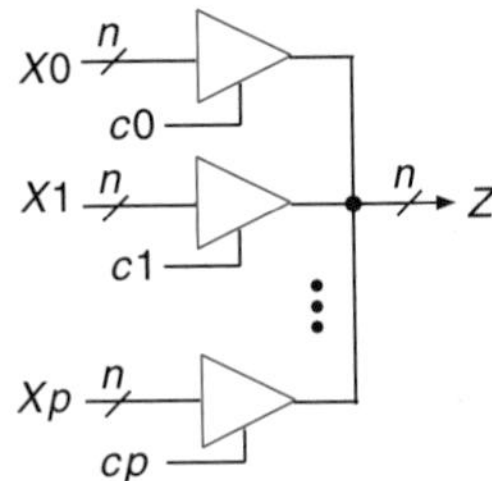

Figure 14.6 Vector gate switches.

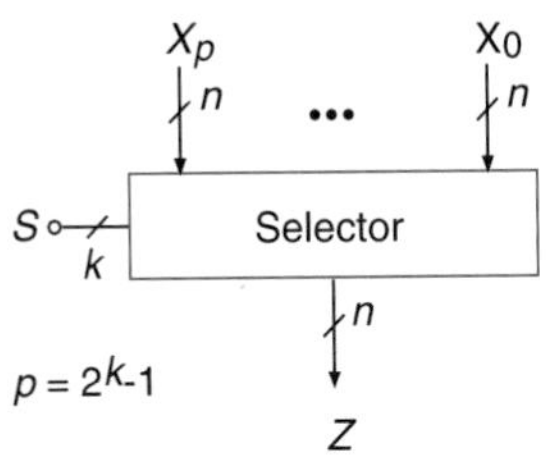


```
PROCESS (Xp,...,X0,S)
BEGIN
  CASE S IS
    WHEN "0..0" => Z <= X0;
    WHEN "0..1" => Z <= X1;
    ....
    WHEN "1..1" => Z <= Xp;
  END CASE;
END PROCESS;
```

Figure 14.7 Vector selector.

The type of datapaths (shared or dedicated, parallel or serial) and their number significantly affect both the speed at which a system can perform a computation and the cost of an implementation. To illustrate this issue, consider the case of a system having m registers of n-bits each, whose datapaths allow transfers between any pair of registers. Two extreme datapath structures for this case are:

Complete interconnection, called **crossbar**, in which m simultaneous transfers are possible. Figure 14.8 illustrates an example for $m = 4$ and $n = 16$. This network becomes quite complex for large m and n, because it requires m vector selectors and at least $m \log_2 m$ selection control signals.

Single bus interconnection (see Figure 14.9), which allows only **one source** to be connected to the bus at a time.

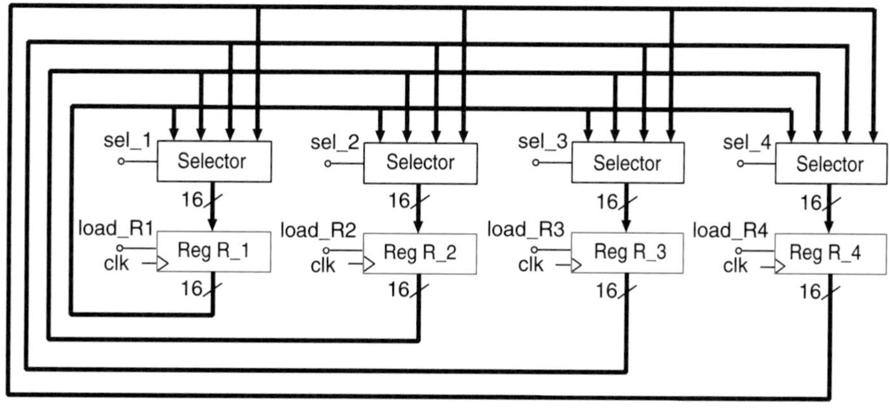


```
  SIGNAL R_1,R_2,R_3,R_4: BIT_VECTOR(15 DOWNTO 0);
PROCESS (clk)
  VARIABLE Sel1,Sel2,Sel3,Sel4: BIT_VECTOR(15 DOWNTO 0);
BEGIN
  CASE sel_1 IS
    WHEN "00" => Sel1:= R1;
    WHEN "01" => Sel1:= R2;
    WHEN "10" => Sel1:= R3;
    WHEN "11" => Sel1:= R4;
  END CASE;
  ....
  CASE sel_4 IS
    WHEN "00" => Sel4:= R1;
    WHEN "01" => Sel4:= R2;
    WHEN "10" => Sel4:= R3;
    WHEN "11" => Sel4:= R4;
  END CASE;

  IF (clk='1') THEN
    IF (load_R1 = '1') THEN R_1 <= Sel1; ENDIF;
    IF (load_R2 = '1') THEN R_2 <= Sel2; ENDIF;
    IF (load_R3 = '1') THEN R_3 <= Sel3; ENDIF;
    IF (load_R4 = '1') THEN R_4 <= Sel4; ENDIF;
  END IF;
END PROCESS;
```

Figure 14.8 A crossbar interconnection network implemented with selectors.

14.2 CONTROL SUBSYSTEM

The control subsystem of a RTL system is a (synchronous) sequential machine. Specifically,

- the inputs are the control inputs to the system and the conditions from the data subsystem;
- the outputs are the control signals;
- there is one state per statement in the register-transfer sequence, and the transition function corresponds to the sequencing in the computation; and
- the output for each state corresponds to the signals that control the activities in that state.

Several alternative schemes for the implementation of sequential systems were considered in Chapters 8, 11, and 12; as discussed there, these alternatives range from fixed

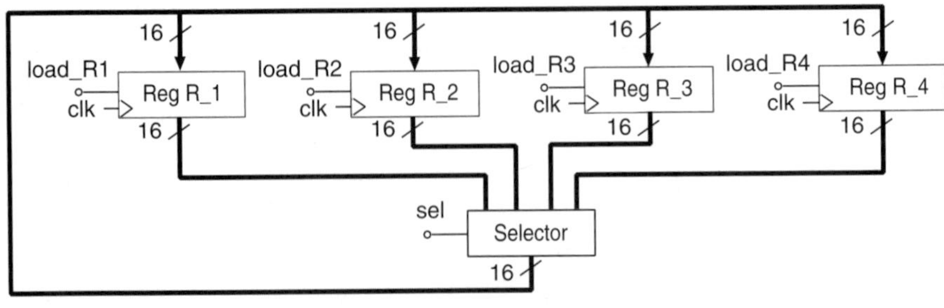


```
  SIGNAL R_1,R_2,R_3,R_4: BIT_VECTOR(15 DOWNTO 0);
PROCESS (clk)
  VARIABLE Sel_out: BIT_VECTOR(15 DOWNTO 0);
BEGIN
  CASE sel IS
    WHEN "00" => Sel_out:= R_1;
    WHEN "01" => Sel_out:= R_2;
    WHEN "10" => Sel_out:= R_3;
    WHEN "11" => Sel_out:= R_4;
  END CASE;

  IF (clk='1') THEN
    IF (load_R1 = '1') THEN R_1 <= Sel_out; ENDIF;
    IF (load_R2 = '1') THEN R_2 <= Sel_out; ENDIF;
    IF (load_R3 = '1') THEN R_3 <= Sel_out; ENDIF;
    IF (load_R4 = '1') THEN R_4 <= Sel_out; ENDIF;
  END IF;
END PROCESS;
```

Figure 14.9 A single bus interconnection network (bus) with vector selector.

networks to programmable modules such as ROMs and PSAs. In the case of RTL systems, this programmability can be extended further, leading to the microprogrammed systems discussed in Section 14.4.

As we already know, implementations with fixed networks can achieve the fastest operation because the control subsystem can be optimized with respect to speed. On the other hand, the use of programmable modules simplifies the design, the correction of design errors, and design modifications. For example, a local change in the transition function may require global modification in the case of an implementation with fixed networks, whereas it might result in a minor reprogramming effort when implemented with programmable modules. This ease of modification is especially important in RTL systems because the design of these systems usually requires several iterations due to their complexity.

State Assignment

The state values are represented by a bit-vector. For this representation, an arbitrary assignment can be used; however, in group-sequential execution graphs there are two types of sequencing:

- unconditional, in which there is only one successor to a state; and
- conditional, in which there are several possible successors depending on the value of a condition.

Because the unconditional case is much more frequent in most execution graphs, a favored implementation of the sequencer consists of using a counter in which consecutive states in

PS	Condition	NS	Count Enable	Parallel Load	Parallel Inputs	Active Control Signals
S0	`start = 0`	S0	0	1	000	`set_done`
S0	`start = 1`	S1	1	0	—	`set_done`
S1	—	S2	1	0	—	`reset_done, ld_arg, ld_rec, ld_eps`
S2	—	S3	1	0	—	`ld_w, selM`
S3	—	S4	1	0	—	`ld_y`
S4	`k = 1`	S2	0	1	010	`ld_rec, selR`
S4	`k = 0`	S0	0	1	000	`ld_rec, selR`

(*a*)

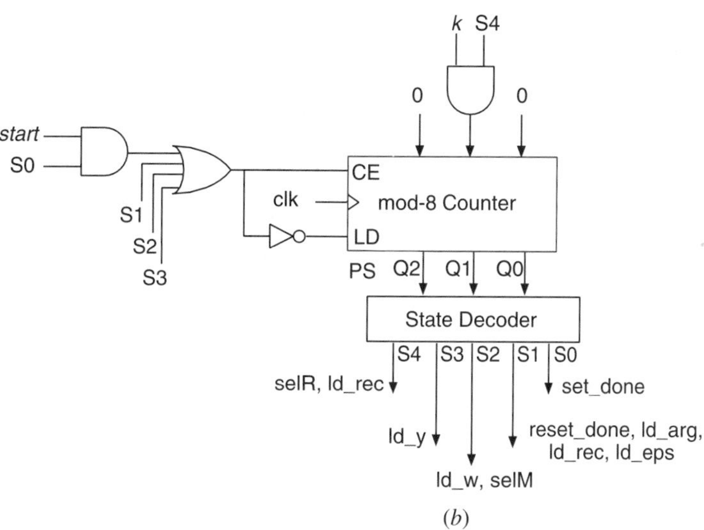

(*b*)

Figure 14.10 Counter-based implementation of control subsystem for Example 13.9. (*a*) Specification of counter control functions. (*b*) Network.

the sequence are assigned to consecutive states of the counter. This approach is illustrated in Figure 14.10 for the system analyzed in Example 13.9.

In addition, if the number of states is small, structures with one flip-flop per state result in a straightforward mapping between the sequence (state diagram) and implementation, as discussed in Chapter 8. These structures also have the advantage that no decoder is required for the generation of the control signals. For convenience, we repeat in Figure 14.11 the two basic cases that occur in state diagrams, and their possible implementations. In the first case, the transition to a next state does not depend on a condition and has an obvious implementation; in the second case, the transition depends on a condition and can be implemented with an OR gate and a demultiplexer. Clearly, a given state diagram can be translated directly into a network of hardware modules of either type. The control subsystem in Figure 13.14 (Example 13.9) illustrates the one flip-flop per state approach.

Control Signals

In general, control signals depend on the state, the conditions, and the external inputs to the system. To reduce the complexity of the combinational network for the generation of

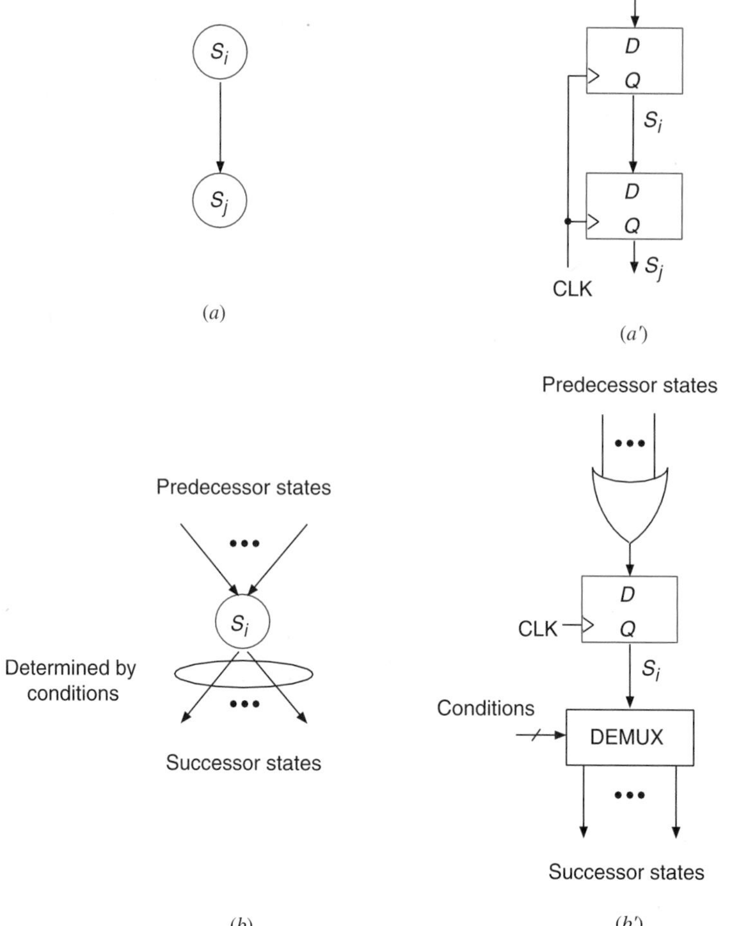

Figure 14.11 Primitives for the one flip-flop per state approach.

control signals, it is often convenient to first decode the state variables and use the decoded states. The conditional control signals can be implemented in two ways, corresponding to the Mealy and Moore models of sequential systems. Consider the following statement

```
IF (sign = '0') THEN A <= B;
ELSE                 C <= D;
END IF;
```

and let C_1 and C_2 be control signals for loading *A* and *C*, respectively. In a Moore-type implementation, a state is introduced for each conditional signal, thus simplifying the output function at the expense of the state-transition function. In a Mealy-type implementation, the conditional control signals are generated as functions of the state and the conditions. Figure 14.12 illustrates these alternatives.

Often a control signal is active during several consecutive states. Instead of generating such a signal in each relevant state, it is possible to introduce a clocked cell that can be set when the signal becomes active and cleared when it becomes inactive, as illustrated in Figure 14.13.

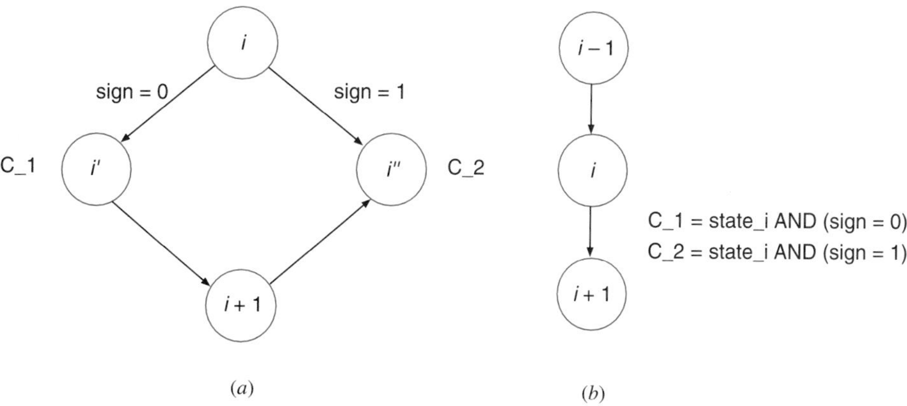

Figure 14.12 Implementation alternatives for control signals. (*a*) Moore-type implementation. (*b*) Mealy-type implementation.

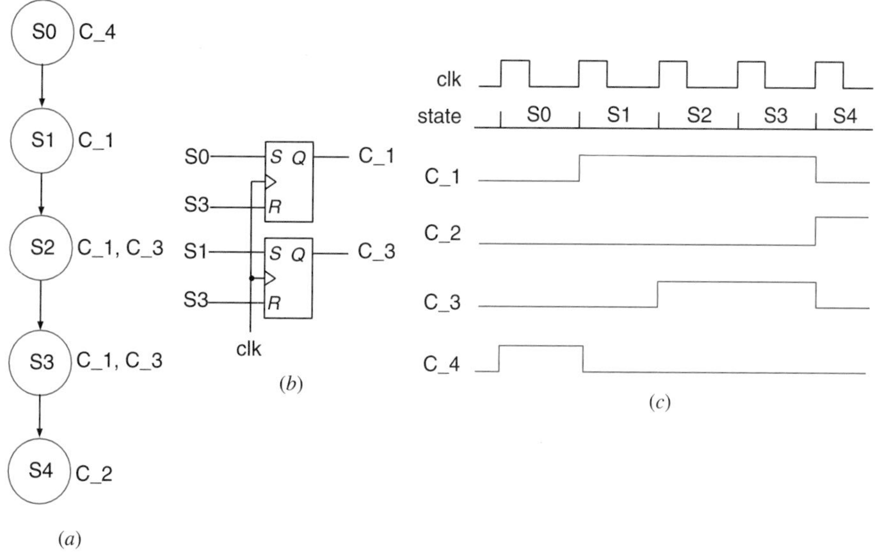

Figure 14.13 Clocked cell. (*a*) State diagram. (*b*) Implementation of signals C_1 and C_3. (*c*) Timing diagram.

14.3 A DESIGN EXAMPLE

Let us now illustrate the use of some of the components discussed in the previous two sections, by developing an implementation of the system specified in Example 13.6. A μVHDL specification of this system, in which we have identified the states and register transfers per state, is given in Figure 14.14.

For an implementation, we need to develop a structural description having as components the data and control subsystems.

Data Subsystem

From Figure 14.14, we determine that the following elements are needed:

- Registers x and y to store x and y, respectively.

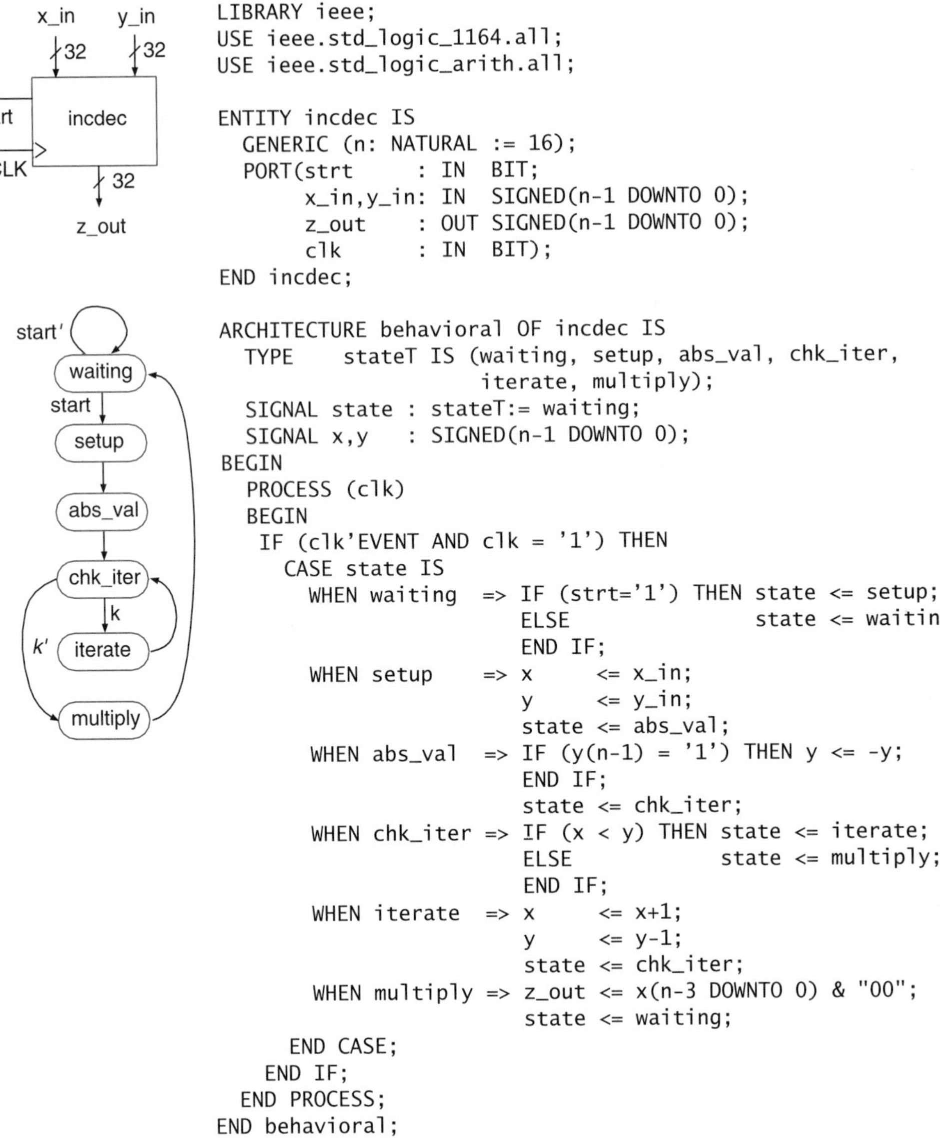


```
LIBRARY ieee;
USE ieee.std_logic_1164.all;
USE ieee.std_logic_arith.all;

ENTITY incdec IS
  GENERIC (n: NATURAL := 16);
  PORT(strt      : IN  BIT;
       x_in,y_in: IN  SIGNED(n-1 DOWNTO 0);
       z_out     : OUT SIGNED(n-1 DOWNTO 0);
       clk       : IN  BIT);
END incdec;

ARCHITECTURE behavioral OF incdec IS
  TYPE    stateT IS (waiting, setup, abs_val, chk_iter,
                     iterate, multiply);
  SIGNAL state : stateT:= waiting;
  SIGNAL x,y   : SIGNED(n-1 DOWNTO 0);
BEGIN
  PROCESS (clk)
  BEGIN
   IF (clk'EVENT AND clk = '1') THEN
     CASE state IS
       WHEN waiting  => IF (strt='1') THEN state <= setup;
                        ELSE               state <= waiting
                        END IF;
       WHEN setup    => x     <= x_in;
                        y     <= y_in;
                        state <= abs_val;
       WHEN abs_val  => IF (y(n-1) = '1') THEN y <= -y;
                        END IF;
                        state <= chk_iter;
       WHEN chk_iter => IF (x < y) THEN state <= iterate;
                        ELSE             state <= multiply;
                        END IF;
       WHEN iterate  => x     <= x+1;
                        y     <= y-1;
                        state <= chk_iter;
       WHEN multiply => z_out <= x(n-3 DOWNTO 0) & "00";
                        state <= waiting;

     END CASE;
   END IF;
  END PROCESS;
END behavioral;
```

Figure 14.14 Specification of incdec system.

- The operators abs, inc, dec, left_shift2, and comp (less_than). We utilize a different module for each operator (that is, an implementation without sharing operators).
- Datapaths to connect the registers and operators. Specifically, connections

  - from x to operators left_shift2, inc, and comp.
  - from y to operators dec, abs, and comp.
  - from inc and x_in to x. This requires a two-input multiplexer.
  - from dec, abs, and y_in to y. This requires a three-input multiplexer.

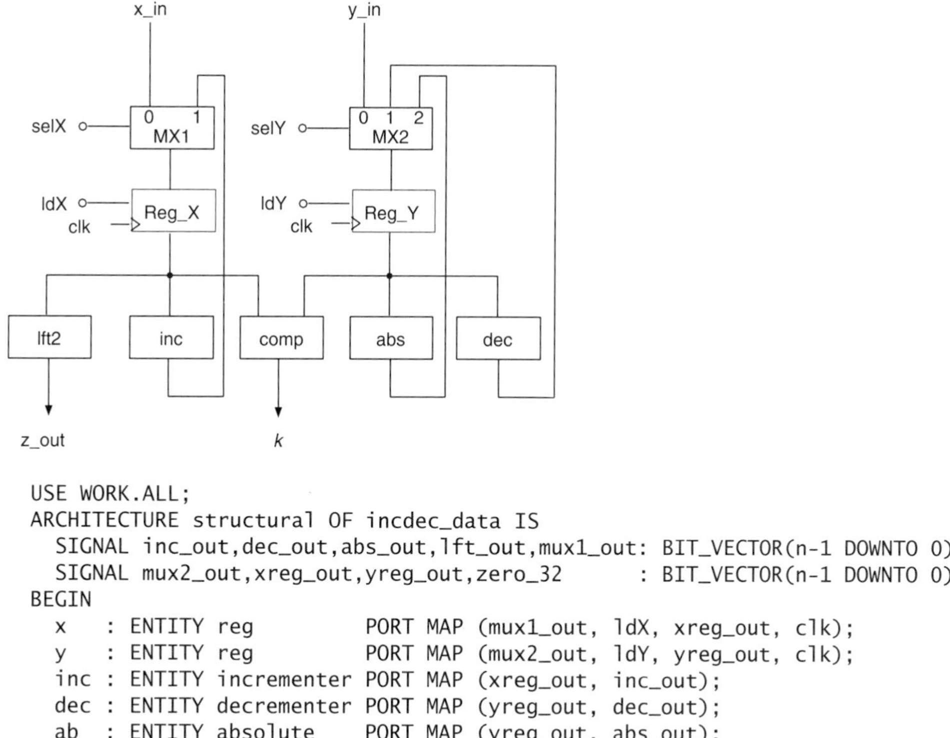


```
USE WORK.ALL;
ARCHITECTURE structural OF incdec_data IS
  SIGNAL inc_out,dec_out,abs_out,lft_out,mux1_out: BIT_VECTOR(n-1 DOWNTO 0);
  SIGNAL mux2_out,xreg_out,yreg_out,zero_32      : BIT_VECTOR(n-1 DOWNTO 0);
BEGIN
  x   : ENTITY reg         PORT MAP (mux1_out, ldX, xreg_out, clk);
  y   : ENTITY reg         PORT MAP (mux2_out, ldY, yreg_out, clk);
  inc : ENTITY incrementer PORT MAP (xreg_out, inc_out);
  dec : ENTITY decrementer PORT MAP (yreg_out, dec_out);
  ab  : ENTITY absolute    PORT MAP (yreg_out, abs_out);
  mx1 : ENTITY mux2        PORT MAP (x_in, inc_out, selX, mx1_out);
  mx2 : ENTITY mux4        PORT MAP (y_in, dec_out, abs_out, zero_32,
                                     selY, mx2_out);
  lft2: ENTITY lft_shift2  PORT MAP (xreg_out, lft_out);
  comp: ENTITY less_than   PORT MAP (xreg_out, yreg_out, k);
END structural;
```

Figure 14.15 Structural description of `incdec` data subsystem.

- The following control points:

Operation	Control Points
`load register x`	`ldX`
`load register y`	`ldY`
`select input to x (1 bit)`	`selX`
`select input to y (2 bit)`	`selY`

  Several control points could correspond to the same control signal. However, in this case we use one control signal per control point with the corresponding name.
- The conditions required by the control subsystem. In this case only one condition is required:

$$k = \begin{cases} 1 & \textbf{if} \quad x < y \\ 0 & \textbf{otherwise} \end{cases}$$

Using this information, we produce the structural description shown in Figure 14.15 and the behavioral description depicted in Figure 14.16, which indicates the various register transfers that occur for the different control signals, and the generation of the condition.

```
ENTITY data_subsystem IS
  GENERIC (n: NATURAL := 16);
  PORT(x_in, y_in : IN  BIT_VECTOR(n-1 DOWNTO 0); -- data inputs
       ldX,ldY    : IN BIT;                       -- control signals
       selX       : IN BIT;
       selY       : IN BIT_VECTOR(1 DOWNTO 0);
       k          : OUT BIT;                      -- condition
       z_out      : OUT BIT_VECTOR(n-1 DOWNTO 0)  -- data outputs
       clk        : IN  BIT);
END data_subsystem;

ARCHITECTURE behavioral OF data_subsystem IS
  SIGNAL x,y,z : BIT_VECTOR(n-1 DOWNTO 0);
BEGIN
  PROCESS (clk)
  BEGIN
    IF (clk = '1') THEN
      IF (ldX = '1') AND (selX = '0')  THEN x <= x_in;   END IF;
      IF (ldX = '1') AND (selX = '1')  THEN x <= inc(x); END IF;
      IF (ldY = '1') AND (selY = '00') THEN y <= y_in;   END IF;
      IF (ldY = '1') AND (selY = '01') THEN y <= dec(y); END IF;
      IF (ldY = '1') AND (selY = '10') THEN y <= ABS(y); END IF;
      IF (x < y) THEN k <= '1';
      ELSE            k <= '0';
      END IF;
      z_out <= shift_left(x,2);
    END IF;
  END PROCESS;
END behavioral;
```

Figure 14.16 Behavioral description of incdec data subsystem.

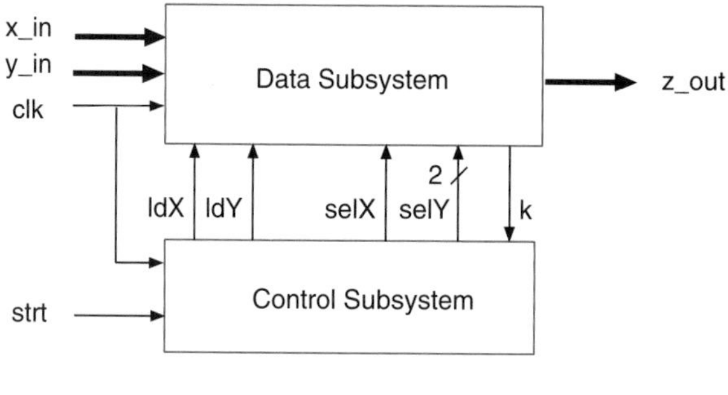


```
USE WORK.ALL;
ARCHITECTURE structural OF incdec IS
  SIGNAL selY          : BIT_VECTOR(1 DOWNTO 0);
  SIGNAL ldX,ldY,selX  : BIT;
  SIGNAL k             : BIT;
BEGIN
  datasub: ENTITY incdec_data
           PORT MAP (x_in,y_in,ldX,ldY,selX,selY,k,z_out,clk);
  ctrlsub: ENTITY incdec_ctrl
           PORT MAP (strt,k,ldX,ldY,selX,selY,clk);
END structural;
```

Figure 14.17 Structural description of incdec system.

Structural Description of the System

From the description of the data subsystem, it follows that the connections between the two subsystems and the corresponding μVHDL description are as shown in Figure 14.17.

Modules in Data Subsystem

The next level of description corresponds to the description of the modules in the data subsystem. As an example, the behavioral description of the absolute value module is given in Figure 14.18 (for representation in the 2's complement system), where we use the ability of the language for describing a module without specifying the number of bits in the ports.

Control Subsystem

Let us now look into the control subsystem. From the RTL sequence and the definition of the control signals, we determine the following table for the control function:

State	ldX	ldY	selX	selY	Next state
waiting	0	0	—	—	setup, waiting
setup	1	1	0	00	abs_val
abs_val	0	1	—	01	chk_iter
chk_iter	0	0	—	—	iterate, multiply
iterate	1	1	1	10	chk_iter
multiply	0	0	—	—	waiting

A behavioral description of the control subsystem is given in Figure 14.19. The corresponding state diagram is depicted in Figure 14.20 together with an implementation using the one flip-flop per state approach.

```
LIBRARY ieee;
USE ieee.std_logic_1164.all;
USE ieee.std_logic_arith.all;

ENTITY absolute IS
  PORT (x_in : IN  SIGNED;
        z_out: OUT SIGNED);
END absolute;

ARCHITECTURE behavioral OF absolute IS
BEGIN
  PROCESS (x_in)
  BEGIN
    IF x_in(x_in'LEFT) = '1' THEN z_out <= -x_in;
    ELSE z_out <=  x_in;
    END IF;
  END PROCESS;
END behavioral;
```

Figure 14.18 Behavioral description of absolute value module.

```
ENTITY incdec_ctrl IS
  PORT(strt,k  : IN  BIT;      -- control input, condition
       ldX, ldY: OUT BIT;      -- control signals
       selX    : OUT BIT;
       selY    : OUT BIT_VECTOR(1 DOWNTO 0);
       clk     : IN  BIT);
END incdec_ctrl ;

ARCHITECTURE behavioral OF incdec_ctrl IS
  TYPE stateT IS (waiting,setup,abs_val,chk_iter,iterate,multiply);
  SIGNAL state : stateT:= waiting;
BEGIN
  PROCESS (clk)                        -- transition function
  BEGIN
    IF (clk'EVENT AND clk = '1') THEN
      CASE state IS
        WHEN waiting  => IF (strt = '1') THEN state <= setup; END IF;
        WHEN setup    => state <= abs_val ;
        WHEN abs_val  => state <= chk_iter;
        WHEN chk_iter => IF (k = '1') THEN state <= iterate ;
                         ELSE              state <= multiply;
                         END IF;
        WHEN iterate  => state <= chk_iter;
        WHEN multiply => state <= waiting ;
      END CASE;
    END IF;
  END PROCESS;

  PROCESS (state)                      -- output function
    VARIABLE ctrls : BIT_VECTOR(4 DOWNTO 0);
  BEGIN
    CASE state IS
      WHEN waiting  => ctrls(4 downto 3):= "00"    ;
      WHEN setup    => ctrls            := "11000";
      WHEN abs_val  => ctrls(4 downto 3):= "01"    ;
                       ctrls(1 downto 0):= "01"    ;
      WHEN chk_iter => ctrls(4 downto 3):= "00"    ;
      WHEN iterate  => ctrls            := "11110";
      WHEN multiply => ctrls(4 downto 3):= "00"    ;
    END CASE;
    ldX  <= ctrls(4); ldY  <= ctrls(3);
    selX <= ctrls(2); selY <= ctrls(1 DOWNTO 0);
  END PROCESS;
END behavioral;
```

Figure 14.19 Behavioral description of `incdec` control subsystem.

14.4 MICROPROGRAMMED CONTROLLER

We now introduce the concept of **microprogrammed controller,** which is a generalization of the ROM-based implementation discussed in Chapter 12. In this approach, the structure of the control subsystem is made more systematic and general so that it can suit a variety of register-transfer sequences.

In a microprogrammed controller, the state-transition and output functions of a sequential system are implemented using table look-up; that is, these functions are stored in a memory. Each statement in the register-transfer sequence (a **microinstruction**) is represented by one word in the memory, which specifies:

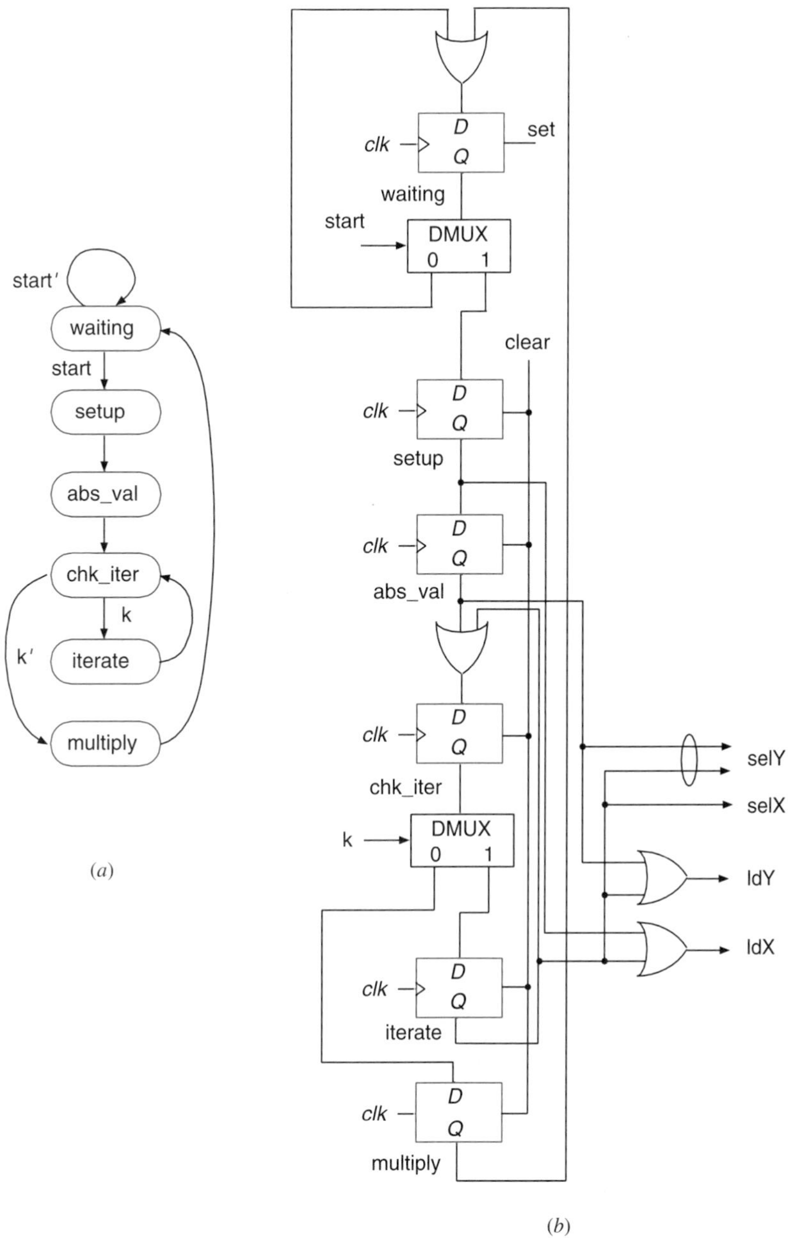

Figure 14.20 Implementation of the control subsystem for `incdec` system.

1. the values of the control signals; and
2. the sequencing information that determines which microinstruction is executed next.

The set of microinstructions for the control of a computation sequence is called a **micro-program**.

14.4.1 Structure of a Microprogrammed Controller

A typical microprogrammed controller is illustrated in Figure 14.21. Such a controller consists of the following modules:

Control store (CS). This module corresponds to a memory containing the microprogram representing the computation sequence; it can be a ROM, PROM, or RAM. A ROM-based implementation is permanent, whereas PROM or RAM-based implementations allow modifying the microprogram. A RAM-based implementation is known as **writable control store.**

Systems with writable control store are called **microprogrammable;** this type of implementation is used when a variety of computation sequences are implemented by the same system.

Control-store address register (CSAR). This register is used to address the memory containing the microprogram. It corresponds to the state register of a sequential system.

CS address generator (CSAGEN). This module computes the address of the next microinstruction to be fetched and executed. As discussed later, the address of such a microinstruction can be specified in several ways, depending on the conditions, external control inputs, and type of sequencing.

Typical functions of the address generator include incrementing the current address by one, transmitting an externally specified address, generating a computed branch address, or specifying an initial address.

Decoder. This module generates controls signals, based on the contents of the microinstruction fetched from the control store.

Microcontroller. This module is the "control unit" of the microprogrammed controller.

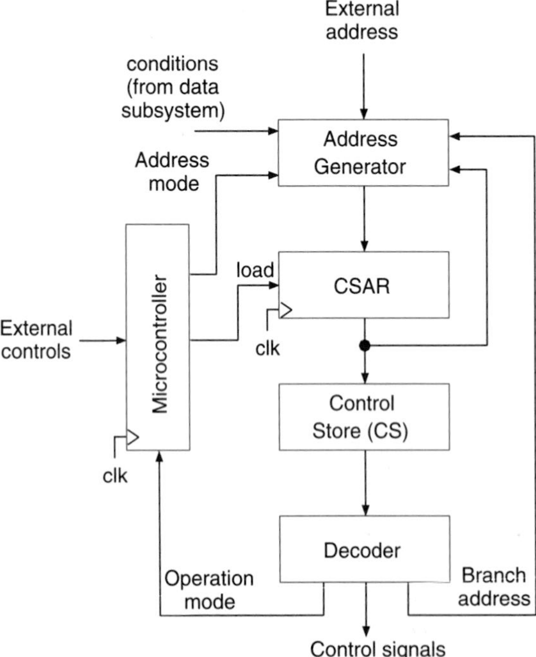

Figure 14.21 A microprogrammed controller.

In some cases, microprogrammed controllers also contain a "microinstruction register" (MIR), which is loaded with the microinstruction fetched from the control store; that is, MIR contains the microinstruction being executed at a given time.

The advantages of a microprogrammed controller with respect to a controller implemented as a fixed network (such as the ones described in previous examples in this chapter) are as follows:

- The structure of the controller is modular, regular, and independent of the particular computation implemented by the system. This simplifies the design, because the modules composing the controller can be used for many different systems.
- The implementation of the controller for a complex computation consists of writing the corresponding microprogram, a task which is simpler and more amenable to verification and/or simulation than the design of a fixed controller. Moreover, the computation sequence can be easily modified by changing the contents of the control store.

The main disadvantage of a microprogrammed controller is that it might lead to a slower implementation than the one resulting from a fixed network of modules, due to higher access time of the ROM and to constraints arising from the regular structure of the controller.

14.4.2 Microinstruction Format

A microinstruction is divided into **fields.** The following fields, which are discussed below, are required as a minimum:

- a **control field,** giving the values of the control signals; and
- a **sequencing field,** specifying the address of the next microinstruction.

Control Field

The **control field** specifies the values of the control signals during the execution of a microinstruction. Two basic formats are used to represent these signals:

Horizontal (unpacked, decoded): in this format, each control signal has a separate subfield indicating the value of the corresponding control signal, as illustrated in Figure 14.22*a*.

Vertical (packed, encoded): in this format, a subfield is used to specify a subset of control signals as illustrated in Figure 14.22*b*. Only one control signal per subfield can be active per microinstruction, and the subfield identifies the active control signal. Consequently, a k-bit subfield can be used to specify one out of 2^k control signals (note that it might be necessary to reserve one encoding for the case in which none of the signals in the subset is active).

A decoder per subfield is used to obtain the control signals. These decoders can be part of the control subsystem or can be incorporated in the modules of the data subsystem. Examples of control signals that are sent encoded to the data subsystem are addresses of register arrays, operation codes of operator modules, and selection signals of multiplexers.

Because only one control signal per subset can be active at a time, it is necessary to select the subfields in such a way that two signals are assigned to the same subfield only if

- the operations they control are not required at the same time in the microprogram; or
- the data subsystem does not allow the simultaneous use of such control signals.

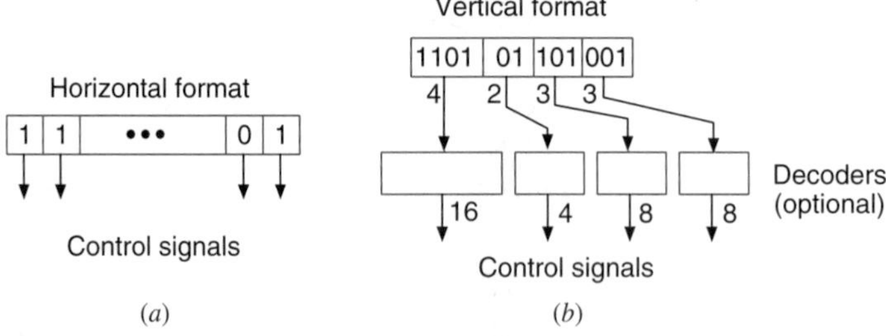

Figure 14.22 Formats of the control field.

EXAMPLE 14.1

An example of horizontal and vertical control-field formats is given in Figure 14.23. Figure 14.23*a* indicates a fragment of a data subsystem with 24 control points; Figure 14.23*b* illustrates a horizontal format, as well as a vertical format; and Figure 14.23*c* shows an example of a register transfer and the corresponding encoding of the control subfields. The horizontal format requires 24-bit words in the control store, whereas the vertical format requires 12-bit words.

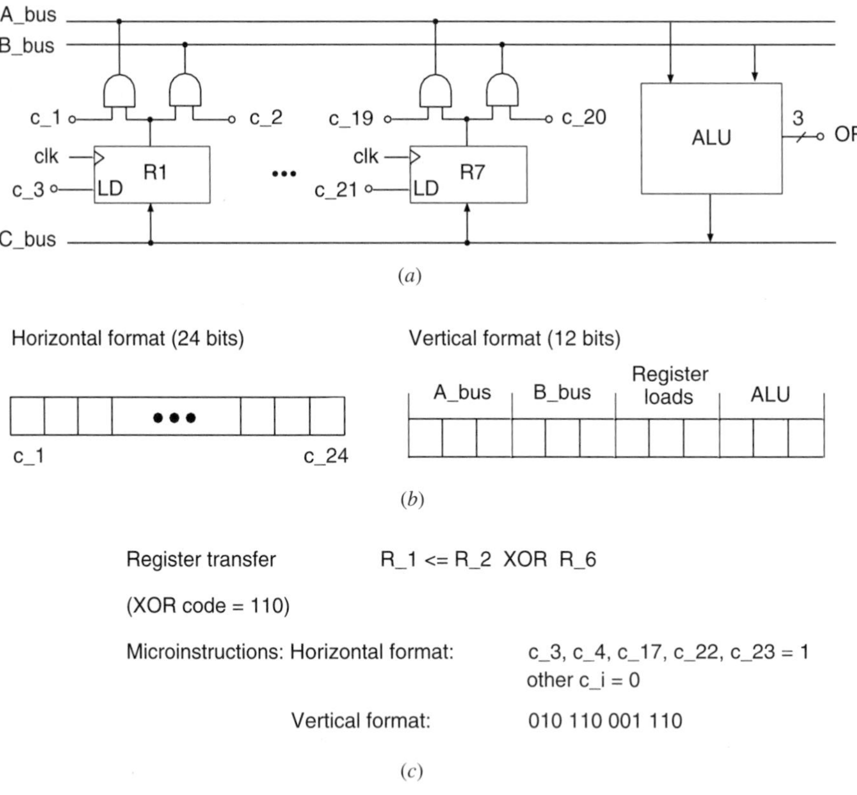

Register transfer R_1 <= R_2 XOR R_6

(XOR code = 110)

Microinstructions: Horizontal format: c_3, c_4, c_17, c_22, c_23 = 1
other c_i = 0

Vertical format: 010 110 001 110

(*c*)

Figure 14.23 Vertical and horizontal encoding of control field for Example 14.1. ■

The horizontal format provides for maximum possible concurrency among control signals because any combination of them can be specified in a microinstruction. In addition, this format results in a faster generation of the control signals because no decoding is necessary. On the other hand, the horizontal format requires long words in the control store, so that the memory space is not used efficiently. Moreover, all control signals are sent decoded to the data subsystem, resulting in a connection between the subsystems having many bits.

The vertical format limits the concurrency among control signals since only one signal of each subset can be specified at a time. However, the concurrency can match the concurrency that the data subsystem can use, as occurs in Example 14.1. This format results in a slower generation of the control signals because of the decoding required. It is also less flexible because signals encoded in the same subfield cannot be used simultaneously, so that a modification of the computation sequence might require a change of the format. Its advantage is the use of shorter words and therefore a smaller control store. The horizontal and vertical formats can be combined for greater efficiency and flexibility. For example, some subfields may be in the horizontal format, whereas other subfields may be in vertical format.

14.4.3 Microinstruction Sequencing

The execution of a microprogram requires a scheme to determine the next microinstruction to be executed. This scheme can be implemented in several ways:

Explicit sequencing. In this scheme, the address of the next microinstruction is specified in a separate field in the microinstruction being executed, as depicted in Figure 14.24*a*. This address is loaded into CSAR. For conditional sequencing, two (or more) addresses are required per microinstruction. Thus, explicit sequencing requires long microinstructions.

Implicit sequencing. In this scheme, microinstructions are executed in the order in which they are stored in the control store. Therefore, no sequencing information is required in the microinstructions, which contains only the control field, as long as the RTL sequence does not contain any conditional branches. If branches are present (as is the case in almost all computation sequences), a special type of microinstruction is required to specify the branch. That is, the implicit sequencing scheme requires two types of microinstructions: one to specify control signals, and another to specify a branch. In the branch type, two fields are required: one for the condition, and another for the branch address. An example of these microinstructions formats is depicted in Figure 14.24*b*. Note the additional bit required to distinguish among the two formats (a mode field).

Explicit addressing scheme:

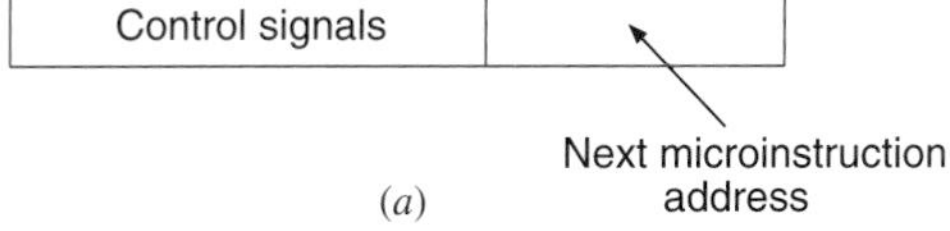

(*a*)

Implicit addressing scheme:

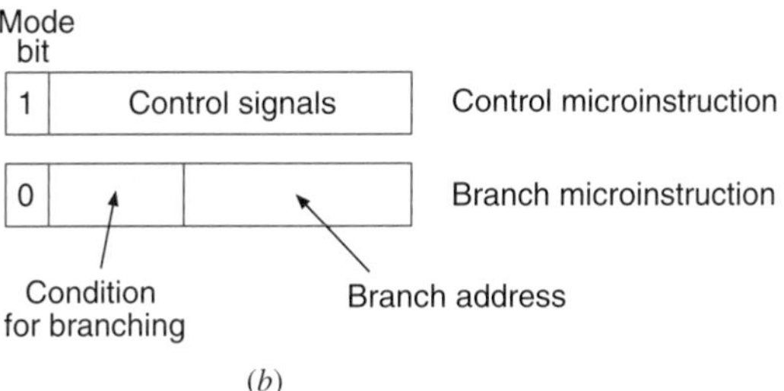

(*b*)

Figure 14.24 Microinstruction addressing schemes. (*a*) Explicit sequencing. (*b*) Implicit sequencing.

For implicit sequencing, two types of control store address calculations are required:

- Increment CSAR if the current microinstruction is not a branch, or if the condition is not satisfied when the current microinstruction is a branch.
- Load CSAR with the branch address if the current microinstruction is a branch and the condition is satisfied.

Implicit sequencing is characterized by shorter microinstructions but longer microprograms than explicit sequencing.

EXAMPLE 14.2

Consider a computation sequence that has 1000 microinstructions (with 30 control signals), and whose sequencing contains 200 conditional branches that specify one of 16 conditions.

Explicit sequencing requires a control store of $1000 \times (30 + 20 + 4) = 54 \times 10^3$ bits, because 10 bits are required to specify each of the two target microinstruction addresses (condition being true and false) and 4 bits to specify a condition. The width of the control store is 54 bits.

On the other hand, implicit sequencing requires $(1000 + 200) \times 31 = 37.2 \times 10^3$ bits, because 200 additional microinstructions are required for the branches, and the width of each microinstruction corresponds to the 30 control signals plus the mode bit. ■

14.4.4 Microinstruction Timing

A microinstruction **execution cycle** consists of (see Figure 14.25):

1. Loading the address of the next microinstruction into CSAR.
2. Fetching (reading) the corresponding microinstruction.
3. Decoding the fields.
4. Executing the microoperations.
5. Calculating the address of the next microinstruction; this calculation can be overlapped with the execution part of the cycle.

The clock signal delimits the microinstruction cycle; the clock pulse synchronizes the loading of the address of the next microinstruction into CSAR; the remaining parts of the microinstruction cycle correspond to combinational modules: the control store, the decoder, and the address generator.

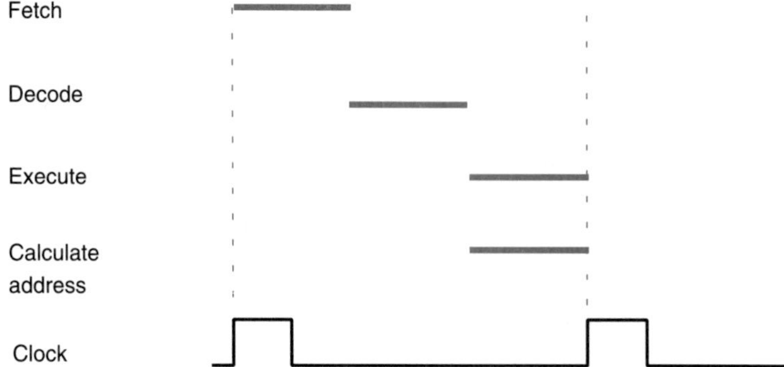

Figure 14.25 Microinstruction cycle.

14.4.5 Example of microprogrammed system

We now describe an example of a microprogrammed system. Instead of having a data subsystem designed specifically for a RTL sequence, we consider the use of a predefined ("general-purpose") data subsystem; this approach requires mapping the elements used by the RTL sequence onto elements available in the data subsystem, as illustrated in the example that follows.

Data Subsystem

Let us consider the data subsystem depicted in Figure 14.26. This is a quite general structure, suitable for a variety of RTL sequences, which consists of the following modules:

- A register file with eight registers of eight bits each. Two read and one write operations can be performed simultaneously.
- An arithmetic-logic unit (ALU) that performs the operations ADD, SUB, XOR and INC; in addition to the result of the operation, this unit also provides conditions ZERO, NEG and CY.
- An eight-bit input register.
- An eight-bit output register.

These modules are connected as shown in Figure 14.26, which also depicts the control points and conditions. The control inputs to the data subsystem are

Control signal	Description
`fld_A`	address for read port A
`fld_B`	address for read port B
`fld_C`	address for write
`ldRF`	load register file (write)
`alu_op`	operation performed in ALU 00 - ADD 01 - SUB 10 - XOR 11 - INC
`ldR_in`	load R_in
`ldR_out`	load R_out
`selR_in`	select R_in 0 - select ALU output 1 - select R_in

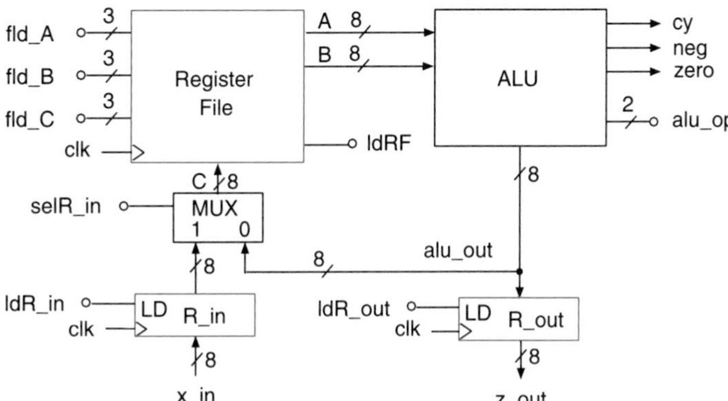

Figure 14.26 Data subsystem.

Moreover, the data subsystem generates the following conditions:

Condition	Signal	Description
`alu_out = 0`	`zero`	result is zero
`alu_out < 0`	`neg`	result is negative
`carry`	`cy`	result generated carry

The behavioral description of this data subsystem is given in Figure 14.27, in which we assume that the description of the function `alu` is available in the package `microp_pkg`.

```
LIBRARY ieee;
USE ieee.std_logic_1164.all;
USE ieee.std_logic_arith.all;

USE WORK.microp_pkg.ALL;
ENTITY microdata IS
  PORT(x_in                      : IN  SIGNED(7 DOWNTO 0);
       fld_A, fld_B, fld_C       : IN  UNSIGNED(2 DOWNTO 0);
       alu_op                    : IN  UNSIGNED(1 DOWNTO 0);
       ldR_in, ldR_out, selR_in  : IN  STD_LOGIC ;
       ldRF                      : IN  STD_LOGIC ;
       zero, neg, cy             : OUT STD_LOGIC ;
       z_out                     : OUT SIGNED(7 DOWNTO 0);
       clk                       : IN  STD_LOGIC);
END microdata;

ARCHITECTURE behavioral OF microdata IS
  TYPE   reg_fileT IS ARRAY(0 TO 7) OF SIGNED(7 DOWNTO 0);
  SIGNAL RF: reg_fileT ;
  SIGNAL R_in: SIGNED(7 DOWNTO 0);
BEGIN
  PROCESS(clk)
    VARIABLE A,B,C  : SIGNED(7 DOWNTO 0);
    VARIABLE alu_out: SIGNED(7 DOWNTO 0);
    VARIABLE zzero,nneg,ccy: STD_LOGIC;
  BEGIN                                   -- combinational modules
    A:= RF(CONV_INTEGER(fld_A));                  -- ALU
    B:= RF(CONV_INTEGER(fld_B));
    CASE alu_op IS
      WHEN "00" => alu(zzero,nneg,ccy,alu_out,A,B,op_add);
      WHEN "01" => alu(zzero,nneg,ccy,alu_out,A,B,op_sub);
      WHEN "10" => alu(zzero,nneg,ccy,alu_out,A,B,op_xor);
      WHEN "11" => alu(zzero,nneg,ccy,alu_out,A,B,op_inc);
      WHEN OTHERS => NULL;
    END CASE;
    zero <= zzero;  neg <= nneg;  cy <= ccy;
    IF (selR_in = '0') THEN C:= alu_out;     -- multiplexer
    ELSE                    C:= R_in ;
    END IF;
                                          -- register modules
    IF (clk'EVENT AND clk = '1') THEN
      IF (ldR_in  = '1') THEN R_in <= x_in    ; END IF;
      IF (ldR_out = '1') THEN z_out<= alu_out; END IF;
      IF (ldRF    = '1') THEN RF(CONV_INTEGER(fld_C))<= C; END IF;
    END IF;
  END PROCESS;
END behavioral;
```

Figure 14.27 Behavioral specification of data subsystem.

Control Subsystem

The microprogrammed control subsystem has the following inputs and outputs:

Inputs:	start
	zero, neg, cy
Outputs:	fld_A, fld_B, fld_C
	alu_op
	ldR_in, ldR_out
	selR_in, ldRF, done

Its implementation has the following characteristics:

- implicit sequencing; and
- two microinstruction formats: operations and branch, as depicted in Figure 14.28.

Field cond in the branch microinstruction format encodes four values, the start input plus the three conditions obtained from the data subsystem, as follows:

Condition	Code
start	00
zero	01
neg	10
cy	11

Field cond_val specifies the value that the corresponding condition must have for the branch operation to be executed; in other words, this field allows testing whether the corresponding condition input is either 0 or 1.

Output done is set and reset by placing a 1 in fields s_d and r_d, respectively, of the microinstruction.

The behavioral description of this control subsystem is shown in Figure 14.29 and Figure 14.30. The connections between the two subsystems are depicted in the structural description given in Figure 14.31.

As stated earlier, we now use this general microprogrammed system to implement a particular computation sequence. For pedagogical reasons, this example is quite simple; real systems consist of much more complex sequences.

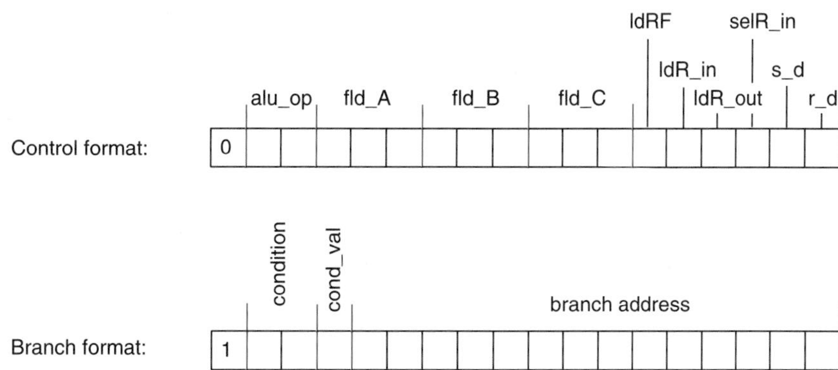

Figure 14.28 Microinstruction formats.

```
LIBRARY ieee;
USE ieee.std_logic_1164.all;
USE ieee.std_logic_arith.all;

ENTITY microctrl IS
  GENERIC(cssize: NATURAL:=16);
  PORT(start,zero,neg,cy: IN  STD_LOGIC       ;
       fld_A,fld_B,fld_C: OUT UNSIGNED(2 DOWNTO 0);
       alu_op           : OUT UNSIGNED(1 DOWNTO 0);
       ldR_in,ldR_out   : OUT STD_LOGIC       ;
       selR_in,ldRF,done: OUT STD_LOGIC       ;
       clk              : IN  STD_LOGIC      );
END microctrl;

ARCHITECTURE behav_microprogr OF microctrl IS
  SIGNAL csar     : NATURAL     ;              -- state
  SIGNAL uinstr   : UNSIGNED(17 DOWNTO 0); -- microinstruction
  ALIAS  mode     : STD_LOGIC IS uinstr(17);        -- branch mode
  ALIAS  condition: UNSIGNED(1 DOWNTO 0) IS uinstr(16 DOWNTO 15);
  ALIAS  cond_val : STD_LOGIC IS uinstr(14);        -- condition value
BEGIN
  PROCESS(clk)
    VARIABLE index: UNSIGNED(13 DOWNTO 0);
  BEGIN
    IF (clk'EVENT AND clk = '1') THEN        -- transition function
      IF (mode = '0') THEN csar <= csar + 1;
      ELSE
        CASE condition IS
          WHEN "00" => IF (start = cond_val) THEN
                         index:= uinstr(13 DOWNTO 0);
                         csar <= CONV_INTEGER(index);
                       ELSE csar <= csar + 1;
                       END IF;
          WHEN "01" => IF (zero = cond_val)  THEN
                         index:= uinstr(13 DOWNTO 0);
                         csar <= CONV_INTEGER(index);
                       ELSE csar <= csar + 1;
                       END IF;
          WHEN "10" => IF (neg = cond_val)   THEN
                         index:= uinstr(13 DOWNTO 0);
                         csar <= CONV_INTEGER(index);
                       ELSE csar <= csar + 1;
                       END IF;
          WHEN "11" => IF (cy = cond_val)    THEN
                         index:= uinstr(13 DOWNTO 0);
                         csar <= CONV_INTEGER(index);
                       ELSE csar <= csar + 1;
                       END IF;
          WHEN OTHERS => NULL;
        END CASE;
      END IF;
    END IF;
  END PROCESS;

  -- Continued in the next figure
```

Figure 14.29 Behavioral description of control subsystem: Part 1.

```
-- Continuation

PROCESS (csar)                  -- output function
  TYPE     csarray IS ARRAY(0 to cssize-1) OF UNSIGNED(17 DOWNTO 0);
  VARIABLE cs: csarray
  -- here the microprogram as initial contents of ARRAY cs
                  := (0 => "001000000000100010",
                      1 => "100000000000000001",
                      2 => "011000000011110001",
                      3 => "000000000010100100",
                      4 => "000000000111100000",
                      5 => "000010010010100000",
                      6 => "111000000000001000",
                      7 => "011111000111100000",
                      8 => "000011011011100000",
                      9 => "111000000000000101",
                     10 => "000111000111101000",
                     11 => "111000000000000000");
BEGIN
  uinstr <= cs(csar);
  CASE uinstr(17) IS           -- check mode
    WHEN '0' => alu_op <= uinstr(16 DOWNTO 15);
                fld_A  <= uinstr(14 DOWNTO 12);
                fld_B  <= uinstr(11 DOWNTO  9);
                fld_C  <= uinstr( 8 DOWNTO  6);
                ldRF   <= uinstr(5); ldR_out <= uinstr(3);
                ldR_in <= uinstr(4); selR_in <= uinstr(2);
                IF (uinstr(1) = '1') THEN done <= '1'; END IF;
                IF (uinstr(0) = '1') THEN done <= '0'; END IF;
    WHEN '1' => ldRF <= '0'; ldR_out <= '0'; ldR_in <= '0';
    WHEN OTHERS => NULL;
  END CASE;
 END PROCESS;
END behav_microprogr;
```

Figure 14.30 Behavioral description of control subsystem: Part 2.

EXAMPLE 14.3

Consider a RTL implementation of a computation to count the number of ones in an eight-bit input vector. For these purposes, let us first develop a RTL sequence and then map it onto the microprogrammed system just presented.

A simple way to count the number of ones in a bit-vector consists of shifting the vector to the left and incrementing a counter whenever the bit shifted out from the most-significant bit of the vector is 1. The corresponding specification is depicted in Figure 14.32.

To use the selected data and control subsystems, we need to

1. map registers and operations in the RTL sequence into the resources available in the data subsystem; and
2. write a microprogram for the sequence, and store it in the control store.

Mapping registers and operations is performed as follows:

- Arbitrarily assign register R2 for x, register R7 for cnt, register R3 for the loop count (variable i in the computation sequence), and register R0 to contain the value 0.
- Perform the left-shift operation of x by adding R2 to itself and storing the result in the same register.

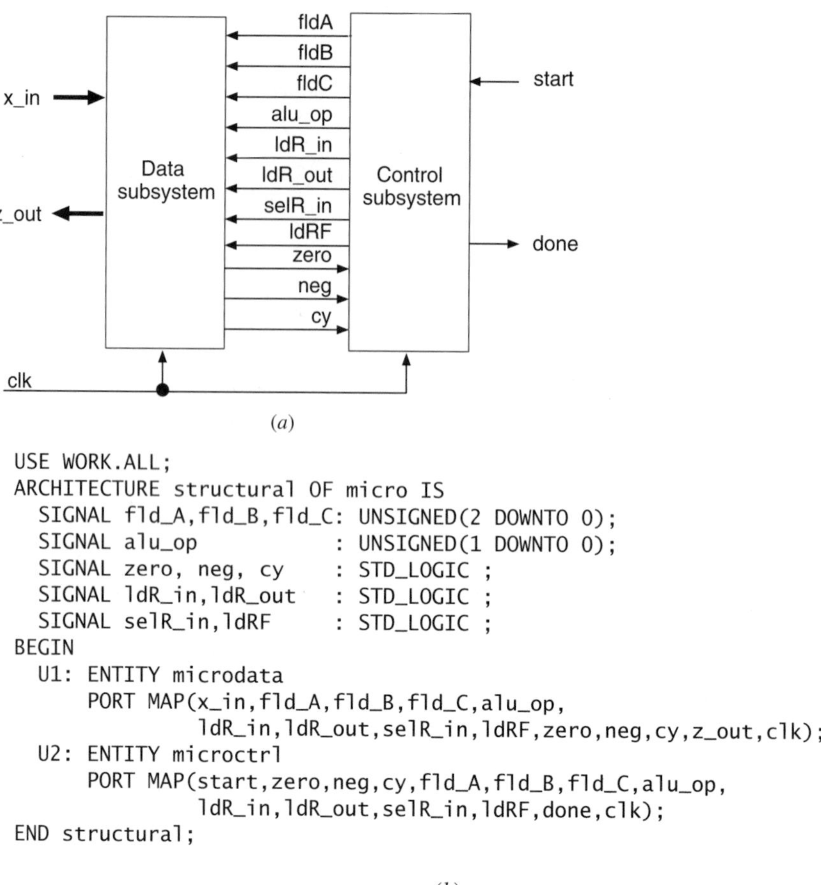

(*a*)

```
USE WORK.ALL;
ARCHITECTURE structural OF micro IS
  SIGNAL fld_A,fld_B,fld_C: UNSIGNED(2 DOWNTO 0);
  SIGNAL alu_op           : UNSIGNED(1 DOWNTO 0);
  SIGNAL zero, neg, cy    : STD_LOGIC ;
  SIGNAL ldR_in,ldR_out   : STD_LOGIC ;
  SIGNAL selR_in,ldRF     : STD_LOGIC ;
BEGIN
  U1: ENTITY microdata
      PORT MAP(x_in,fld_A,fld_B,fld_C,alu_op,
               ldR_in,ldR_out,selR_in,ldRF,zero,neg,cy,z_out,clk);
  U2: ENTITY microctrl
      PORT MAP(start,zero,neg,cy,fld_A,fld_B,fld_C,alu_op,
               ldR_in,ldR_out,selR_in,ldRF,done,clk);
END structural;
```

(*b*)

Figure 14.31 Structural description. (*a*) Block diagram. (*b*) μVHDL.

- To avoid a comparison with the constant 8, implement the loop count with a 1-out-of-8 code; that is, R3 is initialized to 1 and then added to itself (shifted left) each iteration until a carry-out appears.

The corresponding microprogram is depicted in Figure 14.33, which leads to the contents of the control store depicted in Figure 14.34. In this microprogram, microinstruction 0 prepares the system for executing the sequence by setting R0=0 and signal done=0. Microinstruction 1 implements a loop waiting for signal `start` to be 1, microinstructions 2 through 4 load the input value and initialize the count, and microinstructions 5 through 9 implement the counting process. Microinstruction 10 loads the result in the output register, and microinstruction 11 brings the controller back to the initial state. Note that this last microinstruction corresponds to an unconditional branch, implemented as a conditional branch whose condition is the carry-out from the previous operation in the ALU; such previous operation was the addition of R7+0, which never produces a carry-out. ■

```
LIBRARY ieee;
USE ieee.std_logic_1164.all;
USE ieee.std_logic_arith.all;

ENTITY micro IS
  PORT(start: IN  STD_LOGIC          ;   -- start signal
       x_in : IN  SIGNED(7 DOWNTO 0);   -- input vector
       z_out: OUT SIGNED(7 DOWNTO 0);   -- result
       done : OUT STD_LOGIC          ;   -- done signal
       clk  : IN  STD_LOGIC)         ;
END micro;

ARCHITECTURE specif OF micro IS
BEGIN
  PROCESS (start)
    VARIABLE x,cnt: SIGNED(7 DOWNTO 0);
  BEGIN
    IF (start'EVENT AND start = '1') THEN
      done <= '0';
      x:= x_in;  n:= (OTHERS => '0');
      FOR i IN 1 TO 8 LOOP
        IF (x(7) = '1') THEN cnt:= cnt+1; END IF;
        x:= x(6 DOWNTO 0) & '0' ;
      END LOOP;
      z_out <= cnt;
      done  <= '1';
    END IF;
  END PROCESS;
END specif;
```

Figure 14.32 Specification of system in Example 14.3.

	mode	alu_op	fld_			ldRF	ldR_		selR_	s_d	r_d	control format
			A	B	C		in	out	in			
	mode	(cond., cond_val)		branch address								branch format
0:	0	sub=01	0	0	0	1	0	0	0	1	0	R0 <- 0; set done
1:	1	(start,0)=000		1								branch if start = 0
2:	0	inc=11	0	0	3	1	1	0	0	0	1	input x_in; R3 <- 1; clear done
3:	0	add=00	0	0	2	1	0	0	1	0	0	R2 <- Rin;
4:	0	add=00	0	0	7	1	0	0	0	0	0	R7 <- 0;
5:	0	add=00	2	2	2	1	0	0	0	0	0	R2 <- R2+R2;
6:	1	(cy,0)=110		8								branch if cy = 0
7:	0	inc=11	7	0	7	1	0	0	0	0	0	R7 <- R7+1;
8:	0	add=00	3	3	3	1	0	0	0	0	0	R3 <- R3+R3
9:	1	(cy,0)=110		5								branch if cy = 0
10:	0	add=00	7	0	7	1	0	1	0	0	0	Rout <- R7;
11:	1	(cy,0)=110		0								done; branch to 0

Figure 14.33 Microprogram for Example 14.3.

```
-- to be included in description of control subsystem
-- (spaces inserted between fields for clarity)
   VARIABLE cs: csarray                     -- control store
                    := (0 => "0 01 000 000 000 1 00 0 10",
                        1 => "1 000       00000000000001",
                        2 => "0 11 000 000 011 1 10 0 01",
                        3 => "0 00 000 000 010 1 00 1 00",
                        4 => "0 00 000 000 111 1 00 0 00",
                        5 => "0 00 010 010 010 1 00 0 00",
                        6 => "1 110       00000000001000",
                        7 => "0 11 111 000 111 1 00 0 00",
                        8 => "0 00 011 011 011 1 00 0 00",
                        9 => "1 110       00000000000101",
                       10 => "0 00 111 000 111 1 01 0 00",
                       11 => "1 110       00000000000000");
```

Figure 14.34 Control store contents for Example 14.3.

14.5 FURTHER READINGS

Data and control subsystems are discussed in many books on digital design. We mention the following: *Digital Systems and Hardware/Firmware Algorithms* by M. Ercegovac and T. Lang, Wiley, New York, 1985; *The Art of Digital Design* by F. P. Prosser and D. E. Winkel, Prentice-Hall, Englewood Cliffs, NJ, 1987; *Computation Structures* by S. A. Ward and R. H. Halstead, Jr., McGraw-Hill, New York, 1990; *Introduction to Digital Logic Design* by J. P. Hayes, Addison Wesley, Reading, MA, 1993; *Contemporary Logic Design* by R. H. Katz, The Benjamin Cummings Pub. Co., Redwood City, CA, 1994; and *Principles of Digital Design* by D. D. Gajski, Prentice-Hall, Englewood Cliffs, NJ, 1997. A detailed discussion of microprogramming is given in *Principles of Firmware Engineering in Microprogram Control* by M. Andrews, Computer Science Press, Potomac, MD, 1980.

EXERCISES

Data subsystem

Exercise 14.1 Design a 2-read/1-write register file with 16 words of 8 bits each. Use 8-bit registers, 4-input decoders, and NAND gates (if necessary).

Exercise 14.2 A **sequential-access** memory (SAM) stores bit-vectors in such a way that the access time depends on the address of the bit-vector to be operated upon. Specifically, for a SAM of 2^n words, if i is the address of the most-recently accessed word, then the time to access the word at address j is

$$T = C_1((i - j) \bmod 2^n) + C_2$$

where C_1 and C_2 are implementation-dependent constants. In a typical implementation of a SAM, the storage is organized as a shift register and the READ/WRITE operations are performed only on one cell of the register.

a. Give a computation sequence that describes the READ and WRITE operations, taking into account this shift-register organization but no other implementation aspects.
b. Design a data section for this sequence. Make a diagram of all components and connections and give a list of registers, operators, datapaths, control points, and conditions.

Exercise 14.3 The access time of a sequential-access memory depends linearly on the distance between the addresses of two consecutive accesses. Determine the average access time for the following three cases:

a. The distance between addresses of consecutive accesses is uniformly distributed on the whole address space.
b. The distance between addresses of consecutive accesses is always one.
c. The accesses are made in blocks of k words, that is, the distance between addresses of consecutive accesses is one for a block of k accesses, after which another block is accessed, the initial address of the block being uniformly distributed.

Exercise 14.4 A **direct-access** memory has an access mechanism that is a combination of random-access and sequential-access. For an access, the address A is divided into two parts $A_R = A/M$ and $A_S = A \bmod M$. The first part (A_R) is used to select a portion of the memory with a random-access mechanism; within this portion, the access is done sequentially using A_S.

a. Design a direct-access memory with 16K words of eight bits each, for $M = 16$. Use shift-registers, decoders, and NAND gates (if necessary).
b. Determine the average access time for the design of part (a), for the three situations described in Exercise 14.3.

Exercise 14.5 A data section contains four registers `R1` to `R4`, and two operators `P1` and `P2`. Each register has one input and one output, and each operator has two inputs and one output. To distinguish the two inputs of an operator, we call them `LPi` and `RPi`, respectively, where `i` identifies the operator. The computation sequence to be executed in the data section requires the following data transfers (data transfers in one line are done simultaneously):

```
R3  <= R1; LP1 <= R2; RP1 <= R1; R1 <= P1;
LP2 <= R3; RP2 <= R4; R4  <= P2;
R2  <= R4; LP1 <= R2; RP1 <= R1; R1 <= P1;
LP2 <= R2; RP2 <= R3; R2  <= P2;
```

Design the datapaths consisting of the minimum connections required to perform these transfers.

Exercise 14.6 Figure 14.35 shows the datapaths of a data section, where `R3,R4`, and `R5` have three-state outputs. Describe all the statements that can be implemented directly by the datapaths.

Control subsystem

Exercise 14.7 Consider the following system description:

```
ENTITY exercise IS
  PORT (X,Y : IN  Bit_Vector(7 DOWNTO 0) ;
        s   : IN  BIT                    ;
        C   : OUT Bit_Vector(7 DOWNTO 0));
END exercise;
```

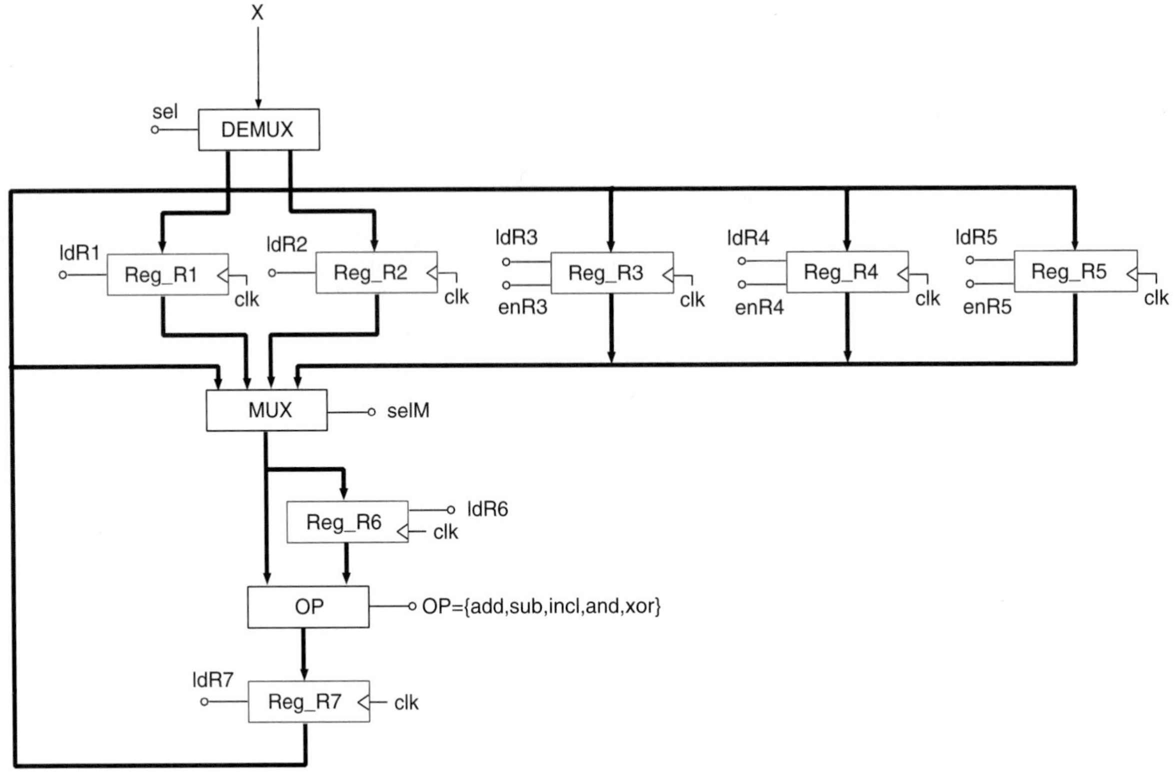

Figure 14.35 Data subsystem for Exercise 14.6.

```
ARCHITECTURE simple OF exercise IS
  SIGNAL state: NATURAL RANGE 0 TO 6:= 0;
  SIGNAL A,B   : Bit_Vector(7 DOWNTO 0)
BEGIN
  PROCESS (clk)
  BEGIN
    CASE state IS
      WHEN 0 => IF (s = '1') THEN state <= 1; END IF;
      WHEN 1 => B <= X; A <= Y; state <= 2;
      WHEN 2 => A <= A + B;
                IF (A(7) = '1') THEN state <= 5;
                ELSE                 state <= 3;
                END IF;
      WHEN 3 => A <= NOT(A); state <= 4;
      WHEN 4 => A <= A + 1 ; state <= 6;
      WHEN 5 => B <= B + 1 ; state <= 6;
      WHEN 6 => C <= A + B ; state <= 0;
    END CASE;
  END PROCESS;
```

a. If the initial values in the registers are X = 00101110 and Y = 11100010, determine the value of A, B, and C after the execution.
b. Design a data section that is adequate to execute the RTL sequence.
c. Give a state diagram of the control subsystem and implement it using a multiplexer, a counter, a decoder, and gates.
d. Repeat the design of the control subsystem using the one-flip-flop-per-state approach.

Design of systems

Exercise 14.8 Determine a RTL sequence, and design the data and control subsections of a system, for the following computation. The control section should be designed using two alternative approaches, one of them being PLA based.

The input is a sequence of positive integers in the range 0 to 127. The value 127 is used as a delimiter to separate sequences. The output is generated at the end of each sequence to indicate the number of elements in the sequence (`COUNT`), the smallest element (`MIN`), and the largest (`MAX`). Assume that the sequence can have, at most, 50 elements.

Exercise 14.9 The following system computes an approximation to the square root of a positive integer.

```
ENTITY square_root IS
  PORT (number_in: IN  INTEGER;
        root_out : OUT REAL);
END square_root;

ARCHITECTURE high_level OF square_root IS
  SIGNAL root: REAL;
BEGIN
  PROCESS (number_in)
    VARIABLE eps : REAL:= 10**(-6);
  BEGIN
    root <= 1.0;
    WHILE (ABS((number_in/(root**2) - 1) < eps) LOOP
      root <= ((number_in/root) + root))/2;
    END LOOP;
  END PROCESS;
END high_level;
```

Design a data section and a control section to implement the system. Assume that the integer is received in register `NUMBER` and the output is left in register `ROOT`. Assume that the following operators are available: `ABS` (absolute value), `DIV`, `ADD`, `MUL`, and `COMPARE`. For the control section use two approaches, one of them PLA based.

Microprogrammed control

Exercise 14.10 An implementation for computing the number of ones in a bit-vector is described in Section 14.4.5. The RTL sequence is based on the fact that the operator in the data section is an adder. Develop alternative sequences and design the data and microprogrammed control subsystem for the following available operators:

a. Two counters and one shift register.
b. One counter and one shift register.
c. Just one counter.

Exercise 14.11 A digital system has the data subsystem shown in Figure 14.36.

a. Obtain a RTL sequence to load in $R0$ the maximum of the values stored in the eight registers. The values in the other registers should be the same at the end of the algorithm as before. The contents of registers $R8$ and $R9$ need not be preserved.
b. Write a microprogram for the RTL sequence in (a) using an horizontal microinstruction format with implicit sequencing.

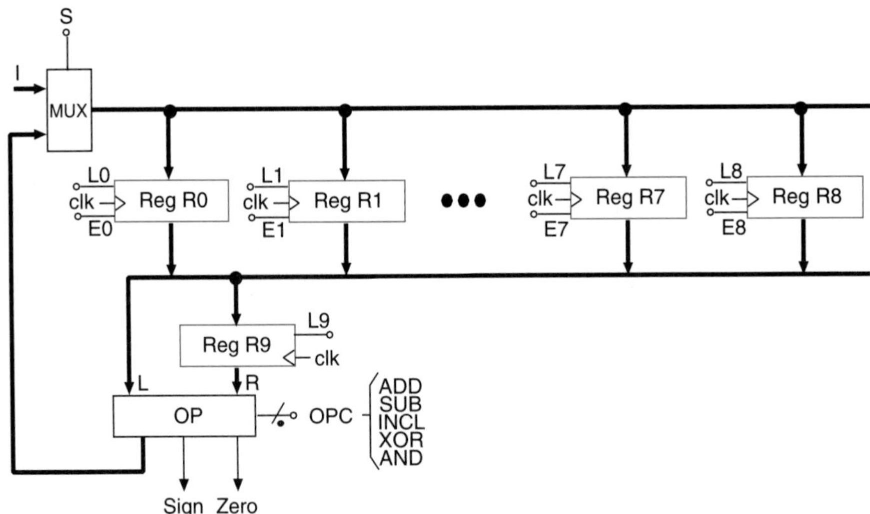

Figure 14.36 Data subsystem for Exercise 14.11.

Exercise 14.12 Use the Bubblesort algorithm to sort n integers stored in locations 0 through $n - 1$ of a RAM. The specification of Bubblesort is

```
BEGIN
  PROCESS (start)
    VARIABLE i,j : INTEGER;
  BEGIN
    j := n-1;
    WHILE (j > 0) LOOP
      i := 0;
      WHILE (i < j) LOOP
        IF (M(i) > M(i+1)) THEN
           Exchange (M(i),M(i+1));
           i := i+1;
        END IF;
        j := j-1;
      END LOOP;
    END LOOP;
  END PROCESS;
```

The n integers are stored in a 256 by eight-bit words RAM. Design the data subsystem for the corresponding RTL sequence. Design the control subsystem using a microprogrammed controller with horizontal format and explicit sequencing.

First-in/first-out (FIFO) memory

Exercise 14.13 A **first-in/first-out (FIFO) memory** or **queue** (see Figure 14.37) performs two operations: write and read. In a write operation, the data are placed at the end of the queue; that is, bit-vectors are stored in the order in which they are written into the memory. On the other hand, data are read from the beginning of the queue and deleted from the memory. Because of this predefined access order, a FIFO does not require an external address. A FIFO memory also provides two conditions, `empty` and `full`, which respectively indicate when `read` and `write` operations cannot be performed. A FIFO would be used, for example, to store data waiting for service at some computing resource; data would then be serviced in the order received.

a. Design the data subsystem.
b. Design the control subsystem.

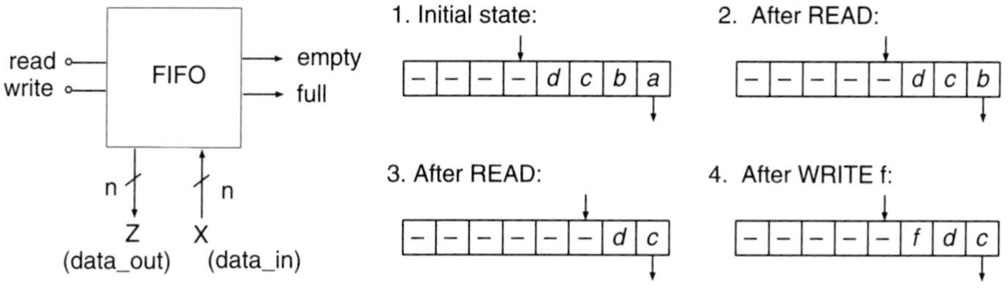

```
ENTITY fifo IS
  GENERIC(n: NATURAL:= 16);          -- FIFO size
  PORT(X          : IN  BIT_VECTOR(15 DOWNTO 0);  -- input bit-vector
       Z          : OUT BIT_VECTOR(15 DOWNTO 0);  -- output bit-vector
       Rd,Wr      : IN  BIT;          -- read,write control signals
       Empty,Full: OUT BIT;          -- condition signals
       Clk        : IN  BIT);
END fifo;

ARCHITECTURE behavioral OF fifo IS
  TYPE   StorageT IS ARRAY(0 TO n-1) OF BIT_VECTOR(15 DOWNTO 0);
  SIGNAL fifo: StorageT;              -- FIFO memory
  SIGNAL last: INTEGER RANGE -1 TO n-1;
BEGIN
  PROCESS (Clk)
  BEGIN
    IF (Clk = '1') AND (Wr = '1') THEN     -- write operation
      IF (last=n-1) THEN NULL;             -- fifo already full
      ELSE
        IF (last=n-2) THEN Full  <= '1'; END IF;
        IF (last=-1 ) THEN Empty <= '0'; END IF;
        fifo(last+1) <= X;
        last         <= last+1;
      END IF;
    ELSIF (Clk = '1') AND (Rd = '1') THEN  -- read operation
      IF (last=-1) THEN NULL;              -- fifo already empty
      ELSE
        Z <= fifo(0);
        FOR i IN 0 TO last-1 LOOP
          fifo(i)<= fifo(i+1);
        END LOOP;
        IF (last = 0) THEN Empty <= '1'; END IF;
        last <= last-1; Full <= '0';
      END IF;
    END IF;
  END PROCESS;
END behavioral;
```

(c)

Figure 14.37 FIFO. (*a*) Module. (*b*) Examples of read/write operations. (*c*) Behavioral description.

Last-in/first-out (LIFO) memory

Exercise 14.14 A **last-in/first-out** (LIFO) memory or **stack memory** (see Figure 14.38) stores bit-vectors in the order in which they were written into the memory; however, in a read operation, the **most-recently entered** vector (the top of the stack, last in) is transferred to the output and deleted from the stack. As in the case of a LIFO, no external address is needed because the access is always

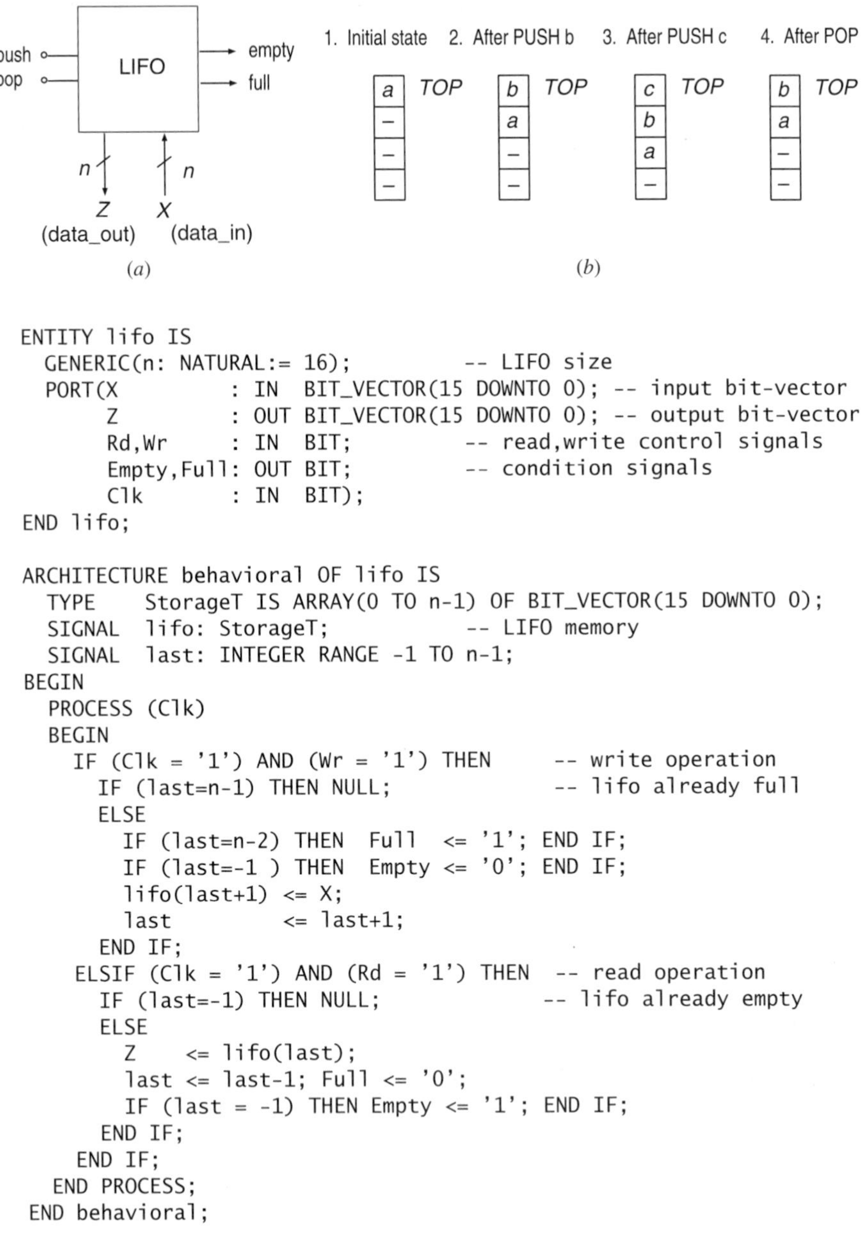


```
ENTITY lifo IS
  GENERIC(n: NATURAL:= 16);           -- LIFO size
  PORT(X          : IN  BIT_VECTOR(15 DOWNTO 0); -- input bit-vector
       Z          : OUT BIT_VECTOR(15 DOWNTO 0); -- output bit-vector
       Rd,Wr      : IN  BIT;          -- read,write control signals
       Empty,Full: OUT BIT;           -- condition signals
       Clk        : IN  BIT);
END lifo;

ARCHITECTURE behavioral OF lifo IS
  TYPE    StorageT IS ARRAY(0 TO n-1) OF BIT_VECTOR(15 DOWNTO 0);
  SIGNAL  lifo: StorageT;             -- LIFO memory
  SIGNAL  last: INTEGER RANGE -1 TO n-1;
BEGIN
  PROCESS (Clk)
  BEGIN
    IF (Clk = '1') AND (Wr = '1') THEN      -- write operation
      IF (last=n-1) THEN NULL;              -- lifo already full
      ELSE
        IF (last=n-2) THEN  Full  <= '1'; END IF;
        IF (last=-1 ) THEN  Empty <= '0'; END IF;
        lifo(last+1) <= X;
        last         <= last+1;
      END IF;
    ELSIF (Clk = '1') AND (Rd = '1') THEN  -- read operation
      IF (last=-1) THEN NULL;              -- lifo already empty
      ELSE
        Z    <= lifo(last);
        last <= last-1; Full <= '0';
        IF (last = -1) THEN Empty <= '1'; END IF;
      END IF;
    END IF;
  END PROCESS;
END behavioral;
```

(c)

Figure 14.38 LIFO. (*a*) Module. (*b*) Examples of read/write operations. (*c*) Behavioral description.

performed to the top of the stack. Read and write operations are usually called `push` and `pop`, respectively. A stack also provides `empty` and `full` conditions. A LIFO memory would be used, for example, when a sequence of events is to be traced in an order that is the reverse of the order of occurrence.

a. Design the data subsystem.
b. Design the control subsystem.

Chapter **15**

Specification and Implementation of a Microcomputer

In this chapter, we discuss

- The basic components of a microcomputer system.
- The informal and μVHDL-based description of the architecture and implementation of a simple microcomputer system.
- The operation of the simple microcomputer system and its cycle time.

A microcomputer[1] is a **general-purpose system;** that is, the system is organized in such a way that it can perform a large variety of computations. To achieve this objective, each computation is represented by a sequence of instructions (a **program**) that is stored in a read-write memory and is **executed** by the microcomputer. The execution of the instructions produces transformations on the data. In this way, changing the computation consists just of loading a different program in the memory.

The main advantage of a microcomputer with respect to the single-computation systems described in previous chapters is its generality. However, for a specific computation, such a generality results in more silicon area in an implementation (more modules) than the single-computation counterpart, and in a degradation of the speed of execution of the computation.

The implementation of a computation using a microcomputer is usually called a **software solution**, because it consists of writing a program and executing it in a computer. In contrast, the implementation of a computation using a dedicated digital system is called a **hardware solution.**

Modern microcomputers are very complex systems, so it is out of the scope of this text to present a comprehensive discussion of their specification, implementation, programming, and use. This chapter presents the basic concepts, and shows that the methods discussed in previous chapters are applicable to digital computers. Thus, this chapter should provide a suitable starting point for further detailed studies.

[1]The term microcomputer reflects the fact that a microprocessor (single chip) is used. Since today most computers use single-chip processors, the term is almost equivalent to computer.

Instead of presenting the concepts in a general fashion, we develop them around the description of a simple microcomputer system. We begin with the specification of the microcomputer system, and the description of how computations are represented for execution by this system. This level of description is called the **architecture** of the system. Then, we present an implementation. We give informal as well as descriptions in μVHDL; moreover, a complete description of the system in μVHDL is given in Section 15.5.

15.1 BASIC COMPONENTS OF A MICROCOMPUTER

A microcomputer system consists of three subsystems, as illustrated in Figure 15.1:

- a **processor;**
- a **memory subsystem;** and
- an **input/output (I/O) subsystem.**

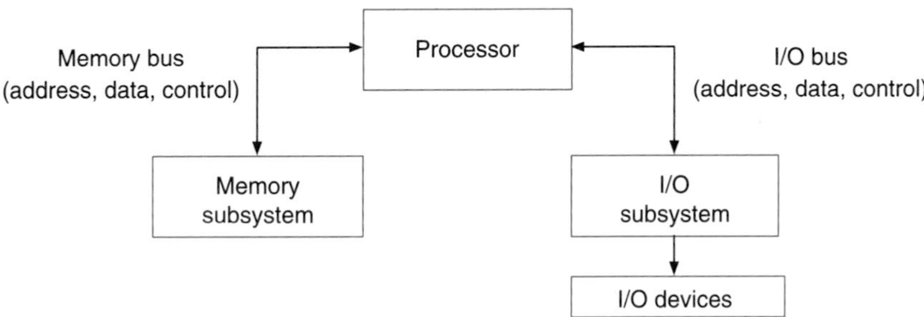

Figure 15.1 Microcomputer system.

The **processor** is the computing engine of the microcomputer: it executes the sequence of instructions, that is, the program. Because it is the fundamental component of a computer system, a processor is also known as the **central processing unit** (CPU).

The **memory subsystem** stores the program as well as the data used by the program. Some computers have separate memory subsystems for the program and for the data, although the prevalent approach used nowadays is one subsystem that is shared for both functions. The memory is divided into **locations**, such as bytes and words; these locations are identified by their **address**.

A memory operation is used to read or write one memory location. In a read operation, the processor provides the address and receives the data read from the location addressed. On the other hand, in a write operation the processor provides both the address and the data to be stored at the corresponding location.

Modern computer systems implement **virtual memory**, in which a very large memory is available to the programmer (2^{32} or 2^{64} locations, each of one byte); such a memory is implemented as a hierarchy of levels ranging from fast semiconductor devices up to disk storage (see Figure 15.2). Because large semiconductor memories have access time equivalent to several processor cycles, using a single level of semiconductor memory for instruction fetch or for load/store operations would degrade the performance of the system (the processor would have to spend cycles waiting for the memory accesses to complete). To reduce this degradation, the semiconductor memory is implemented as two levels of the hierarchy:

- a small (fast) memory (implemented by static RAM), called a **cache memory**, which contains the portions of a program (data and instructions) being used at a given point in time; and

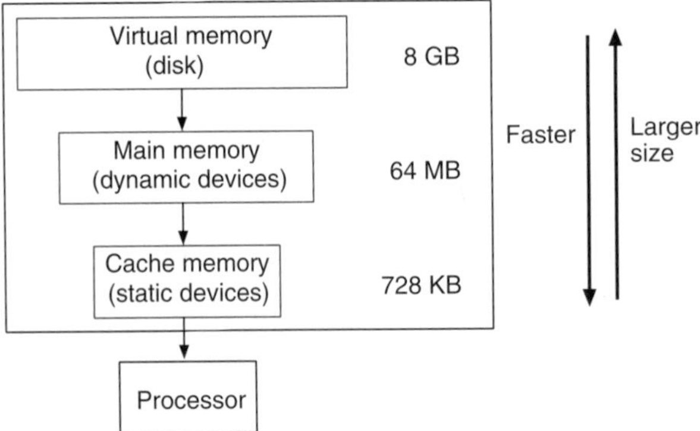

Figure 15.2 Memory hierarchy in a computer.

- a large (slower) memory (implemented by dynamic RAM, which is slower but less expensive per bit), called the **main memory**.

With this structure, the processor finds instructions and data in the cache most of the time, resulting in an overall semiconductor memory subsystem whose size is determined by the dynamic devices but whose average access time approaches that of the static devices (the cache memory). In practice, contemporary systems may have several levels of cache memory.

The **I/O subsystem** contains the interfaces between the microcomputer system and external devices, such as keyboards, monitors, printers, and modems; these interfaces allow the exchange of information between the microcomputer and the external world. In a similar manner as done for memory locations, each specific interface—called an **I/O port**—is identified by an address and the transfer of data is done in units such as bytes or words.

The connections of the processor with the memory and with the I/O subsystem are called the **memory bus** and the **I/O bus**, respectively. These buses consist of sub-buses corresponding to the address, the data, and the control parts.

Note that each of the three subsystems is in itself a sequential system, so that each one can be described and implemented using the techniques for sequential systems studied in previous chapters. Because of the complexity of the systems, register-transfer level descriptions are most suitable.

In terms of these components, the basic operation of a microcomputer consists of the repetition of the following **instruction loop:**

1. The processor reads an instruction from the memory (instruction fetch), by providing an **instruction address.**
2. The processor

   a. performs the operations specified by the instruction, and
   b. determines the location in memory of the next instruction.

   The operations might

   - operate on data that the processor already has internally;
   - bring data from the memory or the I/0 subsystem; or
   - store data in the memory or transfer it to the I/O subsystem.

As stated earlier, the detailed description of the structure of a microcomputer system, including virtual memory, cache memory and I/O devices, is beyond the scope of this text. For simplicity, we do not consider virtual memory in the rest of this chapter; furthermore, we assume that the memory of the microcomputer system described next is composed entirely of static memory whose access time is shorter than one processor cycle. In addition, we do not describe the I/O devices attached to the microcomputer neither the signals connecting to/from those devices.

15.2 SPECIFICATION (ARCHITECTURE) OF A SIMPLE MICROCOMPUTER SYSTEM

We now illustrate the specification of a computer system by presenting a simple microcomputer which we call XMC (eXample MicroComputer). Figure 15.3 shows its components—the processor, memory and input/output subsystems—and the connections between them. The memory bus and I/O bus are composed of the following signals:

- an **address bus**, which identifies the memory location or I/O port being accessed. The memory address bus has 24 lines (to address up to 2^{24} locations) whereas the I/O address bus has 11 lines (to address 2^{11} ports).
- **control signals**, which indicate the type of access being performed (read or write), the length of the operand (byte or word), and an enabling signal;
- a **status signal**, which indicates the state (busy, ready) of the memory or I/O subsystem; and
- a **data bus**, which transfers the data to/from the processor and the memory or I/O subsystem. These data buses have 32 lines for 32-bit data items.

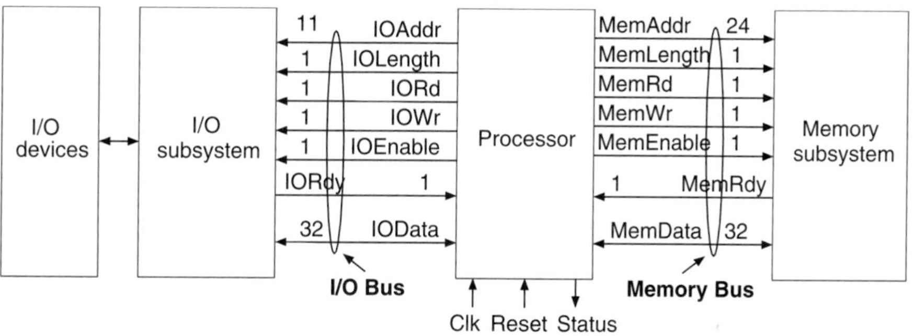

Figure 15.3 Structure of XMC.

The processor also has an output signal called `Status`, which is used to indicate the activity within the instruction cycle (this signal is useful to follow the activity on the processor cycle by cycle). Because we do not describe the I/O devices, the only external inputs to XMC are the clock and reset signals.

The corresponding μVHDL structural description is as follows, in which we use the package `ieee.std_logic_1164` as well as the package `comp_pkg` defined below.

```
LIBRARY ieee;
USE ieee.std_logic_1164.all;

PACKAGE comp_pkg IS
  SUBTYPE WordT   IS STD_LOGIC_VECTOR(31 DOWNTO 0);
  SUBTYPE MAddrT  IS STD_LOGIC_VECTOR(23 DOWNTO 0);
  SUBTYPE IOAddrT IS STD_LOGIC_VECTOR(10 DOWNTO 0);
  SUBTYPE ByteT   IS STD_LOGIC_VECTOR( 7 DOWNTO 0);
  TYPE    StatusT IS (undef, p_reset, fetch, execute, memop, ioop);
```

```
  FUNCTION get_carry(RA_Data,RB_Data,Imm,Opcode: STD_LOGIC_VECTOR)
           RETURN STD_LOGIC;
  FUNCTION get_ovf (RA_Data,RB_Data,Imm,Opcode: STD_LOGIC_VECTOR)
           RETURN STD_LOGIC;
  FUNCTION get_cc  (RA_Data,RB_Data,Opcode: STD_LOGIC_VECTOR)
           RETURN STD_LOGIC_VECTOR;
END comp_pkg;

PACKAGE BODY comp_pkg IS
  FUNCTION get_carry(RA_Data,RB_Data,Imm,Opcode: STD_LOGIC_VECTOR)
           RETURN STD_LOGIC
  IS
    VARIABLE cy: STD_LOGIC:= '0';
  BEGIN
      -- description of carry generation included here
      RETURN(cy);
  END get_carry;

  FUNCTION get_ovf (RA_Data,RB_Data,Imm,Opcode: STD_LOGIC_VECTOR)
           RETURN STD_LOGIC
  IS
      VARIABLE ovf: STD_LOGIC:= '0';
  BEGIN
      -- description of overflow generation included here
      RETURN(ovf);
  END get_ovf;

  FUNCTION get_cc (RA_Data,RB_Data,Opcode: STD_LOGIC_VECTOR)
           RETURN STD_LOGIC_VECTOR
  IS
      VARIABLE cc: STD_LOGIC_VECTOR(3 DOWNTO 0):= "0000";
  BEGIN
      -- description of cc generation included here
      RETURN(cc);
  END get_cc;
END comp_pkg;


LIBRARY ieee;
USE ieee.std_logic_1164.ALL;
USE WORK.ALL, WORK.comp_pkg.ALL;

ENTITY Computer IS
  PORT (Reset, Clk : IN STD_LOGIC);
END Computer;

ARCHITECTURE structural OF Computer IS
  SIGNAL MemAddr           : MAddrT    ;  -- memory address bus
  SIGNAL MemLength, MemRd  : STD_LOGIC;   -- memory control signals
  SIGNAL MemWr, MemEnable  : STD_LOGIC;
  SIGNAL MemRdy            : STD_LOGIC;   -- memory status signal
  SIGNAL MemData           : WordT     ;  -- memory data bus

  SIGNAL IOAddr            : IOAddrT   ;  -- I/O address bus
  SIGNAL IOLength, IORd    : STD_LOGIC;   -- I/O control signals
  SIGNAL IOWr, IOEnable    : STD_LOGIC;
  SIGNAL IORdy             : STD_LOGIC;   -- I/O status signal
  SIGNAL IOData            : WordT     ;  -- I/O data bus

  SIGNAL Status            : StatusT;
```

```
BEGIN
  U1: ENTITY Memory
      PORT MAP (MemAddr, MemLength, MemRd, MemWr, MemEnable,
                MemRdy, MemData);

  U2: ENTITY IO
      PORT MAP (IOAddr, IOLength, IORd, IOWr, IOEnable,
                IORdy, IOData);

  U3: ENTITY Processor
      PORT MAP (MemAddr, MemData, MemLength, MemRd, MemWr,
                MemEnable, MemRdy,
                IOAddr,  IOData,  IOLength,  IORd,  IOWr,
                IOEnable, IORdy,
                Status, Reset, Clk);
END structural;
```

15.2.1 Memory Subsystem

The memory addresses produced by the processor have 24 bits. Consequently, the memory subsystem (see Figure 15.4*a*) is an array of 2^{24} locations, each of one byte, for a total of 16 MB; this is typical for a computer workstation (circa 1997). Memory addresses range from 0 to $2^{24} - 1$.

Memory can be accessed as bytes or as 32-bit words, organized as indicated in Figure 15.4*b*. Successive byte addresses differ by 1, with successive addresses allocated from

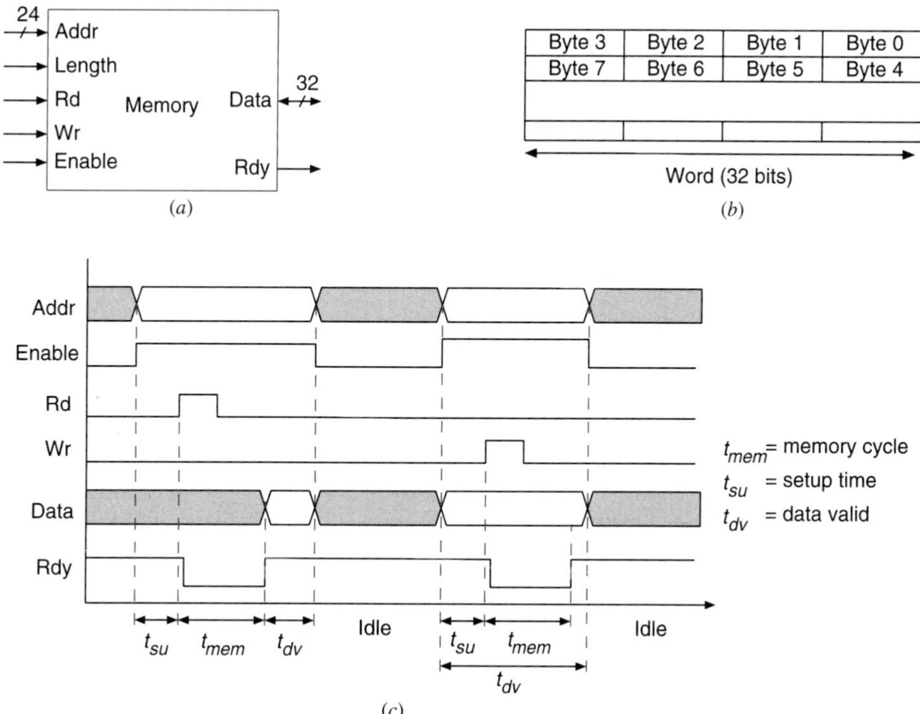

Figure 15.4 Memory subsystem. (*a*) External signals. (*b*) Internal organization. (*c*) Timing diagram.

least-significant to most-significant positions within a word. The address of a word is the address of the least-significant byte within the word.

The data bus to/from the memory is 32-bits wide. In the case of accessing a byte, as indicated by the input signal Length, the 8 least-significant bits of the bus are used to transfer the corresponding data.

The μVHDL entity declaration for this memory subsystem is as follows:

```
LIBRARY ieee;
USE ieee.std_logic_1164.all;
USE WORK.comp_pkg.ALL;

ENTITY Memory IS
  PORT (Addr      : IN     MAddrT    ; -- memory address bus
        Length    : IN     STD_LOGIC; -- byte/word operand
        Rd, Wr    : IN     STD_LOGIC; -- access control signals
        Enable    : IN     STD_LOGIC; -- enable signal
        Rdy       : OUT    STD_LOGIC; -- access completion signal
        Data      : INOUT  WordT   ); -- memory data bus
END Memory;
```

The operation of the memory is as follows (see Figure 15.4*c*):

- for the memory subsystem to be active, the Enable signal has to be set to 1;
- the subsystem responds to an event in either one of the control signals Rd or Wr (which are never active simultaneously); depending on which of these control signal is active, a memory read or a memory write operation is performed for an operand of the length specified in signal Length (0: byte, 1: word);
- the address of the memory location accessed is specified in signal Addr; in case of word accesses, the two lowermost bits of the address are ignored (they are assumed to be 00);
- the data is transferred through signal Data;
- the completion of a memory operation is indicated by signal Rdy; this signal is set to 0 while the operation is in progress and to 1 when the operation finishes.

With respect to the timing of signals,

- signals Addr and Enable must be stable before signals Rd or Wr become active (setup time);
- for a read operation, signals Addr and Enable must be stable until signal Rdy becomes 1; the data accessed from memory remain stable in signal Data until signal Enable becomes 0 (data valid time);
- for a write operation, in addition to signals Addr and Enable, the signal Data must also be stable until Rdy becomes 1.

Finally, with respect to consecutive operations, the following situations have to be distinguished:

- read followed by read, write followed by write, and write followed by read can be performed keeping signal Enable set to 1; for each operation, a pulse is required in the corresponding signal Rd or Wr;
- a read followed by a write requires that signal Enable is set to 0 and then set again to 1; this transition is required to reverse the direction of the data bus and to remove the data placed by the memory in the data bus during read operation.

Note that the operation of the memory subsystem is not synchronized by a clock signal; instead, memory operations are performed in response to the memory control signals. An active control signal (Rd or Wr) initiates the operation of the module; signal Rdy is set to 0 while the module is busy. Furthermore, the module does not accept further requests until the current memory access has completed.

The complete specification of a memory subsystem includes additional timing information such as hold times for the different signals; for simplicity, we do not include those specifications in this description.

A behavioral description of the memory subsystem is given next, which includes the verification of the timing constraints previously given.

```
LIBRARY ieee;
USE ieee.std_logic_unsigned.ALL;

ARCHITECTURE behavioral OF Memory IS
  CONSTANT Tmem   : TIME :=   8 ns;    -- nanoseconds (static memory)
  CONSTANT Td     : TIME := 200 ps;    -- picoseconds
  CONSTANT Tsu    : TIME := 200 ps;    -- picoseconds
BEGIN
PROCESS (Rd, Wr, Enable)
  CONSTANT byte_l: STD_LOGIC:= '0';    -- constant declarations
  CONSTANT word_l: STD_LOGIC:= '1';
                                       -- memory declaration
  CONSTANT MaxMem    : NATURAL := 16#FFFFFF#;  -- 2**24 bytes
  TYPE     MemArrayT IS ARRAY(0 TO MaxMem-1) OF ByteT;
  VARIABLE Mem    : MemArrayT;
                                       -- working variables
  VARIABLE tAddr  : NATURAL;
  VARIABLE tData  : WordT  ;
  VARIABLE tCtrls: STD_LOGIC_VECTOR(2 DOWNTO 0);

  BEGIN
    tCtrls:= Rd & Wr & Enable; -- group signals for simpler decoding
    CASE tCtrls IS
                                             -- output to tri-state
      WHEN "000" => Data <= (OTHERS => 'Z') AFTER Td;

      WHEN "011" =>                          -- write access;
                                             -- indicate module busy
            Rdy <= '0' AFTER Td, '1' AFTER Tmem;
            IF (Length = byte_l) THEN        -- compute address
              tAddr:= CONV_INTEGER(Addr);    -- bit-vector to integer
                                             -- from pkg std_logic_unsigned
            ELSE
              tAddr:= CONV_INTEGER(Addr(23 DOWNTO 2) & "00");
            END IF;
            CASE Length IS
              WHEN byte_l => Mem(tAddr)   := Data( 7 DOWNTO  0);
              WHEN word_l => Mem(tAddr)   := Data( 7 DOWNTO  0);
                             Mem(tAddr+1):= Data(15 DOWNTO  8);
                             Mem(tAddr+2):= Data(23 DOWNTO 16);
                             Mem(tAddr+3):= Data(31 DOWNTO 24);
              WHEN OTHERS => NULL;
            END CASE;

      WHEN "101" =>                          -- read access
                                             -- indicate module busy
```

```
                Rdy <= '0' AFTER Td, '1' AFTER Tmem;
                IF (Length = byte_l) THEN         -- compute address
                  tAddr:= CONV_INTEGER(Addr);     -- bit-vector to integer
                ELSE
                  tAddr:= CONV_INTEGER(Addr(23 DOWNTO 2) & "00");
                END IF;
                CASE Length IS
                  WHEN byte_l => tData( 7 DOWNTO  0):= Mem(tAddr);
                  WHEN word_l => tData( 7 DOWNTO  0):= Mem(tAddr);
                                 tData(15 DOWNTO  8):= Mem(tAddr+1);
                                 tData(23 DOWNTO 16):= Mem(tAddr+2);
                                 tData(31 DOWNTO 24):= Mem(tAddr+3);
                  WHEN OTHERS => NULL;
                END CASE;
                Data <= tData AFTER Tmem; -- deliver data

        WHEN OTHERS => NULL;                 -- memory not enabled
      END CASE;
    END PROCESS;

                                             -- timing verifications
    ASSERT NOT (Rd'EVENT AND Rd='1' AND NOT Addr'STABLE(Tsu))
       REPORT "Read address setup time violation";

    ASSERT NOT (Rd'EVENT AND Rd='1' AND NOT Enable'STABLE(Tsu))
       REPORT "Read enable setup time violation";

    ASSERT NOT (Wr'EVENT AND Wr='1' AND NOT Addr'STABLE(Tsu))
       REPORT "Write address setup time violation";

    ASSERT NOT (Wr'EVENT AND Wr='1' AND NOT Enable'STABLE(Tsu))
       REPORT "Write enable setup time violation";

  END behavioral;
```

15.2.2 Input/output (I/O) Subsystem

The I/O subsystem contains the interfaces to devices that allow transferring data in/out to/from the computer. These interfaces are accessed as an array of 2048 ports (see Figure 15.5), so that I/O addresses range from 0 to $2^{11} - 1$.

The μVHDL entity declaration for this I/O subsystem is as follows:

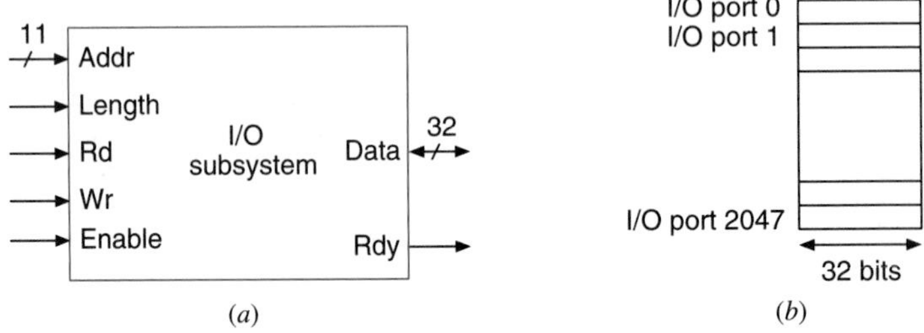

Figure 15.5 Input/output subsystem.

```
LIBRARY ieee;
USE ieee.std_logic_1164.all;
USE WORK.comp_pkg.ALL;
ENTITY IO IS
  PORT (Addr     : IN     IOAddrT   ; -- I/O address bus
        Length   : IN     STD_LOGIC; -- byte/word control
        Rd, Wr   : IN     STD_LOGIC; -- I/O access control
        Enable   : IN     STD_LOGIC; -- I/O enable control
        Rdy      : OUT    STD_LOGIC; -- I/O completion signal
        Data     : INOUT  WordT    ); -- I/O data bus
END IO;
```

The general behavior of the I/O subsystem is the same as that of the memory, except that the address spaces are different. The module responds to an event in either one of the control signals `Rd,Wr` (which we assume are never active simultaneously), after the I/O devices have been enabled by signal `Enable`; depending on which one of the control signals is active, either an I/O read or an I/O write operation is performed for an operand of the length specified in signal `Length`. The address of the external device accessed is specified in signal `Addr`, whereas the data are transferred through signal `Data`.

The behavioral specification of the I/O subsystem is similar to that of the memory, so we do not describe it here.

15.2.3 Processor

The processor architecture is described in terms of the processor state, which corresponds to all the registers that can be referenced (explicitly or implicitly) by the instructions. Moreover, the execution of an instruction is described by the changes it produces to this state.

Processor State

As shown in Figure 15.6, the processor state consists of the following registers:

- 32 general-purpose registers (32-bits wide), called `R0, R1, ..., R31`;
- a 24-bit Program Counter register (`PC`);
- a 4-bit Condition Register (`CR`); and
- a 32-bit Instruction Register (`IR`)

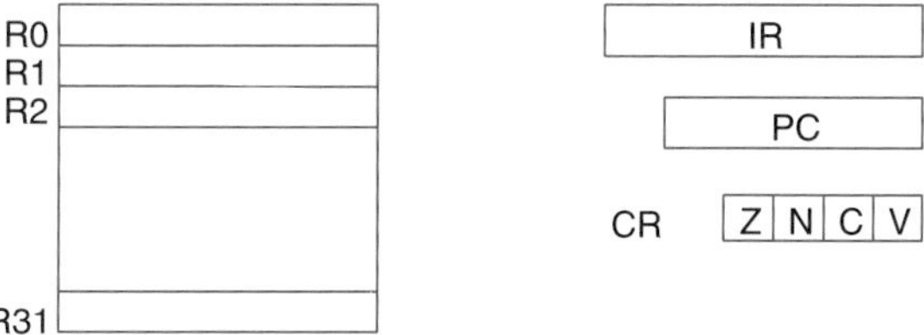

Figure 15.6 Processor state.

Basic Instruction Cycle

The behavior of the processor is as follows:

- Whenever input `RESET` is set to 1, the processor state is cleared (all registers are set to 0).

- Whenever input `Clk` is set to 1, an iteration of the **instruction loop** is performed (see Figure 15.7*a*):

  Fetch an instruction from the memory location specified by register `PC`. The memory access is completed when input `MemRdy=1`, at which point the instruction is placed in register `IR`.

  Execute the instruction contained in `IR`, which includes

  - performing the operations required by the instruction; and
  - computing the address of the next instruction and placing that address in `PC`.

In terms of the two components of the instruction cycle, the timing behavior with respect to the memory bus is shown in Figure 15.7. Figure 15.7*b* depicts the timing for instructions that do not access data from memory, whereas Figure 15.7*c* illustrates the timing for a load operation that brings data from memory into a general-purpose register.

The execution of an instruction modifies the state of the processor; the specific modification depends on the instruction being executed. For example, as depicted in Figure 15.8*a*, executing the instruction `ADD R7,R1,R5` puts in register `R7` the sum of the contents of registers `R1` and `R5`, and puts in `CR` the conditions corresponding to the result of the operation; all other general-purpose registers remain with the same value as before executing the instruction.

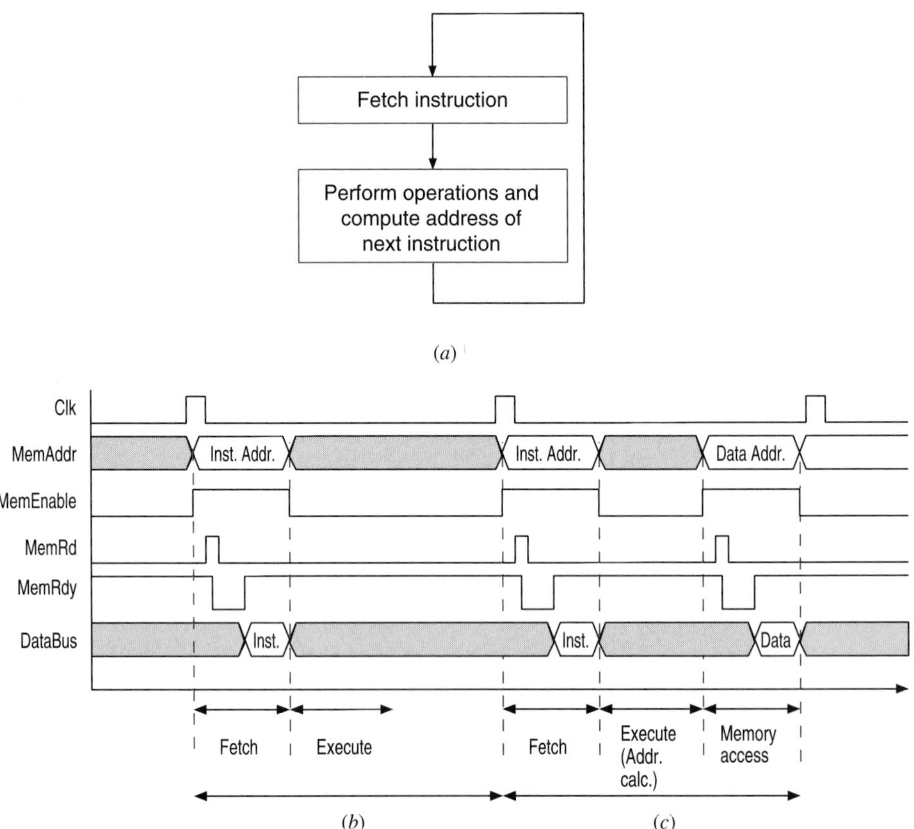

Figure 15.7 Behavior of the processor. (*a*) Instruction loop. (*b*) Memory bus behavior for register operation. (*c*) Memory bus behavior for load operation.

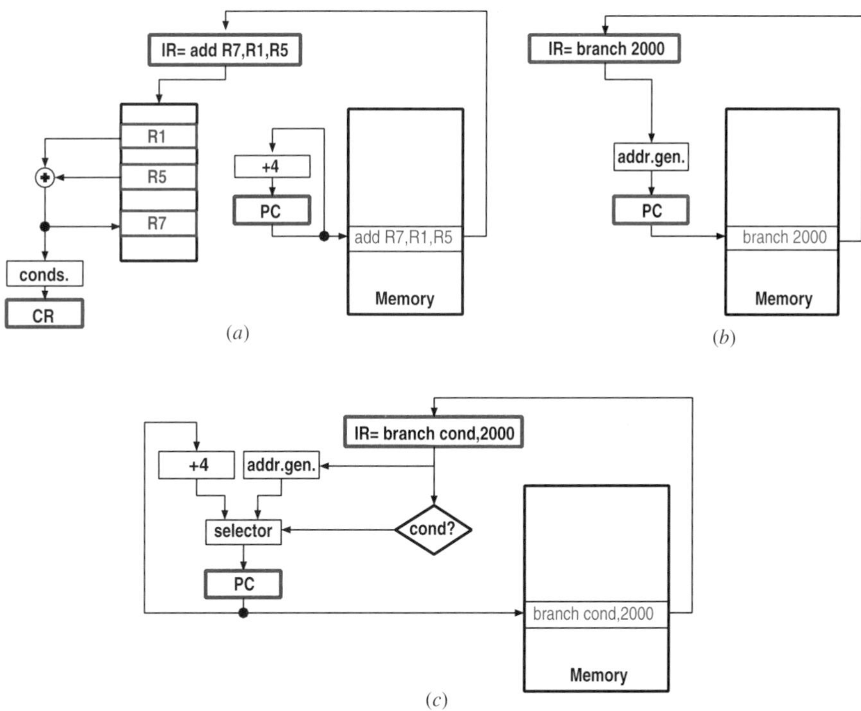

Figure 15.8 Behavior of instructions. (*a*) Add instruction. (*b*) Unconditional branch instruction. (*c*) Conditional branch instruction.

Instruction Sequencing

For all instructions except branches, the instructions are fetched sequentially from memory, in the order in which they are stored (increasing order); that is, if the instruction being executed has address k, the next instruction to be executed has address $k + 4$ (four bytes per instruction). This instruction sequencing is achieved by incrementing register PC by 4.

The sequential execution order is modifiable by branch instructions. Such instructions specify the address of the next instruction, which is loaded in register PC (see Figure 15.8*b*). Two types of branches are typical:

Unconditional branch, in which the branch is always taken.

Conditional branch, in which the instruction specifies an address as well as a **condition** (the value of one specific bit of the Condition Register CR). If the value of the specified CR bit is equal to the value specified in the instruction, then the branch is **taken,** that is, the next instruction is fetched from the address specified in the branch instruction. Otherwise (i.e., if the value of the CR bit is not equal to the value specified in the instruction), the branch is not taken; in this case, the next instruction address is obtained by adding 4 to PC.

Conditional branches allow two types of important sequencing structures:

1. Data dependent sequencing, in which the instructions executed depend on the value of a data item.
2. Loops, in which a portion of the program is executed repeatedly, either a fixed number of times or until a data condition occurs.

Condition Setting

The execution of some instructions set CR (see Table 15.1). The bits of this register are set to reflect the result from the execution of arithmetic or logic operations, as follows:

Zero	Z	set to 1 if the result is 00...00, set to 0 otherwise;
Negative	N	set to 1 if the leftmost bit of the result is 1 (negative in two's complement representation), set to 0 otherwise;
Carry	C	set to 1 if there is a carry-out from the most-significant bit of the adder, set to 0 otherwise; and
Overflow	V	set to the result of XOR between the carry-out from bit 30 and the carry-out from bit 31 (corresponds to overflow in two's complement addition).

Instruction Formats

An instruction is represented by one word (32 bits). These 32 bits have different meaning according to the formats depicted in Figure 15.9. In these formats, instructions are divided into the following **fields**:

- an **opcode field** (Opcode) which is six bits wide and specifies the operation performed by the instruction (up to 64 operations);
- two **register fields** (RT/RS and RA) which are five bits wide. Each specifies one of the 32 general-purpose registers. Registers RA and RS contain operands and register RT specifies the destination register; and
- a 16-bit field that may have different interpretations (depending on the opcode):
  - a 5-bit **register field** (RB) which specifies an additional register used by the instruction (the rest of the bits are unused); or
  - a 16-bit **value** (SI or UI), which specifies the value of an operand used by the instruction. This value can be interpreted as a signed integer, an unsigned integer, or a bit vector, depending on the opcode; or
  - a 16-bit signed **displacement** (D) used to calculate an address in a memory instruction or in a branch; or
  - an 11-bit **port number** (PN) used by I/O access instructions (the rest of the bits are unused).

Note that symbols RT,RS,RA,RB are used to denote the corresponding instruction fields as well as the contents of the registers whose address is specified in those instruction fields; the actual meaning of the symbol is inferred from the context. On the other hand, SI,UI,D,PN denote the contents of the corresponding fields within the instruction, whereas symbols PC,IR,CR denote the contents of those registers.

Instruction Set

The processor has six groups of instructions, which are listed in Table 15.1. For each instruction, the table lists the name, the opcode, the function, whether it sets the Condition

	31	25	20	15	10 0	
RT:= op(RA)	Opcode	RT	RA	-		Unary
RT:= RA op RB	Opcode	RT	RA	RB	-	Binary
RT:= RA op SI	Opcode	RT	RA	SI		
RT:= RA op UI	Opcode	RT	RA	UI		
RT:= M[RA+D]	Opcode	RT	RA	D		Memory
M[RA+D]:= RS	Opcode	RS	RA	D		
RT:= IO[PN]	Opcode	RT	RA	-	PN	I/O
IO[PN]:= RS	Opcode	RS	RA	-	PN	
PC:= PC + 4 + D	Opcode	-		D		Branch
PC:= RA	Opcode	-	RA	-		

Figure 15.9 Instruction formats.

Register (CR), and the representation used in an assembly-language program, as described later. The corresponding instruction groups are:

Unary operations, which have a single operand and produce the corresponding result, including setting the condition register CR.

Binary operations, which have two operands and produce the corresponding result, also setting CR.

Memory operations, which access the memory location whose address (referred to as the **effective address** EA) corresponds to the lowermost 24 bits from the result of adding the sign-extended value specified in field D to the contents of the register specified in field RA. The length of the operand transferred can be one byte or one word (four bytes) (denoted as `Mem(RA+D,1)` and `Mem(RA+D,4)`, respectively, in the table).

I/O operations, which access the I/O port whose address is specified in field PN.

Branch operations, which can be **conditional** or **unconditional**.

The (unconditional) `Branch` instruction forces the next instruction to be fetched from address PC+4+D (24 bits), where D is the signed displacement field in the instruction. This mechanism for specifying the address of the next instruction is known as **PC relative** because the target instruction is located D+4 bytes from the current instruction (which is addressed by PC). Because field D is only 16-bits wide, this approach is limited to branching $\pm 2^{15} + 4$ bytes around the branch instruction.

The (unconditional) `Branch indirect` forces the next instruction fetch to occur from the address contained in the lower 24 bits of the register specified by field RA. Thus, indirect branches are able to branch anywhere in the memory space but they require loading/using a register.

A conditional branch instruction (e.g., `Branch if` N=0) tests a bit in the condition register according to the condition specified by the instruction; if the condition is fulfilled (in the example N=0), the next instruction is fetched from the address PC+4+D, otherwise the next instruction is fetched from address PC+4. Note that, as for unconditional direct branches, the branching range is limited to $\pm 2^{15} + 4$ bytes from the branch itself.

The instruction set listed in Table 15.1 provides a complete description of the capabilities of the processor; any computation sequence executed by this system must be represented as a program written using these instructions.

Table 15.1 Instruction set

Name	Opcode	Function	CR	Assembly Language	
No-op	000000	no operation		nop	
NOT	000010	RT:= not(RA)	Y	not	RT,RA
Left shift	000100	RT:= lshift(RA)	Y	lsh	RT,RA
Right shift	000110	RT:= rshift(RA)	Y	rsh	RT,RA
Left rotate	001000	RT:= lrot(RA)	Y	lrt	RT,RA
Right rotate	001010	RT:= rrot(RA)	Y	rrt	RT,RA
Add	010000	RT:= RA + RB	Y	add	RT,RA,RB
Add immed.	010001	RT:= RA + SI	Y	adi	RT,RA,SI
Subtract	010010	RT:= RA - RB	Y	sub	RT,RA,RB
Sub. immed.	010011	RT:= RA - SI	Y	sbi	RT,RA,SI
AND	010100	RT:= RA and RB	Y	and	RT,RA,RB
AND immed.	010101	RT:= RA and UI	Y	ani	RT,RA,UI
OR	010110	RT:= RA or RB	Y	or	RT,RA,RB
OR immed.	010111	RT:= RA or UI	Y	ori	RT,RA,UI
XOR	011000	RT:= RA xor RB	Y	xor	RT,RA,RB
XOR immed.	011001	RT:= RA xor UI	Y	xri	RT,RA,UI
Load byte	100000	RT(7 to 0):= Mem(RA+D,1)		ldb	RT,D(RA)
Load word	100001	RT(31 to 0):= Mem(RA+D,4)		ldw	RT,D(RA)
Store byte	100010	Mem(RA+D,1):= RS(7 to 0)		stb	RS,D(RA)
Store word	100011	Mem(RA+D,4):= RS(31 to 0)		stw	RS,D(RA)
I/O Rd byte	100100	RT(7 to 0):= IO(PN,1)		irb	RT,PN
I/O Rd word	100101	RT(31 to 0):= IO(PN,4)		irw	RT,PN
I/O Wr byte	100110	IO(PN,1):= RS(7 to 0)		iwb	RS,PN
I/O Wr word	100111	IO(PN,4):= RS(31 to 0)		iww	RS,PN
Branch	111000	PC:= PC + 4 + D		br	D
Branch indirect	111001	PC:= RA		bri	RA
Branch if N=0	110000	If N=0 then PC:= PC+4+D		brp	D
Branch if N=1	110001	If N=1 then PC:= PC+4+D		brn	D
Branch if Z=0	110010	If Z=0 then PC:= PC+4+D		bnz	D
Branch if Z=1	110011	If Z=1 then PC:= PC+4+D		brz	D
Branch if C=0	110100	If C=0 then PC:= PC+4+D		bnc	D
Branch if C=1	110101	If C=1 then PC:= PC+4+D		brc	D
Branch if V=0	110110	If V=0 then PC:= PC+4+D		bnv	D
Branch if V=1	110111	If V=1 then PC:= PC+4+D		brv	D

Data Representation

As it can be observed from the instruction types, a 32-bit data item can represent any of the following data types, the interpretation being given by the type of instruction that uses it:

- Logical data (bit-vectors) used for logical operations, such as AND and XOR.
- Integers (signed) in the two's complement notation; this is used for all arithmetic operations.
- Unsigned integers used for representation of addresses.

In addition, memory and I/O operations use 8-bit (byte) data as unsigned or logical values.

Binary Program and Assembly-language Program

Executing a computation sequence by XMC requires loading the corresponding program—in binary form—into the memory, and setting the program counter to the address of the first instruction. The program is usually extracted from some external device such as a disk, and transferred into the memory under control of another program known as a **loader** (in larger systems, there is an **operating system** that takes care of this as well as many other functions). The loader is always resident in the memory, either in a ROM or loaded when the computer is first powered up (booted).

Because the binary form of a program is difficult to handle by human beings, an **assembly language** is used to simplify writing, debugging, and modifying programs. A program called an **assembler** is used to translate the program into binary form. The assembly language form of the instructions in XMC is shown in the last column of Table 15.1.

Specification of the Processor in μVHDL

We now give a μVHDL-based specification of the processor. The entity declaration is as follows (see Figure 15.3):[2]

```
LIBRARY ieee;
USE ieee.std_logic_1164.all;
USE WORK.comp_pkg.ALL;

ENTITY processor IS
  PORT (MemAddr   : OUT   MAddrT    ;  -- memory address bus
        MemData   : INOUT WordT     ;  -- data bus to/from memory
        MemLength: OUT   STD_LOGIC;  -- memory operand length
        MemRd     : OUT   STD_LOGIC;  -- memory read control signal
        MemWr     : OUT   STD_LOGIC;  -- memory write control signal
        MemEnable: OUT   STD_LOGIC;  -- memory enable signal
        MemRdy    : IN    STD_LOGIC;  -- memory completion signal
        IOAddr    : OUT   IOAddrT   ;  -- I/O address bus
        IOData    : INOUT WordT     ;  -- data bus to/from I/O
        IOLength  : OUT   STD_LOGIC;  -- I/O operand length
        IORd      : OUT   STD_LOGIC;  -- I/O read control signal
        IOWr      : OUT   STD_LOGIC;  -- I/O write control signal
        IOEnable  : OUT   STD_LOGIC;  -- memory enable signal
        IORdy     : IN    STD_LOGIC;  -- I/O completion signal
        Status    : OUT   StatusT   ;  -- processor status signal
        Reset     : IN    STD_LOGIC;  -- reset signal
        Clk       : IN    STD_LOGIC); -- clock signal
END processor;
```

[2]This specification can be skipped without loss of continuity.

The behavior of the processor, summarized in the previous section, is described in μVHDL as follows. This description uses the package `ieee.std_logic_signed` so that bit-vectors are regarded as signed values for arithmetic operations.

```
LIBRARY ieee;
USE ieee.std_logic_arith.all;     -- use definitions and operations
USE ieee.std_logic_signed.all;    -- on signed values

ARCHITECTURE behavioral OF processor IS
  -- registers (processor state)
  TYPE      RegFileT IS ARRAY(0 to 31) OF WordT;
  SIGNAL    GPR: RegFileT              ;  -- general registers
  SIGNAL    PC : MAddrT                ;  -- Program Counter register
  SIGNAL    CR : STD_LOGIC_VECTOR( 3 DOWNTO 0);  -- Condition Register
  SIGNAL    IR : STD_LOGIC_VECTOR(31 DOWNTO 0);  -- Instruction register

  -- signals used by output function
  SIGNAL    Phase: StatusT     ;    -- instr. cycle phase
  SIGNAL    tMemAddr: WordT    ;    -- memory address
  SIGNAL    tData    : WordT   ;    -- memory/io data

  ALIAS     Z  : STD_LOGIC IS CR(0)  ;    -- Condition code Zero
  ALIAS     N  : STD_LOGIC IS CR(1)  ;    -- Condition code Negative
  ALIAS     C  : STD_LOGIC IS CR(2)  ;    -- Condition code Carry
  ALIAS     V  : STD_LOGIC IS CR(3)  ;    -- Condition code Overflow

  ALIAS     Opcode : STD_LOGIC_VECTOR(5 DOWNTO 0)  IS IR(31 DOWNTO 26);
  ALIAS     RT     : STD_LOGIC_VECTOR(4 DOWNTO 0)  IS IR(25 DOWNTO 21);
  ALIAS     RA     : STD_LOGIC_VECTOR(4 DOWNTO 0)  IS IR(20 DOWNTO 16);
  ALIAS     RB     : STD_LOGIC_VECTOR(4 DOWNTO 0)  IS IR(15 DOWNTO 11);
  ALIAS     RS     : STD_LOGIC_VECTOR(4 DOWNTO 0)  IS IR(15 DOWNTO 11);
  ALIAS     Imm    : STD_LOGIC_VECTOR(15 DOWNTO 0) IS IR(15 DOWNTO  0);
  ALIAS     D      : STD_LOGIC_VECTOR(15 DOWNTO 0) IS IR(15 DOWNTO  0);
  ALIAS     PN     : STD_LOGIC_VECTOR(10 DOWNTO 0) IS IR(10 DOWNTO  0);
  ALIAS     dlength: STD_LOGIC                     IS IR(26)         ;

  -- other declarations
  CONSTANT delay      : TIME := 200 ps; -- register delay
  CONSTANT Reset_delay: TIME :=   5 ns;
  CONSTANT Exec_delay : TIME :=  10 ns; -- Execute delay
  CONSTANT Mdelay     : TIME := 600 ps; -- MemEnable signal delay
  CONSTANT Pulse_Width: TIME := 2.6 ns; -- memory signals width
  CONSTANT Fetch_delay: TIME :=   3 ns; -- disable memory after
                                        -- access completed

 BEGIN
  PROCESS                              -- transition function
  -- working variables
  VARIABLE RS_data, RA_data, RB_data          : WordT;
  VARIABLE RT_addr, RA_addr, RB_addr, RS_addr : Natural;

  BEGIN
  WAIT ON Clk,Reset;

  IF (Reset'Event AND Reset = '1') THEN                 -- reset function
     PC <= (OTHERS => '0'); CR <= "0000"; IR <= (OTHERS => '0');

     FOR i IN 0 TO 31 LOOP
       GPR(i) <= (OTHERS => '0');
     END LOOP;
```

```
      Phase  <= p_reset;
      Status <= p_reset;

      WAIT UNTIL (Reset = '0') AND (Clk = '1');
   END IF;

   IF (Clk'Event AND Clk='1') THEN
     -- Instruction cycle
      Status     <= Fetch AFTER delay;
      Phase      <= Fetch AFTER delay;
                                           -- instruction fetch
      PC         <= PC + 4  AFTER Exec_delay;
      WAIT UNTIL MemRdy='1';     -- wait instr. fetch completed
      IR         <= MemData;
      WAIT FOR Fetch_delay;

                                           -- instruction execution
      Status     <= Execute;
      Phase      <= Execute;
      RA_addr := CONV_INTEGER('0' & RA); RB_addr := CONV_INTEGER('0' & RB);
                          -- '0' to force bit-vector to positive value
      RA_data := GPR(RA_addr)    ; RB_data := GPR(RB_addr)  ;
      RT_addr := CONV_INTEGER('0' & RT);
      RS_addr := CONV_INTEGER('0' & RS); -- source reg. for store
      RS_data := GPR(RS_addr)  ; -- or I/O write
      WAIT FOR Exec_delay;

      CASE Opcode IS
      WHEN "000000" => null;                          -- nop
      WHEN "000010" => GPR(RT_Addr)<= not(RA_data);    -- not
      WHEN "000100" => GPR(RT_Addr)<= RA_data(30 DOWNTO 0) & '0'; -- lshift
      WHEN "000110" => GPR(RT_Addr)<= '0' & RA_data(31 DOWNTO 1); -- rshift
                                                              -- lrotate
      WHEN "001000" => GPR(RT_Addr)<= RA_data(30 DOWNTO 0) & RA_data(31);
                                                              -- rrotate
      WHEN "001010" => GPR(RT_Addr)<= RA_DATA(0) & RA_data(31 DOWNTO 1);

      WHEN "010000" => GPR(RT_Addr)<= RA_data + RB_data     ; -- add
      WHEN "010001" => GPR(RT_Addr)<= RA_data + Imm;
      WHEN "010010" => GPR(RT_Addr)<= RA_data - RB_data     ; -- sub
      WHEN "010011" => GPR(RT_Addr)<= RA_data - Imm;
      WHEN "010100" => GPR(RT_Addr)<= RA_data and RB_data   ; -- and
      WHEN "010101" => GPR(RT_Addr)<= RA_data and ext(Imm,RA_data'LENGTH);
                                     -- ext: zero extension from ieee pkg
      WHEN "010110" => GPR(RT_Addr)<= RA_data or  RB_data   ; -- or
      WHEN "010111" => GPR(RT_Addr)<= RA_data or  ext(Imm,RA_data'LENGTH);
      WHEN "011000" => GPR(RT_Addr)<= RA_data xor RB_data   ; -- xor
      WHEN "011001" => GPR(RT_Addr)<= RA_data xor ext(Imm,RA_data'LENGTH);

      WHEN "100000" | "100001" =>                -- ldb, ldw
              Phase      <= MemOp;
              Status     <= MemOp;
              tMemAddr   <= RA_data + D;         -- mem.addr.
              WAIT until MemRdy = '1';

      WHEN "100010" | "100011" =>                -- stb, stw
              Phase      <= MemOp;
              Status     <= MemOp;
              tMemAddr   <= RA_data + D;         -- mem. addr.
              tData      <= RS_data;             -- mem. data
              WAIT until MemRdy = '1';
```

```
WHEN "100100" | "100101" =>                   -- irb, irw
        Phase      <= IOOp;
        Status     <= IOOp;
        WAIT until IORdy = '1' ;

WHEN "100110" | "100111" =>                   -- iwb, iww
        Phase      <= IOOp;
        Status     <= IOOp;
        tData      <= RS_data;                -- io data
        WAIT until IORdy = '1' ;

WHEN "111000" => PC <= PC + D;                -- branch
WHEN "111001" => PC <= RA_data(23 DOWNTO 0);       -- br.ind.
WHEN "110000" | "110001"
              => IF (N = Opcode(0)) THEN            -- br on N
                   PC <= PC + D;
                 END IF;
WHEN "110010" | "110011"
              => IF (Z = Opcode(0)) THEN            -- br on Z
                   PC <= PC + D;
                 END IF;
WHEN "110100" | "110101"
              => IF (C = Opcode(0)) THEN            -- br on C
                   PC <= PC + D;
                 END IF;
WHEN "110110" | "110111"
              => IF (V = Opcode(0)) THEN            -- br on V
                   PC <= PC + D;
                 END IF;
WHEN others   => null;
END CASE;

IF ((Opcode(5 DOWNTO 4) = 0) or (Opcode(5 DOWNTO 4) = 1))
   and (Opcode /= 0) THEN
   -- set condition register
   IF (GPR(RT_Addr) = 0) THEN CR(0) <= '1';        -- zero result
   ELSE                       CR(0) <= '0';
   END IF;
   IF (GPR(RT_Addr)(31) = '1') THEN CR(1) <= '1'; -- negative result
   ELSE                             CR(1) <= '0';
   END IF;
   -- check if operation Opcode generates carry out
   CR(2) <= get_carry(RA_Data,RB_Data,Imm,Opcode);
   -- check if operation Opcode generates overflow
   CR(3) <= get_ovf(RA_Data,RB_Data,Imm,Opcode);
END IF;

WAIT FOR 0 ns;             -- force signals to be updated

IF (Phase = MemOp) THEN
   IF (dlength = '1') THEN                    -- ldw
     GPR(RT_addr) <= MemData;
   ELSE                                       -- ldb
     GPR(RT_addr)( 7 DOWNTO 0) <= MemData(7 DOWNTO 0);
     GPR(RT_addr)(31 DOWNTO 8) <= (OTHERS => '0');
   END IF;
   WAIT FOR Fetch_delay;
END IF;
```

```
   IF (Phase = IOOp) THEN
      IF (dlength = '1') THEN                 -- irw
        GPR(RT_addr) <= IOData;
      ELSE                                    -- irb
        GPR(RT_addr)( 7 DOWNTO 0) <= IOData(7 DOWNTO 0);
        GPR(RT_addr)(31 DOWNTO 8) <= (OTHERS => '0');
      END IF;
      WAIT FOR Fetch_delay;
   END IF;
END  IF;
END PROCESS;

PROCESS                              -- output function
BEGIN
-- Instruction cycle
WAIT ON Phase;
IF (Phase = p_reset) THEN               -- reset
   MemRd <= '0'; MemWr <= '0'; MemEnable <= '0'; MemLength <= '0';
   MemData <= (OTHERS => 'Z');
   IORd  <= '0'; IOWr  <= '0'; IOEnable  <= '0'; IOLength  <= '0';
   IOData <= (OTHERS => 'Z');

ELSIF (Phase = Fetch) THEN              -- instruction fetch
     MemAddr   <= PC  AFTER delay;
     MemEnable <= '1' AFTER delay;
     MemRd     <= '1' AFTER Mdelay, '0' AFTER Pulse_Width;
     MemLength <= '1' AFTER delay;
     WAIT UNTIL MemRdy='1';     -- wait instr. fetch completed
     MemEnable <= '0' AFTER Fetch_delay;

ELSIF (Phase = Execute) THEN NULL;   -- instruction execution
                                     -- no output signals

ELSIF (Phase = MemOp) THEN
     MemAddr   <= tMemAddr(23 DOWNTO 0) AFTER delay;
     MemEnable <= '1' AFTER delay;
     MemLength <= dlength AFTER delay;
     IF ((To_Bitvector(Opcode) = "100000") OR
         (To_Bitvector(Opcode) = "100001")) THEN   -- ldb, ldw
       MemRd     <= '1' AFTER Mdelay, '0' AFTER Pulse_Width;
       WAIT until MemRdy = '1';
       MemEnable  <= '0' AFTER Fetch_delay;
       WAIT FOR Fetch_delay;
     END IF;
     IF ((To_Bitvector(Opcode) = "100010") OR
         (To_Bitvector(Opcode) = "100011")) THEN   -- stb, stw
       MemWr      <= '1' AFTER Mdelay, '0' AFTER Pulse_Width;
       IF (dlength = '1') THEN                 -- stw
         MemData <= tData AFTER delay;
       ELSE                                    -- stb
         MemData(7 DOWNTO 0) <= tData(7 DOWNTO 0) AFTER delay;
       END IF;
       WAIT until MemRdy = '1';
       MemEnable  <= '0' AFTER delay;
       MemData    <= (OTHERS => 'Z') AFTER delay;
       WAIT FOR delay;
     END IF;
```

```
    ELSIF (Phase = IOOp) THEN
          IOAddr      <= PN AFTER delay;
          IOEnable    <= '1' AFTER delay;
          IOLength    <= dlength AFTER delay;
          IF ((To_Bitvector(Opcode) = "100100") OR
              (To_Bitvector(Opcode) = "100101")) THEN    -- irb, irw
             IORd        <= '1' AFTER Mdelay, '0' AFTER Pulse_Width;
             WAIT until IORdy = '1'  ;
             IOEnable    <= '0' AFTER Fetch_delay;
             WAIT FOR Fetch_delay;
          END IF;
          IF ((To_Bitvector(Opcode) = "100110") OR
              (To_Bitvector(Opcode) = "100111")) THEN    -- iwb, iww
             IF (dlength = '1') THEN                   -- iww
               IOData <= tData AFTER delay;
             ELSE                                      -- iwb
               IOData(7 DOWNTO 0) <= tData(7 DOWNTO 0) AFTER delay;
             END IF;
             IOWr        <= '1' AFTER Mdelay, '0' AFTER Pulse_Width;
             WAIT until IORdy = '1';
             IOEnable    <= '0' AFTER delay;
             IOData      <= (OTHERS => 'Z') AFTER delay;
             WAIT FOR delay;
          END IF;
     END  IF;
     END PROCESS;
END behavioral;
```

15.2.4 Specification of the Memory Contents

The μVHDL specification of XMC given in the previous section can be used to simulate the execution of programs. For these purposes, it is necessary to "load" a program in the memory. As described earlier, the actual operation of a computer uses a loader to achieve this function. For simulation purposes, a simpler alternative consists of specifying the program as the initial contents of the memory; moreover, it might be necessary to define a memory smaller than the maximum size indicated earlier. Taking these issues into account, the memory declaration becomes

```
-- memory declaration
CONSTANT MaxMem: NATURAL:= 16#FFF#;    -- 4Kbytes
TYPE     MemArrayT IS ARRAY(0 to MaxMem-1) OF ByteT;
VARIABLE Mem : MemArrayT:=
    (-- program
      3=>"01100000",  2=>"00000000",  1=>"00000000",  0=>"00000000",
      7=>"01000100",  6=>"00100000",  5=>"00000000",  4=>"00110010",
     11=>"10000110", 10=>"10000001",  9=>"00000000",  8=>"00000000",
     15=>"10000110", 14=>"10100001", 13=>"00000000", 12=>"00000100",
     19=>"01000100", 18=>"01000000", 17=>"00000000", 16=>"00111111",
     23=>"10001000", 22=>"01000001", 21=>"00000000", 20=>"00000000",
     -- data
     51=>"00110011", 50=>"00001111", 49=>"11110000", 48=>"11001100",
     55=>"00110011", 54=>"00001111", 53=>"11110000", 52=>"11001100",
     OTHERS => "00000000");
```

where the memory contents corresponds to the following instructions (prefix 0x indicates hexadecimal value):

```
  0x000000: xor R0,R0,R0   ; R0 = 0
  0x000004: adi R1,R0,50   ; R1 = 50
  0x000008: ldw R20,0(R1)  ; R20= Mem(50,4)= Mem(48,4)
                           ; ignore 2
lowermost address bits
  0x00000C: ldw R21,4(R1)  ; R21= Mem(54,4)= Mem(52,4)
  0x000010: adi R2,R0,63   ; R2 = 63
  0x000014: stb R2,0(R1)   ; Mem(50,1) = 63

  0x000048: 0x330FF0CC
  0x000052: 0x330FF0CC
```

In this case, the program starts at memory location 0, so that the program begins execution when input `Reset` changes from 1 to 0.

15.3 IMPLEMENTATION OF A SIMPLE MICROCOMPUTER SYSTEM

According to the specification given in Section 15.2, XMC consists of three subsystems. For an implementation, we need to focus on the structure of these subsystems. For simplicity, we do not discuss the implementation of the I/O subsystem.

15.3.1 Memory Subsystem

The memory subsystem is composed of storage modules (chips), a selector/distributor, and a controller. Let us consider storage chips having a capacity of 4 Mb (2^{22}), with a single-bit output (i.e., each memory chip is organized as an array of $2^{22} \times 1$ bits). Because the processor accesses both words and bytes, the memory must be able to deliver 32-bits-wide data. Consequently, the memory is organized as 32 parallel modules, for a total of 128 Mb (16 MB), as depicted in Figure 15.10. A four-input selector/distributor, controlled by address bits 1,0 and input `Length`, is used to select the entire 32-bits word accessed by address bits 23 down to 2, or a byte within these 32-bits, which is transferred through the

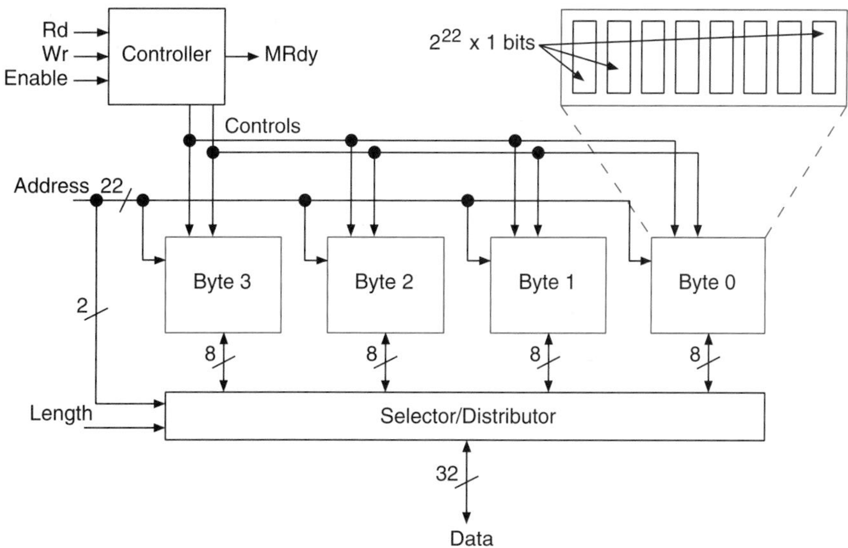

Figure 15.10 Implementation of the memory subsystem.

lowermost 8 bits in the data bus. The memory controller produces control signals for the read and write operations, as well as the `MRdy` signal.

15.3.2 Processor

The processor is a rather complex sequential system, so it is better implemented as a RTL system consisting of two subsystems (see Figure 15.11): the **data subsystem** and the **control subsystem**. The data subsystem contains the registers for the processor state and the operators for data modification, whereas the control subsystem controls the operation of the data subsystem.

The control subsystem generates the **control signals** for the data subsystem as well as for the memory and I/O subsystems; on the other hand, the data subsystem as well as the memory and I/O subsystems generate the **condition signals** used by the control subsystem. In addition, the data subsystem connects with the memory and I/O subsystems via the corresponding buses. The data part of these buses are implemented as bidirectional channels.

We now give an informal description of the implementation of the processor in terms of these two subsystems. The μVHDL description of the implementation is given in Section 15.5. For simplicity, we do not include the I/O signals.

Data Subsystem

A network that implements the requirements of the data subsystem is depicted in Figure 15.12. This network consists of a register file that contains the general-purpose registers, dedicated registers for `PC`, `CR`, and `IR`, an arithmetic-logic unit (ALU), as well as other supporting modules. Each of these modules has control signals that determine its operation. For example, signal `ALUop` determines the function performed by the ALU on the current input values, and signal `WrCR` produces the update of register `CR` with the value at its input. All register write operations are synchronized with signal `Clk`.

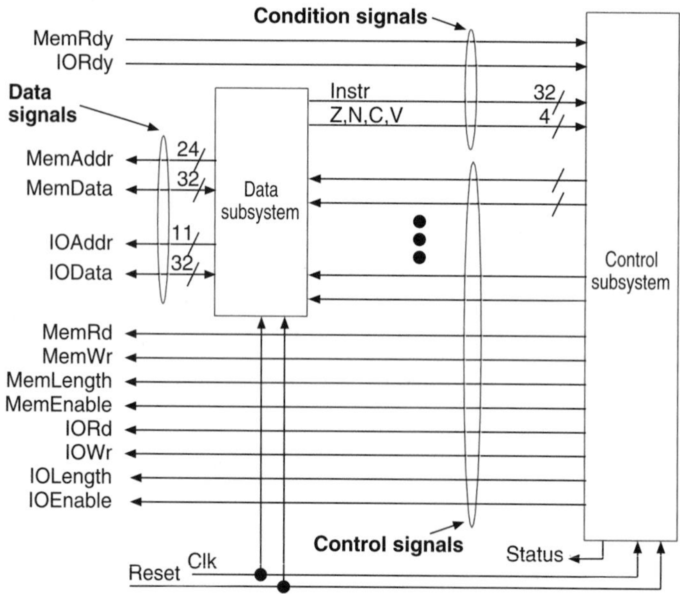

Figure 15.11 Implementation of the processor.

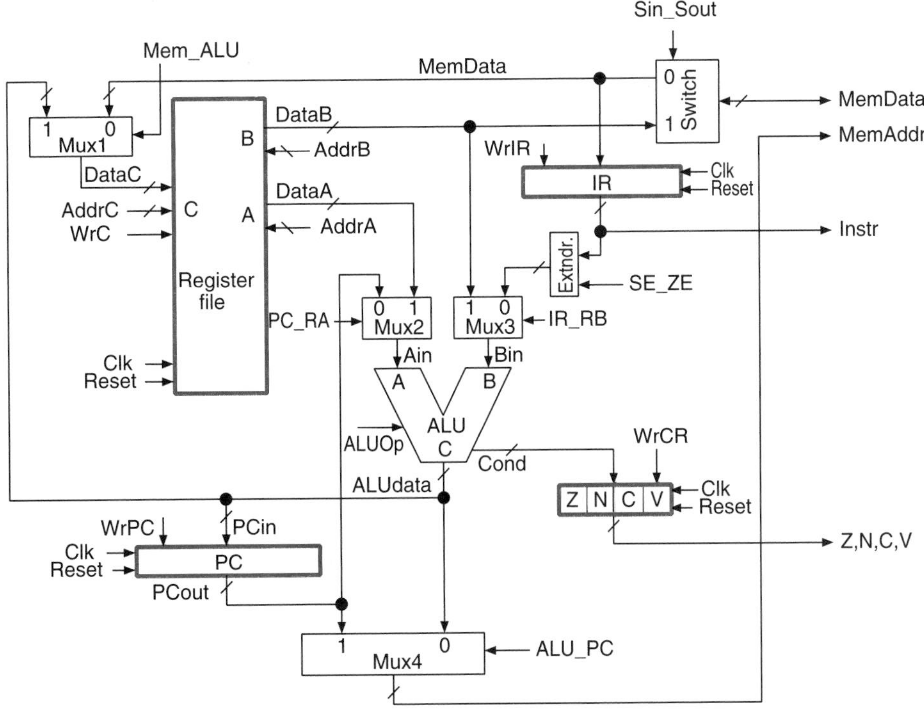

Figure 15.12 Implementation of data subsystem (I/O signals not shown).

Register File

The register file (GPR) contains 32 registers of 32 bits each. It has two **read ports** named A,B, which are used to read up to two operands required by an instruction, and one **write port** named C used to write the result. Each port has its own address (5 bits) and data signals (32 bits); the write port also has a control signal. As a result, two read operations and one write operation can be performed simultaneously. Each read port delivers the data stored in the register selected by the corresponding address signal. The write port stores the data present at the DataC input into the register selected by the AddrC signal, synchronized with signal Clk. Both operations have a delay of RF_delay. All registers are set to zero when the signal Reset is active.

Dedicated Registers

The data subsystem contains dedicated registers for IR,PC, and CR (32 bits, 24 bits, and 4 bits, respectively). To simplify the implementation, register PC is extended at the left with 8 bits that are set to zero; consequently, within the processor PC appears as a 32-bit register. The dedicated registers are loaded whenever the corresponding control input is set to 1 (WrIR,WrPC, and WrCR, respectively), synchronized with signal Clk. The new value is delivered at the output after a register read delay (Reg_delay). The registers are set to zero whenever signal Reset is active.

Arithmetic-logic Unit

The arithmetic-logic unit (ALU) is a combinational module that performs the arithmetic and logic operations; it has two data inputs, one data output, one control input, and one condition output. The data inputs are labeled A and B, whereas the data output is labeled C. The control input ALUop specifies which operation is performed according to the following encoding:

ALUop	Operation
0000	Zero_32
0001	A + B
0010	A − B
0011	−B
0100	A AND B
0101	A OR B
0110	A XOR B
0111	NOT(B)
1000	unused
1001	B
1010	SHIFTL(A)
1011	SHIFTR(A)
1100	ROTL(A)
1101	ROTR(A)
1110	A + 4
1111	unused

The arithmetic operations A + B, A − B, and −B are performed using signed integers in two's complement representation. This is consistent with the representation of the arithmetic instructions Add and Sub (for the operations with an immediate value, SI is sign-extended to 32 bits).

However, the ALU is also used to calculate the effective address in memory operations and the address of the next instruction in branches. In these cases, the content of the registers RA and PC are interpreted as positive integers, and the displacement D is sign-extended to 32 bits. The address is calculated with the ALU operation A + B, and the result is interpreted as a positive integer, which corresponds to (RA+D) mod 2**32 and (PC+4+D) mod 2**32, respectively (the operation PC+4 is done during the Fetch part of the instruction). The address sent to memory correspond to the lowermost 24 bits from the result of this operation.

The logical operations use 32-bit vectors. Therefore, for these operations the 16-bit UI is extended with zeros.

The 4-bit condition output Z,N,C,V reflects the value of the result in terms of the conditions zero, negative, carry, and overflow, respectively.

The data output and condition output are delivered after a delay (ALU_delay) relative to a change in any of the input signals (either data or control).

Other Modules

The data subsystem also contains multiplexers, a zero/sign-extender and a switch; all these are combinational modules. The zero/sign-extender extends a 16-bit input to 32 bits, according to its control signal (0: zero, 1: sign extension); and the switch connects a bidirectional signal either to an input or an output. Each of these modules is characterized by its own delay (Mux_delay, Ext_delay, Switch_delay, respectively).

Interconnections

As shown in Figure 15.12, the interconnections among the modules, as well as with the memory subsystem, have the following characteristics:

- the connection to memory consists of the data bus (MemData) and the address bus (MemAddr); the address corresponds to the lower 24 bits either from the ALU output (for accessing data) or from register PC (for fetching instructions);
- the RF write port is shared by the paths from memory and from the ALU;
- the RF read port B is shared by the paths to memory and to ALU input B;
- ALU input A is shared by RF and PC;
- ALU input B is shared by RF and IR (the 16-bit fields D, SU, IU from IR are sign-extended or zero-extended)

Events and Flow of Data During Execution

Let us consider the events and flows of data that take place in the data subsystem during the Execute part of the instruction loop (e.i., the instruction fetch has already been performed and the instruction has been stored in IR).

Let us first consider an arithmetic-logic instruction; the sequence of events and their timing (as depicted in Figures 15.13 and 15.14) are as follows:

1. Signal Instr (the output from IR) is sent to the control subsystem for decoding.
2. After the instruction decode delay, the signals that control the modules are activated by the control subsystem; this includes the signals to access RF and the signals to control the ALU, the multiplexers, and the storing of the results into the registers.
3. After the RF read delay, the contents of the registers used as operands by the instruction become available and are fed to the ALU through multiplexers Mux2 and Mux3.

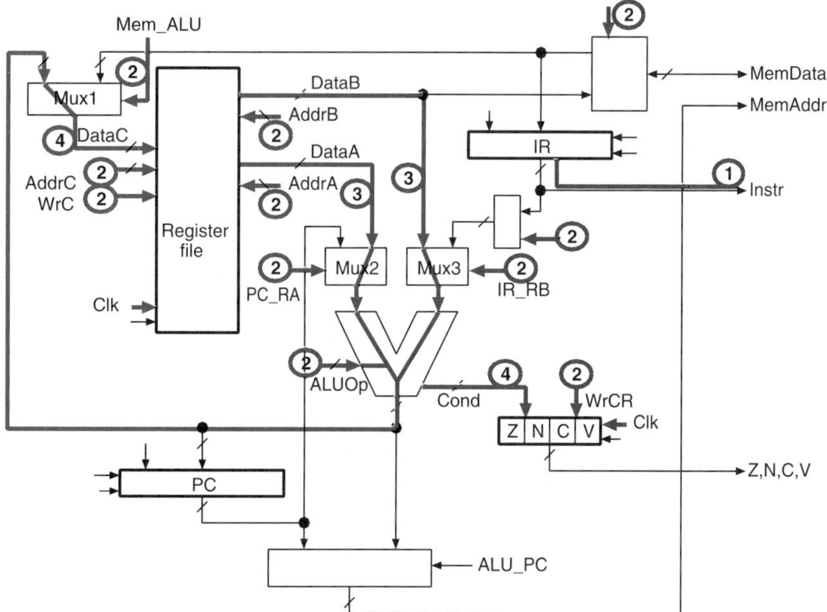

Figure 15.13 Sequence of events in data subsystem for arithmetic-logic instruction.

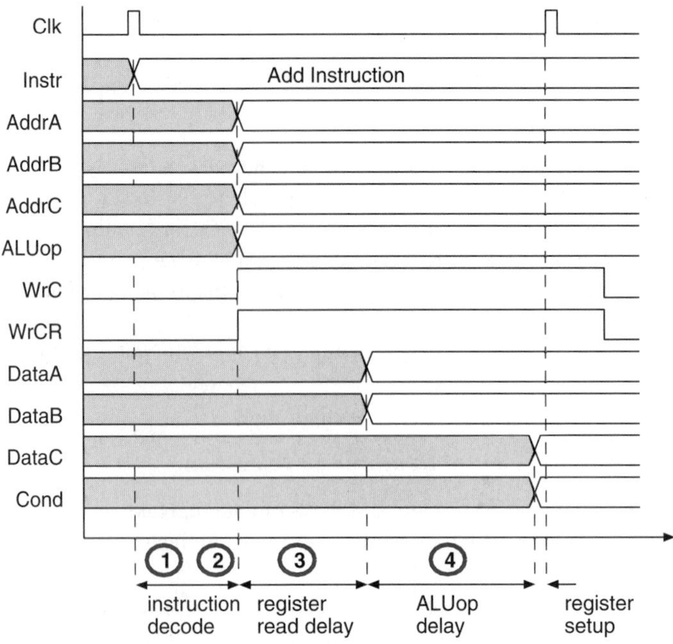

Figure 15.14 Timing diagram in data subsystem for arithmetic-logic instruction.

4. After the ALU delay, the ALU delivers the results from the operation (data and condition); the data result is stored in the RF (through Mux1), and the condition result is stored in CR. These storing operations are synchronized with the clock signal, so that the values must be stable earlier than the setup time of the registers.

The flow is similar for instructions that have an immediate operand SI or UI, except that the second operand is obtained from IR and extended accordingly.

In branch instructions, the branch address is calculated using the ALU and stored in PC instead of in the register file.

In memory operations, the address is calculated in the ALU and sent through the address bus. For a Load instruction the data come through the data bus and are written in RF through port C. In a Store operation, the data are obtained from RF through port B.

All these steps comprise the **critical path** in the execution step of an instruction: the instruction is decoded, the operands read, the operation performed, and the results transmitted to the input of the registers before the arrival of the next clock pulse (complying with the setup time of the registers). Moreover, in memory operations the access to memory has to be included. Depending on the implementation of the control subsystem, this critical path might be required to fit in one or in several clock cycles. We consider one such implementation now.

Control Subsystem

The control subsystem produces the control signals so that the instruction loop is performed in the data subsystem. The control subsystem is a canonical sequential network, as depicted in Figure 15.15.

The first question to be answered in the design of the control subsystem is the number of clock cycles for the instruction loop. Activities are separated into different cycles (control states) for the following reasons:

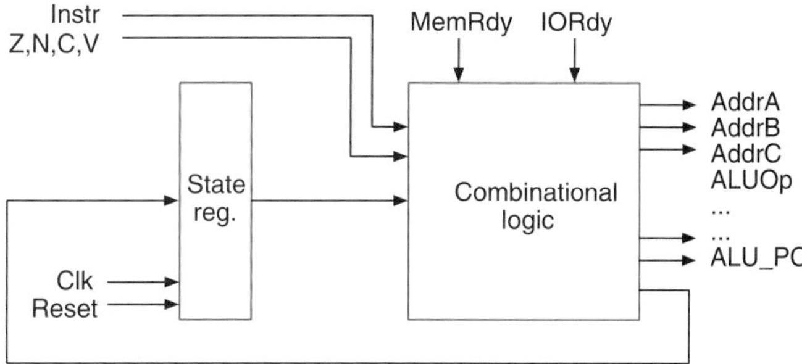

Figure 15.15 Control subsystem.

1. A resource is used more than once in the instruction. This is the case of the ALU, which is used to increment PC and also to perform the operation. It is also the case of the memory in Load and Store operations as it is used twice, once for instruction fetch and once for data read/write.
2. Because different instructions take different times, dividing the execution in several cycles reduces the execution time of the faster instructions. For example, the main delays involved in the execution part of an Add instruction are the delay of reading the operands from RF, the delay of performing the operation in ALU, and the delay of storing the result in RF. On the other hand, the memory instruction Load has these same delays plus the delay of reading the operand from memory. Consequently, it is convenient to divide the execution of the Load instruction into two parts, so that the execution of the Add instruction is done in one cycle whereas the Load is done in two cycles.

The exact number of cycles used for an implementation and the activities that are included in each cycle are complex design decisions. The objectives are using the resources effectively and achieving the best execution time (for the instruction mix of typical programs). In our illustration implementation we use three states, as shown by the state diagram depicted in Figure 15.16. The activities in each of the states are:

Fetch: The instruction is fetched from memory and stored in IR. The address of the next sequential instruction is calculated in the ALU and stored in PC.

Execute: The instruction is decoded, the operands are fetched from registers, the operation is performed in the ALU and the result is stored in the destination register. In memory instructions (Load and Store) as well as in branches, the effective address is calculated. In the case of branch instructions, the effective address is placed in PC.

Memop: In memory instructions, a memory operation (read, write) is performed. Moreover, in Load the data are stored in RF.

As a consequence of this division, two clock cycles are required for instructions other than memory instructions, and three clock cycles for memory instructions.

The state register encodes the three states shown in Figure 15.16 using a 1-out-of-3 code; that is, the state register consists of three flip-flops, with only one of these flip-flops being set to 1 at any given time.

The combinational logic receives as inputs the value in the state register as well as the condition signals from the data section, the memory, and the I/O subsystems (signals `Instr,Z,N,C,V,MemRdy,` and `IORdy`). Based on these inputs, this subsystem produces the signals that control the operation of the entire system, including the generation of the input to the state register (value of the next state). The values of these signals are shown in the

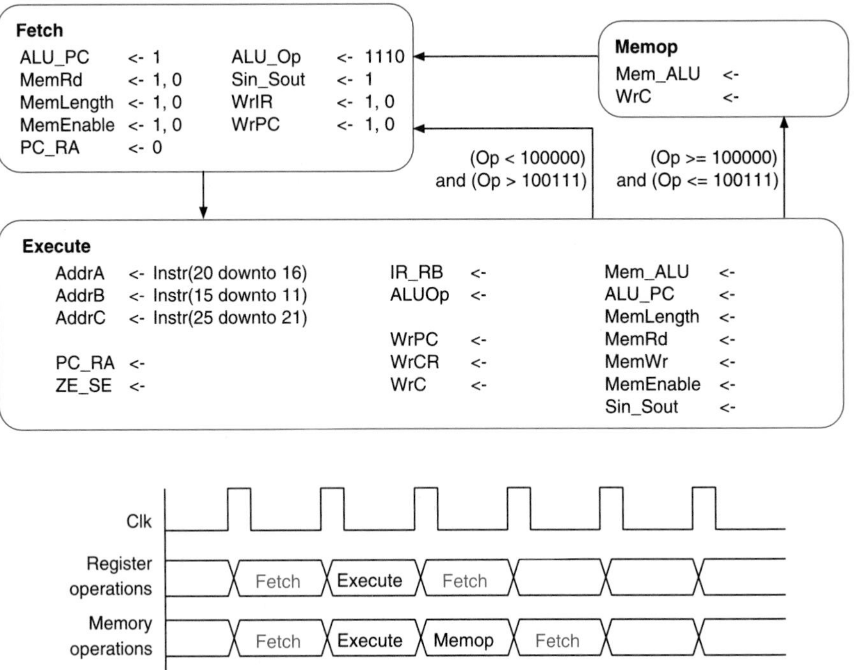

Figure 15.16 State diagram and timing for control subsystem of the processor (signal values not shown depend on instruction executed).

state diagram depicted in Figure 15.16. Most of these signals depend only on the value of the state register, so they are available a short delay after the state register changes value; let us call this `Ctrl_delay`. On the other hand, decoding the instruction requires a few levels of logic, so that the corresponding delay is longer; we refer to this as `Dec_delay`.

15.4 OPERATION OF THE COMPUTER AND CYCLE TIME

Let us consider now the detailed execution of the instruction iteration loop. For simplicity, we ignore the delays arising from transmitting the signals between the modules (we assume that such delays have been incorporated into the modules which generate/use the signals, see Figure 15.12). A dependence diagram is given for each state, indicating the signals that become active at the time shown.

1. **Fetch** (see Figure 15.17):

   a. The iteration begins at time $t_0 = t_{clk} +$ `Reg_delay`, when the output of the state register has been set to the value `Fetch`, that is, `SR_out = (001)`.

   b. At $t_1 = t_0 +$ `Ctrl_delay`, the control subsystem activates the control signals to fetch the next instruction (`ALU_PC=1, MemLength=1, MemEnable=1, Sin_Sout=0, WrIR=1`), and to increment PC (`PC_RA=0, ALUop=1110, WrPC=1`). In addition, the control logic produces the input to SR (next state =`Execute` = 010). Signal `MemRd=1` becomes stable at t_0+`MCtrl_delay`.

   c. At $t_2 = t_1 +$ `Mux_delay`, `Mux4` transmits the value in `PC` to `MemAddrBus`, and `Mux2` transmits the value in `PC` to the ALU input A.

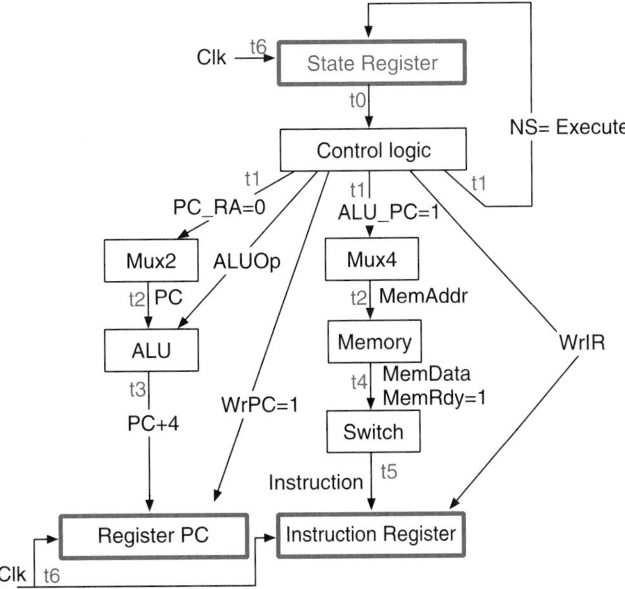

Figure 15.17 Dependencies for state Fetch.

d. At $t_3 = t_2 +$ `ALU_delay`, the ALU delivers the result from the operation A+4. This value is now available at the input of PC.

e. At $t_4 = t_2 +$ `Mem_delay`, signal `MemRdy=1` and `MemData= Instruction`.

f. At $t_5 = t_4 +$ `Switch_delay`, the instruction appears at the output of the switch module and is ready to be loaded in IR.

g. At $t_6 \geq t_5$ the clock pulse arrives, triggering the update of IR, PC, and SR. Note that the signal `MemRdy =1` is not used, because we have assumed that the access to memory always fits in one cycle.

2. **Execute** (see Figure 15.18):

a. At $t_7 = t_{clk} +$ `Reg_delay`, signals `IR_out` = Instruction, `PCout` = updated PC, and `SR_out=Execute`.

b. At $t_8 = t_7 +$ `Ctrl_delay`, control signals AddrA, AddrB, and AddrC are transmitted to the data section. Note that, because the register address fields in the instruction are always in the same position (if they exist), these signals can be extracted from `IR_out` without first decoding the opcode; this is possible even for those instructions that do not use all the register fields, in which case the value(s) read from RF that are not needed are just not used.

c. At $t_9 = t_7 +$ `Dec_delay`, the decoding of the instruction is completed. Signals PC_RA, ZE_SE, IR_RB, ALUop, ALU_PC, WrCR, WrC, and WrPC are set according to the instruction being executed. Also the input value for SR (next state value = `Memop` = 100 or `Fetch` = 001) is produced, depending whether the instruction is a memory operation or not.

d. At $t_{10} = t_8 +$ `RF_delay`, signals DataA and DataB receive the values stored in the registers addressed by signals AddrA and AddrB.

e. At $t_{11} = t_9 +$ `Ext_delay`, the output of the Zero/Sign Extender becomes stable.

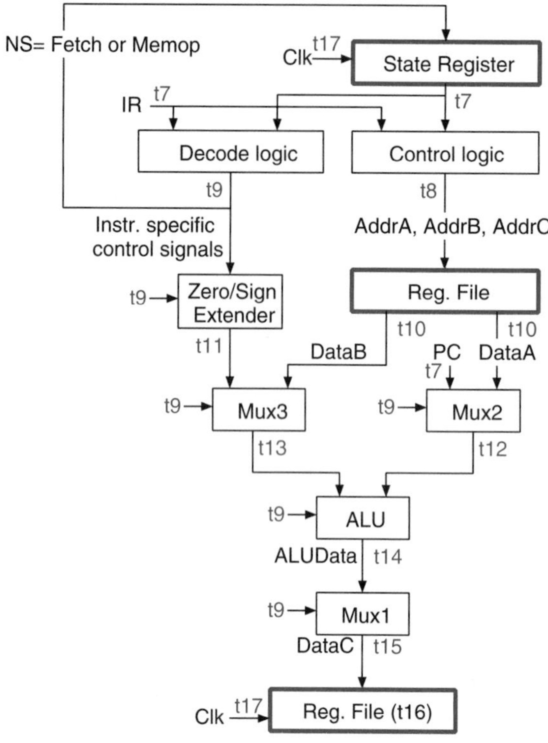

Figure 15.18 Dependencies for state Execute.

f. At $t_{12} = t_{10} +$ `Mux_delay` the output from `Mux2` becomes stable; this assumes that $t_{10} > t_9$.

g. At $t_{13} = t_{11} +$ `Mux_delay`, the output from `Mux3` becomes stable; as previously, this assumes that $t_{10} > t_9$.

   This event completes the signals required by the ALU to perform its operation.

h. At $t_{14} = t_{13} +$ `ALU_delay`, the ALU delivers the results from its operation (data and condition). At this time the value is available also at the input of `PC`.

i. At $t_{15} = t_{14} +$ `Mux_delay`, `Mux1` transmits signal `ALUdata` to the input of `RF` (signal `DataC`). At this time it is also available at `MemAddr`.

j. At $t_{16} = t_{15} +$ `RF_delay` the data are ready to be written in `RF`.

k. At $t_{17} \geq t_{16}$, the next clock pulse arrives, triggering the update of `CR`, `RF`, or `PC` (for branches), and `SR`.

3. If the next state is **Memop** (see Figure 15.19):

   a. At $t_{18} = t_{clk} +$ `Reg_delay`, `SR_out= Memop`.

   b. At $t_{19} = t_{18} +$ `Ctrl_delay`, the control logic sets signals `ALU_PC`, `Mem_ALU`, `MemLength`, `MemEnable`, `Sin_Sout`, and `WrC`, depending whether the operation is a `Load` or a `Store`. `MemRd` or `MemWr` becomes stable at $t_{20} = t_{18} +$ `MCtrl_delay`.

   c. At $t_{21} = t_{20} +$ `Mem_delay`, signal `MemRdy=1` and the memory access is completed.

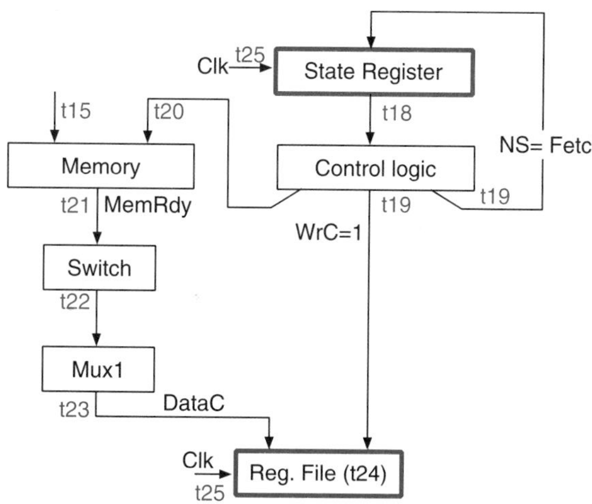

Figure 15.19 Dependencies for state Memop.

d. At $t_{22} = t_{21}$ + Switch_delay, the output from the switch module becomes stable.

e. At $t_{23} = t_{22}$ + Mux_delay, the output from Mux1 becomes stable.

f. At $t_{24} = t_{23}$ + RF_delay, the data are ready to be written in RF.

g. At $t_{25} \geq t_{24}$, the next clock pulse arrives, triggering the update of RF, if the instruction is Load, and SR.

The critical path that determines the minimum clock period corresponds to the maximum of the critical paths among all the states. We now show an example of the calculation of the minimum clock period.

EXAMPLE 15.1

We calculate the minimum clock period using the following values for the delay of the different modules:

Register	Reg_delay	t_R	2 ns (setup and propagation delay)
Register file	RF_delay	t_{RF}	4 ns
ALU	ALU_delay	t_{ALU}	6 ns
Multiplexer	Mux_delay	t_{mux}	0.5 ns
Zero/sign ext.	Ext_delay	t_{ZSE}	0.5 ns
Switch	Switch_delay	t_{sw}	0.5 ns
Control delay	Ctrl_delay	t_{ctl}	0.5 ns
Decode delay	Dec_delay	t_{dec}	3 ns
Memory	Mem_delay	t_{mem}	8 ns (static memory)

From the expressions given before, the following critical paths are obtained:

$$
\begin{aligned}
t_{fetch} &= t_R + t_{ctl} + t_{mux} + t_{mem} + t_{sw} \\
&= 2 + 0.5 + 1 + 8 + 0.5 \\
&= 12 \text{ ns}
\end{aligned}
$$

$$
\begin{aligned}
t_{exec} &= t_R + t_{ctl} + t_{RF} + t_{mux} + t_{\mathrm{ALU}} + t_{mux} + t_{RF} \\
&= 2 + 0.5 + 4 + 0.5 + 6 + 0.5 + 4 \\
&= 17.5 \text{ ns}
\end{aligned}
$$

$$
\begin{aligned}
t_{memop} &= t_R + t_{ctl} + t_{mem} + t_{sw} + t_{mux} + t_{RF} \\
&= 2 + 0.5 + 8 + 0.5 + 0.5 + 4 \\
&= 15 \text{ ns}
\end{aligned}
$$

Note that the delay in decoding the instruction is not present in these expressions, because the addresses for the RF access are obtained directly from IR and, therefore, the decoding is performed at the same time as the RF read.

From the expressions above, the critical path is in state Execute; as a result, the clock cycle is 17.5 ns, the clock frequency is 57 Mhz, and the instruction execution time is $2 \times 17.5 = 35$ ns for register operations (approximately 28 million instructions per second (MIPS)) and $3 \times 17.5 = 52.5$ ns for memory operations (19 MIPS).

The actual instruction rate in the execution of a particular program depends on the instruction mix, that is, on the fraction of memory instructions. For example, for a program that has 20% memory instructions, the average execution instruction time is $35 \times 0.8 + 52.5 \times 0.2 = 38.5$ ns, so the instruction rate is about 26 MIPS. ■

To achieve a higher instruction rate, high-performance processors decode and execute more than one instruction at a time (**multiple-issue processors**), and/or use a technique called **pipelining**, which approaches a maximum rate of one instruction per clock cycle. A pipelined processor divides the instruction iteration loop into stages and overlaps the execution of several instructions, so that at a given time there can be one instruction executing per stage. These stages are similar to the states of the control subsystem discussed earlier. However, to achieve a larger instruction rate, the implementation might have more stages (five or more is typical) so that the critical path per stage is reduced. The detailed study of these techniques is outside the scope of this text.

15.5 DESCRIPTION OF THE PROCESSOR IMPLEMENTATION IN μVHDL

We now give the structural description of the processor and the data subsystem, the description of the modules that compose the data subsystem, and the behavioral description of the control subsystem. In these descriptions, the delays are those considered for Example 15.1.

15.5.1 Structure of Processor

The structure of the processor is described in μVHDL as follows:

```
LIBRARY ieee;
USE ieee.std_logic_1164.ALL;
USE WORK.comp_pkg.ALL, WORK.ALL;

ARCHITECTURE structural OF Processor IS
  SIGNAL Instr                 : WordT;
  SIGNAL ZE, NG, CY, OV        : STD_LOGIC;
  SIGNAL AddrA, AddrB, AddrC   : STD_LOGIC_VECTOR(4 DOWNTO 0);
```

```
  SIGNAL ALUOp                  : STD_LOGIC_VECTOR(3 DOWNTO 0);
  SIGNAL WrC, WrPC, WrCR, WrIR : STD_LOGIC;
  SIGNAL Mem_ALU, PC_RA, IR_RB : STD_LOGIC;
  SIGNAL ALU_PC, ZE_SE, SinSout: STD_LOGIC;

BEGIN
  P1: ENTITY Data_Subsystem
      PORT MAP (MemAddr, MemData, IOAddr, IOData,
                Instr, ZE, NG, CY, OV, AddrA, AddrB, AddrC, ALUOp,
                WrC, WrPC, WrCR, WrIR, Mem_ALU, PC_RA, IR_RB, ALU_PC,
                ZE_SE, SinSout, Clk, Reset);

  P2: ENTITY Ctrl_Subsystem
      PORT MAP (Instr, ZE, NG, CY, OV, AddrA, AddrB, AddrC, ALUOp,
                WrC, WrPC, WrCR, WrIR, Mem_ALU, PC_RA, IR_RB, ALU_PC,
                ZE_SE, SinSout, MemRd, MemWr, MemLength, MemEnable,
                MemRdy, IORd, IOWr, IOLength, IOEnable, IORdy, Status,
                Clk, Reset);
END structural;
```

15.5.2 Data Subsystem

The μVHDL structural description of the data subsystem is as follows:

```
LIBRARY ieee;
USE ieee.std_logic_1164.ALL;
USE WORK.comp_pkg.ALL, WORK.ALL;
ENTITY Data_Subsystem IS
  PORT(MemAddr                 : OUT   MAddrT    ;
       MemData                 : INOUT WordT     ;
       IOAddr                  : OUT   IOAddrT   ;
       IOData                  : INOUT WordT     ;
       Instr                   : OUT   WordT     ;
       ZE, NG, CY, OV          : OUT   STD_LOGIC ;
       AddrA, AddrB, AddrC     : IN    STD_LOGIC_VECTOR(4 DOWNTO 0);
       ALUOp                   : IN    STD_LOGIC_VECTOR(3 DOWNTO 0);
       WrC, WrPC, WrCR, WrIR   : IN    STD_LOGIC ;
       Mem_ALU, PC_RA, IR_RB   : IN    STD_LOGIC ;
       ALU_PC, ZE_SE, Sin_Sout: IN    STD_LOGIC ;
       Clk, Reset              : IN    STD_LOGIC);
END Data_Subsystem;

ARCHITECTURE structural OF Data_Subsystem IS
  SIGNAL DataA, DataB, DataC : WordT     ;
  SIGNAL Ain   , Bin         : WordT     ;
  SIGNAL ALUdata, IRdata     : WordT     ;
  SIGNAL tMemdata            : WordT     ;
  SIGNAL Cond, CRout         : STD_LOGIC_VECTOR(3 DOWNTO 0);
  SIGNAL IRreg, IRext        : WordT     ;
  SIGNAL PCout               : WordT:= (OTHERS => '0');

BEGIN
  ALU1: ENTITY ALU
        PORT MAP(Ain,Bin,ALUop,ALUdata,Cond);
   GPR: ENTITY Reg_File
        PORT MAP(AddrA,AddrB,AddrC,DataA,DataB,DataC,WrC,Reset,Clk);
    PC: ENTITY Reg
```

```
            PORT MAP(ALUdata(23 DOWNTO 0),PCout(23 DOWNTO 0),WrPC,Reset,Clk);
        CR: ENTITY Reg
            PORT MAP(Cond,CRout,WrCR,Reset,Clk);

            ZE <= CRout(0);  CY <= CRout(1);
            NG <= CRout(2);  OV <= CRout(3);

        IR: ENTITY Reg
            PORT MAP(tMemData,IRreg,WrIR,Reset,Clk);

            Instr <= IRreg;

       MX1: ENTITY Mux
            PORT MAP(tMemData,ALUdata,Mem_ALU,DataC);
       MX2: ENTITY Mux
            PORT MAP(PCout,DataA,PC_RA,Ain);
       ZSE: ENTITY Extender
            PORT MAP(IRreg,ZE_SE,IRext);
       MX3: ENTITY Mux
            PORT MAP(IRext,DataB,IR_RB,Bin);
       MX4: ENTITY Mux
            PORT MAP(ALUdata(23 DOWNTO 0),PCout(23 DOWNTO 0),ALU_PC,MemAddr);
       SL : ENTITY Switch
            PORT MAP(MemData,tMemData,DataB,Sin_Sout);
END structural;
```

15.5.3 Register File

The μVHDL description of the register file is as follows:

```
LIBRARY ieee;
USE ieee.std_logic_1164.ALL;
USE ieee.std_logic_unsigned.ALL;
USE WORK.comp_pkg.ALL;

ENTITY Reg_File IS
  PORT(AddrA, AddrB, AddrC : IN  STD_LOGIC_VECTOR(4 DOWNTO 0);
       DataA, DataB        : OUT WordT;
       DataC               : IN  WordT;
       WrC                 : IN  STD_LOGIC ;
       Reset, Clk          : IN  STD_LOGIC);
END Reg_File;

ARCHITECTURE behavioral OF Reg_File IS
  TYPE     RegFileT IS ARRAY(0 to 31) OF WordT;
  SIGNAL   GPR : RegFileT     ;
BEGIN
  PROCESS(AddrA,AddrB)               -- output function
    CONSTANT RF_delay    : TIME := 4 ns;
  BEGIN
    DataA <= GPR(CONV_INTEGER(AddrA)) AFTER RF_delay;
    DataB <= GPR(CONV_INTEGER(AddrB)) AFTER RF_delay;
  END PROCESS;

  PROCESS(Reset,Clk)                 -- transition function
  BEGIN
    IF (Reset'EVENT and (Reset = '1')) THEN
      FOR i IN 0 TO 31 LOOP
```

```
        GPR(i) <= (OTHERS => '0');
      END LOOP;
    END IF;

    IF (Clk'EVENT AND Clk = '1' AND WrC  = '1') THEN
        GPR(CONV_INTEGER(AddrC)) <= DataC;
    END IF;
  END PROCESS;
END behavioral;
```

15.5.4 Arithmetic-logic Unit

The μVHDL description of the ALU is as follows:

```
LIBRARY ieee;
USE ieee.std_logic_1164.ALL;
USE ieee.std_logic_signed.ALL;
USE WORK.comp_pkg.ALL;

ENTITY ALU IS
  PORT(A, B: IN  STD_LOGIC_VECTOR(31 DOWNTO 0);
       Op  : IN  STD_LOGIC_VECTOR( 3 DOWNTO 0);
       C   : OUT STD_LOGIC_VECTOR(31 DOWNTO 0);
       Cond: OUT STD_LOGIC_VECTOR( 3 DOWNTO 0));
END ALU;

ARCHITECTURE behavioral OF ALU IS
BEGIN
  PROCESS(A,B,Op)
    CONSTANT ALU_delay  : TIME := 6 ns;
  BEGIN
    CASE Op IS
      WHEN "0000" => C <= (OTHERS => '0') AFTER ALU_delay;
      WHEN "0001" => C <= A + B           AFTER ALU_delay;
      WHEN "0010" => C <= A - B           AFTER ALU_delay;
      WHEN "0011" => C <= (OTHERS => '0') AFTER ALU_delay;
      WHEN "0100" => C <= A and B         AFTER ALU_delay;
      WHEN "0101" => C <= A or  B         AFTER ALU_delay;
      WHEN "0110" => C <= A xor B         AFTER ALU_delay;
      WHEN "0111" => C <= (OTHERS => '0') AFTER ALU_delay;
      WHEN "1000" => C <= A               AFTER ALU_delay;
      WHEN "1001" => C <= B               AFTER ALU_delay;
      WHEN "1010" => C <= A(30 DOWNTO 0) & '0'   AFTER ALU_delay;
      WHEN "1011" => C <= '0' & A(31 DOWNTO 1)   AFTER ALU_delay;
      WHEN "1100" => C <= A(30 DOWNTO 0) & A(31) AFTER ALU_delay;
      WHEN "1101" => C <= A(0) & A(31 DOWNTO 1)  AFTER ALU_delay;
      WHEN "1110" => C <= A + 4           AFTER ALU_delay;
      WHEN "1111" => C <= not(A)          AFTER ALU_delay;
      WHEN OTHERS => NULL;
    END CASE;
    Cond <= get_cc(A,B,Op) AFTER ALU_delay;
  END PROCESS;
END behavioral;
```

15.5.5 Registers

Registers are described in μVHDL as follows:

```
LIBRARY ieee;
USE ieee.std_logic_1164.ALL;

ENTITY Reg IS
  PORT(Data_in : IN  STD_LOGIC_VECTOR;
       Data_out: OUT STD_LOGIC_VECTOR;
       Wr      : IN  STD_LOGIC ;
       Reset   : IN  STD_LOGIC ;
       Clk     : IN  STD_LOGIC);
END Reg;

ARCHITECTURE behavioral OF Reg IS
BEGIN
  PROCESS(Wr,Reset,Clk)
    CONSTANT Reg_delay: TIME := 2 ns;
    VARIABLE BVZero: STD_LOGIC_VECTOR(Data_in'RANGE):= (OTHERS => '0');
  BEGIN
    IF (Reset = '1') THEN
       Data_out <= BVZero AFTER Reg_delay;
    END IF;

    IF (Clk'EVENT AND Clk = '1' AND Wr = '1') THEN
       Data_out <= Data_in AFTER Reg_delay;
    END IF;
  END PROCESS;
END behavioral;
```

15.5.6 Other Modules in the Data Subsystem

The remaining modules in the data subsystem are described in μVHDL as follows:

```
LIBRARY ieee;
USE ieee.std_logic_1164.ALL;

ENTITY Mux IS
  PORT(A_in,B_in: IN  STD_LOGIC_VECTOR;
       Sel      : IN  STD_LOGIC        ;
       Data_out : OUT STD_LOGIC_VECTOR);
END Mux;

ARCHITECTURE behavioral OF Mux IS
BEGIN
  PROCESS(A_in, B_in, Sel)
    CONSTANT Mux_delay: TIME := 500 ps;
  BEGIN
    IF (Sel = '0') THEN
       Data_out <= A_in AFTER Mux_delay;
    ELSE
       Data_out <= B_in AFTER Mux_delay;
    END IF;
  END PROCESS;
END behavioral;
```

```
LIBRARY ieee;
USE ieee.std_logic_1164.ALL;

ENTITY Extender IS
  PORT(X_in  : IN  STD_LOGIC_VECTOR(31 DOWNTO 0);
       ZE_SE : IN  STD_LOGIC                    ;
       X_out : OUT STD_LOGIC_VECTOR(31 DOWNTO 0));
END Extender;

ARCHITECTURE behavioral OF Extender IS
BEGIN
  PROCESS(X_in, ZE_SE)
    CONSTANT Ext_delay: TIME := 500 ps;
  BEGIN
    IF (ZE_SE = '0') THEN
       X_out(31 DOWNTO 16) <= (OTHERS => '0') AFTER Ext_delay;
       X_out(15 DOWNTO  0) <= X_in(15 DOWNTO 0) AFTER Ext_delay;
    ELSE
       X_out(31 DOWNTO 16) <= (OTHERS => X_in(15)) AFTER Ext_delay;
       X_out(15 DOWNTO  0) <= X_in(15 DOWNTO 0) AFTER Ext_delay;
    END IF;
  END PROCESS;
END behavioral;


LIBRARY ieee;
USE ieee.std_logic_1164.ALL;

ENTITY Switch IS
  PORT(A    : INOUT STD_LOGIC_VECTOR;
       B_out: OUT   STD_LOGIC_VECTOR;
       C_in : IN    STD_LOGIC_VECTOR;
       Sel  : IN    STD_LOGIC      );
END Switch;

ARCHITECTURE behavioral OF Switch IS
BEGIN
  PROCESS(A, C_in, Sel)
    CONSTANT Switch_delay: TIME := 500 ps;
    CONSTANT dataZ: STD_LOGIC_VECTOR(A'RANGE):= (OTHERS => 'Z');
  BEGIN
    IF (Sel = '0') THEN
       B_out <= A AFTER Switch_delay;
       A     <= dataZ;
    ELSE
       A     <= C_in AFTER Switch_delay;
    END IF;
  END PROCESS;
END behavioral;
```

15.5.7 Control Subsystem

The behavioral description of the control subsystem is expressed in μVHDL as follows:

```
LIBRARY ieee;
USE ieee.std_logic_1164.ALL;
USE WORK.comp_pkg.ALL;
```

```
ENTITY Ctrl_Subsystem IS
  PORT(Instr                  : IN    WordT        ;
       ZE, NG, CY, OV         : IN    STD_LOGIC    ;
       AddrA, AddrB, AddrC    : OUT   STD_LOGIC_VECTOR(4 DOWNTO 0);
       ALUOp                  : OUT   STD_LOGIC_VECTOR(3 DOWNTO 0);
       WrC, WrPC, WrCR, WrIR  : OUT   STD_LOGIC    ;
       Mem_ALU, PC_RA, IR_RB  : OUT   STD_LOGIC    ;
       ALU_PC, ZE_SE, Sin_Sout: OUT   STD_LOGIC    ;
       MemRd,MemWr            : OUT   STD_LOGIC    ;
       MemLength              : OUT   STD_LOGIC    ;
       MemEnable              : OUT   STD_LOGIC    ;
       MemRdy                 : IN    STD_LOGIC    ;
       IORd, IOWr             : OUT   STD_LOGIC    ;
       IOLength               : OUT   STD_LOGIC    ;
       IOEnable               : OUT   STD_LOGIC    ;
       IORdy                  : IN    STD_LOGIC    ;
       Status                 : OUT   StatusT      ;
       Clk, Reset             : IN    STD_LOGIC );
END Ctrl_Subsystem;


LIBRARY ieee;
USE ieee.std_logic_signed.ALL;

ARCHITECTURE behavioral OF Ctrl_Subsystem IS
    SIGNAL State: StatusT;
BEGIN
PROCESS                                              -- transition function
    ALIAS    Opcode : STD_LOGIC_VECTOR(5 DOWNTO 0) IS Instr(31 DOWNTO 26);
    CONSTANT Reset_delay: TIME:= 500 ps ;
    CONSTANT Ctrl_delay : TIME:= 500 ps ;
BEGIN
  WAIT ON Clk,Reset;
  IF (Reset'EVENT AND Reset = '1') THEN
      State  <= p_reset AFTER Reset_delay;
      Status <= p_reset AFTER Reset_delay;
      WAIT UNTIL Clk = '1';
  END IF;

  IF (Clk'EVENT) AND (Clk = '1') THEN
     CASE State IS
     WHEN p_reset      => Status <= fetch   AFTER Ctrl_delay;
                          State  <= fetch   AFTER Ctrl_delay;
     WHEN fetch        => Status <= execute AFTER Ctrl_delay;
                          State  <= execute AFTER Ctrl_delay;
     WHEN execute      => CASE Opcode IS
        WHEN "100000" | "100001" => State  <= memop AFTER Ctrl_delay;
                                    Status <= memop AFTER Ctrl_delay;
        WHEN "100010" | "100011" => State  <= memop AFTER Ctrl_delay;
                                    Status <= memop AFTER Ctrl_delay;
        WHEN OTHERS              => State  <= fetch AFTER Ctrl_delay;
                                    Status <= fetch AFTER Ctrl_delay;
                          END CASE;
     WHEN memop | ioop => Status <= fetch   AFTER Ctrl_delay;
                          State  <= fetch   AFTER Ctrl_delay;
     WHEN undef        => NULL;
     END CASE;
  END IF;
 END PROCESS;
```

```
PROCESS(State,Instr,MemRdy)                              -- output function
    ALIAS    Opcode : STD_LOGIC_VECTOR( 5 DOWNTO 0) IS Instr(31 DOWNTO 26);
    ALIAS    Imm    : STD_LOGIC_VECTOR(15 DOWNTO 0) IS Instr(15 DOWNTO  0);
    ALIAS    D      : STD_LOGIC_VECTOR(15 DOWNTO 0) IS Instr(15 DOWNTO  0);
    ALIAS    PN     : STD_LOGIC_VECTOR(10 DOWNTO 0) IS Instr(10 DOWNTO  0);

    CONSTANT Dec_delay  : TIME:=    3 ns;
    CONSTANT Ctrl_delay : TIME:=  500 ps;
    CONSTANT MemRd_delay: TIME:= 2500 ps;
    CONSTANT MemRd_pulse: TIME:= MemRd_delay + 3 ns ;
    CONSTANT MemWr_delay: TIME:= 2500 ps;
    CONSTANT MemWr_pulse: TIME:= MemWr_delay + 3 ns ;

    TYPE     Ctrl_LineT IS
      RECORD
        MemOp, WrMem     : STD_LOGIC;
        RS_RB, IR_RB     : STD_LOGIC;
        WrC, WrPC, WrCR  : STD_LOGIC;
        ZE_SE            : STD_LOGIC;
        ALUop            : STD_LOGIC_VECTOR(3 DOWNTO 0);
      END RECORD;

    VARIABLE Ctrl_Line  : Ctrl_LineT;

    TYPE     Ctrl_TableT IS ARRAY(NATURAL RANGE 0 TO 63) OF Ctrl_LineT;

    CONSTANT Ctrl_Table: Ctrl_TableT:=
     --     Mem  Wr   RS   IR   Wr   Wr   Wr   ZE   ALU
     --     Op   Mem  RB   RB   C    PC   CR   SE   op
     (0 => ('0', '0', '1', '1', '0', '0', '0', '0', "0000"), -- nop
      2 => ('0', '0', '1', '1', '1', '0', '1', '0', "1111"), -- not
      4 => ('0', '0', '1', '1', '1', '0', '1', '0', "1010"), -- lsh
      6 => ('0', '0', '1', '1', '1', '0', '1', '0', "1011"), -- rsh
      8 => ('0', '0', '1', '1', '1', '0', '1', '0', "1100"), -- lrt
      10=> ('0', '0', '1', '1', '1', '0', '1', '0', "1101"), -- rrt

      16=> ('0', '0', '1', '1', '1', '0', '1', '0', "0001"), -- add
      17=> ('0', '0', '1', '0', '1', '0', '1', '1', "0001"), -- adi
      18=> ('0', '0', '1', '1', '1', '0', '1', '0', "0010"), -- sub
      19=> ('0', '0', '1', '0', '1', '0', '1', '1', "0010"), -- sbi
      20=> ('0', '0', '1', '1', '1', '0', '1', '0', "0100"), -- and
      21=> ('0', '0', '1', '0', '1', '0', '1', '0', "0100"), -- ani
      22=> ('0', '0', '1', '1', '1', '0', '1', '0', "0101"), -- or
      23=> ('0', '0', '1', '0', '1', '0', '1', '0', "0101"), -- ori
      24=> ('0', '0', '1', '1', '1', '0', '1', '0', "0110"), -- xor
      25=> ('0', '0', '1', '0', '1', '0', '1', '0', "0110"), -- xri

      32=> ('1', '0', '0', '0', '1', '0', '0', '1', "0001"), -- ldb
      33=> ('1', '0', '0', '0', '1', '0', '0', '1', "0001"), -- ldw
      34=> ('1', '1', '0', '0', '0', '0', '0', '1', "0001"), -- stb
      35=> ('1', '1', '0', '0', '0', '0', '0', '1', "0001"), -- stw
      36=> ('1', '0', '0', '1', '1', '0', '0', '0', "1001"), -- irb
      37=> ('1', '0', '0', '1', '1', '0', '0', '0', "1001"), -- irw
      38=> ('1', '1', '0', '1', '0', '0', '0', '0', "1001"), -- iwb
      39=> ('1', '1', '0', '1', '0', '0', '0', '0', "1001"), -- iww

      56=> ('0', '0', '1', '0', '0', '1', '0', '1', "0001"), -- br
      57=> ('0', '0', '1', '0', '0', '1', '0', '1', "1000"), -- bri
      48=> ('0', '0', '1', '0', '0', '1', '0', '1', "0001"), -- brp
```

```
     49=> ('0', '0', '1', '0', '0', '1', '0', '1', "0001"), -- brn
     50=> ('0', '0', '1', '0', '0', '1', '0', '1', "0001"), -- bnz
     51=> ('0', '0', '1', '0', '0', '1', '0', '1', "0001"), -- brz
     52=> ('0', '0', '1', '0', '0', '1', '0', '1', "0001"), -- bnc
     53=> ('0', '0', '1', '0', '0', '1', '0', '1', "0001"), -- brc
     54=> ('0', '0', '1', '0', '0', '1', '0', '1', "0001"), -- bnv
     55=> ('0', '0', '1', '0', '0', '1', '0', '1', "0001"), -- brv
OTHERS => ('0', '0', '1', '1', '0', '0', '0', '1', "0000")
    );

 BEGIN
 IF (State'EVENT) THEN
    CASE State IS
    WHEN undef     => NULL;
    WHEN p_reset   => ALUOp     <= "0000";
                      MemRd     <= '0';    MemWr   <= '0';
                      MemEnable <= '0'; MemLength <= '0';
                      IORd      <= '0';      IOWr  <= '0';
                      IOEnable  <= '0';  IOLength <= '0';
    WHEN fetch     =>
             -- disable write signals from previous cycle
             WrCR     <= '0' AFTER Ctrl_delay;
             WrC      <= '0' AFTER Ctrl_delay;

             -- fetch instruction
             ALU_PC    <= '1' AFTER Ctrl_delay;
             MemLength<= '1' AFTER Ctrl_delay;
             MemEnable<= '1' AFTER Ctrl_delay;
             MemRd     <= '1' AFTER MemRd_delay, '0' AFTER MemRd_pulse;
             Sin_Sout  <= '0' AFTER Ctrl_delay;              -- switch in

             -- increment PC
             PC_RA     <= '0' AFTER Ctrl_delay;
             ALUop     <= "1110" AFTER Ctrl_delay;           -- PC + 4
             WrIR      <= '1' AFTER Ctrl_delay;
             WrPC      <= '1' AFTER Ctrl_delay;

    WHEN execute  =>
             -- disable signals from fetch cycle
             WrIR      <= '0' AFTER Ctrl_delay;
             WrPC      <= '0' AFTER Ctrl_delay;
             MemEnable<= '0' AFTER Ctrl_delay;

             -- other actions done by Instr'EVENT

    WHEN memop | ioop   =>
             -- initiate memory access
             ALU_PC    <= '0' AFTER Ctrl_delay;        -- address to memory
             MemEnable<= '1' AFTER Ctrl_delay;
             MemLength<= Opcode(0) AFTER Ctrl_delay; -- operand length
             WrC        <= Ctrl_Line.WrC AFTER Ctrl_delay;
             IF (Ctrl_Line.WrMem = '0') THEN
               MemRd      <= '1' AFTER MemRd_delay, '0' AFTER MemRd_pulse;
               Mem_ALU    <= '0' AFTER Ctrl_delay;
             ELSE
               MemWr      <= '1' AFTER MemWr_delay, '0' AFTER MemWr_pulse;
               Sin_Sout   <= '1' AFTER Ctrl_delay;
             END IF;
     END CASE;
```

```
    END IF;

    IF (Instr'EVENT) THEN
       -- decode opcode
       Ctrl_Line:= Ctrl_Table(CONV_INTEGER('0' & Opcode));

       -- decode registers
       AddrA    <= Instr(20 DOWNTO 16) AFTER Dec_delay;
       IF (Ctrl_Line.RS_RB = '0') THEN
         AddrB <= Instr(25 DOWNTO 21) AFTER Dec_delay;
       ELSE
         AddrB <= Instr(15 DOWNTO 11) AFTER Dec_delay;
       END IF;
       AddrC    <= Instr(25 DOWNTO 21) AFTER Dec_delay;

       -- decode control signals
       PC_RA    <= not(Ctrl_Line.WrPC) AFTER Ctrl_delay;
       ZE_SE    <= Ctrl_Line.ZE_SE AFTER Ctrl_delay;
       IR_RB    <= Ctrl_Line.IR_RB AFTER Ctrl_delay;
       ALUOp    <= Ctrl_Line.ALUop AFTER Ctrl_delay;
       WrPC     <= Ctrl_Line.WrPC  AFTER Ctrl_delay;
       WrCR     <= Ctrl_Line.WrCR  AFTER Ctrl_delay;

       IF (Ctrl_Line.MemOp = '0') THEN
         WrC     <= Ctrl_Line.WrC AFTER Ctrl_delay;
         Mem_ALU <= '1' AFTER Ctrl_delay;
       END IF;
    END IF;

    IF (MemRdy'EVENT AND MemRdy='1') THEN
        CASE State IS
          WHEN memop  => IF (Ctrl_Line.WrMem = '1') THEN
                                       -- deactivate data bus
                           Sin_Sout <= '0' AFTER Ctrl_delay;
                         END IF;
          WHEN OTHERS => NULL;
        END CASE;
    END IF;
    END PROCESS;
  END behavioral;
```

15.6 FURTHER READINGS

The specification and design of computers have been standard subjects of books on computer organization and architecture. We mention *Computer Organization and Design: The Hardware/Software Interface* by J. L. Hennessy and D. A. Patterson, Morgan Kaufmann Publishers, Inc., San Francisco, CA, 1994; *Computer Organization* by V. C. Hamacher, Z. G. Vranesic, and S. G. Zaky (Fourth Edition), McGraw-Hill, Inc. New York, 1996, and *Computer Architecture and Organization: Designing for Performance* by W. Stallings (Fourth Edition), Prentice-Hall, Englewood Cliffs, NJ, 1996.

The use of VHDL in specification and design of computer systems is discussed, for example, in *The Designer's Guide to VHDL* by P. J. Ashenden, Morgan Kaufmann Publishers, Inc., San Francisco, CA, 1996; and *VHDL Analysis and Modeling of Digital Systems* by Z. Navabi, McGraw-Hill, Inc., New York, 1993.

EXERCISES

Specification

Exercise 15.1 A memory subsystem has the following timing characteristics:

- the enable signal becomes active at time 0;
- the address must be valid 5 ns before the read or write signal is activated;
- the read signal is active for 30 ns;
- the data become available after 50 ns;
- the data remain available for 10 ns.

Determine the time when Rdy becomes high and when Enable becomes low. Give an upper bound on the number of memory accesses per second.

Exercise 15.2 Give the binary representation of the following XMC instructions:

```
add R5,R7,R9
ldw R7,1200(R8)
brn 1000
```

Exercise 15.3 Determine the effective address for the following XMC instructions

```
stw R5,1300(R7)
brn 1250
bri R7
```

with the following contents of registers:

$$\begin{aligned} \texttt{PC} &= 5321 \\ \texttt{R1} &= 10 \\ \texttt{R5} &= -1250 \\ \texttt{R7} &= -110 \end{aligned}$$

Exercise 15.4 Write a sequence of branches to branch-on-negative a distance of 2^{20} locations from the location of the current instruction.

Exercise 15.5 Write a program in assembly language and translate it to binary, for adding an array of 105 integers stored consecutively beginning in location 1000 and storing the result in location 2000. Try reducing the number of memory accesses and the number of instructions.

Exercise 15.6 Use the μVHDL specification to simulate the behavior of the instructions given in Exercise 15.2.

Exercise 15.7 Give the μVHDL specification of an instruction that is similar to `ldw` but, in addition, it increments by four the register used to calculate the effective address.

Implementation

Exercise 15.8 Show modifications to Figure 15.10 for implementing a 64 MB memory.

Exercise 15.9 Show the sequence of events and values of the signals in Figure 15.12 during execution of the following instructions. The value of register `PC` is 1500 in all cases.

```
add R7,R5,R8
sw  R3,11300(R2)
bn  10000
```

Exercise 15.10 Show timing diagrams similar to that of Figure 15.14 for a load word instruction and for a branch instruction.

Exercise 15.11 Show an implementation of the control unit using the one flip-flop per state approach. Give all control signals required to execute the instructions of Exercise 15.2.

Exercise 15.12 Calculate the cycle time using the same values as in Example 15.1, except for the delay of the arithmetic-logic unit and the memory, which now are 4 ns and 10 ns, respectively.

Exercise 15.13 Consider a modification to XMC in which, to reduce the size of the programs, there are two instruction lengths: two bytes and four bytes.

a. Determine the required length for each of the instruction types depicted in Figure 15.9, and show the corresponding formats.
b. Provide an opcode that makes it easy to determine the length of an instruction.
c. Modify the data subsystem to execute these instruction types. In particular, indicate how the program counter can be updated without increasing the number of cycles per instruction. (Because the instruction length is now variable, it is not possible to update the program counter in the Fetch state; moreover, it is not possible to update the program counter in the Execute state with the current data subsystem because the ALU is utilized for the execution of the operation. You might need to add a special unit to update the PC.)

Exercise 15.14 Suppose that the instruction format is such that it is not possible to read the register file before knowing the instruction class. This would require decoding the instruction before reading the registers. Determine the effect of this additional delay on the cycle time in Example 15.1.

Exercise 15.15 Because the cycle time in Example 15.1 is determined by the `Execute` state, it is possible to reduce the cycle time by decomposing this state into two states. One alternative is to introduce a register (latch) at the output of the ALU so that the first `Execute` state terminates by storing the result in the latch. Then, the second `Execute` state stores this value in the register file.

a. Determine the cycle time in this case.
b. Determine the number of cycles for each instruction type.
c. Determine the execution time for each instruction type and compare with that of Example 15.1.

Exercise 15.16 This is a continuation of Exercise 15.15. Now that the `Execute` state has been split into two, the cycle time might be determined by the `Memop` state. Using the same approach for this state as in Exercise 15.15, determine the cycle time, number of cycles, and execution time for each instruction type.

Exercise 15.17 Most contemporary processors have separate instruction and data caches. This separation is done mainly to be able to fetch the next instruction in the same cycle as data for the current instruction, which is required by pipelined processors. Although we do not discuss pipelined processors in this text, let us consider the case in which the instruction cache is faster ($t_{im} = 6$ ns) than the data cache ($t_{dm} = 8$ ns). Repeat Exercise 15.16 for this situation.

Appendix

Boolean Algebras

Boolean algebras is an important class of algebras that has been studied and used extensively for many purposes (see Section A.5). The **switching algebra,** used in the description of switching expressions discussed in Section 2.4, is an instance (an element) of the class of Boolean algebras. Consequently, theorems developed for Boolean algebras are also applicable to switching algebra, so they can be used for the transformation of switching expressions. Moreover, certain identities from Boolean algebra are the basis for the graphical and tabular techniques used for the minimization of switching expressions.

In this appendix, we present the definition of Boolean algebras as well as theorems that are useful for the transformation of Boolean expressions. We also show the relationship among Boolean and switching algebras; in particular, we show that the switching algebra satisfies the postulates of a Boolean algebra. We also sketch other examples of Boolean algebras, which are helpful to further understand the properties of this class of algebras.

1 BOOLEAN ALGEBRA

A **Boolean algebra** is a tuple $\{B, +, \cdot\}$, where

- B is a set of elements;
- $+$ and $\cdot$ are binary operations applied over the elements of B,

satisfying the following postulates:

P1: If $a, b \in B$, then

i. $a + b = b + a$
ii. $a \cdot b = b \cdot a$

That is, $+$ and $\cdot$ are commutative.

P2: If $a, b, c \in B$, then

i. $a + (b \cdot c) = (a + b) \cdot (a + c)$
ii. $a \cdot (b + c) = (a \cdot b) + (a \cdot c)$

P3: The set B has two distinct **identity elements,** denoted as 0 and 1, such that for every element in B

i. $0 + a = a + 0 = a$
ii. $1 \cdot a = a \cdot 1 = a$

The elements 0 and 1 are called the **additive identity element** and the **multiplicative identity element**, respectively. (These elements should not be confused with the integers 0 and 1.)

P4: For every element $a \in B$ there exists an element a', called the **complement** of a, such that

i. $a + a' = 1$
ii. $a \cdot a' = 0$

The symbols $+$ and $\cdot$ should not be confused with the arithmetic addition and multiplication symbols. However, for convenience $+$ and $\cdot$ are often called "plus" and "times," and the expressions $a + b$ and $a \cdot b$ are called "sum" and "product," respectively. Moreover, $+$ and $\cdot$ are also called "OR" and "AND," respectively.

The elements of the set B are called **constants.** Symbols representing arbitrary elements of B are **variables.** The symbols a, b, and c in the postulates above are variables, whereas 0 and 1 are constants.

A **precedence ordering** is defined on the operators: $\cdot$ has precedence over $+$. Therefore, parentheses can be eliminated from products. Moreover, whenever single symbols are used for variables, the symbol $\cdot$ can be eliminated in products. For example,

$$a + (b \cdot c) \quad \text{can be written as} \quad a + bc$$

2 SWITCHING ALGEBRA

Switching algebra is an algebraic system used to describe switching functions by means of switching expressions. In this sense, a switching algebra serves the same role for switching functions as the ordinary algebra does for arithmetic functions.

The switching algebra consists of the set of two elements $B = \{0, 1\}$, and two operations AND and OR defined as follows:

AND	0	1
0	0	0
1	0	1

OR	0	1
0	0	1
1	1	1

These operations are used to evaluate switching expressions, as indicated in Section 2.4.

Theorem 1

The switching algebra is a Boolean algebra

Proof We show that the switching algebra satisfies the postulates of a Boolean algebra.

P1: Commutativity of (+), (·). This is shown by inspection of the operation tables. The commutativity property holds if a table is symmetric about the main diagonal.

P2: Distributivity of (+) and (·). Shown by **perfect induction,** that is, by considering all possible values for the elements a, b, and c. Consider the following table:

abc	$a + bc$	$(a + b)(a + c)$
000	0	0
001	0	0
010	0	0
011	1	1
100	1	1
101	1	1
110	1	1
111	1	1

Because $a + bc = (a + b)(a + c)$ for all cases, P2(i) is satisfied. A similar proof shows that P2(ii) is also satisfied.

P3: Existence of additive and multiplicative identity element. From the operation tables

$$0 + 1 = 1 + 0 = 1$$

Therefore, 0 is the additive identity. Similarly

$$0 \cdot 1 = 1 \cdot 0 = 0$$

so that 1 is the multiplicative identity.

P4: Existence of the complement. By perfect induction:

a	a'	$a + a'$	$a \cdot a'$
1	0	1	0
0	1	1	0

Consequently, 1 is the complement of 0 and 0 is the complement of 1.

Because all postulates are satisfied, the switching algebra is a Boolean algebra. As a result, all theorems true for Boolean algebras are also true for the switching algebra. ■

3 IMPORTANT THEOREMS IN BOOLEAN ALGEBRA

We now present some important theorems in Boolean algebra; these theorems can be applied to the transformation of switching expressions.

Theorem 2 Principle of Duality

Every algebraic identity deducible from the postulates of a Boolean algebra remains valid if

- the operations $+$ and $\cdot$ are interchanged throughout; and
- the identity elements 0 and 1 are also interchanged throughout.

Proof The proof follows at once from the fact that for each of the postulates there is another one (the dual) that is obtained by interchanging $+$ and $\cdot$ as well as 0 and 1. ■

This theorem is useful because it reduces the number of different theorems that must be proven: every theorem has its dual.

Theorem 3

Every element in B has a **unique** complement.

Proof Let $a \in B$; let us assume that a_1' and a_2' are both complements of a. Then, using the postulates we can perform the following transformations:

$a_1' = a_1' \cdot 1$	by P3(ii)	(identity)
$= a_1' \cdot (a + a_2')$	by hypothesis	(a_2' is the complement of a)
$= a_1' \cdot a + a_1' \cdot a_2'$	by P2(ii)	(distributivity)
$= a \cdot a_1' + a_1' \cdot a_2'$	by P1(ii)	(commutativity)
$= 0 + a_1' \cdot a_2'$	by hypothesis	(a_1' is complement of a)
$= a_1' \cdot a_2'$	by P3(i)	(identity)

Changing the index 1 for 2 and vice versa, and repeating all steps for a_2', we get

$$\begin{aligned} a_2' &= a_2' \cdot a_1' \\ &= a_1' \cdot a_2' \qquad \text{by P1(ii)} \end{aligned}$$

and therefore $a_2' = a_1'$. ■

The uniqueness of the complement of an element allows considering $'$ as a unary operation called **complementation.**

Theorem 4

For any $a \in B$:

1. $a + 1 = 1$
2. $a \cdot 0 = 0$

Proof Using the postulates, we can perform the following transformations:

Case (1):

$$\begin{aligned} a + 1 &= 1 \cdot (a + 1) && \text{by P3 (ii)} \\ &= (a + a') \cdot (a + 1) && \text{P4 (i)} \\ &= a + (a' \cdot 1) && \text{P2 (i)} \\ &= a + a' && \text{P3 (ii)} \\ &= 1 && \text{P4 (i)} \end{aligned}$$

Case (2):

$$\begin{aligned} a \cdot 0 &= 0 + (a \cdot 0) && \text{by P3 (i)} \\ &= (a \cdot a') + (a \cdot 0) && \text{P4 (ii)} \\ &= a \cdot (a' + 0) && \text{P2 (ii)} \\ &= a \cdot a' && \text{P3 (i)} \\ &= 0 && \text{P4 (ii)} \end{aligned}$$

Case (2) can also be proven by means of Case (1) and the principle of duality. ■

Theorem 5

The complement of the element 1 is 0, and vice versa. That is,

1. $0' = 1$
2. $1' = 0$

Proof By Theorem 4,

$$0 + 1 = 1 \quad \text{and}$$

$$0 \cdot 1 = 0$$

Because, by Theorem 3, the complement of an element is unique, Theorem 5 follows. ■

Theorem 6 Idempotent Law

For every $a \in B$

1. $a + a = a$
2. $a \cdot a = a$

Proof

		by
(1):	$a + a = (a + a) \cdot 1$	P3 (ii)
	$= (a + a) \cdot (a + a')$	P4 (i)
	$= (a + (a \cdot a'))$	P2 (i)
	$= a + 0$	P4 (ii)
	$= a$	P3 (i)
(2):		duality

■

Theorem 7 Involution Law

For every $a \in B$,

$$(a')' = a$$

Proof From the definition of complement $(a')'$ and a are both complements of a'. But, by Theorem 3, the complement of an element is unique, which proves the theorem. ■

Theorem 8 Absorption Law

For every pair of elements $a, b \in B$,

1. $a + a \cdot b = a$
2. $a \cdot (a + b) = a$

Proof

		by
(1):	$a + ab = a \cdot 1 + ab$	P3 (ii)
	$= a(1 + b)$	P2 (ii)
	$= a(b + 1)$	P1 (i)
	$= a \cdot 1$	Theorem 4 (1)
	$= a$	P3 (ii)
(2)		duality

■

Theorem 9

For every pair of elements $a, b \in B$,

1. $a + a'b = a + b$
2. $a(a' + b) = ab$

Proof

		by
(1):	$a + a'b = (a + a')(a + b)$	P2 (i)
	$= 1 \cdot (a + b)$	P4 (i)
	$= a + b$	P3 (ii)
(2):		duality

■

Theorem 10

In a Boolean algebra, each of the binary operations (+) and $(\cdot)$ is associative. That is, for every $a, b, c \in B$,

1. $a + (b + c) = (a + b) + c$
2. $a(bc) = (ab)c$

The proof of this theorem is quite lengthy. The interested reader should consult the further readings suggested at the end of this appendix.

Corollary 1

1. The order in applying the + operator among n elements does not matter. For example,

$$\begin{aligned} a + \{b + [c + (d + e)]\} &= \{[(a + b) + c] + d\} + e \\ &= \{a + [(b + c) + d]\} + e \\ &= a + b + c + d + e \end{aligned}$$

2. The order in applying the $\cdot$ operator among n elements does not matter.

Theorem 11 DeMorgan's Law

For every pair of elements $a, b \in B$:

1. $(a + b)' = a'b'$
2. $(ab)' = a' + b'$

Proof We first prove that $(a + b)$ is the complement of $a'b'$. By the definition of complement (P4) and its uniqueness (Theorem 3), this corresponds to showing that $(a + b) + a'b' = 1$ and $(a + b)a'b' = 0$. We do this proof by the following transformations:

$$\begin{aligned} (a + b) + a'b' &= [(a + b) + a'][(a + b) + b'] && \text{by P2(i)} \\ &= [(b + a) + a'][(a + b) + b'] && \text{P1(i)} \\ &= [b + (a + a')][a + (b + b')] && \text{associativity} \\ &= (b + 1)(a + 1) && \text{P4(i)} \\ &= 1 \cdot 1 && \text{Theorem 3(1)} \\ &= 1 && \text{idempotency} \end{aligned}$$

$$\begin{aligned} (a + b)(a'b') &= (a'b')(a + b) && \text{commutativity} \\ &= (a'b')a + (a'b')b && \text{distributivity} \\ &= (b'a')a + (a'b')b && \text{commutativity} \\ &= b'(a'a) + a'(b'b) && \text{associativity} \\ &= b'(aa') + a'(bb') && \text{commutativity} \\ &= b' \cdot 0 + a' \cdot 0 && \text{P4(ii)} \\ &= 0 + 0 && \text{Theorem 3(2)} \\ &= 0 && \text{Theorem 5(1)} \end{aligned}$$

By duality,

$$(a \cdot b)' = a' + b'$$

■

Theorem 12 Generalized DeMorgan's Law

Let $\{a, b, \ldots, c, d\}$ be a set of elements in a Boolean algebra. Then, the following identities hold:

1. $(a + b \ldots + c + d)' = a'b' \ldots c'd'$
2. $(ab \ldots cd)' = a' + b' + \ldots + c' + d'$

Proof By the method of **finite induction.** The basis is provided by Theorem 11, which corresponds to the case with two elements.
Inductive step: Let us assume that DeMorgan's law is true for n elements, and show that it is true for $n + 1$ elements. Let $a, b, \ldots, c$ be the n elements, and d be the $(n + 1)$st element. Then, by associativity and the basis,

$$\begin{aligned}(a + b + \ldots + c + d)' &= [(a + b + \ldots + c) + d]' \\ &= (a + b + \ldots + c)'d'\end{aligned}$$

By the induction hypothesis

$$(a + b + \ldots c)' = a'b' \ldots c'$$

Thus

$$(a + b + \ldots c + d)' = a'b' \ldots c'd'$$ ■

DeMorgan's theorems are useful in manipulating switching expressions. For example, finding the complement of a switching expression containing parentheses is achieved by applying DeMorgan's law and the Involution law repeatedly to bring all (′) inside the parentheses. That is,

$$\begin{aligned}[(a + b')(c' + d') + (f' + g)']' &= [(a + b')(c' + d')]'[(f' + g)']' \\ &= [(a + b')' + (c' + d')'](f' + g) \\ &= (a'b + cd)(f' + g)\end{aligned}$$

The symbols $a, b, c, \ldots$ appearing in theorems and postulates are **generic variables.** That is, they can be substituted by complemented variables or expressions (formulas) without changing the meaning of these theorems. For example, DeMorgan's law can read as

$$(a' + b')' = ab$$

or

$$[(a + b)' + c']' = (a + b)c$$

We have described a general mathematical system, called Boolean algebra, and established a basic set of algebraic identities, true for any Boolean algebra, without actually specifying the nature of the two binary operations, (+) and (·). In Chapter 2, we presented an algebra useful for the representation of switching functions by switching expressions.

4 OTHER EXAMPLES OF BOOLEAN ALGEBRAS

There are other algebras that are also instances of Boolean algebras. We now summarize the two most commonly used ones.

Algebra of Sets. The elements of B are all subsets of a set S (the set of all subsets of S is denoted by $P(S)$), and the operations are set-union ($\cup$) and set-intersection ($\cap$). That is,

$$M = (P(S), \cup, \cap)$$

The additive identity is the empty set, denoted by ϕ, and the multiplicative identity is the set S. The set $P(S)$ has $2^{|S|}$ elements, where $|S|$ is the number of elements of S.

It can be shown that every Boolean algebra is isomorphic to an algebra of sets. Consequently, every Boolean algebra has 2^n elements for some value $n > 0$.

Venn diagrams are used to represent sets as well as and the operations of union and intersection. Consequently, since the algebra of sets is a Boolean algebra, Venn diagrams can be used to illustrate the theorems of a Boolean algebra.

Algebra of Logic (Propositional Calculus). In this algebra, the elements are T and F (true and false), and the operations are LOGICAL AND and LOGICAL OR. It is used to evaluate logical propositions. This algebra is isomorphic with the switching algebra.

5 FURTHER READINGS

The topic of Boolean algebras has been extensively studied, and many good books on the subject exist. The following is a partial list, in which the reader can obtain additional material that goes significantly beyond the limited treatment of this appendix: *Boolean Reasoning: The Logic of Boolean Equations* by F. M. Brown, Kluwer Academic Publishers, Boston, MA, 1990; *Introduction to Switching and Automata Theory* by M. A. Harrison, McGraw-Hill, New York, 1965; *Switching and Automata Theory* by Z. Kohavi, 2nd. ed., McGraw-Hill, New York, 1978; *Switching Theory* by R. E. Miller, Vols. 1 and 2. Wiley, New York, 1965; *Introduction to Discrete Structures* by F. Preparata and R. Yeh, Addison-Wesley, Reading, MA, 1973; and *Discrete Mathematical Structures* by H. S. Stone, Science Research Associates, Chicago, IL, 1973.

Index

D